When We're Singin'
The Partridge Family & Their Music

When We're Singin'

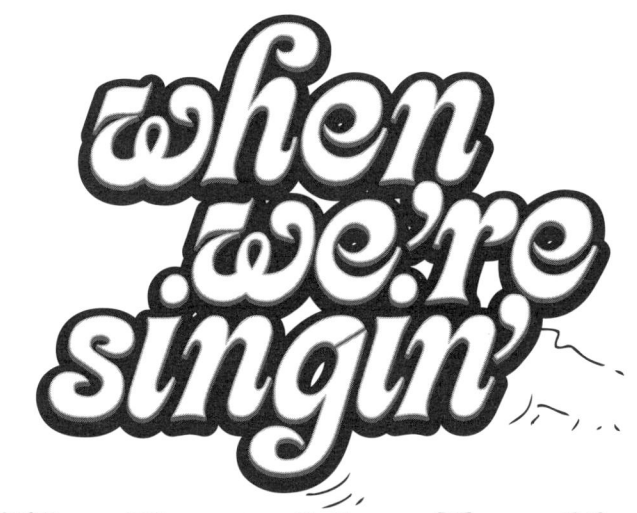

The Partridge Family & Their Music

Johnny Ray Miller

Copyright ©2016 by Johnny Ray Miller. All rights reserved. Unauthorized duplication of material contained in this book is a violation of copyright law. If you would like to use material contained herein for any purpose other than review, please contact the publisher at JohnnyRayMiller1@gmail.com.

Second Printing 2020

Published by
When We're Singin' LLC
9020 Kiowa Cove
Negley, Ohio 44441

Edited by Donna Spencer
Cover art and book design by Kristina Danklef, Sourballpython
Printed in the United States of America – Signature Book Printing

---

For further information on *When We're Singin'* Books' publications and availability visit our website at whenweresingin.com.

Miller, Johnny Ray, 1965–
When We're Singin': The Partridge Family & Their Music

ISBN: 978-0-692-75075-9

*For Mom and Dad.
I can feel your heartbeat.*

CONTENTS

Foreword by David Cassidy xii
Preface xiii
Author's Note xvii

Prologue

Three Birdseeds xix
Connie Partridge, Divorcée? xx
More Family Business xxiii
A Visit with the Cowsills xxv
What Are *You* Doing Here? xxvi
Casting xxvii
What Happens in Vegas xxxii
Green Light xxxiii

Chapter 1
The Breezy Beginning *or ... **The Partridge Family Album***

To Produce, or Not to Produce 3
Voices Singing 4
Monkee Business 9
What a Day 10
Enter Wes Farrell 11
David Can Sing! 13
Tracy's Voice 14
The Search for Songwriters 15
The Wrecking Crew 17
The Vocal Sessions 18
We're Better Together 20
I Really, *Really* Think I Love You 21
A Mini-Movie 21
A Theme Song 24
On the Air 25
Liner Notes: *The Partridge Family Album* 25

Chapter 2
Made for TV *or ... **The Partridge Family Up to Date***

Instant Fame 47
I'm on the Road? 48
Getting Together 50
Goodbye, Jeremy 52
Moving Mondrian 53
Nervous Mother Driving 55
Bus Sightings 55
Bus Legends 56
The Mystery of the Partridge Family Bus 57
Bus Stop: The Fanatic's Guide to the Partridge Family Bus 61
Matching Songs to Episodes 66
Liner Notes: *The Partridge Family Up to Date* 67

Chapter 3
The Defining Moment *or ... **The Partridge Family Sound Magazine***

Season 2: The Times They Are A-Changin' 87
Hello, Hello Brian! 90
Teens and Magazines 92
Bus Stop: *Tiger Beat's Official Partridge Family Magazine* 95
Posters and Pinups: The Friend Behind the Lens 102
The Smile Contest 105
Come On Get Happy! 106
On Location: Saving the Whales 107
Liner Notes: *The Partridge Family Sound Magazine* 110

Chapter 4
Generation X-mas *or ... **A Partridge Family Christmas Card***

A Unanimous Favorite 133
Bus Stop: Tony Romeo: A Christmas Baby 136
Christmas 1971 146
Yes, Virginia, There Is a Partridge Family 148
Liner Notes: *A Partridge Family Christmas Card* 148

Chapter 5
The Secret Formula *or … **The Partridge Family Shopping Bag***

The Merchandising Machine. 163
Patti/Kate, Patti/Kate 165
From the Personal Collection of…. 166
Cherish-ed 167
"Naked Lunch Box" 172
Bus Stop: The Memorabilia Store 175
Liner Notes: *The Partridge Family Shopping Bag* 181

Chapter 6
Keeping Up Is Hard to Do
*or … **The Partridge Family at Home with Their Greatest Hits***

A Real TV Family. 195
Branching Out. 201
The Partridge Family Neighborhood 202
Bus Stop: Wes Farrell: The Man with the Golden Ear 204
Liner Notes: *The Partridge Family at Home with Their Greatest Hits*. 215

Chapter 7
White Covers *or … **The Partridge Family Notebook***

Season 3: Status Quo 223
On Location: Roller Coasters 224
The Writer's Voice. 227
Bus Stop: Partridge Family Diaries 230
Rock Us, Baby 235
Liner Notes: *The Partridge Family Notebook*. 238

Chapter 8
Mellow Yellow *or … **The Partridge Family Crossword Puzzle***

Shirley Goes Solo 255
Danny's Turn. 258
Susan Dey's Recording Deal?. 259
Music Videos. 259
Western Recorders, Studio 2 264

Weekend at Wembley 268
Bus Stop: The Musicality of David Cassidy 269
The Price of Fame 276
Liner Notes: *The Partridge Family Crossword Puzzle* 277

Chapter 9
The Funky Finale *or ... The Partridge Family Bulletin Board*

Season 4: Reinvention. 289
The Boy Shirley Temple. 293
Bus Stop: *Ricky Segall & the Segalls* 296
On Location: The Cruise 299
Dreams and Wishes. 301
Liner Notes: *The Partridge Family Bulletin Board*. 304

Chapter 10
Across the Pond, Down Under, and Back
or ... The World of the Partridge Family

Cancellation 321
Bus Stop: Laughing with Dave Madden 324
To Australia, with Love 334
Cassidy Live! and *David Cassidy's Greatest Hits* 337
Bus Stop: The Most Inspired Fan Club. 338
Liner Notes: *The World of the Partridge Family* 342

Chapter 11
The Album Covers *or ... The Partridge Family TV Dinner*

Bell Records 349
The Music Agency. 352
The Album Designs. 353

Chapter 12
The Lost Songs *or ... The Partridge Family Garage Sale*

The Recording Sessions. 373
The Screen Gems Records 378

Colagé 379
Liner Notes: The Partridge Family Garage Sale (Lost Recordings) 380

Chapter 13
Life After Partridge *or ... The Partridge Family Time Capsule*

Moving On 409
The '80s: Partridge Who? 413
Partridges vs. Bradys 414
The Lost Reunion 415
'90s Retro 417
Nick at Nite New Year's Eve 419
Danny! 419
Partridge Pop Culture 420
Bus Stop: Sound Magazine, the Tribute Band 420
David Cassidy in the New Century 424
In Search of the Partridge Family 426
Ruby & the Rockits 428
The Partridge Family Live in Concert? 428
Becoming Classic TV 430
Becoming Classic Music 433
Where Are They Now? 437
What Is the Legacy of the Partridge Family? 438

Epilogue by Wes Farrell Jr. 443
Afterword by Brian Forster 445
Discography 447
Suggested Reading 451
Acknowledgments 452
Sources 456
Photo Credits 462

FOREWORD

As someone who was nineteen, inexperienced and working with professional musicians and songwriters, I was blessed to work with some of the greatest of all time.

I could never possibly replace the opportunity I was given during those years. It changed my life—they taught me so much.

I loved every moment of the experience and I shall never forget them or the music that still thrills me today.

Thanks, John, for your work with the book and your passions for the music.

David Cassidy
May, 2016

PREFACE

One of my earliest memories of buying records is the purchase of my first Partridge Family album. I was nine years old and my mother had taken me to Clarkins, a local department store in Canton, Ohio, long since out of business. I can still envision it. I picked up two Partridge Family albums from the bin, but I was only permitted to have one. I took it home and played it to death. I was discovering my love of music for the very first time. Luckily, the music that caught my attention was good music. *Really* good. And over 45 years later it has a loyal fan base who still loves it. The Partridge Family, as it turns out, has staying power.

I listened to those albums over and over, and I didn't understand why they sounded so much better than the other so-called teenybopper fare that was popular at the time. As an adult I came to understand the concept of artistic chemistry, and the layers of musical talent that went into making these records. I came to understand the power of marketing and its ability to create an image. While the image sold records, it also colored the perception of the music. The '70s cool cats and the musical elite wanted nothing to do with it, denying it as legitimate music.

But underneath its marketing stigma, the Partridge Family's music proved to be easy listening–adult contemporary music at its core, flavored for the early '70s pop scene, and it came at a time when easy listening was at its best. As a kid, I connected with the image that was cleverly marketed to my age bracket. Packaged deep within was the newly discovered lead vocalist that took the world by storm. David Cassidy has entranced millions with his musical versatility, both then and now. Cassidy's voice, so underrated, is among the greats of his generation. You know it the minute you hear it. But he was faced with a challenge in being taken seriously if he wanted a musical career of longevity.

When I first set out to write a book on the Partridge Family's music, I felt that tearing down the marketing image, revealing David Cassidy and all the other musicians, singers, and songwriters behind that image, must be the sole focus. But as I began to concentrate on the pure essence of the music, I came to realize that the image is actually part of what we love. It's nostalgic, and it's a very real part of the story, and it needed to be included as long as it could be broken down and examined separately for what it is.

The Partridge Family's image helps provide that escape and return to innocence I often crave. The advent of the Internet, social media, and the explosion of reality TV nearly forbids innocence today. In a world filled with skepticism and cynicism, I feel grateful that the Partridge Family music is as worthwhile as the projected innocence of their identity.

The marketing image is the easy part of the story. Digging deeper, I searched to unearth the stories and inspiration of nearly all the surviving songwriters who wrote for the Partridge Family. The real background singers also tell their stories with great pride for the music. The musicians, known as the Wrecking Crew, were an elite nucleus of Hollywood talent who worked on the greatest records of that era, including recordings by the Beach Boys, Elvis—and, yes, the Partridge Family. Many of them have also shared their insights and memories of creating the sound of the Partridge Family.

The idea for the book began as a result of the fans' desire (myself included) to have a well-researched book on the Partridge Family and their musical influence on the '70s. In 2009 I worked with David Cassidy on a concert booking in Franklin, Pennsylvania. I found him to be exactly the man he says he is—a man who, at heart, is just a normal guy. He was kind, grateful to his fans, and very personable and professional. But the mark he made on a generation supersedes normal in every aspect of the word. His talent and charisma, mixed with his normal-guy persona, make him the complicated man he really is. During my time with David he spoke of his work and his passions, and his love for his family. That conversation served as the catalyst which inspired me to begin work on this book.

The successful concert with David opened the next door for me: Shirley Jones. I needed her involvement if I was to continue forward. After an initial email sent to her office, I corresponded back and forth with her husband, Marty Ingels. Several weeks went by. Then one day I was standing at a grocery store checkout line, putting my items down on the conveyer belt, and my phone rang. On the other end I heard this voice say, "Hi, John. This is Shirley Jones." How do I explain to you exactly what that felt like? I dropped my groceries (unpaid) and literally walked away from the checkout line and went outside to the sidewalk. Trying to hold my quickly crumbling composure, I had a short conversation that ended with an invitation from Shirley to come to her home for the interview. Struggling to keep my cool, I said, "Sure, I'd love to," as I mouthed silently to myself *Oh my God!* So I hopped a flight very quickly, and before I knew it I was knocking at her front door. When she answered the door she was wearing casual clothes, no makeup, and she said, "Hi, John. Come on in. Please excuse me, I just came back from the gym." It was exactly like one of the greetings she made as Shirley Partridge when someone came to the door—I felt like I was walking into the Partridge Family home! Her dogs also greeted me, and then we sat in the living room for two or three hours just chatting about her memories of the show, the music, and the phenomenon of it all. She is one of the most graceful, elegant, and welcoming human beings one could ever hope to meet. She was everything you'd hope she might be. A class act. A true star. With that, the next door opened.

Dave Madden was so funny that I decided his interview would be most entertaining just as it is. I have included almost all of it in its original form. He joked about death, life, youth and aging. He also poked fun (lovingly) at his former castmates. At the end of the interview, he told me that he emailed with Susan Dey almost daily and he offered to contact her for me. In a very short time he got back to me and said, "Talked to Susan … She's not interested. I think when I told her you wanted a nude picture of her it turned her off. Don't feel rejected … She wouldn't pose for me either." *Yep, that's Dave!*

Danny Bonaduce spoke with me one morning after going off the air from one of his radio programs. He was very excited about the interview and the potential for a Partridge Family book. Only two days prior he had performed live in concert with David Cassidy, playing bass for real and singing "Doesn't Somebody Want to be Wanted" alongside Cassidy for the very first time in his life. He was even wearing crushed red velvet! When we spoke he was still on a high from the concert, and you could hear both the boy and the man in his voice as he talked about the Partridge Family, David Cassidy, and how special that time in his life was to him.

Brian Forster was very personal and grounded, and he had the clearest memories of filming the show. He is a great storyteller, able to create vivid pictures with his words. He even took photos of his Screen Gems records and rare acetates for use in this book. His tribute to Suzanne Crough is one of the most heartfelt you will ever read. The "two little kids," as they have often been dismissively called, mattered.

Jeremy Gelbwaks, the "first Chris," was also a pleasure. Even though he is probably the furthest removed from all things Partridge, he still had insightful comments and strong memories of his time on the show. He especially remembered his young friendship with Suzanne Crough, and asked me to put him in touch with her in hopes of reconnecting.

I probably spoke with Suzanne five or six times during the research phase, and the thing I remember most was the way she made me feel she'd known me her whole life. Like Danny, she was unguarded, as though she'd love to hang out and shoot the breeze on the back porch with you all evening long. During my first conversation with her I can still hear her telling me, "I just pulled up to the drive-through at Starbucks. Hang on a second." There was something casual and real about her that made me laugh, and I dropped my professional formality very quickly. I came to know her as a friend. I was astonished at her sudden passing. It is a tragedy that we lost her at such a young age.

Getting to know the real background vocalists was powerful. It put faces to the music that I have never seen before. When I hear the music of the Partridge Family now, I can actually envision Jackie Ward, Ron Hicklin, and John and Tom Bahler singing in the studio. I can see their voices in the music. John Bahler alone must have contributed over 10 hours of time in interviews with me, and countless emails. We first spoke when he was in his car traveling across the country with his wife, former Lennon Sister Janet. They had an entire day of travel ahead of them after playing a gig. He had Janet do the driving so he could talk to me in the car. He spent that entire drive talking in detail about his work as vocal arranger and everything that went into the making of these albums. We took a break about four hours in so he could stop at TGI Fridays for a bite to eat, and then he was back on the road and back on the phone with me for another three hours. Every so often I could hear Janet in the background singing "I Think I Love You" during a couple of his comments.

By summer of 2014 it came time to look for a book publisher. My good friend Ken Sharp suggested I take a look at Kickstarter.com. I had no idea what Kickstarter was. Ken felt I could raise funds based on the demand by the fans, who have always wanted a book about the Partridge Family. In doing so, I would keep control of production and offer up the book everyone wanted—one of substance and detail rather than an excess of commercialism. I spent nine months preparing for the campaign. Hundreds of items were signed by actors, singers, songwriters, musicians, producers, photographers, even Bell Records VPs. They were offered to the fans as campaign donation rewards. On June 1, 2015, we won the campaign, raising over $27,000 to produce this limited edition book in hard cover, with 64 color photo pages included. The fans had spoken.

For all the stories behind the music, I have also included countless stories of the show as told by the producers and cast, many of them for the first time. The music is as much a part of the show as the show is part of the music. Longevity proves the music stands on its own, but together with its warm television image, the Partridge Family is truly America's first and foremost TV family garage band.

Johnny Ray Miller
October, 2016

AUTHOR'S NOTE

The bulk of this work is based on interviews conducted by the author between 2009 and 2015. Quotations from these interviews are presented in present tense. Quotations from all other sources, including interviews, magazines, newspapers, and videos—are presented in past tense.

Sadly, several people interviewed for this book have since passed away, including Dave Madden, Mike Melvoin, Larry Rosen, and Suzanne Crough. For the purposes of clarity, their stories are quoted in the present tense along with the other primary interviews.

PROLOGUE

Before there was music, there was a family. Then the family made music—or seemingly so. Before we heard the music, we met the family. Or was it the other way around?

Three Birdseeds

Series creator Bernard Slade is originally from Canada, where he began his career writing variety shows. "I did a [variety] show up in Canada called *The Big Coin Sound*, which was about a musical group," recalls Slade. "It was about three guys and a girl doing music together. The idea for *The Partridge Family* maybe started there, somewhere," he says. "I started thinking that it would be a good idea to mix situation comedy with music." The idea of a singing family as the basis for a sitcom had not been done before.

The Sound of Music was all the rage in the theater and at the movies during the 1960s. The film version was released in 1965, adapted from the 1959 Broadway play by Richard Rogers and Oscar Hammerstein II—who, coincidentally, had made Shirley Jones a star in musical film adaptations of *Oklahoma!* (1955), *Carousel* (1956), and *The Music Man* (1962). *The Sound of Music* showcased Julie Andrews in one of the most memorable performances of her career. It tells the story of the Trapp Family Singers, a real-life singing family from Salzburg, Austria. Bernard Slade took notice. His singing-family seed was now further pollinated. The idea he had been toying with was beginning to take root, and when Slade moved to the States that root began to grow deeper.

"One night I was watching *The Tonight Show* and there was this group on," says Slade. "They were a real family." That family was the real-life singing and recording act known as the Cowsills. Different from the Trapp Family Singers, this was a U.S. pop group with a real-life mom singing hit pop tunes alongside her six children, while yet another sibling worked as manager. This group was most notable to Slade because they made records.

The Cowsills were all over the pop charts during the late 1960s. They were also popping up on television everywhere, appearing on *The Dick Cavett Show*, *The*

Johnny Cash Show, *The Hollywood Palace*, and *Kraft Music Hall*, all in 1969 alone. They even starred in their own television special in 1968, *A Family Thing*.

Slade was contracted to come up with three pilot submissions each year for Screen Gems, the television subsidiary of Columbia Pictures Industries. "I thought that this was a good idea for a show—a family group involved in doing records," says Slade. "So I put it all together and presented it to Screen Gems." And Screen Gems liked it. They liked it a lot! After all, Slade had given them hits like *The Flying Nun* (1967–1970) and *Love on a Rooftop* (1966–1967). He was given the green light on his proposed singing family, which he originally titled *Family Business*.

The first scene he envisioned for the show involved middle child Danny trying to convince the yet-to-be manager, Reuben Kincaid, to sign the family on as a client. The scene takes place in an airport men's bathroom, in which Danny knocks on all the stalls until he locates the right one, then slips a tape recorder with the family's first recording, "Let the Good Times In," underneath the door.

Slade's stylistic vision would resurface in many of the scripts he wrote for the show, which usually involved Danny. Slade says he works fast once he gets started, and he gets bored quickly with writing too many scripts for one series. He looks forward to moving on to the next project. Slade wrote short of a dozen scripts for *The Partridge Family*. It was Dale McRaven, story editor through most of the series' four-year run, who would bring consistency as the style and characters developed.

It's often been said that *The Partridge Family* was based on the Cowsills, but it was really more thought out than that. "It really *wasn't* based on the Cowsills," says Slade. "I just happened to see this group on *The Tonight Show* and I thought that it wouldn't be a bad idea to do a family thing." For Slade, the fact remains that the Cowsills was merely one of three inspirations—along with *The Big Coin Sound* and the Trapp Family Singers—merging together into the final idea and the impetus to write the pilot script.

Connie Partridge, Divorcée?

Slade came up with the name Partridge for his soon-to-be famous family, based on a friendship with a childhood soccer buddy. "Partridge was a kid I went to school with in England," he says. "I thought it was an unusual name and I wanted a name like that—something that would stick. So we used that name and it sort of took off."

His next order of business was to sit down and flesh out the characters for his new Screen Gems assignment. First on deck was the role of the mother. Originally the character's name was intended to be Connie. Slade also envisioned the Partridge matriarch as a divorced woman—not because he was trying to make a statement, but simply because it was different. It opened up the possibilities for storylines in ways a married couple could not. "If you have someone's husband hanging around it gets in the way of the plots," Slade explains. "It was always the same setup during those days—that someone had died—and we didn't want to do that again, so we thought we'd make her divorced."

But the divorced mother was a bit too risky by network standards in 1969, so mother Partridge joined the ranks of widowed television moms. Paul Junger Witt, who would soon join the team as a producer, reflects back on the early months of preproduction. "Were talking about 40-plus years ago," Witt says. "There were not many divorced people on television. Norman Lear [*All in the Family*] was just getting new shows on the air, so we had yet to see television begin to reflect the realities of the time, although that lag was made up quickly. I'm sure advertisers, the studio, and everyone felt more secure with a widow than a divorcée."

The originality of Shirley Partridge was still groundbreaking, representing one of the first single working mothers on television. She would sing with her children, both out on the road and locally, in and around the fictional San Pueblo, a small town in northern California, where the Partridge Family home was set. Slade wrote the part of Shirley Partridge as a grounding force for the kids—the glue that would hold the family together—which Shirley Jones took very seriously.

Eldest son Keith was envisioned as a kind, sweet boy, dependable enough for his mom to lean on from time to time. The character's name had its roots within Slade's own family ties. "Keith was the name of my daughter's boyfriend at the time," says Slade. "That's where that name came about." The character of Keith was developed with more vision by Dale McRaven as the first season went along. The producers, with the guidance of McRaven, worked hard at keeping Keith's character human. They didn't want Keith to be a super-successful teen idol in the real-life way it eventually began playing out for David Cassidy.

Daughter Laurie, named after Slade's daughter, was intended as a sort of intellectual, reflecting the times as the nation headed into the free-spirited '70s. Feminism was beginning to take hold in the mainstream, and Laurie would represent that section of youth screaming for recognition as individuals, with their own new ideas of freedom, liberty, and personal identity. From a commercial standpoint, Slade also knew Laurie—played by 17-year-old model Susan Dey—would appeal to young boys, just as Keith would to the girls.

The infamous middle child, 10-year-old Danny, was written as the centerpiece for wit and sarcasm. He was given lines that were far beyond the mindset of any normal 10-year old, and the character was clearly the focal point of the comedy during the freshman year of the show. Danny was the brains behind the business of getting the family discovered. The "40-year-old midget" worried about money, fame, and success more than the average fifth grader, always giving his mom constant impetus to reign him in.

when we're singin'

"Danny was the main focus of this play simply because he was funny," says Slade. Danny was originally envisioned with dark, wiry hair, based on a child actor named Barry Gordon, who Slade saw in a stage production of *A Thousand Clowns*. (Gordon is most notable for his childhood recording of "Nuttin' for Christmas," which hit No. 6 on the *Billboard* charts in 1955.) The original vision for Danny was a far cry from the sarcastic, sharp-witted character that was soon to emerge through the talents of the young and undiscovered Danny Bonaduce.

When executive producer Bob Claver was familiarizing himself with the script and characters, it was easy for him to imagine the family without the two youngest children, Chris and Tracy. Claver would have been happy with only three children. But Slade's vision included five children, and that vision was kept intact. Chris (named after another of Slade's children) and Tracy filled the picture out nicely.

"Bernie wanted, and kind of copied, the causes and structure," according to Claver, meaning that the show was intended to draw the biggest audience possible. "Bernie felt we shouldn't do the show with just three kids." Slade admits the design of the show was commercially planned so there would be something for everyone. One could have hoped for more story lines focused on Chris and Tracy, but the other actors quickly broke out as stars in their own right. Outside writers submitted script ideas based on the characters that inspired them, which most of the time involved Danny. The demand for attention on Shirley, David, Susan, and Danny left little screen time for the two little ones.

Rounding out the pack was neurotic manager Reuben Kincaid, who would be played by Dave Madden. "I wanted somebody who would cut the sweetness a bit," recalls Slade. "So we came up with Reuben, and he and Danny would have this relationship together that would be fostered." Between the wisecracking Danny and the cynical Reuben, there was no shortage of comedy. The characters of Shirley, Reuben, and Danny were well-developed from the very beginning, but the breakout star power of David Cassidy and Susan Dey was soon to take hold, and subsequently their characters began to develop.

Simone the dog was tossed in as well. Slade had a dog named Simon, so he changed the name slightly because the Partridge pooch was female-later replaced by a male! Simone was featured primarily on the first season, though she can be spotted briefly during the second season by die-hard fans who know where to look. Simone was given her single starring performance in episode 8, "The Memory Lingers On," in which she would do battle (and lose) with a skunk. It was also the episode that introduced "I Think I Love You," which was already at No. 7 on the *Billboard* charts when the show aired. Slade wrote the episode based on an incident that happened in his own family. But the difficulty of working with animals on the set, together with the realization that story lines were going to be plentiful without Simone, led producers to eliminate the pet.

PROLOGUE

A few recurring characters appeared on the show from time to time, including Reuben's on-and-off girlfriend, Bonnie Kleinschmidt (Elaine Giftos, four appearances); Danny's best friend, Punky Lazaar (Gary Dubin, six appearances); and Danny's first sweetheart, Gloria Hickey (Patti Cohoon, two appearances). Most notable were the occasional appearances of Grandma and Grandpa (Rosemary DeCamp, four appearances, and Ray Bolger, three appearances). Slade wrote the part of Grandpa based on his own father. Bolger and DeCamp were prominent and celebrated actors in their day. They made their first appearance on episode 3, "Whatever Happened to the Old Songs?"

While Rosemary DeCamp appeared as Grandma in all four guest spots, Ray Bolger appeared in only three, with Jackie Coogan replacing him in the final season's appearance. Most famous for his role as the Scarecrow in *The Wizard of Oz*, Bolger brought a lot of excitement to the set, especially for the child actors.

Bernie Applebaum (Gerald Hiken, two appearances) was the family doctor, showing a romantic interest in Shirley, but it was based in the comedy that it was his idea more than Shirley's. Bert Convy also appeared twice as Shirley's love interest Richard Lawrence.

Despite the fleshing out of the characters and premise, at this point little thought had been given to the element of the show that was about to claim stardom in its own right—the music.

More Family Business

In the meantime, what would eventually become one of the biggest real-life musical families in Hollywood was beginning to emerge: the Cassidy family. The patriarch was the legendary Jack Cassidy, from Richmond Hill, New York, who had established himself as a Broadway actor (most notably in the 1963 production of *She Loves Me*). He was married to actress Evelyn Ward, and they had one child together. They named him David.

Life in the theater can present challenges to relationships and families, and Jack Cassidy was not immune to those influences. He was on the road a lot, trying to make a living, when he found himself taken by a young, beautiful emerging talent. Cassidy eventually fell in love with the sparkling actress, who was beginning to take America by storm. Her name was Shirley Jones. She was from Smithton, Pennsylvania, and received her first big break as Laurey in the film version of *Oklahoma!*

The two married after carrying out an old-fashioned courtship amid the glamour of the 1950s movie industry. Together, Shirley and Jack had three children, all boys. Shaun was the first, born in 1958 in Los Angeles. He was soon followed by Patrick, born in 1962, and finally the youngest, Ryan, who came along in 1966.

when we're singin'

When *The Partridge Family* was on the air, Shaun, Patrick, and Ryan were all quite young and impressionable. "Oh, they loved the show!" recalls Shirley Jones. "Shaun was on the set all the time. He was very interested in what David was doing and obviously it hit home for him because he went right on to do the same thing," she says with great pride, although she admits she strongly discouraged her children from pursuing show business careers.

Shaun Cassidy eventually landed the role of Joe Hardy in the ABC television series *The Hardy Boys/Nancy Drew Mysteries*, which premiered in 1977 and ran for three seasons. The influence of David's musical success with *The Partridge Family* inspired Shaun, and he was soon launching his own musical career as the next Cassidy teen idol during the latter part of the 1970s. Patrick and Ryan also grew up to establish successful careers within the entertainment industry.

Young David Cassidy lived his adolescence on the East Coast with his mother until they both moved to Los Angeles in 1961. Like many children from divorced families, David never really knew his father's second wife. He initially figured her as an evil stepmother, but from the moment he met her he could not help liking her. "I first met Shirley when I was about seven," said Cassidy in 1971. "I was all prepared not to like her, but it was impossible because Shirley was like a fairy godmother to me. And the more we work together, the more I respect her. She's so thoroughly professional. We're really good friends. I would feel the same way if she were not married to my father." Cassidy had no idea what he was about to embark on during his wild run from 1970 to 1974, and Jones would be a grounding force, a go-to person when he needed support and stability amid the craziness of sudden fame, superstardom, and a distant father from whom he craved approval.

Jones rounded out the late 1960s looking for a way to be home with her children. Family always was—and still is—the most important thing to her. In early 1969 she began to put the word on the street that she was looking for work that would allow her to be home in the evenings on a regular basis. That would mean television work.

In the late 1960s movie stars did not often do television, and most of Jones' industry friends and business cohorts discouraged her from doing so. "To do a television series at that time was a big no-no for film actors," she explains. "Agents, managers, everybody said, 'Shirley, don't do a television series! You're a movie star!' That's the way they felt then and talked then, you know. They said that if it is successful, I would be that character for the rest of my life. 'You'll never do another film!' they said. Well, they were somewhat right about that!" She laughs as she looks back with a genuine sense of humor and humility.

Jones had her priorities and she knew what mattered to her. Sure, she says, doing a television sitcom halted her movie career for a long while, but what she received instead was two families. She came to think of her television family with great love, respect, and care for all of the people who were involved, just as if they were her own. How she handled that over the course of *The Partridge Family*'s four-year run would prove to be the glue for everyone involved. As times have changed and the advent of independent filmmaking has taken hold, Shirley Jones has recaptured an audience for her work on the big screen as well as the small.

A Visit with the Cowsills

It's easy to understand why the Cowsills are often cited as the creative inspiration for *The Partridge Family*, because the team producing the pilot initially visited the Cowsills to see if they might be suitable contenders as actors for the Partridge Family characters. Even more importantly, their musical sound would be a huge influence on that of the Partridge Family. The Cowsills were scoring big on the pop music charts during the late '60s with hits like "Indian Lake," written by future Partridge Family hitmaker Tony Romeo. Other hits included "The Rain, the Park and Other Things," "We Can Fly," and their biggest smash, "Hair," the title song from the groundbreaking Broadway musical of the same name, which reached No. 2 on *Billboard* and No. 1 on *Cash Box* in 1969. The Cowsills' chart-topping status with pop songs like these led ABC executives to encourage the producers developing *The Partridge Family* to pay them a visit.

The Cowsills began their career in Newport, Rhode Island, and lived there at the time the *Partridge Family* pilot was in the works. Bob Claver left no stone unturned during the casting of the show. "Bernie Slade and I actually went back East to see them," he says.

The mission was to see if this successful singing family's acting skills and screen charisma were as appealing as their harmonic voices, potentially springing a television show onto the airwaves featuring the real-life family in the roles of the Partridges. But the Cowsills were primarily singers. In the end, the producers felt they needed to cast real actors, leaving the singing to be dubbed by studio singers. "The show was supposed to *be* the Cowsills," recalls Shirley Jones. "But what the producers came to learn was that they weren't actors. You see, that was the problem. They were wonderful as the singers and as the band, but they just weren't actors."

Bob Claver emphasizes the point. "After spending very little time with them we realized there was only one person with any [screen] talent and that was the little girl. The rest of them were not actors, so we got in the car and said, 'We just have to forget this forever.'" It would have been a brilliant marketing coup if such clever casting had been possible.

Convincing the network executives to leave the producers alone to do their thing isn't always easy during the early development of a series. "When management gets its hand into things, first of all they usually don't know what they're talking about," says Claver. "But in this case they finally walked away from it once we got some tape with the real family on it. The Cowsills were nice kids and a nice family. They were just not talented actors." Claver and Slade returned to Hollywood and went on the search for actors.

"I think there were some disagreements and they were obviously very upset in the beginning," says Shirley Jones on the initial reaction of the Cowsills, a family she clearly holds in affection. "I got to know them later on," she adds. "As a matter of fact, I once did a benefit for their older brother, who had cancer. They were raising money for him. I have a big picture of them and they signed it to me!"

What Are *You* Doing Here?

Surprises were plentiful during the casting of *The Partridge Family*. The casting search seemed to bring one twist after another.

"I was the first person cast for the show," begins Shirley Jones. "They wanted me to read with all of the little kids and do a tape on them and so forth. So they came to me one day while I was sitting in the dressing room. I had been taping with all of the little kids that day and they said, 'Shirley, how do you feel about your stepson, David Cassidy?' And I said, 'What do you mean, how do I feel about him?' They said, 'Do you have a good relationship with him?' I said, 'Oh, yes! In fact I have a better relationship with him now that he's grown up than I did when he was little, because it was a sad time for him then, and he didn't know why his father left his mother and all of that. He's a very talented young man!' They said, 'We're very happy to hear that because we think we're going to cast him in the role of Keith Partridge.' I said, 'That would be great!'

"Now, he didn't know that I was cast. So I came on the set and he was waiting to do a test with the kids. They didn't tell him, you know, and he looked at me and said, 'What are *you* doing here?' I said, 'I'm your mama!'" Shirley laughs, wide and broad. "He said, 'What?'"

The *Partridge Family* casting director and former vice president of casting at Columbia Pictures, Renée Valente, has her own memories of this situation. Valente was a relatively new casting director on the scene in Los Angeles at the time *The Partridge Family* was being put together. She had come from New York, where she had begun her career. Valente was the first person to read David Cassidy for the part.

"When David got the show, the interesting story is that I did not know he was the son of Jack Cassidy and Shirley Jones," recalls Valente. "Shirley and I were certainly good friends, not social friends but rather business friends."

PROLOGUE

Valente was just getting to know the faces and names on the West Coast. "I found out a bit later that David's manager, Ruth Aarons, was also the manager for Shirley Jones," she continues. "So Ruth called me and she says she has another client she thinks would be great for the show, and his name is David Cassidy. You know, Cassidy is a very common name, and I didn't put the two together. So David came to see me, and he was just delicious! He was just cute as could be! I read him and he did very, very well. So I screen-tested him, and when the powers that be saw the test, they wanted him.

"It was then, after that, that Shirley came to me and said, 'I've got to trust you with something.' I said OK, and she told me that he was her son. She knew that we who were vice presidents, or people who worked for the company, were not allowed to use anybody's relatives. That was in all contracts, not just Columbia. You couldn't hire anyone in your family. So I said to Shirley, 'You know if anyone finds out, my job is over, and God knows what would happen to David.' So we could never tell anybody this. And we didn't!"

The story then turns even further. "David didn't tell me he was related to Shirley when he came in to read, so when it was finally over, I called David and I said, 'You kept it very well hidden. Now you have to keep it even more hidden!'

"The thing that comes to mind every time I think of *The Partridge Family* is that we went through with this ruse and no one ever found out. It was this whole thing we decided to do so that heads would not roll. And then, when it got out of the bag somehow, everybody was just so happy with the success and what Screen Gems and everyone else was making off of it financially. It was just a major, major hit!" The studio got a lot of mileage out of publicizing the fact that David and Shirley were real-life mom and stepson, to the point that the facts were being blurred over the reality that David was Shirley's stepson, and his real mother was actually Evelyn Ward, a dancer and actress in her own right.

Casting

In the early stages of development, Bob Claver and Bernard Slade worked closely together. Once the Cowsills had been eliminated as a casting possibility, the giant task of assembling a brew of kids to work with Shirley Jones was under way. Claver brought on the young, enthusiastic Paul Junger Witt as a producer for the show. Witt was in the early stages of his career, having previously worked as producer under Claver on the Bobby Sherman smash *Here Come the Brides* (1968–1970). He was now working closely with Slade and Claver on the huge task of casting *The Partridge Family*.

when we're singin'

Shirley Jones

"Shirley was a major Hollywood star," recalls Paul Witt. "We were thrilled that she would even consider doing television. It was not a time when many movie stars were making that move. But Shirley found the material appealing, and we were thrilled to have her, and also—she could sing! That helped with our credibility in that area."

Shirley Jones was a major box-office draw during the '50s and '60s. She even won an Oscar as Best Supporting Actress for *Elmer Gantry* in 1960, but *The Partridge Family* brought Shirley pop culture notoriety like she had never imagined. "She could sing, she had the look, and you could believe her as a mother," says Renée Valente. "She had all the prerequisites. It was just fortunate that she loved the idea, and she was ready. I first saw her in *Carousel*, and I knew her from New York so it was easy for me to contact her. She was really the first and only choice. That normally doesn't happen."

"Jack and I went back to New York to do a play together called *Maggie Flynn*," begins Jones. "It was the late '60s, and we lived in New York for four or five months. Unfortunately the play only lasted about seven months, and then I came home to California. I remember I did a television show, and that's when the offer for the series happened."

Just prior to *The Partridge Family*, Jones had starred in an NBC made-for-TV Christmas movie, *Silent Night, Lonely Night*, which aired in December 1969. It garnered her an Emmy nomination—a first for Jones, and something that would not happen again until 2006. Incidentally, it is one of her favorite movies of her film career. Jones worked on three more films before *The Partridge Family* began airing.

"They offered me *The Brady Bunch* first and I turned that down," Jones says. "There wasn't anything in it for me that I hadn't done before. Then the offer for *The Partridge Family* came. Now that was interesting to me because, number one, it had music in it. I was also the first working mother on television. I wouldn't just be wearing the apron bringing the roast out of the oven, you know? It was a more interesting character. The fact that she was trying to keep family together any way she could was something I found interesting."

Jones was also impressed with the way the kids' roles were written. "The kids were today's kids," she says. "They were kids that had their own personalities and did their own thing, and yet still had to be mothered. The other big reason for doing it was that I had been all over the world on movie locations for so long, and I had three young children. They were school age now, and I just couldn't go away any more. I just had to settle down and be a mom. I wanted to go to the meetings. I wanted to help. It was very important to me. I knew the show would give me the opportunity, if it was successful, to stay home and work."

PROLOGUE

The role wasn't much of a stretch for Jones. She had children of her own; she worked in show business and still put her family values first. As Shirley Partridge, she treated her fictional children in much the same way Shirley Jones, the actress, was raising her own kids. She was so much the perfect choice that other legendary actresses who wanted the part, allegedly including Jane Powell, were turned down. "I'm sure we considered other people," says Paul Witt, "but I do remember how thrilled we were when Shirley came into the picture. Once she entered the picture we didn't consider anyone else."

Despite Jones' celebrity status, Bob Claver had his own quiet thoughts on the matter. "I had reservations for a while that Shirley would be right, because she's just a nice lady," he says. "Sometimes you want to have somebody with a little fire and she didn't have that, but she was perfect for this show." Perfect she was, indeed—so much so that once the series took off, children across the country would travel to California, figure out where she lived, camp out on her lawn and ask Shirley if she would become their mother.

David Cassidy

While Shirley and Jack Cassidy were out on the road doing *Maggie Flynn*, Jack's son David was back East landing his first Broadway show in *The Fig Leaves Are Falling*, which opened on January 2, 1969, and closed two days later. But it was enough to get him seen by a casting director, and back to Los Angeles he went to audition for a film role that he lost to Michael Douglas. But David Cassidy was just getting started.

Jack set David up under the guidance and management of Ruth Aarons, who had successfully managed both Jack and Shirley's careers. David immediately began to get work in the West Coast television scene, establishing himself as a serious young actor with some legitimate television roles on various hour-long dramas. His first TV appearance was on the short-lived nighttime soap *The Survivors*, airing in 1969 and starring Lana Turner. It was modeled after the success of *Peyton Place* but never grabbed the public's solid interest. He then landed roles on *Ironside; The FBI; Marcus Welby, M.D.; Adam-12; Bonanza; Medical Center;* and *Mod Squad*. Reluctant to take the part of Keith Partridge and get into situation comedy, Cassidy had a serious sit-down with both his father and Ruth Aarons.

He wanted to do more sophisticated work like his recent TV guest star appearances. He wanted to be taken as a serious actor and he was absolutely opposed to the character of Keith. Both his manager and father convinced him to do the show because they felt it was a great opportunity for him. Through the years, Cassidy has famously joked about the simplistic dialogue that didn't go beyond asking mom

when we're singin'

to borrow the keys to the bus. He had no idea what a musical superstar he would become and what a bus ride it would be!

Susan Dey

Susan Dey was cast as Laurie after an extensive search that went all the way back to New York City. Bob Claver wasn't finding what he wanted in L.A., so he sent Paul Witt out on the hunt. "We were delighted to have found Susan," says Witt. "New York always had this extraordinary and rich base of actors—adults and children." Dey had been working in New York as a teenage model and had appeared in various commercials and magazines for girls. She appeared on the covers of *Seventeen, American Girl,* and *Simplicity.*

Renée Valente shares her early memories of the young beauty. "Susan was from New York and she came to L.A. to see if anything could happen. Somebody had her meet with me, and I really thought she was terrific. We tested her because we thought she would fit in with the family so well. Susan lived with her father in Westchester County, New York, and her father did not want her to stay in L.A. and go into a series," adds Valente. "I think he wanted her to continue with her education. She was maybe 17 at the time. I had to talk to her father and assure him I would look after her, have her at my home, and just make sure she had someone to come to that was not only a VP but also a friend."

Valente cared for all the actors as both people as well as professionals, and would always lend her support, making every effort to be there on a personal level. "I had both Susan and David Cassidy at the house many, many times," she says.

Since Dey was underage, Jane Joyce, a friend from her hometown of Mount Kisko, New York, shared a two-bedroom house with Dey and went to the set with her as her legal guardian until she turned 18 in December 1970.

Danny Bonaduce

It seemed as if the role of Danny Partridge was written specifically for Danny Bonaduce, with his comic timing and uncanny ability to deliver very adult lines—often without really knowing what he was saying.

But the perfect casting didn't come without a lot of effort on the producers' part. "We saw massive numbers of people for the kids' parts," recalls Paul Junger Witt. It all boiled down to two groups of kids in the end. Danny Bonaduce was part of the group they decided against, but Bob Claver saw the talent of this young boy and believed in him fiercely. Bernard Slade, also very involved with the casting, agreed wholeheartedly with Claver. So Claver pulled Bonaduce from one group and put him with the other group he wanted to use, which took some convincing. "Everybody liked the other kid," recounts Claver. "I forget his name—Joe something-or-other—and I thought they were all nuts. I said, 'That kid's never going to make you laugh. Danny's funny!' And he was funny! Finally, the head of the jury at Screen Gems said, 'I'm giving you your way. You're the executive producer. It's your show. If you're wrong, it's your fault.' But when we went on the air, Danny was gold."

"I knew I had that job," says Danny Bonaduce. "I only had about five television jobs before that. They were like one-time episodes on the *The Ghost and Mrs. Muir, Mayberry R.F.D.,* and *Bewitched*. I had maybe one or two lines on those shows. By this time I was 12. When I walked in there and did the audition, I walked out and I told my mom, 'We've got this one.' I said, 'I want to stop at the motorcycle store,' because she and my dad promised me a minibike if I got the part. I said, 'We should just stop off and pick one out, cause we've got it.' When we got home the phone was ringing. 'You got it!' they said. There was no missing I had this one."

Jeremy Gelbwaks and Suzanne Crough

Young Jeremy Gelbwaks was cast in the role of the family drummer, little Chris Partridge, having had only a small taste of show business before landing the role. "I remember poking around and auditioning," says Gelbwaks. "I had a couple of commercials, including a Pringles commercial where we dressed like the Founding Fathers! It was the introduction for Pringles potato chips. They shot the commercial in two days and it was a big, big production. I don't know whether the product was pulled or the commercial was pulled, but in any case it never aired. The only other thing I ever did [before *The Partridge Family*] was a bit on a variety show.

"There was a comedian named Pat Paulsen, and *[Pat Paulsen's Half a Comedy Hour]* was done in the style of *Rowan & Martin's Laugh-In*. There was a scene where Pat was playing the husband or television repairman, and Angie Dickinson was the housewife. Paulsen was fussing with the TV, and all of a sudden there was a big electrical shock. Then he emerged in the next scene, short, and without any teeth!" Jeremy laughs. "I was the little him. They put me in a bald wig, and gave me candy teeth to spit out! I enjoyed that!"

As it turns out, Gelbwaks' casting for *The Partridge Family* had a bit of a twist to it. "During the screen test, I actually tested for the tambourine player, and there was a girl playing the drums," he says. "I was eventually cast as the drummer."

Suzanne Crough was the youngest to be cast, at only age six. Her memories of the audition process are understandably sketchy, but fun for her to recount. "I do remember the audition process," says Crough. "I just remember that it got down to a couple of girls after going back so many times, and I remember

when we're singin'

I knew, when they were talking, that I already had the job. I don't know if someone said so, but I remember sitting on one of the guys' laps and I knew I had the job, even though the other girl was there. The memory of it is all kind of bizarre. I don't know who told me this, but I heard that there was possibly a girl before me that was cast for two days or so, and it didn't work out, but I never had that confirmed."

Though Chris and Tracy were important to the show, they ultimately didn't get many story lines. "They were very young and inexperienced," recalls Paul Witt, "and so you write to the people you know can deliver the most, especially on that kind of shooting schedule." Bob Claver agrees. "We got these two kids—nice kids. They couldn't be more likeable, and they were fine for our needs."

Dave Madden

Bernard Slade knew Dave Madden prior to casting. Slade thought of Madden right away and figured he'd be great for the part of the haphazard manager and Danny's comedic sidekick, Reuben Kincaid. "They needed someone ugly because Susan and David were so good-looking," jokes Madden. Paul Witt praised Madden's professionalism on the show. "Here was this pro, this consummate pro, working mostly with kids. He worked great with Shirley. They were almost equal in experience. But Dave's patience in working with the kids—especially the comedic relationship he developed with Danny—was a gift. He was also temperamentally suited in that he was a sweet, patient man." Dave Madden was a regular on *Rowan & Martin's Laugh-In* in 1969, just prior to landing the Partridge gig. He was also a regular on the mid-'60s series *Camp Runamuck*.

The casting of *The Partridge Family* was now done. Executive producer Bob Claver had got his way. There were five kids, all unknown, the experienced Dave Madden, and the superstar Shirley Jones, who was the only one with any known ability to actually sing. There was no musical audition, vocal or instrumental, for any of the actors cast in the show. The plan for the music strictly involved lip-syncing.

What Happens in Vegas...

In the pilot episode, the cast makes their musical debut at Caesars Palace in Las Vegas. The comedy behind the premise was unmistakable, but finding a casino that would agree to work with them was very difficult for the producers.

"I remember going to Las Vegas and talking to casino managers," recalls Paul Witt, "most of whom said, 'This isn't what we do.'" Witt was scoping out a family-friendly location they could use to shoot part of the pilot. Las Vegas in 1969 was still very much geared to adult lifestyles. "'No. We don't want to do it.' That was our initial response," says Witt, "but the people at Caesars came through for us."

"The only memories I have of the pilot are the scenes we shot in Las Vegas," says Jeremy Gelbwaks. "I distinctly remember driving down what was the Strip in those days, which is quite different than it is now. The marquees were the old-style marquees with the plastic letters, and I remember seeing "The Partridge Family" on one of them. It was a long time ago, in the old Las Vegas of that era, when someone had to go up a ladder to put those letters on the marquee. Of course it was all totally fictional, but they needed it for the establishing shot. Pretty cool."

Proving to management that the Cowsills were not appropriate to fill the roles of the children was only one of several battles Bob Claver faced as he shaped the look and feel of the series. What else did they want—or not want, as the case may be? "They didn't want Danny in the pilot, is what they didn't want," says Claver. "They wanted the other kid. But there were people in management on my side too, obviously, because I did win that argument. If they were going to be stubborn about it, all I could have said was that I wouldn't do the show—and that's not going to win you anything, because they'll say 'big deal.' That's how the business works.

"People don't realize that all of these production companies were family-owned and family-oriented in that era," he says. "It was the Paramounts, the Warner Brothers, the Columbias, and all of the rest of them. It was a whole different thing then. That's not necessarily always good, but that's what it was. Television was a new leg up for an industry that already existed. In other words, you had a production company, you had lots of soundstages, you had lots of people that were working for you, and they just moved television into it. It moved in very easily for them because they were already in that business. Those companies that started out were major motion picture production companies, and still are in many cases."

Claver had a long list of credits by the time he was signed on to *The Partridge Family*. He was coming right off the successful Bobby Sherman series *Here Come the Brides* as executive producer. He served as producer on several shows during the '60s, including *Occasional Wife, The Second Hundred Years,* and *The Farmer's Daughter*. Claver also served as executive producer for *The Interns,* premiering the same fall as *The Partridge Family,* but it was canceled fairly quickly. Ironically, Claver thought *The Interns* would be the one to succeed over *The Partridge Family*.

Green Light

According to Paul Witt, the screenings for a TV pilot usually happen at the network. The executives and decision makers sit down, watch the proposed program, and decide its fate. Bob Claver worked hard at putting the pilot together, which was the period of development where the studios haven't yet handed complete control over to the producers. When a show starts off, the network executives who consider giving it the green light are watching closely. But once the series took hold, Claver says, there wasn't much attempt at interference. "The most attempt at interference was when we were casting the pilot," he recalls. "That was really tough. Once we got on the air and they saw the kind of reviews and ratings we received, they didn't want to bother us at all." Ironically, it was Danny's performance—the very performance Claver believed in and fought for—that was one of the most likeable and marketable factors. Paul Witt recalls the higher-ups wanting much more of him.

"Danny was a truly gifted comedic actor," says Witt. "As such, he had an almost disproportionate load to carry in the first year. We depended on him as our go-to funny guy, along with Dave Madden and their on-screen relationship. Danny was truly gifted in comedy for his age. For kids to have timing, to understand, to have an instinct for comedy, is very unusual."

Shirley Jones agrees. "Danny and Ron Howard were the two best child actors I've ever worked with," she says. "Danny was brilliant. His sense of comedy at that young age was so extraordinary that I would just stand back and say 'wow,' and his onscreen relationship with the family manager was so great."

Even Susan Dey has commented on this, during a touching moment when she called in for a short interview with Bonaduce on the premiere episode of his short-lived talk show, *Danny!*, in 1995. "I can remember the pilot," Dey told him. "You know those executives that use to stand around in the suits? I can remember them shaking their heads and talking about you. 'That kid,' they'd say. 'That kid—he is so funny. His timing is so great.' I think you had a lot to do with selling that pilot."

Shirley Jones had more than a lot to do with selling the pilot—she had everything to do with it. The suits knew very well that the middle-age demographic would tune in for Jones. She was a Hollywood heavyweight. David Cassidy was still relatively unknown, but that was about to change quite dramatically.

The original unaired pilot ran about three-and-a-half minutes longer than actual air time, so a few cuts and changes were made. Once the green light was given, 14 episodes were initially slated for filming. The pilot cuts included editing out a few of Laurie's lines, including a reference to dad at Christmas. It was the only reference to the late Mr. Partridge, aside from Shirley's opening narration used to set up the premise of the show. According to Bob Claver, it was unnecessary for the characters to mention the father after the first episode, because they didn't want any looking back. It was fine to show it to the executives in order to sell the premise, but Claver felt it would limit the possibilities for Jones' character and story lines once the show hit the airwaves.

The last scene on the pilot episode—the tag—was originally a montage of scenes, narrated by Jones, which included a quick appearance by her real-life

PROLOGUE

husband and David's real-life father, Jack Cassidy. Claver remembers it as a move for some good publicity for the show. "I think we hired him on that one for obvious reasons," says Claver. "If you go on the air, that's another little piece of publicity you could put together, and for that it's fine. Jack was a working actor, and people knew of him."

Shirley Jones remembers it as a bit of fun. "I don't think it was ever intended to be part of the show," she says. "He knew it too. They talked to him about it and said, 'Why don't you just appear in the pilot?' It was a thing that they did more as a joke for me, and of course for David too. It was intended as a surprise for the both of us."

Jack Cassidy's cameo appearance was edited out before airing. "One of the problems with pilots," says Paul Witt, "is taking it from pilot stage to airing it. Pilots are usually delivered a bit long. You want to give the network as much information as possible to make their decision." Cutting the scene from the closing tag was probably a question of running time more than anything else, according to Witt.

"What a Day," a song recorded for the pilot, was also cut. A few other subtle changes were made, including the mother's name. Connie Partridge, as the character was initially named, became Shirley Partridge as a courtesy to Shirley Jones. In those days it was a common thing to name the lead character after the star who was playing that character, according to Bernard Slade. The decision to do so was made very late in the game, and the name Connie appeared with Shirley Jones' photo on one of the early trade ads for the first Partridge Family record, *The Partridge Family Album*.

Ohio was the original setting for the family's home, but it was changed to northern California. Though Witt couldn't remember why they made the change, he could speculate. "California is a lot easier to shoot in Los Angeles than an Ohio setting, although the industry had been shooting the entire world within the confines of Hollywood and the Valley for many years. I think it was just easier to utilize the back lot, the existing sets, the houses on the back lot, and the Columbia Ranch," says Witt. "I thought under the circumstances it was very well done, and most importantly it sold! Pilots are labor-intensive. You're making discoveries as you go along. Any mistakes in a pilot can really be pronounced. Not only does it have to be good, but it has to be considered commercial enough to get put on a schedule. That's the acid test, and we all felt very good about passing that test."

Witt continues on the stronger points of the pilot in terms of selling it to the network. "The music played a big role in it," he says. "At that particular moment the music business was the most exciting part of show business. It was creating more stories than anything else, and certainly getting more press. The show was placed in a family setting to get a younger audience. It was less hip, both in terms of style and content, than *The Monkees,* but we were going for a broader audience. We wanted more parents. We wanted more families. That's how that came to be."

when we're singin'

In early press releases Bob Claver described the comedic style of the show as "neither soft nor ingenuous." He told reporters, "We don't have a birthday show and we're steering clear of the overly sentimental. We are aiming for a much more sophisticated kind of program. Children, like adults, are more aware and hip today, and the Partridges' exchanges are fast and funny." On the music, he added, "Music, of course, is a major part of every episode. The songs will be integrated into the shows, but we never stop the action to do one. Music is used to further the story or help set a specific mood; occasionally as a bridge over an action montage. We believe our music will have a wide appeal. Wes Farrell, who is producing the musical numbers, works closely with me on every script before he and his staff create the songs."

The pilot was presented and sold in early 1970 and quickly given the green light by the ABC Network. The actors found themselves back in the studio in no time. Meanwhile, the story of the music was only just beginning.

"I Think I Love You" was out on radio stations even before the pilot aired. The recordings for the show would require a staff as big as the television side of it, and a leader as strong as Claver. The music America heard in the pilot episode, and the music the executives approved, did not include the voice of David Cassidy. While the four seasons of *The Partridge Family* never rose into the top 10 as measured by end-of-season Nielsen ratings, the music that climbed the *Billboard* charts over those four years did. The television show spawned 10 record singles, 10 albums, and a teen idol who broke attendance records in concert sales and fan clubs that have yet to be topped—and that was in America alone.

This is where our story begins...

THE BREEZY BEGINNING
or ... *The Partridge Family Album*

To Produce, or Not to Produce

With the pilot of a new musical series approved for production, *Partridge Family* creator Bernard Slade needed … well, music. But with no preconception of what that music should be, he left it to the studio to come up with the sound and style. Current pop music wasn't something executive producer Bob Claver could relate to, either. "I'm a Frank Sinatra kind of guy," Claver says. "I'm from a whole different era."

Tommy Boyce and Bobby Hart had made a name for themselves producing and writing for the Monkees, and they were already signed with Screen Gems as contract players. The duo seemed a perfect fit for the upcoming Partridge Family project and were approached about producing the music for the Partridge Family. But Screen Gems was grooming them for a musical series of their own. They had just been given an unprecedented multimillion-dollar agreement to star in their own show, making records on their own label—Aquarian Records, to be distributed by Bell Records—so they turned down the Partridge Family offer.

Claver turned to his old buddy Shorty Rogers. "I worked with Shorty on a number of series," recalls Claver. Rogers was known as one of the best jazz musicians in the business. Just as important, he was temperamentally suited to work in film and television, with his laid-back attitude and no-worries disposition. Rogers was signed to do the music for the pilot.

We loved Shorty Rogers," says Tom Bahler, the vocalist and arranger who would become a central part of the Partridge Family's music. "First of all, he was a jazz player, and he was also cool. We used to say that Shorty talked in quarter triplets. He was like [in hippie voice], 'Hey man, how are you doing, man, it's so good to see you.' That was just Shorty. He was a great arranger, and a hell of a trumpet player. But he wasn't a pop dude, you know? He was great. He kind of went from being a jazz player to scoring shows and being a music director, and he was great at all of those things, but to be a hit record producer you've got to know a hit when you hear it."

Screen Gems then approached Chip Douglas to co-produce the music for the series with Rogers. Douglas, a native of Hawaii, was a hot commodity in Hollywood, having produced the Monkees' *Headquarters* album. He was even better known for his work with the Turtles, for which he produced the giant No. 1 hit "Happy Together." But Douglas was hesitant about the Partridge Family gig.

"I had a couple of records on the charts, and Screen Gems asked me if I wanted to produce the music for the Partridge Family—and I thought about it, but I was kind of wanting to go back to Hawaii because I had grown a little tired of Hollywood," he says. "The other thing was that they said, 'You know, it's a TV show, and you'll be responsible for getting us the hits,' and I thought *hmmm*. All they had was Shirley Jones at the time. I don't think David Cassidy had been cast yet, and I thought, *Well, gee, I don't know if I can get any hit records with Shirley Jones' voice,* because she was more of a Broadway person. That was the sticking point for me.

"I also had my own approach to things," continues Douglas, "which was loosely based on what I had started doing with the Turtles. Had I produced the Partridge Family, though, it probably would have been very similar in style to the way it ended up sounding. Shorty Rogers was going to be co-producing and doing the arrangements," he says. "The other thing was that I was used to working with groups.

"The fact that I would have to put together a studio band with people I didn't know was very different for me. In a situation where you've got studio musicians, you've got to get in there and put it together in the time allotted at the recording studio. You don't get to practice on the side. You've got to have it all figured out when you go in there. And you couldn't always get the same musicians from one session to another because people were busy, and they might have another session that same day.

"When I produced 'Happy Together,' we worked that song on the road for about two or three months. This process was not going to work for the Partridge Family because of the sheer number of songs that would be needed on a weekly basis. It was the difference between a studio band, which was what the Partridge Family required, and a non-studio band."

Douglas continues: "So I thought, *Well, I think I just might turn this one down.* No one could believe at Screen Gems that I turned it down."

In the meantime, Shorty Rogers began to assemble his musical team. The first call he made was to session vocalist Ron Hicklin.

Voices Singing

Ron Hicklin

Ron Hicklin was the first background singer signed to the Partridge Family. Hicklin was the top session vocalist that every musical producer in Hollywood had in his little black book. Hicklin was not only a vocalist himself but also a vocal contractor with a list of other talented singers that he could quickly assemble. "As a studio singer, when you're working for scale, the only way that you can really be assured of getting the call in the first place is to try and work yourself into a position where you are first call on things," he says. Studio singers were in high demand and short supply. There was a very small group of people considered the best, and Hicklin was not only one of them, but a key player in finding equally talented colleagues.

"Once I had done 'This Diamond Ring,' which was my first No. 1 record as a session vocalist, things began to break for me. I became a first-call person. Then I was in a position where people wanted me, and one way they made sure they got me was to put me in charge vocally. They would hire me and I would, in turn, hire the other singers," continues Hicklin. "Hopeful singers would come into town wanting to work in the industry, and they would contact me. I would audition them and find out what they could do. This way I could always go into a work environment with the best group I could possibly put together. I felt that our longevity as session singers would be based upon our ability to continually do hits and compete. That's how I began using John Bahler, and later his brother Tom."

"Then, when I started contracting voices, I began bringing in females when in a mixed-group situation," continues Hicklin. "Jackie Ward was already established. Jackie, to me, was my No. 1 alto."

With the first Partridge Family background singer now locked down, Hicklin was given double duty to contract the other voices.

Jackie Ward

Jackie Ward was the second voice hired. Known for her vocal precision and dependability, having begun in the industry at a very young age, Ward had a hit in 1963 with a single called "Wonderful Summer," right around the time the Beatles broke in America. She was 21 when she recorded "Wonderful Summer," but it was recorded and mixed to make her voice sound like a young teenager's. She even used her daughter's name, Robin Ward, on the record label rather than her own. "Wonderful Summer" climbed its way up the *Billboard* charts to No. 14.

Ward had been one of the regular singers on *The Danny Kaye Show*, *The Red Skelton Show*, and *The Carol Burnett Show*. She did commercials, jingles, movies, solos, choir calls, and just about every other possible singing engagement, establishing herself as a top session vocalist. Ron Hicklin called in four women to potentially sing for the *Partridge Family* pilot, but he ended up contracting only Jackie Ward and Sally Stevens.

when we're singin'

John and Tom Bahler

Two brothers became the third and fourth Partridge Family background vocalists, and vocal arrangers. Their intertwined career paths prepared them perfectly for the major role they would play in the Partridge Family's music.

Both John and Tom Bahler grew up with a lot of musical training behind them. John had been active in the music business up until he went into the Navy. During that time, his brother Tom was going to the University of Southern California. Tom turned down an offer to sing on *The Andy Williams Show* with the program's Good Time Singers because he was in school. In a twist of fate, his brother John, whose term with the Navy was coming to an end, landed the job. Andy Williams had decided he was going to end his show that year, so they all knew it would be just a one-year gig.

As a result of his work on *The Andy Williams Show,* John was offered his next job as music director on a 1966 show, a Dick Clark production called *Swingin' Country.* "It was on during the daytime," recalls John Bahler, who thought Dick Clark was innovative—a trailblazer of sorts. "It was on five days a week on NBC. Rusty Draper, Molly Bee, and Roy Clark were the headliners. We were cast as the Hometown Singers. When *Hee Haw* came out with Roy Clark, they did the exact same kind of show in prime time that we were doing, yet theirs was a hit! We were only on 13 weeks. It was really sad." But John was now learning how to work as a musical director, a skill that would eventually play a key role in his work with the Partridge Family vocal arrangements.

Meanwhile, John hired Tom as a member of the Hometown Singers. "My brother John said, 'I'm going to put you on the show because you can do the show and still go to school,'" says Tom Bahler. "'Just work your classes around it.' I was in my early 20s and they wanted young people, so John thought I would fit in fine. But after the audition they told John he couldn't use me because I looked too young!" Tom laughs. "John said, 'You wanted young people!' And they said, 'Yeah, but not 12-year-olds!' So they wouldn't let me on camera, but John used me for prerecords. It became kind of a group—the kids on camera and me!"

Suddenly and unexpectedly, John and Tom were offered a record deal and found themselves signing a contract. They called themselves the Love Generation, a title based on the media's portrayal of '60s youth, "like Generation X is today," says John. Their music was very much a reflection of the blended harmonic sound coming out of the '60s pop scene at the time. The music was upbeat, clean-cut, and beautifully arranged. It was their work on the Love Generation albums that laid further groundwork for the Partridge Family project.

"The Love Generation came about totally by accident," explains Tom Bahler. Someone familiar with the Hometown Singers had decided the group should have a record deal. "I think he was an attorney who dated one of the girls on the show," says Tom. "So all of a sudden, John called me and said, 'Hey, man, looks like we have a record deal with Imperial Records.' I said, 'Huh?' Then we realized it was a great opportunity. We had been arranging and singing all our lives, and we were both trumpet players. We felt this was a good opportunity to have some fun. We never really thought about starting a band before this, because we didn't want to tour."

"I couldn't travel," says John Bahler. "I was trying to save my marriage, and every time I went out of town she freaked out. That put a kibosh on our career, unfortunately, and it didn't save my marriage. If I have one regret, I regret that I didn't go out on the road and see what might have happened. There was a lot of interest in us from a certain segment of the population, but it wasn't enough to put us over the top because they didn't see us live."

The Love Generation's sound was in sync with the times. The vocal lead featured a group sound, harmonically blended, akin to the sound of the Mamas & the Papas or the Byrds. The Love Generation released three albums between 1967 and 1969: *The Love Generation, A Generation of Love,* and *Montage*—the last with "Let the Good Times In," a song that was reworked for the *Partridge Family* pilot.

"It was a great blossoming time for John and me," says Tom Bahler. "All of a sudden we were signed to a record deal, and it was just like getting pregnant when you weren't planning on it!" Tom laughs; he has a genuine sense of humor about himself and life.

"Back then I had only written songs for girls. That was my way of getting famous," jokes Tom. Then their record producer approached him to write some songs. "John and I didn't really write together very much. I guess, being brothers, we just had different ideas on how things should go. So I had a roommate in college, a fraternity brother, and I went to him and said, 'Hey, they've been asking me to write some songs for this new group, and I haven't got a clue, man.' He said he wanted to write some lyrics for me, so he wrote a lyric called 'Groovy Springtime,' and I took a look at it. The moment I looked at it, the melody came.

"I showed it to Tommy [Oliver, their producer], and he said, 'I love it, but by the time this record comes out, springtime will likely be over. Let's make it 'Summertime.' Suddenly we were on the radio with it! We were really surprised. It didn't go that high up the charts, but for a debut single I think it rose into the 70s, and in some cities it was a hit. That was our very first release."

"Groovy Summertime" peaked at No. 74 in 1967.

The next significant turn came when they landed an account with Ford Motors. "It was in the summer of '68," recalls Tom. "They kicked off their fall schedule, and Henry Ford II had said, 'You can sell a young man's car to an old man, but you can't sell an old man's car to a young man. I want a group!' The group sound and look was really popular then. He said, 'I want a group to represent this company that looks young and clean and sings great.' During that era, most of the bands that were really selling records were not likely bands to represent Ford Motor Company, so those in charge were looking through the record albums on a store shelf one day and came across the Love Generation. They said, 'God, they look so clean, and they sound so good!' So they called us and asked if we would put a group together for Ford."

Ford passed on a few members of the group, and some of the singers passed on the project, so Tom and John held auditions to replace them. "My brother had seen this one group on a television battle of the bands program that was really very good," says Tom. "They were on a local Channel 9 TV show and John called the station and said, 'Man, I want their number!' It was actually Richard and Karen Carpenter! They came and took the job, and then they asked us later to help get them out of their contract because they wanted to sign with A&M, so we did. Consequently those friendships have lasted for years." The Bahler brothers, Jackie Ward, and Ron Hicklin all worked on and off with the Carpenters throughout the years.

"With the Ford account, all of a sudden John and I watched our career take off. When J. Walter Thompson saw that we knew what we were doing, it made it easy for them. Advertising people are always going 75 miles an hour in a 25-mile-an-hour zone. They began to say, 'Hey, man, why don't you arrange this? Why don't you arrange that?' Then they asked us to produce a session. They sent us copy and said, 'Hey, man, you know what to do, just do it!'"

Tom Bahler continues, "All of a sudden we went from being studio singers to being involved with the ideas as well. All of a sudden we were doing national commercials. Not only were we singing, but now we were arranging and even writing. When we came out of the Ford account two years later, we were now producers, arrangers, and singers, and we had cornered a market. It was funny, man. I mean, all of these things just fell into place."

Then along came the Partridge Family. "The sound of the Partridge Family kind of followed the style we had created," explains Tom. "The Love Generation was a pop group all of its own. It wasn't a family. It wasn't a type of story. Once you have a story like the Partridge Family, then you start to take a look at that. We took a look at these kids, and they were little kids. We were all in our 20s, and we thought we were the coolest things ever."

Tom laughs again. "When we were looking at the Partridge Family it took on a different flavor just by looking at the recipe of people. That's where the tweaking came in. I didn't change that much in my approach. It just became a little lighter-textured. We were working with Mike Melvoin, who was doing the band arrangements, and we worked together seamlessly. It was great fun. The sound of the Partridge Family kind of followed the style we had created."

THE BREEZY BEGINNING

Monkee Business

The Monkees had come to television as a direct result of the Beatles and the musical revolution they brought to America. *The Monkees* was the first TV program that successfully manufactured music to match an image. Rather than a group that emerged from their musical skills, hits, and likeability factors, the Monkees were manufactured and created as part of a complete package—a product—created by Screen Gems. Ron Hicklin's skill with this kind of specialized singing and image building was instrumental to its success.

"One of the things that really kicked off my work with the Partridge Family came from my association with the Monkees," says Hicklin. "While we were doing *Shindig* (another popular television show during the 1960s), the British Invasion with the Beatles and all of the other groups from Britain were coming in, so we were doing sound-alikes."

As session singers they were expected to work like chameleons, replicating all kinds of sounds, accents, and ethnicities within their vocal performances to create a musical sound matching the desired image for any kind of group, whether British Invasion or Motown. "So they put this group together called the Monkees, but they weren't necessarily group singers. They were a group of personalities," explains Hicklin. "They didn't just come in and suddenly start singing together, like a group might do. What really happened is that they featured different people on lead, like Mickey Dolenz and Davy Jones, and then I was brought in as a session vocalist.

"On my first session, I came in with two of my singers, and we did the backgrounds on the first three songs. We did three songs in 20 minutes. The producers felt the best thing to do was hire me to come in and sing *with* the Monkees, so the group would be more than just studio singers. Basically, Micky Dolenz, Davy Jones, and I did most of the songs, along with Tommy Boyce and Bobby Hart, who also wrote a lot of the stuff. I was called the ringer, meaning that I was, in effect, anonymous. I was in there singing with the others, uncredited and anonymously, to help get the sound we wanted.

"As it progressed, there was a kind of bumping of heads because I was paid for the records but never the television shows—and I was on *everything*, including the theme song. Because I was a member of the Screen Actors Guild, I should have been paid to scale. But the Screen Actors Guild made an agreement with Colgems that they could have my services for all time, getting paid something like a $1,400 flat fee, which was just ridiculous. Finally I just had to sign off. I was never paid for any reuse on anything. On top of it there was this 'don't hire' out on me from Columbia Pictures. See, there's this old saying that goes *I never want to see that son-of-a-bitch again … until I need him,* which is the reason I mention this."

when we're singin'

Fast forward to the *Partridge Family* pilot. "Here was a case where they thought, *Well, OK, Ron is who we need to put the group together.* So I got the call from Shorty Rogers," continues Hicklin. "He said the show would star Shirley Jones. I said 'Shorty, after what I've been through with the Monkees, I don't want to work with any actors. I don't want to go in there with people who don't sing in the musical bag we're recording in.'"

Hicklin liked and respected Shirley Jones. He thought she was a magnificent talent, but he really wanted to work with singers who were strictly singers because of his bad experience with the Monkees. But Shorty Rogers managed to talk Hicklin into working with him, and soon Hicklin was lined up as vocal contractor for the project.

What a Day

The first vocal session for the *Partridge Family* pilot was held on December 18, 1969. "We just walked in, and the arrangements were there from Shorty and we did them," says Hicklin. It was as simple as that. The initial group of Partridge Family vocalists was made up of Ron Hicklin, Jackie Ward, and John and Tom Bahler—the four who would end up staying for the entire series—in addition to Stan Farber and Sally Stevens, session singers who worked frequently with the others. Two other vocalists were there, but only six voices were actually used in the final recordings for the pilot. The group recorded an original composition by Shorty Rogers with lyrics by Kelly Gordon, "Together (Havin' a Ball)." It was used in the pilot episode as both the theme song and one of the family's featured concert performance songs.

The viewing audience received their first glimpse of the *Partridge Family* cast lip-syncing during the garage session in a video sequence shot for the pilot. The song was a minimally altered redo of the Love Generation's "Let the Good Times In," also recorded that same day. Some vocal arrangements were altered a bit from the original and the tempo was tweaked, but it bore a very close resemblance to John Bahler's original arrangement. Shorty Rogers and company reconvened three days later and worked on a third song for the show, titled "What a Day." It was recorded and completed for use on the pilot, but ultimately never used.

Ron Hicklin recognized the potential for this group of session singers to work together in perfect harmony should the pilot get picked up. The chemistry was unmistakable. "Tom Bahler was writing material, and he had success with certain songs that made it on the charts," says Hicklin. Bahler had just scored with Bobby Sherman's biggest hit—"Julie, Do You Love Me?"—which clocked in at No. 5 on *Billboard* in early 1970. I thought this would be ideal," says Hicklin, "because John could arrange the vocals, and Tom could write material, and I would handle the vocal contracting. Together we would all go in and sing it, and I could run interference in the booth to make sure that we could do our thing without a lot of distraction."

THE BREEZY BEGINNING

Once David Cassidy came on board as the lead singer, the extra session vocalists who worked on the pilot were not used on a regular basis, but they were called in from time to time when one of the regulars had a conflict. Jerry Whitman, Sally Stevens, Stan Farber, and several other session singers made up the substitute list. Shirley Jones, who was also contracted as an added background vocalist, brought the total number of singers heard on the Partridge Family albums to six. By coincidence, the actual number of singers matched up with the number of actors portraying the family members in the show.

Enter Wes Farrell

The producers never planned on featuring Shirley Jones as the lead singer, but they offered her the option to sing on all the records—giving her a chance to have a little fun doing what she loved to do and make a few extra bucks. She was thrilled, and also hoped there would be a few solo opportunities for her on the show from time to time. Ultimately Jones would sing a full uninterrupted solo only three times on the show and once on the Partridge Family records. Her stepson, however, was about to wreak havoc on the pop music scene. At the Columbia Ranch—now the Warner Brothers Ranch—production was well under way for the series. Minimal changes occurred on the television side of things once the pilot was given the green light. But it was a different story over at Western Recorders Studio 2, where the recording sessions were being held. Ron Hicklin recalls it well: "We did the pilot, and the next thing I know I get a call later from Shorty Rogers. He says 'Ron! The show's going to go! The pilot received the highest ratings since *Mission: Impossible*!' So I was waiting for the next shoe to drop, and suddenly Columbia replaced Shorty Rogers with Wes Farrell." Getting the music right became the most important focus for producer Paul Witt.

"We had worked with Shorty on a few projects and loved him," explains Witt. "Shorty scored the pilot and the series. You know, if a pilot doesn't sell, it's unlikely that you're going to sell any of the music from it, either. If it is picked up, then Screen Gems Music would start to bring in people they felt could generate hits in that young market. We're talking about 1970–71, when the record business was exploding with groups like the Stones and the Beatles. It was just huge. It was the most important aspect, and certainly the template for the cultural revolution that was going on."

Witt continues, "Wes Farrell was our music guy. Wes had this great track record with contemporary popular music, and Shorty was more of a jazz guy. Screen Gems Music was one of the biggest powers in the business. Part of the reason the Partridge Family came to be was a result of the music division's enormous success with the Monkees. The Partridge Family was another opportunity to take advantage of that marketplace."

when we're singin'

Wes Farrell brought a completely different kind of energy when he came on board. "Wes Farrell was hyper–New York," remembers Jackie Ward. "Typical of someone who has the Brooklyn accent, and if he didn't like something he didn't mince words. This was totally opposite from Shorty Rogers. They were like night and day." Ward says Rogers was "the sweetest man you could ever want to know. He was very soft-spoken. He would talk to you and talk kind of slow, and he was never in a hurry, and there was never a problem." Ward chuckles as she imitates Rogers' slow, easygoing speech pattern. "He was just easy to be around."

Wes Farrell was a prominent force in the music business—especially music oriented toward teens. Farrell had just come out of the 1960s with a successful pop hit, "Come a Little Bit Closer," and his earlier smash "Hang On, Sloopy." He had also produced Every Mother's Son, a short-lived pop band whose "Come On Down to My Boat," a Farrell-penned pop song, hit No. 6 on the *Billboard* charts in 1967. Their image was squeaky clean. Every Mother's Son appeared on a two-part episode of *The Man From U.N.C.L.E.* singing their own music, then released a second album before disbanding in 1968.

In 1969 Farrell was also heavily promoting Elephant's Memory and Brooklyn Bridge, two other bands with albums produced by Farrell. Farrell's protégé Tony Romeo had written songs for Brooklyn Bridge as well as commercial jingles for Farrell's commercial division, Commercial Management Group Inc.

John Bahler remembers seeing Farrell hanging around the studio while they were working on the pilot episode. "We got through that first session and the pilot went," he recalls. "I remember Wes Farrell was there for the mixing, and basically I found out later that Wes went to the producers and said, 'Do you want hit records out of this, or do you just want the trash you've been doing?'" Bahler laughs as he reflects fondly on the bold and brash Wes Farrell. "They said, 'We want hit records!' Wes said, 'Then hire me!' And they did! Wes was quite a character," says Bahler. "Wes didn't really think it was trash. It was just his New York way of getting the job."

"The project was offered to me by Larry Uttal," said Farrell (who passed away in 1996) in a 1993 interview with Ken Sharp. Uttal was the president of Bell Records, a subsidiary of Screen Gems Television/Columbia Pictures. "Larry and I had known each other for some time, and he had a feeling this would be a project to my liking. We had successes that paralleled it in several ways with Every Mother's Son and the Cowsills. We knew how to have Top 40–oriented projects put together. The image matching the music was the name of the game. Larry showed me the pilot and the rest is history—the pilot was filled with possibilities. You had a young guy named David Cassidy who had star image written all over him like a hundred-dollar bill. You had a perfect family situation. You had all the elements. We had been trying to do what *The Partridge Family* had done on the pilot with Every Mother's Son.

"We tried to have *The Adventures of Every Mother's Son,* said Farrell of a potential show for the group. "We had talked about it and were in advanced stages of being involved with something for the Cowsills, and that never panned out. So when I saw the pilot, it was kind of something I had wanted to do that had been done for me."

David Can Sing!

Speaking of the pilot, Farrell said, "That music had already been done and was planned for programming." Farrell had his own ideas and a vision for a teen idol sensation. "Paul Witt was a pretty sharp dude at that time and still is one of the finest of all the people out there. I said 'Who sings?' and Paul said 'Shirley sings.' At my request they called David Cassidy and asked him if he knew how to sing, because they really didn't know if he could or couldn't."

Though Cassidy wasn't signed to sing on the records yet, his contract allowed him the option to audition. He was already expressing to the producers that he felt foolish lip-syncing, so when he discovered that Farrell wanted to meet with him, he asked Bob Claver if he could audition. Claver says that quite a bit of time had actually passed before Cassidy stepped forward and expressed interest in singing. "It was later than people think," says Claver. "I remember I asked him the question 'What were you waiting for to start with?' I think he and Jack, his dad, talked about it a lot. I think Jack probably said 'If you agree to sing on this show and it doesn't work out for you, you're not going to have much of a singing career after that.' That was probably true, but it did work out for him and I think he made a good choice. He's a pretty good singer, and he's very, very good looking. That whole thing just worked out well." So the young David Cassidy went into the studio and sang for Wes Farrell.

"He didn't really have a formidable background as a singer," Farrell said of Cassidy. "He came down within a short period of that conversation taking place and he sang to a couple of records—Crosby, Stills, and Nash and Chicago. I had a clue from that particular meeting what he was capable of and what we could possibly get accomplished."

"We needed a front person," recalls John Bahler. "What we were doing was good musically, but it wasn't what it could be, and Wes knew it. A big part of what made the show a hit," adds Bahler, "was David and the sound of the group. That was Wes Farrell's baby."

When Shirley Jones began to see the writing on the wall, she embraced it wholeheartedly. "Well, you know the truth is they didn't tell me anything in the beginning," she says. "I think, to be very honest with you, that they thought I was going to be the singer in the show. But when they saw David and heard him play that guitar, and when they saw the kind of music that was being written, automatically they said, 'Wait a minute. We love Shirley, but this is our star for the music.' So they knew it right away. They knew it from the beginning because of the kind of music that it was. I was in my 40s then and this was young be-bop stuff for kids, and they knew it wasn't my style but it certainly was his. The way he came across to the public put them in shock. Then they laid it out for me. They said, 'Do you understand?' And I said, 'I understand perfectly. Just give me a song or two once in a while,' which is exactly what they did."

Tracy's Voice

Now that David Cassidy was placed as the lead singer, Farrell needed to lock down the background vocalists as a permanent act. Once again, he had his own vision. "We auditioned about 50 background singers who were all top studio singers," he said, although he ended up calling back the six original singers from the pilot recording sessions: John and Tom Bahler, Ron Hicklin, Jackie Ward, Sally Stevens and Stan Farber. "We were looking for a sound, and we picked what turned out to be four of the best background singers that have ever lived. They were just incredible. They were the very best background singers on the West Coast."

Jackie Ward vividly remembers the final round of the audition: "Originally, Shorty Rogers did the music off of a demo when they were trying to sell the idea. There was a group. I believe there were eight of us—four girls and four guys. Wes Farrell felt that the original sound was too much of a typical background group to be singing behind a solo artist, and he didn't want that. He wanted something that sounded more like a group that sang together all the time and functioned as a group on the road, that sort of thing. He wanted a different sound than the typical studio sound. So he started trying different combinations with the studio singers he called in, so he could come up with something he liked.

"For example, he might first try two guys and two girls as a combination, then only guys, then only girls. He also tried different sounds to find what he wanted. While we were experimenting with different sounds, I remembered that the actors who were hired to do the show were mostly younger boys—David Cassidy, Danny Bonaduce. But then there was this very young little girl. Somehow, in my mind, I thought *Wait a minute!* In 1963–64 I had a hit record singing like a little 15-year-old, and I used my daughter's name, and I thought *You know what? I think with the three boys—the three tenors—I should use that voice! I should go into that voice when I'm singing with them because then I would* be *that little girl!* So that's what I did. I tried using that sound, and Wes said 'Yes! That's it!'

"I think we all knew, when we were in the studio, the exact moment we hit on that sound," continues Ward. "Even we could hear it, because Wes played it back to us when we were trying things out. It just had a hot sound. You know what I'm saying? It was like how people would say during that era—*That's in the pocket! That's tight! That's got it!* It had a sound that made listeners stop long enough to say to themselves, *Boy, that's interesting.*"

Ward elaborates: "You no longer have eight voices. You don't have four girls and four guys. You have four voices—three tenors and a little girl sound. Right there you're going to have a different sound, and with that few voices, the voicing is going to be different. It was written more like a small group sound rather than a choral sound, which is what Shorty Rogers had originally written. It makes for a totally different sound. It just does. It's the difference between having a choir of voices and having a trio.

"And this is what John Bahler would be able to do well. John knew the tenors' voices very well, and he was very familiar with my voice, too. He knew what my range was, and what would be comfortable for us, and it all jelled. It just so happened to be when I was singing for that little girl alongside the other three tenors."

The Search for Songwriters

"From there we then went to the drawing board," said Wes Farrell. "We literally had about five screenings of the pilot for just about every writer that I could remember ever talking to, so we could get as much input as possible in terms of compositions for the show. Most of the people walked away thinking it was not going to be a big success. It was very disappointing. However, we had our own team of writers, including myself—but I wasn't looking at myself as the focal point for composition for the show.

"At that stage in my life," continued Farrell, "my business [the Wes Farrell Organization] had really started to grow and become very big. I was dedicating my time to other creative writers and broadening that base. As it turns out, a lot of people were betting against it. Very few people were betting for it. I had some very competent people on my staff. We had Levine and Brown, Levine and Wine. We had Tony Romeo, for whom I held the highest regard. We had a number of other people, too."

Songwriters Mike Appel and Jim Cretecos were very young and just starting out when they signed with Pocket Full of Tunes, the publishing arm of the Wes Farrell Organization. They would become some of the recruits to the Partridge Family project. "I remember Lester Sill of Screen Gems Music calling Wes Farrell up and telling him that he had the pilot episode at their offices," says Appel, "and to bring all his staff writers over to see it so we knew what to write. We all went over and watched the pilot, and we knew immediately that David Cassidy was going to be a teen idol overnight. Nobody was fooled or had any doubts. So we went back to our writer rooms over at 3 East 54th Street in Manhattan, on the 14th floor, and began to kick around ideas."

Many notable songwriters who came on board to write for the Partridge Family were not signed to Farrell but instead wrote songs under their own publishing label. One notable team was singer-songwriter-producers Terry Cashman and Tommy West. "Wes was on 55th Street in Manhattan," says Cashman. "His offices were across the street from us. We became friendly over the years, being in the same business. Around 1969–70 Wes produced a couple of singles with Cashman, Pistilli, and West. That's how we met him."

Farrell approached Cashman and West and pitched his newfound Partridge Family project. Cashman recalls, "He needed songs, so right from the beginning he contacted Tommy and myself and asked if we would like to come to a screening of the pilot for this new show. We went, along with a lot of other new songwriters at the time. This was 1970 and the basic reaction from most people was that this was very square, and not hip enough. They thought nobody would really get into this, and the audience wouldn't be there. A lot of writers didn't want to be involved with something that was so white-bread. But I said to Tommy, 'This is going to be a big hit. Not everybody in the world smokes pot and gets into anti-war causes. There are a lot of middle Americans out there that will like this show, and I think it has a chance to be very successful.' So we got in touch with Wes. We said that we'd be glad to be involved and write songs.

"It was obvious that this was a down-the-middle, American family show," says Cashman. "We certainly weren't going to write anything too risqué or anti-war or that type of thing." Cashman and West were in touch with America's pulse. Even the trade magazines were now coining the acronym MOR—Middle of the Road—in reference to the large audience out there demanding a specific type of music.

Despite those who declined, Farrell soon had a massive group of songwriters submitting demos for the Partridge Family. He narrowed the field to the absolute best submissions: "For every song that we recorded we went through 50 or a hundred songs. "We had tremendous overage in terms of listening. And that may not be songs in their completed state, but bits and pieces."

Farrell also contributed as a songwriter, always with a co-writer. "The idea and the melody are really my forte," he said. "That's where I can best indulge myself. However, in certain instances, and depending on who I wrote with, an idea would always be considered. I never closed the door on listening to others. I would write songs for the Partridge Family in David's vocal range. Everything was written with him in mind. Nothing was written to see what it was going to sound like later."

THE BREEZY BEGINNING

The Wrecking Crew

Farrell said of the production process, "At my request they provided me with storyboards for 15 episodes at a time and everything was recorded almost a year in advance of it being released, because we had to have everything in the can 13 weeks before they started shooting, so it was pretty crazy, man!"

To keep the pace, Farrell recruited musicians from the unofficial group that has since come to be known as the Wrecking Crew. These first-call studio musicians were the crème de la crème of that era and, some would argue, of all time. They were playing on records for artists of all genres—Motown, folk, country, rock, and pop—and were in high demand by every recording studio in L.A. Like the top session vocalists who made up much of the Partridge Family sound, they knew how to adapt to the kind of sounds needed to fit any style of music. It was a small handful of musicians, and their reputation for perfection kept them working nonstop.

"There were about four rhythm sections working virtually around the clock," says Mike Melvoin, who was musical arranger for seven of the eight Partridge Family studio albums. "It simply meant that if someone couldn't do it on one particular day, you'd just get another one. As a matter of fact, I think that almost all of it was as simple as that. We were just so busy, we took each other's work, and at the same time we were handing each other work."

Legendary percussionist Hal Blaine, who played drums on every Partridge Family album, recalls the origins of the name Wrecking Crew. "We started working with Phil Spector in about 1960–61. A lot of his songs were all major hits, and the people were saying, 'Who are those guys?' I literally named us 'the Wrecking Crew' because all of these older musicians who wore the three-piece suits, or the blue blazers, would look at us in our Levis and T-shirts and they'd say 'These kids are going to wreck the business!' But after a very short time, these same guys were all calling us, wanting to come to our sessions and see what we do." The name has come to represent the wider group of first-call session musicians who played on the greatest albums of the day.

Blaine has more than 5,000 songs credited to his name as a drummer, including all the Partridge Family titles. While little Jeremy Gelbwaks and later his replacement, Brian Forster, were viewed by the television audience playing the drums as Chris Partridge, it was Hal Blaine who did the real work.

Legendary bass player Joe Osborn also played on the Partridge Family albums, behind the image of Danny Partridge. Osborn spoke about the way these musicians could morph their sound into whatever was needed. "We were going out to sessions with new sounds, and we were able to create these sounds for the new writers coming in, becoming specialists for different kinds of sounds. For instance, the beautiful harmonies of the Carpenters contrasted in sound with a group like the Mamas & the Papas and their out-of-tune harmonies. They're equally as great, but not the same.

"One guy in Nashville asked me one time about some of the different groups we played for, so I named a few of them. He hadn't realized it was so many of the same musicians playing on so many different records and he said, 'I just found out my five favorite bands are all the same guys!'" Osborn laughs. "We were able to adapt to whatever situation was needed and give them their sound. I don't know if we even realized that was happening until later. We came in with a new way to do things, not even realizing it. Hal Blaine calls himself 'your 10 favorite drummers.'"

"I really enjoyed the music," Osborn says of the Partridge Family. "I think a lot of that has to do with the people that were there—working with Hal Blaine, Dennis Budimir, Larry Knechtel, and those guys. Our calls came individually from the producers, so when you went in to a session you never knew who you were going to be with because we weren't a group. You would go in and see Hal Blaine's drums set up and you'd think *Wow*. Now you're already 50 percent relaxed. We just wound up together a lot of the time. The producers figured out that when this certain group of musicians was there, they were very likely to come out with a hit record."

Louie Shelton played guitar on most of the Partridge Family albums, as did Dennis Budimir, Larry Carlton, and the late, great Tommy Tedesco. More than 25 musicians were credited on the Partridge Family albums, collectively.

The Vocal Sessions

The background vocalists recorded their parts at the very end of the process. Leading up to it, Wes Farrell's job was to get the rhythm charts done and Cassidy's vocals in place, although it didn't always happen in the order it was intended because of filming schedules for the show. The merger of television and music was still unrefined in its approach.

"I used to go in and generally have two and three sessions, and I'd do tracks," Farrell said. "I'd do the vocals myself. I'd do scratch vocals because we didn't have the use of David. He was doing the TV show while I was cutting the tracks. We'd sandwich in these little bits and pieces where I'd give him one verse and a chorus, and he'd learn that. We'd then get a key, and very often he learned the songs after the fact or while we were moving through the project. If I heard the song and I believed in it, and if I knew where the song was going, it was pretty easy to cut the track and get at least the first verse, chorus, and the bridge out of the way.

"Once that was completed we would then tailor words, sometimes rewriting them on the spot. I would go into the studio at two in the afternoon and come out about midnight. Then I'd go back to the Beverly Hills Hotel, and I'd go into the dining room there and I'd lock the door and work on the piano there till three or four in the morning. Then I'd fall asleep at the piano, and the bellboy would come and wake me up. 'Mr. Farrell! Mr. Farrell! You fell asleep!' 'Oh, I fell asleep?' Then I'd go up to the room and go to sleep for four or five hours and do it again."

On May 5, 1970, Farrell, Cassidy and the new group of family singers all met for the first vocal session. It was at this very first session that the megahit "I Think I Love You" was recorded, along with two other tunes. But the structure of the first session with Farrell was quite different from the pilot sessions with Shorty Rogers.

"On that first session [with Farrell], I remember there were no charts for us," says John Bahler. "That used to happen to us a lot. We'd walk into a session, and there'd be no vocal charts where the vocal charts should be. There'd be six people on three parts, or five people on three parts, and I had a choice of either waiting it out and staying there all night trying to figure out what we were going to do or just grabbing some paper and writing something—which is what I did." John literally wrote the charts for "I Think I Love You" on the spot, during the actual recording session. Billy Strange was there, too, working on musical arrangements with Mike Melvoin and Don Peake. Though Melvoin was the arranger who stayed on board through the entire run of the Partridge Family, it is Billy Strange who is credited as arranger on the single of "I Think I Love You."

John Bahler explains his collaboration with Farrell in coming up with vocal arrangements: "Under normal circumstances I'd be given a demo, and Wes and I would sit together and listen to the demo. Very often I had a rhythm track that Wes had already made with the band, and sometimes there was a guide vocal by David. Then Wes would tell me where he thought the backing vocals should happen."

By the time the background singers came in to record their part, most of the band arrangements were already done. The basic track was there, including most of Cassidy's lead vocals, and the background singers would sing to Cassidy's lead, layering in vocals to match his inflections. Sometimes the work involved sweetening and sometimes it was straight overdub.

Jackie Ward remembers the process well. "When John would write the vocal charts based on what David was singing, we would come in and sometimes we would have to change the phrasing just slightly because David didn't sing it that way. We had to hear how he sang it so we could phrase everything right with him, so that we were all singing together. If we were simply doing background responses, *ahhhs* and *oooohs,* it didn't matter. But when we were singing a phrase with the same words that had to match him, we had to do it right with him. Wes had to be happy with his delivery before we came in and did ours."

Farrell always looked at every song as a potential hit. That was his focus. He knew that music was needed for the TV show, but a hit record was his primary goal. There were occasions when he had to produce songs specifically tailored for a certain episode. Sometimes those songs would end up on a record and sometimes not. When the songs needed to be shortened for the show by cutting out a verse or a phrase, or when they might require an alternate ending, Farrell would usually put John Bahler in charge of recording those and leave for the day. He was not too concerned with the alternate takes and alternate endings; he trusted Bahler's decisions for that.

We're Better Together

Before the recording sessions began to pick up pace, another snag developed over Ron Hicklin's involvement. Hicklin found himself facing a situation he had feared earlier—his old issue with the Monkees coming back to haunt him. "There was some politics going on at the time," he says, "and one day I got a call from John saying that Screen Gems had requested I not be a part of the Partridge Family sessions.

"You cut off the head, as they say, and then you can do what you will," continues Hicklin. "Screen Gems felt the job was done. They got the sale on the show and the music, and now they didn't want to deal with me. Shorty Rogers was gone and now suddenly I was gone."

But Hicklin's story wasn't over after all. "Because of the relationship I had with the rest of the singers, they refused to do the Partridge Family without me. I'll never forget that feeling of support from my colleagues," he says. It was John Bahler who adamantly took the lead in supporting Hicklin.

"Billy Strange called me," he remembers, "and said, 'We're doing another session for the Partridge Family but we've got to cut the size of the crew down, and you can't use Ron Hicklin.' I said, 'What?' He said, 'We're really concerned because Ron's so close to the union and there's going to be double-tracking and all this stuff.' So I said, 'You know what? You ought to call somebody else. If you call me to put together a crew, I want to put the best singers together that I know. If you're telling me I can't use somebody, then I'm not interested.' So he said he would think about it. He went back to the producers and told them the story. He called me back and said, 'Use anybody you want.'"

Bahler was young, ambitious, and able to make a lot of money by signing on to this project, but loyalty to his colleagues came first. He was determined to keep the group intact. "John Bahler was quite a gentleman," says Jackie Ward, recalling the situation.

"I was then included back in with the group," says Hicklin. "At that point, John became the vocal arranger, like I had intended originally. So John worked with Wes. Wes would pick material and produce us, and Mike Melvoin would do the charts for the band, and John would write the vocal arrangements for the vocal group and work to establish the sound that we were after. Then Jackie, Tom, and I would sing the parts with John."

To keep Hicklin under the radar, John Bahler became more of a front man for the group. Like a real family, the Partridge Family singers stuck together. The fictional story portrayed on screen was also playing out in real time at Western Recorders Studio 2, but without any spotlight or fame.

I Really, *Really,* Think I Love You

Wes Farrell put his mind to promoting "I Think I Love You" as the Partridge Family's first single with relentless determination.

"Shirley and David went on the road to 15 cities," said Farrell. "The record was shipped and not a person in the country played the record. It looked like a living damn nightmare. So the record company and I were very close, and we were talking every day. We had our own promotion division within my production company and we paid very close attention to the marketing, and primarily the promotion of the record. Larry Uttal felt strongly about it. I credit him with a tremendous amount of ability for the project being successful and succeeding as it did. He agreed to ship the record a second time because we had a lot of preorders and a lot of pre-energy and input on this, but we weren't selling records. Still nothing was happening, and Screen Gems on the West Coast was starting to give us a lot of heat. This was several weeks ahead of the show's first airing. One thing led to another.

"I kept believing in 'I Think I Love You,' and I kept persisting. My friendship with Larry Uttal prevailed. Larry wasn't losing his interest, but he was also getting a lot of heat. I said, 'Let's just give it two more weeks.' I had a promotion guy by the name of Bob Harrington. He was the director of promotion out of Columbus, Ohio. I said, 'Bob, beg on this one. I'll go to the wall with it. If this record isn't a hit, just tell somebody they never have to play another one of my records. Find somebody that will give this record a shot!'

"A guy out of Grand Rapids picked the record to play, and 'I Think I Love You' went from the pick to No. 1!" Farrell laughed. "Just right to No. 1, man! And I said, 'That's it! The record's history!' We were about 60 or 70 with a bullet several weeks before the show aired."

A Mini-Movie

The one thing left to do was create the opening sequence for the show. The producers decided to go with an animated opening, a popular style of the era that had been used on such shows as *I Dream of Jeannie* and *Bewitched*.

when we're singin'

Sandy Dvore, who originally hailed from Chicago, was an artist who had established himself as an illustrator and was turning up consistently in *Variety* and other trade magazines. Dvore created original illustrations of Rock Hudson, Steve McQueen, Natalie Wood, Henry Fonda, Judy Garland, and just about anybody who was somebody in the industry during the 1960s. His first foray into prime-time television began with *The Partridge Family.*

"I got a telephone call from the head of postproduction at Columbia Television and I was asked to take a meeting with a man named Paul Junger Witt," begins Dvore. "I had never met the man before. I went into his office and he started telling me that they were working on a new show, and they wanted to dress up the front of it with something a little bit more colorful than the usual yellow typeface that was used on most everything back then. He said it was about a mother and her children who decide to form a rock and roll band as a family. Well, my love for popular music ended with Sarah Vaughan, Jack Jones, and Vic Damone, and the kind of music where you could get a chance to dance cheek to cheek. So the idea of doing a show about rock and roll didn't really thrill me to death, because I didn't care about rock and roll. I had no idea what the Beatles were doing. That part of my life—music—was very 1940s and 1950s.

"I asked him about the name of the show, and he said it was called *The Partridge Family.* He said 'I was told that you're really good, and I thought maybe you could come up with something that would be interesting for the beginning.' I thought that I had fallen into something so unique and so different. I mean, where do you get called in and asked to do something as simple as this? So I decided I wouldn't make it *look* simple!

"I stopped for a second, and I actually put on a bit of a performance. I closed my eyes and I made believe I was going into this creative trance based on what he had just said to me. In reality, the minute he said it I had the idea, for pity's sake! I mean, *The Partridge Family*? He didn't even have to finish the word *family* and I knew exactly what the screen was going to look like. I used to walk through the fields in Champaign, Illinois, during the winter, and I used to watch the pheasants. I knew that partridges were just smaller versions of those kinds of game birds. I had seen so many illustrations of partridges that had to do with Christmas books and so forth, so I knew exactly what they looked like.

"I finally said to him, 'I know what I'll do!' Witt had a wooden desk with some ornamentation at the end of it so things wouldn't fall off the edge. It was like a little wooden rollercoaster. So I reached my hand out and I said, 'I'll just make a family of partridges, and I'll have them walk across the screen!' With my fingers, I walked across the edge of his desk, from one side to the other, as if it were happening on the screen, because it was a pretty wide desk. Then I told him that, since color television was pretty new, I would just use the basic colors that make up television—green, blue, red, yellow, and another form of red. He leaned back in this big swivel leather rocking chair. It was one of those original La-Z-Boys that goes all the way back. He put his hands over his head like he had just discovered something big, and he said, 'God, they told me you were great—and you are!' I thought he was going to go over backwards in his chair, he got so excited. I thought, *Please, God,* you know? This kind of job and this kind of money was not something you could find back in Chicago.

"I thought, *You better make hay while the sun shines,* because this couldn't possibly go on. So I went home and I did a storyboard. The bus already existed, and they gave me a picture of it and some film on it. The bus was made up of colors and sections much like a Mondrian painting. Since I was getting away with just about any idea I wanted, I thought about the painted bus, and I thought to myself *Partridges come from eggs. I'll just make a mini-movie of the mother coming out of an egg. I'm going to make an egg out of this Mondrian!* When I broke that egg in half, just off center and down the middle, I was so jazzed with myself! Then I thought it would be cute if she kicked both parts of the egg off the screen, then suddenly she'd turn around and look back to her family to follow her—and they did!" Dvore began to put it together.

"They gave me some film of the bus turning around a corner," he says. "As it turned around and came towards the center of the screen, I had the little guys turn around and look back—as if a bus were suddenly coming up behind them. They would look at it, and think *Whoops! Let's get going!* And that was it!"

Dvore created the artwork that represented each of the actors in the main title as well. "I went to Columbia publicity and looked through all of the pictures that were shot on the set. I found the exact kind of pictures I wanted. I could tell what pictures would translate into their simplest form and still keep the character and the personality of the person. We decided not to do it with painted animation cels. Instead we did it with colored paper cutouts. This way, there would be no possibility for any signs of streaking. Everything would be flat, without any ridges, and then photographed.

"I went to the top title house in town, which was Pacific Title, and I met a man there named Chuck McKinson. He was an animator from the old *Bambi* days.

"I showed him the storyboard and I told him how I wanted them to walk across the screen. In those days there were no computers, so when you wanted to time, for example, how fast the legs moved, or how long the little faces would look back at the bus, you simply imagined it, picturing in your mind what it should look like on a screen. So Chuck would say 'How long do you want that first kick to take place?' He had this glass-top cover on his desk, and so I took a No. 2 pencil and I would just tap on his desk as timing, indicating how long I wanted it kicking off until the image of the egg flew off the screen. I did this with every movement of the partridges.

when we're singin'

When they turned their heads to see the bus coming, McKinson would say 'How fast do you want their heads to turn?' I'd just respond with my pencil. *Tap, tap.* He'd say 'And when they're walking across following the mother, how long do you want that procession to be?' I'd respond with the pencil. *Tap, tap, tap, tap.* After we were finished, he added up the taps of the pencil. With his genius in understanding every single thing, and from the storyboard and my explanation of it, he laid out the sheet." McKinson's timing for the first section exactly matched the planned 30 seconds.

Dvore explains how he created the middle section of the piece. "I used very fast dissolves that looked like cuts, but I didn't want to make it dramatic. It was fun. It was moving. So when Shirley's red and black portrait came on followed by Cassidy and the others, McKinson would again ask 'How long do you want them on the screen until they go out?' I'd respond with *tap, tap, tap.* 'How long's the reading type?' *Tap, tap, tap.* That was the way it was done, and it was done right on the first try."

"*The Partridge Family* took about three weeks. I learned how to work very, very fast because I liked making short half-minute or minute movies. I don't have much of a middle. Some people have patience with the middle of things. I like the high of getting an idea and seeing it come to life as quick as I can, so I made a career out of making very short films and integrating them with my art, and putting them into other people's projects."

Dvore went on to create opening title sequences for several more hit television programs, including *The Waltons, Knots Landing,* and *The Young and the Restless.*

"I loved making that egg look like a Mondrian painting!" he exclaims. "It was a way of making the bus mean something rather than having it simply look like just a bunch of hippies who painted a bus. I tell this story and the story of my little acting performance in front of Paul Witt to everybody," he laughs. "That little opening title was just as easy as magic … just as easy as magic."

"I was in the Big Bon supermarket a couple of years ago and for the first time I saw Shirley Jones shopping in the aisle. I walked up to her and introduced myself and told her I was the one who designed the opening animation for the show. She was so friendly and sweet. She gave me her address and I sent her a print of the original artwork and signed it. That was the last I had anything to do with *The Partridge Family,* and it sort of made it complete."

A Theme Song

Shorty Rogers' theme song for the pilot did not match Wes Farrell's vision. Farrell had to come up with something that set up the story and did so by matching it up to the 60-second mini-movie. Farrell had been listening intently to several different songs submitted specifically as theme song contenders by many of the songwriters who had attended the initial viewing. Though several great songs were written specifically for the theme song, the mechanicals of setting up a premise through lyrics and music—and doing so in only 60 seconds—were constraining.

Farrell finally decided to compose one himself, and he enlisted the help of young songwriter Diane Hildebrand. Probably the most recognizable song that identifies the Partridge Family, even more than "I Think I Love You," is the smiling anthem "Come On Get Happy." As big as it was, and as indelibly woven into the psyche of American pop culture as the definitive Partridge Family theme song, it was not the original. The song specifically written and recorded as a theme song—and ultimately used for the entire first season—is "When We're Singin'." Layered in behind the animated opening sequence, it is the often-forgotten story-chant exclaiming to the world, "There's nothin' better than bein' together … when we're singin'."

On the Air

The egg cracked open and out popped *The Partridge Family*. The show premiered on Friday, September 25, 1970, at 8:30 p.m. on ABC. *The Partridge Family* followed *The Brady Bunch*, which had been on the air since the year before.

The critics hated it. "Looks like it was made for Saturday morning," reported *Variety*. The review goes on to skewer the show's premise ("beyond adult belief"), the acting, the singing, and the music ("nondescript bubblegum tunes"), finding positive things to say only about Shirley Jones and Danny Bonaduce. It concluded, "Even the teenage girls who buy records will see through the flimsy premise that the 'Partridge' kids could make it in today's record market. Show's chances look slim."

But what the critics didn't count on was the public craving for escape and acceptance of implausibility. And all those soon-to-be screaming teens were about to discover their own music while ushering in a fresh teen idol for the new decade.

Liner Notes: *The Partridge Family Album*

On May 4, 1970, the country was devastated when the National Guard opened fire on students at Kent State University who were protesting the Vietnam War. The late 1960s had been a radical time in terms of change. The youth of that era believed they could bring a better, brighter future by eliminating war and exchanging violence for peace; hate for love; and prejudice for equality. The yet-to-be discovered David Cassidy was part of the counterculture and believed in these ideals. He had been known as one of the first guys at his school to grow long hair as a symbol of rebellion.

But the movement had been building emotionally until it became violent and out of control. May 4, 1970, was the day it began to stop. It was a day the nation went into shock.

when we're singin'

The next day, David Cassidy, Wes Farrell, and the new group of singers behind the Partridge Family came together for the first time and recorded their first three songs. One of them—the first song David Cassidy ever recorded—was "I Think I Love You," which would become the television band's biggest hit.

"*I don't know what I'm up against; I don't know what it's all about; I've got so much to think about ...*" So go the lyrics written about the innocence of love and the wondrous moment you feel it for the first time. It speaks to feelings often dismissed as unattainable idealism. But this is not just youthful music to be written off and forgotten. It retains its fans for many reasons, but the biggest is our need to keep a bit of our own innocence preserved—or, at the very least, remembered.

Both the song and the album happened exactly when we needed to turn the dark storm of 1970 into the perfect sunny day. "I Think I Love You" is brilliant in many ways, beginning with the hidden complexities in its musical structure. These were the kind of things the artists would perfect on the Partridge Family albums as they figured out the groove and the groovy, moving forward as musicians, arrangers, singers, songwriters, producers, and even marketers.

By the time the album reviews came out on October 10, 1970, "I Think I Love You" was already rising in the charts, having been launched in August. The show helped the song sell records, and the song helped the show gain viewers. An easy argument can be made for either side of the question: Which came first—the Partridge or the egg?

By the new year of 1971, *The Partridge Family Album* had powered its way into the No. 4 spot on the *Billboard* charts, where it peaked on January 2, 1971, and remained for a second week.

Packed full of potential hits, the album showcases some incredible songs and brilliantly layered harmonies. Its songs are breezy and hopeful, reflecting only good vibes. The nostalgic sound captures what was left of the late 1960s harmonies that popularized such acts as the Byrds, the Mamas & the Papas, and the Cowsills, but with enough new identity to signal that this was something fresh.

The Partridge Family captured an audience from the tail end of the baby boomer generation and the early edge of Generation X. Finding the perfect sound for this segment of the youth—experimenting, preparing, and discovering—is where it all began. Much of that success began with vocal arranger John Bahler.

"Getting the Partridge sound didn't really start until after Wes came on board and we were getting prepared for the first album," he says. "I remember it very well. I was in the middle of a divorce, living in a one-room place over in Burbank called the Equestri-Inn. I remember pulling out all my records and listening to them. Every minute I wasn't working, I sat in that little one-room apartment with all the shades drawn and the lights out, and listened. I listened to the Mamas & the Papas, the

THE BREEZY BEGINNING

Cowsills, the Osmonds, and everything else I could find." Bahler says these three groups were the most influential in developing the Partridge Family's sound. "After I did that for about a week, I just let it go," he says. "I didn't listen to anything more. So when I sat down to write, I came up with a mixture of vocal ideas that were hot during the day, and I found a family sound."

Bahler worked hand in hand with Wes Farrell to establish what would become a distinct sound. David Cassidy was right on board—eager, energetic, very serious, and professional in his approach, according to everyone who worked with him. Shirley Jones took a musical back seat but remained very excited and full of enthusiasm. "Shirley and David really wanted the music to be good," remembers Paul Witt. "They wanted it to be credible, and credible on two levels. First, that this family could conceivably be singing it. David wanted them to be musically credible as well. David loved the music, loved the music business, loved rock and roll, and didn't want simplistic stuff. He wanted credible stuff."

The Partridge Family Album is unique in that the sound—the feel of it—was never repeated in any of the group's subsequent albums. In the beginning of any musical project, there is a search for identity. The sound of the group's first record reflects this quality. There is a little bit of old and a little bit of new in this album, as it combines a nostalgic '60s vibe and the energy of a new beginning with the breakout vocals from David Cassidy.

"You have, or you think you have, all the right answers," says Jackie Ward, "but you don't know for sure. There are certain things you hear to which you say, *That's it!* There are other things you hear and, though you're not quite so sure of it, you still decide to go with it. You may realize later on that something else might have been a little better. Next time you're doing a similar record you might change that piece a little bit. It's searching." Ward thinks quietly for a moment and then adds, "That's the right word—*searching*."

The Partridge Family Album has a long list of credits, including three prominent arrangers—Billy Strange, Don Peake, and Mike Melvoin, each with an amazing background of individual experience. Strange and Peake were primarily guitar players, while Melvoin was first and foremost a keyboard player. The combination of these three individually talented musicians all working on the same album is reflected, overall and in the arrangements of each individual track, in ways that no subsequent Partridge Family album would ever repeat. "A guitar player certainly envisions a musical arrangement differently than a keyboard player," says Jackie Ward. *The Partridge Family Album* is unique in that it exemplifies the unified craft of these three brilliant arrangers and their individual ways of thinking.

During the 1960s the legendary Phil Spector developed his famous "wall of sound" effect. "Spector kind of pushed everything back in the mix," explains John

when we're singin'

Bahler, "and then surrounded it with echo." This technique was invoked by all sorts of bands, and it plays a big role in this album, giving it a significant piece of its identity. *The Partridge Family Album* has a feeling of distance and nostalgia while at the same time filling the entire room with sound.

Background vocalist Ron Hicklin recalls some of the ideas that came into play. "There were certain things we did that were recording techniques of the day. If David needed to sound a little bit younger to reach a certain demographic, we could put a quarter wrap on the capstan and it would speed his voice up just a tad. It made him sound just a little bit younger."

The background vocalists also knew how to enhance Cassidy's voice with their own voices, unnoticed. "At that time David Cassidy's voice was still pretty young," recalls Jackie Ward. "He couldn't sing some of the lower notes, and yet the key was right. It was a good key for him. On some of the songs, Tom Bahler would record a track and sing some of that lower stuff so that they could push those couple of notes that were a little too low for David."

Wes Farrell experimented with lead vocals for the album. David Cassidy sang lead on eight of the 11 tracks, while the remaining three were done with the background vocalists. They sang in blended harmonies, complex throughout, reflecting some of the original sound created by Shorty Rogers. Neither "I'm on the Road" nor "I Really Want to Know You" has any sign of Cassidy's voice, and he has only a short refrain on "To Be Lovers."

It was a brilliant move on Farrell's part. The executives who had given the pilot a green light did so based on Shorty Rogers' original arrangements. By sprinkling Rogers' sound here and there throughout the album, Farrell kept the nervous executives at bay while providing variety and experimentation. "Maybe he thought that if for some reason David wasn't a hit, then maybe he could make the group a hit," speculates Jackie Ward. "That's the way he thought. He didn't think about television shows. He thought about making hit records. *Will this sell on the street? Is it popular? Is it today's sound?* That was his whole perspective. It had nothing to do with anything else. Knowing him, he was trying to cover all his bases. If one thing didn't turn out too well, maybe he could make the other thing happen."

The Partridge Family Album shook up the music industry, making David Cassidy a pop music sensation. It entered the *Billboard* Top 200 charts at No. 98 on October 13, 1970, and stayed on the charts for 68 weeks.

All the songs on *The Partridge Family Album* were used on the television show during the first season. By March 1971 *Cash Box* reported that the album had sold more than a million units: "The Partridge Family, produced by Wes Farrell, have become the hottest TV/recording phenomenon in the music business today." It was

THE BREEZY BEGINNING

one of Bell Records' first three gold albums, and by the new year of 1971, "I Think I Love You" had sold more than two-and-a-half-million copies.

Partridge Family insiders suddenly began receiving persistent calls asking how to book the family for gigs. Shirley Jones was constantly asked where they would be playing next and was always trying to explain that there really was no Partridge Family.

The album credits made the band's identity even more mysterious. "I know there was a period of time where they didn't want anybody to know it was us," says John Bahler. The credits on the back of the album were vaguely worded, reading "Vocal arrangements by John Bahler, Tom Bahler, Jackie Ward and Ron Hicklin." It was never made clear that the actors were not really singing. The credits at the end of the television show were also vague, reading "the voices and music of the Partridge Family were augmented by other performers."

Paul Witt acknowledges the pressure to hide the truth. "We had to," he says. "The marketing called for it. Once David became a hit, it was a different story. When David emerged, we publicized that as much as possible."

Once the cat was out of the bag and both the show and the band had become success stories, the need to keep secrets quickly dissipated, according to Witt. Good music is good music, and that's all that mattered. Despite the initial ploy to hide the real vocalists, Witt has nothing but respect for those singers and their extraordinary voices heard on the albums. "They were the best in the business," he proudly states. "They were professional musicians, and they were amazing."

As session singers, these vocalists were present on hundreds of albums during this era and, like the musicians, never credited. Jackie Ward remembers how fans specifically reacted when they found out the truth about the singers. "They thought everybody on the show did it," she says. "'You're kidding!' they would say. I'd say, 'Nope! We were it!' They were surprised."

A lot of people were also surprised to learn that Shirley Jones had such a small part in the actual recordings. "She is a wonderful singer, but the sound she produced was not the kind of sound that would make that kind of a hit record," says Ward. "She is a marvelous singer in her own right and a wonderful actress."

The Partridge Family Album is gentle, breezy, and full of musical experimentation. Its flavor is eclectic. It contains the most noticeable and frequent use of reverb on any of the Partridge Family albums, as well as the most obvious use of pitch-altering techniques on David Cassidy's voice.

The album was so favored by one '90s filmmaker, Brian Sloan, that he used four songs from it as part of the soundtrack for his 1997 romantic comedy, *I Think I Do*: "I Think I Love You" (both the original Partridge Family version and a cover by Voice of the Beehive); "Somebody Wants to Love You" and "Only a Moment Ago," which are heard as montage music; and "Brand New Me" in the final scene, as the lead

when we're singin'

character peeks at his cassette version of *The Partridge Family Album*. There is even a joke from a character who receives a real partridge (yes, the bird) as a wedding gift: "Barbara said you love partridges."

To say that timing played a role in the magic of this very real band packaged underneath a brilliant marketing image is more than an understatement. In the wake of the period that culminated with the Kent State shootings, it seemed the nation was changing dramatically. It was a new free-spirited time. People wanted to have fun. The 1970s brought plenty of innocent kitsch, including love beads and lava lamps, mood rings and elevator shoes—and let's not forget shag haircuts! Pet rocks and yellow smiley faces both moved into the neighborhood, too. Luckily, some of these things decided to stay. :)

Brand New Me, 2:33, Wes Farrell–Eddie Singleton

"Brand New Me" opens the album with the intimate me-and-you songwriting style that became synonymous with David Cassidy's success. It reflects the narrator's imperfect nature as he professes his deep-hearted promises to change.

"I love this song," said Wes Farrell. "I wrote that with Eddie Singleton. I hadn't seen Eddie in many, many years. I was just at Midem [an international music trade event] in the south of France, and I was standing at the Majestic Hotel waiting to be seated for lunch with my wife. I saw him coming across the patio with his wife and son, who is now grown. I said to my wife, 'Watch this! Wait until he sees me!' His eyes caught mine about 50 feet away. I've very rarely seen people smile that brightly as they approach, step by step. It was the most amazing thing, because I would like to think that we really enjoyed that collaboration, however brief it was. His roots were more R&B, and he really got a big kick out of writing for a pop project. I hadn't seen him in over 20 years. I could not believe time went by like that."

Singleton was most notably remembered for his work in R&B and soul. He had a short-lived record company, Shrine Records, from 1964 to 1967. Singleton co-wrote two Partridge Family songs, both on this album.

The opening hook grabs listeners instantaneously with a strong electric guitar lick. Cassidy's voice is overdubbed and tracked twice on this song and it is sped up, heightening his pitch to make the song feel younger. The track also premieres the complex harmonies of the background vocalists, a key factor as the Partridge Family sound begins its development.

Appears On: Season 1, episode 8, "But the Memory Lingers On"
(November 13, 1970)

Point Me in the Direction of Albuquerque, 3:47, Tony Romeo

One of the first story songs of the 1970s, "Albuquerque" was written before the show ever aired. It was so captivating that an episode of the show was written around the song, rather than the other way around. Capturing a certain effervescence of the '70s, this song by Tony Romeo demonstrates all the elements of that early Partridge sound. Reverb is used on Cassidy's voice most effectively here, creating a mesmerizing haziness along with entrancing instrumental arrangements.

"Albuquerque" is full of the horns, strings, and brass that would come to define the sound of the Partridge Family over the next four years. The song opens with a beautiful piano lick. Acoustic guitar is woven heavily throughout and the vocal harmonies are layered, rich, and full.

"This was one of the first three songs I initially submitted for *The Partridge Family* TV show, having just heard David Cassidy's voice," said Romeo. "The other two were 'I Think I Love You' and 'Morning Rider on the Road.' The difference in style and tone with all three show how little I, or any of us, knew what direction we'd be taking musically. The song's story actually occurred one summer night in New York City. I was browsing a newspaper kiosk when I first laid eyes on the angelic waif.

"I wasn't satisfied with this song when I turned it in. It was written in haste and rushed out, without the fine-tuning I think it needed. That would never happen again. Meanwhile, it was out there and I suffered through it. And in spite of all the flaws, it became one of the most popular and successful Partridge songs. To this day, whenever I hear the song I recall that night, and I see that face. Wherever you are, darlin', I hope you made it OK to Albuquerque."

"At the time, I didn't like this song because I thought it was redundant," says Tony Romeo's brother Frank Romeo. "Then, I thought this song was irrelevant. Now, I think it's a fantastic song. I think it was very influenced by 'Wichita Lineman.' I always thought that."

The passing of time has revealed "Albuquerque" as a fan favorite, though it was never released as a single. When David Cassidy went back out on the road performing concerts again in 2000, he ran a fan poll on his website asking what fans would like to hear him play. "Albuquerque" was one of the top five songs chosen. Since then, Cassidy has nearly always included it in his concert repertoire, and he has conceded it to be one of his favorite Partridge Family songs.

John Bahler responds affectionately as well. "Man, I've probably got about 10 favorite Partridge Family songs, and I've been asked about this before. For whatever reason, I come up with "Albuquerque," probably because it was so much fun to sing. We did things on there that we hadn't really done before. There were little sounds, and little licks, and things we did that only black groups were doing back then."

One of the most engaging performances of the song happened in September 1991 on an episode of daytime talk show *Regis & Kathy Lee*. Cassidy was promoting his first concert tour since 1974, and he sat down and played the song on broadcast television for the first time with only an acoustic guitar and piano accompaniment.

> **Appears On: Season 1, episode 3, "Whatever Happened to the Old Songs?" (October 9, 1970); Season 1, episode 22, "Road Song" (February 26, 1971)**
> **Favorite Partridge Family song of David Cassidy (one of several), Jeremy Gelbwaks, John Bahler, Paul Witt**

Bandala, 2:24, Eddie Singleton–Wes Farrell

When the *Partridge Family* writers created an episode involving racial integration, they came up with "Soul Club," a story in which the family finds themselves booked at a venue where the Temptations were supposed to perform. Richard Prior and Louis Gossett Jr. guest starred.

Wes Farrell needed a song specifically tailored for this episode. He put a few demos together, including a Joerey Ortiz cut from the 1960s titled "Warm My Soul," but it was "Bandala" that ultimately won the spot. Oddly, "Warm My Soul" had far more actual soul and grit, but it was considered a bit too edgy for the image of the Partridge Family. "Bandala" is a great song with a reggae feel, and reflects the fresh thinking and experimental spirit of the group's first album.

"Bandala" is totally different from the songs that came before it. It features violins, cowbells, congas, and more overall percussion than usual, not the typical recipe for blues and soul. So what is it that gives this track its soulful edge? David Cassidy's impassioned voice. A lover of the blues, Cassidy began to make his own personal mark on the Partridge Family music from the early beginnings.

"Soul Club" became so popular with fans throughout the syndicated years that *TV Guide* named it No. 78 on its 1997 list of the 100 greatest TV episodes of all time. When David Cassidy appeared on *The Arsenio Hall Show* on July 13, 1993, Hall played a clip of the episode. An embarrassed Cassidy began to sink in his chair over his character's line "It's sort of an Afro thing." But Hall told Cassidy that it was one of his favorite television episodes.

Paul Witt, who served as director on this episode, also names it as his favorite. "We discussed the music for every episode," says Witt, "and this was an episode that involved the family playing in a primarily African-American nightclub, so we wanted their music to be credible in the sense that an ethnically diverse audience might enjoy it. All of these things were part of the consideration for the musical choices."

The success of "Soul Club" laid the groundwork for *The Partridge Family* to take on other social issues in later episodes, including stories about the environment, women's rights, and the diversity of religion and other cultures.

"'Bandala' was really fun to sing," remembers John Bahler, "but just weird, you know? I remember when Wes wrote it, he wrote it on the spot. He was good at that.

He loved the reggae stuff. I don't think it had anything to do with the show. It was all about feel. He liked the way that song felt."

"'Bandala' fits into the roots of many of the hits I had that came out of rhythm and blues," said Wes Farrell, "and the Afro-Cuban chords, which I used in 'Hang On, Sloopy' and 'Come a Little Bit Closer.' I've written a lot of things in that genre. This just came together, although I had to go a lot softer with this one and a lot sweeter because of the theme of the show. I cleaned it up a little bit."

"Bandala"—or Ban-da-lay-la, as it is actually sung on the recording—is the name of a girl.

Appears On: Season 1, episode 18, "Soul Club" (January 29, 1971)

I Really Want to Know You, 2:55, Barry Mann–Cynthia Weil

With the similarities between the premise of *The Partridge Family* and the success of the real-life Cowsills, it is no wonder Wes Farrell chose this song. Written specifically for the Cowsills, "I Really Want to Know You" is the first cover tune by the Partridge Family and the only one on the album. Experimenting with style, Farrell left off Cassidy's lead vocal and featured his background singers, adding variety to the album's track list.

"I Really Want to Know You" first appeared on *The Cowsills II by II*, released earlier the same year on the MGM label. The original version features a female lead vocal and an even slower tempo, giving it a churchlike quality. Both the Partridge Family's and the Cowsills' versions perfectly reflect the late 1960s peace, love, and happiness vibe. With a couple of acoustic guitars, strings, piano, and more gorgeous harmonies, Melvoin and Bahler showcase their abilities as arrangers. According to songwriter Cynthia Weil, "I Really Want to Know You" was written with the help of Russ Titelman, although he is not credited.

When John Bahler was working with the Ford group, they recorded this song. "We used a parody of that to open our show because the writer we had at the time was really good at writing parodies. He wrote this, and we basically came out and to say to the audience, 'We really want to know you. We want to get to know you.'"

Appears On: Season 1, episode 5, "When Mother Gets Married"
(October 23, 1970)
Favorite Partridge Family song of Shirley Jones (one of several)

Only a Moment Ago, 2:33, Terry Cashman–Tommy West

Both Terry Cashman and Tommy West remember having written this song for episode 4, "See Here, Private Partridge," but Farrell and the television producers decided to place it in another episode after it was completed.

when we're singin'

"When we started writing songs for the show, the first two we wrote were 'Only a Moment Ago' and 'She'd Rather Have the Rain,' and they were accepted very quickly," says West. "'Only a Moment Ago' was the first," recalls Cashman, adding, "It's a very nice song. Sometimes Wes would say to us, 'We need a song for this situation' or 'This is what's going on in this episode.' Then there were other times we would just write what we thought were good pop songs and give them to Wes. He would pass them along to the television producers and they would fit them into whatever episode they wanted to."

The lyric for this song is strong, and the beautiful string arrangements become a recurring theme on the album. "Only a Moment Ago," with its noticeable use of reverb, evokes a feeling of nostalgia, a gentle longing for the old days and the sentiment of good times past. Cashman and West were enjoying success at the top of their game during this period. "Cashman was very, very good at coming up with titles," recalls West. "We would write songs as easy as eating a sandwich," he says. Cashman often found a strong lyric and West would play a bigger role in writing the melody, though both songwriters crossed over. A song like this would only take them a couple of hours at most.

Appears On: Season 1, episode 10, "Go Directly to Jail" (November 27, 1970)

I Can Feel Your Heartbeat, 2:05,
Wes Farrell–Mike Appel–Jim Cretecos

"Sometimes titles just come to you out of the air," recalls songwriter Mike Appel. "This was such a case. I mean we knew that David would become a heartthrob for God knows how many kids, but the title just came to us." So often a good pop song emerges in this way. "As much as I love Wes Farrell—and I do—he had nothing to do with any of our songs written for the Partridge Family except for 'Doesn't Somebody Want to Be Wanted.' Jim and I knew if we included Wes' name on all our songs, they would have a better shot at getting recorded—and we were right."

"Heartbeat" was recognized as a potential hit single very early on. It is driving, pulsating, and builds to a powerful climax. The use of the synthesizer creates a spooky, almost haunting, rock vibe. From the opening drumbeats to the harmonies filling it out later on, this song is penetrating. It is the first high-energy song on *The Partridge Family Album*. David Cassidy belts it out, showing us for the first time his power to rock.

In the episode music videos, Cassidy is very animated in his performance on this number. It's obvious he connects to it with the same enthusiasm as his fans. In fact, Cassidy chose to open his first concert, in March 1971, with "Heartbeat." It made its mark that evening with such an impression that it became a standard opener for nearly all of his concerts up to the present day.

THE BREEZY BEGINNING

Songwriter Mike Appel never knew of Cassidy's concert tradition with this song and was pleasantly surprised. "Somehow this song is more sentimental than the others for me," he says. "I always liked that particular song because it reminded me of Herman's Hermits' "Can't You Hear My Heart Beat."

The original title of the song was actually "I Can Hear Your Heartbeat," which is the way it reads on the back of the *Partridge Family Album* cover. Despite the listing, the actual lyric heard on the record is "I can feel your heartbeat." One version was likely replaced by the other at the last second, leaving no time for a title correction on the cover before going to print. "It was always 'I can *hear* your heartbeat," says Appel, "but they changed [the lyrics] for the record." Wes Farrell consistently referred to it as "I Can Hear Your Heartbeat" in his 1993 interview with Ken Sharp.

"All the albums sold well," explained Farrell as he began his story on "Heartbeat." "People talk about selling a million units today. We were selling millions of units. We were selling 50,000 records a day! It was incredible! It was beyond anybody's comprehension. But I tell you, I made one mistake: I made a decision, not totally on my own, but in agreement with Larry Uttal. The first album was so big in terms of volume and sales; it was my feeling that if we put out another single it would water down the album sales, so we purposely didn't release another single from the first album. However, I think that 'I Can Hear Your Heartbeat' probably would have been another top five record. I had a couple versions of it, too. Now that I listen to it, in that time period, it probably would have been another top five record for us. So if we had one oversight I think that was it. 'I Can Hear Your Heartbeat,' incidentally, was a top five record in a lot of markets."

Danny Bonaduce has special affection for this song as well. "If I'm out on the street, or in public, or the mall, or the grocery store, or whatever it is in a 24-hour day, the Partridge Family comes up in the life of this 50-year-old man at least 20 times a day—most times from people coming up to me and talking to me about it. But sometimes it's my wife and I laying in bed. I like to sing in bed. Sometimes I lay my head on her shoulder and I say, 'Honey, I can feel your heartbeat,' casually, almost romantically, and then I'll go '... and you didn't even say a word!' Then we both crack up. I know every word to it!"

The use of drums creates the opening hook as the song builds, filling it out with growing harmonies later on. There is also some use of the electric guitar here. The late-'70s disco smash "Jive Talkin'" by the Bee Gees opens with the same kind of guitar techniques.

"I Can Feel Your Heartbeat" was used on the series a total of four times, making it the most utilized Partridge Family song that appeared on both an album and the show.

***Appears On**: Season 1, episode 14, "The Red Woodloe Story"*
(January 1, 1971); Season 1, episode 15, "Mom Drops Out" (January 8, 1971);

when we're singin'

Season 1, episode 17, "Why Did the Music Stop?" (January 22, 1971);
Season 1, episode 24, "A Partridge by Any Other Name" (March 12, 1971)
Favorite Partridge Family song of Danny Bonaduce, Mike Appel

I'm on the Road, 2:50, Barry Mann–Cynthia Weil

When Wes Farrell organized the pilot viewing for his songwriter friends, the successful songwriting couple Barry Mann and Cynthia Weil attended. Farrell said he needed songs for the show, but he was also looking for something else. He needed the perfect theme song. Mann and Weil caught on to the free and easy feeling of a family working together as musicians, and they were inspired.

"I'm on the Road" was written as Mann and Weil's vision for the show's theme song. While several other writers at the pilot screening that day also contributed prospective theme songs for *The Partridge Family*, "I'm on the Road" became Farrell's first choice. On June 27, 1970, Bell Records and Screen Gems sent out a press release announcing that "I'm on the Road" would be the official theme song. The song was also announced as the intended second single to be released, following the release of "I Think I Love You."

"I'm on the Road" was worked on intensively during the early recording sessions, some five months before the show premiered. It was initially completed on May 16, 1970, and re-recorded on June 11. The final version was triple-tracked and it is laden with complex chords, including a lot of major seventh and major sixth chords. The effect is loungey, distant, and smoky, with an echo-chamber-like effect.

"I'm on the Road" is colored with vivid imagery and very lyrical in nature. It's loaded with the hopeful quality for which the Partridge Family sound would become known. The tune is also surprisingly bluesy, with its "gotta get on" refrains, and it captures an ethereal quality, with lyrics that speak of the past and the present, and the hope of finding what they are looking for somewhere on the road.

In another twist, "I'm on the Road" became one of only three songs on the album featuring the blended harmonies of the background singers as the lead vocal, rather than David Cassidy. At least four versions of the track were completed, including at least one with Cassidy singing lead. Bold in delivery, the Cassidy version produces a very different feeling.

In the end, both the theme song version and the plans for a single release were mysteriously shelved. The powers that be decided to use the version with the blended voices for the album, and the TV producers did the same for the show. The version with Cassidy's lead vocal was lost in the vaults at Screen Gems and has remained there through all these years, making it one of the most sought-after unreleased Partridge Family songs in the entire catalog.

"I'm on the Road" is the only track on the album put down in mono rather than stereo, leaving suspicion of a late switch—possibly a decision at the very last second to replace the Cassidy lead vocal with the harmonic version.

The Partridge Family recorded four songs written by this accomplished team, but "I'm on the Road" was the only Mann–Weil song composed specifically for the group.

Appears On: Season 1, episode 3, "Whatever Happened to the Old Songs?" (October 9, 1970); Season 1, episode 4, "See Here, Private Partridge" (October 16, 1970)

To Be Lovers, 2:44, Mark Charron

This is the only Partridge offering by songwriter Mark Charron, who wrote several songs for pop sensation B.J. Thomas during the '60s. The arrangement is Latin in flavor, with horns and a classical nylon-string Spanish guitar—typical of that transitional era and reflective of artists such as the impeccable Herb Alpert.

The fluid vocal harmonies are again obvious as they work like a through line for the emerging Partridge sound. Farrell, for the third time, goes with a vocal track made up primarily of the four background vocalists, with only a hint of David Cassidy singing on one short refrain. The hands of the many musical masters enlisted for this project were clearly in full control of the Partridge Family's musical destiny. *Olé!*

Appears On: Season 1, episode 11, "This is My Song" (December 4, 1970)

Somebody Wants to Love You, 2:33, Wes Farrell–Mike Appel–Jim Cretecos

The earliest seeds for the composition of this song date much further back than Partridge Family days, according to songwriter Mike Appel. "We had the title long before the Partridge Family project but never gave it a thought for David until Wes said he liked it," explains Appel. "We weren't sure about 'Somebody Wants to Love You' as a song that was right for David Cassidy at the time. Wes Farrell heard me singing it and jumped in the writers' room with Jim and I and said that he wanted that song for David—and that was it! Wes was the boss!"

Farrell liked it so much he decided to make it the B-side on the single release of "I Think I Love You." Once again, the arrangers toy with various sounds so subtly that the listener doesn't really know what's going on. In this case, they slip a little country into the opening hook with a 12-string acoustic guitar. Cassidy's voice is sped up here, with a little reverb. The result is a catchy tune with a hint of twang. The guitar part is country-flavored, and that lick shows up again right before the first chorus. Full of Bahler's strong vocal arrangements, it successfully mixes pop and country, giving us another delightful experiment in sound. David Cassidy is strong on this track.

when we're singin'

Appears On: Season 1, episode 6, "Love at First Slight" (October 30, 1970)
Season 1, episode 9, "Did You Hear the One About Danny Partridge?" (November 20, 1970)

I Think I Love You, 2:52, Tony Romeo

To say that this song is anything less than brilliant would be foolish. The Partridge Family's all-time biggest hit is packed with clever phrases, catchy hooks, and intelligent arrangements.

It opens with a fast 12-string acoustic guitar, starting out in a minor chord and staying there until the first chorus. This is also the first appearance of the harpsichord that would become a signature sound for the Partridge Family up through the last album. The way the harpsichord is used brings out a subtle baroque nuance.

The lyric is dark and mysterious, and doesn't resolve until the lead singer shouts the reason for his consternation at the climax of the first verse. He's in love! And Cassidy, as interpreter, blurts it out with the kind of energetic complexity and self-discovery that suggest it scares him as much as it excites him.

"I Think I Love You" was released to this review from *Cash Box*: "In the beginning was the Nelson family. Came the Monkees and Cowsills and now the Partridge Family. Attractive sound side and material curries favorable attention from all types of pop programmers: teen, adult and in between."

It entered the *Billboard* Top 100 charts on October 10 at No. 75 and steadily began climbing—No. 60, No. 41, No. 17, No. 7. It made its first appearance on the television show on November 13 and showed up on the *Billboard* charts the next day at No. 4. A week later, on November 21, it landed into the No. 1 position, bumping out the Jackson 5's "I'll Be There" and staying for three weeks.

It was ranked by *Billboard* as No. 6 for the year 1970, and in the Casey Kasem radio countdown on January 5, 1980, the top 50 hits of the 1970s includes "I Think I Love You" at number 46.

"'I Think I Love You' was take one," said Wes Farrell. "I really liked the way it felt, and because it was take one I rehearsed it for about half an hour. When we got to the instrumental solo it took on its own measure of balance. It was out there all by itself. Larry Knechtel thought the take was breaking down and he laughed about halfway through the middle of it. I was in the studio with headsets on, and I was directing what was taking place. He looked at me in the middle of his laugh, and I had a serious look on my face, and I waved to him to keep going. Don't stop! That's when it hit him that he shouldn't have laughed! Meanwhile we did take two, and take three, and take four, and take five, and take six, and I said to my engineer, 'I think I got the right take back at the beginning of this whole thing.'

"After you rehearse everybody there's a certain level of energy, and when it settles down there's that magic moment that happens in the studio where everything's live. It's really very difficult to recreate that. I felt it had gone by us. It took me, realistically, about two hours to do the track, and it took me five hours to filter out the laugh, because when I went back to take one, the problem was that the laugh was on the master tape all over the place! After all kinds of fooling around and no other take could be spliced in because it, just again, breathed. When something breathes like that it works."

The trademark Partridge Family harpsichord sound also found its footing in this song. "I just liked it," said Farrell. "It lent well to the balance of that particular tune and it added a little element to it of change, as the bass voice did. Larry Knechtel played the harpsichord on 'I Think I Love You,' and Mike Melvoin did a lot of the keyboard work and Michael Omartian did some of it."

"I think the great thing about 'I Think I Love You' is the vocal interlude where we did this two-part fugue in the middle of the song. It was very baroque. David couldn't sing the musical interlude," remembers John Bahler. "He was only 19 years old. It was too low for him, so that was done by Ron Hicklin, Tom, and I. Jackie sang the youngest kid, and I sang the next youngest kid. Ron Hicklin sang the next youngest, and then we called my brother the teenage bass because his part was so high." (So according to this account, Jackie Ward was in essence the voice of Tracy, John Bahler was Chris, Ron Hicklin was Danny, and Tom Bahler was Laurie!)

Ron Hicklin recalls, "Tom and I were singing the bottom part where it was too low for David. John, Tom, and I were basically tenors, and Jackie was an alto. We all had very similar ranges, and we could extend down low and do all this younger stuff that way. We were actually overdubbing that part."

Bahler continues, "Every time I listen to that I think, man, that's one of the early ones. It's one of them that I wrote on the session. That just came from the heavens, you know? We just jotted it down, and we just sang it. I remember doing things like that, and when I listen to it, it just puts a smile on my face. I remember how much fun it was; how much fun it was to write, and how much fun it was to perform. And even more fun to have people love it, you know?"

Tony Romeo often spent time with his friend and fellow Partridge Family songwriter Tommy West and his family. "My wife and I were living in Nashville for a while and sometimes Tony came down and stayed with us for a few days," says West. It was during one of those stays that Romeo confided to West his story behind this song. As West recalls, "'I Think I Love You' was based on a '50s song called 'Kiss of Fire' which was out in the early '50s before rock and roll kind of pop songs." The song was recorded by Toni Arden, a pop singer who emerged out of the 1940s big-band era.

"Space would not allow what can be said about the effect of this song on my life," Romeo said. "It's been loved, loathed, covered by other artists, clobbered by the press, satirized, instrumentalized, camped, tramped, revamped, Muzaked, film-scored, be-bopped, and hip-hopped. It's been Frenched, Dutched, Italianated, Germanicized, Japanified, Hispanicated and Down-Undered. It sold global millions. Sudden millions. At one point there were six LPs on the top 100 chart containing the song, three of which were certified gold.

"And what a life-changer! It was my third gold single in two years and the one that made me feel like I'd be around a while. With one, you worry about being a one-hit wonder. With two, it's 'Sing me a medley of both your hits.' With three, you got what you came for—you have a career. Thank you, everybody. Thank you, Wes, for going with it. And most of all you, David, our gifted messenger who lifted us off and sailed us away to strange and extraordinary places."

Extraordinary places, indeed. The pop culture references to this song are unending. One of the most memorable is a cleverly placed reference in the 1994 British film *Four Weddings and a Funeral*, in which Hugh Grant's character quotes the song title while professing his love to the woman of his dreams. "I Think I Love You" also inspired the title of the 1997 feature film *I Think I Do*. As recently as 2015 "I Think I Love You" is still popping up—played at a critical moment in the comedy *Trainwreck*. The song also provided author Allison Pearson the title for her novel *I Think I Love You*, released in 2011, an upbeat fun-loving adventure about two middle-aged women from England who travel across the Atlantic in a quest to meet their childhood idol, David Cassidy.

Partridge Family songwriters hail "I Think I Love You" as one of the greatest works of pop songwriting ever put to verse, and many of those interviewed for this book brought the subject up without ever being asked. "Before I hang up, let me talk about my favorite Partridge Family song that I didn't write," adds L. Russell Brown at the end of a telephone conversation. "It is by a man who died early in life—Tony Romeo, my late friend and brother songwriter. He most certainly wrote the Partridge Family's greatest hit song. The instant I heard 'I Think I Love You,' I told Wes, 'This is a No. 1 record! It's a smash!'

"The song has a haunting melody and a lyric that touches you," continues Brown. "It starts out in a minor and goes to a major in the hook. Every part of the song is hooky, just like a Bee Gees song. The song will live on even after the Partridge Family is forgotten and someone else in the future makes it a hit again."

There have been many attempts, but so far no one has outdone the Partridge Family's original version. "I Think I Love You" has been recorded countless times through the years, including a bouncy 1991 alternative rendition by UK girl group Voice of the Beehive. Less Than Jake covered it in 2003, and their version was used in the horror film *Scream 2*.

Cassidy himself re-recorded it a number of times in different styles. In 1986 he released a live version as part of the double album *His Greatest Hits Live*. Cassidy also jazzed it up a bit in 1998 on *Old Trick New Dog*, and even went techno–dance with it on his 2007 CD *David Cassidy—Part II The Remix* (also known as *Dance Party Remix*). In 2002 he released a new version on his platinum-selling *Then and Now* album, meticulously recreating it right down to the original background vocals exactly as they were done the first time around, and with the same singers except for Ron Hicklin. These new versions were also heard on his self-produced television movie, *The David Cassidy Story*, which premiered January 9, 2000, on NBC. He went on to record a slow, bluesy version for his 2003 album *Touch of Blue*, but it was ultimately not included on the CD track list and currently remains unreleased. His daughter, Katie Cassidy, offered up a take in her own attempt at a recording career in 2002. And it hardly stops there.

The crooners of the era were jumping on board within weeks of the original song's debut. As early as November of 1970, while "I Think I Love You" was reigning on the charts, Perry Como recorded his own version of it, and by 1971 Andy Williams had followed suit. "I Think I Love You" received a hip-hop nod in 1992 by Nice & Smooth on their album *Hip Hop Junkies*. Clam Abuse covered it in 1999. Solo artist Kaci did it in 2002. Paul Westerberg in 2004. Declan Galbraith in 2007. The list goes on and on, and it will surely continue to grow.

"Tony Romeo's 'I Think I Love You' was the song that made it all possible for the rest of us to ride his coattails a bit," says songwriter and producer Mike Appel. "It was such a huge success. When you looked at Tony Romeo, he looked like he came out of the back country, but he wrote the most poppy kind of melodies. Tony got the ball rolling big time. That was his biggest contribution, as I see it."

"Tony used to come up and visit," says Romeo's good friend and Partridge Family songwriting collaborator Ken Jacobson. "We talked about songs all the time. Once he came up and said he wanted me to hear something that had been recorded. It was the first recording of 'I Think I Love You' by the Partridge Family, but it wasn't out yet. We played it and he said, 'What do you think?' I said, 'First of all, I love the song, but it dies in the middle and then comes back.' And he said, 'Oh my God, that's exactly what I think!' How wrong were we? It couldn't have been more successful!"

Bassist Joe Osborn also hails the tune as one of the greats. "The one song that stands out, that I really still love, is 'I Think I Love You,'" he says. "I just love that record."

The cast members remember its powerful impact and sudden explosion on the music scene. "The first time I heard it was in the recording studio," says Shirley Jones. "I have to say, when I heard him sing it in the recording studio I thought, *Wow!* I knew it was a great song for him. I thought, *Yeah! This is going to be something!*"

"This is actually one of those sitcom moments," reflects Danny Bonaduce. "The first time I ever heard 'I Think I Love You' I was in a car with some friends. I can't remember why or where because we were all too young to drive, but I heard it on

AM radio. I remember the song was probably 30 or 40 seconds in, and I had never heard it because they recorded it before the airing of *The Partridge Family*. So when the DJ said 'the Partridge Family,' my ears perked up. I mean they were playing a song by a band that I'm supposed to be in—even though I wasn't really—and now it's on the radio! It was like that big moment in movies when a band first hears their song on the car radio and they flip out. *We've made it!* you shout. But it took like 30 seconds for it all to sink in.

"It was really weird because it was supposedly me in there somewhere, but it really wasn't. We were several weeks into shooting the show, and I remember one day I went back to work and there were 500 people in my front yard with signs—most of them for David Cassidy, by the way, which was very annoying! But people with signs saying *We Love Danny! We Love David! I Think I Love You!* It was pretty amazing. It's one of those skyrocket stories!"

"I thought 'I Think I Love You' was a brilliant song because it was a young teenage song and yet it had depth to it," John Bahler explains. "It was vulnerable for me. He's talking, and then he just pours it out. It was so sweet! Every guy knows what it feels like. It's just that very awkward moment when all of a sudden you just go I THINK I LOVE YOU! And then you go, *Oops*."

On March 13, 1971, *Cash Box* reported that "I Think I Love You" had sold 3.1 million copies, and by the following week that report was at 3.5 million copies. "I Think I Love You" was voted single of the year for 1970 at the National Association of Recording Merchandisers conference. It was the fastest selling single of the year. It also won the BMI Award for the most performed song of 1970.

"It was the first record I ever made," said David Cassidy. "We made some good records and that one was one of the best."

> *Appears On*: *Season 1, episode 8, "But the Memory Lingers On" (November 13, 1970); Season 1, episode 12, "My Son, the Feminist" (December 11, 1970); Season 4, episode 77, "Beethoven, Brahms, and Partridge" (September 29, 1973) Favorite Partridge Family song of David Cassidy (one of several), L. Russell Brown*

Singing My Song, 2:10, Diane Hildebrand

Aside from the season one theme song, this is the only Partridge offering by Diane Hildebrand. It's certainly the most edgy song on the album, opening powerfully with a prominent electric guitar accentuated with a fuzz pedal.

Diane Hildebrand was a young songwriter and one of the only single women signed to Screen Gems at the time. Hildebrand had written countless lyrics with Jack Keller. She was considered very good at her craft and very fast. She won several gold records, including three for the Monkees. Hildebrand released her own solo album on Elecktra titled *Early Morning Blues and Greens*, and she wrote or co-wrote every song on the album, an exciting endeavor given that she had primarily written for other artists up to that point. She had written countless lyrics for various artists. This particular lyric, though written for the Partridge Family, also spoke to her personal passions.

"I always wanted to sing my own song," says Hildebrand. "I didn't want to sing what they wanted me to write. You see, I was a flower child and I really believed that the world needed to change, and that we could make everything all right. I didn't think it was going to take so long, and I didn't think it was going to get this bad, but eventually I think everything will be all right. I still have the same belief system that I had then. People have confused those of us who believed that greed really needed to leave the world, and that we need to really love more, with those that were into drugs, free sex, and all of that. It was a time and a chance to express myself—to love more. I was always like that. That was more of what the '60s were about for me."

David Cassidy clearly taps into those ideas when he belts this lyric. His voice shows its strength, climbing out of the distance and pushing past the reverb. It is a precurser of Cassidy's own personal vocal evolution, his capabilities, and what was yet to come.

Appears On: Season 1, episode 10, "Go Directly to Jail" (November 27, 1970); Season 1, episode 13, "Star Quality" (December 18, 1970)

Album Summary and Reviews

Total Time: 27:26
Original Release: September 1970, Bell 9050

Having made their television debut, the Partridge Family featuring Shirley Jones and David Cassidy now makes their album debut. They've a well blended sound, and the impact of the TV series is sure to bolster sales of this LP. Along with their current single "I Think I Love You," they offer top treatments of "Singing My Song," "I Really Want to Know You" and "Brand New Me." *Billboard, October 10, 1970*

With their own ABC television series, a single on the charts, and thousands of fans across the country, the Partridge Family's album can't miss. Of the 11 tracks on the album, "Brand New Me," "I Really Want to Know You," "Singing My Song," and "Point Me in the Direction of Albuquerque" are among the more interesting. *Cash Box, October 10, 1970*

First Chart Appearance: October 31, 1970 (**Billboard,** *No.* **98; Record World,** *No.* **84; Cash Box,** *No.* **55**)

MADE FOR TV
*or ... **The Partridge Family Up to Date***

Instant Fame

The Partridge Family became a household name overnight. Headlines in *Cash Box* declared "Bell Sees Biggest Single in 'Partridge,'" with 300,000 copies of "I Think I Love You" sold in the first three weeks of its release. The article continues, "The Partridge Family disking of 'I Think I Love You' is shaping up as the biggest singles seller in Bell Records' history." By December 26, full-page thank-you ads from Bell Records were running in the trades reading "Thanks for Making Our First Record First!" In addition, *The Partridge Family Album* was among the top-selling albums of the year, and its reign continued into 1971.

The show was holding the lead against NBC and CBS for the time slot. By December 6, only three weeks after "I Think I Love You" hit No. 1, ABC announced that *The Partridge Family* would be renewed for the remaining batch of episodes filling out the entire first season. The actors had completed 14 episodes by Christmas and were given a month off so the writers could get a little bit ahead with the new round of scripts.

Despite the record-breaking success of the music from Bell Records, the show's initial overall ratings were respectable but modest. While *Billboard* and *Cash Box* reported No. 1 rankings for the music, Neilson ranked *The Partridge Family* in a three-way tie at No. 25 with *The Carol Burnett Show* and the *NBC Friday Night Movie of the Week*. For quite some time during the airing of the first season, the producers were not sure whether the show would be renewed for a second season. But as the audience grew and fans latched on, they did so with intensity. The music, and the launching of the first single, had much to do with that.

The Partridge Family's music hit the pop scene with a thunderbolt of success—sudden and unequivocal. Even before the green-light renewal for another season of the show was given, there was no question that another album would come, and come fast.

David Cassidy's star was about to launch. "I remember watching the first episode of *The Partridge Family* at the Breckys' house," recalls Danny Bonaduce. "They were the neighbors at the corner. We lived on a cul de sac with kids that ranged from my age, 10, to my brother's age, 17, and about 10 of us got together. If you went to school in San

when we're singin'

Fernando Valley, or Hollywood, or L.A., there were at least three child actors in your school, so it was nothing super novel to see one of the kids in your neighborhood on TV.

"So we watched it, and we all thought it was pretty cool. There were some that just didn't really care. Then we went outside and played. The next day, all of a sudden there were cars that nobody recognized lining up in front of our house! People were honking horns and holding signs! It happened literally overnight."

The show's success was instantly felt by all the actors, especially David Cassidy. The onslaught of sudden attention brought out some new ego in the kids.

"When the pilot became the giant success that it was, we signed up for more shows," says Shirley Jones. "Right after that, everybody—Danny, David, and Susan—were suddenly saying, 'The next episode better be mine.' They were arguing over who would get the next episode, who was going to be written about first, that kind of thing. And that's when I thought, *Uh-oh. We have trouble here.* So I literally sat them all down on the set and I stood up and I lectured. I said 'Guys, we have what looks like a big hit show here, but I want to tell you something. We're not going to have a hit show if this attitude continues. You can't do this,' I said. 'We'll have good writers, good directors, and we have a wonderful producer in Bob Claver. He will choose. Everybody will have their moment, but none of us can dictate that. None of us can play the star. We have to go along with whatever happens. If there's something you don't like in the script, of course you can talk to the director or the producer, but nobody's going to be the star of this show. Each one of us will have our own time. You better get that now.'"

"Shirley had extraordinary patience," says producer Paul Witt. "She's a great actress who had done some extraordinary films, and for her to do this series with a bunch of inexperienced kids was remarkable. She had grace. She had charm. She had equilibrium and a good humor. She was a saint."

"Shirley was like a mom," says Suzanne Crough. "Very much so. If we were out of check, she'd get us in check. She didn't want to put up with our crap. She was, and is, a very professional, very classy lady. I have the utmost respect for her." Susan Dey also spoke to the jealousies that almost arose at the time, particularly in the wake of Cassidy's success. "We resented the totem-pole status," she said. "But mainly the resentment that was felt for a time was not because David had become an overnight superstar, but because he was so busy, and so very much with it. That was great! We all wanted that. I think it was a sign of maturity that we outgrew it." According to Jones, they outgrew it very quickly, and supported one another like a real family.

I'm on the Road?

By the new year of 1971, David Cassidy started thinking about going out on the road. At this point the only music he had to pull from was the songs from the first album and some of the new songs that were about to appear on the second album, *Up to Date*, scheduled for release in March. There was not yet any completed solo music from Cassidy himself.

David Cassidy opened his first concert at 8:30 on Friday night, March 26, 1971, at the Seattle Coliseum, and the teenyboppers nearly shred their vocal cords in ecstasy. The headline in the *Seattle Times* read "David Cassidy Scores Hit in Concert Debut at Arena." The article opens with a description of the frenzied excitement as "a scream that would make a banshee turn in his union card."

Attendance was estimated at 5,400 fans with an average age of seven. Cassidy's legacy began that day—his lifelong imprint on members of an impressionable age group who, in many cases, would truly love him for the rest of their lives. "Cassidy didn't have to do anything but be there to be a rousing success," says the review. "For those of us who were lucky to be close enough to the amplifiers to hear his music, Cassidy actually put on a good show." The review goes on to describe Cassidy as a performer with poise and an "as yet unpolished magnetism."

The show opened with a local group, Chinook, followed by two additional acts, soloist Brooks Hunnicut and the duo of Kim Carnes and Dave Ellingson, who also performed backup for Cassidy. Carnes and Ellingson's performance was likened to gospel-style rock, with Carnes' voice drawing particular praise. There was also an impressive array of orchestral instruments behind Cassidy. The review closes, "We attended the concert reluctantly (we're over 15), and although our ears will probably ring for a month, we must admit that the concert was fun. And David Cassidy seems to have successfully launched his first concert tour."

The next concert scheduled was in Portland, Oregon, the following night and it was met with the same energetic response. A solo career for David Cassidy was born.

Having finished his first weekend of concert gigs, Cassidy returned to the set on Monday to begin taping for the show. The success of the initial performances demanded additional dates. An entire roster of cities across the country was now scheduling concerts for summer of 1971. It was the first official David Cassidy concert tour.

He was back out on the road in May for two more dates, playing an amusement park venue in Detroit and another date in Canton, Ohio. By June he was touring regularly. He returned to Ohio first, playing dates in Cincinnati, Columbus, and Cleveland. It was an adventurous summer, interrupted with a gall bladder attack and surgery in July. More dates were booked for August, ending the month with another Ohio date at Idora Park, a small amusement park in Youngstown. The mayor officially declared the concert date (August 29, 1971) David Cassidy Day.

Meanwhile, Wes Farrell began to plan the obvious next move—a David Cassidy solo album. At the same time he was in full gear planning the music for season

2, part of which would debut on the third Partridge Family album—*The Partridge Family Sound Magazine*—scheduled for release in August.

Farrell was thrilled with Cassidy's success. "David *was* the Partridge Family," said Farrell. "And Shirley, because of the magnitude of her talent as a vocalist—but David was the front man and he deserved to get the recognition. His shows were dynamite, man! He would walk on that stage and explode! The band did a wonderful job."

There was no doubt that David Cassidy had found a way to make this music his own, but he couldn't see it at the time. The marketing of the television image was so well done that Cassidy felt most of the public was looking at him as Keith Partridge. The longevity of his career would later suggest otherwise, but it was difficult for him to believe at the time. He began to crave the free expression of his own musical identity.

Getting Together

As *The Partridge Family* was heading toward the end of the first season, the show was now among the highest rated of ABC's new programs—and the response to the music was phenomenal.

Both *The Partridge Family Album* and *Up to Date* were riding the top of the pop charts. *Cash Box* touted "New Partridge LP Spotlights Bell's Diversified Release," and *Up to Date* was declared gold only a few days after its release. Irv Biegel, vice president of Bell Records, called the *Up to Date* certification "the fastest and most exciting for our company." "Doesn't Somebody Want to Be Wanted" was also dominating the charts, and the Partridge Family was nominated for a Grammy Award for best new artist. By spring, "I'll Meet You Halfway" became the second single from *Up to Date*—hot on the rise on both the pop and the easy listening charts.

The trades were also announcing the group as a global winner. Australia loved Cassidy and the Partridge Family, and "I Think I Love You" was a hit in Ireland, Japan, and South Africa. Biegel credited the Partridge Family as an example of artists who were proving "the validity of music as a universal means of communication." From the network's standpoint, the music-to-television crossover plan was working, as it had with the Monkees, and Screen Gems began developing more of the same. The newest brainstorm was titled *Getting Together*, a proposed spinoff from *The Partridge Family*'s season 1 finale guest starring Bobby Sherman.

It was rumored that *Getting Together* had been loosely based on Tommy Boyce and Bobby Hart, who were best known as writers and producers for the Monkees. According to Hart, *Getting Together* wasn't just based on Boyce and Hart but was originally developed to star the two. "Screen Gems had cast us on all the shows they had running at the time," says Hart. "We guest starred on *Bewitched* and *The Flying Nun*. They were giving us acting lessons, and it was developed right up to that point. Then it just ended abruptly because Tommy quit the business. We had our own record label, which was distributed by Bell, and when we signed with them we made big commitments that I was not able to fulfill without Tommy. So we had to give back a whole bunch of money they'd given us, and that became this Bobby Sherman project."

Having found success on the charts with "Julie, Do You Love Me?" and other hits in addition to his two years on *Here Come the Brides*, Sherman was an established teen idol with a devoted fan base and a reputation as a down-to-earth guy—"the nicest kid ever," in Bob Claver's words. "He was wonderful, and he was popular with that particular age group. He wasn't nearly as good a singer as David, but he was easy to work with."

The pilot, called "A Night In Shining Armor," slated Sherman as a young songwriter and Wes Stern as an eccentric lyricist. "That was a good example of a backdoor pilot," says associate producer Mel Swope. A backdoor pilot is written to put the weight of the episode on the proposed new series, keeping the stars of the established show in the background.

True to its usual format, the *Partridge Family* episode featured a song, with Bobby Sherman singing the opening bars and David Cassidy carrying it through. The song, "Stephanie," was a reused melody with a reworked lyric from another song, "All of the Things," that had aired earlier in the first season. Neither song was ever released on a studio album by either the Partridge Family or Bobby Sherman.

At the time, Cassidy felt this episode was poorly executed. "I think it's soft," he said. "It hasn't got the machinery. That pilot was the worst show we ever did." Having said that, he really wanted the Sherman show to succeed. He and Shirley Jones both owned a piece of the new Bobby Sherman program and could only benefit by its success.

Suzanne Crough, who was only eight years old at the time, shares her perspective: "OK, I never had a crush on David because it always sounded very routine," she laughs. "All of my friends did, though, and I thought, *No! He's like my brother! Are you kidding?* If I were to say I had a crush on someone it would have probably been Bobby Sherman." Crough chuckles as she finally confesses her real heartthrob: John Wayne!

Producer Paul Witt, who had worked with Sherman on *Here Come the Brides*, left *The Partridge Family* to produce *Getting Together*. The new show was slated for Saturday nights at 8 p.m., competing against the explosive new hit *All in the Family*, and was quickly annihilated. *Getting Together* was canceled after shooting only 14 episodes.

"It was another attempt by a studio that had a strong television division and an incredibly successful music publishing division to put something on the air that could be successful and maybe sell some records," says Witt. "There was a lot of success with the convergence of music and television, and television bands getting on the air during those days. It all goes back to the Beatles and *A Hard Day's Night*, which kind of stylistically inspired the Monkees and their success. *Getting Together* was yet another attempt at the trend, but it didn't take off."

when we're singin'

An album titled *Getting Together* was released in 1971 to correspond with the show, and the debut single was "Jennifer"—titled after a girl's name, like "Stephanie" from the pilot.

Tom Bahler praises Sherman for his realistic understanding of the nature of fame. "Bobby is a paramedic today and he gives his check back to the city. He's got his own starship, man. He was the first guy to have a 727 jet for rock and rollers to lease!"

It wasn't the last attempt at this style of show, either. On Christmas Day 1971, the cover of *Billboard* announced the next Partridge-inspired venture, a half-hour series called *Bobby Jo and the Big Apple Goodtime Band*. It was stated that the likelihood of success was a "foregone conclusion based on the success of *The Partridge Family*." Again Paul Witt teamed with Bell Records president Larry Uttal, this time with CBS. The show's storyline involved a recording group whose members came from all over the nation. They would meet in Nashville and begin their adventures from there. As with *The Partridge Family*, new music was planned for every show. But again, the show never took off.

Goodbye, Jeremy

Young Jeremy Gelbwaks was also not returning to the show after the first season, and he was leaving show business for good. Jeremy was 10 years old at the time, and his parents were calling the shots the best they knew how for their child's future.

Many accounts of Gelbwaks' departure have cited different reasons for the cast change, including one that he was fired over bad behavior. That was absolutely not true, although it did make for good press. Reports of fighting between Danny Bonaduce and Gelbwaks on the set were true but manipulated, as is most Hollywood chatter, and used as an unfair shot against Gelbwaks.

Danny Bonaduce has always recounted his time on *The Partridge Family* with blunt honesty. Bonaduce wasn't above instigating a fight, and, as it turned out, Gelbwaks was the type who would fight back. There's nothing unusual about children fighting. The real test comes back to the parents and their role. According to Bob Claver, Gelbwaks' parents had no experience or knowledge of show business or what was expected of them on the set. While no one faulted them for that lack of knowledge, it was a contributing factor in the childrens' situation.

Paul Witt remembers Gelbwaks very well and emphatically states that he was "a very nice boy." He explains, "Children working on that kind of schedule are under enormous stress. I think the Gelbwaks family decided that he didn't need it, they didn't need it, and they sought a more normal childhood for him and a more normal family life for themselves. I know it wasn't an easy decision for them, but they felt very strongly that they were doing the right thing."

"The reason I left the show, to the best of my recollection, was that my father was offered a position in Virginia and wanted to take it," says Jeremy Gelbwaks. "He was all of 29 years old at the time, maybe 30. It's hard to fault them for taking it. It was a good opportunity in a government agency for which he was exactly suited." According to Bob Claver, Gelbwaks' father approached Claver partway through the filming of the first season, asked him if he thought the show would renew, and was told there was no guarantee that it would happen. He then made the best decision for his family that he could make, and they moved on.

"We followed his career around for a while, and lived in a bunch of places," remembers Gelbwaks, who ultimately grew up back East. Gelbwaks says he has enjoyed his non–show business life path. He likes to look back and reflect on his year as a Partridge, and from time to time he has joined the others in reunion appearances. Interestingly, he became good friends with the Cowsill family in his adult life and enjoys those relationships to this day.

Moving Mondrian

By the time *Up to Date* was released, the visually captivating Partridge Family bus had become its own character in the show. It grabbed the television audience quickly, identifying the show and the band with a colorful and bright image.

During the 1960s the look of the "psychedelic bus" was an image tied to the hippest music of the era. It was a look that series creator Bernard Slade originally envisioned for the Partridges on something about the size of a family van.

But getting away from 1960s psychedelia was a way to appeal more broadly to the family audience. *The Partridge Family* was packaged to be a family show. At a time when the phrase *generation gap* had just been coined, the network's goal was to hook the entire family on the Partridges and delicately bridge the ideas of youth and those of the middle class.

Paul Witt had a big influence on the design of the now-famous Partridge Family bus. "I was, and continue to be, very much into contemporary art that was inspired by French modernist Piet Mondrian," says Witt. Mondrian produced a number of paintings beginning in 1919 that used only vertical and horizontal lines and primary colors making up block designs, a style known as neoplasticism. It is the work for which he became most famous, *Composition II with Red, Blue and Yellow*, created in 1930, along with similar paintings, that served as the model for the Partridge Family bus. According to Witt, the look of the bus was very much an intentional homage to Mondrian.

Once a design was established, the task of getting the bus painted began. "In a studio like Screen Gems, which had so many series on the air, time was critical," says

when we're singin'

Witt. "Clearly, we wanted a bus that was believable, that they could buy and paint. There were creative elements to that choice, and you had a transportation department, a prop department, and an art department. All of these people were pros. It was done well, and done quickly." Ross Bellah, who had served as art director for *The Monkees, Here Come the Brides*, and many other shows, was responsible for the final look of the bus.

In a twist of fate, the already famous Mondrian would find revived fame because of the visibility and popularity of the Partridge Family bus. By and large, young fans of that era had no idea who Mondrian even was, so they began to associate his artwork with the Partridge Family bus rather than vice versa.

The cast's memories of the bus focus on the many challenges it presented to filming. "The bus was a horror show!" says Danny Bonaduce. "There was almost a Broadway setup for the lights inside the back of the bus. There was this theatrical-looking rack for upholding lights behind Shirley that would shoot down on the cast of *The Partridge Family* who were sitting behind her. These lights were excruciatingly hot. It would easily get to be 120 degrees inside that bus."

"Ah, the infamous bus," reminisces Brian Forster. "The bus was usually parked next to our stage and it would be there for months and months and months. So whenever it came time to fire it up, it always put out clouds of smoke! It was already old anyway, and it was not tuned up well, but they'd get it running and then off we'd go somewhere. Once we were driving back and forth by Forest Lawn Cemetery, shooting something that was supposed to be on the road. They had these portable lights that were run by battery banks or something, and we're in the very back of the bus, and it's Burbank, so it's already hot. Then you have all these lights behind us, like nine lights in a panel, and they are *really* hot! So the back of the bus is really cooking, and all the kids were back there really close to the lights. I remember suddenly smelling something like burning rubber. I thought *what's that*? I turned around and it was my shoe up against the equipment, starting to melt! Part of me thought it was fun, because we were out of the studio and getting to ride around in the bus, but on the other hand it was like being in an oven, going back and forth and back and forth."

Mel Swope recalls the technical challenges. "Shooting on the moving bus was difficult," he begins. "If we could get away with it, we'd shoot at nighttime. That way we'd be in the bus and it wouldn't be moving."

The bus was very popular with the audience and played a big role in establishing the show as a sitcom that was fresh and out of the ordinary. In the years to follow, the bus never received as much screen time as it does in the first season, with the family out on the road. It quickly became the single most visual identifier of *The Partridge Family* as a show about music.

Nervous Mother Driving

Though it was no stretch for Jones to play a mother of five, she was given her biggest challenge when she had to learn to drive the bus. Jones, in her adventurous, positive way, stepped up with enthusiasm. "Well, you know, I had never driven a stick shift before," she says with a laugh. "I mean, I grew up on a hydromatic thing, so I didn't know how to drive with a clutch. And particularly—that was an old bus.

"So they taught me—the Teamsters union! They worked with me and worked with me and finally I drove it! That's actually when I first learned to drive a stick shift. And at the end of the show, when we finished the four-year run, the Teamsters union gave me a badge of honor. They said, 'You are a Teamster now—you're in the union!' It was great! I was very proud of myself."

Brian Forster remembers being on the bus with Jones. "I wasn't around for Shirley learning how to drive it," he says," but I do remember the few times she drove it. They would have her trying to make a corner with that difficult power steering. And the steering wheel was the size of a pizza! It took, like, 25 turns of the steering wheel to actually make a turn. Shirley was used to her nice Mercedes, and the bus was a far cry from that," he laughs. "But she was a typical professional. Here she is trying to turn this thing and realizing that she had to keep turning in order to make this corner, and she's just laughing and laughing and going 'Oh my God!' She had a great sense of humor about it."

Bus Sightings

Fascination with the bus was widespread throughout the run of the show. In June 1973, the summer after the third season, a Pennsylvania high school's senior class prank involved painting a school bus overnight to look like the Partridge Family bus. Because the teens had the foresight to use washable paint, the prank was celebrated rather than punished. In a letter to the editor of the local paper, the bus driver reported, "I saw more smiles and laughter on more faces than I have seen in a long time. One man, stopped at a traffic light, actually applauded as the bus passed by."

In the years since, the bus has become a pop culture symbol of the 1970s, and there have been many replicas. During the 1990s, the '70s were finding a resurgence in popularity. The term "retro" moved into common usage. The Have a Nice Day Cafe, a nightclub franchise, decorated its interiors with wall-to-wall '70s nostalgia, complete with a lighted disco ball and dance floor. The gem of the franchise was a version of the Partridge Family bus that was available for private rentals. Have A Nice Day Cafe had locations all around the country, including Pittsburgh, Boston, and Indianapolis.

when we're singin'

"I once went to Mason City, Iowa, with regard to *The Music Man*, and down the street came a Partridge bus," says Shirley Jones. "'Look! We have a Partridge bus!' someone shouted. I've been several other places where they have had a Partridge bus, too."

From time to time, different television talk shows bring on Partridge Family cast members for a little nostalgic fun, and once in a while a bus appears as part of the reunion. "A couple years ago when they did the first *Today* show Partridge reunion, they brought a Partridge Family bus, which, of course, wasn't the original one," says Brian Forster. "It was just something they bought and made up to look like the original. Anyway, I had this great idea. They were doing a tour with the bus to promote the newest Partridge Family thing, so I found out who the guy was at transportation and I said I was thinking of buying the bus. I would then lease it back to them for the tour, and when the tour was over I'd own the bus. Then I could sell it or do whatever. Well, it turns out I was one step behind. When I talked to the transportation guy he told me someone had already done that! I think it was the studio. They figured it was stupid to lease it from somebody else when they could own it themselves. Even though it wasn't the original, I thought it would be kind of fun, you know?"

When Danny Bonaduce launched his short-lived talk show, *Danny!*, the pilot episode was a Partridge Family reunion, and the cast arrived in yet another variation of the bus. This time it was a convertible. "That one wasn't even close!" laughs Forster. "It didn't even have a top on it! At least the one from the *Today* show had a top on it. A few years ago I did a Google search looking for a 1957 Blue Bird school bus, thinking maybe there's one around somewhere. Yeah, there's a couple around—and they're rotting in the kudzu of Georgia!"

Bus Legends

For decades people have laid claim to having owned or spotted the original Partridge Family bus. From Vermont to Washington State, down to Texas and back to L.A., the sightings continue to this day. Hundreds of pictures and postings on the topic exist online.

The most widely believed tale is that the original bus sat parked at Lucy's, a Los Angeles Mexican restaurant. After the cancellation of the series and up through the late '80s, sightings and photos of this bus were plentiful. Even Partridge Family producers remember seeing it parked there.

The same bus was captured on screen in a 1982 episode of *ChIPS* (episode 18, titled "In the Best of Families"). A big sign advertising Lucy's is also visible in the shot.

In 1987 this bus disappeared when the building behind Lucy's was demolished and replaced with a parking lot. The question of where it went has hung on for years in the belief that it was the true Partridge bus. But was it really? The answer—

emphatically and without any shadow of any doubt— is no. The bus at Lucy's was a 1956 Chevrolet 6800 with a bus coach by Carpenter—the wrong make and model, yet very close—a good attempt at a match. The *real* Partridge Family bus is a 1955 Chevrolet 6800 Second Series Task force with a coach by Superior.

The Mystery of the Partridge Family Bus

The make and model of the Partridge Family bus have been incorrectly documented so many times over the years it's no wonder there's a mystery behind it!

The 1955 Superior coach for the Partridge Family bus was manufactured only at Superior's Lima, Ohio plant. The Chevrolet 6800 chassis was made in Norwood, Ohio; the bus was assembled in Lima and likely delivered new to the Los Angeles County School District in time for the beginning of the school year in fall 1955. This particular bus was produced in small numbers, and the make and model characteristics make it easy to spot the correct design once you know what to look for.

In the mid-1950s, Superior was the biggest maker of bus coaches in the country. Models remained much the same from 1955 to 1957, making confusion more likely.

In the pilot episode, Danny and Shirley are seen negotiating for the purchase of the bus at Al's Used Cars. The bus in that shot is a 1957 Chevrolet 6700 with a body by Carpenter, which has marked differences from the bus that was actually used. Most notably, it's shorter, with only seven windows on each side. The actual Partridge Family bus was already painted and ready to go—and it had eight windows on each side.

A later shot in the pilot shows the family painting their new bus. Pausing the DVD reveals that the art department placed a yellow covering made to look like a section of the bus was still unpainted. They were actually filming the scene with the already-painted 1955 Superior 6800 Chevrolet Series II Task Force—the *real* Partridge Family bus.

Superior's branding is all over it. The company name is branded into the metal on both sides of the bus as well as the front end. Publicity shots of the cast reveal the branding just above Jeremy Gelbwaks' head as he hangs out the window with the rest of the cast.

The eight windows running down the side, finished with a half-size (D-shaped) ribbed metal piece at the end rather than a glass window, is one of the most significant identifiers. The bus paint job has also never been precisely replicated on any of the lookalike buses, including the one at Lucy's.

When the show was picked up, the producers decided that the interior of the bus was bland. Since they were going to do a lot of interior shooting on the bus, they spiced it up by recovering the seats with a pseudo-psychedelic fabric in shades of orange and repainting the interior ceiling and front end in yellow and orange.

when we're singin'

Shooting actual scenes on the bus while Shirley Jones was driving required a lot of modification to accommodate a crew, a power source, batteries and lights, and a means of controlling surface noise.

Belly boxes rigged underneath the bus held the batteries that powered the lights on the inside. Even disguised by the paint job, the compartment is clearly visible.

Other modifications included hand-grabs throughout the interior of the bus so the cast and crew could have something to hold on to while driving and shooting. Many of the seats in the back of the bus were removed, leaving only three rows intact, with one additional seat turned sideways. This configuration was the same on both passenger sides. A hitch was placed at the back of the bus so that a generator could be pulled behind the bus to power the batteries without making noise inside the bus. A roof rack was also added.

In a twist responsible for a lot of the later confusion, the studio decided early on to create a duplicate Partridge Family bus to be used by Bell Records for promotional purposes on the East Coast. This bus was never to be used for shooting, so no modifications were necessary—just a make and model as close as they could get to the original, with a similar paint job. But the plan didn't go so well and the use of the Bell Records promotional bus was short-lived.

John Rosica, executive director of West Coast operations for Bell Records, tells the story: "We had a replica made. Painted the exact colors. Somebody bought it thinking it was a great idea and it wasn't a great idea! But the reason they bought it was to promote *The Partridge Family*, except they bought the exact same bus that was on the show—which meant it was 20 years old!" Actually it wasn't exactly the same bus, or the same paint job, but it was a very close match. The replica ran as poorly as the original.

"I picked it up one Friday afternoon when it was ready. The problem with the bus was that it was created by the public relations people at the television studio, and they had planned to send it back east. And how are you going to drive it across the country? The bus could never have made it. It was not very reliable.

"So then they checked to see if they could put it on a flat car, a train, but it was too high for many of the bridges going across the country. So by default, I inherited the bus." The duplicate bus now had a new home in John Rosica's driveway.

"So when we had the opening party for the actors and for the producers of the show at what use to be the Gene Autry Hotel, on Sunset right at La Cienega, I drove it from Tarzana over the mountains and to the hotel to park it for the day." The bus was to serve as a kind of visual—a billboard for the party.

"I parked right in front of the hotel," Rosica recalls. "But the problem was that I wasn't really familiar with driving a big vehicle through the canyon, and I just remember not being able to slow it down. I thought I was going to die! I mean it was a long trip and at one point it got so violent that I was thrown out of the driver's seat, still holding on to the steering wheel! I ultimately made it and didn't die. But it was an interesting experience.

"I used to take the neighbors to the beach in it, or go to the airport and pick people up. The problem with the bus was you put a dozen people in it and try to go to the beach and go through another canyon, the bus had a problem getting up a hill. I had to literally stop the bus and put it in first gear.

"And because of its unreliability it sat in my driveway and became a planter! We referred to it in our driveway as 'the planter.' So the kids use to play in it and it was a highlight. It made us famous in the neighborhood.

"Still to this day people talk about that planter we had in front of our house, which was that bus," says Rosica. "I didn't know what to do with it! My kids still talk about it. We had a good time. The bus … ah well, as a promotion it was a mistake; as a toy it was a success!"

Harvey Cooper was the West Coast promotional manager for Bell Records and a good friend of Rosica's. He used to take turns with Rosica using the bus on weekends for fun.

"Eventually we got bored with the bus," says Rosica, "and we really didn't need it, because by then 'I Think I Love You' was really establishing the show and the records. The bus was so unreliable that I left it at a gas station. We parked it at a gas station after it was a planter! It was in Tarzana on Ventura Boulevard. I don't remember specifically which gas station. Then, shortly after that, I resigned from Bell to move back East, and have no idea what happened after that."

Both Rosica and Cooper think the bus at Lucy's taco stand was likely the Bell Records promotional bus, but their suspicion remains unconfirmed. And the current whereabouts of that bus are also unconfirmed, with rumors of its appearance in junkyards around Los Angeles.

But the bigger question still remains: What happened to the *real* Partridge Family bus?

The story can be traced up to a point. In early 1974, *Apple's Way*, a new series produced by the same company as *The Partridge Family*, was launched. In the months between *The Partridge Family*'s final episode in March 1974 and the start of the second season of *Apple's Way*, the original Partridge Family bus was pulled from storage, painted over in a bland light yellow/off-white, and used in the new show.

The bus is featured in *Apple's Way* season 2, episode 7, "The Candy Drive." There is no mistaking the bus as it pulls into a full-frame shot during the opening scene. It's portrayed as a run-down bus purchased by Mr. Apple for restoration. The rack on top and the specially designed battery compartment underneath are still there, the hand-grabs along with the unmistakable pseudo-psychedelic seat covers on the

when we're singin'

few remaining seats inside are also present, along with a host of other identifiers that prove it to be the original Partridge Family bus.

The bus went into hiding for another year and then reappeared in the 1976 made-for-TV movie *Helter Skelter*. Again, specific identifiers can be seen, notably the covers on the few remaining seats. What happened to the bus after the *Helter Skelter* appearance remains a mystery.

Colin Strayer is a restoration expert who has returned three diners to their original historic specifications and restored the original car driven by John-Boy Walton in the long-running series *The Waltons*. Strayer has been researching the missing bus for years in hopes of finding the original and restoring it. The likelihood that it escaped the scrapyard is slim, although he continues to search.

As an alternative to finding the original, Strayer set out to find an identical model in hopes of recreating the bus. Buses of that make and model have proven to be extremely rare—almost as elusive as the original bus itself.

"The 1955 model was rare when new," explains Strayer. "Today, finding one is extremely rare. To date, and after 10 years of searching, I have never seen a 1955 Chevrolet 6800 Superior Coach on eBay or Craigslist. Not one. Not anywhere on the Internet. Ever. It is possible there is not one surviving. That is how rare the Partridge Family bus is."

It was this rare chassis that was the Partridge Family bus—a bus purchased by the studio in 1969 for $500 from the Los Angeles County School District.

To give an idea of exactly how rare the make and model of the Partridge Family bus is, Strayer elaborates: "Total school bus industry output from the 10 major school bus makers in 1957 was approximately 18,000 buses, fewer in 1956 and 1955. Of these, Chevrolet may have represented approximately 25 percent of the total school bus chassis used. Breaking this down further, that would mean approximately 4,500 Chevrolet school bus chassis would have been built in 1956 and 1957, representing all chassis model numbers. Further breaking this down, for the 1955 Second Series chassis—the year and model of the Partridge Family bus chassis—the output is small. As explained, the 1955 Chevrolet Second Series Task Force school bus chassis was a midyear replacement, introduced on March 25, 1955.

"My guess is there would have been fewer than 2,000, 1955 Second Series Chevrolet school bus chassis made during their approximate five months of production. Of these, perhaps only half (approximately 1,000) would have been the 6800 Model. Of these, I would estimate fewer than 20 survive in 2015.

"The PF bus was a significant object worthy of museum preservation by Smithsonian or Henry Ford Museum," says Strayer. "Amazing that no one saw its value. Odd too because of California car culture. You'd think someone in Southern California would have appreciated it."

MADE FOR TV

Strayer continues, "The bus would be a less interesting story today if it just existed in someone's collection. The fact that such an iconic object completely disappeared makes it worthy of pursuing."

Strayer wrote and directed the 1996 documentary *Rod Serling: Writer*, and he's interested in producing another documentary, titled *In Search of the Partridge Family Bus*. "Everyone loves a good mystery!" he says.

Bus Stop ...

The Fanatic's Guide to the Partridge Family Bus

"The average person typically thinks of school buses as being boxy and without any distinguishing features," says Colin Strayer. "Reality is, they are as easy to identify as the difference between a 1955 Chevrolet or Ford or DeSoto. One just needs to know what the differences are." With the high number of modifications made to the bus by the Screen Gems art department, the actual Partridge Family bus is even more identifiable.

The following is a list of specific identifiers of the real Partridge Family bus, should anyone happen to be browsing their local junkyards for the real thing:

1. Hood emblem. The Partridge Family bus had a Chevrolet "bowtie" hood emblem that was unique to the Second Series Task Force for 1955, located center front on the hood. This badging was only used briefly for a few months as part of the mid-season design change by Chevrolet.

2. 6800 Series designation fender badge. Also used only for a few months in 1955, 6800 Series badges were attached on the right and left side front fenders. From the beginning of the series, the Partridge Family bus was missing its left side 6800 badge. The right side badge, painted over in yellow, can be seen on the front fender near the bus door entrance.

when we're singin'

3. Windows. The Partridge Family bus had a two-piece windshield, and the glass was flat throughout the bus. The front door had four windows, each a different size. The bus had eight windows on each side—one of the most obvious identifers of the Superior coach—and the first window was 32 inches wide, nine inches wider than the rest.

There were three windows on the upper portion of the rear end of the Partridge Family bus: D-shaped windows on the right and left side, again with flat glass, and a middle window that formed the upper half of the rear emergency exit door.

4. D-shaped fluted panel. At the rear, after the eighth window on either side, was a painted and ribbed stamped-steel D-shaped rear quarter panel, a unique feature on Superior Coach school buses of this period.

5. "Superior" name stamped in metal. "Superior" was stamped into the metal roof directly above the gutter over the first window on either side, and into the panel directly below the rear door window. This feature was common for Superior buses of the era, but not universal. The "Superior" name is seen on the Partridge Family bus numerous times, including early publicity shots where you can see the word above Jeremy Gelbwaks' head. In the opening sequence, the rear of the bus is seen with the name "Superior" clearly visible.

6. "Superior" tread entrance. The name "Superior" appears on the edge of the flooring on the top step of the entrance.

7. Roof-mounted stop light housings. The bus originally had two lights in front and two at the rear. These were—and still are—a standard feature on every school bus, usually (but not always) removed from old buses that are sold to the public. At the front and rear of the Partridge Family bus you can clearly see where the four roof-mounted red stop light housings had once been attached.

8. Belly Boxes. After the pilot, compartments were installed underneath the bus body so that batteries and other film-related equipment could be carried while driving and filming. These compartments had flip-down hinged doors and could be accessed from either the left or right sides.

The doors on these belly boxes had a habit of flopping open during filming, and shots with the open compartments can sometimes be seen. Because these were custom-built add-ons, they are unique to the Partridge Family bus. The repainted compartments remained intact and can still be seen in both *Apple's Way* and *Helter Skelter*.

9. Exterior roof grab handles. Four hand-grabs appeared during the first season after the pilot. Two were installed on each side—one midway, just ahead of the rear wheel, and the other at the back, above the exterior side windows. These were used to tie things to the bus.

10. **Roof rack**. A custom-made roof rack was attached to the bus after the pilot episode was shot. This remained on the bus throughout its post-*Partridge Family* use in *Apple's Way* and *Helter Skelter*.

11. Window blinds. Blinds, hand-painted with the same Mondrian-inspired design, were installed above all of the side windows. Similarly painted pull-down blinds appeared on the Lucy's Tacos bus, supporting the theory that it was the Bell Records promotional bus.

12. Trailer hitch. After the pilot was shot, a trailer hitch was added to the rear bumper of the bus. This enabled the bus to pull a gas-electric generator to power lights. Mounted on the rear bumper to the left of the hitch was a plug-in receptor for the wiring harness. This connected to the bus wiring system to operate trailer brake and signal lights.

13. Seating and upholstery. The driver's seat seen in the show was the original seat installed on the bus when delivered new. The seat frame was painted and decorated with flower stickers in the pilot. After the pilot, the seat was re-upholstered with the same upholstery as the bench seats.

when we're singin'

The bus originally had eight rows of bench seats—two seats per row with a center aisle, for a total of 16 seats. As configured for the show, there were three forward-facing bench seats on each side with a center aisle, and behind them an additional inward-facing bench seat on each side.

The distinctive orange and yellow psychedelic fabric used on the driver's seat and bench seats for *The Partridge Family* can still be seen in *Apple's Way* and *Helter Skelter*.

14. Front rigging frame. A steel frame added under the front bumper served as a mounting point, allowing the production crew to attach a framework so the camera and/or lights could be securely attached to the front of the bus. It was installed sometime in the first season. Like much of the front bumper, the frame was painted gray.

15. Electric power tracks. Two custom-installed electrical tracks were added, running the length of the bus interior above the windows. They permitted the film crew to plug in lights and electrical equipment anywhere on the bus.

16. Stop sign mechanism. Throughout the show, the bus still had the remnants of the original stop sign. Although the actual sign had been removed, the base mount and mechanism to operate the sign could still be seen on the outside directly below the driver's window.

17. Dimensions and weight. The bus measured just short of 30 feet in length. (The Superior Coach body was about 24 feet, and the Chevrolet chassis front end was about five feet six inches from the windshield to the front bumper. The addition of the trailer hitch lengthened the bus by another five inches.) The width, including the rub rails, was eight feet, and the overall height was nine feet. The bus weighed approximately five tons empty.

18. Rub rails. Two rub rails—metal reinforcement strips, approximately three inches wide—run the length of both sides of the Partridge Family bus. The unique design was used by Superior from 1953 to 1963. Although some Superior buses had rail rubs that wrapped around the back end, the Partridge Family bus did not.

19. Interior headroom. The bus had a floor-to-ceiling interior headroom of 72 inches. Anyone over six feet tall would have to duck the ceiling limitation, which is likely why Dave Madden wasn't seen in many of the bus scenes.

20. Fluted steel side panels. The bus had a row of fluted, stamped galvanized steel side paneling running the length of the bus. This horizontally mounted panel had five ridges and added rigidity to the side of the bus. The panel was located directly below the side windows, above the rub rail. Below that was another panel extending to the bottom edge of the body. This lower panel was flat, without flutes. After 1955, all Superior Coach school buses had fluted panels running the entire length of the side of the body, from under the window to the bottom edge.

21. Body type. The bus had a school bus body built by Superior Coach of Lima, Ohio. In contrast, the bus parked at Lucy's Tacos had a school bus body built by Carpenter Body Works of Mitchell, Indiana.

22. Wheelbase. The 1955 Chevrolet 6800 Second Series Task Force school bus chassis had a wheelbase of 220 inches.

23. Wheels. The bus had six standard factory-installed 1955 Chevrolet wheels with five round holes.

24. Doors. The bus had a right front door and rear-end emergency exit with a window on the top half and the lower half painted with the inscription "CAUTION NERVOUS MOTHER DRIVING."

25. Steering wheel. The bus had a Chevrolet Task Force Second Series steering wheel that was unique for 1955.

26. Windsplits/hood spears. This is a major identifier of the bus as a 1955 model. Beginning in 1957, Chevrolet added two hood spears, officially known as windsplits, to all truck models. These added rigidity and reduced hood vibration. The windsplits are introduced on page 15 of the 1957 Chevrolet "Engineering Features" publication: "The hood panels of all models are strengthened and distinguished by two high windsplits which extend rearward at each side of the hood along its full horizontal length." In contrast, the sheet metal on the top of the hood of the Partridge Family bus was flat, which rules out 1957 as its model year.

27. Front clip. The front end or "front clip" of a school bus is distinctive to the chassis maker—Chevrolet, Ford, Dodge, International Harvester, etc. The Partridge Family bus had a front end unique to a 1955 Chevrolet Task Force Second Series 6800 chassis.

28. Rear wheel well surrounds. Superior had two standard styles for rear wheel wells between 1953 and 1963. The Partridge Family bus had the plain "standard" style that is seen only in buses made until 1955. This style has a stamped two-inch band around a semicircular rear wheel well. Beginning in 1956, Superior buses had a flared, streamlined design wheel well.

29. Intake vent. At the front end on the driver's side of the bus, just under and ahead of the driver's window, is an air intake vent. On a 1953–1955 Superior, the air intake is a pronounced smooth-surface rounded curved scoop. From 1956 to 1963 the air intake was rectangular-shaped, clad with a ribbed fluted steel panel on the side matching the surrounding ribbed fluted side panels running the length of the bus.

30. Front fender turn signals. On the top of the left and right front fenders were turn signals. These were installed by Superior Coach at the factory and remained on the bus throughout the show. The lenses were round, with amber-colored arrows. These same lights can also be seen in *Apple's Way*; in *Helter Skelter* the camera does not show this area of the bus.

31. License plates. In the pilot and early publicity stills and passby traveling shots, the bus displayed a cardboard license plate, 4A689. All the cars at Al's Used Cars had the same nondescript red-and-white cardboard plates. Even Shirley Partridge's blue car had a cardboard plate in the pilot. These plates did not specify a state name.

The temporary license plate was replaced with the 1963 series California black-and-gold plate NLX 590 for the remainder of the show.

The early use of the temporary plate created continuity problems. By the time the pilot aired in 1970, the opening sequence featured both 4A689 and the later NLX 590 plate on the back of the bus. In the scenes that follow, the plate reverts back and forth.

Matching Songs to Episodes

The Partridge Family's music was married to the television show. Especially in the first season, great effort was made to match the songs to the episodes. There were also occasions where the television producers needed something written specifically for an episode. "I never spoke to them personally," says John Bahler of the television producers. "I remember Bob Claver and the other producers being there only in the very beginning. They never came to our sessions. After the first song hit so big, so fast, Wes followed it up with the second hit ["Doesn't Somebody Want to Be Wanted"], which was the hardest, most difficult thing to do. They figured, *Ah, this guy obviously knows what he's doing, and he's making us money so we'll leave him alone to do what he does.* That's what they did, and I'm really happy about it!"

The third smash hit followed very quickly on the heels of "Doesn't Somebody Want to Be Wanted." "I'll Meet You Halfway" skyrocketed into the top 10, further cementing confidence in Wes Farrell—confidence that was never again questioned by either Bell Records or the show's producers. When the songs were completed, they had to be matched up with episodes. Bob Claver left it up to

Farrell most of the time: "I had the right to pick them, but I never thought I was as good at that as Wes."

Farrell took time to watch the episodes. If he had a particular song ready to go, he might offer it up to Claver. In some instances he would need to think about it for a while. "They'd go into a recording session, and they'd make *x* number of songs," Claver explains, "and for the most part they weren't necessarily positioned until we had done the episode. Sometimes there was one that played to the episode more specifically, but most of the time they were just there, and we used them. But what they gave us all the time were songs that we could easily fit in.

Claver continues, "Sometimes they were specific things. If the characters were having some kind of personal problem, we would try to get the song to fit the occasion. But you can only get so many of those, you know? Writing those ahead is not so easy, and you can really end up with a lot of bad music that way.

"Sometimes Wes would look at the episode and then he'd go away and come back, because you just don't suddenly say 'I have a great idea for a song.' Sometimes they were slower, so we didn't schedule our recording sessions like the army. We wanted to give him all the time we could possibly give him, because sometimes you get into a bad place. The episodes may be good, but if they couldn't find the right kind of music then they might start forcing it. And when you start forcing it, it's just not good. I'll tell you what, we cut a lot of songs! If you work in the theater, you know that people spend years of their lives writing musicals, and sometimes they just don't work for whatever the reason." Claver understood what the television magic is all about and how hard it is to achieve.

Liner Notes: *The Partridge Family Up to Date*

The second album by the new group is possibly the most pop-sounding of them all, and the album jacket is much more visually commercial that its predecessor. The television image plays a stronger role in the sound and look of the record, with its colorful cover featuring the cast's smiling faces and block designs that reflect the look of the Mondrian-inspired bus. Incidentally, the cover design is the only time Jeremy Gelbwaks appears on the front of an album cover. The design established the primary branding of the Partridge Family, and the multicolored block design is still featured in articles and DVD releases.

The album is much more made-for-television in its musical construction as well, with its sound masterfully refined to match TV viewers' image of the fictional band.

Up to Date reflects the next stage in the development of Wes Farrell, John Bahler, and Mike Melvoin into a team. They were refining and honing their skills, and developing their knowledge of how best to work together. Describing the changes in sound between the first and second album, Bahler says, "I think there were at least two things involved. One was Wes' choice of songs, and the other was me coming of age and maturing as the writer for the Partridge Family sound. Those are the two things that I recall really starting to happen in the second album.

"The second album has more *presence*, as we call it in the music business. The more you put something in echo, the less presence it has, and the more you start approaching the Phil Spector 'wall of sound.' When Wes came on, he and I were of the same mind. We liked the vocals and certain other things to be very, very present, and we never put a lot of juice, as we used to call it, on the band, because it took the pop out of it. It took the power out of it and kind of washed things out. So we made things as present as we could.

"The other reason behind it was that, when you see it on television, you wouldn't have that much echo in the garage, or even in a stadium. You would have what we call room noise—the normal sound of somebody singing in a room, or inside a house. We used that, and enough schmootz on it to make it sound professional, because most demos are real dry."

Bahler continues, "Wes use to do something else that was very interesting. We all love toys, you know? Well, Wes found a little gadget that would transmit on an FM wavelength from his tape recorder or his sound system in his house out to his car. That's the way we tested mixes! This is back in the days when people just didn't do things like this.

"When I finished mixing, I would take the material over to Wes. Wes mixed the first ones, but once we got it going I mixed all the rest of them with Bob Kovach. I'd bring the mixes to Wes, and he put them on his tape recorder. I don't think we used acetates. I think we used tapes. And his little gadget would broadcast it to an FM station that wasn't being used. We'd go out in his car and he'd tune it in and we'd listen to it. That's how we could tell what the mixes would sound like on the radio. Very often, in the beginning, we'd both look at each other and say, 'There's not enough bass, is there?' Or 'There's too much bass' or 'Not enough this' or 'Too much of that,' and I'd go back and fix it.

"That was a very, very interesting technique," says Bahler, "and it really worked! It really, really worked! In fact we, meaning me and my cohorts, used that idea for years. We didn't go out in our car, but we would test mixes on this German machine. It was a Studer 2-track. It was about the size of a lot of radios that were out in those days, like a car radio speaker. They had a little teeny speaker on them, just a little mono speaker, and we used to test mixes listening to them at a low level on that speaker. We could tell if it sounded great on that little speaker." TV set speakers in that era were small and didn't deliver great sound. "We wanted to make sure that the mono tracks which went over a TV speaker sounded good coming over television."

"This is when most guys were mixing on huge monitors at ear-splitting levels to check their mixes. We went the opposite way and listened on the worst little rotten speaker we could find, which was on this machine, at a real low level. If we got it to sound great on that speaker, we could put it on the big speakers and turn it up to an ear-splitting level and it sounded great! It was just one of those tricks I learned from Wes. I took his idea and just went a different direction with it."

Mike Melvoin, originally recruited by Shorty Rogers, became the sole arranger beginning with *Up to Date*; Don Peake and Billy Strange were no longer involved. Bell Records, Wes Farrell, and company had begun to figure out exactly what they needed as they refined the sound of the second album, and the large staff credited on the first album was no longer necessary so they cut back on the number of musicians.

Melvoin had offered to take over doing the arrangements when the original collaborative process proved ungainly and time-consuming.

"The piano player has the entire graphic system right in front of him, and is generally better trained technically than the guitar players. So finally I went to Wes one day and said, 'You know all the time we spend doing that? I could arrange it. I just don't want to have to keep answering all those pesky little questions. I can turn your one tune a day into three tunes a day.' And he went 'Oooh!' So I would actually write out the charts from the sheets answering all of those musical questions and all of the technical questions, so when a real musician would open that page the first part would be about content and nuance.

"So the idea of getting three tunes in three hours—a tune an hour—was very feasible. That's what we started doing, and I got a reputation for being able to do that. And when those tracks were done, they'd say, 'Now let's get a string arranger in here to do the strings.' I would say, 'Those parts were generated by lines that I conceived! Why not let me do that?' And they'd say, 'Of course, you're right!' So I started doing the strings as well. John Bahler and myself—we're responsible for every note on the record.

"Once I had control," Melvoin continues, "I made sure that there were no blind changes that didn't resolve forward—no bad time, no bad tuning, no bad performances, no bad anything. I took great pains to create charts that had references to the entire history of music. There are quotes from Brahms on the string parts. These are things, frankly, that Wes knew nothing about, and that I was doing under the radar. John and I did the same thing, and the more power we had over the notes the better the material got." Melvoin says he feels the music holds up well, and that it is much more reflective of easy listening or adult contemporary music from the early 1970s than the bubblegum image under which it was marketed. "I am very proud of that body of work," he says.

Up to Date benefited from excellent songwriting. "I remember the extraordinary songwriters that were signed to Screen Gems music at the time," recalls Paul Witt. "We had some brilliant songwriters doing Partridge Family material. If you look at the names of the songwriters in the first couple of years, they are people that had major hits over a long period of time."

when we're singin'

The team of Appel and Cretecos wrote a total of six songs for the Partridge Family, two of them appearing on *Up to Date*. Despite any quarreling behind the scenes over "Doesn't Somebody Want to Be Wanted," the song zoomed up the charts, peaking at No. 6 in *Billboard* on March 27, 1971 (the day of Cassidy's second concert). In both *Cash Box* and *Record World* the single rose to No. 1.

Appel and Cretecos were just starting out when they signed on with Wes Farrell. Mike Appel thought the world of Farrell and he looks back with great fondness on the time they spent together. "He always had a smile on his face," says Appel. "He always kidded us. It was exciting to be around him. He was the guy that first took me to California to record as Mike Appel on Capitol Records.

"I've got to tell you this story because it was so funny when it happened," continues Appel. "Wes and I were driving up Cahuenga Boulevard in L.A. and we stopped at a light. Two guys got out of a car behind us and they were carrying a red-colored plastic toy dial telephone. It was Boyce and Hart—two of the biggest song-writing-producing names in the world at the time! They walked right up to Wes' side of our convertible Cadillac and said, 'Mr. Farrell, there is a telephone call for you.' We all laughed out loud because it was so funny and it caught us completely off guard!"

Up to Date boasts several other legendary songwriters. Farrell managed to get the brilliant Gerry Goffin on board to write four songs for the Partridge Family, three of which appear on *Up to Date*.

Goffin had made his name with his former girlfriend and songwriting partner, Carole King. Together they had written some of the greatest songs ever recorded. His involvement is another demonstration of the high level of talent brought in to work on these records and Wes Farrell's fierce motivation to make the Partridge Family succeed.

Goffin and King were signed to Screen Gems at the time. They wrote together although they had been signed individually. He would write poems and King would put them to music. But Goffin was known to be a bit of an eccentric and eventually suffered a painful breakup with King. He continued to write, sometimes by himself and sometimes with other writers.

Gerry Goffin was intense and highly driven by his craft, obsessing over lyrics until he felt they were perfect. That songwriting perfection is demonstrated on *Up to Date*, with Goffin's submissions "I'm Here, You're Here," "There's No Doubt in My Mind," and what would be the next Partridge Family top 10 hit, "I'll Meet You Halfway," penned with Wes Farrell.

Up to Date also made use of three new songs by Tony Romeo. Romeo's diverse contributions include the folky "Morning Rider on the Road," the straightforward pop song "You Are Always on My Mind," and the celebratory anthem "That'll Be the Day."

Cashman and West saw their second Partridge Family song—and, many feel, the best of their eight that were recorded by the group—appear on *Up to Date*. "She'd Rather Have the Rain" is a beautiful tune full of sentiment.

Last but not least, *Up to Date* debuts a new songwriter with an uncanny ear for writing songs but literally no background in music. "I'll Leave Myself a Little Time" is Steve Dossick's only officially released Partridge Family cut. He seemed to be poised for much more success in the music business, but as it turned out, the kind of music Dossick wanted to write was much more rock-oriented—like many of his peers, he had been impressed by the sounds of such groups as the Rolling Stones, the Doors, and Cream.

Nine of the 11 cuts on *Up to Date* were used on the show, all during the first season. When the final episode of the season aired on March 19, 1971, *The Partridge Family Album* was still on the charts, at No. 16 on *Billboard*. "Doesn't Somebody Want to Be Wanted" was sitting at No. 9 on the singles charts, with the upcoming release of "I'll Meet You Halfway" imminent. Reviews of *Up to Date* appeared in the trades the next day, and the album was quickly released by Bell Records just in time for Cassidy's first concert outing. *Up to Date* was declared gold only a few days after its release. Within four weeks of its debut on the charts, it reached its peak position at No. 3 and held for three weeks, becoming the highest-charting Partridge Family album of them all. It stayed on the *Billboard* Top 200 album charts for a total of 53 weeks.

I'll Meet You Halfway, 3:47, Gerry Goffin–Wes Farrell

Sometimes things happen in threes. Released as the family's third single, "Halfway" also hit as their third top 10 record in a row, peaking at No. 9 within a month of release. It entered the Billboard Top 100 on May 8, 1971, and stayed there for nine weeks, peaking at No. 9 for two weeks beginning June 12, 1971.

Infectious right off the bat, "Halfway" opens with a gorgeous piano intro and captivating lyric that asks *"Will there come a day?"* This song is mesmerizing. Wes Farrell knew it, too. "I love that song," he said affectionately in his 1993 interview with Ken Sharp. "Gerry's from the great writing team of Goffin and King, and one of the great lyricists that has ever been put on this earth. Our collaboration is one I really enjoyed. Gerry and I spent about a month or so writing as often as was possible. I would throw ideas at him with melodies and he would come back with titles and with words. I thoroughly enjoyed this one, and I must credit him with his contribution. I loved that melody, too. All my ideas come from the piano. I don't care who you write with, certain things will have different levels of meaning. 'I'll Meet You Halfway' made an impression on me."

As the first track on *Up to Date*, the song marks the discovery of David Cassidy's breathy voice, a quality that quickly became identified with his sound. Greatly reduced are the heightened pitch and distant reverb. He sings on a very personal level here, and the blend of his voice with the touching lyric and gorgeous arrangement is a new "perfect" for the Partridge Family. "Halfway" was so ear-grabbing it caught the attention of the US military, which licensed it for use in an Army recruitment commercial that aired in the mid-'70s.

It is also an evolution, though subtle, in musical style. A prominent string section indicates the new solo control of Mike Melvoin as musical arranger. Melvoin uses his piano background to full advantage here. The tune is filled with beautiful strings and piano, pulling back on the guitar that was so prominent in the first album. The entire song is made of only one verse repeated three times. *Cash Box* called it the strongest single to date.

"'I'll Meet You Halfway' is just a great song," says John Bahler, "and it's got so much energy. I remember singing it and having so much fun. I hope it came out on the record. It was one of my favorites, one of everybody's favorites." Though Wes Farrell never commented on his favorite Partridge Family song, his widow, Jean Farrell, feels it was "I'll Meet You Halfway."

It was proving to be a favorite of the buying public, too. "I'll Meet You Halfway" aired on the television show toward the end of the first season, carrying fans into the summer of 1971 from hot atop the *Billboard* charts. It was the last *Billboard* Top 10 single for the Partridge Family, even though their success had just begun.

Appears On: Season 1, episode 23,
"Not with My Sister, You Don't" (March 5, 1971)
Favorite Partridge Family song of Suzanne Crough,
David Cassidy (one of several)

You Are Always on My Mind, 2:53, Tony Romeo

David Cassidy has said he always loved this song, especially the opening lyric: *"I wake up in the morning feeling all right till I recall, you're gone from my life and I stare like a dummy against the wall...."* Staying with the intimate "you and I" lyrics designed to make teenage girls swoon, this song has tons of layered background vocals throughout thanks to vocal arranger John Bahler. Mike Melvoin employs electric guitar and a tremolo guitar sound, an effect used frequently on the Everly Brothers' records. As a result, the song reflects a slight country influence. Songwriter Tony Romeo's lyrics and David Cassidy's delivery come together to create Wes Farrell's perfect singer-and-songwriter confection.

"By now David Cassidy was a phenomenon," said Romeo in 1993. "Notwithstanding fanzine image, he was an excellent singer for whom I was lucky to be writing—which I did for five years. Knowing him personally made it possible to write not only for his sound, but more importantly, his psyche. I was able to project what I instinctively felt he wanted to communicate in a song. 'I Am a Clown' from his first solo LP, *Cherish*, was also an example of that."

Romeo continues, "'You Are Always on My Mind' seemed to satisfy everyone in charge. I thought the demo was craggy but truly haunting. So did Wes. So did David. The song came from a temporary dent in the same relationship in my life that inspired 'I Think I Love You.' Three-chord turnaround harmonic hooks always seem to work."

Appears On: Season 1, episode 21, "Partridge Up a Pear Tree" (February 19, 1971)

Doesn't Somebody Want to Be Wanted, 2:46, Mike Appel–Jim Cretecos–Wes Farrell

Spoken lyrics had been proven successful time and time again in pop music during the 1950s and 1960s. Elvis had done it, and there were a lot of Elvis comparisons going on with David Cassidy at the time. It is no coincidence that the white jumpsuit that came to define Elvis also became part of Cassidy's look when he began performing live as a solo artist in 1971—in fact, a designer who made several of his concert costumes also designed for Elvis. Even so, Cassidy was staunchly opposed to the release of this song as his follow-up Partridge Family single because he felt the talking section was yesterday's news.

In the early recording sessions, before anyone had seen the show or heard the records, Cassidy described the music they were recording up to this point as "sophisticated blues rock," that, "at times gets right down to it, right there, and at other times its Mamas & Papas–type stuff with lots of harmony and flow." It was a good assessment of the early Partridge Family sound, and the blues rock element is plentiful during the first season of the show. But this song doesn't fit either of those descriptions. The musical style took a sharp right turn, and it threw Cassidy. He didn't intend to change the world and sing music with strong messages. "I'm not trying to preach anything, or right anyone else's wrongs," he said. "I'll leave that to other people." But he did want credible music, and he didn't think this song fit the bill.

His reluctance to do the spoken section of this song was an early sign of the conflicts that were beginning to emerge between Cassidy and Wes Farrell. Cassidy was only 20 years old at the time and just beginning to establish himself in the industry. Farrell was in his mid-30s with tremendous success fueling his ideas. A musical generation gap did exist between the two.

Farrell and Cassidy liked each other. They spent a lot of time together, especially during the early sessions for the Partridge Family. "Doesn't Somebody Want to Be Wanted" was a sort of crossroads for the two talents; Cassidy had his own ideas, quite different from Farrell's, about where he wanted his musical career to go. But Farrell was steering the boat, and Cassidy was only able to toss in ideas and get approval from time to time—and to hold to his own vocal interpretations.

when we're singin'

The combination of the two conflicting visions, as different they may have been, lent itself to the unique sound that belongs to the Partridge Family. They were creating their own unexpected sound because of their differing opinions and ideas, not in spite of them. *Cash Box* had this to say: "Knocking out some of the tinsel that adorned the group's first single, the Partridge Family returns with an even more intriguing bit of material to advance the act's hold on Top 40 and MOR playlists. Strong ballad follow-up to 'I Think I Love You.'"

When asked if it was true that Cassidy abhorred this song, Farrell responded, "Yeah, sure. He wasn't thrilled with that." He continued with a laugh, "He hated it. He disliked it immensely. But I thought it worked for, not against, the message we were trying to pass through the market we were attracting…. So I guess it was my doing. It certainly wasn't his doing, and it didn't thrill him to death, but it worked."

Cassidy liked the blues and the '60s rock being explored by Cream and Jimi Hendrix, and continues to say so consistently. At the same time "Doesn't Somebody Want to Be Wanted" was finding its way into America's heart, Cassidy was also putting down a romping guitar-fuzzed track titled "Warm My Soul." It was considered for a potential Partridge Family single release, but ultimately they went with "Doesn't Somebody Want to Be Wanted."

It's not hard to imagine the disappointment young Cassidy must have felt with the realization that marketing would play such a huge role in his musical career and much of the decision-making would be outside his control. Is it any wonder that a 20-year-old newcomer with sudden fame would retaliate? Nonetheless, he found himself back on the charts as the lead vocalist on the No. 6 song in America in March 1971. It had entered the *Billboard* Top 100 on February 13 and remained there for 12 weeks—not a bad tradeoff.

Songwriter Mike Appel remembers the song's origins vividly. "Wes came into the writer's room and started playing this chorus with the title 'Doesn't Somebody Want To Be Wanted,' he says. "He then turned to us and said, 'Do you think you can finish it?' We said sure and he left. Jimmy hated the song and I didn't think anything of it at the time either. However, I was signed to Wes and had to try and please him, so I finished the music and all the lyrics and stuck everybody's name on the record. I have no regrets about that, either. Wes wrote the musical chorus for this song, but nothing else. I wrote the verse and I wrote all the lyrics.

"I remember after Wes had recorded the song with David in L.A., when he came back to the office in New York he asked me to come in to hear it. Wes played the record, and that was the first time I heard the recitation part in the middle of the song. It was all Wes' idea, and that was it! It was our first million-selling single! It went to number one here in the States!" "Doesn't Somebody" hit No. 1 on April 3, 1971, in *Cash Box*, less than a week after Cassidy's first concert.

The huge success of this song was quite different from the reception of the episode on which it aired. The storyline involves Danny, who comes to think he is adopted after being teased by his siblings that he doesn't look anything like them. The episode caused a stir with children who were frightened by the suggestion that Danny may not have been a "real" Partridge, and the producers received letters of discontent from parents and fans. Even executive producer Bob Claver has expressed regrets over the episode, and when the series went into syndication it was left out of the package for some time. It was later included back into the package and appears along with all the other uncut episodes on the official DVD releases. The song plays over a montage rather than in a concert sequence, and it was never used on any other episode despite its hit status.

Musically, "Doesn't Somebody" has a free-spirited, searching quality to it, accentuated by Cassidy's vocal interpretation. Some congas can be heard, but otherwise it is pretty standard pop fare.

Twenty years after the song's release David Cassidy described his youthful feelings about it, how important a musical identity was to the youth of his era, and how this song affected him. It was "like fingernails down a chalkboard for me," he said. "I think it sold a million, seven hundred thousand copies. You can't knock something that sells that much, except if you have to sing something that you are diametrically opposed to—which is talking in the middle of a record. I almost left the show over it. It threatened my whole essence of being cool. At that time I was still holding on to 'OK, I'm acting and I'm singing this part, but I'm not going to be doing something like that 'cause people are going to think it's not Keith. It's David Cassidy singing it."

Cassidy's opinion mellowed out over the decades. In 1991 he revived it live in concert at Hershey Park, Pennsylvania, at his first live US concert in over 15 years. He told the audience that when he played this song for the last time in the early '70s, he'd sworn he would never play it again, but his fans had convinced him otherwise.

The song again disappeared from the concert set list, then reappeared in 2009 at the Barrow-Civic Theatre in Franklin, Pennsylvania. Cassidy told the audience he hadn't played "Doesn't Somebody" in years but had been told many times by fans that the song was important to them. One story that really affected him came from an unnamed actor who told him that the spoken section of the song best captured how he felt.

In a 2012 concert performance in Alexandria, Virginia, he shared a few spirited comments with the audience during the intro to the song. He said he'd thought talking in the middle of a song was outdated, even for the '70s. "But now," he joked, "it fits like a Nehru jacket."

Appears On: Season 1, episode 24,
"A Partridge by Any Other Name" (March 12, 1971)

when we're singin'

I'm Here, You're Here, 2:51, Gerry Goffin–Wes Farrell
Among Gerry Goffin's contributions to the Partridge catalog, "I'm Here, You're Here" comes off as the most rock and roll in nature, slightly reminiscent of "I Can Feel Your Heartbeat." It opens strong and immediate, with absolutely no vocal harmonies or hooks from the background singers, just Cassidy's attention-grabbing vocal and a heavy dose of keyboard. There's a haunting quality to this song.

Appears On: Season 1, episode 17, "Why Did the Music Stop?" (January 22, 1971)

Umbrella Man, 2:44, Mike Appel–Jim Cretecos
Though none of the other songwriters interviewed can remember being given parameters within which a David Cassidy song should be written, Mike Appel says he and Jim Cretecos were, with the intention of matching the songs to the intended image of the television show. Even so, the construct of "Umbrella Man" hints at the edge that excited the two creatively—and that found fuller expression in their next career move once they left the Partridge Family—discovering and managing the early career of Bruce Springsteen.

"Jim and I had already musically left the teen pop world to develop what we considered real artists—artists who wrote their own songs and weren't necessarily dependent on songwriters like us," says Appel. "David and Wes loved this song and made it better than Jim and I would have because somehow, by this stage of the game, our hearts weren't really in it." The title of the song came first, and it served as inspiration for the rest of the composition. This time we get a harpsichord and triangle intro, with a bluesy feel throughout, enhanced by David Cassidy's vocal interpretation.

Appears On: Season 1, episode 19, "To Play or Not to Play" (February 5, 1971)

Lay It on the Line, 2:34, David Cassidy–Wes Farrell
David Cassidy penned three songs that made it onto Partridge Family albums, and "Lay It on the Line" is the first. It is without a doubt the rocker on this album. No chord progressions, no major sevenths (an arranger's delight, heard often in the Partridge catalog), and a song like nothing that the group had done before. Much like the straightforward nature of the title, the song is a very direct rock tune, with only three or four chords running throughout and a very deliberate rock guitar sound. The Wurlitzer electric piano is also prominent.

"It was a lot of fun," said Wes Farrell of the songwriting collaboration with Cassidy. "I remember David had the idea. He played me a little bit of it and I put it on a cassette machine, and I was at that time doing a lot of commuting between the East Coast and the West Coast. While I was on vacation in Palm Beach, I sat down and carved it out. The contribution was an equal one. We both collaborated on it. We tossed it back and forth for a number of weeks. It was like a lot of songs—you don't know whether you want to finish it because you don't know whether you have an idea that you're going to be pleased with."

Cassidy remembered it differently. In 2013, he told Ken Sharp, "I wrote 'Lay It on the Line' in my dressing room really quickly. Some of the songs that were more successful took years to write and some took a minute and a half. 'Lay it on the Line' was one of those that happened very quickly and took a minute and a half. Wes' name is listed as co-writer but he wrote none of it—not a word, not a note."

"Lay It on the Line" is the first Partridge Family song to appear on an album but not on an episode of the show.

Morning Rider on the Road, 3:01, Tony Romeo

No one wrote for the Partridges better than Tony Romeo. Filled with his masterful imagery, this easy-listening tune points toward the up-and-coming lyrical sounds of the '70s. "Morning Rider on the Road" is one of his first three songs demoed for the Partridge Family, and the last of those songs to appear on an album.

"As I look back now at the direction the group eventually took and the audience targeted, I wonder what possessed me to pitch this song for the group," said Romeo. "It would seem to be a casting disaster. But it turned out well, thanks to producer, arranger, and artist. I wrote it for Glen Campbell and demoed it accordingly. Fact is, it's a faint countermelody to 'By the Time I Get to Phoenix,' a timeless classic by Jim Webb to which no candle should even be lit, let alone held. The lineup on the original LP—side 2, band 1—tells you how close this cut came to being the group's second single."

The folk influence is an obvious one. "This song was very autobiographical, very erotic, very double entendre," explains Frank Romeo, Tony's brother. "There's a whole lot going on in there. My brother adored Jimmy Webb. He freaked out on him. Webb was a big influence on him. Tony's songs grew more mature through the influence of Jimmy Webb."

"Tony Romeo was just an unbelievable writer," reflects John Bahler. "I never got to meet him because he was in New York, although we spoke on the phone. He was the perfect kind of writer for us. He wrote such out-of-the-box stuff. 'Morning Rider on the Road,' that one alone, is a perfect example. There were so many of his songs that were just so very outside the box. That's the kind of material Wes found. It challenged David. It challenged Mike Melvoin. It challenged me. By the time we got past this album, Mike Melvoin and I could finish each other's phrases."

"Rider" was never used on an episode of the show, but Romeo would see it retitled "Morning Rider" and recorded again by his friend Lou Christie.

That'll Be the Day, 2:45, Tony Romeo

A hopeful, uplifting number, "That'll Be the Day" is a declaration that shouts out to its audience all the way through. Like "Morning Rider on the Road," it has an obvious folk influence. The lyrics suggest that we dream of a perfect day when each one of us can join together with our perfect mate.

Musically, a type of guitar, much like a steel guitar, creates a sort of banjo effect. Intricate synthesizer instrumentation and a bluesy harpsichord lick are also included.

"I'd started this in the turbulent late '60s and put it aside," Romeo said. "The interplay between background group and solo made me think to finish it for the Partridge project. Really a song about tolerance, self-actualization—you should pardon the expression."

Appears On: Season 1, episode 7, "Danny and the Mob" (November 6, 1970)

There's No Doubt in My Mind, 2:29, Gerry Goffin

With the new Partridge sound still being adjusted, a bit of musical experimentation goes on here, bringing out the saxophone and clarinet for the first time. It's another reflection of the Melvoin-Bahler nuances slipped into these arrangements, building substance, sophistication, subtlety, and complexity. David Cassidy's vocals, though still pitch-altered, are much more prominent on the album as a whole, and definitely so on this tune. "There's No Doubt in My Mind" is another lyrically visual song delivered with confidence, and Gerry Goffin scores three in a row for Cassidy.

Appears On: Season 1, episode 19, "To Play or Not to Play" (February 5, 1971)

She'd Rather Have the Rain, 3:17, Terry Cashman–Tommy West

There's a lot to be said for songs inspired by something intimately personal—or in this case, some*one*.

This bittersweet and beautiful romantic standout comes from songwriter Terry Cashman. It manages to retain a gentleness and sense of innocence within the emotional complexity behind the song. It opens with a gorgeous piano hook, using the flute and triangle to enhance the sentimentality.

"I think this was the best song we wrote," says Cashman, rating it among the eight Partridge songs he wrote with Tommy West. "This was actually a more personal song. It was written about my first wife, and it just happened to fit in with one of the shows they were doing. I just thought it was a clever lyric and it had a really good melody. Of the songs we wrote for the Partridge Family, I thought this one, as well as 'Only a Moment Ago,' was above the others, both musically and lyrically. The others were all nice songs, but I don't think they compared with these two songs."

Cashman's songwriting partner, Tommy West, agrees wholeheartedly. "This song's also my favorite. Honestly, I think if the Partridge Family would have released 'She'd Rather Have the Rain' as a single it would have been a No. 1 record."

"She'd Rather Have the Rain" was considered for a single release but passed up. The craftsmanship was obvious, though, and the song ended up on the *Greatest Hits* album despite its lack of a single release.

The song was released later in 1971 by a group called Heaven Bound on the MGM label, with the title and lyric altered to "*He'd* Rather Have the Rain." The single failed to chart, despite Heaven Bound's beautiful rendition.

Appears On: Season 1, episode 20,
"They Shoot Managers, Don't They?" (February 12, 1971)
Favorite Partridge Family song of Shirley Jones (one of several),
Terry Cashman, Tommy West

I'll Leave Myself a Little Time, 2:27, Steve Dossick

"Carly Simon sang my demos for me," says songwriter Steve Dossick. A tremendous storyteller, he knows how to rivet a listener's attention with a single sentence. "And she sang the demo for this song."

"I never studied music," says Dossick, recalling his youth in Florida. "I didn't play music. It just wasn't in me. Fifteen months before I wrote this song, I had never even thought about writing a song.

"When I was in college, literally all we did was smoke pot and listen to rock and roll!" He laughs. "That was it. And yes, we did have lava lamps! It was the kind of thing where we'd ask each other, 'Are we psychologically addicted?' That's the kind of thing we did instead of going to class. I don't even remember college," he jokes. "I was listening to all the rock and roll—the Stones, the Doors, Cream. I was more of a Stones person than a Beatles person. I was very influenced by Leonard Cohen and his very first album.

"It was Christmas, 1968. I'm 21. I'm home for Christmas in Miami where I had grown up, and I'm out with some friends. I'm looking at this band, and they had this lead singer who looked to me like his job was to shake a tambourine and scream into a microphone every 10 or 15 seconds. So I said to my friend, 'That's the job I want!' Since I didn't sing and didn't play music, I just started writing songs." Dossick laughs again as he soberly looks back on his youth. "It was the kind of thing you do when you're really young. You just go off on a thing. It makes no sense."

Dossick jumped into songwriting. He wrote a couple of lyrics over the course of a few weeks, finding some affirmation from a few of his friends in a band who thought he had a talent for writing. He made a recording and found that he had a natural gift for it.

"I had just finished college, and the draft was looming on me," he reflects. "I worked hard to stay out of the draft. I had grown up in Miami Beach, and back then, when you finished with school it was about six weeks before they sent you a notice

when we're singin'

for a physical. If you passed your physical you just went around the building and got on the bus. So I determined that if, somehow, I could work it so that I never take a physical, then there's obviously no way I'm going to get drafted. They can't recruit you if you never had a physical!

"So my plan was to go to New York. Back then it took about seven months for them to transfer the physical up there. Other people did all kinds of things to avoid the draft. I had many friends who went to the draft board and said 'My psychiatrist tells me I'm a latent homosexual.' We had a real enemy and they were trying to ship us off and get us killed.

"I wanted a life in New York, but I didn't know exactly what. Initially, I didn't have confidence in myself as a songwriter because I didn't play. I'd hear the melodies in my head, and I wrote the songs in my head with the use of a tape recorder. I didn't know what I would do, so I tried some things, and one thing led to another. Every time I did something with music, something good would happen, despite the fact I had no business doing any of this. Over the course of a few months it started to occur to me that the only way I can get out of this (the draft) is to write my way out."

Dossick soon found himself involved in the development of an independent film, and he saw an opportunity.

"A friend of a friend who was making this movie that Judy Collins was going to be in took an interest in me. I had written some good songs and I wanted to record one of them for this movie." The director wanted a singer who sounded like Judy Collins, and it became Dossick's mission to find her. "So I'm hanging out at this bar in the Village," he continues, "and I meet this guitar player. I say 'I need a singer that sounds like Judy Collins.' The first female singer he sent me wasn't right. The second was Carly Simon.

"That's about the time she was working on her first album. Carly had actually once been involved with Wes Farrell. She was in a band called the Elephant's Memory that was heard in the soundtrack of *Midnight Cowboy*. Carly liked what I was doing, and I recorded a couple of my songs with her." The movie was eventually made without Dossick's music. But with a strong new vocalist to sing on his demos, Dossick pressed on.

"I was soon referred to a music lawyer who gave me a couple of names and a couple of doors to knock on. The second door I knocked on was Wes Farrell's. This was March of 1970. The guy that I talked to was Steve Bedell. He was Wes' lieutenant. He called me back into the office and said that Wes really liked the demo. It was just a couple of guitars, and Carly, and some voiceovers. These were not records, but they sounded like they were. They were really good. Wes really liked them. He said that I reminded him of Jimmy Webb, who he had just hung out with in Las Vegas. He told his lieutenant, 'Get him a contract!'

"So I'm waiting for my contract and a couple of weeks had gone by. I was invited to the screening at Screen Gems for the *Partridge Family* pilot, but my contract still wasn't coming, and while this is all going on, Wes approaches me and makes up this scenario: He says, 'I've got a perfect *Partridge Family* episode that needs a song. I know you could write a perfect song for this.'

"So he tells me this storyline where Keith is riding along in the school bus, and he's looking for his sister and stops at a mall or a shopping center. He goes in this lingerie store, and he's smitten with the salesgirl. She won't give him the time of day. She doesn't know who he is. She doesn't realize who he is or that he's a star, so he feels dejected, and he gets back in the school bus, drives down this alley." At that point the song played as underscore to the scene. "It was like *The Sound of Music* or something!" Dossick had no idea what to expect of the yet-to-be seen *Partridge Family* series except for what Wes Farrell was telling him. "All any of us had seen at that time, in the very beginning, was the pilot," he says.

"The inspiration for 'I'll Leave Myself a Little Time' was simply that I wanted a signed contract," says Dossick matter-of-factly. "Now remember, this is five years after the heyday of the Brill Building in 1965, '66, '67, you know, it was just a great time. A contract back then was something like $100 a week and you were supposed to just write songs.

"So I'd walk to the subway from the West Side, dowtown, in Soho before there was Soho, and I was always kind of in a trance. When you're writing you can't really do anything else. You always have something playing in your head. So I was walking to the subway, and I think this song had something to do with B. J. Thomas' 'Raindrops Keep Falling on My Head.' I was sort of hearing, almost like B. J. Thomas' voice in a way that, if you just slow down the tempo of 'I'll Leave Myself a Little Time'"—he sings the opening lyric, *"Not long ago you'd find me feelin' so low"*—"you will hear it. In that loping-along kind of way, you can actually kind of see it. It had a little bit of that to it and a little bit of Fred Neil's influence." (Neil was an established Florida-based folk singer.)

"I was very much influenced by Fred Neil, who wrote 'Everybody's Talkin',' though my influence for this was not specifically from that song but rather the body of his work."

Meanwhile, Dossick pursued Wes Farrell about the delays on his contract, and Farrell kept putting him off. "Since I was waiting for my contract and still hanging out, I figured the best thing I could do was to finish this song. He says, 'Go to the studio. I'll pay for it. Just do what you do.'

"Some of the things that were different about all of this was—one, while he was doing the demo, I could not play any music! I would hear the music in my head and I would sing it into the tape recorder and I would bring it to him."

when we're singin'

Dossick recalled being with friends in New York and seeing the episode that included his song, which was not the story Farrell had described but one in which the Partridges are in an auto accident with a dubious character called Whiplash Willie, played by Harry Morgan. "Now remember, I'm an *artist!* I'm *serious!* And at the end of the episode, when it's all over, they sing my song to keep this guy from suing them! I mean, my life had passed before my eyes! Here's this schlocky story with Harry Morgan, here's my song, and there's like a four-year old drummer and they're using my song to serenade Whiplash Willie? So to me, when I finally saw the episode on TV, as I said, sitting around with my questionable friends, it was like, *Oh my God, what's my life come to?* I mean Wes literally had to lie to me to get me to write this song."

Dossick's song aired on the second episode of the series. What he never knew until this interview was that the episode storyline Farrell had first presented to him was actually written, filmed, and aired as episode 6, "Love at First Slight," just with a different song ("Somebody Wants to Love You"). Dossick, who was convinced Farrell had made up a ridiculous plot to get him to write the song, was floored by the revelation: "So he didn't just completely make this up? I never knew that!"

With plenty of harpsichord in the arrangement, the song is carefree and introspective, giving the feeling of a daydreamer and roamer. Cassidy connected with that searching nature, mixing simplicity and complexity in an uncanny way through his delivery.

"I looked online some years ago, maybe eight, nine years ago," says Dossick, "and I saw some woman in Ohio who had said that whenever she feels bad she listens to this song. I really wanted to send her an anonymous copy of it with Carly singing it, but I couldn't do that to Carly."

Appears On: Season 1, episode 2, "The Sound of Money" (October 2, 1970)

Album Summary and Reviews

Total Running Time: 29:34
Original Release: March 1971, Bell 6059

The TV stars' first LP took them right into the Top 10 of the album chart. This follow up, with the spotlight on their current Top 10 single, "Doesn't Somebody Want to Be Wanted," has all the play and sales appeal to equal the success of their initial entry. Other strong cuts are "I'll Meet You Halfway," "Morning Rider on the Road," and "That'll Be the Day." *Billboard, March 27, 1971*

The Partridge Family is currently riding high both on TV and disks. Here is their latest LP effort and it should be another giant. The Family's single, "Doesn't Somebody Want to be Wanted," sets the pace for an assortment of tunes which are sure to find a ready welcome among the group's millions of fans. We liked the bouncing "Umbrella Man" and "There's No Doubt in My Mind," a catchy song written by Wes Farrell (who produced the set) and Gerry Goffin. Album should blossom into a substantial charter. *Cash Box, March 20, 1971*

The Partridge Family continues their initial disk momentum in this outing. This is a highly pleasant songalog in a variety of rhythmic grooves, but without any rough spots. The TV group effectively delivers such numbers as "You Are Always on My Mind," "I'm Here, You're Here," "Lay It on the Line," "Morning Rider on the Road," "She'd Rather Have the Rain" and "I'll Leave Myself a Little Time." *Variety, March 31, 1971*

First Chart Appearance: April 3, 1971
(Billboard, *No. 36;* **Cash Box,** *No. 47;* **Record World,** *No. 80)*

THE DEFINING MOMENT
*or ... **The Partridge Family Sound Magazine***

Season 2: The Times They Are A-Changin'

During the summer of 1971 the show was gearing up for its second season. Several changes were in store, and they had everything to do with David Cassidy's success as a musical chart-topper. With Paul Witt leaving, executive producer Bob Claver brought on Larry Rosen as a new producer.

In the 1960s, Rosen had worked as an associate producer on *The Outcast* and *Mr. Deeds Goes to Town* and as a producer on *The Mike Douglas Show*. He credits the top executive at Screen Gems, Jackie Cooper, for taking notice of his talents, having offered him the opportunity to work on scripts. Claver recognized his talent as a perfect fit for *The Partridge Family*.

Rosen was already familiar with the show, and he was more than enthusiastic when offered the position. "I said, 'Hell, yes, I'm up for that!'" exclaims an animated Rosen. "I *loved* the show in the first year. It had not been a major hit, but over the first summer, from broadcasting the reruns, the show just took off. By the time the second season came around it was a hit. It was a major, major hit. I was thrilled to be on it."

As big as *The Partridge Family Album* and *Up to Date* had been, the summer release of *The Partridge Family Sound Magazine* was equally as hot. By August 1971 there were three Partridge Family albums available on the market, all of them selling like hotcakes. The show, on the other hand, had completed only one season, which illustrates the speed at which these albums were being put together.

In preparation for the second season, producers sat down and made some decisions on the look and feel of the show. During season 1, most of the episodes depicted the family out on the road, with stories intertwined around each concert venue. Beginning with season 2, the family would be seen much more frequently at home, performing concerts locally more often than going out on the road. Consequently, the bus became less visible, even though the music, in real life, was becoming larger than anyone had ever dreamed.

"The producers and people involved felt the show would be more appealing," explains Shirley Jones. "Even though we were in show business, the audience still wanted to see us as a normal family. They wanted to see the 'real' mother and kids, school, girlfriends, and even boyfriends for Mom. Initially the priorities were the music and the bus, and then they just switched it around and decided the family was more important. We would still do a song every week, maybe a concert or a show, but they felt this change would be more relatable for 'Mr. and Mrs. America.'"

Depending on whom you ask, you get a different opinion on which approach was best. Dave Madden, for one, felt the first season of the show was the best. He came to make jokes about his appearances becoming relegated to the opening and closing tags, especially beginning season 2 when the comedic structure shifted a bit.

The focus on the characters' storylines also changed noticeably in season 2. They moved away from giving so much attention to Danny Bonaduce and developed the other characters a bit more—especially Cassidy's. Bob Claver, who had gone to bat for Bonaduce during casting, found himself continually pushing back during the first season as the network was pressing for Bonaduce to be used as much as possible. Claver argued that too much of Danny's character would begin to get annoying after a while. But very quickly it was the rising star of David Cassidy who took center stage, ready or not.

By now Cassidy had established himself as a singer and musician, playing sold-out concerts on weekends to thousands of screaming young fans. Cassidy discovered he could make a lot more money on weekends doing concerts than he could on the show. Unhappy with the situation, he went to his manager, Ruth Aarons.

Larry Rosen recalls the tension surrounding the situation: "There was a mistake made by one of the attorneys at Screen Gems that allowed David's contract to lapse, so we had David Cassidy with no contract and a hit show on our hands. This is what managers and agents live for. He was making pennies an episode when he started, but that changed rapidly. Ruth Aarons told me she didn't kill them too much," laughs Rosen, "but they took good care of David. It was a very tenuous time where we thought we might lose the kid, but there was no way we could lose him because the show was such a hit. Ruth knew that, so the ball was completely in her court."

Cassidy had been only 19 when he was signed to do the pilot episode and had turned 21 in spring 1971, as the first season was coming to a close. In those days he was considered a minor as long as he was under 21. When Aarons caught the mistake, his contract was open to be renegotiated. The new deal included a pay increase from $600 to $4,000 a week and an opt-out after four years rather than seven. Even with the new contract, Cassidy still made far more money on the weekend concert gigs—as much as $50,000 per show.

Cassidy's popularity with the public was unmistakable. During season 2 he had the highest Q rating of anyone on television, and the scripts began to favor Keith much more. Suddenly viewers began to see the role of Keith Partridge develop. He was also being paired more with Danny as part of the shifting comedic formula. Dale McRaven was the show's story editor, responsible for the development of the characters as well as the consistency of the scripts submitted by outside writers. By season 2, McRaven was given double duty as a producer. "We kind of wanted to keep the show as it was," he explains. "It was a hit the way it was. We didn't want to make too many changes because it seemed to be working. When you have a show and you're making big changes, the show's in trouble. It was my first job at producing, and Larry sort of taught me the ropes."

The records and concert tours were causing Cassidy's popularity to grow faster than anyone could imagine. Fans were so entranced that a second concert tour was already being scheduled before the first one had ended. "The ratings were showing that David was the one coming out as the attractive male lead," says Rosen. "Danny was the foil. Danny was the manipulator and the financier. He was the kid that was brighter than his years, and even brighter than his brother sometimes. But he was not the lead. It was the adorable David Cassidy. He was the attractive kind-of-safe-yet-sexual guy that started to emerge as the star of the show, so we started to write the show towards him."

Producers were careful in handling the character of Keith for fear he would appear too perfect, potentially turning off some of the viewing audience. So they made sure he always had flaws. As a result, the character was not only loved by girls but relatable to boys as well. "Young boys wanted to possess the same attraction to girls that David had," continues Rosen. "They wanted to be as funny as he was, and as confident in his own innocence and his own inexperience. Keith felt he knew everything, and he didn't—but feeling always confident in that, and always being caught in the middle of saying and doing things that were inappropriate, he would learn from his siblings that he was out of line. He would always manage to handle it. He never pouted. He wasn't shy. He had an opinion. He participated in the family operations and had a self-confidence in himself that males were attracted to, and the idea that he could attract so many girls would appeal to any young man at that age."

The comedy was sometimes at Keith's expense, often the butt of the jokes from Danny, and opinions vary on whether or not they sometimes went too far. But he would come out on top when he was at the microphone singing. It was always his winning hand. The musical success of the Partridge Family was, by now, reflected both on screen and in David Cassidy's live performances. He captured an audience that was making him the biggest teen idol of all time. His fan club would eventually top both Elvis Presley's and the Beatles'.

The producers had special plans for Shirley Jones this season as well. She was given solos to sing on two different episodes, one of them the special location episode filmed at Marineland.

Some the show's best episodes appeared in the fall of 1971, including "I Can Get It for You Retail," culminating with a concert performance from atop the bus, and

when we're singin'

the Christmas episode, "Don't Bring Your Guns to Town, Santa." Ray Bolger and Rosemary DeCamp were back as Grandpa and Grandma. Rob Reiner and a host of other impressive guest stars also appeared.

Though still mostly in the background, Susan Dey also began to see a few more storylines develop for her character. Even the two little ones were featured during season 2, in their only starring episode.

David Cassidy was now sporting the feathered shag hairstyle that went mainstream faster than hairdressers could clip. Cassidy is credited for popularizing the shag during the early '70s as much as Farrah Fawcett for her famous flipped bangs later in the decade.

"I Woke Up in Love This Morning" debuted on the show with the first episode of the second season. Both the song and its parent album, *Sound Magazine*, were already riding high when season 2 began, and the first signs of respect began to come from within the music industry. Insiders began mumbling that the album was better than its bubblegum image may have suggested. But while the music was growing, the image created by the marketers was still growing faster. *Tiger Beat's Official Partridge Family Magazine* increased its schedule to monthly beginning with the October 1971 issue, which was available on the stands to coincide with the start of the second season.

The theme song lyrics were also changed, from *"When we're singin'"* to *"Come on, get happy,"* (set to the same music), and the role of youngest son, Chris, was now played by Brian Forster, picking up where Jeremy Gelbwaks left off.

Hello, Hello Brian!

Brian Forster had been working as a child actor from a very young age. Forster had deep roots in the entertainment industry. Both his parents were actors, and his grandfather was Alan Napier, best known for his role as Alfred on the 1966 *Batman* series. His great-great-grandfather was the British novelist Charles Dickens.

Forster clearly remembers his first interview for *The Partridge Family*: "It was a very strange interview because I was used to the usual cattle call interviews, and this was a case where it was just me and my mom. I guess they had already heard about me and they had viewed the work I had already done. I think a big part of it was not only interviewing the kid but also the parents. They wanted to make sure the parents were somebody they could deal with.

"So here I am, and *The Partridge Family* had already been on for a year. I had already been watching it, too. I was in fourth grade the year before, and one time we were having a little classroom party and we were all dancing around to 'I Think I Love You.'" Forster laughs. "I knew the show was big before I was ever on it, but I didn't know quite what to expect." His first meeting with the other cast members happened at a photo shoot before filming began for the second season.

THE DEFINING MOMENT

"I remember the first photo shoot very well," he says. "Here I was with all the cast members and it was all very cool. I remember thinking *Susan Dey! She IS hot!* It was a lot of fun. I can always identify pictures from the first photo shoot because there was this shirt. It was a blue and white shirt that my mom used to have me wear. It was kind of a good-luck shirt I wore to interviews, because I almost always got the part if I was wearing that shirt. And there I am in that shirt, because I didn't have my own wardrobe yet!"

The show-business atmosphere was familiar to Forster, but this was something new. "I had been doing commercials and other things," he recalls, "so I was used to being around crew and other actors, but this was on a much larger scale. The show was already big and it was kind of overwhelming and much larger in every way."

Forster was sentimental about his on-screen mother. "Shirley sort of adopted me from the get-go," he says. "I can see it in those shots from the first photo shoot. You look at the two of us and we're both blonde, and realistically I could totally be her offspring. I don't know where that redhead came from," he jokes of Danny Bonaduce. "It must have been the mailman."

Larry Rosen remembers the replacement of Jeremy Gelbwaks with Brian Forster as one of the showbiz lessons he learned from the experienced Bob Claver. "I was a novice producer. I had never done a TV show in my life. One of the first things Claver told me was that Jeremy Gelbwaks was going to be leaving the show because his parents felt that it was not something they wanted their son to stay involved with. They felt he could do better, and that he's only getting one or two lines so it wasn't worth keeping him on the show. They'd rather take him back east and give him a good education. Claver agreed, and I said, 'My God, Bob, this show is becoming a hit! You're taking one of the characters out! What do we do?' He said, 'We put another kid in.' I said, 'Just like that?' And he said, 'Yeah, just like that. Nobody will know and nobody will care.'

"It shattered me because I'm taking over this show, and I didn't want anything to change because it worked so well in the first year. But Jeremy left and we put Brian Forster in, and we didn't get a letter. It was like *Bewitched*. That was on the air for years with Elizabeth Montgomery. Dick York initially played her husband. Then they eventually replaced him with Dick Sargent, and it didn't make a dent. It was experience that I didn't have. Bob was absolutely right, and the show worked just fine with Brian."

Rosen continues, "Brian was adorable, and we'd give him a line or two on the show, and I remember Brian's mother sat me down one day on the soundstage and said, 'This is sad. Brian's here all day long and all he gets is a line or two. Can't we give him more to do? Because if he's not going to have a heck of a lot more to do, I think we may pull him off the show because it's just not the best thing for him.' So I remembered what Bob had told me, and I said, 'Mrs. Forster, you know, it just isn't going to change. We're not going to give him many more lines than he already has, so if that's not acceptable to you, I think you should seriously consider taking him off the show.' I never heard from her again."

Forster appeared on the cover of *Sound Magazine*, even though the season 2 episodes introducing him had not yet aired. To get the teen audience fired up about the new Chris Partridge, *Tiger Beat's Official Partridge Family Magazine* featured an introductory article in the August 1971 issue. The headline read "Meet the new Partridge—Brian Forster!" *Tiger Beat* laid claim that Forster was cast after being spotted on an airline commercial, and that he didn't even have to do a screen test or an interview. Forster says the article was true. "They came to my house and they interviewed me. My mom use to raise cats, and so they took pictures of me with our cats, and a picture of my stepdad. In fact, I think that was about the only time you saw my stepdad on anything I did with *The Partridge Family*. I seem to remember I'm wearing that same damn shirt again, the blue one I was telling you about." He laughs.

Suzanne Crough remembers the casting change as no big deal. "I just remember, 'Here's your new brother. His name's Brian,'" says Crough. "The impact on the whole dynamic of the show wasn't risky, because nothing they could have done besides kill us off in a tragic train accident would have changed the dynamics as far as it pertained to Chris and Tracy," Crough jokes. "If the show had killed us off, that could have been sad, really. I mean, I *do* still have some fan mail!"

Teens and Magazines

Tiger Beat's Official Partridge Family Magazine provided a goody-goody portrayal of the actors, adding even more momentum to the rise of the show as well as album sales. The magazine, an offshoot of the highly successful *Tiger Beat* magazine, had launched in December 1970 and was playing a significant role in the manufactured image of the show, the actors, and the music. The cover of the first issue featured the entire family with their Partridge pooch, Simone, and declared itself to be the only official Partridge Family magazine. The first issue was 67 pages long and came with introductory stories on every cast member compiled from individual interviews and visits to their homes. Of course it came with a few color photos of Cassidy, including a shirtless head-and-shoulder shot for the centerfold.

Chuck Laufer owned the *Tiger Beat* corporation, having started the popular teen magazine in 1965. Laufer was very successful, making millions of dollars providing magazines to teens and preteens featuring all their favorite television and pop music stars of the day.

David Cassidy was already showing up briefly in the teen mags before he ever landed the role of Keith Partridge. His guest appearances on some of the hot prime-time shows prior to *The Partridge Family* had caught Laufer's attention even then. Once Cassidy landed the role of Keith, his face became larger on each of the magazine covers, while Monkees star Davy Jones and teen heartthrob Bobby Sherman found their images growing smaller.

The teen magazines captured viewers and helped build the financial success of the show. Bob Claver reflects, "I think that all of us in that business are open-minded about things that are going to help the show. *Tiger Beat,* believe it or not, was a very successful magazine for kids. It was like *Variety* for kids, so it was a very big deal."

The outside effects of the teen magazines were huge. Memberships in the Partridge Family Official Fan Club were being pushed not only through the magazines but also through cross-marketing on the back of the album covers. Millions of dollars were being made on the fictional family band.

The effects on the cast varied. David Cassidy was uncomfortable with it from the get-go. He has spoken about it frequently and quite candidly through the years. Cassidy, at one point, asked Laufer to stop featuring him, and Laufer laughed at him. Cassidy felt the magazine was rooted in greed.

Susan Dey was marketed to male preteens and to the young girls who were the primary buyers of the magazines, so she played a big role in the content of each issue. By the time *Tiger Beat's Official Partridge Family Magazine* came out, the entire television family, with Cassidy at the head, found themselves as part of a mega-marketing campaign.

The influence of the magazines on the younger cast members was much different than it was for Cassidy, Dey, and the others. "They'd come out to my house, and they'd take pictures, and they'd write a little article," says Suzanne Crough. "I didn't live through my childhood without it, so I don't really know how it would have been without it, versus with it," she says. "David was growing up as a teenager without it, and then all of a sudden he had it. The magazine exposure started for me when I was five, you know?" Crough doesn't feel she suffered any negative effects from the magazine's influence.

The articles ranged from stories that were truly rooted in fact to complete fabrications. "There was definitely some bit of truth in them—" says Crough, "a picture of me and my mom taking a trip, or a picture of my backyard and the swimming pool—but a lot of it was written by the magazine. There were some things where I thought *Where did they get that?* Even at that age, I noticed. But it wasn't malicious so it didn't matter."

The teen magazines were not tabloids, and there was no intent to exploit shocking images or negativity. In fact, it was quite the opposite. They piped up the wholesome image as much as they could, because they worked in conjunction with the show as a marketing tool. The studio and networks benefited as much as the magazines. The audience for *Tiger Beat* and similar teen magazines was young readers, and during those days no one wanted to shock the youth with questionable stories of morality about their favorite television stars. The teen magazines promoted the image of middle America and the dreams of its youth. They were focused on idealism rather than scandal, even if that idealism was not grounded in reality. Nonetheless, Partridge viewers and readers began to fantasize about the perceived perfect family. They wanted badly to be a part of it. While Shirley Jones had children asking her if they could join her family, David Cassidy had 10 times as many fans—but they were more interested in marrying him.

Don Glut was a young, aspiring writer-musician-filmmaker who wrote for the teen magazines to earn some extra cash. Glut knew Laudi Powell, an editor of *Fave,* another popular teen magazine owned by Laufer. "I had already written some published articles that appeared in various monster movie magazines, so I had some writing experience," he begins. "I gave her a call, and I said, 'Hey, could I get some work writing freelance for you?' So I came down and she gave me my first assignment, which was making up a story about David Cassidy's past. She said, 'Write a story—it doesn't have to be true—just write a story with this title, 'The Girl That Taught David to Love.' And since I wasn't sure if I was going to get a name credit or not, one thing I always did (even if I did know I was getting a byline) was fill it with all kinds of little in-jokes so I could say, 'Hey, I wrote that.'

"So anyway, I was a big comic book fan at the time, and I was just getting into comic book writing. And so Betty Dean was a girlfriend of Sub Mariner in *Sub Mariner* comics, so I called her Betty Dean. That was the beginning of it, and then Laudi liked my writing and the fact that I could turn out these things quickly, and she started giving me a lot of work."

Glut had roots with the Monkees and knew Brendan Cahill, who had worked with the Monkees and served as a music coordinator on the first season of *The Partridge Family*. Before the series had even aired, Cahill suggested Glut work on a comic strip based on *The Partridge Family*. Cahill predicted this show would be bigger than *The Monkees.*

"He sent me some photos of the actors, and at the time I was writing comics for the Warren Publishing Company," says Glut. So he put together some sample pages, took them to the set, and shared his drawings with the cast. There were 21 issues produced of *The Partridge Family* comic books by Charlton Comics, and a separate 14 David Cassidy comics. Glut went on to become best known for writing the novel for the *Star Wars* sequel *The Empire Strikes Back,* and has since gone on to work as an independent filmmaker.

Plenty of photo shoots went along with the publicity generated by *Tiger Beat*, all intended to perpetuate the wholesome image. "The photo shoots weren't tied to the contract of the show," explains Suzanne Crough. "It was simply publicity. They had photographers on the set, and they would take pictures of us with our Michelin bikes. We had bikes at the lot, swing sets, and other things. They'd take different pictures of Brian, Danny, and I getting ready to bike ride, and things like that. They were just candid spontaneous shots. When they came to my house on the weekend or during hiatus, it was more of a scheduled type of thing. Of course my parents were very welcoming, and they probably cooked them dinner, too!" she laughs.

"Kenny Lieu, the photographer for *Tiger Beat,* continued to take my pictures for years afterwards," says Crough.

Tiger Beat produced the first four issues of *The Official Partridge Family Magazine* between December 1970 and September 1971 on a near-bi-monthly release schedule. It was issued monthly from October 1971 to June 1972, and wrapped up in the fall with two special issues. The magazine's popularity peaked in the summer of 1971 during the release of the *Sound Magazine* album.

Cassidy's face alone was on the cover of thousands of teen magazines worldwide. *Tiger Beat* featured his face on the cover of every issue for more than two years. But he and the Partridge Family were certainly not restricted to teen magazines. The family graced the cover of *TV Guide* twice, while David Cassidy sported the cover as a solo artist another two times. Both Cassidy and the Partridge Family were individually featured on covers of *Cash Box,* and Cassidy himself appeared on the covers of *Life* and *Rolling Stone*—all within a four-year span. That was a lot of coverage to be generated by one TV show in those days.

Bus Stop ...

Tiger Beat's Official Partridge Family Magazine

The *Tiger Beat Official* volumes mostly featured syrupy articles on each individual cast member, geared toward a female audience of about eight to 15 years old. A journalist and photographer visited the home of each actor, collecting images and information. The articles were harmless, mostly serving as an advertisement for the show. There were contests, collectible booklets and items, color centerfolds of David Cassidy in each issue, and little tidbits of information, now historical in context (Did you know Cassidy was on *The Dating Game?*). The magazine, which ran for 15 issues, provides

when we're singin'

an innocently portrayed behind-the-scenes chronology. Here's an issue-by-issue summary—excluding all the syrup!

Issue No. 1, December 1970

Jack Cassidy hand-wrote some notes about David, and comments from Shaun Cassidy are also featured. There are pictures and information on some of the stand-ins, especially Susan Dey's. Many of the issues feature stories of Dey and her guardian, Jane Joyce. Song lyrics for songs on *The Partridge Family Album* are included.

The new Partridge Family Fan Club kit is advertised heavily with full color ads. There are 19 different mail-away items offered throughout the run of the magazine, not including subscription offers for other Laufer-owned magazines such as *Fave, Tiger Beat,* and *Tiger Beat Spectacular.* Nearly half of the entire set of mail-aways are offered in the first issue:

- *Fan Club Kit No. 1 (the very first Partridge Family fan club). Contents include a "Private Lives of the Partridge Family" booklet, Partridge mini-poster, autographed photos of each star, red stickers, wallet-size photos of each star, a membership card, a "groovy stuffer," and an address-of-the-stars sheet.*
- *David Cassidy's Super Luv Stickers (a variation of the fan club kit stickers)*
- *David's Choker Luv Beads (small red, white, and blue beads with a needle to string them)*
- *"The Secret of David Cassidy" booklet*
- *"1001 Secret Facts about The Partridge Family" booklet*
- *"David's Private Photo Album" booklet*
- *"Dynamic David Cassidy" booklet*
- *"Susan Dey's Private Journal" booklet*

Issue No. 2, March 1971

Includes a teaser for the upcoming Smile Contest; the first part of a rare two-part interview with Wes Farrell; baby pictures of the actors; more song lyrics from *The Partridge Family Album;* and an article by Juel Anderson, the on-set tutor for the children. A childhood picture of David Cassidy reveals that he used to be called Smilin' Sam!

Issue No. 3, May 1971

David Cassidy's birth certificate appears at the beginning. Photos and tidbits about Cassidy's move from Laurel Canyon to his new house in Beverly Hills are included. Susan Dey talks about the cast teasing her over eating a lot of carrots. Danny Bonaduce's older sister, Cecelia Bonaduce, is noted as the president of the official Partridge Family Fan Club, with regular columns appearing throughout the upcoming issues. This issue also includes the Smile Contest entry form and part two of the Wes Farrell interview with comments from Farrell about the next album, *Up To Date*. New mail-away items:

- *The David Cassidy Love Charm (a piece of jewelry with Cassidy's autograph on the back)*
- *"Daring Danny Bonaduce" booklet*
- Susan Dey's Secrets on Boys Beauty & Popularity *paperback book*

Issue No. 4, August 1971

This issue focuses on returning to the set to begin filming for season 2 and what each cast member did while on hiatus. Susan Dey's lease had expired early, so she moved in briefly with Danny Bonaduce's family before going back to New York for a visit with her own family. There's a mention of Dey dating Dino Martin Jr.—something Jeremy Gelbwaks says he remembers! A few tidbits about the early part of David Cassidy's tour was featured. Dave Madden went to Vegas. Photos of Cassidy's concerts in Detroit and in Canton, Ohio, along with photos of his background singers, are included. A watered-down version of the hysteria in Detroit is mentioned. *Tiger Beat's* staff threw a birthday party for Cassidy's 21st birthday and cashed in on some photo ops of him opening presents. A new contest offers the chance to win a *Partridge Family* script.

Also included is a good-bye message from Jeremy Gelbwaks and an introduction of Brian Forster. Smile Contest winner Karen Lee Bowman is announced with a full-page photo. A secret decoder is added to the item list for fan club subscribers, and new mail-aways are added:

- *"David Cassidy's Concert Tour" booklet*
- *Full color wallet-size photos of the cast (available exclusively to fan club members)*

when we're singin'

Issue No. 5, October 1971

The magazine is now issued monthly and is available by subscription. The episode "Whatever Happened to Moby Dick?" filmed at Marineland is detailed, with pictures of Orky the whale. The cast reportedly stayed overnight at Marineland's motel. An interview with Brooks Hunnicut, who opened Cassidy's concerts, is also featured. Also included are David Cassidy's emergency gall bladder surgery; lyrics promoting the newest single, "I Woke Up in Love This Morning"; and the claim that Shirley Jones' favorite Partridge Family song is "She'd Rather Have the Rain." New mail-away items:

- *Four posters of David Cassidy, purchased separately, that can be combined to create the "Largest David Cassidy Poster in the World" (32x42 inches) on the reverse side*
- *Four different autographed 8x10 head shots of Cassidy*

Issue No. 6, November 1971

Details and stories of Smile Contest winner Karen Lee Bowman dominate the issue. Details are revealed about her trip to Hollywood and guest appearance on the season 2 episode "A Tale of Two Hamsters." Many more contests ran throughout the remaining issues. Brooks Hunnicut now has her own column reporting on Cassidy concert news, and song lyrics for *The Partridge Family Sound Magazine* are included. New mail-aways:

- *Fan Club Kit No. 2, for 1972. Contents are similar to those in the first kit, now with Brian Forster as the new Chris Partridge. The secret decoder is deleted from the ad, the black welcome record is changed to hot pink, and the red stickers are now green. The new membership card includes David Cassidy's autograph, and a "huge, living, kissable all-color" 17x22-inch poster of Cassidy is added.*
- *For Girls Only, a new Susan Dey paperback (which she didn't really write)*
- *"Life, Love and David Cassidy," a new booklet by Shirley Jones (which she didn't really write)*

Issue No. 7, December 1971

A Susan Dey lookalike contest is announced, and the issue features photos of Dey as a child and teen. Photos are included of David Cassidy singing

"Danny Boy" with his father on *The Merv Griffin Show*, with a note that Shirley Jones also appeared. Photos and captions about Cassidy's November 2 appearance on *The Glen Campbell Goodtime Hour* are also featured. "Set Side with Cecelia" continues with news of Danny Bonaduce's first personal appearance tour in Atlantic City, where he served as MC for a musical performance by Dawn and performed with them in concert.

Issue No. 8, January 1972

Handwritten Christmas wishes from the cast are featured. A two-page spread announces the newest contest, "Win a Phone Call from the Partridges." Handwritten notes from Evelyn Ward, David Cassidy's mom, appear in a series that begins with this issue and runs through several more. "Set Side with Cecelia" documents stories and behind-the-scenes anecdotes on "H-e-l-l-l-l-p!" a season 2 episode about a weekend camping trip gone amok. Dave Madden is quoted on his ideas of the "generation gap" in the most saccharine of ways, and a full-page promotion of *A Partridge Family Christmas Card* with lyrics to the only original song, "My Christmas Card to You," is featured. The issue has artwork of Cassidy on the back cover, designed for Christmas, rather than the usual photo.

Issue No. 9, February 1972

Kim Carnes and Dave Ellingson begin a column called "Let's Tour with David," a simplistic view of being on the road with Cassidy. (Did you know he once chartered a jet to get to a concert on time and offered rides to others at the airport who had missed their flight?) The column picks up where Brooks Hunnicut left off, explaining that Hunnicut is working on a new recording deal. Carnes and Ellingson once toured with the New Christy Minstrels; Bell Records reportedly called them to tour with Cassidy. Kim Carnes' first album, *Rest of Me*, is plugged in the column. Cassidy's friend Al Rhodes is also given a column to report on Cassidy.

The Partridge Family mystery books are heavily advertised. The first six are available to order. More contests are promised and winners from previous contests, including the Susan Dey lookalikes, are announced and featured with photos. Suzanne Crough poses in outfits by Kate Greenaway, announced as "coming soon." Documentation of Cassidy moving again is also featured, and *Tiger Beat* announces that they moved their offices closer to the studio.

when we're singin'

New mail-away: The David Cassidy Fan Club kit—the first fan club offered by Tiger Beat focusing on just Cassidy. Contents include a blue introductory record, a personalized membership card, David Luv Stickers, Secret Decoder, and a poster-size calendar including important dates about Cassidy marked throughout the year. "David's Photo Album" and a special full-color autographed photo are also part of the kit.

Issue No. 10, March 1972

The issue notes that the cast hiatus is December 13 to April, and that the cast had a Christmas wrap party in which the crew put together a blooper reel and played it as a surprise for the cast. The newest contest, "Where Are the Partridges?" asks readers to find six partridge birds hiding in a coloring picture. "Let's Tour With David" shares more reports on touring, noting that Cassidy is afraid of fans rushing the stage and getting hurt.

Two new contests begin. The first offers a chance to win a trip to Hollywood, dinner, and a kiss from David Cassidy. The second offers five dollars and an autographed cast photo. A track list for Cassidy's upcoming *Cherish* album is included, noting that "I'm Running the Opposite Way" and "It's All In Your Mind" were planned for the album, though neither were included. "The Mystery of Echo Park," an ongoing mystery story resulting from the popularity of the paperback mystery books, debuts.

Issue No. 11, April 1972

This issue focuses on the cast packing up their dressing rooms for hiatus, and their personal plans. There are reports of David Cassidy returning from Europe, where his camera was stolen. Reports of Susan Dey's first acting work on *Airborne* with James Brolin (later released as *Skyjacked*) is mentioned. Al Rhodes' column "David's Open House" notes that "I'll Meet You Halfway" remains Cassidy's favorite Partridge Family song to date.

A monthly column by Susan Dey, "Sharing Secrets with Susan," is introduced, though it is quite superficial and obviously ghostwritten. The "Fly to Hollywood and Kiss David" contest is announced. Fans are asked to count the number of pictures of Cassidy in *Tiger Beat* from January 1971 to January 1972 and send the answer in, with the winner chosen from a drawing of those who answered correctly. Song lyrics for *The Partridge Family Shopping Bag* are included and previous contest winners are announced.

Issue No. 12, May 1972

A month out from the start of filming for season 3, this issue updates readers on the cast. Danny Bonaduce has a new horse named Chief; Susan Dey moved from her house to an apartment; Shirley Jones and Jack Cassidy separated; Suzanne Crough is taking organ lessons (which she remembers vividly, although it was short-lived). A last-chance offer is made to enter the "Fly to Hollywood and Kiss David" contest.

With more focus than ever on Cassidy, we get a new contest offer to win his bicycle. The issue documents a few April concert dates tentatively planned for the U.S. John Raine, Cassidy's drummer, and Sam Hymen, the friend and business partner in charge of his concert merchandising, are also mentioned. Fans learn that "Life Love and Happiness" is inscribed on a family crest ring that was given to Cassidy by his father on his 21st birthday. (Cassidy heart-wrenchingly lost the ring decades later, offering a reward for it, but to no avail. It was the only piece of jewelry he wore, other than a medallion given to him by his mother.)

Issue No. 13, June 1972

The last regular monthly issue describes several internal shifts in the editorial department: Editor Sharon Lee was promoted to editor of *Tiger Beat*, replacing Ann Moses, who had moved to northern California. With Loudy Powell, editor of *Fave*, leaving to get married, Liz Dagucon was named editor of both *Fave* and *The Official Partridge Family Magazine*.

Ten U.S. concert dates for David Cassidy are announced as tentative, with shows planned from April 30 to June 25. Another contest is announced: "David's Personal Towel Can Be Yours!" Contestants are asked to state the number of concerts David performed from February 1971 to April 30, 1972. The winner, chosen from a drawing of correct entries, would receive a towel Cassidy used to wipe his face during concerts (yuck!). A second contest, "Susan Needs Your Help," offers another coloring page picture search, this time for girls' beauty items. Winners received five dollars and the Partridge Family album of their choice. *Tiger Beat*'s series of teen paperback books is announced.

when we're singin'

Issue No. 14, August 1972

The issue reports on Susan Dey, who had gone to Europe after filming finished on *Skyjacked* and was just returning, and provides an update on Jeremy Gelbwaks. The "Mystery of Echo Park" serial concludes, and three new contests are offered: "Design a Partridge Family Costume" promises that the winner's photo and design will be featured in the next issue, while another "Find the Partridges" hidden-image contest offers the chance to win a copy of the next Partridge Family album, *At Home with Their Greatest Hits,* and a signed cast photo. A third contest, "Win a Gift from a Partridge," asks only for an entry form to be filled out and mailed in, with the winner to receive a prize chosen by one of the cast members. Photos show a party thrown by the magazine for David Cassidy's 22nd birthday. Clothing fashions from Suzanne Crough and Susan Dey are pushed as part of the Kate Greenaway collection.

Issue No. 15, Fall 1972

The undated final issue has 114 pages and is billed as a double issue. It includes David Cassidy's concert schedule and photos of contest winners, and mentions Cassidy's now-famous puka shell necklace made of shells he gathered from the beaches of Hawaii. Susan Dey, returning from Europe, is reported to be upset that she put on 15 pounds while vacationing. As with other issues there are plenty of photos and articles. A final contest, "Do What You Wanta Do," contest is announced, and winners of the "Design a Partridge Family Costume" contest are pictured along with their designs.

Posters and Pinups: The Friend Behind the Lens

A strong element contributing to David Cassidy's success in print media was his friendship with famed photographer Henry Diltz. Diltz eventually became Cassidy's personal photographer, and the photos he took of Cassidy during the early '70s became some of the most popular, iconic images of David Cassidy seen throughout the world.

"I became a photographer in 1966 as a folk musician who picked up a camera on the road, and sort of got bitten by the bug of photography," begins Diltz. "I got this camera in '66 and started photographing all my friends who were musicians—like

THE DEFINING MOMENT

David Crosby, Neil Young, Stephen Stills, Mama Cass, people like that—and eventually did a bunch of album covers. In '67 I got a call from *Tiger Beat* magazine and they wanted to know if I would spend a day photographing the Monkees on their TV show. From the first day on, I became their photographer. I was their age. I was their generation. I had the long hair and the love beads, and so I fit the mold of what they needed. They didn't like the older AP photographers who had been photographing them, so I got the job doing that for a couple years.

"Then I went to England, and spent four months in England with Stephen Stills. I was working with him and had done two of his album covers, and on the way back from England I was reading about this group called the Partridge Family. This would have been the end of 1970, the beginning of '71. I was reading about this group, and as soon as I got home to my little house in Laurel Canyon the phone rang. It was *Tiger Beat* again, asking me if I would spend a day on the set of *The Partridge Family*. They would pay me a day rate, and I would photograph everything and then they would take the film and use it for magazine covers, posters, and stories. That's my favorite kind of photography because I'm kind of a fly on the wall. I'm a documentary-style photographer. I shoot what's happening rather than setting up shots, so the TV show setting was perfect for me.

"On the very first day, I met David. Once again, I was a few years older than him but more or less his age. I told him I had just come back from living with Stephen Stills for four months in England. He says, 'Wow. Well, come to my dressing room. I've got a guitar—I'll play you some songs I've written.' That had pushed his button about wanting to be a rock and roller, you know. When I arrived, it was the second season of *The Partridge Family,* and David was stuck in the role of Keith Partridge. It was a good job for an actor, and they were very popular. But basically he was a frustrated rock and roller. Right? He wanted to get out there and be a rock and roll star, not Keith Partridge. So we kind of instantly hit it off because I was in the music business and I knew all these people, and we were just these kindred spirits. We started talking and we just got to be really good friends.

"I would go down to that set maybe three days a week, so I was there a lot of the time. Hanging out with David on the set, in the dressing room, at lunchtime, and of course when they would film outside—those were the best days because everybody would be outside and you could shoot—I would not only shoot pictures of the Partridge Family but the crew and the director and visitors. Anything that went on. And my pictures began to appear on the covers of magazines, and then on the posters that little girls would hang on their walls. Of course I would shoot Susan, and Danny and Shirley, and everybody, really. I was a part of that family, just hanging out on the set. A kind of on-set family."

when we're singin'

Diltz took hundreds of photos of the *Partridge Family* cast, but it was the face of David Cassidy with which he became most familiar. He intrinsically knew what qualities he was after when shooting photos of Cassidy. "First of all there are several kinds of photos," begins Diltz. "One was a portrait. Most portraits of him were shot on the set or outside at lunchtime. When I started working, there was another magazine called *Star Magazine* and David was on the cover of the first issue of that, and my friend Don Berrigan was the editor.

"That magazine was interesting because Don Berrigan was a schemer. David and I went to Hawaii once and we stayed in this beach house for a week, and at one point I took a picture of David sitting under a tree with a little puppy that came wandering over. So he's sitting there in kind of a maroon T-shirt with a puppy, and Don Berrigan put that picture full page in the magazine and made up a whole story about the little girl next door who comes over—the puppy loves David and David loves the puppy, and she ends up giving it to David. She loves the puppy, but she loves David more. He made up a name for her, like Little Kalani or something. He was real good at making up stories.

"What *Star Magazine* wanted, of course, was a bunch of really nice portraits of David, but they wanted him in a lot of different shirts because they couldn't print month after month with David in the same clothes. So Berrigan worked out this deal where he had his secretary come over with a tray full of sandwiches for lunch and five or six shirts, and we'd do maybe 10 or 20 shots in each shirt. He'd quickly change shirts, we'd do another half a roll, then he'd change shirts and we'd do some more. And we'd eat lunch. It was a nice lunch, and she was a pretty secretary, and Berrigan would get these great portraits of David all in one day in six different outfits. So he could use that over a period of time. Berrigan was really quite a schemer. He was really good at doing odd things.

"I grew to know David's face very well. It was very familiar to me, as was Donnie Osmond's face, and Micky Dolenz, and Davy Jones. These are people I have looked at through my viewfinder literally thousands and thousands of times, so you get to know that face. It's familiar. It's comfortable to see them through the frame in the lens. I just knew how he looked the best.

"Then there were the trips—like on the ship, or out in the western lot for the Christmas show—where you could take pictures all day long. When you were inside you could only shoot when people were in the light.

"Then there were the concert stage shots. On stage, of course, I would try to get the heroic shots. Full length. Very often waist-up. And I would not usually be in the audience. I would be at the side of the stage looking straight across the stage because then I could get a side shot of David holding the microphone in a certain way, his head thrown back, you know, something that looked really heroic and beautiful. Or maybe he'd bend down and be taking flowers from the front row."

Cassidy loved his fans but wrestled with the image that was being created through the same magazines that brought him fame. Diltz says, "The writers from *Tiger Beat* would come down to the set and hang out, and write about what was happening. So maybe that was a bigger problem—that he didn't want to be identified all his life as Keith Partridge. But certainly *Tiger Beat* helped him become as popular as he was. The main thing about the Partridge Family was those young girls. They were 9, 10, 11, 12, 13, 14-year-old girls. That's who came to his concerts. That's who loved him. That's who loved him when he stopped being Keith Partridge and was just David Cassidy. Those girls are his fan base. Of course they first found out about him through the TV show and the records, but those magazines were really where they got all the glossy color photos that went on their walls. They enshrined him on their walls."

The Smile Contest

Tiger Beat ran promotions of all kinds. The fan clubs offered through the magazine were enormously successful. During the Partridges' four-year run, *Tiger Beat* offered at least two different Partridge Family fan club kits and a separate David Cassidy fan club.

The magazines also ran contests. The Smile Contest was the first for the Partridge Family, and it was a huge success. The May 1971 issue of *Tiger Beat's Official Partridge Family Magazine* included a full-page announcement that laid out its simple rules: send a snapshot that shows you smiling and explain in 25 words or less why the Partridge Family makes you smile. The contest stressed that it wasn't about having a perfect smile, looking good, or having any acting ability, but the sincerity behind the photo and the words. The winner would travel to L.A., meet the cast, and appear on an episode of the show.

According to the ad, the seven judges included Shirley Jones, David Cassidy, Bob Claver, Paul Witt, and the editors of *Tiger Beat, Fave,* and *The Official Partridge Family Magazine*. In summer 1971 the winner was announced: 16-year-old Karen Lee Bowman from Indianapolis. Details of her visit with all the actors on *The Partridge Family* were shared with readers nationwide.

"She was kind of sweet, actually," says Brian Forster, who remembers it vividly. "She was not all star-struck, but she was having a good time. I know she enjoyed it. It wasn't like she was totally jaded, but she wasn't silly about it, either."

Bowman made her appearance in episode 34, "A Tale of Two Hamsters." In this episode, Chris and Tracy take a bigger role than usual, helping Danny manage his new business scheme—breeding hamsters. "I remember a lot about the episode because I finally had something to do," says Forster. Then he reveals the inside scoop: "I got bit by the hamster!" he laughs. "I think Danny got bit first, so we shut down for the afternoon long enough to take care of the bites. Danny went to first aid, and

when we're singin'

then we got going again. Then the same thing happened to me! So we didn't have too much fun with the hamsters." Bowman appears toward the end of the episode, during a scene depicting a record-signing publicity stunt to get rid of the hamsters. The new *Sound Magazine* album is featured in the shot, as well as the first two albums. The popularity of this contest was so huge that *Tiger Beat* began to run regular contests. The second episode of the new season, "In 25 Words or Less," was also conceived as a result of the popularity of the Smile Contest.

Come On Get Happy!

Wes Farrell had been unhappy with the theme song from the beginning. He liked the music but had the lyrics rewritten. Along with the rewrite came a re-recording featuring David Cassidy's natural-sounding voice, as opposed to the pitch-altered sound on the first season's theme song. The new recording also matched the sound and style of Cassidy's voice on the new album, *Sound Magazine*.

Farrell met with Lester Sill, head of the music division at Screen Gems, and together they decided to employ the talents of established songwriter Danny Janssen for the task of rewriting the lyrics.

Janssen was a successful songwriter who was working with Bobby Hart writing songs for a number of different pop acts. Together, they had done all the songs for the chase sequences featured in the Saturday-morning breakout cartoon *Scooby Doo, Where Are You!*, which aired in its original two-season run during 1969 and 1970. Janssen was also recruited to work on *Josie and the Pussycats* not long after that. In fact, he is credited for bringing the first African-American cartoon character to life in the *Pussycat* series.

Janssen was already financially successful long before he started as a songwriter, having made a fortune in real estate, so he wrote music not for the money but because he loved it. He actually began at the insistence of his brothers, who all felt that he had a knack for songwriting and that his writing always seemed to reflect positivity. By the time he signed on to the Partridge Family project, Danny had already co-written several big hits, including Bobby Sherman's "La La La (If I Had You)." He was a natural for something like the Partridge Family.

Janssen never had any kids of his own, but he had a couple of nephews of whom he was very fond. One day, he promised his nephews he would take them to Disneyland. It happened to be the day before the new Partridge Family theme song lyric was due. Janssen usually had a personal driver who worked for him, but that day his nephews really wanted Uncle Danny to drive. Here is his account:

"So here I am, driving down to Disneyland, and I don't know how to find it, you know, 'cause the driver always found it. So I get down there, and about an hour after

I'm there I hear 'Danny Janssen! Telephone!' I think *Oh, shit, what's that?* So I say to this guy who works at the park, 'What's the deal?' He says, 'Oooh … I'm sorry.' I said, 'What are you sorry about?' He says, 'Well, they never call anybody to the phone unless it's for a death in the family or something.' And I said, 'Oh, crap!'

"So I get to the phone and it's Lester Sill—you know, president of Screen Gems/Columbia. He says, 'Danny, what the hell are you doing down at Disneyland?' And I said, 'Well, my nephews wanted to come down here. What about it?' He says, 'Did you get the *Partridge Family* theme song ready? I said, 'Yeah!' I had forgotten all about it! He says, 'Listen, Danny, I don't believe you, but if we're going to be in the studio tomorrow morning for this, we'll meet you first at Dupar's, OK?' I said, 'Yeah!' He says, 'Will you go home right now?' I said, 'Oh yeah, sure!' We stayed till 1:30 in the morning.

"So we're on our way back home, and I still haven't written the lyrics for the *Partridge Family* theme song, and so I thought about what to do. Well, my nephews wanted to sit up front with me, so one lays on my lap and the other one lays on his brothers' back. They're only like nine and seven or something at the time. And so we're driving home, and I'm driving with one hand, and I take a piece of paper out and I write on my nephew's back: *"Hello world, hear the song that we're singing, Come on, get happy!"*

"Brought it down to Lester the next morning. He says, 'You have that song done, Danny?' I said, 'Of course! I'd never let you down!' And that is how it happened!"

"Come On Get Happy," as it was later titled, became synonymous with *The Partridge Family* forever after.

On Location: Saving the Whales

Bob Claver and the other producers and writers always favored the chance to take on causes. Earth Day had just been established as a national holiday in 1970, and by 1971 the top 10 list of the earth's most vanishing species was being addressed in student classrooms across America. The white whale was on that list.

The second season included an episode about the growing extinction of whales. This episode included something special for Shirley Jones—her first opportunity to sing lead vocal on the show. "Whale Song" was written specifically for her and tailored to the script.

The episode was shot at Marineland of the Pacific, a popular aquarium in Palos Verdes, California. It showcased aquatic life, especially killer whales. Marineland was very popular in those days. Families took day trips and brought their children to see the dolphins, whales, and other types of marine life. Several television shows from the '60s, including *The Beverly Hillbillies* and *The Munsters*, had shot episodes there. It seemed a perfect fit for *The Partridge Family*.

when we're singin'

"That was a good episode," Claver says, "and it had some positive things to say. It had a pro-animal kick to it. It was more typical of *The Partridge Family* because we were standing for something, and that's the stuff that everybody liked best on the show—in this particular instance, that you were not going to let people kill animals. That's not a bad thing to teach kids."

The episode featured guest star Howard Cosell. Though Cosell wasn't an actor, he was instantly recognizable as the most prominent TV sportscaster during the early '70s. Cosell was a journalist and sports commentator who had an unmistakable voice. "Howard Cosell!" blurts Bob Claver, when asked about his memories of the show. "God forbid I should forget his name! One of the two good pains in the ass in this world," he jokes. Claver says that using Cosell made things a little bit harder than usual. "Charm doesn't float around him easily," he laughs, "but it was very good."

"My biggest memory of that episode was having Howard Cosell there," says producer Mel Swope, "because he was always fun to joke about. At that time, when you would have somebody from another world in television—from the sports world—come on your show, it helps promote the show. You might draw a few more people into the audience. That's a good example of using a guest star in the best possible way."

E.W. Swackhammer, a frequent guest director, was at the helm for the episode. Swackhammer had a reputation for being diligent and perfectionistic. "There was a structure that had an elevator in it and it kind of gave you a view of the park from up high," remembers Brian Forster. "Swackhammer's looking on it from the ground, going, 'I want a shot from up there,' and I think the rest of the crew was thinking, *You've got to be kidding me, right?* They all went off and shot some film from up in this elevator to get the overhead shot. Swackhammer was a real perfectionist. He could be firm, too, and he definitely got the quality out of everyone.

"It's funny. I'll never forget that guy's name, because it's such a name. My mom used to joke, and I don't know if she actually did it, but I think there were times when we would make a reservation for a restaurant, especially a real popular one, and we'd use his name, because everybody knew that name. It's like, 'Hi, I'm *Swackhammer*,' you know?" Forster laughs.

"Whale Song" was written by Marty Kaniger and Dan Peyton, a couple of struggling young songwriters who were into surf guitars and the folk scene.

The building elevator was one of the best places to meet people, according to Peyton, who remembers hopping on the elevator at Screen Gems just to meet Lester Sill. "He signed us," says Kaniger, "and that started our relationship with Screen Gems Columbia Music. We were writing mostly for ourselves, and Lester Sill put David Gates on to produce us as an act, which was great." Peyton and Kaniger's band was called P.K. Limited. But eventually, it was songwriting that moved to the forefront of their career.

"We didn't have Partridge Family particularly in mind," says Kaniger. "But Lester was a very powerful man there at Screen Gems, and we wanted very much to write songs, along with all the other great people they had there—Barry Mann, Cynthia Weil, Tommy Boyce, Bobby Hart, Carole King. They had a great stable of writers who wrote a large portion of the hits at that time."

Peyton adds, "Writing for the Partridge Family came about just by our being in the right place at the right time. We'd been writing our own songs—kind of ballad-y songs. The fact that the Partridge Family popped up for us was really just a lucky circumstance.

"Marty and I were pretty good at writing music for scripts. I took a lot of pride in being given a script and then coming up with something right for it." Kaniger agrees. "I always found that was kind of easier," he says. "You've got the subject so you don't have to start thinking about what to write. At that point I was playing 12-string mostly. I had a little chord progression I had been playing, and this was just a thing that sounded so nice on the 12-string. So I thought, *Why don't we start with this?* I think I came up with a chorus and a verse, and then we just sat down and it all came pretty quickly."

"When the cast and crew heard "Whale Song" for the first time, they were mesmerized. The songwriters were invited to the set. The music video sequence was shot on location, just around the corner from the oceanarium. "They had picked these typical places to shoot, with a giant tank in the middle," says Peyton. "They had a trainer who was going to make the killer whales jump at appropriate times and they had big speakers to play back the song. Shirley took her position and they ran through it a number of times. After the final go-round, Shirley was sitting in a chair and I remember going over to her and introducing myself. She was so gracious and sweet. She said it was a really a pretty song and she enjoyed singing it, and thanked us. She's just a wonderful person. It was a real treat, because we were thinking, *My God, she's an Academy Award winner.* And here she was singing one of our songs!"

Brian Forster and Suzanne Crough were very young, and Forster had just joined the cast, so he was not yet familiar with the extraordinary vocal talent his TV mom had to offer. "I just remember thinking, *Wow, this woman really can sing,*" says Forster. "I can be a sensitive guy, and this song kind of made me weep a little bit. It was so pretty. And always being a bit of an environmentalist I thought it was really cool the way they overdubbed the whales on the recording. *Song of the whale,* I thought. *Yeah ... this is really cool.* Shirley's singing was the perfect complement to it." Suzanne Crough felt the same way: "I thought, *Why doesn't she sing more?*"

"Afterward, I remember the trainer coming up to us and he was kind of teary," says Peyton, flattered by the reaction to their song. "He said, 'You're the guys who wrote this song?' He said it really got to him. He asked if we wanted to meet 'the boys,' so he took us to the training area, brought us to the killer whales, and he had them pop their heads out from the edge of the pool there. He gave them a command, and told us to scratch their tongues, because I guess they really like that. So we were reaching in their mouths and scratching their tongues! It was a special treat."

Meanwhile, Danny Bonaduce—always dependable for a good dose of trouble—struck again. "The thing I remember most ..." says Crough. "OK, I don't know if I should tell this out of context, because anything I tell you, you might actually print," she laughs.

"They had these whale performances. It was cool because we were able to go where the public doesn't usually get to go. We were treated like royalty. So Danny went over to the whale tank and gave the commands to the whale to do certain things, and the whale did it! But the whale didn't get fed any fish for his reward! So during the next show, the rider gets on the back of the whale, and the whale was kind of agitated and doing things it wasn't supposed to do, and it dove down and wouldn't come back up!"

"Danny, devious as always, was watching the trainer and figuring out how to make the whales do the tricks," adds Forster. "Then he went back when no one was around and started making the whales jump. He knew the signals! And when he got caught, it wasn't just 'Oh, come on, Danny, don't do that.' He was in some *serious* trouble for that one!"

"Whale Song" was so well received that press reports began suggesting a single would soon follow. The press announced: "The record will probably be released if The New York Zoological Society, which owns the rights to the whales' sounds, gives permission to use them." Sadly, "Whale Song" was never released on either a Partridge Family or Shirley Jones record, but it remains one of the most requested songs from the Partridge Family's body of unreleased recordings.

Liner Notes: *The Partridge Family Sound Magazine*

Despite the fanzine image, the Partridge Family's body of work was built on a complex and solid musical foundation. It is this underlying and seldom recognized credibility that has driven the passion of the group's fans, who have stood by the Partridges' music for decades. Today, as that original audience has grown and matured, it can be fun to look back at the image that was so cleverly built and manipulated to target them as preteens. But the music itself showcases the talented professionals who were behind it—every note, every pitch, every phrase, and every dynamic—giving it longevity and making the Partridge Family one of the most overlooked pop bands of the 1970s. That principle is especially evident on the band's third album, *Sound Magazine*, which represents their greatest moment.

Sound Magazine hit the sales racks in August 1971 and was certified gold for the third album in a row. *Sound Magazine* sold millions, and the Partridge Family reached the peak of their critical success with this intricately woven masterpiece. The arrangers had finally arrived at the definitive Partridge Family sound. Fans worldwide credit it as one of the best, if not *the* best, of the entire Partridge Family repertoire. Most of the artists who worked on it agree, including David Cassidy. The album had such impact on a generation that even musicians were inspired; a Partridge Family tribute band that emerged in the '90s named themselves Sound Magazine.

When *Sound Magazine* came out, it quickly had insiders talking. David Cassidy had just turned down an invitation to perform at Madison Square Garden on Thanksgiving weekend 1971, and his manager suggested the buzz on *Sound Magazine* had much to do with it: "It's a little too early to go in there. We know we'd get 10,000, but we want to sell it out. We're starting to get a big underground from the music magazines. *Rolling Stone* and *Creem* and others back East gave great reviews to his *Sound Magazine* album."

John Bahler and the group were peaking with energy on this album. You can hear it in every song. The arranger's precision and the vocal energy rival those of any other pop album from this era. The arrangers and producers felt they had really hit on the perfect sound. And the songs had not been composed on the basis of television episodes as with the previous two albums, so they stand out with more individuality as pop songs.

The producers still put serious thought and planning into the placement of songs into the weekly episodes. All 11 songs on the album were used on the show. Ten were showcased during season 2, with many appearing on more than one episode, while "One Night Stand" was held for season 3.

"By the end of the second album we had it nailed," says John Bahler. "We had figured it out. Wes had figured out what songs would go. I had figured out what the Partridge Family was, and although I hate to use the term formula, that's kind of what it was." Still, the songs were tightly devised and executed. The arrangements were always clever, imaginative, and attention-grabbing.

"The thing that brought the ideas out of me and Wes Farrell was the songs," says Bahler. "The reason I never wrote like this for anybody else was because nobody else had these kinds of songs. I wrote a lot of music over the years, and you write what it is that you hear for any particular song. It was really Wes' thing—finding hits and writing hits.

"What was really strange was that, except in the very, very, very beginning, I don't ever remember a TV producer or a writer ever suggesting a style, or suggesting anything. I think that's because of Wes. When Wes came in, he was able to prove himself. He was able to follow up what he said with his mouth, and he had a big mouth! He said, 'You want hits? OK, I'll give you hits!' And he did."

The Partridge Family recording sessions were refined in their approach as time went on. Bahler says, "For the earlier two albums, we would have a session where

when we're singin'

we only did two or three songs, but one of them we'd do twice, or even three times, depending on what things they wanted for the TV show. They may have asked for a particular ending, or whatever. So we'd do the record version and then we'd do the show version. But later on we got that down to a science, so we could do less sessions and get more product done, because by then we pretty much knew what we had to do for the show going in. By the third album, we always went in there with the idea that we're doing an album, you know? We were going in there to do an album, and any other incidental music that the show needed. That was our mindset."

Adding to the scheduling nightmares, David Cassidy was now coming back from his first tour, with his own solo album in the works. But fearless Wes Farrell never missed a beat. "He did it all," says Bahler, "except when they wanted something specific for an episode. He was kind of bored with those things, because that wasn't what he did. Usually, after we did the record version we had to do a special version for an episode, and he'd just say 'I'll see you guys.' Then he'd leave and we would just do it."

Sound Magazine flows beautifully from song to song. David Cassidy's voice is brought front and center like never before, although there are still traces of pitch altering and bits of echo used here and there. It was a significantly different sound than that of the two earlier albums, establishing the second musical phase of the Partridge Family and the signature sound that every fan recognizes.

Sound Magazine is more heavily produced than the earlier albums, and it reflects a much tighter pan in the mix. "Wes and I used to mix on headphones," explains John Bahler, "and everybody always said, 'You're crazy, man! You can't hear!' Well, 20 years later, that's what everybody's doing! We mixed on headphones because we could really get the stereo correct, for want of a better word. By listening on headphones you could really hear the placement of things. I always hated when they took a vocal group and spread it out left to right. It used to make me crazy. I never spread the group more than ten o'clock to two o'clock behind David. We would pan them to the left speaker or the right speaker, and of course I left David in the center.

"What a lot of engineers do with vocals is they pan hard left or hard right, and that's not normally the way you hear it if you were to hear it live. For example, when you go and hear a choir concert you don't hear all of the people on the left just in your left ear, and all of the people on the right just in your right ear. You know what I mean? It doesn't make for one sound, but it's still in stereo. Bob Kovach was a great mixer, and he took care of the pan and I took care of the vocals. Kovach was a great guy with a great personality and he never became rattled. He and I really had some fun together."

Bahler adds, "My favorite album would probably be a toss-up between *Shopping Bag* and *Sound Magazine*, because by then we were really into it. But if I had to pick, I'd probably have to say *Sound Magazine*." Mike Melvoin agrees: "*Sound Magazine* is the flush of success: *They know me and they like me.* Production values went up. Everything went up. I am most proud of this album. I thought the songs were all good."

The commercial success of *Sound Magazine* reflected the arrival of Irwin Levine and L. Russell Brown. These two songwriters were already legendary when they came on board. Their first co-written song was the chart-topper "Knock Three Times," and they went on to write the '70s pop smash "Tie a Yellow Ribbon Round the Ole Oak Tree," which hit No. 1 in April 1973. In between, there was the Partridge Family.

Brown, like Farrell, had a knack for recognizing potential hits. "Elvis was who I wanted to be," he says. "I wanted to be a Bobby Darin, a Dino, or a Sinatra. I never wanted to be just a songwriter. I only wrote songs so that I could sing them."

But it was Brown's talent as a songwriter that took him to the top. Brown had been writing for producer Bob Crewe, including the top 10 hit for the Crewe-produced Four Seasons hit "C'mon Marianne." He also produced a few songs that were local hits in Detroit and Cleveland before hitting it big with Irwin Levine and "Knock Three Times." At one point, in 1966, Motown wanted to sign Brown and made a very lucrative offer, but Brown was determined to have a career in New York.

At the same time that L. Russell Brown was signed to Bob Crewe, Irwin Levine was signed to Wes Farrell. "Bob Crewe was in disarray," says Brown. "He was selling off his things, and he sold off all his writers. So he sold the publishing rights for "Knock Three Times," along with my contract, to Wes Farrell. Levine and I were signed to Wes for just less than a year, and our contracts terminated the exact same day. I would be free when Irwin terminated, and that was in six months, so I went along with the deal. That's how I came to be working for Wes."

Levine and Brown wrote six songs for the Partridge Family, starting with "I Woke Up in Love This Morning." After the single skyrocketed up the charts, the Levine-Brown train began to speed up.

The duo also penned "I'll Be Your Magician" for *Sound Magazine,* but it ended up an unreleased outtake. It resurfaced later, with a little bit of syrup and a lot of overdub, on Danny Bonaduce's solo album.

"My biggest hits were written in less than half an hour," says Brown. "I usually have my ear open for anything that is said, anything that I think might make a great title or an idea for a song. I write those ideas down on little pieces of paper, tuck them in my wallet, and when it's time to write again, I open my wallet and look for all the little notes on the back of business cards."

The Partridge Family was now the group for which every aspiring songwriter hoped to write, and even established songwriters jumped on board. Paul Anka was a superstar in his own right and a friend of Wes Farrell's. "One Night Stand" was his sole Partridge Family contribution. It opened the album strongly and has been remembered by fans over the years as a standout. When David Cassidy began performing live again in 1991, his set list included this well-crafted pop song.

Rupert Holmes wrote the fan favorite "Echo Valley 2-6809." Like Paul Anka, Holmes was a one-time contributor to the Partridge Family, although his credits were plentiful.

Tony Romeo was back again with some powerful writing. *Sound Magazine* includes three Romeo-penned songs: "You Don't Have to Tell Me," "I Would Have Loved You Anyway," and the orchestral showcase "Summer Days."

The team of Mike Appel and Jim Cretecos contributed the last of their Partridge Family offerings, "Rainmaker."

Sound Magazine showcases the arrival of Danny Janssen with the innocent "Twenty-Four Hours a Day," and Cassidy's up-close-and-personal vocal interpretation of "Brown Eyes." Janssen becomes a central force in shaping the lyrical evolution of the Partridge Family on this album.

Janssen was already poised for recognition as the new theme song lyric, *"Come on, get happy,"* was about to premiere at the start of the second season. He developed meaningful relationships with Bobby Hart and Wes Farrell during the upcoming second half of the Partridge Family years, and grew to know Wes Farrell like a brother. Though intrinsically different, they became the best of friends. Janssen has story after story of his days in the music business. He reflects on how he left his job as a master teacher because of the industry's demand for his songwriting talent.

"One day, doggone it, somebody put a picture out there of me with Bobby Sherman, who had his arm around my shoulder," reflects Janssen. He had been writing for Sherman while holding down his teaching job. "I couldn't get to the parking lot anymore because they wanted to know who wrote those songs. So I thought I'd take a leave of absence, but I never went back. When I left, the principal said to me 'Danny, would you just promise me something? Will you not forget the kids?' I told him that every year I would do something in music for the children."

Janssen had songs on the charts that were hitting gold and platinum, selling millions of copies. An energetic personality with a fun spirit, he shares his colorful story on the first time he met Wes Farrell: "One day Bobby says, 'We have to go down and see Wes Farrell. He's going to have this meeting.' I thought, *Who the hell does this Farrell think he is?* You know? I was maybe one of the richest guys in the music business and this little shit gets up there and he has 200 people there to write his songs! I said, 'You Wes Farrell?' I won't tell you what I *really* said, though. You couldn't print it! He says 'Are you Danny?' I said, 'Yeah, I'm Danny.' He said, 'What do you want?' I said, 'You know what, Wes? You just eat shit! If you ever want to see me I'll be at such-and-such a studio. You come down and see me.'

"So he came down there! He was curious about someone who would tell off old Wes Farrell! So we get down there and I say to him, 'You're such an arrogant shit, you oughta name your company the Wes Farrell Organization.' And so he did! I said, 'Then you need Tommy and Johnny Bahler, Bobby Hart, me, yourself and then we can write the music, see?'"

Janssen has a great capacity for the dramatic, and he can get anyone laughing with his storytelling. Listening to him is like sitting on an old movie set listening to the best of the best reminisce, razzing and roasting his peers, all with a wink and a nod.

Of David Cassidy's three Partridge Family contributions as a songwriter, the second surfaces here on *Sound Magazine*, co-credited to Wes Farrell: the soulful and expressive "Love Is All That I Ever Needed."

The album also includes a song from the great Jack Keller, who teamed up with Bobby Hart on "I'm On My Way Back Home." As Hart came off his ride with the Monkees, he found himself often paired with other songwriters on different projects, including this one—his first for the Partridge Family.

Keller was another legendary songwriter with roots dating back to early years of the Brill Building. He had penned "Venus in Blue Jeans" and "Everbody's Somebody's Fool," a big hit for Connie Francis. He was contracted to Aldon Music, which was purchased by Screen Gems in 1963, leading Keller to television.

Keller scored a lot of television shows, including *Bewitched, Hazel,* and *Gidget.* He also wrote "Seattle," the theme song for Bobby Sherman's *Here Come the Brides,* and his name is credited to Sherman's pop single "Easy Come, Easy Go." Keller wrote his own musical arrangements. He eventually formed a songwriting relationship with Bobby Hart beginning with their collaboration on "I'm on My Way Back Home," one of the most sentimental songs ever written for the Partridge Family.

With a full jukebox of potential hits to choose from, Farrell decided to release "I Woke Up in Love This Morning" as the first and only single from *Sound Magazine.* It spent 11 weeks in the *Billboard* Top 100, peaking at No. 13 on September 25, 1971, and holding there for a second week. One could argue that almost every song from this album could have worked as a successful single.

The Partridge Family Sound Magazine was the Partridge Family at its peak. During the summer of '71, *Love Story* and *Summer of '42* were topping box office sales; cigarette advertising on television ended and Greenpeace was formally established; Nixon signed the 26th Amendment lowering the voting age to 18, and the Partridge Family was permeating the psyches of millions of impressionable young music fans all over the world.

The end of summer left teen magazine images of Suzanne, Danny, and Brian riding bikes and playing with whales; David Cassidy blowing kisses to the cameras of staff photographers for the publicity machine while selling out concerts nationwide,

when we're singin'

and Susan Dey only months away from signing on to her first feature film. Meanwhile, the musicians of the Wrecking Crew were working around the clock to keep those Partridge Family albums coming. The image and the reality were distinctively different, but the image was unbreakable.

One Night Stand, 3:01, Paul Anka

Paul Anka and Wes Farrell had worked and partied together for many years. One day they decided it was time to dream up a Partridge Family song together.

"Wes Farrell and I had so many great times," begins Anka. "We socialized a lot. We met each other in the early '60s. His mother lived in my building. He was very professional. Had a lot of energy. He wanted to hook up with me and talk about publishing and doing songwriting, and we continued on that path, and he produced a couple of albums of mine later on. We wrote, as you know, a couple of songs together. We were friends for many, many years. Even after—professionally he went one way and I went the other, but he was just one of these viable, energetic, good publishers with a lot of enthusiasm and a lot of passion about what he did.

Anka describes the origin of "One Night Stand": "We just decided to write. I had the title, and it was the creative process, just like I have done with everybody, right down to Michael Jackson. Wes was creative, and he was a little different than anyone because he wasn't a singer," Anka laughs. "But he was an idea guy. I worked with an eclectic array of people. So I invited him, and he sat down and he liked it.

"We knew where we were going to go with it. Cassidy and that whole gang were all hot, and he wanted to write something for them, so I think it was kind of aimed at Cassidy.

The lyrics happened on the spot, says Anka. "You're in the moment. You're throwing stuff at each other. We probably both had a little brandy or schnapps. We were always drinking something. So we were just in the moment and we sat down and just bounced ideas and laughed at each other and got excited, and I can't tell you—it just rolled out. We probably got the core of it in one day, but I nursed it good for about a week, back and forth, polished it, the bridge, all that kind of stuff."

The song was written specifically for the album rather than the TV show. Anka says his favorite aspect of the song is the energy that resulted from the final cut.

"Even as a songwriter, the unsung heroes for me are the arrangers," says Anka. "Nobody ever hears about the brilliance of how they come in and take a lead sheet of one note, look at the artist, look at the writer, look at the song, and then they marry it all together so it comes together with the great framework that allows the consumer to feel it emotionally.

"It's important that the fans see the other side of it, keeping in mind that success has many fathers, and they have to realize that they can't idolize and look up at all of us as artists and think that it just happens. It happens with a team of people. But the creative part, the creative dynamic, is what really counts because that's what makes us—whether we are actors or singers—that's what makes us what we are."

Right out of the gate, "One Night Stand" opens the album to pop perfection. The lyric is strong and the arrangement more tightly blended than on earlier albums, making it much more evenly woven. There's also much less stereo spread than on previous albums. David Cassidy's voice is his own, with no sign of reverb or pitch altering.

Some reverb is present in the background vocals, though, and Mike Melvoin throws in a muted trumpet and strong brass support. "One Night Stand" represents a new sound that is perfect for David Cassidy and the Partridge Family. The song's theme itself is a relatable subject for a pop superstar, and Cassidy sings the number with passion.

"I love that song," said Wes Farrell in 1993. "I loved writing with Paul. Paul is one of the great writers in contemporary music. We've been very close friends for a long time. Paul got a big kick out of writing a song for the Partridge Family. It was something that he hadn't done. I had produced a couple of albums with Paul, and it was kind of fun to be sharing something with him that wasn't tied to him.

"This song had a lot of energy. Once you got it started you couldn't stop. It kept building and building. I loved seeing David do it live again a few years ago," Farrell added, referring to David Cassidy's concert revival tour in 1991 It was fun because it took on another sense of energy and life."

Danny Bonaduce, who at Cassidy's invitation did a stand-up routine as the opening act for the same tour, recalls, "I tried to write jokes, but I discovered I don't write jokes. I write stories. So I told one about a song called 'One Night Stand.'" "I didn't even remember it, and when David played it, I thought, *This is the exact same song as 'Wanted Dead or Alive' by Bon Jovi, except better! David Cassidy's version is better!*

"My wife is the one that turned me on to the quality of the Partridge Family music," says Bonaduce. "I had pictures of Led Zeppelin and Jimi Hendrix on my wall while we were playing these Partridge Family tunes, so I didn't like them. David didn't like most of them either, even though he recognized the quality of them. I did not."

Appears On: Season 3, episode 73, *"Diary of a Mad Millionaire" (March 23, 1973)*

Brown Eyes, 2:44, Danny Janssen–Wes Farrell

In 1993 Wes Farrell described "Brown Eyes" as a very important song for the group, and that the first CD hits compilation released in 1989, *The Partridge Family's Greatest Hits*, overlooked its inclusion. "Brown Eyes" is the strongest early showcase for David Cassidy's new breathy vocal style, with an interpretation that resonates beyond the lyrics. Here we discover a new facet of Cassidy's talent, something even better than a good voice: He has the rare ability to *communicate* a lyric.

when we're singin'

He can make the listener identify with him through the presence in his voice. That presence and intimacy, together with the conversational way Cassidy handles lyrics, rival any of his contemporaries. There's a sincerity, an innocence in both the lyric and arrangement, rather than the distance of the first two albums. The background vocals are also phenomenal. What girl wouldn't swoon? What boy couldn't relate? The song opens with a Wurlitzer piano and ends with a cold stop rather than a fade.

"I wrote that with Danny Janssen," Farrell told Ken Sharp in 1993. "He's a very fine writer who really had some energy to last it out with me. He would get the West Coast side of me where I'd come in there and record all night, then write the rest of the night. Danny was a real hard-working composer. It was a good collaboration."

Appears On: *Season 2, episode 29, "The Undergraduate" (October 8, 1971)*

Echo Valley 2-6809, 3:05, Rupert Holmes–Kathy Cooper

Theatricality plays well in pop music, but only if delivered capably. Cassidy's interpretation of "Echo Valley 2-6809" and the way it captures the listener reaches back to his early theatrical roots and points toward the success he would find on the stage later in life.

A story song by singer-songwriter and theatrical writer Rupert Holmes, "Echo Valley 2-6809" was intentionally listed second on the cover design of *Sound Magazine* because it was going to be the next single, but in the end Farrell and Larry Uttal decided against a second single and remained focused on album sales.

The theme reflects the past and looks back nostalgically. Discovered to be a fan favorite as the years have passed, it is usually included in David Cassidy's current concert appearances.

"My own style as a songwriter was still evolving at that time," Holmes told Ken Sharp in an interview. "I'd had a couple of minor hit records and I was working in the industry with a lot of nonexistent studio groups. By that time I had become the new voice for the Cuff Links. Ron Dante was the voice behind that group. He was one of the greatest session singers of all time and a great producer for Barry Manilow. He left the group and I sort of took over. Ted Cooper was a record producer and songwriter person who worked for Wes Farrell. I'd worked with him in different capacities—him as a producer and me as a songwriter. One day he said to me, 'I think I can get a song placed with the Partridge Family if it gets written the right way.' I spent an awful lot of time with Ted Cooper, who gave me his and his wife Kathy's input on this song. I credit Kathy in providing a tremendous artistic overview on the song.

"'Echo Valley 2-6809' was written specifically for the Partridge Family. We wanted to write something that didn't feel as bouncy-bubblegummy. We wanted to write a more grown-up song, and wanted it to be a more sophisticated song for the Partridge Family. We wanted it to be a little wistful and we wanted it to be a little poignant. Together we started thinking about the idea of somebody trying to find a love they had lost. With that premise, I started vamping on chords—the thought being that we grew up together and our life had been very idyllic, and now we're apart. That sort of came through.

"I did all the music, and my writing partner came up with lots of the key ideas such as *'ferris wheels and sunshine laughter.'* That's not what I would have written. By then I was a little too cynical to have written something like that. The line *'I've become a lonely runner'* may have been me, because at that time I was very into the movie *The Loneliness of the Long Distance Runner*. The line *'I can't face the sunrise, lighting up a road to nowhere/Where you are, I have to go there, are you waiting? I've got to know,'* I felt, was about coming to the end-title part of the movie that we were telling in this song. The line *'lighten up a road to nowhere,'* is, to me, the last shot of the movie where the hero's going off toward the sunset, but he's forlorn, with the guitar strapped over his back. *Nowhere* was just within spitting distance of the rhyme *go there*, so without trying to get overly pompous and analytical, it was just an attempt to make a song that could be on a Partridge Family album and yet one that an adult could sing and for whom it could be totally relevant.

"As for the song title, I knew it was going to be a phone number. All I did was think about picking a phone number that sounds mellifluous. The numbers mean nothing. They just seem to sing well—*'Echo Valley 2-6809.'* I wasn't going to say *seven* as that would have screwed up everything," he laughs. "As for the exact phone number, I know that I came up with the numbers *2-6809*, and I think I may have also come up with *Echo Valley*, portraying the idea of the past returning, the way something from the past reverberates with you—like an echo, or a ricochet.

"In terms of the musical construction of the song, I knew I wanted to start the song with a major seventh chord because that immediately says we're not in a folk or old rock and roll vocabulary. We're more in a Beatles vocabulary. The song definitely has a melancholy and plaintive feel. We were trying to write something that would be as smooth and satiny as a Carpenters record.

"I played a lot of different instruments, so when I made a demo, I'd lay down all the instruments myself and it would be pretty sparse-sounding. On the demo for this song, I did a vocal harmony on the choruses because I thought that was an important part of the structure of the song. I made the demo and sang it. When I heard the Partridge Family version, I was flattered because it seemed there were a few times where David Cassidy copied my phrasing. He had a much better voice that I did, and he had a lot of things that were uniquely his, but it just made me feel really good that whatever I'd done on the demo, there were a couple of little nuances that he copied.

"The idea of the phone operator on the song sounds like something I would have come up with, and bears all my earmarks because I was the fellow in the late '70s and '80s who did twist endings. I recorded a song called 'Answering Machine' where the message ran out after 30 seconds, and 'Escape (The Piña Colada Song)' also has a twist ending. In all fairness, it was Ted Cooper's suggestion we include a recording of an operator on the song. I think he felt it was something that Wes Farrell would really like. Wes liked the cut a lot as it was being done for the Partridge Family, and he went on to produce a version of the song by Wayne Newton, which was the B-side of his hit single, 'Daddy Don't You Walk So Fast.' In those days, if you had a song and you thought it might be a hit song, and you were working with a few different artists, you might record it with several of them, thinking that someone's version among your roster will have a hit with it.

"I really enjoyed the Partridge Family's version of the song. I loved all of the production. The musicians that played on it were a lot of the same musicians that played on the theme for *Love, American Style.* That unit of players was able to come up with a sound that epitomizes commercial pop music in the '70s that's slick and smooth, and I don't mean that in a negative way. Some people might have looked at groups like the Partridge Family as being elevator music. But the truth of the matter is that when something is really well thought-out musically, you don't judge it. Duke Ellington said there's only two types of music—good and bad. And when something's good, no matter what category it falls into, whether it's the Beatles or the Partridge Family, you're still talking about whether there's good musical ideas in there and if it's executed well.

"I thought the Partridge Family's third album, *Sound Magazine,* was the best album they ever did. It was done so well compared to some of the really mindless stuff that was out there, and it was done with musicality. Plus David was, and is, a fantastic singer. With that song, considering the fact that David was barely old enough to wax nostalgic, he really gave you that sense of somebody regretting a fork in the road and which path they'd chosen, and wishing that he could go home again."

In 2005 *Cast of Characters: The Rupert Holmes Songbook* was released on CD with a re-recorded version of "Echo Valley 2-6809." "I'm extremely proud of 'Echo Valley 2-6809.' It was a sweet song. Musically, it was interesting and David did a great vocal on it. I've noticed that it seems to be a Partridge Family song that's liked, even by people that don't like the idea of the Partridge Family."

Appears On: Season 2, episode 27, "In 25 Words or Less" (September 24, 1971)

You Don't Have to Tell Me, 3:53, *Tony Romeo*

John Bahler says this song reflects his best work as vocal arranger for the Partridge Family. Returning to the Phil Spector "wall of sound," the concert hall effect is full and all-encompassing. A cymbal flare at the top of the song grows dynamically throughout.

In 1993, Tony Romeo elaborated on his Partridge Family sleeper: "After the success of our first single, I received a brief and ominous phone call from Bell

Records. 'Listen, Tony. I want you to re-write 'I Think I Love You' sideways. You understand?' the undertaker voice said. I recognized the specter and told him I couldn't do that; that I had other songs I felt were stronger than any rehash, material that could allow the group to grow with the audience. 'Well, if you don't, someone else will,' he responded. 'Let them,' I said, and hung up. And someone else did, and in my opinion (which I respect) it stunk! I then submitted 'You Don't Have to Tell Me.' I wrote it for David Cassidy the actor, the communicator. I was actually surprised that it got recorded. I thought it would be shot down for being a little too bluesy for the group. It was a welcome peek out of the teeny-bop woods, where little trees hidden from the light are rarely permitted to grow. David prevailed."

"This was one song I was super proud of that I don't think was ever a hit," says John Bahler. "I was able to write jazz harmonies for us. When I'm talking about jazz harmonies, I'm talking about plus 11/13, just really jazzy voicings on top of the band that to my knowledge hadn't been done at that time. I remember the song and I remember singing it." Bahler breaks out into the full chorus, remembering every beat.

"There were so many of those Partridge Family songs that I love. You have to believe in your own stuff, you know what I mean? This one was probably my favorite arrangement, only because I was so excited to be able to do something that I never heard anybody do. I was so excited to get some jazz chords on a rock and roll song, because we were singing notes out of the realm of what was going on in those days."

"David was singing the lead, and we sang some really hot chords on top of what he did. That was due to my knowledge of the Freshmen, the Hi-Lo's, and all of that stuff. It was my jazz side coming out. I got away with it and Wes loved it. I didn't know going in that particular day, whether he was going to like it or not. I never did. Although I learned that the stuff he didn't like was the stuff I had trouble writing—meaning that it wasn't inspired. It was just the journeyman pounding nails in a piece of wood. It was OK, but it wasn't special. And when that happened, Wes was always there with some ideas, and we always came up with something. Ron always had ideas. Jackie always had ideas. There were times when it was a complete collaboration. I always thought of it as a collaboration because I couldn't have written what I did without those people. The more I challenged them, the more they stepped up to the plate, and the more exciting the sound became, you know? I mean, you're talking about 250 percent concentration and energy in that stuff. That's very disciplined work to do. We didn't think of it that way. We just went in and did our job. But when it was right—man, you could cut the energy with a knife in that room." Bahler says he wishes this song had been released as a single. "I always loved this one, but Wes just didn't feel it was going to be a smash, and he was probably right."

Appears On: Season 2, episode 49, "Who Is Max Ledbetter and Why Is He Saying All Those Terrible Things?" (March 17, 1972—last episode of season 2)

when we're singin'

Rainmaker, 2:27, Mike Appel–Jim Cretecos–Wes Farrell

The last of the six Partridge Family songs written by Mike Appel and Jim Cretecos, "Rainmaker" was another inspiration stemming from a catchy title. It provides another strong lead vocal for David Cassidy with intrinsic vocal contrasts throughout. Cassidy's new breathy style and his earlier bold, belting style are integrated in this song, again demonstrating a dynamic vocal performance. Full and rich with orchestration, it pulls out all the stops.

"Jim and I were very interested in the music of the late '60s," says Mike Appel. "We had discovered a new band called Sir Lord Baltimore, a heavy-metal act that we placed on Mercury Records at the time. They toured with Humble Pie and Black Sabbath when Ozzy Osbourne was the lead singer of the group. We also discovered a young Bruce Springsteen, which we brought to Wes, but Wes was a teen-oriented guy and did not see the new music coming, so he passed. That's when I left Wes Farrell, as much as I loved that guy.

"Although David did a good job on 'Rainmaker,' we let it be known to David, through Wes, that we would not be contributing any more songs. David was also trying to grow up musically and wanted to start experimenting with the kind of stuff Jim and I had gravitated toward, but Wes was the boss and that just wasn't in the cards. However, 'Rainmaker' made a great teen song and everybody loved it."

Appears On: Season 2, episode 37, "Guess Who's Coming to Drive" (December 10, 1971); Season 2, episode 48, "All's War in Love and Fairs" (March 10, 1972)

I'm on My Way Back Home, 3:32, Bobby Hart–Jack Keller

Self-discovery. Love. Home. The one you miss the most. Unlike so many songs where the lyric reflects a lost, searching narrator, this one plays out as a moment of personal growth and a sense of self-realization. The singer is growing up in front of the listener.

The breakup of Boyce and Hart in 1969 led Bobby Hart on a new path, and one of the stops along the way was writing for the Partridge Family. In fact, he is credited as songwriter on more songs by the Partridge Family than any other songwriter except Wes Farrell. The remarkable thing about the number of cuts from Hart is that his songs didn't even enter the game until the third album, *Sound Magazine*. "I'm on My Way Back Home" was the first lyric he wrote specifically for the Partridge Family and was also his first time writing with Jack Keller.

Hart shares the story: "Near the end of the Boyce and Hart tenure at Screen Gems, Lester Sill, who ran the company on the West Coast, came to Tommy and I one time and said, 'I got news of this great songwriting team, Jack Keller and Howard Greenfield, a New York team who's had a whole bunch of hits and they're coming out to California. I want to split you guys up, and to welcome them out here, I want Bobby to write a lyric with Jack, and Tommy to write a melody with Howard.' So we did it kind of as a lark.

"It was a whole new experience for me after Tommy left, because we always collaborated, and we both wrote music and we both wrote lyrics, and we would just jam in a room together and knock them out."

Hart continues, "I always liked this song. Jack was another real high-energy guy, and he would sit down at a piano and rip out a melody that'd just blow you away."

The collaboration led Hart to develop his talents as a lyricist, working with film score composer Dominque Frontiere. "I started writing the lyrics to the theme songs he put in his movies. For the first time I learned that you have to write one syllable per note, and make it sound conversational, make it sound singable, and make it rhyme—like a jigsaw puzzle. Before that, I'd started the first time with Jack. Jack was exclusively a melody writer. Starting in the '70s I became known more as a lyricist than a melody writer."

Jack Keller assembled a sampling of his own musical legacy on a homemade CD that he affectionately titled "Music for All Occasions" in memory of his father's orchestra. That CD, along with his handwritten notes, is now in the hands of Keller's children. His son Russ Keller found the notes during our interview and read his father's 1969 thoughts on "I'm on My Way Back Home" directly from the CD: "This song was the result of two longstanding collaborations splitting up. When Tommy Boyce and Howie Greenfield decided to write a song together, Bobby Hart and I figured we might as well do the same. I've always felt this cut was great, and would make a wonderful airline commercial."

"That's the end of the quote," says Russ Keller. "Now here's the part that makes me laugh. You know that Tommy and Bobby are the guys behind the Monkees, right? And of course Howie Greenfield was my father's collaborator on things like the theme for *Bewitched*, and the early '60s hits 'Venus in Blue Jeans,' 'Everybody's Somebody's Fool,' and a lot of other great songs. The funny thing is that the song Howie and Tommy wrote as a first-time collaboration was called 'You Can't Make a U-Turn on a One-Way Street.' I don't think it was ever cut. The joke here is that it's a terrible title, you know? It's kind of an inside joke that the Greenfield-Boyce collaboration didn't go very well—at the same time Bobby and Dad wrote this great song for the Partridge Family that a lot of people know and remember."

The demo for "I'm on My Way Back Home" was recorded by a female vocalist named Charlene.

"The demo is very cool because you get to hear the arrangement that the Partridge Family received when they recorded 'I'm on My Way Back Home,'" says Keller. "My dad produced the demo at home, and you can see the influences where they [Wes Farrell and team] basically took the original demo and copied directly from it, even though Jack's name is not credited as a producer of that song. What's cool about the demo is this little vocal thing at the very end." Keller sings the vocal part, emphasizing the short answer-back effect at the end of the song.

"He was very proud of this. I remember driving in the car with him and listening to the Partridge Family version, and I remember him saying to me, 'I came up with that!' He was like 'That's me!'

"He was very proud that it found its way into the actual recording, even though he wasn't there as a producer and he wasn't in the Partridge Family session. That backing vocal in the recording is also on the original home demo, which is the only demo that exists."

"You know, it really was a mystery with Wes," says John Bahler. "Pretty much every idea he had about what song was going to be a hit was a hit. There were a lot of songs that I wished had been released as singles just because I loved them. This was one of them."

Appears On: Season 2, episode 33, "Days of Acne and Roses" (November 5, 1971); Season 2, episode 35, "The Forty-Year Itch" (November 19, 1971); Season 2, episode 45, "Hel-l-l-l-p!" (February 11, 1972)

Summer Days, 3:12, Tony Romeo

The biggest production number on the album, "Summer Days" carries full orchestration and a Phil Spector-esque "wall of sound" delivery, including a harpsichord—used frequently since the success of "I Think I Love You." The song also makes good use of key changes, a technique that appears more frequently on *Sound Magazine* than on earlier albums. "Summer Days" reflects the band's new polished sound, contrasting with the raw, searching quality of the earlier two albums.

"Summer Days" was originally intended for David Cassidy's first solo album as the featured production number and first single. When reassigned to the Partridge Family, it went through a couple of re-records. "It's a little different-sounding than the other songs," says background vocalist Ron Hicklin, "because it's very much featuring David with minimal background vocals." Wes Farrell ultimately felt it was better suited as a Partridge Family song, though Cassidy and songwriter Tony Romeo disagreed. The song later reappeared on Cassidy's third solo album, *Dreams Are Nuthin' More Than Wishes,* in a much slower introspective interpretation. Romeo's friend Lou Christie also released it as a single in 1975.

David Cassidy's website poll ranked this song in the top five most requested songs. Time and reflection have proven that "Summer Days" is truly one of the band's greatest tracks, and David Cassidy still performs it in concert. One of the most memorable performances happened in Orange County, California, during two

THE DEFINING MOMENT

concerts performed with the Pacific Symphony on November 21 and 22, 2003. The performance brought out the strings and horns, which were key ingredients to the Partridge Family music.

"Summer Days" builds with an almost overwhelming type of energy. Again, the imagery is vivid, painting the pictures Tony Romeo composed so well. It showcases Cassidy's voice and perfectly captures the essence of a Melvoin-Bahler arrangement.

"My favorite of all the Partridge records and the unanimous choice for David Cassidy's first solo single," Tony Romeo told Ken Sharp in 1993. "Shipping date set, group in orbit, summer in gear, it seemed the perfect vehicle to launch our wonder boy. But politics prevailed. The single was killed. I would be sued if I told you why. I was shattered. The low point of my affiliation with the project. It's hard enough getting your song recorded. Rare when the arrangement, production, performance, turn out as exciting as this did. It had a certain ether beyond all its components which screamed 'HITSKY!' David fought just as hard as I did for this one. He redeemed his fury by later re-recording it solo. But for me, still, 'Summer Days' is the one that got away.

"I left L.A. ecstatic over the record, counting the hours till its release. It was a few days later when I was back in New York that I received a curious phone call at 2 a.m. It was Wes Farrell, indefatigable producer. 'Sorry to wake you, man. Listen, what's one of the most popular ballads of the last 10 years that's never been revived?' Without missing a beat, the self-defeating show-off musicologist he knew me to be mumbled, 'Cherish.' I told him how it was always number one on those annual top 500 countdowns. He started gathering the song in his memory. '*Cherish is the word … that one?*' 'Uh-huh,' I said suspiciously. 'Hmmm, 'Cherish,' great! Thanks, man! Talk to you soon—get some sleep!' I did.

"And while I dreamed, a group of brilliant musicians assembled in a recording studio 3,000 miles away and laid the tracks for what became David Cassidy's first solo release. 'Summer Days' never dawned. But at least I had an unwitting hand in picking its replacement. Now there's a dubious achievement!"

Appears On: Season 2, episode 32, "Dr. Jekyll and Mr. Partridge" (October 29, 1971); Season 2, episode 40, "Home Is Where the Heart Was" (January 7, 1972)
Favorite Partridge Family song of Brian Forster, Tony Romeo

I Would Have Loved You Anyway, 2:34, Tony Romeo

Wes Farrell returns to using reverb on this track, having abandoned the technique for the most part. But Farrell played it safe, knowing what elements delivered success on the first two albums. Cassidy's voice is also double-tracked. The title is catchy, and the song was memorably used on an episode featuring Danny's recurring girlfriend, Gloria Hickey. Tony Romeo commented only briefly: "Minor verse, minor song, major hook, European feel. It worked for 'I Think I Love You,' and I saw this particular style as one the group could draw from now and then. Fortunately, they didn't."

Appears On: Season 2, episode 40, "Home Is Where the Heart Was" (January 7, 1972); Season 2, episode 46, "Promise Her Anything but Give Her a Punch" (February 18, 1972)

Twenty-Four Hours a Day, 3:16, Wes Farrell–Danny Janssen

A vocal interpretation can tell you so much about the artist. This is the second song from Wes Farrell and Danny Janssen, and another exceptional delivery. Janssen's lyrics reflect the happy upbeat style of someone used to writing for a very young audience. "I enjoyed kids," says Janssen. "I think that's what you hear in any of those songs I wrote. They were just happy lyrics because I really did enjoy the kids."

The vibe here is happy, light, and innocently romantic. What lends maturity to this song is the underrated and mispackaged David Cassidy. His vocal interpretation is heartfelt and layered with emotion and intimacy. Cassidy was growing into a great vocal artist, and he was also poising himself with his solo material to fight hard against his now-ingrained image.

Cassidy seems to be singing at the upper range of his vocals on this number. The track is slightly sped up, sifting out a touch of the breathy quality and adding subtle variation to the album. Farrell liked the song so much he used it as the B-side for the single release of "I Woke Up in Love This Morning."

"I think the song fit the circumstances, but I think it was tailored to fit a particular episode," commented Farrell.

Appears On: Season 2, episode 34, "A Tale of Two Hamsters" (November 12, 1971)

I Woke Up in Love This Morning, 2:41, L. Russell Brown–Irwin Levine

Cash Box predicted: "Teen Idol David Cassidy leads the Partridge Family towards another gold record with this splendidly commerial outing." They were right on the money.

"The songwriter, in order for him to create the right song which will be a hit for any particular artist, has to get inside of the artist's head," says L. Russell Brown. "He has to become the artist. He has to understand what the artist not only wants to sing to people, but what his audience wants to hear from him. A song has to be carved out in such a way that it's something you can't seem to *forget*—not *remember*—but can't seem to *forget*. Tony Romeo's "I Think I Love You" is one of those songs I heard just one time, and it drove me crazy! I couldn't get it out of my head! Tony understood. And it was Wes Farrell who really understood what his artist should sing to the people—that he sings what they want to hear."

THE DEFINING MOMENT

Arranger Mike Melvoin says "I Woke Up" is the single Partridge Family song of which he is most proud. With another harpischord intro and a driving melody, the song features a slightly more spread-out stereo mix than other songs on the album. It became the next megahit for the band, and David Cassidy knew how to make it rock.

"I Woke Up" was written specifically for the Partridge Family. L. Russell Brown tells the story of its creation:

"Wes Farrell says, 'Now that you're signed to me, Brown, and I own "Knock Three Times," I want you to write me songs for David Cassidy.' So we sat down and we wrote what we felt was kind of a Beatles-esque song. You know, a young song for kids, but with lasting virtue. Irwin and I used what we learned from great writers like Bob Crewe. He learned from Phil Spector, and his teacher was Aaron Shroeder [who wrote for Elvis].

"I wanna be careful how I say this," says Brown. "OK, so people who write one hit are called one-hit wonders. They got lucky. They made a record. Two hits, you might be lucky. Three, who knows? After you've written a dozen hit songs, it's no longer luck. Obviously, you must know something about it. You're doing a formula.

"What I was trying to do is write a song like 'She Loves You,' says Brown. "Listen to the chorus of 'I Woke Up in Love This Morning.' He breaks out and sings: *"I woke up in love this morning, I woke up in love this morning..."* "She loves you, yeah, yeah, yeah! She loves you, yeah yeah, yeah."

"Listen to the chorus of 'I Woke Up in Love This Morning,' he instructs, "and if you are a musician you will recognize the same chord progressions. Now think about it. We wanted something that had that Beatles-esque feeling to it, right? So we wrote a song kind of like 'She Loves You'—very much like it. That was the thing we were trying to emulate. We didn't copy the notes or anything. We just got the feel of that song."

But the influences do not stop there. "I think that this song has a beautiful, beautiful melody in the front," he explains, "and if you listen to it, it's kind of Eastern. If you sing the melody of 'I Woke Up in Love This Morning,' you will feel the Eastern melodic strains contained in the score from *Fiddler on the Roof*." *Fiddler on the Roof* was huge on Broadway during this time, and the musical soundtrack was selling wildly to the public. Brown now begins to sing a few notes from the musical. Again, he weaves the phrases back and forth, demonstrating the influences while showcasing the originality of the song.

"So, in other words," he says, "we hit—like the Beatles did—we hit with a *great* song, instead of a *rock and roll* song. It's a beautiful melody, and it has lasting virtue, obviously, because people are still playing it today. A lot of people have told me that it's their favorite Partridge Family song.

when we're singin'

"It would be a cool idea for David Cassidy to do a medley of 'She Loves You' and 'I Woke Up in Love This Morning' in concert," he adds.

Brown clearly had a blast during his brief time writing for the Partridge Family. "It's gratifying, no matter how long ago it was. I only wrote one major hit for them, but the million-selling 'I Woke Up in Love This Morning' only added fuel to a fire we had going, and it made us hotter than ever. David nailed the lead vocal on that song and Wes made the consummate pop hit record of that day. So my experience with the Partridge Family was an integral part of my career. 'I Woke Up in Love This Morning' was a hell of a good song!" he exclaims.

David Cassidy has re-recorded "I Woke Up" at least three times since 1971. In 2002, Burger King used it for a campaign ad.

Appears On: Season 2, episode 26, "Dora, Dora, Dora" (September 17, 1971—first show of season 2); Season 2, episode 34, "A Tale of Two Hamsters" (November 12, 1971)

Favorite Partridge Family song of Shirley Jones (one of several), Mike Melvoin

Love Is All That I Ever Needed, 2:54, David Cassidy–Wes Farrell

Sometimes songs will undergo complete changes in lyrics. That was the case with the second of three David Cassidy–penned Partridge Family songs. An alternate version of this song was titled "Love Is All That *You* Ever Needed," with completely different lyrics. The change from "You" to "I" makes the song more personal to the listener, reflecting more feeling and vulnerability. With a bluesy guitar opening and a very bluesy-African feel to the pop chorus, the song emulates Motown in its delivery, especially with the bass guitar and Cassidy pushing the upper range of his vocals.

Mike Melvoin recalls it as one of the greatest Partridge Family songs. David Cassidy recalls the sources and effects of the song: "I wrote that one totally by myself. I don't remember much about writing that one except the hook. On that particular day I was scheduled to record 'Love Is All That I Ever Needed' and two other songs that I'd written. There was a group of musicians there but they'd left. I said to the engineer—I can remember this so vividly—I said, 'Look, I've got this idea for a song, can I just sing it with me playing guitar as a demo? Just run the take.' That was 'Ricky's Song,' which I wrote in about 30 seconds. I did it in one take. It's a really nice little song. I like it."

Appears On: Season 2, episode 30, "Anatomy of a Tonsil" (October 15, 1971); Season 2, episode 39, "Where Do Mermaids Go?" (December 31, 1971)

THE DEFINING MOMENT

Album Summary and Reviews

Total Running Time: 31:19
Original Release: August, 1971, Bell 6064

For their third album, the TV family come up with more dynamite rock material with the help of producer Wes Farrell, and it features the current hot single, "I Woke Up in Love This Morning." Other strong cuts that feature Shirley Jones and David Cassidy are "Summer Days," "One Night Stand" and "I'm on My Way Back Home." Chalk up another chart topper for the group. *Billboard, August 21, 1971*

The third album from the popular TV family is in the tradition of the first two. The songs bounce right along, a feeling of exuberance is constantly in the air, and, as an added bonus, a top single, "I Woke Up in Love This Morning," is included. With Shirley Jones and David Cassidy handling the vocals in their inimitable fashions, and with the slick production work of Wes Farrell, how can anything go wrong? It doesn't and this will be another spectacular best-seller for the family. *Cash Box, August 21, 1971*

The TV series The Partridge Family continues to spin off click albums. The billing on this is shared by Shirley Jones and David Cassidy, but the latter carries the burden of songs, doing very well on such numbers as "One Night Stand," "Echo Valley," "I'm On My Way Back Home," "Summer Days" and "I Woke Up in Love This Morning." *Variety, September 22, 1971*

> *First Chart Appearance: August 28, 1971* **(Record World,** *No. 49;* **Cash Box,** *No. 53;* **Billboard,** *No. 159)*

GENERATION X-MAS
or ... A Partridge Family Christmas Card

A Unanimous Favorite

The cast has been asked many times, "What is your favorite episode?" At one point or another, every single cast member has listed the Christmas episode as their favorite. It has long been a favorite too among fans and even the producers. Its success, both commercially and artistically, went hand in hand with the new Christmas album.

"My favorite episode was the Christmas show, because it was so expansive," says producer Larry Rosen. "It gave us a chance to put these actors into characters that they never played before, and to work with a guy like Dean Jagger, and to create sets and costumes and the atmosphere that we never had an opportunity to do before. That's what made this episode so special.

"Sometimes we would get a little stir crazy being on the lot all of the time, and we would want to go off the lot to shoot somewhere else and breathe a little air into the show. So on a few episodes we might occasionally go out into the woods or somewhere and give the actors a chance to be outside. Shirley was fun because she'd help us. We'd say, 'Shirley, we may need you here. If they give us any trouble will you help us?' And she'd say, 'Absolutely!' So we'd say we want to go out for a few days and they'd say, 'No, we can't afford it,' and I'd call and say, 'Shirley's catching a cold!' It was kind of like code for suggesting that Shirley might not show up for work that day—not that she would ever have done that—but we used that trick as a fun way of saying 'Give us a break here.'

"'OK! We'll let you go outside,' they'd say. We were on the lot 30 weeks of the year, and we just wanted to get out and do some things that give the show a little bit more scope, and more opportunity for expanded stories and characters. We didn't do it often, but we did it occasionally. We used to tease Seymour Friedman, who was the head of production. We'd say 'Shirley's coughing!'" Rosen laughs an ornery laugh. "They'd say 'OK! We'll let you go outside!'"

This particular episode was going to call for a lot more than just going outside. Rosen continues, "Susan Harris pitched a show to us about a Christmas story, and I don't know how much she gave us, but what came out of it was a fantasy idea that Dale [story editor Dale McRaven] and I were working on with Bob.

when we're singin'

"We said, 'Wouldn't this be wonderful, if they were stranded in a town with an old crusty gold miner who told the story about Christmas in a town that he had lived through during the great days of the wild West?' Then that fantasy would turn into all of our characters—Shirley as the 'Kitty' character (à la *Gunsmoke*) at the saloon, Danny the bad guy, and David the good guy. We had roles for all of them. We did this show with these great costumes—gowns and outfits and everything. Bob, Dale, and I sat and we reworked everything that Susan Harris had done and turned it into this fantasy. Then we turned the script in to the production department. We had this great Western street at Columbia where *High Noon* was shot. That street still sat there. So we had the whole exterior set from that film to use, and we just built the saloon.

"Seymour Friedman screamed at me. He said, 'Are you kidding me? This show will be $20,000 over budget! You have new costumes and new sets! Are you guys crazy?' I said, 'We'll save it on other episodes. We're going to do this show!' We fought like crazy to get the money for that show. It wasn't easy, because the studio was not happy about this at all. It was way out of budget. We never had costumes and major sets, period things, and horses, too. We never did that. Most of our shows were interior."

Shirley Jones had known and worked with legendary actor Dean Jagger in *Elmer Gantry*. Jagger guest starred on the *Partridge Family* Christmas episode as the lonely old miner. "He was a great actor," says Rosen. "We sent the script to his agent, and I think he had recently suffered a stroke but he was still able to work, and he did this beautiful job as the storyteller for us. He was a wonderful, wonderful character actor who had done multiple movies, and he was very well known. Dean was a delight to work with and fully able, despite his stroke. He didn't have any voice deficiency and he wasn't limping or anything, though he was slightly weak—but he was wonderful."

Bob Claver agrees. "To have Dean was a very special treat. We hired him, and I'm sure we paid him more than we usually paid, though we were never cheap. Shirley had a good relationship with him and that made it even better. That particular episode was built around that. You've got to care for the guy. You've got to worry and fret over him. You have to care if he's living a lonely life, and that kind of thing. I'm sure he had a good time doing that show. It was a sweet show. When you do shows like that families get a good feeling from it."

"Dean Jagger is one of those kinds of actors that's been around for so long you want to kneel at his altar," adds producer Mel Swope. "There's nothing but respect."

"Everyone flipped out because Dean Jagger was on the show," says Danny Bonaduce. "I had never heard of Dean Jagger in my whole life. Everybody was paying their respects to this guy, and I didn't understand why. I just wanted to ride horses and shoot my gun, but Dean Jagger couldn't have been more into it. He was older, but he just said to me, 'Don't settle down, son. This is your time. Go ride that horse! Go shoot your gun!'"

Bonaduce continues: "I was an excellent horseback rider. Unfortunately, they gave me the real Trigger, who was still alive, and he was so incredibly well trained. I had horses at that time, and most of them were freakin' thugs. If they didn't do what you wanted them to do you had to outmuscle them. And so here I had Trigger, and you'd touch back on the reins, and Trigger would go into 'Hi-Ho Silver!' But I was a really good rider, so I liked showing off. I put Trigger away, because Trigger was more famous than I was at the time, and I'd pick up one of the other set horses, and I'd be jumping over barrels, and you know, we're all wearing six-shooters and dressed up. That was one of the most fun episodes."

With high production demands on the episode, the entire cast was used more than usual, which meant that the small children were being worked harder. "This episode was really tough because we were doing night shooting on a Friday night," says Mel Swope, "and whatever the cutoff time was, you had to stop because of the kids. You always put the kids' scenes first. It's very complicated. That show had a little more music and costume changes than most of them. It wasn't your normal episode.

"I had talked to the kids' teacher, and I said, 'I need another half-hour and I need your blessing.' We needed to finish the shots with the kids before they left, and I had to make a phone call to the board of education on Monday morning to explain the circumstances. They set limits for kids, but I told them what the circumstances were. Over the years you build a reputation and they know who you are. If you're someone who takes advantage, you're in trouble. I could go to jail. But they understood and said 'Don't let it happen again,' and it didn't. The law is so strict, but I totally support that. This episode turned out to be a lovely show. David sang 'I think I'll lick my lolly later,' laughs Swope. "It's very funny! I loved it."

The musical bits Cassidy sang were hysterical. This episode really showcased his comedic ability, which has always been underrated, even to this day.

The two youngest actors especially recall this episode with fond memories as children on the studio back lots. "I think we've all said that we loved that episode," says Brian Forster. "The plot was good. It didn't fall into the same formula, and we had that part of Columbia Ranch that was the western town to play on. The studio had bought us bicycles and Danny, Suzanne, and I got to ride around. That western set was one of our favorite playgrounds. To be able to actually film on it, watching them paint all the facades and all those fun colors—and then to have Dean Jagger on the set—was great. It seemed like a lot more care went into it than other episodes. There were more retakes, not because we messed up, but because they were more focused on getting it just right." Richard Kinon, a frequent director on the series, directed this episode, titled "Don't Bring Your Guns to Town, Santa."

when we're singin'

Bus Stop ...

Tony Romeo: A Christmas Baby

"I was thinking about him today," says Tony Romeo's older brother and only surviving relative, Frank Romeo, his voice raw. "Christmas morning, five o'clock, the bells were ringing and Tony was born," he says.

Tony Romeo was born on Christmas Day 1939, and beyond any shadow of a doubt he loved Christmas. He and Frank grew up in Watervliet, New York, with a strong Italian heritage. Their grandparents never spoke English, and although their father was born in the US, their mother had arrived in the States when she was six months old.

Both Frank and Tony were singing as early as they could remember. They were brought up on old Italian folk music, and they used to sing and harmonize together all the time. "When we were kids our mother would get us to sing with her while we did housework," says Frank Romeo. "We always sang Italian songs while we were doing the dishes or sweeping the floor. We would find these gorgeous harmonies and sing them together. My mother sounded like Skeeter Davis. I would take the lead, and my brother would take the high harmony, and we would just sing our way through all the chores. I just remember how lovely that was."

Tony and Frank both took accordion lessons at a very young age, sparked by a cousin who was an accordion teacher. Tony took to it and loved it, while Frank despised it. Eventually Tony transferred his talent to the piano. "From the seventh grade on we'd come home from school, go into the bedroom, and he would take out the accordion. We'd have the *Hit Parader,* which was a music magazine that came out every month. We had hundreds of them. We'd start from number one and sing the whole damn *Hit Parader.* I'd be the singer. He'd play the accordion, and we'd be doing the arrangements exactly the way the records were done. That was our whole routine when we came home from school."

Tony enrolled at Syracuse University in 1956 and majored in journalism. It was during that period that he started writing songs. Right after college, both brothers moved to New York City. Tony landed a job at MGM Records in the engineering department, during which time he started really getting serious about writing. He was making the rounds and trying to get heard.

Tony Romeo was heavily influenced by the music of Les Paul and Mary Ford, Patti Page, Kay Starr, and the pre-'50s crooners. But most of all he loved Joni James, an MGM artist who was a big star during this time. Romeo adored every song she ever recorded and dreamed of writing a song for her. These influences, along with the songs of his Mediterranean background and his love of Broadway show tunes, inspired Romeo as a songwriter.

It was in his early New York days that Romeo met Ken Jacobson, another young songwriter, who would become his best friend for life. Jacobson's own career had begun with a great stroke of luck. "I was in New York for a week and a half, and I got a call from Joni James—who heard, quite by accident, a song I had written in college," he says. "It ended up being my first record. It was a song called "Every Day" and it was released in the '50s. The song was featured as the B-side on James' huge hit "Why Don't You Believe Me?"

Romeo asked a mutual friend to introduce him to Jacobson, eager to meet a songwriter who had actually had a song recorded by Joni James. When the two met, Jacobson recalls, one of the first things Romeo said to him was "June is Joni James Month!"—a slogan that had been used to promote "Why Don't You Believe Me?"—drawn from his encyclopedic knowledge of music from the early '50s. Jacobson was flabbergasted: "How on earth did he know that?"

"He told me once that he used to go around saying he wrote that song because he loved it so much," laughs Jacobson. Romeo asked Jacobson to listen to some songs he had written. "I listened to some of his songs and I thought, *My God, these are wonderful.* I remember one of them he wrote when he first came to New York was called "Gin Buddy." It was later recorded by Richard Harris on *Slides*. It's a wonderful album," says Jacobson. "I told Tony, 'You're going to make a fortune writing songs.' He looks at me and says 'Do you think so?'

"We were great, great friends," says Jacobson. "We were friends forever."

The Trout

Frank Romeo recalls how he and Tony finally got through to Wes Farrell. "We had done a lot of demos, always with the hope and the dream that Wes Farrell was going to say, 'Holy geez, forget about them! Who are *these* people?'"

Broadway actress Cass Morgan, who has since risen to fame with the popular musical comedy *Pump Boys and Dinettes*, was a friend of Frank's. Frank convinced Tony that they needed to do a record together, and he persuaded Morgan to be part of it. "It was almost like setting a trap for Wes," laughs Frank. "We started doing these demos together, and we played them for Wes. Then Wes finally said the unbelievable thing: 'Holy mackerel, why don't we do an album with these people! Who are they?' Frank then broke it to Wes that it was the three of them—Tony, Frank, and Cass Morgan. "Wes said, 'Damn, let's do it!'

Frank continues, "At the time, there were about three different groups of this kind—two guys and a girl—and we were sort of right there at that moment. We got great reviews from *Billboard*, and we thought good things were gonna happen."

But timing proved problematic for the album; MGM was shaking things up internally. "All of a sudden there was a change in leadership," says Frank Romeo. "After having spent a treacherous two hours in a room with about 30 A&R people figuring out how they were going to move with this record, everything just died because of a change in personnel."

The record can still be found on auction sites and in vintage record stores all over the world. It has a strong cult following.

The Partridge Years and Beyond

The success of the Partridge Family was certainly good to Tony Romeo. He broke out of the gate with "I Think I Love You," and became a songwriting superstar in his own right. His brother Frank says, "I'll never forget it. We both came home for the weekend to see our mom, and all of a sudden the radio comes on. We're all sitting down to dinner and the radio DJ says, 'At No. 1, "I Think I Love You."' The song came on and Tony just started crying. I just looked at him and I saw in his eyes. I saw everything in his eyes. Then the whole table started it. I started crying. My mother started crying. We're all crying. It was this beautiful moment where we actually got to be with our family when that radio said, 'At No.1 this week is "I Think I Love You!"'"

Over the years, the two hot-headed Italian brothers had their share of arguments, disagreements, and professional differences, but Frank always loved his brother fiercely. Frank was interested in jazz and jazz theater at the time, and he was critical of the music Tony was writing. Though Frank really didn't like any of the music that was being recorded by the Partridge Family at the time, age and distance have given him the opportunity to listen and re-examine the music.

"It took me some time to understand," he explains. "One time I started breaking these lyrics down, and I thought, *Holy mackerel, these are just amazing!* Line for line it's truly amazing, even theatrical."

The Partridge Family years were filled with a lot of success and fun for Tony Romeo. "He brought Bruce Springsteen to the house one time," says Frank. Tony had known Mike Appel, who was producing Springsteen. Tony told Frank he was bringing company to the house one day, and he wanted Frank to be there. It was intended as a surprise. When Bruce Springsteen showed up, he was wowed beyond belief. "Springsteen was so incredible! That was amazing to me!"

Tony enjoyed a great relationship with Wes Farrell. "He adored Wes and Wes adored him," says Frank. "They were like kindred spirits. Wes would see Tony coming and he'd say 'Tony!' with a big enthusiastic smile. Tony was the same way toward Wes. They were born around the same time, and ironically they died within six months of each other. Wes was very kind to Tony. Wes was what we now call a personality. You can't keep up with their enthusiasm, and you could never sort out what was real and true and, what was just dreams and fantasies. But Wes clicked onto to Tony's talent. He saw it immediately, and that marriage was totally perfect for both of them."

Tony also developed a meaningful friendship with David Cassidy. He worked hard at his songwriting craft to find words that Cassidy could find relatable, bringing his own musical vision through his delivery and interpretation. There was definite chemistry in the trio of producer Farrell, songwriter Romeo, and vocalist Cassidy. For his part, Cassidy has always been fond of Tony and his talents. "My cousin went to the Sarasota race track and saw David," Frank says. "It's one of the oldest race tracks, and David comes here every year. My cousin went up to him and introduced himself and David was so excited that he took him in his booth, had champagne, and talked for an hour. He said David was just incredibly kind to him."

In 1972 Richard Harris released *Slides*. The album was conceived and produced by Tony Romeo, who also wrote 11 of the 12 songs, two of them co-written with Ken Jacobson and Ralph Landis—also both contributors to the Partridge Family. The album was released by ABC/Dunhill and produced under the umbrella of the Wes Farrell Organization. "We all went to London to record it," recalls Frank Romeo. "I did background vocals, and it was another unbelievable record of Tony's. The songs on that album are magnificent."

when we're singin'

"I liked the *Slides* album," agrees Jacobson. "It's more typical of Tony than a lot of the pop material he wrote. There's more of the solo Tony in that album. It's very imaginative, poetic, and Americana, which is what Tony was really into." But *Slides* was only the precurser to songwriting that would come to reflect who Tony Romeo really was.

Moonwagon

Once the Partridge Family reign was over, Tony Romeo teamed up with two other former Partridge songwriters, Terry Cashman and Tommy West. Cashman and West had a label called Lifesong and were producers in their own right. They had hit big producing Jim Croce during the Partridge years.

West said that Romeo was the kind of person who went into a studio, found things, and then put something amazing together. He went off, wrote, sang, and recorded an entire solo album, then pitched it to Cashman and West. The album, titled *Moonwagon*, failed to get a release, but it lives on for those closest to Romeo as the most personally reflective album of his life.

Moonwagon was introspective and personal. It was designed in four parts, each tied to periods in Romeo's life. Frank Romeo acquired the music from the album just a few days before being interviewed for this book, and the timing made for a bittersweet, heartfelt, and sentimental conversation.

"The songs making up part one are all about when he gets to New York, his nights in the town, his fantasies and his dreams," says Frank. "The second part is about trying to become a songwriter and begging people to listen to his music. The third part is about having success and what it felt like, and the fourth part is about coming home and reflecting on the past."

He continues, "Ken and I were talking about it the other night, because I had emailed him all the songs from that album, and Ken wrote back and said, 'This is Tony's soul. This is the Tony that we didn't know then and the puzzle we now see, 17 years after his death.' *Moonwagon* is really from the heart. I was very emotional when I first heard it, and it has been that way for the last 10 days.

"The last words from the last song, titled 'My, My, My, How the Years Go By,' are very, very moving," Frank continues. "I insist that you find 40 minutes sometime and go on YouTube and start the first song. In fact, it's imperative that you do so if you want to write anything about Tony, because everything I could ever tell you, he will tell you in this record. You will know everything."

Moonwagon was completed in 1976. "I'll never understand why they didn't put it out, but it was terribly disappointing to Tony because he put so much of himself into it," says Frank. "There was even talk of Lou Christie putting it out and doing overdubs, but that never happened. The melody on the very last song begins with the first eight bars Tony ever wrote on the piano of 'I Think I Love You.' In other words, he is saying 'I made it!' Then he goes into the song called, 'My, My, My, How Time Goes By.' He made the juxtaposition of the 'I Think I Love You' melody into finality. Even though he did this years before his death, it was almost as if there was something he knew." Frank Romeo has uploaded all 13 tracks from *Moonwagon* onto YouTube so friends and fans can listen to his brother's most intimate work.

Romeo Does Disco!

The late '70s brought Tony Romeo a different kind of opportunity.

People, an entertainment news magazine program that was an early predecessor of *Entertainment Tonight,* was being developed by David Susskind Productions. Jacobson and Romeo teamed up to write the theme song. "It was the disco era, and we wrote a disco song called 'People,'" says Jacobson, noting that it shouldn't be confused with the Barbra Streisand song of the same name.

"They asked me to be the musical director for the show, but I couldn't because I was writing another show at the time. So I suggested they talk to Tony. They contacted Tony and he ended up being the musical director. He was writer and supervisor for all the music in the show, almost all of which were sections from, and variations of, the recording of 'People' that we recorded up front. Like many disco records of the era, it was seven or eight minutes long.

"The name of the song had to be the name of the show, because it was intended to promote the show. Lou Christie recorded it and they did use it on the show, except Lou Christie recorded it under a different name. 'People' was actually released in Europe and it was somewhat of a hit, but it was never released here as a single. It became a bit of a hit in Scandinavia and those Northern European countries." The show, whose full title was *People on TV with Phyllis George,* debuted September 28, 1978, and didn't get much of a run before cancellation.

The 1980s

"We were both out of the country all the time in the '80s," says Jacobson. "Tony was a character! We went to Europe together at one point. One time I was going to go to Europe for the summer and stay as long as my money lasted. I went in the beginning of June, and Tony said 'I'll meet you August first in Vienna.' So I was running around Europe all through July and August, and ended up in Vienna on August first, not knowing if Tony would be there or not because we weren't in touch since I had left. He had said 'I'll meet you wherever the biggest American Express is in the central part. So I'm walking around Vienna, and went over to the American Express, and there's Tony sitting right across the street in the café. Then we traveled into Eastern Europe together! That was Tony!"

Lou Christie

Tony Romeo produced two albums for pop sensation Lou Christie. They had a hit with "Beyond the Blue Horizon." Christie also sang with the Romeo brothers on many demos that were submitted for the Partridge Family and other acts. Tony was always working a song up. "Tony had swarms of melodies and lyrics in his head," Frank says. "He could have five or six songs he was writing at the same time, all oozing from him at once. He'd be there with a tape recorder, his head up in the air, eyes closed, at the piano, and he'd come up with a melody, and he'd work it till it was more profound than it was the hour prior. There were songs that were offered up and never accepted, too. Tony wrote like crazy. He has a couple of hundred songs that were recorded. He was an incredibly prolific writer."

"Both of us were writers," says Lou Christie of his artistic chemistry with Romeo. "We visualized things. It's part of who a writer is. That's what Tony did. He would ride around in his truck, and he literally kept a pen and paper with him. He was always honing his songs, making them finer and better.

"Once Tony and I got together, the musicality was ridiculous because we were raised with the same musical head," says Christie. "Musically he was sort of like a brother. We would sit around and sing these songs—songs that everyone made in the early '50s prior to rock and roll. Frank has a great voice, too. It was a whole musical family. Frank and I and Tony just sat around singing the first couple weeks we met. Then we started working on a project and we worked together for years."

Sudden Death

As brothers, Tony and Frank Romeo were sometimes distant throughout the years, but there was never any doubt that they were connected in very deep ways. Above all, Frank wants his brother's life and work to be celebrated.

Shortly before Tony's sudden death, Frank says, he wanted to address some relationship issues. "I had written him a letter because I was really, really upset over a lot of things that were going on with us. I was incredibly honest to the point that I was really scared when I put it in the mailbox, because I said some things that nobody had ever said to him before. He never, ever once responded to that letter—until the next time I saw him. Making small talk, I said to him, 'Oh, I love that shirt.' He took it off and said, 'Well, I think it would look a lot better on you than it does on me,' and he handed it to me." Frank Romeo chokes up as he reflects on the encounter, one that may be impenetrable to outsiders but clearly carried deep meaning for the two of them.

"The day he died, I happened to be with him that morning. He lived in Pleasant Valley, which was 60 miles from me, and it was early. I went up to meet him. He was trying to get some songs out. They were country songs and he had just come back from Nashville, where he was trying to get them heard. We were in the car together. We always had very philosophical talks. We had many deep conversations. I remember he said, 'You know, people like to say life is short. I don't think so. I think life is long. How many more years do I have? Ten?' We were at the mall by the post office in Pleasant Valley, and as he was leaving, and as I was driving away, I happened to catch sight of him in the mirror through my car window. He was walking into the post office, and I swear to God I had this feeling I would never see him again. He was dead 10 hours later." Tony Romeo died of a heart attack on June 23, 1995. He had just been to the doctor that week and received a good report of solid health.

"Tony was just filled with possibility," continues Frank. "He believed if things weren't so bright today, it could all get better tomorrow." Like most artists, he had his melancholy side, too. *"Is that all there is?* was always a question in his mind," adds Frank, "but mostly he was very upbeat. He was a leader." Frank pauses and reflects. "I'll never forget the morning I went to his apartment after the funeral. It was a couple of days later and I went into the kitchen and there was a scratch pad. Tony always wrote lyrics and ideas for songs on scratch pads. He had written a line on it and it said *Even a broken heart can heal*. I used that on his gravestone, because I figured that was the last lyric he ever wrote. It was his last words."

Remembering Tony

Frank Romeo: Tony was a "do it" type of guy. When he got his first Mercedes, he said "Let's go to the Kentucky Derby—it's the day after tomorrow!" So about six of us piled into the car and went to the Kentucky Derby. It was always like that. You wanted to be on his trip.

He was a very optimistic guy. He loved life. He adored his friends. In fact, every Friday night he'd have dinner for all his friends. He did so the night before he passed away.

Our voices were very similar. My mother could never tell us apart when we called. Tony's nickname was Babe—because he was the baby of the family—so I would call her up and she'd say "Babe?" I'd say, "No, it's Frank."

Ken Jacobson: Christmas was a big, big deal to Tony. Big! We had a friend who became very, very sick and he went into the hospital. He also lived upstate, and he was coming home for Christmas, so Tony went over to his house before he arrived home, and filled it with Christmas decorations! He loaded it with the Christmas tree, wreaths, candles, decorated the windows and everything.

He had the biggest truck on the road, and it was red! Tony would always run out of gas, because he always wanted to see how far he could go in his truck. There were people who would not get into that truck with Tony, because it was always running out of gas. And you'd say, "Tony, the gas is low," and he'd say, "Yeah, I know." He was a daredevil.

When I think about it, I don't know if he was really shy or if it was just an act, because he was ballsy. I'll tell you a funny Tony story: Joni James was giving a concert in New York, and Tony got tickets. We went to the concert, and when the concert was all over, Tony says "Let's go back and see her!" Well, Tony didn't even know her—I did! So we started back. There was a guy at the door before you get upstairs where the dressing room is, and he stopped us and said, "No, you can't go up there." And Tony says to him, "He's with me," and we went right up through! Ballsy, right? Now we are in Joni James' dressing room, and Joni James says "Oh! Ken, how are you?" Tony went into a corner and never said a word! All of a sudden he turned into this shy little thing! It was the only time I'd seen him like that since the early days.

John Bahler: I never really got to know him except through his music, and he was exceptional. Tony Romeo wrote so outside the box. He was very instrumental in creating the Partridge sound, because his songs were just out there. They weren't like songs that anyone else was writing. If I had to pick a favorite Partridge Family songwriter, it would be Tony. He just got it from the beginning. So many of the Partridge Family songs that make you go "wow"s were Tony's.

Tony was to music in his day what Burt Bacharach was to music in his day. In other words, what Burt did was so much different than anybody else that he was one of a kind. As soon as Wes would play one of Tony's songs for me, almost without exception I'd know it was Tony Romeo, just because he wrote so differently. All his music was simply not what was going on during that era, and that gave us a leg up. It certainly helped me a lot because it gave me something new to key off of. So many of the other writers were just writing the hits, and there's nothing wrong with that—but then all of a sudden Wes comes along with Tony Romeo and he breaks the mold. He challenged me like no other writer had challenged me up to that point. It was really exciting.

Tommy West: We met at the screening of the pilot episode. He was a gentle soul. Tony was a very sensitive, deep, lovely man. As a writer, he was a real craftsman. His style was eclectic. He was Italian, like me, and he was very lyrical, very melodic. Tony had really nailed down what it was like to live in small-town America. He was a big Beach Boys fan, so those kind of harmonies would pipe in every now and then. He would take time to write a good song, like "Point Me in the Direction of Albuquerque." Who would ever come up with a title like that? Tony Romeo, that's who!

Tony was very influential in pushing me to do an album with Anne Murray. He was very much influenced by records of Les Paul and Mary Ford. He and I both loved the pre-rock and roll crooners of the '50s. We were talking about those kinds of songs one time, and he said, "You ought to do

when we're singin'

> an album like that". "With who?" I said. Then all of a sudden Anne Murray came into the picture, and I did an album with her called *Crooning*.
>
> Tony and I used to get together about once or twice a year. My wife and I were living in Nashville for a while, and sometimes Tony came down and stayed with us for a few days. When I found out he died, I was lying in bed in my mother-in-law's house in Arlington, Virginia. I just had eye surgery a couple days before, and I had fallen asleep in the bed. I woke up and the news was on. I heard, "… and also in the news, Partridge Family songwriter Tony Romeo dead at 56." I felt like a bowling ball had hit me in my stomach.
>
> **Jean Farrell:** Wes and Tony had reconnected when Wes bought Benson Records, which was in Nashville. I think they were talking about collaborating. Wes was always interested in what Tony had going on music-wise because he was a big fan of Tony's.
>
> Tony was brilliant. I spent one day with him when he came up to visit us at Lake George. We rented a house there every summer. I still have a clear picture of Tony standing there on our deck. He was overlooking the water and playing all his new songs. He and Wes were just so excited. It was this moment in time where you see the creator actually exposing his work for the first time, and he wanted Wes' opinion. It was a great day.
>
> When Tony Romeo died, I got the call. Wes was traveling, and he was on a plane from New York to Miami. I picked him up, and he got in the car, and I told him I had some sad news. I told him that Tony had died. I never saw Wes break down like that. I mean he just sobbed in the car. He just sobbed. He really loved Tony.

Christmas 1971

Christmastime was always special on the set of *The Partridge Family*. Each year the cast and crew had Christmas parties. Brian Forster says, "I remember a kind of funny story there. We'd give gifts to each other for Christmas, and I got this gift from David, along with everybody else. It turned out to be a bottle of scotch! So my mom goes up to David and says 'Hey, David, thanks for the Christmas gift. Do you know what you gave Brian?' All of a sudden I guess his eyes opened up real wide and he goes, 'Oh my God! I'm so sorry! My personal assistant did that.' And she said, 'Yeah, we kind of figured that.' So David went out himself and personally bought me a Swiss army knife."

The TV family had a lot to celebrate during Christmas of 1971. The show was now a bona fide hit, ranking No. 16 on the Neilson ratings during its second season. David Cassidy's first single, "Cherish," had just been released and was climbing the charts. To celebrate, he played the song for everyone at the wrap party that year, and the crew put together a blooper reel of collected outtakes of the cast which they all watched together.

It was an especially merry Christmas for Cassidy, whose first solo single reached its peak position at No. 9 on Christmas Day and remained there into the New Year. Cassidy was featured on the cover of *Cash Box* on Christmas Day 1971. His first solo album was set for release in the new year, with the fifth Partridge Family album, *Shopping Bag,* not far behind. In addition, the next Partridge Family single, "It's One of Those Nights (Yes, Love)" made its first chart appearance on December 18, showing up at No. 57 on *Billboard* and No. 37 on *Cash Box.* The trades predicted it to be a top 20 hit.

Bell Records was also riding high in the holiday season. As early as September 11, Bell announced *A Partridge Family Christmas Card* as one of eight packages planned for full-scale promotion, including personal visits to retailers from the executives. "This is by far the most impressive album release since we began concentrating on LP product a year and a half ago," said Gordon Bossin, vice president of LP sales.

A *Cash Box* year-end summary listed the Partridge Family as the No. 3 best artist of 1971, beating out the Rolling Stones, Creedence Clearwater Revival, Bread, and Chicago. David Cassidy was listed as best new male artist among a list that included George Harrison, Cat Stevens, Stephen Stills, John Denver, Rod Stewart, Elton John, and Michael Jackson. The Partridge Family was listed as the No. 1 top vocal group of 1971 over Three Dog Night, Grand Funk Railroad, the Rolling Stones, the Doors, the Guess Who, the Jackson 5, the Bee Gees, the Beach Boys, Deep Purple, and a long list of others. Best albums of 1971 included *Up to Date* at No. 11; *The Partridge Family Album* at No. 19, and *Sound Magazine* at No. 54. During the Christmas season, the Partridge Family had all four of their albums ranking on the top album charts at the same time.

The issue also featured an article headlined "Bell's Best Xmas Sales Assisted by Partridge Bonanza." Gordon Bossin said the label was going through its best Christmas sales in history, sparked by Partridge Family LPs—each of which had sold more than a million units for total sales of 5.5 million copies.

In another year-end article, in the *Anderson (Indiana) Herald,* Bossin says many retailers had declared December to be Partridge Family Month. The same story reported that during the 1971 holiday shopping season, the four Partridge Family albums available on the market sold a combined total of 200,000 copies on one day alone.

when we're singin'

Yes, Virginia, There Is a Partridge Family

In 1897 the editor of the *New York Sun,* Francis Pharcellus Church, replied to a letter from a young girl with an editorial that included the famous phrase, "Yes, Virginia, there is a Santa Claus." What is real, he said, goes beyond what we can perceive.

So was the Partridge Family "real" music? After all, most of the actors didn't sing. The editor of *Cash Box* thought so, and in an editorial dated December 11, 1971, "The Necessity of Pre-Teen Stars" he relates his thoughts:

There is a world of rock music alien to many "mature" rock fans which probably first generated their interest in rock in the first place. It is a world of so-called teeny-bop or bubblegum music generally inhabited by artists who may not be much older or somewhat younger than the audience they appeal to.

To many older rock fans, acts like the Jackson 5, the Partridge Family, and the Osmonds represent a too simple, unsophisticated rock format, sugar-coated with a sentimentality they would rather not admit a fondness for. Perhaps with the exception of record companies that do a land office business in this type of music, the industry, including radio, also tends to shy away from this field.

Yet, it would seem to us, it is the very simplicity and uncluttered approach to rock, performed in a thoroughly professional and winning manner, that justifies their superstardom within the range of their audience. That audience, if you happened to drop by at one of the concerts, is as dedicated a musical audience as you're apt to find in any area of music. They do not bear the burden of forced 'coolness' and openly express their joy at the musical pleasures set before them.

To amplify a statement made earlier, these acts serve a vital function. They are the introductory vehicle to 'heavier' forms of rock, educating as well as entertaining tomorrow's adult music fans. Certainly to the music business, they reach, as no other musical attraction can, a massive group of eager new record fans, as a continuous flow of gold albums and singles will testify to. And there is good reason to believe that their sounds reach out into older age groups. This is for the simple reason that it's difficult not to be delighted by the engaging quality of youthful spirit and melodies you can hum as you cheerfully leave the concert hall or listen to a record player.

It would seem to us that those who put down rock acts who delight the younger audiences are engaging in a form of snobbism without reflecting on the true musical merit of these performers.

Liner Notes: *A Partridge Family Christmas Card*

Christmas has been a huge part of pop culture since the early 1800s, and so has the power of marketing. "A Visit from Saint Nicholas" (also known as "Twas the Night

Before Christmas"), written in 1823 by Clement Clarke Moore, is often credited as the biggest influence for the marketing images and visuals attached to Christmas and Santa Claus as we know them today.

Year after year, decade after decade, musical stars come out with a Christmas album at one point or another. It was a smart move for Bell Records to issue a Christmas album by the Partridge Family, even though the idea was frantically carried out at the last minute. "Somebody thought, 'Hey, I bet you a Christmas album would sell a lot of records!'" says John Bahler.

According to series producer Larry Rosen, that somebody was likely Wes Farrell. "Wes was pretty dedicated to making the songs into hits. 'Whale Song' didn't excite him because he didn't see a hit in that. A Christmas album for the Partridge Family? Yeah! Now *that* made sense, because he could sell that!" Choosing the most marketable songs and time-tested Christmas tunes, Farrell quickly gathered a slate of commercially proven Christmas hits to work with and seventies-ified them with grooviness. The short time frame for pulling the album together, however, complicated the sessions for *Christmas Card*.

John Bahler's reaction to the short deadline was typical of his adventurous spirit. He knew how to roll with just about anything Wes threw at him. "Ok, well—let's do it! It needs to be released tomorrow," he laughs. "That happened in the business all the time."

Bahler continues, "This was one album where we were so up against it that Wes didn't have time to get the album finished, so we worked up a plan. Mike Melvoin said to me, 'You do the rhythm parts on this song, and I'll do the rhythm parts on that song, and when we're finished, we'll switch. You do the strings and horns and I'll do the strings and horns.' We split it up that way. It got to be so much fun because there were things that he'd pick out of my rhythm chart to use with the horns and strings that he said he never would have thought up otherwise, and the same was true for me. I'd pick a bass line, or something he had written, and use it in the horns or the strings. Then I'd get an idea from something he had written, and vice versa with him. We used to laugh about it because we came out with ideas that never would have arisen individually. Together, it was just magic. We had many, many all-nighters where I would be running over to his house and he'd be running over to my house. This was at like five o'clock in the morning, you know? It was so much fun, and we just laughed and laughed."

Despite the speed and focus of both John Bahler and Mike Melvoin, they needed more help. Tom Bahler decided to jump in and write some of the vocal arrangements, trying to help them meet the impossible demands of the deadline. It was the first album that he'd ever written background vocals for. "I just couldn't get it all done," explains John. "He may have done about half of them, and he did a wonderful job. Tom wrote a lot differently than I did, and he also has a lot more hits than I do. That album was really Keystone Cops."

when we're singin'

Tom Bahler was a strong songwriter and had also written "Goin' Home (Sing a Song of Christmas Cheer)" for Bobby Sherman at around the same time. He and his brother John were in sync musically. "He and I are very much alike, but we also have nuances," elaborates Tom. "We know each other very well and we know who's who. When I do vocal arrangements, I tend to play off the lead and either repeat what the lead is saying or comment on what the lead is saying. I remember as soon as I heard those Partridge Family Christmas songs I went, *Oh yeah … YEAH!* I remember Wes getting such a big kick out of it."

Wes Farrell had a blast, even under duress. Tom Bahler remembers him running around the studio singing, 'He's comin', comin', poking fun at Tom's arrangement on "Santa Claus Is Coming to Town," yet really loving everything the two brothers did. "Wes really dug us," says Tom Bahler.

"This album was like *Just get it done, get it done, get it done!* But you know, we were never going to be any less than everything we had, so the quality was always going to be there. I ended up taking the lead as vocal arranger on this album because my brother was overworked. John had become such a popular vocal arranger, so at that time people didn't come to me for that kind of work very often."

Shortly afterward, Tom Bahler earned the critics' respect for his vocal arranging when he scored big with the No. 3 hit single "Precious and Few," recorded and released by Climax in 1972, only one year after his work as vocal arranger on *Christmas Card*.

The Bahlers and Melvoin were pulling out every Partridge Christmas jingle they could come up with to fill the required number of *oohs, ahhhs,* and *la-la-las* needed for their hip holiday Partridge in a pear tree. The sessions for *Christmas Card* were combined with those that made up *Shopping Bag* and the latter half of season 2.

Just when it seemed impossible to deal with any more hurdles, David Cassidy began to show signs of getting sick. "He was singing incorrectly," remembers John Bahler. "By then David was taping the show four or five days a week, then flying out on Friday afternoon and doing concerts on the weekend." Cassidy had to cancel two summer concert dates (July 17 and 24) when he had to have an emergency gall bladder removal. His doctor told him to take it easy, but he was out on the road again in no time. In the coming weeks, Cassidy would have to begin recording the Christmas album, which wasn't originally planned.

"White Christmas" is the first Christmas song listed as complete on Ron Hicklin's session notes dated August 28. That same day the studio announced that Cassidy would be "making his variety show debut as the special guest star on 'The Glen Campbell Show' taping September 14th at CBS-TV, for airing November 2nd. Cassidy will take a day's hiatus from the Partridge Family series to tape the 60-minute show."

Fall of 1971 was, without any doubt, much more stressful for Cassidy than the first year of the show. In addition, he had to return to taping for season 2, while doing the concert tour through December. "He was burning the candle at all ends, and he was killing himself," says John Bahler. "He was killing his voice, killing himself physically, and he ultimately had a lot of vocal problems." Cassidy was maxed. They needed a plan.

Farrell and the team had to come up with a way to successfully get the record out, and none of them was willing to settle for less than perfection. If one thing can be said about Wes Farrell, it is that he never approved any music for release that he didn't feel 100 percent good about. He knew what a seller this album could be if it landed under every preteen's Christmas tree that year. He also knew that good Christmas albums have repeat business each year if they stand the test of time. They talked about the situation. They brainstormed. They gave up sleeping. Then visions of sugarplums danced in their heads—the obvious finally hit them in the face.

"They'll buy this simply because it's the Partridge Family," explains Tom. "David was exhausted, so John and I and the others decided that he didn't have to be on all the lead vocals. As long as he's on there enough to make it authentic, he didn't have to be on every track." After all, they had Shirley Jones and their own blended harmonic sound, both of which could be featured without question on a holiday album and still keep sales at their prime.

Larry Rosen reflects, "At that point it didn't matter so much that David was the featured singer as much as it was about the Christmas songs, you know? David on lead vocal was important for hit songs like "I Woke Up in Love This Morning," because it's David Cassidy's lead that made the song work. When you're singing 'Have Yourself a Merry Little Christmas,' it doesn't matter."

Cassidy still worked hard on the album, shuffling in and out of the studio with every free second he had. Jackie Ward says, "Usually when we were doing our singing for the group David had already done his singing. He was usually leaving the studio as we were coming in. On rare occasions, like the Christmas album, he was there when we were all there. He would sing a phrase, and then we would sing a phrase, because of the rush in getting it out. This was not normally the way we recorded. Normally, he would finish his part, and we would go in and do what we had to do."

Shirley Jones was also a soloist on this album because she was absolutely perfect for Christmas music, despite the established pop sound of the Partridge Family. *Christmas Card* was a perfect chance to spotlight Jones, with her musical theater background. "We finally got into a genre in which she could sing and, at the same time, find acceptance by the Partridge fans," says John Bahler. "None of the other Partridge music was right for her talent," says Tom Bahler. "She was Broadway, man, and she beat on it! She was great at what she did, but it didn't fit the Partridge Family sound at all. So now we were doing a Christmas album and that was right up her alley. That was a perfect time to let her shine." Jones took the lead vocal on the holiday standard "The Christmas Song."

when we're singin'

Wes Farrell commented, "She was so impossibly smooth about everything. She never gave us a bit of anything but pleasure. Shirley is one of the great joys on this earth. A first-class person beginning to end. She's such an immense talent."

John Bahler speaks to the ongoing question on whether or not she sang on the Partridge Family albums: "That's the biggest question I get when people find out I was involved with the Partridge Family. The answer is yes, absolutely! She sang on every single record. However, we had her on a separate track, so when we mixed the records we mixed her down so that she wasn't really noticeable. I mixed her low not because she wasn't a great singer. She was. But her vocal style did not fit the family sound. It also gave the producers some elements to work with on the music videos. Because she was on a separate track, they could raise her up a little bit when they did a close-up of Shirley, and then drop her back down in the mix when they cut away from her." This tactic was employed throughout all four years of *The Partridge Family*. It is especially noticeable on the television version of "Have Yourself a Merry Little Christmas" featured on the Christmas episode "Don't Bring Your Guns to Town, Santa."

"She was great," says Tom Bahler. "Her voice was such a different style. Her power colored the sound to a place where Wes said, 'That's not what the audience wants to hear.' So they dialed her down for that reason only, but she sang on every song. I was listening to 'The Christmas Song' before I talked to you, and she sounds so good on that, man, because she wasn't going into her stage voice. It was really pretty." Jones usually recorded all of her parts for an entire album in one single session.

One good idea led to another. Wes Farrell knew the gorgeous harmonic sound of his background vocalists also had winning potential with Partridge Family fans. The first record, *The Partridge Family Album,* had proven so in the very beginning. The newly revamped Christmas plan was put into motion. John and Tom Bahler, Jackie Ward, and Ron Hicklin took the lead with their blended harmonies on two tracks for the album. "Sleigh Ride" is traditionally a very difficult song to sing, but the four pull it off effortlessly. They also take lead vocals on "Have Yourself a Merry Little Christmas," with a brief solo bit from Jones, who can be heard on the refrain. In another one-time-only performance, David Cassidy and Shirley Jones sang a duet together on "Winter Wonderland." It appears on both the episode and the album.

In spite of his vocal exhaustion and scheduling issues, Cassidy still provides the lead vocal on seven of the 11 songs on *Christmas Card*. The album contains only one original song, "My Christmas Card to You," written by Tony Romeo, which appears as the first cut.

A Partridge Family Christmas Card is entirely secular. There are no songs reflective of any single religious belief, nor do any of the Farrell-chosen standards play to the origins of the Christmas holiday. None of that matters. *Christmas Card* has proven itself as an album with holiday staying power. It was produced with originality, reflecting the musical styles and trends of its day. The overall sound of the album keeps with the rest of the Partridge Family sound, although its pop style seems more pronounced because of the familiarity of the songs.

Christmas Card was the best-selling Christmas album in the United States during the Christmas season of 1971. It was No. 1 each week of *Billboard*'s special four-week Christmas album sales chart. A *Cash Box* headline from October 16, 1971, reads "Bell: Pre-Order Gold For 'Family.'" The article states, "For the first time in Bell Records' history, an album has qualified as a gold record on the basis of pre-release orders. 'A Partridge Family Christmas Card' has received an initial order topping the Partridge Family's previous album, 'The Partridge Family Sound Magazine,' which reached gold record status two weeks after release. The album, which shipped last week, comes with an actual Christmas card featuring a photo of the Family and signatures of the individual members slipped onto the front cover. 'Our distributors tell me that the enthusiasm among dealers is unbelievable. Orders for it have exceeded anything they ever had for any other Christmas album they've handled,' said Gordon Bossin, director of LP sales."

Christmas Card was released in November, making its showing on the pop charts right out of the gate. The album was so popular it was reissued in 1972 and went to No. 9 on the *Billboard* Christmas chart.

Both the TV episode and the album were so well received that one might have expected more of the same over the decades from Shirley Jones and David Cassidy. They appeared together on a Canadian Christmas broadcast in 1982 called *Frank Mills' Christmas Special*. They sang "The Twelve Days of Christmas" with Barbara Eden and reprised their duet of "Winter Wonderland." Cassidy also performed "White Christmas" as a solo number. To date, David Cassidy has never released a solo Christmas album, but he has long said that he would love to. Shirley Jones recorded *A Touch of Christmas* in 2010, released on Encore Music Presents Records.

One of the most endearing reflections of *A Partridge Family Christmas Card* is the family of colleagues behind the music who worked together and stuck together, determined to get the album out on deadline. Even in all the stressful moments, they had fun. Tom Bahler's personality shines in his lighthearted and loving jokes about his brother John and his friend Mike Melvoin (who he nicknamed "Mickey Milquetoast" because it was, as he says, "antithetical to his persona"). He reminisces about being a fan of David Cassidy, and Cassidy's admiration of him and his brother.

"David never had an opinion, I don't think, in any way other than the love for his artistry, because David trusted those around him, which I think smart artists do," he says. "And you know he used to come—Ollie Mitchell and I had a group that we called the Good Stuff, which was all people that played on the Partridge stuff—

the horn sections, and all the stuff. And we played at Dante's, which was this very cool music place on Lankershim, and it was very, very popular. We put together this 16-piece band, Mike Melvoin on piano—I mean it was just amazing, and then these hot horn sections, and anyway, we just had a ball.

"David used to wear dark glasses and a beard, man, and a hat pulled over his head in friggin' August, and he would come and listen to us because he loved our music so much. He was the coolest guy. He couldn't go to the market because 50 little girls would jump him. He also saw that for what it was. He was very cool. He never lost it. He was very, very cool."

Despite the schedule, *Christmas Card* prevailed. The album comes off with spirit, and it is exceptionally done. Tom Bahler explains it this way: "I was just watching *Casablanca* for the hundredth time, and because it's on DVD now, you can listen to everybody's commentary. The script wasn't done when they were shooting. They didn't know from day to day what they were going to do. Ingrid Bergman wasn't ever sure who she was supposed to be in love with! The point is, sometimes when things are so helter-skelter, as Quincy Jones used to say, you end up having to leave a little room for God, instead of trying to control everything, because, you know, we are only as good as what we can't control."

He continues, "Somehow these conversations bring back memories. I'm standing in the studio right now. I'm in Studio 2. I mean, it's wild. Talking about it again just really puts you there, especially when the memories are so happy. I think part of the reason the Partridge Family, musically, was so glowing, was because everybody knew what they were doing. They were into what they were doing, and they were fun people. I used to say, as a studio singer, 'Man, if I wake up in the morning and I'm depressed, or whatever dark mood I might be in, as soon as I get on the mike singing next to my brother and Ron, and standing across from Sally and Jackie and Sue, it's just impossible to be in a funk.'"

That spirit is what the Partridge Family is all about. The cast felt it. The musicians felt it. The fans felt it. There is feeling and passion and spirit pressed deep into those vinyl grooves that reflect the heart and soul of those albums. It is the quality that makes them live on. And so, as the album's opening lyric proclaims, and with the same goodwill:

May peace and love surround you—
at Christmastime and all the whole year through.

For those who favor the Christmas TV episode, it could also be put another way: Meh-eh-eh-eh-erry Christmas!

My Christmas Card to You, 2:35, Tony Romeo

The story goes that every passing year after the initial release of *Christmas Card*, David Cassidy would call up Tony Romeo on Christmas day and break into the opening lyric of "My Christmas Card to You" the second he answered the phone. Written as the centerpiece for this album, it is truly one of the great Partridge Family songs and one of the most underrated. Although planned as the album showstopper, it was never released as a single in the U.S. Bell Records domestic staff felt there was not enough time for the promotion team to get DJs fired up about it in time for the holiday season. It eventually found at least one international release in New Zealand. Many fans, along with David Cassidy, believe this song is one of the great all-time Christmas classics. Cassidy has said publicly many times that he would like to re-record it on a solo album, and that it also deserves an annual place on radio DJs' slate of classic Christmas rotations.

The musical layers are complex. It is the big production number on the album, opening with the trademark harpsichord and a little french horn, clarinet, and flute tossed in. The entire essence celebrates the sound of the holidays, painting a very Norman Rockwell image of Christmas. Lyrics are personalized and relatable, reflecting Tony Romeo's talent for creating visual imagery. The chord progressions are interesting, and slightly different for Romeo's style. The song wraps up with a flute and cello, closing out with a cold stop ending.

"Nobody did Christmas like Tony," reflects Frank Romeo. "He'd have a Christmas party at his house, and there'd be 50 people there. He'd sit at the piano, and Lou Christie and I would be there, and we would start singing. Pretty soon the whole room would be singing Christmas songs, and Tony would be in his glory.

"Tony loved to write Christmas songs. He must have written 10 Christmas songs. He wrote Christmas songs for the Cowsills, though I'm not sure if they ever recorded one. When he had an opportunity to write a Christmas song for the Partridge Family, it was the best thing that could have ever have happened for him. "My Christmas Card to You" was written specifically for their Christmas album. There was never any doubt that it was going to be on it."

White Christmas, 2:38, Irving Berlin

Irving Berlin wrote "White Christmas" in 1940. He dictated it to his secretary, and felt it was the best song he had ever written. Bing Crosby was first heard singing it on the NBC radio show *The Kraft Music Hall* on Christmas Day 1941. Crosby later recorded it in 1942 and "White Christmas" made its feature debut in the film *Holiday Inn*, released the same year. It won an Academy Award for best original song of 1942, and some 12 years later appeared as the title song for the famous movie of the same name. The song captured the hearts of Americans during wartime, keeping it alive year after year. In the '50s Elvis Presley-fied the song. By the '60s, it was included on practically every mainstream Christmas album. It is the biggest-selling and most recorded Christmas song of all time.

when we're singin'

The Partridge Family recording is a pleasant easy-listening arrangement that captures the laid-back vibe of the times. In place of the opening lyric, Mike Melvoin arranged a beautiful musical introduction, giving it a Partridge Family identity from the first note. The opening lick is reflective of Harry Nilsson's "Everybody's Talkin'," and the easygoing picking style of artists like Glen Campbell. Cassidy's breathy vocal emphasizes the serenity we all crave at Christmas.

Santa Claus Is Coming to Town, 2:24, John Frederick Coots–Haven Gillespie

First sung on Eddie Cantor's radio show in November 1934, this holiday favorite began as a sheet music sensation, selling 100,000 copies the day after it debuted. When the recording came out, it sold more than 30,000 records in the first 24 hours.

In 1970, just a year before the release of *Christmas Card,* Rankin/Bass produced the TV Christmas special *Santa Claus is Coming to Town* with Fred Astaire, molded into their famous stop motion animation style, singing the title song and narrating the story. The audience was similar to that targeted for the Partridge Family, so including the song on the Christmas album was an easy decision.

Both the vocal and musical arrangements on this version are true to their time. The beat is rock and roll with a sugary pop flavor. The vocal arrangement is original, done by Tom Bahler, with whistling tossed into the middle of the song. Cassidy's vocal adds style and hipness with the usual *whoa*s and *why-hy*s.

Blue Christmas, 3:22, Billy Hayes–Jay Johnson

"Blue Christmas" is a tale of unrequited love during the holidays and a longstanding staple of Christmas music, especially in the country genre. It was first recorded by Doye O'Dell in 1948, but it was Elvis Presley who really established it as a rock and roll holiday classic, in 1957.

Following the success of Presley's version, the song began to be recorded by mainstream rock and country artists. David Cassidy loved the blues, and this gem clearly showcases his abilities in that style. With the addition of Bahler's harmonies, the possibilities were endless for this arrangement. The Partridge arrangement makes heavy use of electric piano, giving the rendition a solid dose of the '60s blues, à la Ray Charles. The arrangers were leaving subtlety behind and taking the blues to the extreme.

Jingle Bells, 2:48, Traditional—arranged by Wes Farrell

Written by James Lord Pierpont and first published as "One Horse Open Sleigh" in 1857, this famous Christmas tune was originally composed to celebrate Thanksgiving, first performed at a church concert. Medford, Massachusetts, has a plaque in the center of the town square claiming Pierpont wrote the song and first published it in 1850 at the local pub Simpson Tavern, supposedly inspired by the town's popular sleigh races during the 19th century. "One Horse Open Sleigh" was republished in 1857 as "Jingle Bells."

Given its age, the public domain status makes this song free to record. Its secular nature and popularity with children of all ages made it another easy choice for Wes Farrell.

The vocal and musical arrangement here, in all its '70s glory, gives originality to the piece. The arrangement's opening is a little reflective of '60s pop group Free Design, and their sunshine pop sound, and Cassidy's opportunity to sing a few bluesy runs ("laughin' all the way…") makes it his own.

The Christmas Song, 2:25, Mel Tormé–Robert Wells

"The Christmas Song" was originally subtitled "Merry Christmas to You." It is a classic Christmas song written in 1944 by Mel Tormé and Bob Wells. According to Tormé, the song was originally written during a heat wave in the summer of 1944. He and Wells wrote the song together to distract them from the heat, and they finished it in 45 minutes.

The Nat King Cole Trio first recorded the song early in 1946. Cole recorded the song again in 1953 and again in 1961—the version best known as the annual holiday standard. It has been recorded by countless artists, including the Carpenters, Rosemary Clooney, Natalie Cole, and Doris Day. Judy Garland sang the song in a duet with Tormé on a Christmas-themed episode of her television show in December 1963.

Shirley Jones makes her lead vocal debut on a Partridge Family album here, and it is the only album recording in the entire Partridge Family catalog that she would ever get to call her own. Strings and faint bells add plenty of holiday atmosphere. Jones' vocals are heartfelt, and clarinets round out the arrangement toward the end.

Rockin' Around the Christmas Tree, 2:30, Johnny Marks

Written by Johnny Marks and recorded by Brenda Lee in 1958, "Rockin' Around the Christmas Tree" was recorded when Lee was only 13 years old. A lot of county elements are included in the arrangement. The song didn't take off at first, but as Brenda Lee became a bigger star, it followed suit.

The pop-rock nature of the song reflects the Partridge Family style more than any other of the Christmas songs. The Partridge version shows up from time to time on Christmas compilation albums, no doubt because the arrangement captures the sound of the Partridge Family as it is best remembered. The arrangement is pure '70s pop, with echoing phrases from background vocalists and a fun opening guitar lick at the top amid plenty of electric guitar and organ.

when we're singin'

Winter Wonderland, 2:16, Felix Bernard–Dick Smith

There is no mention of Christmas in this song because it was written as a mere reflection of wintertime. Written in 1934, its lyrics were inspired by Central Park in Dick Smith's hometown of Honesdale, Pennsylvania. He wrote the lyrics while staying at the West Mountain Sanitarium, where he was being treated for tuberculosis. The first hit recording of "Winter Wonderland" is credited to Guy Lombardo and His Orchestra in 1934.

David Cassidy and Shirley Jones sing this song as a duet, making it a special musical pairing for fans who are drawn to the real-life stepmother-stepson relationship these two stars share. Jones is double-tracked in her parts, and the style makes her sound more pop-contemporary, matching Cassidy's style. The arrangement is again very '70s, especially the ending. The period stands out so much on this album because the songs were all traditional in their most familiar format, so when Bahler and company made the sound their own, they gave us a musical moment in time.

Appears On: Season 2, episode 38, "Don't Bring Your Guns to Town, Santa" (December 17, 1971)

Frosty the Snowman, 3:47, Steve Nelson–Jack Rollins

"Frosty the Snowman" was first recorded by Gene Autry in 1950 after the success of Autry's recording of "Rudolph the Red-Nosed Reindeer" the year before. Rollins and Nelson shipped the new song to Autry, who recorded it in search of another seasonal hit. In 1969, the Rankin-Bass company came out with a televised Christmas special based on the song, featuring the voices of Jimmy Durante and Jackie Vernon. The town of Armonk, New York, where Nelson lived much of his life, claims it is the inspiration for the lyrics.

It seemed another good choice for the buying audience of the Partridge Family. A highlight of this album, "Frosty" is treated with a well-thought-out stylized arrangement focused on its storytelling nature. David Cassidy's voice is up front, with beautiful complementary backing vocals. The arrangement showcases Cassidy's voice, tapping into its complex nature and longing, searching, soulful qualities, and a slowed-down tempo turns a poppy children's song into a heartfelt ballad. The arrangement and vocal interpretation capture the bittersweet ending to this song, typically overlooked, as they focus heavily on Frosty's story. The theme is especially accentuated at the end of the song, taking the already slow tempo down by half. The concept was a brainstorm of Wes Farrell, Mike Melvoin, and John and Tom Bahler. "Wes was always looking for a different way of doing something," says Tom Bahler. "I remember talking about what we could do to make this more interesting. I remember just really enjoying this one. I thought it was very cool."

Sleigh Ride, 2:37, Leroy Anderson–Mitchell Parish

"Sleigh Ride" is a light orchestral piece composed by Leroy Anderson. The composer had the original idea for the piece during a heat wave in July 1946, finishing the song in February 1948. Lyrics that set up the image of riding in a sleigh on a winter's day were written by Mitchell Parish in 1949. With no hint of any holiday, the mention of pumpkin pie in the last verse might suggest an association with Thanksgiving rather than Christmas. It has been recorded countless times by a wide range of artists, including the Andrews Sisters with their harmonic sound, the Ventures with their California surf vibe, Henry Mancini with his sophisticated orchestral sound, Herb Alpert with his '60s pop-brass instrumentals—and the Partridge Family in all their '70s happiness.

This time all four background vocalists take the front, providing a harmonized blended vocal to serve as lead, with no sign of David Cassidy, but Bahler and company pull it off in true Christmas spirit, complete with harpsichord, and minus any signs of strings and horns. There was a lot of focus put on this one, with the vocalists reconvening in the studio a second time to do a re-record.

Have Yourself a Merry Little Christmas, 2:22, Hugh Martin–Ralph Blane

"Have Yourself a Merry Little Christmas" was introduced by Judy Garland in the 1944 MGM musical *Meet Me in St. Louis*. The lyrics have been modified several times. Some of the original lyrics penned by Hugh Martin were rejected before the musical was finished for being too depressing, and he made the song more upbeat at Garland's request. Her version of the song became popular among United States troops serving in World War II, and her performance at the Hollywood Canteen brought many soldiers to tears.

Frank Sinatra asked for another rewrite for his album *A Jolly Christmas*, and he too wanted something even more upbeat. The resulting version is the one most often recorded since. In 2001, Martin, then 86 years old, wrote an entirely new set of religious lyrics and titled the song "Have Yourself a Blessed Little Christmas."

The Partridge Family version ends the album with another gorgeous harmonically blended group vocal by the background singers, again minus David Cassidy. Other than a short refrain briefly spotlighting the voice of Shirley Jones, the group vocalists carry this one. It was featured prominently in the final scene of the Christmas episode. The televised version uses a cappella harmonies at the top of the song, also bringing Jones' track up a bit, while the record version is more blended and instrumental. Flute, acoustic guitar, and classical guitar are all heard, with a slightly different guitar mix on the record. It was the last time that any Partridge Family record contained a lead vocal by anyone other than David Cassidy.

Appears On: Season 2, episode 38, "Don't Bring Your Guns to Town, Santa" (December 17, 1971)

Album Summary and Reviews

Total Running Time: 27:44
Original Release: November 1971, Bell 6066

The best selling family is here with a terrific Christmas package. Included are the usual favorites ("White Christmas" "Frosty the Snowman" "Blue Christmas") done by the Partridges in a lovely style which will surely attract much December programming. There is a Christmas card included with signatures and a family picture. A dynamite LP which will be an immediate smash and prove a very popular Christmas present. *Billboard, December 4, 1971*

Christmas is traditionally a family affair and what better family to help us celebrate than television's first family—the Partridge Family. David Cassidy, Shirley Jones and company let fly on "Jingle Bells," "Winter Wonderland," "Rockin' Around the Christmas Tree," "Have Yourself A Merry Little Christmas" and others. We especially liked the group's slowed down version of "Frosty The Snowman." This should be a highly successful Xmas LP. *Cash Box, November 20, 1971*

*First Chart Appearance: November 27, 1971 (***Cash Box***, No. 114); December 4, 1971 (***Billboard*** Christmas List—peaked at No. 1 for four weeks and appeared again in 1972 at No. 9); December 4, 1971 (***Record World***, No. 130)*

THE SECRET FORMULA
or ... The Partridge Family Shopping Bag

The Merchandising Machine

By 1972, it was a shopper's paradise for Partridge Family fans as department stores and supermarkets filled up with toys and trinkets bearing the images of their favorite cast members. Bubblegum cards, clothing, school supplies, and just about anything else the marketers could reach were all embellished with images of the Partridge Family—especially David Cassidy.

In the pre-Internet era, the only hope of getting close to a favorite celebrity was through fantasy—realized, if not through teen magazines, then by an endless supply of merchandising. The Partridge Family operation was so huge it was nicknamed "the merchandising machine." *TV Guide* went one step further and revealed that a Screen Gems higher up coined it "the money machine." According to the article, profits on Partridge Family bubblegum cards alone were over $100,000.

The teen magazines were working in tandem with merchandising contracts. *16* magazine had a circulation of 1,200,000 in 1972. They sold the David Cassidy Luv Kit for $2 each and made a killing. Likewise, *Tiger Beat* was selling memberships to the Partridge Family and David Cassidy fan clubs for $2 each—and one fan club alone had membership upwards of 200,000. Regular issues of *Tiger Beat* sold for 50 cents each, and they sold about 400,000 of them monthly. *Tiger Beat* licensed their image and had a staff of approximately 30 to help move product. They paid Screen Gems 5 percent of profits.

"Oh, God, the marketing on the Partridge Family was phenomenal!" says Beverly Weinstein, who was vice president in charge of art direction for Bell Records. "They were owned by Columbia Pictures, and they really had a wonderful marketing department. It was like walking into a wonderful toy store. Posters, whistles, you name it!"

When the cast members were signed for the show, part of their contract gave the studio the right to their face and likeness. This meant that products using their images could be an extremely lucrative deal for the studio, and not so much for the actors. According to his business manager at the time, David Cassidy's income was derived 60 to 70 percent from concert sales, 20 to 30 percent from the records, 10 percent from his TV salary, and less than 1 percent from merchandising.

when we're singin'

For the most part, Screen Gems used photos from the regularly scheduled session shoots held by the studio each season. They could make whatever deal they wanted to with the photos they already possessed.

"The photo shoots were for different elements," explains executive producer Bob Claver. "Sometimes it was for *Tiger Beat*. Sometimes it was for other kids' merchandise. I'm thinking we had a lot of products out on the street, but we [the producers] had very little dealings with them. You might think that maybe they wanted Cassidy or the rest of the cast to take pictures with whatever object they were trying to sell, but we didn't spend a lot of time fooling with that stuff. Nobody wanted to do it, and Screen Gems got all of the money, so that didn't help. It's so hard to explain sometimes why you behave the way you do, but other elements take priority." Claver's priority was the quality of the show.

David Cassidy was more affected by the merchandising than any other cast member because of his larger-than-life image as the newest teen idol. The companies selling products would frequently set up special mail-order promotions available only through a magazine. Others came directly from manufacturers. They sometimes showed the various products to Cassidy. He had the same criticism as he did for the products offered through the fan clubs—he was dismayed by the quality in relation to the cost. Cassidy, despite the fact that he never aspired to be a teen idol in the first place, genuinely cared for his innocent and impressionable fans. Though not really comfortable with the merchandising, he felt that, at minimum, fans should have well-made collectibles.

Cassidy told Ken Sharp, "The thing that I always felt about fans was that if they were going to pay five bucks for something they should get five bucks' worth of stuff.... So when I started making complaints to them is when they stopped sending it to me. And of course they owned my name and my likeness. I just wanted the fans to get a fair shot." Of the memorabilia itself he said, "It was fun. That's what they're intended to be." Some products focused on the entire family or on other cast members.

Remco produced two items in 1973: a Laurie Partridge doll and a Partridge Family toy bus. Neither fared well, possibly because they were released after the merchandising era had peaked. A giant 31-inch David Cassidy doll was announced by Remco but never produced. Many other companies had their hand in the Partridge Family shopping bag as well, producing everything from a life-size David Cassidy jigsaw puzzle to View-Master reels to bubblegum cards and a Partridge Family cookbook. It was the biggest TV merchandising success to that point in history.

The toy bus and record cabinet are the rarest and most prized items for collectors. One version of the bus sold for $1,500 in the late '90s.

THE SECRET FORMULA

Patti/Kate, Patti/Kate

Years earlier, the 1960s television series *Family Affair* had made Mrs. Beasley—the beloved baby doll of Buffy, played by eight-year-old Anissa Jones—a madly desired Christmas gift by little girls nationwide. *The Brady Bunch* later followed suit by setting up the youngest daughter with her own cherished doll, Kitty Karry-All, who also gave merchandisers a financial field day. Dolls were a proven success in television-inspired toys, and it wasn't long before the Partridge marketers jumped on board.

The youngest Partridge, Tracy, was given a doll to promote as they led into the second season of the show. A photo shoot was done with Suzanne Crough, who appears on the box cover with the doll. Patti Partridge, as the doll was named, had flaming red hair and was billed as "Tracy's very own performing doll," able to yawn, blink, and play patty-cake. She appeared in the first episode of season 2, but without much focus and literally no mention. Crough can be seen holding her in only a handful of episodes. Bob Claver adamantly refused to produce a script around a toy to create a marketing frenzy, and Patti Partridge was not much of a success.

But where the Patti Partridge doll didn't catch on, the clothing line did. The Partridge Family collection was produced for girls' clothing brand Kate Greenaway. Greenaway was a Victorian-era writer and illustrator of children's books. The clothes were inspired by her illustrations, with old-fashioned smocked dresses and other girls' clothing from the era. While it was marketed heavily that both Susan Dey and Suzanne Crough wore these clothes, it was mostly only Crough who was promoting them. The clothing line was expected to bring in about $10,000 a month. "The clothing line actually had more of an effect on me than the Patti Partridge doll," says Crough. "I'd have to go kick off the clothing line at I. Magnin in San Francisco, and that would be my weekend thing. I'd do a fashion show, and that would create more frenzy pertaining to me, personally. Every little dress, and every little thing, had a little Partridge Izod-like emblem on it. So it was kind of interesting.

"I didn't necessarily model it as much I was there as the special guest. Even though I didn't have to model the stuff, I did get a bunch of outfits. It turned out that I didn't wear any of it. I wasn't going to wear it on the show, though I guess they could have costumed me in it. But they gave me a bunch of clothes, dresses and other things, and I ended up giving them to my nieces, who are six years behind me in age. I think they still have some of the outfits. They actually wore them. It was pretty high-quality clothing. It wasn't low-end department store quality, by any means. That was interesting to me, because the merchandising of the clothing line solely involved me, and not anybody else." The clothing designs were also featured as paper clothing for the Susan Dey paper doll sets featuring Susan Dey.

when we're singin'

From the Personal Collection of...

Nostalgia is a powerful thing. No one had the foresight back in the '70s to see that videotape was about to define home entertainment in the upcoming decade and DVDs would take it a step further in the late '90s. This new technology began to make it possible for fans to record their favorite old shows and eventually purchase them as complete series sets. The Internet also redefined fans' access to entertainment in ways that no one could have imagined.

The new availability of websites and online auctions fueled interest in all things nostalgic. Vintage television shows and the products marketed from them were experienced all over again by fans, now middle-aged, who began repurchasing those old items they had thrown away or sold in a garage sale.

"There were no VHS tapes or DVDs then," says Suzanne Crough. "There was nothing in the contracts for any of the kids regarding merchandising, except for Shirley and David. You received your 10 years' syndication payoff and that was it. Hindsight's always 20/20. I can't complain. I mean, I was making good money at six years old, you know?" Crough laughs.

But Brian Forster did some digging and found his old contracts. "There were two contracts," he says. "One was a record contract which covered merchandising. My mom actually went to the producers and reminded them of this, and we got a check, probably for 47 cents…. However, Shirley and I talked a few years ago about the 'future technologies' clause, which she didn't seem to think was there. A number of years ago, however, I did get paid for all the episodes that were put on DVD for seasons 2-3-4. Of course, I didn't get anything for season 1; I hope Jeremy did!"

Crough says, "When I was 12, if you had asked me in 40 years whether it would still be around, I'd have said 'Yeah, right!' We finished the show when I was 11 or 11 and a half, and I don't know what happened but when I was about 12 years old I threw everything out. I kept a few things, but I threw all the scripts out the door. I wish at some point that some of that hadn't been tossed. I think I kept the back to my chair, and I kept my parking space sign."

She continues, "When we went to Ohio for the King's Island episode the governor presented all of us with the keys to the state. I have that, and I have a lot of the plaques for the charity events we did, jewelry they give you, and stuff like that, but virtually that's all I kept. Then friends started giving me albums they'd find in garage sales or wherever. I actually had one fan send me the Patti Partridge doll in the box in really good shape. I don't have the thermos or the lunchbox—but I'm on the bottom side, so who cares?" she jokes.

Jeremy Gelbwaks, even though he was gone from the show after the first season, saved two of the lunchboxes and has them on a shelf. Shirley Jones saved her paper dolls. Danny Bonaduce has held on to a few things: "I have the *Up to Date* album and *Sound Magazine*. I've got the original *Danny Bonaduce* album. I'm sure I have a lunchbox somewhere. I'm not a collector of things. I'm just a collector of memories."

Brian Forster's mother was sentimental enough to save many of the things that are still in his collection. "I have a feeling when the Partridge creators came out with marketing products, they had this idea in their head that it wasn't just going to be the show, it was going to be about the whole packaging and the merchandising. That kind of bugs me," says Forster.

The issue of product sales has brewed for Cassidy over the years far more intensely than for the others because it was primarily his face and likeness cashed in on for profits. Cassidy was deeply troubled by the greed he perceived was driving those product sales, not to mention the problems they created for him as he struggled to break free of the squeaky-clean Keith Partridge image. Cassidy filed a lawsuit in 2011 for money owed him from the Partridge Family days, and a court ruling was finally made in 2015 granting Cassidy approximately $158,000.

Cassidy continues to autograph items for fans and pokes fun at some of the vintage merchandising during concerts, taking it all in stride. In concert today, he still smiles every time someone holds up a paper doll with his smiling face and shagged-out hair posed atop a hand-drawn cardboard body. He jokes with the fans and says how happy he is that these things brought happiness.

Producer Larry Rosen remembers the craze. "David's name and face were on everything besides Tampax, I think. I don't know what the deals were, but I certainly didn't get a nickel out of any of that. I was a contract player at Columbia, so I got paid a salary and no royalties for anything on those episodes."

David Cassidy actually saved a lot of things over the years. He had a Partridge Family lunch box, board game, jigsaw puzzles, and even a red toy guitar. In 2006 he had a public auction with Julien's, a Los Angeles–based auction house specializing in entertainment memorabilia. Among other items, he sold many of his original concert outfits—which went for $1,500 and up—including several one-of-a-kind jumpsuits designed for him by Manuel, the same man who designed performance costumes for Elvis Presley, Little Richard, Johnny Cash, and Tom Jones.

After the passing of his mother in December 2012, Cassidy held a second auction in May 2013 in support of Alzheimer's research. He felt it was time that more of his personal memorabilia move on to longtime fans while making money for a cause that was meaningful to him. All things, including merchandising, come full circle.

Cherish-ed

David Cassidy made his first solo album with youthful hope and a bit of innocence about the music business. He hoped his music would evolve and his image would change.

when we're singin'

On October 30, 1971, *Cash Box* predicted great things for the album: "There's no question about the success of this record at all. David Cassidy, performing one of the most beautiful love ballads ever written, will make his solo appearance a memorable one. Vintage Association material is strikingly delivered."

In the very early stages of the album's development, Tony Romeo was hard at work on songs that would resonate and connect with Cassidy on a more mature level, and he was as eager as Cassidy himself to see this evolution. "Summer Days" was Romeo's masterpiece, written especially for Cassidy. It was planned as the album's title and first single. But at the 11th hour, Wes Farrell began having second thoughts. He decided he wanted to play it safe—*really* safe—so he replaced it with "Cherish." It had been a megahit for the Association that went quickly to No. 1 in 1966.

"Cherish" would go on to become a huge success for Cassidy—as a single, an album, and his introduction to international superstardom—but in the United States his manufactured image would still dominate in the eyes of the public.

Even with "Summer Days" out and "Cherish" in, Cassidy remained excited about the release. It was his first solo album and he worked incredibly hard in the studio. Asked which of Cassidy's recordings he thought was his best, Partridge Family included, John Bahler says, "Oddly enough, *Cherish* comes to mind, because that was his first solo album and solo outing. It was about him, and not about the family. That's what pops into my mind. David always did his best. He never did anything halfway. But when it was finally about him, he sang his butt off, man. He really, really did. We loved doing the background parts, too. They were pretty much a rip-off of what the Association had done, but it was still fun singing it."

"Cherish," the single, was released in October 1971 and rose to No. 9 on the *Billboard* charts, peaking on Christmas Day and holding firm for three weeks into the new year. It hit No. 3 in *Cash Box* and No. 5 in *Record World.*

The album was released in early 1972, entering the *Billboard* charts on February 12 at No. 85. It peaked at No. 14 on March 4 and remained on the charts for 23 weeks, through July 15. "Could It Be Forever" was also released as a single on the heels of the album. Early reviews predicted another smash hit. *Cash Box* stated, "Exceptionally beautiful material and production help David excel as never before: A future No. 1." But the single peaked at No. 37.

The release of the album was planned to coincide with Cassidy's second U.S. concert tour. The tour announcement and album review both appeared in the same issue of *Cash Box,* on February 5, 1972. The review stated, "'Cherish,' his big selling single, leads the way but the trip is nicely laden with the sort of tunes David does best. 'My First Night Alone Without You' and 'We Could Never Be Friends' stands out, as does 'Being Together.' Should be a high charter."

THE SECRET FORMULA

The Cassidy promotional team went all out. There was a nationwide merchandising campaign by Bell Records as part of the newly coined "David Cassidy Month" in February 1972 celebrating the release of *Cherish*. Melody Records, a chain of stores based in New Jersey, plastered their store windows with David Cassidy posters and a giant "DAVID" spelled out in their window display using more than 35 *Cherish* albums to create the letters. Displays like this were happening all over the country. The response was pandemonium. Young girls were lining up at the checkout line, holding back tears of joy while waiting to pay for their heartthrob's first solo album. Boys were also crazy for him.

Cassidy had hoped this album might break his image a bit with the television show and that he would be able to express himself more freely as an artist. But that didn't happen. This album, like the Partridge Family albums, was done under the guidance of Wes Farrell as producer and Bell Records as the label, so the same powers were calling the shots.

Farrell was struggling to define the differences between the Partridge Family sound and the emerging sound of David Cassidy the solo artist. "There were a number of ways to do that," Farrell said in his 1993 interview with Ken Sharp. "Some songs ended up bleeding over and slipping into the Partridge Family. It beats the hell out of me how that happened, because they were two different concepts."

One of the ways Farrell would distinguish the sound from the Partridge Family albums was by pulling back on the background vocals. John Bahler wrote background vocals, but they were mixed much further in the distance than on the Partridge Family albums.

Songwriting newcomer Adam Miller was signed to write for Farrell, and he ended up contributing substantial work to both the David Cassidy projects and the Partridge Family. Miller brought some great songs to the table for Cassidy, and three of his tracks appear on *Cherish*—"I Lost My Chance," "Where Is the Morning," and "Blind Hope."

"'Blind Hope' was actually a song that I put on my second album, produced by Cashman and West," explains Miller. "It was actually a song that I wrote for me, but I think—and this is the kind of thing that happened sometimes with Wes—I think they actually changed the slant of the lyric in the tune, if I'm not mistaken. And also, you know Wes was into big choruses, and I think that he kind of changed that tune pretty dramatically. But I was very thrilled to be involved and have anybody do my stuff, so there's no complaints in that regard.

"For me the song was a little bit about being in a rut in a relationship, and *Let's not get stuck here, let's get going,* and somehow with David's version, 'Blind Hope' was a very positive thing. But I was thrilled, and I remember when I went to David's concert at Madison Square Garden, when he was at the top of everything, Wes must have told him that I was in the audience and he announced my name and that was quite a kick." Miller's recording appeared on his album *Westwind Circus*.

Miller continues, "'I Lost My Chance' was something I remember Wes thinking was good and that it would work for David. Wes brought over the Brill Building approach, and even though he was on the East Side we had little cubicles with pianos in them, and this was one of the ones I just kind of cranked out.

"I think I wrote 'Where Is the Morning' after we recorded my first album, and I was still out in California. I had driven up the coast to San Francisco, and if I'm not mistaken I was in a motel room someplace on the road. I wrote 'Where is the Morning' because I guess I had insomnia or something, and then I turned it into a love thing—a boy-girl thing. I remember Tony liked that song a lot. Tony Romeo—he gave me a lot of compliments about that.

"Wes didn't like the way it came out so he turned up the amps and rocked it there a little in the chorus. Originally the chorus was kind of a soft, nice little melodic change."

Tony Romeo's writings were also at the forefront of the album, further showcasing his artistic connection with Cassidy on three original songs written specifically for him: "Being Together," which opens the album, "We Could Never Be Friends ('Cause We've Been Lovers Too Long)," and the deep and revealing "I Am a Clown," which did very well as a single in the overseas market.

Cassidy's first solo songwriting effort appears on this album. "Ricky's Tune" was a farewell to a dog he loved, also serving as a metaphor for the end of an imagined relationship.

"Could It Be Forever" was the result of a songwriting collaboration between Wes Farrell and Danny Janssen. "I think God meant it to be done," begins Janssen as he reflects on the song, its origins, and its tremendous success. "Do you know where the Polo Lounge is? It's a very famous place. It goes down three stories into the ground. Up in the main bar area there, every day at that time, Elton John was there, and everybody was there, you know? We used to go downstairs and write. So I get down there, and next door all these ladies are there. They were all old ladies, but they were beautiful. They were all Ziegfeld girls. They were having a reunion, and they heard us playing and they wanted to hear what we were writing, so they came over. We were writing (he sings) *'Could it be forever, or is my mind just a-ramblin' on….'*" Janssen jokes, "There's a Wes Farrell lyric for you! What the hell does that mean?"

The album was filled out nicely with a cover of Kin Vassy's "My First Night Alone Without You" and "I Just Wanna Make You Happy," a Farrell-Hart number.

Wes Farrell and company were now planning their strategy and focus on launching Cassidy with full force into the overseas market. *Cash Box* announced that Cassidy would be in England doing a promotional tour in February, including a special appearance on *Top of the Pops.*

Danny Janssen was committed to helping Cassidy and Farrell succeed internationally. Janssen had played a part in the release of the Association's original recording of "Cherish." He loved the song and saw the hit value behind it. But when Cassidy's version was released in the States and it came time to decide on a single release in England, Janssen advised Farrell against releasing "Cherish," because he was worried the word *cherish* would be less emotionally resonant to U.K. audiences. So Farrell instead released "Could It Be Forever" with "Cherish" on the flip side. In spite of Janssen's reservations, both songs scored big in England, with the single rising to No. 2 on the British pop charts.

The success of "Cherish" in the U.K. was unprecedented. "I Think I Love You" had made a small dent in England compared to Cassidy's solo releases. The first season of the show was just beginning to air there around the time *Cherish* was released. *Cherish* was huge in England, topping its success in the U.S. The album rose to No. 2 in the U.K.

The cover photo of David Cassidy used on *Cherish* has become synonymous with Cassidy's trendsetting look of the 1970s. It is a perfect example of the power of simplicity, and how sometimes great art is created without overthinking it. "I think that was just a picture I took on the Partridge Family set," says Henry Diltz. "It was just a picture I took for the magazines. I was always taking those kind of beautiful head shots of him. You know, for posters and magazine covers. We just had a whole bunch of those and somebody saw that one and pulled it out for that record, you know? I mean they didn't say, 'Hey, here, do an album cover for *Cherish.*'"

Diltz shot the photo on the back lot at Columbia Ranch in Burbank, where *The Partridge Family* was being filmed. The shots chosen for the back of the cover were also shot by Diltz—some in Hawaii and some at the house next door to Cassidy's publicist, Ruth Aarons.

Despite Cassidy's attempts at maturity and the overwhelming financial and commercial success of *Cherish,* he remained pigeonholed by his image in the United States. But he was determined to move his music forward. He wanted more control.

In March of 1972, he announced that he and his management team, Aarons Management, had formed their own publishing company, Ru-Da Music. The announcement stated that Cassidy would be not only publishing his own music but also licensing music from other songwriters. "Ricky's Tune," although it had already appeared on *Cherish,* was included under his company. It was one of the first substantial moves on Cassidy's part to gain control of his music and his public persona.

The impact of "Cherish" resonates with fans even today. When Cassidy sought public opinion on his website before going back out on the road around 2000,

"Cherish" was the most requested song by a landslide. Its endurance is a testament to the power of Cassidy as a solo artist—even if he wasn't feeling any separation from his TV image in the '70s.

"Naked Lunch Box"

When *Rolling Stone*—the hippest magazine in the music business—asked him to pose nude as part of a lengthy exposé, Cassidy said yes.

It all happened during the early stages of Cassidy's second U.S. tour, promoting *Cherish*. Respected photographer Annie Liebovitz took the photos and *Rolling Stone*'s Robin Green wrote the article.

Green followed Cassidy around for five days and a couple of concerts, hoping to gather material for a story that was new, different and revealing—something that dug a little deeper. But from the first sentences of the article, she suggested that Cassidy was doing drugs.

Cassidy has said openly that he did drugs in the '60s. But he has also stated that during the Partridge Family years he never messed with drugs, and that he was disappointed in that slip on Green's part. He had nothing to hide.

Cassidy gave Green full access to everything and everyone around him. The article begins with Cassidy's record-breaking Madison Square Garden appearance, which sold more than 20,000 tickets, and ends when his plane pulls into the next concert stop in Bangor, Maine. She reports on Cassidy's screaming fans, eager groupies, naked sunbathing—and the professionalism of the band, which was made up of studio musicians, all over 30 years old, dressed in matching red velvet blazers. Cassidy was also fighting off the flu.

The Madison Square Garden concert was the first time that Shirley Jones saw Cassidy perform live. In fact, nearly all of Cassidy's family was there: his mother, Evelyn Ward, his brothers Shaun and Patrick, and even his 83-year-old grandfather. Cassidy has said that concert meant more to him than any other concert for that reason alone.

The tour had already broken attendance records at the Astrodome in Houston, with more than 56,000 turning out for two matinee performances. *Rolling Stone* reported that Madison Square Garden had sold out in three days, with tickets on sale three weeks before the concert, though many fans remember it selling out in less than 24 hours. Fans were so crazed that six limousines were crushed in an attempt to find Cassidy after the show. He ended up in a dumpy motel somewhere in Queens because none of the posh hotels in NYC could chance having him. The event, and the status of David Cassidy as a superstar, was record-breaking in many ways.

The concert tour was rigorous, with more than 50 dates scheduled between February and October, including at least two shows in Canada.

After the article was written, Annie Liebovitz, who Cassidy regarded as the best photographer of all time, approached him about the photo shoot. Cassidy was all in. He wanted the world to see him as real and unexposed. The nude photos were taken at Cassidy's home in Encino, out in a field of grass.

"Naked Lunch Box" was the cover story of the May 11, 1972, issue, which remained the magazine's best-selling issue until John Lennon's death.

The photos were tastefully done, but like the story, they ran counter to the image of Cassidy's innocent appeal. There were reports of young girls denying that it was actually him. The desired older fan base was not won over, and certainly parents of youthful fans were unhappy.

The article didn't help his career much, either, and may have actually done some damage. Coca-Cola backed out as the sponsor of a planned TV special, as did guest star Bob Hope, who had agreed to appear on Cassidy's special after Cassidy appeared on his. General Mills threatened to stop using him as a spokesperson for their products. But Cassidy has always been extremely proud of it. That's a completely different kind of success.

"He was just tired of being pushed into the mold Wes wanted him in," said Mike Melvoin. "He just wanted to be himself. The business partners wanted him to remain the David Cassidy of the Partridge Family, because it made a lot of money and a lot of show-business sense and it had a great arc to it. If he would have had more patience, he could have seen that through more, but he became very impatient with it and started to express himself."

"I think David was thrilled with it," says Shirley Jones. "That was his moment. I don't think it hurt the show. I'm not sure that it helped the show, but I think it was a good thing for him, definitely. Everybody said, 'Go ahead—play your other music. Do your other thing. But when you're here you're going to do what we do.' It was that kind of thing."

The nude layout didn't really faze the producers or the devoted fans. It seemed that the image as the clean-cut boy next door was so powerful that most fans dismissed the real Cassidy and held on to the image. That's a strong testament to fantasy and the needs of America's youth at the time.

"I remember the nude layout, but I don't recall a lot of flak about it," says Larry Rosen. "I really don't. The thing that appealed so much with David was that he was charming. He was innocent looking and nonthreatening. I think that was the big key thing. He wasn't the kind of guy that girls thought might get aggressive with them if they were with him alone, you know? They just wanted to be with him, and to touch him, and to love him, and they felt totally non-threatened by him.

when we're singin'

"That's the persona that he played. His TV character was kind of this goofy guy who was always talking about things he didn't know anything about, having opinions that didn't make any sense. It was Susan's character who was always the one to bring him back to earth. So a nude layout wasn't going to give David more fans, because it wasn't so much about what a hot lay he would make. It was just that he was accessible to these kids, and they felt that they could be his friend, be his girlfriend, and still be safe at the same time. That's always the feeling I had about David.

"His character was never that sexy hot guy that, if you're going to spend an evening with him, you're going to wind up in bed. They were going to spend an evening, maybe have dinner, and he might take them home and kiss them goodnight at the door, you know? They wouldn't feel terribly threatened, even though I'm sure lots of them wanted to sleep with him. But I think in those days it wasn't so much about that as it was about this sexual energy that was kind of unexpressed and not acted upon, but always there, and always safe. It was a safety thing about David. I think that's what made the show work so well. His character was just a kid, a little bit full of himself, but not dangerous, and not malicious."

Danny Janssen, who worked exclusively with the music side of the Partridge Family, remembers it differently from conversations he had with Wes Farrell at the time. Janssen says there was plenty of fallout in terms of record sales. "It cost us millions of dollars. That killed the Partridge Family. People wanted their money back for albums. That's a fact. They were so angry with him."

It could be argued either way. Sales for *The Partridge Family Shopping Bag* were solid, even though it dropped off the charts in only 17 weeks—about half the time of the previous albums.

Despite any problem the public may or may not have had with the *Rolling Stone* exposé, few would disagree with his right to live his life outside the studio any way he wanted to. Associate producer Mel Swope says, "If you want to go out and ride a motorcycle for 48 hours on your weekend, that's your business. If you want to go and play a concert, then that's your business, too. I don't think it's much different today. It still happens."

David Cassidy's music, both solo and with the Partridge Family, still holds its fan base 45 years later, despite the *Rolling Stone* story or anything else in the press. Cassidy knew the strength of his material and its ability to communicate, even then. He told Green of the story behind "I Think I Love You" and its rise on the charts, pointing out that Percy Faith and the Boston Pops were beginning to play the song— "and it was written for me," he emphasized. "I've got good writers writing for *me*. I want people to know that I like to sing that song. I stand naked—that's the best word I can think of and say—'this is how I am.'"

THE SECRET FORMULA

Bus Stop ...

The Memorabilia Store

Collectors worldwide have come to realize there is no end to collecting Partridge Family memorabilia. Regardless of whether the production quality was good or bad, collecting toys and memorabilia offers a pleasant escape back to childhood and innocence. Here is an overview of some of the Partridge Family memorabilia collected by fans around the world.

Toys and Games

Board game: Milton Bradley produced a simple roll-the-dice-draw-a-card-and-move-around-the-board game geared for kids ages seven to 12. A Greek version was also produced overseas.

Toy buses: The Remco toy bus, one of the most valuable Partridge Family toys released in 1973, is a plastic bus with a door that opens and closes. Six small character figures of the cast and two musical instruments fit into the seats, and the roof is removable. The box opened up like barn doors to act as a garage. Two versions of the bus were available—one with black wheels and one with blue.

In 1998 Playing Mantis Inc. released a Johnny Lighting 1:64 scale Partridge family bus with several different collector cards available. It was reissued in 2001 with a rubber magnet of the bus instead of a card. In 2001 a Johnny Lighting die cast model kit of the Partridge Family bus, with a mini screwdriver for assembly, was also released by Playing Mantis. It was reissued in 2002. All miniature versions of the bus were incorrect replicas of the actual Partridge Family bus make and model.

Colorforms: The David Cassidy Dress Up Set by Colorforms, a popular toy of the era, features a cardboard stand-up figure with Cassidy's real face superimposed. The figure can be dressed in one of several outfits with magnetic-like clothes that stick directly to the stand-up figure.

Toy guitars: Two versions were available—a white one with four strings (making it technically a ukulele) and a bigger red one with the standard six strings. The red version came with a small music book.

when we're singin'

Jigsaw puzzles: Two jigsaw puzzles were released in the U.S. The more popular one, a 500-piece puzzle of David Cassidy's face, was widely available. The other, an 84-piece life-size photo of Cassidy from the waist up is more rare. The pieces are almost as big as an adults' hand. Different puzzles were available in other countries.

Laurie doll: Produced by Remco, the Laurie doll is unusually tall (19 inches). It was sold along with a mini-poster of David Cassidy and Susan Dey.

Paper dolls: Four box sets of Partridge Family paper dolls and two booklet versions all come with groovy '70s clothing for each character, represented by cardboard figures that barely resemble the cast. Two Susan Dey box sets feature costumes promoting the Kate Greenaway clothing line, much more conservative than the wardrobe for the Partridge dolls. The Susan Dey set also comes with paper pendants, rings, and headbands for girls to assemble with ribbons and wear, and can be supplemented with expansion booklets.

Patti Partridge doll: Inspired by other TV-inspired dolls like Mrs. Beasley and Kitty Karry-All, Patti Partridge features a puppet-like control gizmo hidden under the back of her poncho, giving kids the opportunity to make her blink and play pattycake. Patti is seen only briefly a few times on the show and never caught on like her predecessors.

Slide puzzle: A very early Partridge Family toy, this 15-piece slide puzzle features a black-and-white drawing of David Cassidy that looks nothing like him! Produced by Roalex, these puzzles were very popular with kids of the era.

View-Master reels: A trilogy of sets were available. The first is titled "The Money Manager," with slides taken from stills of season 1, episode 21, "Partridge up a Pear Tree." The second set, "The Male Chauvinist," features stills from the season 3 opener, "This Male Chauvinist Piggy Went to Market." A Talking View-Master set was also available for "The Money Manager."

Books and Publications

Activity books: *The Partridge Family Fun Book* features various activities and fictional stories, much like a comic book. The same book appeared as one of the hardback *Partridge Family Annuals* in England. *The Partridge Family Pictorial Activity Album* and *David Cassidy Paint and Color Album* are similar in nature and slightly oversized.

Coloring books: At least five different coloring books were produced by Artcraft and Saalfield between 1970 and 1973. Additional coloring books and puzzle books were sold internationally.

Comic books: Twenty-one issues of the Partridge Family comic books were issued. Two versions of the first issue were available—one with a color photo and one with a black-and-white photo. No. 5 featured a removable pinup to color. The series spawned a separate David Cassidy comic book series, which produced 14 issues in 1972 and 1973.

Cookbook: A rare Partridge Family paperback.

Music books and sheet music: Screen Gems announced the release of complete Partridge Family folios in the trade magazines. *The Partridge Family Album, Up to Date, Sound Magazine, Shopping Bag, At Home with Their Greatest Hits,* and *Notebook* were all made available in the U.S. One collection featuring all the songs from the first three albums is titled *The Partridge Family Complete*. These three-album collections feature guitar arrangements by Dan Fox. Richard Bradley arrangements were also available. *Simply Bradley,* another Richard Bradley collection, features arrangements for eight songs.

In Canada, *The Partridge Family's Biggest Hits* features 14 Partridge Family and David Cassidy song arrangements, and *The Partridge Family Deluxe* is a collection of all 22 songs from *Album* and *Up to Date*. In the U.K., *The David Cassidy Song Book* and *The David Cassidy Book* were both available with the same cover. The first features 16 song arrangements from Cassidy's first three solo albums, and the other provides only the lyrics. Both versions include a reprint of the *Rolling Stone* article and outtake photos from Cassidy's photo shoot with Annie Liebovitz.

Countless issues of sheet music were available for individual songs of both the Partridge Family and David Cassidy's solo music. Several Cassidy solo albums were also released as music book collections.

Paperback fan books: Several paperback books on David Cassidy were produced, some of them the same story packaged under different titles and covers. *Meet David Cassidy, The David Cassidy Story, Young Mr. Cassidy,* and *David, David, David* were all released in 1972.

Tiger Beat offered two Susan Dey paperbacks, *Susan Dey's Secrets on Boys, Beauty and Popularity* and *For Girls Only; 16 Magazine*'s was titled *Cooking, Cleaning & Falling in Love*. Though they were marketed as authored by Dey herself, they were really written by the magazines' editors.

when we're singin'

Paperback mysteries: With one of the early paperback mysteries selling over one million copies, it's no wonder so many were produced—17 in all. Each is a fictionalized mystery adventure along the lines of the Hardy Boys and Nancy Drew books, featuring the Partridge Family. The books were written between 1970 and 1973 by six different authors: Michael Avallone, Vic Crume, Paul W. Fairman, Edward Fenton, Lee Hays, and Vance Stanton. These popular books were sold through Scholastic, a company that markets inexpensive books in schools.

Music Accessories

Record cabinet: Commonly referred to as the holy grail of Partridge Family collectibles, the record cabinet has appeared on Internet auction sites less than a dozen times as of this printing. The cabinet opens up in the front and has space for records, and two additional shelves. Four 7x6-inch photo stickers came with the cabinet, one of them a rare photo of the bus taken before it was modified, between the pilot and regular series shooting. The cabinet was made of thin wood and came in a long, thin box, requiring assembly. Boxed versions are the rarest.

Radio: Made in the U.K., the David Cassidy AM pendant radio features a removable plastic cover so that the included photo of David Cassidy could be swapped out for other photos. It was sold with a 29-inch chain so kids had the option to wear it around their neck.

Buttons, Badges, Cards, and Posters

Bubblegum cards: Topps produced 55 blue-border cards in the first series, 55 yellow-border cards in the second, and 88 green-border cards (considered the rarest) in the third and final series. Card No. 9A, "Electrifying Performance" from the blue series, was reissued in 2013 as part of Topps' 75th anniversary rainbow-foil-edition bubblegum cards. It is No. 56 in the anniversary edition.

Partridge "family tree": Creatively packaged on a colorful display board, this item (also known as a flicker badge set) featured round lenticular 3-D images of each cast member that could be worn inside a button which was displayed as the package centerpiece. Individual buttons of each cast member could also be purchased separately. This item is so rare it sold for over $1,000 on one auction offered by Just Kids Nostalgia in 2012.

Photo cards: At least two different 11x14-inch lenticular 3-D photo cards were available in the U.S. along with smaller postcard-size versions. Various types and sizes were also produced internationally.

Poster packs: Mini-posters measuring 9½x18-inch, made of thin paper, were folded down to the size of a bubblegum package and sold individually in packs. Topps produced a total of 24 posters.

Posters and pinups: Endless posters and pin-ups were produced in the U.S. and internationally.

Sticker-posters: Called "personality prints," these photos were actually sticker-backed mini-posters of David Cassidy measuring 8x13 inches. At least five different packages were available.

Recordings

Music and video formats: All the Partridge Family albums were released on vinyl, cassette and eight-track. Ampex reel-to-reel was also offered for *Album, Up to Date, Sound Magazine, Shopping Bag, At Home with Their Greatest Hits,* and *Notebook.*

The first round of VHS home video was released in 1997 and 1998 by Columbia Tri-Star Home Video—four VHS tapes with four episodes on each. In 2000 Columbia House released a mail-order set of 20 VHS tapes with four episodes on each. The show was released on DVD by season between 2005 and 2009; a set of the complete series was released in 2013 and reissued in 2015. The season 1 final episode, "A Night in Shining Armor" with Bobby Sherman, was clipped short on the DVD releases. The full episode is available only on the Columbia House VHS collection.

"Talking" records: Spoken-word recordings of the era included "Everything You Wanted to Know about David Cassidy" and "The Girl Scouts of America," with a short promo by Susan Dey. Other product-oriented spoken records were also produced, including one for each of *Tiger Beat*'s fan club kits.

Other Items

Beach towel: When fruit drink manufacturer Hi-C wanted to promote a Partridge Family premium, a Screen Gems associate came up with the idea of a beach towel while he was doing laps in his pool. The towel features a life-size caricature of David Cassidy, drawn a little better than some of the other merchandising but still not capturing Cassidy's essence. The beach towel offer began in 1972 and expired March 31, 1973, or "until supply is exhausted." It cost two dollars plus six Hi-C can labels as proof of purchase.

Order forms were on the inside of the Hi-C label, along with a collectible Partridge Family photo. Collectors could obtain eight different photos from the labels of 46-ounce cans of Hi-C or by ordering a set of uncut photo labels for 25 cents.

Bulletin board: Two versions of a Partridge Family bulletin board were produced—one tan, the other red, both with white wooden frames. The pinboard was made of a burlap-like fabric, and the board came with a handful of David Cassidy push pins.

Calendars: David Cassidy calendars by APC were available for 1973 and 1974. David Cassidy calendars were also produced in the U.K. for 2004, 2005, 2006, and 2008. Cassidy produced his own 2012 calendar, which sold through his website.

Cereal box: David Cassidy's face appeared on boxes of Post Raisin Bran cereal. The back of the box offered "Snip-n-Pin" collectible photos that could be cut out. Two Partridge Family versions and two David Cassidy versions were available.

Christmas items: In England and Australia several Partridge Family and David Cassidy Christmas cards were available. In 2003 Carlton Cards produced a commemorative Christmas ornament of the bus, which plays "Come On Get Happy."

Clocks: Two clocks were issued by Time Setters, one with David Cassidy's face and one with the Partridge Family. Clock hands, frames, and cords were sold separately.

Clothing line: The Kate Greenaway Partridge Family clothing line for girls (which Cassidy once called the strangest idea of all the merchandising) launched in 1972 and sold nationally in high-end stores like Bonwit Teller stores. The line included blazers, short dresses, long dresses with pinafores, jeans, jumpshirts, printed shirts, sleeveless dresses, handbags, and sew-on patches. Collectible stickers were included, and sales tags featured cast photos.

Halloween costume: Released by Kusan, a Nashville-based company that produced a variety of Halloween costumes, the David Cassidy Halloween costume looks nothing like the man himself but is noted as one of the rarest of collectibles.

Jewelry: Charm bracelets, rings, necklaces, and other items were readily available in retail stores and mail-away offers through teen magazines. Two wristwatches were produced, one of David Cassidy and the other of the

Partridge Family, using the same images as the clocks. Much of the memorabilia featured the same photos on individual items.

Lunchbox: The metal lunchbox was originally issued in 1971 with a metal Thermos, then re-issued in 1973 with a plastic Thermos.

Pencil case: Available only in the U.K., the Partridge Family pencil case has a zippered top and comes in multiple colors.

Pillowcases: A pillowcase with a black and white photo of David Cassidy was available in the U.S. during 1972. Another, with an inscription reading "Always Remember I Love You, David Cassidy," was available in Australia in 1973 as a mail-order premium through *TV Talk*, a weekly magazine.

Three-ring binder and spiral notebooks: A three-ring binder with David Cassidy's face on the cover features four concert shots on the back. Individual spiral notebooks with paper covers were also available.

Miscellaneous items: T-shirts with iron-on images of David Cassidy were also available through mail order and came wrapped and sealed on a square sheet of cardboard. A special book cover was also offered in pairs. It was manufactured by APC for Lever Brothers and it was only available with the purchase of Lever Brothers–owned soap, including Dove Bar, Lifebuoy, Lux Bar, or Phase III.

International items include scarves (which were waved at concerts), flags, and an array of badges. In the U.K., fan club kits were known as wallets, with contents that varied slightly from the U.S. kits, including stationery and collector stamps. U.K. fans could buy hardback activity books, called annuals: at least three Partridge Family annuals and two David Cassidy annuals were produced. Cigar bands in different colors were also popular items. Embroidered clothing patches, stickers, and buttons were available worldwide. Anabus produced stickers, stationery and envelope packs, and individual memo pads.

Liner Notes: *The Partridge Family Shopping Bag*

Wes Farrell amped up the background vocals and Bell Records amped up the package design, spending more money on *The Partridge Family Shopping Bag* than on any other Partridge Family album. This decision said a lot about the way Bell Records was looking at the selling power of this group. The Partridge Family was selling very, very well, and Bell Records President Larry Uttal, who usually felt package design was not the place to put money, decided to invest a bit more on this one.

The title of the album alone is a nod to the success of the merchandising machine and its millions of Partridge products. The jacket was full color, front and back, with

when we're singin'

a fold-down flap as the cover. The album theme was the perfect tie-in to what was going on with the young shoppers' frenzy. Fans needed a shopping bag for all their Partridge Family memorabilia, right? So Bell Records, along with the creative minds at the Music Agency, thought up this clever package design, complete with a plastic shopping bag inserted inside the album cover. It was a great way to keep the records connected to the merchandising. But the bigger question remained: Was the image itself beginning to overshadow the music?

Just as the image of David Cassidy couldn't be torn down even by Cassidy himself, the image of the Partridge Family was by this time possibly a stronger sell than the actual music. Proving this point, Mike Melvoin said of *Shopping Bag*, "I don't remember the inception, but I remember the packaging being one of the most clever things I'd seen."

The U.K. version sported handles at the top of the album so fans could carry it like a real shopping bag. With Cassidy's star rising in England, the mania had only just begun over there. *The Partridge Family* had been canceled by the BBC in December 1971 after airing only the initial 13 episodes, and fans went berserk. "More than 1000 irate teenage girls staged a march on the BBC-TV Centre on May 13 demanding the return of The Partridge Family TV series and its star David Cassidy," announced *Cash Box*. With more than 13,000 letters received by the BBC making the case for the show's return, fans made themselves heard. They loudly protested to bring the show back on, and though the BBC didn't pick it up, another station did. Meanwhile, "Could It Be Forever," Cassidy's second solo single, was breaking at No. 3 on the U.K. charts.

The first *Shopping Bag* single, "It's One of Those Nights (Yes, Love)" peaked at No. 20 on the *Billboard* charts. The second single, the high-energy "Am I Losing You," was the first Partridge Family single to stop short of the top 40 in *Billboard*, settling in at number 59. But the album as a whole sold well. "That was a huge seller," says Beverly Weinstein.

The sound and style heard on *Shopping Bag* are like a mirror reflection of its predecessor, *Sound Magazine*. The first three albums all had subtle changes and differences as the team continually refined the sound, but they seem to have found what they were looking for with *Sound Magazine*. Rather than experimenting further, they decided to lock it down and stay with it. *Shopping Bag* was an attempted twin. "I think by then we really knew what we were doing," says John Bahler. "Wes gave us the right songs, and we were able to give him the right performances, as was David. We were pretty much shut as far as what the sound had to be, and so we just did what we did."

If the Partridge Family had a formula, it included Mike Melvoin's easy-listening instrumental arrangements, David Cassidy's breathy vocals, Wes Farrell's pick of songs that fit both the show and the pop music charts, and, most notably, John

Bahler's background vocal arrangements that created the distinctive group sound. Bahler's arrangements included a lot of harmonic opening hooks, and Farrell loved them. The number of vocal intros went from three on *Sound Magazine* to seven on *Shopping Bag,* and remains at seven or more for the next two albums. This increase, along with an emphasis on background vocals, helps distinguish the Partridge sound from Cassidy's solo work. It is also a significant, if subtle, identifier of the differences in *Shopping Bag* from its predecessor.

John Bahler reflects, "All those vocal intros came out of nowhere. I have no idea where they came from, but they ended up being a signature for the group. As soon as people heard the intros for any of the songs, it was obviously Partridge Family, and that became the signature."

Shopping Bag starts off with a great song from Tommy Boyce and Bobby Hart. The well-established duo had contributed many songs for the Monkees, but they show up as a team for the Partridge Family only this once, with the well-crafted "Girl, You Make My Day."

Boyce and Hart had received their first big break from Wes Farrell in the early '60s. "Wes was great," begins Bobby Hart. "I met Wes in 1964. It was a break for me when we wrote 'Come a Little Bit Closer.' We were friends then, and we would be so until the day he died."

Hart recounts his first introduction to Farrell: "We got on an elevator at the 1650 Building—which was the other big music business building, across the street from the Brill Building on Penn Alley—and there was Wes. Tommy introduced us, and in the time it took us to get up to Wes' floor, Wes said 'You guys have anything for Chubby Checker? I'm going out to Philly on Thursday to play him some songs.' So we pushed the down button and went back to my little room and we wrote a song for Chubby. We brought it back to Wes, then he took it to Chubby and that's the song he picked for his next single. That was our first Tommy Boyce and Bobby Hart single, of about 40 singles."

One of them was the smash hit "Come a Little Bit Closer" by Jay & the Americans.

"Tommy signed with Screen Gems/Columbia music near the end of '65 and I came over near the beginning of '66. We became pretty much exclusive writers, in the sense that he and I wrote only with each other. That lasted from '65 till the end of the decade, and I found myself without a writing partner at the beginning of the '70s.

"After Tommy and I had finished the Monkees, they asked us to move on to the Partridge Family, but Tommy had decided to quit the business at the end of '69 so we walked away from our deal as contract writers at Screen Gems. Tommy and I basically stopped working exclusively together as writers and decided not to do any of the projects Screen Gems had offered us."

when we're singin'

Hart says, "In early 1970 Wes landed the project to produce the Partridge Family. Wes was always a fun guy to be with, fun to write with, fun to hang out with. We were good friends with Wes, and we had written with him on not only 'Come a Little Bit Closer' but probably a dozen or so others back in those days, before we got our Screen Gems deal.

"Around that time, I got a call from a guy named Danny Janssen, who was having success with a string of hits by Bobby Sherman. Danny was doing a lot of cartoon work for Hanna-Barbara, so he called me up and said he was doing this show called *Josie and the Pussycats* and also *Scooby-Doo,* and wanted to know if I'd like to co-write with him on some of those songs. Danny and I started writing and hit it off, and a couple of writing sessions into it Danny said to me, 'Well, I've got all these great singers that do the cartoon vocals. One in particular is a guy named Austin Roberts.' So Danny said, 'He's got a great voice, and he sang on records just as buyouts and with other group names and so on—they had hits. I'd like to write some stuff for him, so if you're into it you and I can write and produce some stuff, and then maybe take it to Wes.'

"So that's what we did, and we had a top 10 hit with Austin called 'Something's Wrong with Me.' After that Wes kept Danny and me busy writing during the first half of the '70s, and we would give him the publishing—and in return, he would keep us busy in the studio with production work. We produced a whole bunch of people for Wes, and wrote a bunch of songs for Wes."

Wes Farrell was getting busier than ever as his own musical star rose. He launched Chelsea Records in January 1972, at the same time he was producing *Shopping Bag*. The umbrella company known as the Wes Farrell Organization was now at the forefront of the music industry, and Farrell was cranking out music at the speed of a blender.

"Wes had writing cubicles, which were the rage for publishers in those days," says Hart. "He would have maybe three or four rooms of pianos, and he'd have people writing in each room. He'd go from room to room for a few minutes and stop in each cubicle and get his name on all the songs that were written at that time," Hart chuckles. "He would do four rooms at once sometimes. He was working them pretty good. I don't want to make it sound like he didn't contribute, because in our cases he contributed to whatever his name was on, but there were those momentary visits—five minutes in one room, then on to the next."

It's plausible to say that the pace at which these guys were working wore on the originality of the songwriting to some degree, but their tight crafting and expertise are always solidly evident. "Hell on wheels" is how Mike Melvoin describes meeting the deadlines for the Partridge Family albums.

In his interview with Ken Sharp, Farrell spoke of collaborating with Tony Romeo on three songs that ended up on *Shopping Bag*. "I think when you get thrown into commitment and demands tied to the insurmountable pressures of having to deliver, deliver, deliver—what happens when you end up doing a project like this—is that there are a great many demands that have to be met. Tony had his approach and I had mine. Mine was a lot more compulsive, at least in terms of *write 'em, get 'em done*. Tony would exhaust himself on an idea until he had it exactly to the point where it was to his liking, and I guess we started collaborating moreso when we moved forward, in order to elevate the process."

"Bobby was like a fix-it man," says Danny Janssen of his co-writer Bobby Hart. "He could take a top 20-er and turn it into a top 5-er—he was that good." Hart could deliver high-quality songwriting very quickly, and he had studied with piercing focus just how to do that. "Tommy and I were basically short-order cooks who tried to write for whoever was coming up, and write what we thought was commercial," Hart says. "Some of it holds up, some of it doesn't. Some of it just sounds like it's very manufactured and trite. Sometimes the songs were done justice, and sometimes the production was better than the songs."

If the launch of Chelsea Records wasn't enough to put Farrell into overdrive, *The Partridge Family Shopping Bag* was coming out just after the release of *Cherish*. "We were starting to do David Cassidy records," he told Ken Sharp. "So there was not a conflict, but there were now two artists involved—in the same voice," he laughed. "If you think that was easy, man, let me tell you!"

Had Cassidy recorded under a different producer for his solo albums, perhaps he may have had a sound that was more distinct from the Partridge Family recordings, but it's questionable whether fans would have accepted it, especially so early in his recording career.

Farrell felt strongly that any effort to mix it up, change the direction, or experiment outside the established image was simply too much too soon for the fan base. He was careful not to test the innocence of the young and extremely loyal Partridge Family fans. *Shopping Bag* was delivered to fans with the same ferocity with which Bell Records had marketed the previous albums. It was released in March 1972 and entered the *Billboard* chart on March 25. It stayed for 17 weeks, through June 17, peaking at No. 18. Even without the chart longevity of the earlier albums, it was a smash hit, becoming the fifth gold record album in a row for the Partridge Family.

Girl, You Make My Day, 3:11, Tommy Boyce–Bobby Hart

When Tommy Boyce became disillusioned with the business and decided to quit in 1969, the departure turned out to be only a brief hiatus. He dropped by one day in 1970 and soon joined the new team.

Of "Girl, You Make My Day," Hart says, "This is a song we wrote near the end of our tenure at Screen Gems. We had already written it back in '69 and we just pulled it back out. It was Tommy's thought that this was something David could do a good job with. So we pitched it to Wes.

"There was a weekend of concerts Tommy and I did in Alabama in '69, and Screen Gems was developing Tommy and me for our own sitcom at that point. They sent a camera crew along with us for that weekend. As we're flying to Birmingham, sitting on the plane, Tommy pulls out his guitar and starts singing 'New York Mining Disaster 1941' by the Bee Gees. I'm harmonizing with him, sitting next to him, and then suddenly he morphs into 'Girl You Make My Day' at the same beat." All of this was taped on the plane that day.

"I was reviewing some of the tapes recently and this song really sounds good! I mean it's rough, because it's just a recorder and there's the sound of the plane in the background. But it had a lot of energy, and I really loved the changes and the way he was singing it. That's the version I always remembered." The Partridge Family arrangement, with its harpsichord, was different from both the original version and the altered Tommy Boyce version from the plane.

"Tommy, with just his acoustic guitar, was much more of a driving kind of a thing," says Hart, "especially that time on the plane. I think that it had a certain energy. I think I remember it more for what it could have been rather than for what it ended up being. I think it could've been a single if they'd spent more time on it in the studio. Actually, it's probably my favorite of the Partridge Family songs that my name is on."

The song was prominently featured on the season 3 location episode "I Left My Heart in Cincinnati," shot at King's Island amusement park in Cincinnati, Ohio. Hart never knew it was used on that episode, and he waxed nostalgic for a moment. "I played there!" he says. "At the end of the first half of the '70s, Danny and I stopped writing together and I started working again with Tommy, Davy Jones, and Micky Dolenz of the Monkees. We toured for two years as Dolenz, Jones, Boyce, and Hart, and we played every amusement park known to man, I think!" He laughs. "We played King's Island!"

Appears On: Season 3, episode 66, "I Left My Heart in Cincinnati" (January 26, 1973)
Favorite Partridge Family song of Bobby Hart

***Every Little Bit O' You**, 3:02, Irwin Levine–L. Russell Brown*

A little variation of sound is going on in this track, with an electric piano opening lick and a little fuzz guitar on the bridge toward the end. The fade-out is interesting, with a doubling up of downbeats at the end of the song.

"'Every Little Bit O' You' is probably my favorite Partridge Family Levine and Brown song," says L. Russell Brown. "This is another song of ours that I thought could have been a top 10 single. We felt it had that magic. And it played well to the girl in the front row. It was a song that had that universal message, talking to every girl who had her heart set on David Cassidy. I just thought it was the most interesting song. It is one of our best melodies, along with an enduring lyric that holds up today.

Brown continues, "A lot of politics were involved with what songs were cut and what songs were made into singles. The ownership of the music publishing played a major role in those decisions. One other interesting tidbit is that Irwin Levine enjoyed using interesting words in a title to make the title stand out—'Every Little Bit O' You,' 'Tie a Yellow Ribbon Round the *Ole* Oak Tree ….'"

Appears On: Season 2, episode 36, "I Can Get It for You Retail" (November 26, 1971)

Something New Got Old, 2:54, Wes Farrell–Bobby Hart

This is the songwriting debut from Wes Farrell and Bobby Hart, and the result is pure pop formula, with an early-'70s sound that includes a flute solo. Otherwise it's more classic guitar, piano, and strings—Farrell's version of Phil Spector's "wall of sound," complete with lush harmonies from Bahler and the other singers.

"I remember very little," says Hart of his Partridge Family songwriting credits. "It was a factory of turning out songs during those years. Danny and I averaged 50 songs a year that we were writing and producing. Almost every one of them was recorded. So it was a really busy time, writing about one song a week and producing in the studio from ten to five, five days a week, for almost that whole period as well."

Appears On: Season 3, episode 56, "The Mod Father" (October 27, 1972)

Am I Losing You, 2:22, Irwin Levine–L. Russell Brown

"We wrote this song because we were trying to write a follow-up to 'I Woke Up in Love This Morning,'" says L. Russell Brown. "One premise Levine and I constantly always kept in mind when writing a song for David was that we should always have a lyric he could sing to the girls in the first row of the audience."

This energetic pop song is played at a faster tempo than usual. Guitar, tambourines, and banjo make up the opening hook, and light traces of harpsichord can be heard throughout. It is somewhat reflective of the material Levine and Brown wrote for Tony Orlando and Dawn. "Sweet Gypsy Rose" comes to mind, with a similar old-fashioned sound. Even though this song was chosen for single release, it marks the Partridge Family's downslide on the *Billboard* charts.

Brown was never happy with the title. "I had my regrets about using that title because there were so many hit songs—especially some big country songs—called 'Am I Losing You.' The problem with it, is when the song gets played [on radio] it's difficult to log it properly because there are so many different songs with the same name by so many different writers."

when we're singin'

This was the last commercially released Partridge song written by Levine and Brown. Their songs appeared only on two Partridge Family albums—*Sound Magazine* and *Shopping Bag*. Their contract with Farrell expired and they moved on to publishing their own songs. This meant that even more pressure would be put on the Partridge Family songwriting mainstays of Farrell, Hart, and Janssen.

Appears On: Season 3, episode 55 "You're Only Young Twice" (October 20, 1972); Season 3, episode 60 "Whatever Happened To Keith Partridge?" (November 24, 1972)

Last Night, 2:43, Tony Romeo–Wes Farrell

This is Tony Romeo's first appearance as part of a songwriting team and the first of his three collaborations with Wes Farrell that appear on the album. Even Farrell was beginning to feel overwhelmed at this point; when Ken Sharp asked him about his memory of this particular song he said, "I think we started to rush the process a bit by then."

Romeo said, "Wes had a God-given killer instinct for catchy hooks—'Hang On Sloopy,' 'Come a Little Bit Closer.' This wasn't one of them, but it worked for me. I built a frame around it, set the lyric, and together we polished off the edges. My tendency was to write more on the serious side—ironic, considering my biggest successes were frantic. Collaboration was a welcome relief now and then. I knew I'd get to satisfy my own creative aims on David Cassidy's solo albums with songs like 'I Am a Clown' from the *Cherish* LP or 'Sing Me' from *Dreams Are Nuthin' More Than Wishes*—two of my favorites."

Appears On: Season 2, episode 44 "My Heart Belongs To a Two-Car Garage" (February 4, 1972)

It's All in Your Mind, 2:21, Peggy Clinger–Johnny Cymbal

As announced in the March 1972 issue of *Tiger Beat's Official Partridge Family Magazine*, the song was originally planned for David Cassidy's solo album *Cherish*. The lyrics are printed in the magazine along with those of the other tracks planned for the album, but Wes Farrell decided at the last minute it would make a better Partridge Family song.

This is the first Partridge Family song from the Clinger–Cymbal camp. Johnny Cymbal and Peggy Clinger were not only a songwriting team but also a couple. They were signed to Wes Farrell's Chelsea Records and recorded an album of their own with Chelsea that included a cover of "Rock Me Baby." But Cymbal always considered himself a songwriter first.

This is another great pop song, for sure. We get some harpsichord and piano; by now a lot of songs are sounding similar. Brass is more prominent and there are some short bursts of trumpet, somewhat unusual for a pop song.

Appears On: Season 3, episode 53 "Each Dawn I Diet" (October 6, 1972)

Hello, Hello, 3:57, Tony Romeo–Wes Farrell

There are some who consider "Hello, Hello" the worst song in the entire Partridge Family catalog. But even if it doesn't work, no one can deny that it's an unusual and risky cut—and maybe a little more risk is what the album needed. John Bahler continually describes Tony Romeo's songs as out-of-the-box and unlike any other songwriter's work, and Romeo achieves that unique quality on this second Romeo–Farrell pairing.

A Dixieland opening interlude with a tuba solo makes up the opening sequence of the song. It runs about 38 seconds and fades out almost entirely before the next part of the song actually begins—a style that had not been tried before. Muted trumpets and strings throughout demonstrate that a lot is happening here. There's even a wood block. The execution ends up merging pop with Dixieland.

There is a noticeable difference between the TV and album versions of the song. The album version omits the "answer back" second echo effect from the opening and mutes the background vocals. The version used on the show does not include the opening tuba passage.

Romeo spares no feelings for his thoughts on this one. "I must apologize for my part in this, whatever it may have been," he told Ken Sharp. "Doesn't work for me. Maybe the Hotbox Girls from *Guys and Dolls* could have pulled it off. I sure don't think any of us did. A dog."

Wes Farrell felt differently. "I love it!" he exclaimed. "I really like that song! That was a song that had a lot of happiness in it. I had churned that melody for some time and had tried to write it in a lot of different ways and just never got it nailed down. Tony grabbed onto it and finished it. Collaboration is exactly what was needed. It's two efforts combined to make one element from them."

Love it or hate it, "Hello, Hello" opens side B of the album. On the show, it was performed in a live concert setting with a large-screen video of Keith's home movie playing in the background. It fits well for the episode, in which Keith's first attempt at filmmaking is mostly left on the cutting room floor, leaving only happy faces waving at the camera.

Appears On: Season 2, episode 41 "Fellini, Bergman, and Partridge" (January 14, 1972)

There'll Come a Time, 2:49, David Cassidy

For the last of his three offerings as songwriter for his TV family, David Cassidy gives us the best. An autobiographical plea for acceptance, this song showcases a prominent lead vocal by Cassidy. He belts it out with full expression of feeling, capturing the angst and trappings of the height of his mind-blowing fame and pleading for his fans to let him be just a normal guy. Cassidy would struggle with this in the years to come while wrestling with the talent that made him famous in the first place.

when we're singin'

This emotionally charged song is a standout on the album and a missed opportunity for a single.

"At the time I was a very sad and lonely guy," Cassidy told Ken Sharp. "And there was a part of me that would write stuff, and sometimes it would be music and sometimes it would be writing lyrics.

"When I say I was lonely, it wasn't like I couldn't get a date," he laughs. "I was just isolated, and that sadness is reflected in 'There'll Come a Time.' I wasn't a happy-go-lucky guy. I was working 18 hours a day, seven days a week, for five continuous years. You'd be a happier guy if you got a day off. With this song, it was me speaking to the world and my fans about who I really was, as opposed to them perceiving me as my character on TV. I know that a lot of my true fans knew a lot more about me, but the general public just thought 'Well, he's that guy on *The Partridge Family*.' That was their general perception. This song was me speaking to the general public and to my fans, saying 'You have no idea how empty and lonely I feel.'"

Appears On: Season 3, episode 72 "The Selling of the Partridges"
(March 16, 1973)

If You Ever Go, 3:21, Wes Farrell–Tony Romeo

The third of the Farrell–Romeo songs, this pleasant little ditty offers a catchy use of the upbeat and builds well to the chorus. While Farrell remembered very little about this song, Romeo certainly recalled it. "This was a matter of two writers each having half a song that got wedded into one," he said. "We worked it up together, polished off the lyrics and smiled a whole lot. Came close to being a single. Ended up a B-side."

Appears On: Season 2, episode 43, "I Am Curious Partridge"
(January 28, 1972)

Every Song Is You, 3:32, Terry Cashman–Tommy West

Another Farrell-ized production number, "Every Song Is You" contains an homage to an earlier work of its creators hidden in the lyrics, much like an Alfred Hitchcock appearance in one of his own movies.

Both Cashman and West were at the initial viewing of the *Partridge Family* pilot that Wes Farrell organized in early 1970 when he was looking for songwriters. Farrell asked everyone at the viewing to come up with a proposed song for the show's theme, and Cashman and West's offering was titled "Six Man Song Band." Farrell ended up using his own song, "When We're Singin.'" Cashman and West really liked "Six Man Song Band" and felt it was a real miss for the Partridge Family, so when it was passed up, they recorded it themselves and put it onto their album titled *A Song or Two*, released in 1972 on the Dunhill label. As an homage to the lost *Partridge*

Family theme song, the title appears here in the second verse: *"singin' man with a six piece song band, answer to my dreams."*

"Every Song Is You" was written as a David Cassidy love song. The arrangement is heavy with piano, strings, and flute. It's a beautiful up-tempo ballad with Cassidy's voice at the forefront.

Appears On: Season 2, episode 42, "Waiting For Bolero" (January 21, 1972)

It's One of Those Nights (Yes, Love), 3:24, Tony Romeo

Tony Romeo writes solo again, and the result speaks for itself. This is a lovely ballad with visual lyrics delivered rapidly, one thought after another. *Cash Box* reviewed: "America's first musical family follows up 'I Woke Up in Love This Morning' with this Nilsson-influenced ballad—and again, some more gold for their pear tree of hits." The delivery is intimate, with Cassidy's vocal complemented by quintessential John Bahler harmonies and a perfect Mike Melvoin arrangement.

In layered steps, the song describes love and pain, showcasing the chemistry of all the artists—musicians, singers, songwriters, and arrangers—who went uncredited for their work as the fictional Partridge Family garage band. This deep connection reveals itself again with this masterful production number. Cassidy sings it like he wrote it.

Tony Romeo elaborated with fondness. "A sentimental favorite for all of us at the time. I remember being in the studio late at night, sitting around listening to the umpteenth playback after the session. 'Don't you wish it would be as big as 'I Think I Love You?' David said. His voice was foggy, exhausted from an impossible schedule. I could never expect anything to be that big, but I knew how he felt. It represented a kind of peak for my involvement in the project. It was my 16th Partridge–David Cassidy cut. Sweet 16.

"'It's One of Those Nights' made us all glad to be part of one of the hottest groups in the business and the most popular teen idol on the planet. The record came out around Christmastime. I guess the season's spirit was indistinguishable from the glow we felt for a time in our lives we recognized as special. Even the promotion and sales crew at Bell Records were smitten by this one. Dave Carrico called me up and said the entire workhorse gang wanted to take me out for this lavish gratitude bash. These guys were the best in the business—Dave, Steve Wax, John Rosica—all had as much to do with the success of all Bell Records artists as any song, singer, or producer you could name. It was a great honor."

"This may be my favorite Partridge Family song," says Ken Jacobson. "I love it! I love it because it's so typically Tony. It's unpretentious and it's like a conversation instead of a lyric, you know? It's terrific for that song. That song was actually bigger in England than it ever got to be here." It peaked at No. 11 in England.

"It's One of Those Nights (Yes, Love)" was released as a single in December 1971, entering the *Billboard* charts at No. 57 on December 18, only seven days before

when we're singin'

Christmas. It stayed on the charts for eight weeks, peaking at No. 20 on January 22 of the new year, and fell off the charts after February 5.

Appears On: Season 2, episode 47 "The Partridge Papers" (March 3, 1972)
Favorite Partridge Family song of Ken Jacobson

Album Summary and Reviews

Total running time: 31:26
Original Release: March 1972, Bell 6072

America's favorite family is here again with another LP performance sure to go right to the top. Produced by Wes Farrell and backed by some of the finest session musicians in the business, this dynamite package will move over the counter with speed and fervor. Includes their last hit "It's One of Those Nights," their current single "Am I Losing You," "There'll Come a Time" (penned by Cassidy) and a beautiful ballad "Every Song Is You." *Billboard, March 25, 1972*

Actually it's a record. (But the shopping bag comes with it.) And it takes approximately one listen to know that the tube's first family has done it again—concocted still another smooth blend of uptempo type tunes, seasoning it with a proven chart winner, "It's One of Those Nights (Yes Love)," and their newest single, "Am I Losing You." David Cassidy, who has recently blossomed into a formidable solo artist, shares the vocal honors with Shirley Jones as per usual. It all adds up to another sure fire winner for this ensemble. *Cash Box, March 18, 1972*

A spinoff of the "Partridge Family" TV show, David Cassidy has become one of the hot disk properties on the current scene. In this set, Cassidy gets no special billing, but he's the star of the session with lead vocalizing of a group of bouncy ballads. It's well-produced bubblegum music with an easy rhythm and straightforward lyrics, highlighted by "Girl, You Make My Day," "Last Night," "Hello, Hello" and "Every Song Is You." *Variety, April 12, 1972*

*First Chart Appearance: March 25, 1972 (*Billboard, *No. 172;* Cash Box, *No. 68;* Record World, *No. 49)*

KEEPING UP IS HARD TO DO
or ... The Partridge Family at Home with Their Greatest Hits

A Real TV Family

While the musicians and background vocalists were all working closely together like a musical family, the cast and production team were equally close, lifting each other up and developing personal relationships that have lasted a lifetime. That kind of rapport happens only when the guy at the top does his job right. In this instance, executive producer Bob Claver was that guy.

Claver came to the show with a strong background in producing family shows and shows for children, having started his career on *Captain Kangaroo*. He was a respected Hollywood producer both inside and outside the entertainment industry. In fact, President Richard Nixon invited him to the White House only months before *The Partridge Family* began airing as part of his proposed war on drugs. Claver had done a few cause-oriented shows on *Here Come the Brides* and, though not a Nixon supporter, was happy to be part of the meeting.

Of all his co-workers on the set, Claver says he felt the closest to Shirley Jones. "You've got to remember most all of the actors were very young except Dave Madden," says Claver, "and I liked Dave, but I liked Shirley, too. Shirley understood the word grown-up. She knew if something was ever really bugging her, which was very rare, that I would change it. That woman asked for nothing. She was always on time. She made the whole thing go easy, and everybody had a sense of humor on the show. When you're going to work, that makes such a difference. It was a pretty good deal on that show. It was a very peaceful place and a very easy show to do from the standpoint of personalities. We didn't have arguments and fights. *I don't like my part* and *I don't like my dress*—we didn't have any of that."

Shirley Jones was equally fond of Claver. She recalls, "The show began with a Monday morning reading. Then we would start shooting on Tuesday and go through Friday. When David became so popular he was out doing concerts all weekend and sometimes he wouldn't show up for the reading or he'd show up late, and I wouldn't have that. Everyone was so excited about David, you know? They wanted him, and so nobody would say a word to him. So I went to Bob Claver and I said, 'If you don't talk to him, I'm going to, because I won't have this. There are other people waiting for him. We have a show to do. I know he has concerts, and I know he's a big star now, but we still have a show to do.' He said, 'Shirley, you're absolutely right.' Bob was always in tune with everything that the actors needed and wanted. Sometimes producers are not. They go along with what the studio says. They go along with what the director says. But he really had great empathy for the actor, and it was so wonderful for all of us because if there was a problem I could go to Bob and he would deal with it. I had great respect for him. He was one of the best producers I've ever worked with."

The unity of the cast and production team was something everyone enjoyed during the run of the show. Jones' marriage to Jack Cassidy was difficult during these years, and the producers, who were all friends of hers, lent support on several occasions. "Every once in a while I'd do a stand-in part when she needed somebody to go to some kind of event or something. It was that part of her life, her relationship with Jack that was a little up and down. I was married at the time, and my wife liked Shirley, too," Claver says. Just before the start of the third season, Jones announced that she and Jack Cassidy were entering into a trial separation.

Producer Larry Rosen was also very close with Jones. They were around the same age and were social peers as well as co-workers. Rosen respected her in the same way as Claver and also had a special closeness with her.

Jones was the respected matriarch off set as well as on. She cared about the younger actors on the show and she displayed her affection by watching out for them and teaching them how to conduct themselves in the world of show business. "She set a standard for the show," says Rosen. "She was always on time, always on her mark, and always knew her lines. Rarely did you have to do take two with Shirley. That set the model for everybody. They had to meet that standard, and they did."

"Shirley is good old working stock," says Brian Forster. "She feels like you owe it to the fans because you make a living off of this."

Suzanne Crough says, "Back then, growing up around Shirley, you have that whole Hollywood flair to it. You have class about yourself. You go about yourself the right way. You grow up learning that everything comes with the job.

"I remember this kid asking me for my autograph. This boy was a couple years older than me. So I signed an autograph to him, and he ripped it up right there and said to me, 'Why would you think I want your autograph?' That's just one story of many, but the point is, back then, you didn't say anything to them. Your feelings are kind of hurt, but you don't pop them in the face because in old Hollywood you don't talk back. You just keep your mouth shut and move on.

"As far as acting goes I still have the same belief that if you're going to do the business, you're going to do the time. Which means don't give me all this crap about how you don't want to sign autographs, and you don't want to be out there in the public.

It's part of the job. I still have the true belief that as long as the fan is not obnoxious or being unruly, then it's part of your job to have your dinner interrupted, or have your fun time or family time interrupted to sign an autograph."

"We would have talks a lot," Jones says about her relationship with the younger actors. That was especially true of David Cassidy. Cassidy's relationship with his stepmother grew strong during the years of *The Partridge Family*. His father was a troubled man whose personal demons affected the lives of everyone around him. During these years, David spent most of his time trying to get Jack's approval, only to find that his father was jealous of his success. David's youth and the pressures of fame made it hard for him to see things clearly.

"David and I had the same manager," begins Jones. "She was a woman by the name of Ruth Aarons. I have to say she was brilliant. I think she had a great deal of influence with David. He had great respect for her. For a while he was very influenced by his father, but they became estranged. His mother didn't have much influence on him at all. He'll say to you that during the Partridge Family years I had an influence on him, too. 'You helped me so much during that time,' he has said to me. So I think it was a combination of influences for David, you know?"

When the series started, Cassidy lived in a modestly furnished home in Laurel Canyon with his best friend, Sam Hymen. Their lifestyle was bare bones, with mattresses on the floor and few material goods. Once the show hit, fans discovered where he was living and began following him to both the studio and his home. He and Sam moved to a house off Sunset Plaza Drive in Hollywood Hills, but again the fans were constantly at his doorstep. In 1971 they moved again, and this time bought a house in Encino that became a nice escape for him, a retreat of sorts. Even though the fans were still able to track him down, a security system kept them at a distance.

The Partridge Family created a kind of double life for Cassidy. As different as his own personality was from his character's, he was aware that children were looking up to him. He had a long, troubling time dealing with the image that was, by now, glued onto his real persona. The music and the teen idol status defined *The Partridge Family* as different from any other show that had come before or after it, and it was that element of the show that also helped bring the hysteria of the young girls who followed Cassidy around.

On weekends he became a rock star, complete with roadies, groupies, and plenty of sex. Then on Monday he would return to the controlled environment of the set. The two worlds were extremely different, and hopping back and forth between them affected Cassidy immensely. He enjoyed his work on the show and never showed any signs of ego with the other actors.

Cassidy liked photography, as did Dave Madden, and they would tinker with cameras together during down time on the set. Madden was a comedian and a lot of fun, and he and Cassidy would often become caught up in laughter during filming, getting slap-happy from time to time. "David was a lot of fun," says Brian Forster. "Off camera we used to do a lot of joking around and he was always in pretty good spirits. I think toward the end they were kind of driving him on that concert tour, and he would drag in on Mondays, not being quite as lighthearted as he had been."

Cassidy developed a close relationship with Susan Dey as well. She was close to him in age and became his number one confidant and a sort of real-life sister with whom he would share stories of being out on the road. They provided support for one another and valued each other like real-life siblings.

"*The Partridge Family* was the first thing Susan Dey ever did," recalls Jones. "She was 17 years old and she had been a model in New York. She was a beautiful girl. Just beautiful. She and I talked girl talk a lot." Dey was shy but quickly made friends and built a support base. Dey initially roomed with two other girls who worked for Screen Gems—Sally Powers and Shelley Ellison. Ellison worked for Renee Valente as one of the casting directors on the show. "She was the sweetest girl you could ever imagine," recalls Ellison. "It didn't take her long to get herself set up. She was fun. She was exactly what you saw in the Partridge Family— she was a sweet girl who could've come right from the Midwest. She was more mature in real life. She grew up to be a lovely woman—a really lovely woman."

Dey, like everyone, had her personal troubles. She had been a model and had grown accustomed to dieting. At one point Cassidy and Jones were both aware that she wasn't eating much of anything but carrots for lunch. Jones spoke with her about it out of concern. "She got better as time went on," she says. Dey has since acknowledged that she had an eating disorder during the Partridge Family years and for many years after. In 1993 she told *Woman's Day,* "An eating disorder is nothing to be ashamed of. But it's not until you stop hiding it that you can really start getting well." Coming forward about it helped a lot of young girls with the same issues tackle their own problems with eating disorders.

She had many men interested in her, but like Cassidy, experienced a lot of loneliness during her newfound television fame. Eventually she dated script story editor Dale McRaven long-term during the run of the show. "They were an item when I got on the show," says Brian Forster. "He was very much a hippie of that era—the long hair, the beard, flashing peace signs, that kind of thing—and here he is dating America's sweetheart. They were an interesting couple."

Dey impressed the producers with her talent very quickly. "We wrote Laurie as smart, and Susan was smart. I liked the whole concept of that," says Bob Claver. "Smart people are more fun. They say funnier things. They do funnier things. Susan's pretty and all that, but being able to be funny is the territory of the bright. It's hard to do." By all accounts, Claver felt Dey grew as an actor more than anyone else on the show.

"Susan was just this young, fresh, wonderful spirit on the set," reminisces producer Paul Witt. "And I only worked the first year, but she was very easy to work with. She was learning very, very quickly, and I liked working with her."

"We had a standing order on the set for any guest director that, in any scene that Susan Dey was in, she would get a close-up, whether she had a line or not," says producer Larry Rosen. "She got a single close-up in every scene that she did because she was so good. You could always cut to Susan and get these wonderful eye rolls or facial expressions, especially when David was on. Her takes were just wonderful. We knew she was so good that we didn't want to miss an opportunity to be able to cut to her and accentuate a joke, or a moment in the show. We cut to her for everything."

Claver adds, "Here was a woman with no background, no experience, nothing, and we used her, believe it or not, because we couldn't find anybody in Los Angeles. Paul Witt went to New York and found her, and we took a chance with her. When I look at all those silent reactions of hers, which are really tough, I'm impressed. She was wonderful in that series."

The youngest actors spent four crucial years growing up on the set of *The Partridge Family*. Danny Bonaduce expresses gratitude for his role, and is quick to participate and pay tribute to the show in any way he can. "None of us, with the possible exception of Shirley, would be doing what we're doing now without *The Partridge Family*. I wouldn't be on the radio and I wouldn't be doing this interview if I hadn't been the guy on *The Partridge Family*. None of this happens without *The Partridge Family*, so I don't have anything but the fondest memories of it, and that's why I would do a reunion anytime."

"Danny was a very bright and intuitive young boy," says Rosen. "He was also very troubled. He didn't have the best home life. When we wrapped the show at the end of the season, he would cry. He was so depressed because he had to go home for three to four months, when the family that he loved was the Partridge Family. He loved hanging on the set." Bonaduce has always been open about the troubles he had in his home life. He cites his Partridge Family ties as helping him get through. Shirley Jones, David Cassidy, and Dave Madden all did everything they could to help the young boy, with Jones and Madden taking Bonaduce home with them on many weekends. He got to know Jones' real-life sons, Shaun, Patrick, and Ryan, and spent a lot of time with them.

"I spent time talking with Danny, too, about his own family relationships," says Jones. "He had a terrible family. I would bring him to my house on weekends to stay with me and play with my kids, you know. Dave Madden was also wonderful that way. He would take Danny in, too. He would take him for a weekend and then I'd take him the next weekend, and so forth.

when we're singin'

"I certainly didn't care for my dad," says Bonaduce. "And David didn't care for my dad either, and said so. I mean David was really tired of watching me come to work and have to spend an extra hour in makeup to cover my black eyes."

Dave Madden felt a strong fatherly connection to Bonaduce. At that point Madden had no children of his own, and his character's on-screen relationship with Danny Partridge had become a comic centerpiece of the show. When asked what it was that especially connected him with Dave Madden, Bonaduce very quickly responded, "The fact that *he* wanted to be connected to *me*. The fact that I was having a difficult home life was something he was well aware of. Everybody was well aware of it. There was no missing it." Bonaduce grew very close with Madden. "I just started spending all weekends of the summer at his beach house, and even on work nights, he would say, 'You know what? I live closer. Why doesn't he go home with me and we'll bring him to work in the morning?' He was very funny, very nice, a tad mischievous."

"I remember one time he said, 'You know how you got this job, Danny?' I'm 10 years old, right? I said, 'No. How?' He goes, ''Cause you're ugly!' I said, 'WHAT?' He said, 'Look at Shirley. Look at Susan. Look at David. Look at the two adorable kids, and then look at you. Nobody would believe a family that adorable, so they needed some ugly. And they hired you.' But even at 10 years old you know when a guy is kidding. Even a 10-year-old would know that an adult is not really calling you ugly to your face and meaning it. I knew he was kidding! Although I look back at the tapes and I think there's no way we would ever be a family. Dude, I *was* ugly!

"Dave was playful, and he spent time with me. I hate the expression *need to talk,* because I never needed to talk. More often than not I needed a reason to hide, and Dave Madden's dressing room was always open, and I'd go in there. Dave and I were probably the closest on the set of *The Partridge Family*." Madden stayed in close touch, emailing Bonaduce daily up to the time of the older actor's death in 2014.

Bonaduce badgered Cassidy relentlessly, challenging and pestering him like a real-life little brother. Larry Rosen remembers there was always a competitive edge toward Cassidy, but the relationship between the two of them has been a lasting one. "David Cassidy was a godlike figure to me. He was to be worshipped from a distance. David's work schedule was grueling. David would come in exhausted, and everybody knew it was in their best interest to stay out of David's way. Luckily, even at 10, I understood. I understood that we have to have a song every Monday that matches some sort of theme of the show. Somebody had to write it. Somebody had to record it. I was working till I was so tired I couldn't move, which means David Cassidy is going to the studio after the show to record these songs, and then on the weekends, he's actually paying his bills by playing Madison Square Garden. It must have been tortuous for him." Bonaduce's relationships with the other cast members remain important to him. "Shirley Jones is a sweet, sweet woman, but her word was also law," he said of his TV mom on the set. "Susan Dey and I were fairly close, too. Everybody was fairly close."

Brian Forster and Suzanne Crough were very young at the time. Forster came from a show-business family, and his mother was very involved in everything he did, having worked as an actress herself. Crough, while her show-biz roots were not as deep, came from a large, well-adjusted family. Her parents taught her to be grounded and disciplined, with middle-class values that were to be upheld regardless of fame. With little to do on most episodes, both Forster and Crough spent most of their free time on the set riding their bikes around the back lot. They also had school lessons on set, which were held inside an old train car parked not far from the sound stage. In fact, many of the cast publicity shots were taken next to the train car.

Forster says he always felt a strong sense of connection with Shirley Jones. "Shirley was literally like our mom," he says. "She took us in, and she especially bonded with me. I think she really thought of me as her son in a lot of ways. She had three boys at that time who were all around my age. I think she kind of looked at me like *Since I'm not home, here's my son for today.*" He laughs. "Dave Madden was so much fun, too. He was a magician and he was a member of a club in Hollywood, a Magic Store, and he was always entertaining us. Danny and I alternated between him trying to kick my ass to other times where he was just sort of practical joking me. Suzanne and I were pretty close because we were the young ones, both in the same boat together."

Crough looked up to television sister Susan Dey, and through the years continued to feel the kinship that developed during those impressionable early years. "I think the last time I saw Susan she was doing *Mary Jane Harper Cried Last Night,* and I was probably 15 or so. At the same time she was doing that movie, the producer on that show was also the producer on a TV series I was on [*Mulligan's Stew,* 1977], and it was just a fluke that I actually ran into her. She was filming at a location down the street, and I came across the location one day, and it said *Susan Dey* on the door. We sat and visited for a while. Susan hadn't changed. I was just a little girl on the set of *The Partridge Family,* but I remember that she would come over to my family's house for dinner sometimes. We had a great relationship back then, and we had a great visit this particular day. To this day I still admire her." When asked what she would say to Dey if she had the chance, she spoke directly: "It's been a long time, Susan, and I think about you often. You were a great 'sister,' and I love you!"

Branching Out

Most of the cast managed to do a few other artistic things and make a few appearances on talk and variety shows during the four-year run of the show.

when we're singin'

Early in 1971 Shirley Jones was spotted as a presenter for both the Emmy Awards and Academy Awards. She guest starred on *The Bob Hope Show*, and the full cast of *The Partridge Family*, along with her real-life children and husband Jack Cassidy, were all part of a surprise tribute on *This is Your Life: Shirley Jones*. She also appeared that year on *The Jim Nabors Hour*, *The Pet Set*, and *The Glen Campbell Goodtime Hour*.

David Cassidy attended the Emmy Awards with Jones that year, and both of them were seen on the 13th Annual Grammy Awards as presenters and Best New Artist nominees (which the Partridge Family lost to the Carpenters). He also did two episodes of *The Glen Campbell Goodtime Hour*—the second with Jones and Susan Dey—and appeared as the featured guest on a Bob Hope special.

In 1972 Dey landed her first movie role, in *Skyjacked*, and appeared on *The Hollywood Squares* and *The Gloria Graham Show*—an early Oprah-esque talk show out of Chicago. In 1973 she did a made-for-TV thriller, *Terror on the Beach*, and a guest appearance on *Circle of Fear*, the short-lived anthology series originally titled *Ghost Story*, narrated by Sebastian Cabot.

Jones spread her wings a little bit in a made-for-TV movie, *The Girls of Huntington House*, which aired early in 1973 as an ABC Movie of the Week and co-starred a very young Sissy Spacek.

Danny Bonaduce was also working off the set of *The Partridge Family*. In 1972 he appeared on *Call Holme*, a proposed mystery-comedy series starring Arte Johnson, who had also guest-starred on *The Partridge Family*. Bonaduce showed up again on the made-for-TV movie *Invitation to a March*, adapted from the stage play. In 1973 both he and Dave Madden lent their voices to animation in the full-length animated movie *Charlotte's Web*.

Madden guest-starred on two episodes of *Love, American Style*, which was running on ABC at the same time as *The Partridge Family*. He also appeared in *The Girl Who Came Gift-Wrapped*, a 1974 made-for TV comedy starring Karen Valentine and Farrah Fawcett—who was still two years away from finding her own superstardom on *Charlie's Angels*.

Cassidy was considered for roles in the 1973 film version of *Jesus Christ Superstar* (as was Monkee Mickey Dolenz) and the 1974 made-for-TV movie *The Dove*, a dramatic romance starring Deborah Raffen and (in the role that did not go to Cassidy) Joseph Bottoms. His TV appearances during the years of *The Partridge Family* were mostly focused on music rather than acting.

The Partridge Family Neighborhood

The Partridges were residents of the fictional town of San Pueblo, California. The family's interior scenes were shot on soundstage 30 at the Columbia Ranch, known today as the Warner Ranch, with exteriors of the house and neighborhood shot nearby on the back lot.

The Columbia Ranch was the home of many great movie sets and television shows. It was a 40-acre plot of land purchased by the studio in 1934 to accommodate the studio's need for an expanded back lot. A very few soundstages were constructed for use at the back lot. *The Partridge Family* is one of the few shows to be shot on a soundstage there with the back lot exteriors within walking distance.

The Partridge Family house was built in 1953, a Cape Cod reportedly modeled after a plan by Sears, Roebuck & Co. It was first seen in 1955 in *Father Knows Best* and was Mrs. Elkins' house in *Dennis the Menace*. After some modification it was used in the mid-'60s for *Bewitched* as the home of Samantha Stevens' nosy neighbors, the Kravitzes. In fact, the first two years of *The Partridge Family* overlap with the last two years of *Bewitched,* so technically the Kravitzes and the Partridges were living together!

The house facade is located on the back lot's Blondie Street (named after the studio's serial based on the comic book character) along with others used in countless television shows and movies. The Blondie house itself neighbors the Partridge Family house on the right and is occasionally seen on the show. Had the family moved in to the neighborhood during the '60s, their next-door neighbors would have been Jeannie and Major Nelson of *I Dream of Jeannie*. The next house down was the home of Donna Reed *(The Donna Reed Show)*, and quick shots from the *Partridge Family* pilot suggest that the Partridges lived here for their first episode.

The home of Darren and Samantha Stevens on *Bewitched,* across the street, can be seen in many of *The Partridge Family*'s exterior shots. The original Deeds Mansion built for Frank Capra's film *Mr. Deeds Goes to Town* was used as the high school for Laurie and Keith Partridge.

During 1970, while the first season of shooting for *The Partridge Family* was underway, the Columbia Ranch suffered several devastating fires. The first happened on January 30, 1970, and destroyed 17 sets, including the Blondie House, totaling approximately $2 million in damages. Bobby Sherman's series *Here Come the Brides* was shooting at the time, and Sherman can be seen helping fight the fire in photos of the blaze—images that seem to predict his later career educating first responders. A reported quarter to a third of the ranch was lost. The Blondie house (located next door to the Partridge Family house) and other areas were reconstructed based on the original blueprints. It was reported that the fire began from the sun shining through a lamp, causing dry wood nearby to ignite.

The second fire, on April 9, 1970, destroyed as many as five sets—including those used for *The Partridge Family* and *The Young Rebels,* which had to be rebuilt. The fire's cause was deemed suspicious. On April 28 a third fire broke out on Columbia's Stage 4 and destroyed all the sets for *Bewitched.*

when we're singin'

In August yet another big fire broke out, this time completely destroying the Partridge Family home and the adjoining Corner Church. Both structures were rebuilt. Very few changes were made to the Partridge Family house, although detail-oriented viewers can pick them out. A tree that had been in the yard burned in the fire and is noticeably missing. The Corner Church was relocated back a bit and a small nondescript house put up next to the Partridge Family house. Five episodes of *The Partridge Family* had been shot before the fire destroyed the house.

By 1971, the Columbia Ranch had become a combined ranch with Warner in an attempt to combat budget issues caused from the fires. Just after the cancellation of the show in 1974, another fire struck the back lot and the studio lost more sets, causing them to finally sell off eight acres.

Other house facades on Blondie Street were used for shows including *Gidget, The Monkees,* and *The Flying Nun.* A gorgeous fountain that sits on one section of the back lot can also be seen in episodes of *The Partridge Family,* though it is most recognized today as the centerpiece for the opening theme of *Friends*.

The Partridge Family house was modified for use in *Scarecrow and Mrs. King* in 1983 and then put back to its original design. It was again remodeled with a blue paint scheme in 1989 for *Life Goes On*. In 1999, when Danny Bonaduce produced the TV special *Come On Get Happy: The Partridge Family Story,* the house was repainted to its Partridge yellow and the white picket fence, which had been gone for years was put back up. The house facade is still used by the studio. It was also the focus of a Lowe's commercial and can also be seen in exterior shots of current series including *The Middle,* set in the house next door. Despite its many uses, it's still most commonly known as the Partridge Family house.

Bus Stop ...

Wes Farrell: The Man with the Golden Ear

Wes Farrell was born on December 21, 1939, in New York City. With no college education, Farrell began his career working for music publishers. Like so many other songwriters of the day, he had writing space at the Brill Building during the 1960s. It was evident very early on that Farrell had a golden ear combined with an entrepreneurial business mind. He was frustrated working for someone else, and it was only a very short time before he set out on his own.

One of the other young songwriters also working at the Brill Building at the same time was the then-undiscovered Neil Diamond, who was strictly a songwriter then. Farrell was enamored with Diamond's talents, paying close attention to his writing style.

Jean Farrell, Wes' widow, recalls stories shared with her by Wes from his early years: "Wes was working for other publishers at that time. He left them and started out on his own because they wouldn't pay Neil Diamond $15 more a week, and Neil needed it for bus fare to get back and forth to Brooklyn. Talk about shortsighted! After that, Wes said he would never work for anybody again. It was the only time in his career that he ever had a job working for someone else. That's when he started his own publishing company. Wes signed Neil, paid him, and provided him with space to write."

Farrell named his new company Pocket Full of Tunes. "He would write songs and go around to the various record companies trying to tap them," says Jean, "and that's how the name of his company came about—because he had a pocket full of tunes for them!" Soon Farrell began to build a network of hopeful songwriters.

"He would bring in all of these artists and give them space to write," Jean Farrell continues. "Wes had an office but he couldn't afford to get a phone. So he came up with this idea to call the phone company and have a pay phone put in. The only phone in his first office was a pay phone!"

Wes Farrell wasted no time when he spotted talent. "You could be on the radio in two weeks," says Jean. "Wes would hire singers right off the street and book studio time. He never had time to rehearse them in the studio, so he'd rehearse them outside of the studio and then bring them in to the studio once the artist was rehearsed, and he'd pay them something like five dollars an hour. Then he'd shop the recordings around the next day, trying to sell them to the various record companies. Sometimes he'd be composing a song the week before they recorded it, and two weeks later it'd be on television. A month later it would be a big hit."

Farrell lived and breathed music. He kept track of what was on the charts and he went after songwriters and artists with relentless persistence. His interests were broad, but he was always looking for hits. "Wes never stopped listening to music," says Jean. "He always said, 'If you stop listening, you stop learning,' so he was very open to finding the next great songwriter."

Wes loved all kinds of music. Some of his favorite songs were "(Sittin' on) The Dock of the Bay" and "MacArthur Park."

"He also loved the old songs," says Jean. "He especially loved 'My Funny Valentine.'"

Farrell continued to grow his business, and soon some of the up-and-coming talents that were about to be discovered began knocking on his door—along with some relatively established songwriters, such as Tony Romeo.

"He *loved* Tony Romeo," continues Jean. "He thought Tony was really talented. Soon he was bringing in other writers and working with them personally. Wes wrote with a lot of his writers, because that's how he got what he wanted. Being a composer himself, Wes was able to get the best out of the good talent that he placed around him. Bringing in the talent to create the music was his other stroke of genius. He brought in not just studio musicians, but people like John and Tom Bahler who were super talented—*wildy* talented people."

The Jingle Company

Farrell began to expand his business. He opened up rooms for all kinds of writers, including another yet-to-be discovered star. "Wes started a company that just wrote jingles," says Jean, "and he used Barry Manilow. He made money as a jingle writer from the beginning." Commercial jingles not only proved lucrative for Farrell, but they became a very successful avenue for Manilow, too, who sang and wrote jingles for all kinds of companies including State Farm Insurance, Band-Aid, and McDonalds during the '70s.

Hitting Big

In 1965 Wes Farrell's "Hang On, Sloopy," co-written with Bert Russell Berns, rose to No. 1, making the McCoys famous as a one-hit wonder.

"'Hang On, Sloopy' was released by about 11 different artists before it hit big with the McCoys," says Jean Farrell, adding that one of the earlier versions was pulled from radio over the line "Sloopy let your hair down girl, let it run down on me…."

Today "Sloopy" is most frequently heard at sporting events all around Ohio, most notably for The Ohio State University, and in 1985 it became the official rock song for the state for Ohio.

"The first time that Wes heard 'Hang On, Sloopy' on the TV, he was watching an Ohio State ball game," says Jean, who particularly enjoyed this story. "He was back in California, and he used to get up early and bet on football games.

He was in his bathrobe, walking around, and suddenly he heard them singing it on the television. He said he did a double take, and then marched around his room in his bathrobe chanting, 'I feel like John Phillip Sousa!'"

Farrell's next big smash was "Come a Little Bit Closer," recorded by Jay & the Americans. Farrell had co-written "Closer" with new fellow songwriters Tommy Boyce and Bobby Hart.

He followed it up with "Come on Down to My Boat," which was recorded by Every Mother's Son, reaching No. 6 on *Billboard*. Just before he broke with the Partridge Family, he was having moderate success producing albums for Elephant's Memory, Brooklyn Bridge, Beacon Street Union and Dry Dock County.

The Partridge Family Years

When the early buzz about a TV show reached Farrell's ears, he was immediately interested. By this time, he had an excellent track record for making hits, and the proposed series was exactly the kind of vehicle he had been searching for and attempting to create on his own.

"He was already at the stage where he was well known as a producer and songwriter," says Jean Farrell, "so they brought him in, sat him down, and showed him the pilot episode of *The Partridge Family*. The first thing that Wes said was 'Does that kid David Cassidy sing?' Wes recognized the potential of what he called sighting to sound, referring to music television. This was a brand-new concept and Wes recognized it immediately as a vehicle for selling a lot of records, which was really his forte. So they brought David down."

Farrell knew immediately he could make Cassidy into a teen sensation, but he needed the right music for him. His intention went far beyond filling shows with music—he set out to produce quality songs, any of which might surface as a potential hit record.

David Cassidy became the front man for the band, and Wes Farrell began scoring big with *The Partridge Family*. He made an exhaustive effort to assure that all the songs for the television show were the best he had.

Farrell had many individual companies that he developed through the '60s and '70s. Chelsea Records, Roxbury Records, Pocket Full of Tunes, and others were all organized underneath an umbrella company, the Wes Farrell Organization.

when we're singin'

With *The Partridge Family* project making millions, Farrell set out to fulfill his dream of owning a label. "He took his first paycheck and started Chelsea Records," says John Bahler, who went to work for him at the new label.

"He started Chelsea Records with his first release, which was a song by Wayne Newton," says Jean. "Nobody else wanted to release it because they didn't believe Newton could become a star. The song was 'Daddy Don't You Walk So Fast.' Nobody wanted his record, so Wes went ahead and released it and proved everybody wrong. It became a big hit, and that was the beginning of Chelsea. It was release number 001 on Chelsea."

After *The Partridge Family* was canceled in 1974, Farrell continued on with Chelsea Records for another three years. Chelsea Records dissolved in 1977, and by 1978 a tired Wes Farrell went into temporary retirement, left Los Angeles, and moved to Florida. He sold most of his companies and closed down shop. His marriage to Tina Sinatra during the Partridge Family years had been short-lived, and his third marriage to Pamela Hensley also lasted very briefly. Farrell was ready to begin anew. That's when he met Jean Inman. They married in 1981 and had two children together—a boy, Wesley Jr., and a girl, Sky. The two remained together until Farrell's untimely passing in 1996 from cancer. Farrell also had a child, named Dawn, with his first wife, Joan Arthurs.

Reinvention

After relocating to Florida, Farrell regrouped, and soon was back on the trail producing music once again. "While we were married he worked on several different groups, and he never stopped working," says Jean. "His next big success came when he brought in a partner, Warburg Pincus, which was one of the largest venture capital companies in the world. They outlined their goal to buy music. Mainly they were looking for publishing interests. As it turned out it was pretty hard to find the size of publishing interests they wanted, because it was a big company and they had minimum amounts. If it wasn't $10 million and above, they didn't want to buy it. So Wes went on a search and found a company called Benson Music, which owned something like 48,000 copyrights.

"It was a Christian music company, and in order to get all of those copyrights they had to buy the whole company, which had a roster of about 75 artists. Wes was trying to decide whether or not he wanted to buy this, and he had them send all of the product to them. He'd hole up for the entire weekend just listening, listening, listening to everything. He came out and he said, 'Well, this is easy. Christian music is every kind of music I want it to be. I can do this.' So he bought that company and it became instrumental to him. His goal was to cross over a lot of the Christian music, like Amy Grant had done, and one of his first missions was a group called For Him. Wes believed in this group and he brought in pop producers, and he oversaw everything."

Jean Farrell continues, "Wes acquired another company called Diadem because they owned Yolanda Adams, and she's gone on to be very successful. He spotted her right away. Wes is the one who originally told them to record 'Butterfly Kisses,' and that became a really big song after Wes died. The president of that company called me and said 'I just want you to know that Wes is the one that identified that song and that's why we did it,' so he was still picking hits after he was gone! 'Butterfly Kisses' was huge.

"He stayed very involved in the music realm until he died. He was with Benson and he was about to buy another big company, but unfortunately he became sick and they had to cancel the deal. He was building up a portfolio of music entities and his goal was to work with these investment bankers to sell it."

"I remember when the Beatles catalog came for sale," Jean says. "Wes tried to get Wayne Newton to buy it, and we were working with Wayne on an album at that time. It was around 1984, and it was approximately $45 million. Wes was begging Wayne to buy into it with him, but Wayne didn't want to do it. Michael Jackson did it, and it went from being $45 million to $450 million, or whatever it's worth today. Wes was always a visionary. He was ahead of his time. He had a lot of ideas that didn't work out because they were ahead of their time."

In Search of the Singing Cowboy was another of those ideas. It looked something like *American Idol*, only for country music. "He put together this whole thing, complete with auditions," says Jean. "He said that when he drove up to the location that day, there were guys standing in line for a mile and a half with their guitars in hand." Farrell worked closely with music giant Don Kirshner in 1974 on this project, but it didn't catch on.

"Wes really never talked that much about the past," continues Jean. "He was always into the future. We had a guest house, and we did the wall with two dozen of his gold records, but he always called them old medals. It was nice to show everybody, but Wes didn't live for past achievements. He was always going forward."

Farrell was also quick to tune in to rap music. At one point he was asked to go out to L.A. and meet with some artists who were up and coming in the rap and hip-hop genres. "Wes came back and said, 'This is the next big thing in music.' He recognized rap when most people were poo-pooing rap. He looked at me and said, 'This is urban music. This is going to be huge and it's going to be around for a long time.'"

Other opportunities presented themselves, as well. "One night we were looking at the talent down here in Florida," says Jean. "Wes had been called to come and see this artist, and we went to this little dive in Fort Lauderdale. It was weird. They carried this artist up on the stage and poured chocolate syrup all over him. It turned out to be Marilyn Manson! They wanted Wes to sign him. Now, Wes was just at the point where he was getting involved in Christian music, and he said, 'You know, I can't do both. This guy's going to be a big star but not with me. I can't do it.'"

Wes Farrell left a legacy of great music behind him, and the Partridge Family was a giant piece of that legacy. Those who knew Farrell have story after story about him that reflect his insatiable zest for life.

"I wish I could have been able to know him a lot better," says Wes Farrell Jr., who was only 12 years old when his father passed away. "But I certainly have a lot of pride and respect for what he accomplished, and he was an incredible father to me when he was here. We, my whole family, we're very proud of what he accomplished."

Remembering Wes

Jean Farrell: Wes got a call one day and was asked to produce an album for the Everly Brothers. He was ecstatic because he was such a big fan. He said, "Hold on a minute," got off the phone, jumped around all over the place shouting "Woo hoo!" then went back and calmly said, "Yeah, I'd be very interested." But unfortunately that's when they had their big breakup, so he was never able to do it.

Wes knew a hit song when he heard it. That was his strongest suit. He could eliminate things that wouldn't be hits. He just had that uncanny ability to know a hit song. Over the years we were married he'd hear a song on the radio, and he'd look at me and say "Number 1 song of the year," and every year he would pick the Number 1 song the first time he heard it. He would just know.

Tommy West: He and Don Kirshner were very much alike. Wes had an ear for what was commercial. When we were on Capitol as Cashman, Pistilli and

West, Wes was one of our producers toward the end of our stay there. He would come to the session with a suit and tie, immaculately turned out, and he would sit there with a pencil and a pen and memo paper, and he would doodle on it the whole session. He was almost manic with his energy.

Wes had a child's heart. He called Cashman and me to come up to his office to play his new Tony Orlando single, "Knock Three Times." He said, "Watch what I'm gonna do." And he'd start playin' the song, and then he took a little piece of metal and banged it twice on a pipe and that was his big production idea. To make a sound effect out of a pipe. If you listen to the record you'll hear it. He was a good guy.

John Bahler: I agreed with every choice he made. The guy was brilliant. I learned a lot from him. He really, really knew on a gut level what was a hit and what wasn't, and he was rarely wrong. Wes was a great producer. He knew what he wanted, and he was a wild man.

I said, "How in the hell did you write 'Sloopy?'" He said, "I don't know. I was just playing this riff on the piano, and I just started singing 'Hang on, Sloopy, Sloopy, hang on!'" I said, "Where in the hell did that come from?" He said, "I don't know, but I'll take the money anyways!" That was Wes' claim to fame.

Sometimes producers would sing things to me. Wes always tried to sing things to me and it was hysterical because it wasn't even close! (He laughs and imitates Farrell's bad singing.) That's what he sounded like when he tried to sing a background vocal! It was really funny, but a lot of times he had really, really great ideas. I loved working with him.

Frank Romeo: I remember when I first saw Wes, I was so impressed I couldn't even speak. His office reminded me of an incredible Christmas gift. The walls were like wrapping paper. The secretary had a skirt that was so short, and she was so beautiful and everybody was so gorgeous. It was intimidating just to go into the office.

Larry Rosen: I remember Wes when he bought his first Lamborghini. He picked me up at the Columbia Studios and we drove 98 miles an hour down one of the side streets. Oh Jesus, he loved that car. He was a terrific guy.

We did an episode about saving the whales and it was obvious we needed a song about whales. Judy Collins had put out this song about whales, and in those times everybody was a conservationist and wanted to save the whales. I remember Wes said, "You want me to do a song about fucking whales? Are you kidding?" Wes produced it, reluctantly. I don't think it ever sold a record, because that's all he was interested in was selling records, as he should have been.

I loved Wes. I use to fight with him all the time about what song would go into what show. There'd be songs where Wes would say, "I think this is a winner, so pick a good episode to put this into," but we would just pick them because they sounded good, and the message within the song fit the show, whether it was a song about unrequited love or the end of a romance. I don't recall any time where Wes was pushing something that we would ultimately resist.

L. Russell Brown: Wes Farrell was a fascinating person. I was once at his apartment on 57th Street. He had no chairs, and no furniture of any kind. It was a wide open, penthouse apartment, and all he had was like 10 suits hanging in his closet. Strangest thing I ever saw. I spent a lot of time with Wes Farrell. He was a first-class gentleman. I truly liked him and loved his dynamic. He was a top-flight producer, a fine songwriter in his own right, and he knew a hit song when he heard it.

Wes Farrell Jr.: Growing up, I remember the first time I was watching the show. I think my mom had me watching it. And seeing my dad's name at the end, that kind of gave me chills. I was too young to understand the music, but I remember the first time I told somebody that my dad wrote the songs and music for the Partridge Family and they said, "Whoa, I love that music!" Just getting that reaction from people really kind of indicated to me as a child that it was something cool, that people were really responding to it and enjoying it.

Tom Bahler: Wes was very smart. I loved Wes. Sometimes he had more balls than brains, and I appreciate that too. He walked into Screen Gems when he read something about the development of *The Partridge Family*, and he said, "Hey man, I think that you guys need me," and they said, "Well, we've got somebody else [Shorty Rogers]." He said, "Yeah, man, I'm a huge fan of Shorty's, but name me one of his hits. OK, now listen to my hits." They thought, *Well, maybe we better take this dude.*

When Wes came in he brought in all of the writers he loved. That's really what Wes brought to it. It wasn't so much the sound, yet he loved what he was hearing. I had a great music teacher that also taught Quincy Jones and

Randy Newman and a bunch of other artists. His name was George Tremblay and he used to say "It takes talent to recognize genius," and that was Wes' strong suit.

He was a great song picker. He had a great team around him, and he knew it. He always had his own ideas, too, because producers do, and they were good ideas.

The thing that was really funny was when he'd try to sing a part to us. It was like changing stations on a funky radio, man! We'd say, 'Yeah, Wes, thanks, man, got it!' Ha!

He was such a street dude, man. I think he probably went through third grade, but his brain wasn't third grade. Thomas Edison also went only through third grade. I put Wes up there with Edison. They were brilliant men.

Jackie Ward: None of us would ever go in and make suggestions to Wes, because he would usually have such strong opinions of his own, and he knew exactly what he wanted, so you didn't have to. You just didn't go in that direction. Sometimes he would tell us what to do over the speakers in the studio. He would say "You're not doing it right!" He'd try to sing: "Da da da da! That's what I want! Da da da da!" And we were supposed to translate what that meant! Oh, God, the stuff that would come out of his mouth! We still kind of knew what he was doing—whether there was a rhythm thing he wanted us to emphasize differently, or something else—but it was hilarious. I had a hard time keeping a straight face!

Danny Janssen: I was with him once when we were coming back from Topanga Plaza. It was the day before Thanksgiving, and he was driving his Maserati, and I said, "I can't work tomorrow. My boy is sick." I was just giving him shit, you know, because we got to be good friends. He says, "What are you talking about?" I said, "Tomorrow's Thanksgiving, you dumb shit! Can't we just take Thanksgiving Day off?" He pulls over in two lanes of traffic, damn near hits people, stops the car, hits the steering wheel and says, "It just pisses me off so bad that people take these damn holidays off! Christmas! Thanksgiving! What right have they got to do that?" He was really serious about this stuff. But me—I just thought it was a lot of fun!

Paul Anka: Wes Farrell and I had so many great times. We socialized a lot. I think one of the great memories was—we ran into a very sad Jimmy Webb, the writer, way back when. We went into Vegas, tried to cheer him up. I don't know what Jimmy was going through at the time, but Wes came to see me at Caesars. We wound up with about 10 girls in the health club at the hotel—all nude! Room service was coming in and out. We locked the place up. It must have been about eight, 10 hours. That's the other side of it, to the best of my memory.

Steve Dossick: One of the key things about Wes was that he was a guy who everything he touched turned to gold. So about 10 years ago, it had been forever since I heard anything about him, so I Googled him and found that he had died in '96. That same night I happened to come upon a page—it was one of those bizarre Internet things about the luckiest people in history based on astrology, and Wes was there! It listed 20 or 30 people, and Wes was there as one of the luckiest people in history! Because, you know, a lot of things just opened up for him.

Excerpts from Ken Sharp's 1993 interview with Wes Farrell

Did you ever do an album as a solo artist?

No. I recorded a couple of records before I had success as a writer. I recorded for insignificant companies and I recorded for Capitol Records as Wes Farrell. The one session I really was excited about, Jay & the Americans, I sang background. Everybody that I was having hits with contributed and we thought that Wes Farrell was going to have a hit record. It was a song called "The Letter." I wrote it with Bert Berns, the same guy who worked with me on "Hang On, Sloopy." Then I wrote some other things with Chip Taylor. My loves are always greater than me. My love for the idea of music and where it would end up going and how many dimensions one could be intrigued by discovering was far greater than the concept of me as an artist. When I realized you could have ten artists record your songs at one time, and as an artist you could only record one at a time, the idea of being an artist didn't drive me as much as it drove other people.

What ingredients made up the Partridge Family sound?

That's a good one. That's a tough call. I think the formula … jeez, a hit song's a hit song's a hit song. Those were the three things that we were always looking for. Again, when you're dealing with that kind of quantity and deadlines it's not like you can sit around and say, 'We'll record it in six months when we find the right song.' We didn't have those kind of luxuries to deal with. In this case, less was more rather than more was less. I guess if we had been subjected to some of the luxuries which prevail in today's marketplace the Partridge Family records would have been twice as big, three times as big as it was. There are no regrets. Just reflections.

Are you amazed at the amount of work and material that, not only as a producer but as a writer, you churned out in a small period of time for the Partridge Family?

That was something I trained myself to do. Listen, I come from a school that if you don't know how to do it, don't do it. A writer is exactly what he is—he's a writer. If he doesn't know how to write, get out of the process. If you're going to visit it, forget about it. But there are different kinds of writers with different kinds of styles and my choices were never limited, and my interests were never limited. My style was that, if you're going to write, write until you get it right. I'm pleased that the music stands up.

Are you still writing today?

Today I have interests in a number of important music-driven entities, and although I still write, I don't write like I did. My focus is not on writing. Being a writer is part of your life. It never leaves your hands. It never leaves your mind. It never leaves me. I have hundreds of beginnings, but that's for me to enjoy more than anything else, and you do that because it's always part of your person.

Liner Notes: *Keeping Up Is Hard to Do*

The inexhaustible Wes Farrell had an idea. If a tried and true cover tune like "Cherish" could bring such huge success for David Cassidy as a solo artist, certainly an equally recognizable and successful cover tune could work for the Partridge Family, too. And sure enough, it did.

"Breaking Up Is Hard to Do" is one of the most recorded songs ever written. In fact, Neil Sedaka recorded it twice and had a hit with it both times! It was Sedaka's first No. 1 song, hitting on August 11, 1962, and his slow version gave him another Top 10 hit in December 1975. Sedaka, at one point, recorded a special Italian version of it.

The infectious hook and melody make this one of the most instantly recognizable songs in the history of modern pop music. It has been covered by countless artists including the Four Seasons, Tom Jones, Carole King, the Carpenters, and even Alvin and the Chipmunks! The song still has legs, with more current renditions covered by contemporary artists such as Gloria Estefan and Clay Aiken.

when we're singin'

Wes Farrell suspected "Breaking Up" could be another gold mine for the Partridge Family and went quickly to work. John Bahler and company came up with an arrangement that was lively and upbeat—original, yet reminiscent of the first Sedaka release.

As season 2 reached the midway point, Farrell was now juggling his new label, Chelsea Records, in addition to the Partridge Family's demands. He also had David Cassidy's second solo album, *Rock Me, Baby,* in the works for a fall release. He needed all the shortcuts he could get, and with the show winding down its second season and a plate full of established hits, Farrell, together with Bell Records, decided to do a greatest hits album. Not only were there already plenty of hits to put on the collection, but the two-year point in which teen idol sensations had proven to peak was quickly approaching, and it seemed ideal for potentially good sales on a hits LP. During the summer of '72, the Partridge Family was still very much alive with the buying public. The move would also buy him a little more time to get his next set of two Partridge Family albums ready for release during the show's third season.

It was unusual for Farrell to plan a Partridge Family single without a new album of original material to go with it, but it seemed a no-brainer to put a greatest hits package out and feature the newest chart success, "Breaking Up Is Hard To Do," as part of the collection. "Breaking Up Is Hard to Do" was placed as the final song on side B of *At Home With Their Greatest Hits.* The power of the song to finish the album speaks for itself.

The second season was wrapping up when "Breaking Up Is Hard to Do" was released as a single. But the initial release of the single to the radio station DJs had unexpected glitches. About 1,200 DJ copies of another recording were shipped out to the stations with the Partridge Family "Breaking Up Is Hard to Do" label on them. Irv Biegel, Bell Records executive vice president, explained in a press release running June 24, 1972, in *Cash Box*: "The mistake was made at the factory. In order to be sure that there is absolutely no possibility of error at the radio stations, we are shipping out regular label copies. We advise everyone who has received a deejay copy to listen to it to be sure that they have the Partridge Family record."

Despite the backstage fumble, "Breaking Up Is Hard to Do" was pumped out to radio stations just in time for summer airplay in 1972. On June 17, *Cash Box* predicted, "Neil Sedaka's biggie sound tailor made for the family will be their biggest in a long while, and deservedly so." The single entered the charts on July 1 (exactly ten years to the month in which Sedaka's version hit big) and stayed until September 2—a total of ten weeks. It charted respectably on *Billboard,* peaking at No. 28 on August 19. The chart ranking for this song reflected the first *Billboard* chart rise in popularity for the Partridge Family, which had been slipping very slowly, most notably with the previous single, "Am I Losing You." The July 1 issue of *Cash Box* listed the Partridge Family as the No. 1 vocal group for the first half of 1972, and David Cassidy as the No. 5 "newcomer" male vocalist.

"Breaking Up Is Hard to Do" was also extraordinarily popular in the U.K., where the Partridge Family and David Cassidy were continuing to grow in popularity. It captured the British excitement, shooting all the way up to No. 3 on the British charts—a significant peak for the Partridge Family overseas. In fact, "Breaking Up" is the all-time highest chart ranking Partridge Family song in the U.K.

In the early '70s singles were still being released primarily in mono, while stereo was the preferred mix for album cuts. Certain labels moved to the stereo format more quickly than others, but Bell Records, for the most part, had been sticking with mono for singles. "Breaking Up Is Hard to Do" was mixed in mono and released as a single, and it was also used on the television show—which was always mono.

When it came time to assemble the album, Farrell decided to use "Breaking Up" in its mono mix, even though it would be the only song on the album not in stereo. It would have been a waste of money and time to open the track back up and re-mix the song in stereo. "Breaking Up Is Hard to Do" is one of only two songs in the entire Partridge Family catalog that was released on an LP set strictly in mono—the other one is "I'm on the Road" from *The Partridge Family Album*.

Bell Records heavily promoted "Breaking Up Is Hard to Do" and really believed in it. A full-page ad was featured in the trades—the last time a full page Partridge Family ad would ever be placed. As the upcoming fall release of *At Home With Their Greatest Hits* was planning to showcase the newest Partridge Family hit up front on the collection, the graphic artist who designed the cover art was instructed to prominently feature the song title on the cover in accented bold type.

David Cassidy was also very taken with the song and has played it live in concert many times. He included it on his 1974 album *Cassidy Live!* and again in 1986 on *His Greatest Hits Live,* released only in England, this time splitting the tempo between fast and slow. David has played around with this track in concert, sometimes giving it a poignant, bittersweet touch, mellowing the tune out and finding its soul, while other times keeping to the original, uptempo rendition.

In 2004, David Cassidy officially re-recorded "Breaking Up Is Hard to Do" in his own soulful arrangement for his *Touch of Blue* album, which features classic cover tunes recorded in a bluesy style. Oddly enough, "Breaking Up Is Hard to Do" was not featured on the 1989 CD release *The Partridge Family Greatest Hits*. It appeared on the second CD hits collection, *David Cassidy and the Partridge Family: The Definitive Collection,* but was dropped again in 2005 for the third U.S. CD hits package, *Come On Get Happy: The Very Best of the Partridge Family.* Devoted Partridge Family fans have always wanted a stereo version of the song, and finally, in 2013, it was remixed in stereo for the very first time in over 40 years, and included on the fourth U.S. hits collection, *Playlist: The Very Best of the Partridge Family.*

when we're singin'

Weeks before *At Home* was released, Bell announced plans for an aggressive and extensive promotional campaign as part of a 10-LP release for fall—the largest release by Bell Records in its entire history. David Cassidy's *Rock Me, Baby* was also among the lot. Planned use of consumer publication ads and radio spots, T-shirt giveaways, and selected market focus plans for certain LPs, including *At Home*, were executed with precision, especially focusing on regions where the Partridge Family showed strength.

Significant executive shifts were going on at Bell Records that summer, for the first time since the Partridge Family albums were released. Such movement within the company was sure to have an impact on the way all future Partridge Family albums would be handled. *Cash Box* called it "a sweeping restructuring," of promotional and merchandising concepts. The new shift put the control of all merchandising procedures through one single executive for the first time in Bell's history, and the sales activities for both LP's and singles were also combined under that same structure—notable to the second half of the Partridge Family's reign.

At Home with Their Greatest Hits was released in late August, just as "Breaking Up Is Hard to Do" began to cool. It entered the Billboard Hot 100 on September 16 and stayed on the charts for 23 weeks (a longer stay than *Shopping Bag*), peaking at No. 21.

Farrell, together with Bell Records, chose the tracks that were included on this package—every Partridge Family single that had charted the top 40 up to this point in time, plus a few other tracks that were, for the most part, "near-miss" single releases. Fans snatched up the album with enthusiasm.

In addition to "Breaking Up," the album contains two songs from *The Partridge Family Album;* three from *Up To Date;* three from *Sound Magazine*, and two from their most recent album, *Shopping Bag*.

Predictably, "I Think I Love You" opens this collection, followed by 10 other tracks. Wes Farrell believed that placing six songs on side one of the album, followed by five songs on the second side would subconsciously suggest to listeners that they were missing a track, prompting them to turn the album back over to side A and replay it. The idea was calculated to get the listener wanting more. He used this technique on every Partridge Family album except the final compilation LP, *The World of the Partridge Family*.

It was a big deal for a songwriter to have an album cut with the Partridge Family. There was a lot of money to be made, and the exposure was phenomenal. "Wes' tentacles reached very far," says songwriter Tommy West. "He knew everybody. He had a lot of energy, and that energy got out to everyone in the business. Everyone knew that if you had a Partridge Family cut it was kind of like having one with Elvis—you knew you were going to make some money. Wes could almost *will* a record to be commercial."

The Partridge Family at Home with Their Greatest Hits reflects only the early Partridge Family hits. It is a well-done collection, but there were still three more studio albums left to go and two seasons of the show. The bus ride was only half over!

I Think I Love You, 2:52, Tony Romeo
Billboard: *Peaked at No. 1 for three weeks in a row; 19 weeks on the charts.*
Cash Box: *Peaked at No. 1 for three weeks in a row; 19 weeks on the charts.*
Record World: *Peaked at No. 1 for four weeks in a row; 18 weeks on the charts.*

I'll Meet You Halfway, 3:47, Wes Farrell–Gerry Goffin
Billboard: *Peaked at No. 9; nine weeks on the charts.*
Cash Box: *Peaked at No. 2; 10 weeks on the charts.*
Record World: *Peaked at No. 4; 11 weeks on the charts.*

It's One of Those Nights (Yes, Love), 3:47, Tony Romeo
Billboard: *Peaked at No. 20; 8 weeks on the charts.*
Cash Box: *Peaked at No. 13; 9 weeks on the charts.*
Record World: *Peaked at No. 14; 10 weeks on the charts.*

Echo Valley 2-6809, 3:05, Kathy Cooper–Rupert Holmes
Considered, but never released as a single.

I Woke Up in Love This Morning, 2:41, Irwin Levine–L. Russell Brown
Billboard: *Peaked at No. 13; 11 weeks on the charts.*
Cash Box: *Peaked at No. 9; 12 weeks on the charts.*
Record World: *Peaked at No. 14; 10 weeks on the charts.*

I Can Feel Your Heartbeat, 2:05, Wes Farrell–Jim Cretecos–Mike Appel
Considered, but never released as a single.

Doesn't Somebody Want to Be Wanted, 2:46, Wes Farrell–Jim Cretecos–Mike Appel
Billboard: *Peaked at No. 6; 12 weeks on the charts.*
Cash Box: *Peaked at No. 1 for one week; 13 weeks on the charts.*
Record World: *Peaked at No. 1 for one week; 14 weeks on the charts.*

Am I Losing You, 2:22, Irwin Levine–L.Russell Brown
Billboard: *Peaked at No. 59; 7 weeks on the charts.*
Cash Box: *Peaked at No. 31; 8 weeks on the charts.*
Record World: *Peaked at No. 35; 7 weeks on the charts.*

Brown Eyes, 2:44, Wes Farrell–Danny Janssen
Never considered for single release.

when we're singin'

She'd Rather Have the Rain, 3:17, Terry Cashman–T.P. West
Considered, but never released as a single.

Breaking Up Is Hard to Do, 2:30, Neil Sedaka–Howard Greenfield
Billboard: *Peaked at No. 28; 10 weeks on the charts.*
Cash Box: *Peaked at No. 25; 10 weeks on the charts.*
Record World: *Peaked at No. 24; 11 weeks on the charts.*
Appears On: Season 3, episode 61, "Nag, Nag, Nag" (December 8, 1972)

Album Summary and Reviews

Total running time: 29:56
Original Release: August 1972, Bell 1107

A dealer's delight is this powerhouse sales package containing all the hits of the Partridge Family! They're all here: "I Think I Love You," "I'll Meet You Halfway," "I Woke Up In Love This Morning," "She'd Rather Have the Rain," and their recent chart item, "Breaking Up Is Hard to Do." *Billboard, September 16, 1972*

This is destined to be one of the biggest selling LPs of this year. It features the TV and record favorites' seven chart singles from "I Think I Love You" to their most recent "Breaking Up is Hard To Do." To round out the set, four of their most requested LP tracks have been added, including Cashman & West's "She'd Rather Have the Rain" and "Echo Valley 2-6809." The titles and their tremendous following speak for themselves. *Cash Box, September 2, 1972*

The Partridge Family is a TV "family" that has rocked up many disk biggies in a comparatively short time with strong vocals, especially by David Cassidy. Leading happy winners are "Breaking Up Is Hard To Do," "I Think I Love You," "I Can Feel Your Heartbeat," "Doesn't Somebody Want To Be Wanted" and "I Woke Up In Love This Morning." *Variety, September 13, 1972*

First Chart Appearance: September 2, 1972 (Record World, No. 74); September 9, 1972 (Cash Box, No. 63); September 16, 1972 (Billboard, No. 114)

WHITE COVERS
or ... The Partridge Family Notebook

Season 3: Status Quo

The fall of 1972 brought *The Partridge Family* back for its third season. There was little change in the show format or the sound of the music during season 3. For the most part, fans could return to their Friday nights and pick right back up with more of the same. Season 3 was an important year for the business of the TV show. "This, as almost everyone knows, is the money year for a series," reported a nationally syndicated article from the *Washington Post*. "By the third year all major costs have been amortized, and good heavens how the money rolls in. A third season, also, means that the series will have enough episodes for a mass kind of syndication for the reruns." The ratings for season 3 were still solid. *The Partridge Family* came in at No. 19, tying with *The Waltons* and *Medical Center*.

During the third year the cast made two commercials for Rice Krispies cereal. One featured the full cast and the other, only Shirley Jones and David Cassidy.

Season 3 brought another string of impressive guest stars, including Bert Convy, who played Richard Lawrence, a suitor for Shirley on two episodes—the second of which also showcased future Oscar winner Jodie Foster, who played Lawrence's daughter. To borrow a phrase from one of his episode titles, if ever there was a most likely candidate for a potential Mr. Partridge, it was Richard Lawrence.

Other guest characters returned this year, including Punky Lazaar, Gloria Hickey, Grandma and Grandpa, Bonnie Kleinschmidt, and Dr. Bernie Applebaum. The popular Snake the biker, played the previous year by Rob Reiner, returned played by Stuart Margolin, best known from *Love, American Style*. Charlotte Rae, Bruce Kimmel, Tony Geary, Nancy Walker, Arte Johnson, Miss America 1959 Mary Ann Mobley, and even baseball's Johnny Bench all visited the Partridges during season 3.

The type of stories and the homebound settings also remained the same. "So many of the episode stories were taken right from my own house," says Shirley Jones. "From that standpoint I was dealing with the same child-rearing situations at home that I was portraying on the set with the kids of the Partridge Family. The fact that I had been a singer and David was a singer; the fact that David was my stepson and that we were together playing a show business family on TV; the fact that Jack was in show business, I was in show business, and David's mother was in show business—it was all relatable. That's why I needed to be Mrs. Partridge and not Mrs. Brady. Because the element was part of my whole life, you know? As well as being a mother and a wife, my life was show business from the time I was 17. That's what I loved about being Mrs. Partridge. That was a part of her life, too, and so I understood it. I felt a real kinship with the character."

The musical style and sound also remained the same, although David Cassidy's recording schedule nearly doubled. The Partridge Family saw the release of two more albums during the 72–73 season with *The Partridge Family Notebook* in the fall and *The Partridge Family Crossword Puzzle* early the following summer. Also following the September release of *At Home With Their Greatest Hits* was the October release of Cassidy's second solo album, *Rock Me Baby*. The market was truly saturated with plenty of Cassidy and Partridge Family albums to pick from.

On Location: Roller Coasters

For the season 3 location shoot, the cast and crew traveled 2,200 miles across the midwest to the brand-new King's Island Amusement Park just 20 miles outside Cincinnati, Ohio.

"We got this call from King's Island Amusement Park, and they were interested in having the Partridge Family come down to inaugurate the park before it opened," says producer Larry Rosen. "They called Claver, and so Bob, Dale McRaven and I flew down to Cincinnati. The park had not even opened yet, and we spent three days walking through the park looking at everything. Then, at the end of the trip, the three of us sat in the hotel room in Cincinnati for a day and a half and came up with a story for the episode, which was about Keith falling in love with the park guide. Once we came up with the script idea we went back to L.A. and pitched it to the network, and they approved it."

Mary Ann Mobley played the park guide, and the producers landed Johnny Bench of the Cincinnati Reds to make a cameo appearance. Bench was big in his day; he had made his Major League Baseball debut in 1967 and became the youngest player to win the league's MVP award in 1970. "He was right there, and that made a lot of sense," says associate producer Mel Swope. "Johnny Bench played the waiter and we gave him one line," says Rosen. "I had this idea about how I wanted to run the credits at the end. Johnny Bench had just one line in the show, and instead of putting the character name down in the closing credits, we put his entire line that he had spoken. It was a special little thing we did for Johnny Bench."

"King's Island paid all of our expenses," says Rosen. "It was the only way we could have gone down there. I'll never forget this one. We were all on the same plane, and we flew in to Cincinnati, and there were crowds of people. It was the first time that we had ever left Los Angeles, and the concept of walking into Ohio, or someplace far away, was new. Suddenly there were mobs of people! It made our sense of success sink in. *My God,* I thought. *We're being seen everywhere! These people love us!* What was amazing about the people is the way they kind of saw the characters as real people. They would come up to me and say, 'Does Danny sleep with Shirley in her room? Do all of the kids stay with their mom?' It was so touching and so beautiful. These people were just wonderful. We stayed at a hotel right across the street from the park, and every night there would be a thousand kids there."

With real people instead of actors being used in the crowd shots, "the first word that comes to mind is *security,*" says Swope. "That was just to be smart. When we brought the cast from the dressing room area to wherever we were shooting in King's Island, they were surrounded by six to eight security police, and everything was fine. We isolated an area in the hotel in case the groupies found out about David Cassidy or the cast staying there."

There were some tense moments for the producers, who feared that overly excited fans used as extras might lose control of themselves, particularly during the musical performance. "The place had just opened," says Rosen, "and the last segment of the show was David singing a song. We put David in the middle of this crowd, and I remember being in that crowd when David was singing. When the camera pulled back you would see something like 3,000 people around him. Part of those people standing closest to David were guards dressed as tourists. When the song was over, David and I had to walk through that crowd to get him out of there. It was a long walk through this crowd and they were cheering and wanting to touch him. There were guards all around him and I remember saying, 'Aw, fuck, David, we have to get out of here!' There were thousands of screaming kids, and you felt at any second it was going to explode. If it had, and somebody reached for him, we could never have saved him. I held him and kept walking and walking and walking until we got him out of there."

"This one was actually scary in a lot of ways," says Brian Forster. "We had motor homes for dressing rooms, and basically the boys had one dressing room and the girls had the other. We were in this motor home and I was fascinated by motor homes and machinery and that kind of thing, and I saw this ladder, and I thought I would check it out. I go up the ladder, and it led to the roof. I popped my head out, and all of a sudden there's thousands of shrieking fans! I looked around and thought *Oh my God!* I felt like I was at Woodstock! There were people for as far as I could see. They saw my head pop out, and they started shrieking! I felt like the mole that immediately dropped his head back into his hole again. I thought, *This is insane!* And this was just me! What would have happened if David had done this? There would have been a riot!"

when we're singin'

Wes Farrell was always keeping tabs on high-profile opportunities to place certain songs into the show that he felt could be potential hits. In this case, Farrell used the previously released *Shopping Bag* offering "Girl, You Make My Day," written by Tommy Boyce and Bobby Hart, and the upcoming *Notebook* standout, "Together We're Better," by Tony Romeo and Ken Jacobson.

The cast had a blast with this episode. It meant getting out of L.A. for a while and breaking up the routine. It was especially memorable for the younger ones, as any amusement park venture was likely to be. The second they arrived, Danny Bonaduce was already off and running. "The park sound system blazed 'Will Danny Bonaduce report to the set please?'" begins one report of the elusive Bonaduce, who slipped off several times when no one was looking so he could ride the roller coaster. Staff assistants were sent off to look for him because Claver needed him for a scene. The night before, when they arrived, he had ridden the roller coaster three times, and was prowling the park at 3 a.m. By the following evening, he had ridden the coaster at least 22 times. "These rides are better than Disneyland!" he told reporters. The exhausted park deputy had to ride with him when he was free from shooting (and not sneaking off) and reported that Bonaduce had ridden every ride. By the following day, he slipped out at lunch—this time because he met a girl!

"I cannot tell you what happened on the show, but I can tell you we got to ride any ride we wanted, as many times as we wanted, and that was the great part," Suzanne Crough says, laughing. "We rode that roller coaster I don't know how many times straight in a row, in the front seat, or wherever we wanted to sit. That was the best part of it all—that's why kids make a wish! We were there all week, and if school was done and we weren't filming, we would ride the rides. We'd do it as a group—Danny, Brian, and I."

"I was afraid of roller coasters," admits Brian Forster with a chuckle. "I could feel it getting light and I thought we were going to fly off the track until somebody on the set told me they have wheels under the track that keeps them from flying off. From that point on Suzanne, Danny, and I went on this roller coaster about 20 times in a row. I think we were the only ones on it except our security guards. I don't know if those security guards thought this was the best deal they'd ever gotten or the worst! There's a picture of us somewhere looking thrilled as hell, but the security guards are looking a little gray," he laughs.

"The other highlight was that I met a girl," continues Forster. "It was an instant crush, and I was spending as much time with her as I could. We ended up writing letters back and forth and having a little romance for some time after that. The chances of seeing her again were pretty remote, but at that age you think *Oh yeah, we're going to see each other next week.* That's when Danny and I really got into it, because Danny also had a crush on her. That was another time we almost came to blows. He did not like that somebody wasn't paying attention to him. The last time we were all together on *Today* I had everybody sign this picture of all of us, and Danny signed *You got the girl, you little bastard!*" Forster laughs. "He wrote about it in his book, too. He wrote about how much it pissed him off because I was the cute kid and he was the ugly one. Now ask me what the plot was, and I can't tell you!"

Dale McRaven remembers sneaking out of the park with Susan Dey. "You know, we didn't have to wait in line," says McRaven. "They'd let us in at the front of the lines. We decided to sneak out of the park and not carry the bodyguards and all of that stuff, and Susan Dey went with us. I mean we didn't need the bodyguards, but Susan Dey went with us, and she wanted to just sneak out and not make a big deal out of it, and so we were going through the park and we start moving, and when people did recognize us—we were gone. But it was funny because we were sneaking around and having a good time and then we saw Danny Bonaduce with all of the bodyguards coming through, with this army of bodyguards protecting him! And we just sort of walked by and waved, and he kind of did a double take, because there was no one with us! It was kind of funny."

Executive producer Bob Claver says, "I loved going to the amusement park. I think that was good for all of us, and the people—they were very nice. Not only the people at the amusement park, but the people at the hotel, too. I remember sitting outside talking with someone, and this lady comes along with her daughter. We needed something for the episode—I can't remember what—but this lady says, 'If you'll introduce my daughter to David Cassidy, I'll get it for you!' She was the sweetest lady. The Midwest is full of all kinds of mellow people. If we were nice to their kids it was all you needed to do. That trip was amazing. I enjoyed that whole thing. It was a lot of work, and not easy, but we got a good episode out of it, and we had fun doing it."

The publicity was also phenomenal. *TV Guide* did a feature and photo layout for the episode. "I still have this photo on my wall," says Rosen. "It's a *TV Guide* spread of me, David, and Susan walking with an armed guard. Then there's a picture of Shirley on a scale, and Danny on the roller coaster, and a couple of other little pictures. But the biggest picture in the article is me," he laughs. "Shirley said to me, 'Nice going, Rosen! You got the biggest picture in the whole article!' We used to joke about that."

King's Island opened in April 1972 and remains in business. While the episode was shot as part of the Park's inaugural season, it was held for broadcast until January 26, 1973. *The Brady Bunch* shot an episode at King's Island later the same year.

The Writer's Voice

Story editor and producer Dale McRaven became known for his work on *Perfect Strangers* and *Mork and Mindy*, among other successful TV shows. Before that was *The Partridge Family*.

when we're singin'

"Dale McRaven was as close to a genius as you can get in terms of delivering scripts for *The Partridge Family*," begins Larry Rosen. "We had all these great writers come in and pitch stories to us. They would do the first draft and we would give them notes. They would do a second draft and then we'd give them more notes. Then we'd sit there with the final draft, Bob, Dale and I, and we'd decide what works and what doesn't. They never did that because these writers didn't live with the show as we did. So Bob, and I, and sometimes Mel, would sit down with all of our notes, and we'd give them to Dale. We'd point out what has to change, what story arc doesn't work, and all these other notes. Dale would sit there and just stroke his beard with his right hand, and listen. He'd take notes and take notes and then he would disappear on like a Thursday, and we wouldn't see him. He would go home, and he would sit in the bathtub all Thursday night, and he rewrote the scripts by hand. He would come in Friday morning with water-stained pages from the bathtub and give us all these crappy, rumpled pages, but it was a script you could put on a soundstage the next day. It was brilliant. Of course we would polish a little thing here and there, but he was an incredible writer and story editor. He was the genius behind making those scripts work when they didn't work. Without Dale I don't know how we would have ever done that show. He was just incredible, and he did it in his own style, and when it came back to us it was exactly what we needed."

"I had a couple of job offers at the time," says McRaven. "Garry Marshall and Jerry Belson were doing *The Odd Couple* and they offered that job to me. It was tempting. But my agent made a good point. He said, 'If you do the Marshall-Belson project, they're going to get more credit than you're going to get, and if you're the only writer involved on *The Partridge Family* you'll get all of the credit, good or bad." This appealed to McRaven, knowing he could potentially build his career.

"At the time family shows were pretty unrealistic and pretty pure. They were about kids who never had an argument and just loved each other to death. So I said 'I'll do the show if you let me let the kids act like real kids.' Sometimes they'd argue, sometimes they'd hate each other, but they really, basically, all loved each other." McRaven wanted some honest conflict. "It's the old thing—I can call my sister a bitch, but you can't. I'll kick the shit out of you if you call her a bitch. There's a lot of that in there. There hadn't been any of that up to that point, and they let me do it, and that's why I took the show."

McRaven began as a writer and an editor on the show from the very first season but he wasn't involved in the pilot episode. "Bernie Slade did a really good job on the pilot, but the characters he introduced and developed most were Danny and Reuben Kincaid, and their relationship. David didn't have much of a character beyond being some guy that could sing, and neither did Susan, and Shirley was Shirley. So I actually filled in and developed most of the characters after Danny and Reuben.

Despite storylines that focused on Shirley going out on a date from time to time, there was never any intention to bring a permanent romantic figure into her life. "It would have screwed with the premise of the show," explains McRaven. "If we felt like we needed a male figure we would have brought one in, but no one ever felt that. She was a strong mother and did a good job raising the kids. She didn't care if she had jokes. In fact she preferred not to have jokes. She demanded it. She said, 'I want to be a good mother first,' and she was very adamant about it. It also took a lot of pressure off me as the writer, not to have to make her funny. She could deliver a joke, but she wasn't the one you go to for delivering a joke, so it was better. Her instincts were good."

Writers often have one character in their stories that they identify with or relate to in some way. They put a little bit of their own personality into this character more than any other and write the role with some self-reflection or a personalized point of view. For McRaven, that character was Keith.

"I did dumb things," explains McRaven, "so I had him doing dumb things, and I enjoyed that. Keith wasn't a dumb person, though.

"David was hard to convince. It was hard to do stuff with David at first. He had this image of what he should be doing, and what he wanted to be doing, which was making out with every girl," laughs McRaven. "One of the things we had to watch with him in the beginning was coming off as lecherous. Suddenly it's not a comedy anymore. It's this guy just leching after a girl. So I started writing away from that, and that's where his character came from. David was good, too. I don't think he got as much credit as he should have.

"Danny and Dave Madden always had a little thing going, and those were fun to write, but again, you had to be careful not to go over the line with Danny, or write a joke that he could take over the line, because he was still a 10-year-old kid, even though he was a smartass. If he got too smartassed people would hate him, and I wouldn't let him do jokes that would make me hate him."

Of Laurie's introduction in the pilot, he says, "She was nothing at that point. She didn't have a character, really, just lines setting her up as a protester, which hadn't been done all that much at that time. But it gave her an instant attitude. It was a quality that set her up so she could argue with Danny or David about something and still do it in a funny way.

"Susan was really good, without overreacting. She was really modest. She didn't make any demands, and she knew what her position was on the show. We always tried to spread the stories around, and she was treated fairly." Laurie comes off as a very mature teenager, able to have adult conversations with mom and displaying a lot of strength. "That was just Susan's character," says McRaven. "That's her. She is a strong person."

McRaven feels that Dey was the most underrated of the actors. "There was a lot of people that thought she couldn't do anything other than *The Partridge Family*, and then she went on to do *L.A. Law* and other shows, and it just proved that she could act."

when we're singin'

McRaven's script ideas came in all sorts of ways. "Some of them come from beginning to end—two minutes and it's all there—and some of them you work on for weeks and weeks and you never get them right. It's usually the ones that come fast that are the best ones. I just enjoyed turning out a good show. If I turned out a show that made me laugh, I considered it an accomplishment. Ideas are precious, and you stick them in your back pocket and use the good ones when you can."

Bus Stop ...

Partridge Family Diaries: Behind-the-Scenes Stories

Cash, Nelson, and Bonaduce

Danny Bonaduce: I was 10 or 11 years old. I didn't hang out with David Cassidy's friends, but the one person I remember from David Cassidy's inner circle was a photographer named Henry Diltz. There was this calendar of "The World's Greatest," all giving people the finger. It was Johnny Cash, Willie Nelson, and me! Well, along with nine other people. But Henry Diltz took that picture when I was 11 years old, just flipping people off. It's one of my favorite possessions. I'm up there with Johnny Cash, man! That's on t-shirts everywhere now!

Sinatra's Car Wash

Danny Janssen: Just a funny thing that happened with David one day. I don't know if he'd even remember it or not. We were all going to meet at Wes' house and go to the studio at ten o'clock. Wes was going to drive. Anyway, my driver leaves me off right there on Sunset behind Wes' house. I always looked so darn young, and I started walking up the driveway and there's Frank Sinatra out there washing a car and he says, "Hey kid, you work here?" I said, "Yeah." He says, "Well, start working!" So we're washing his Rolls Royce, and I'm asking him questions and he's answering me. We were just jabbering away. Then all of a sudden Wes comes out and says, "Damn it, Janssen, we've got to be at the studio!" Frank looks at me and he says, "I thought you said you work here," and I said, "We do. We do *The Partridge Family*." He said, "That's not what

I meant!" I said, "Hey, let me tell you something. Anybody can work for the Partridge Family, but how many guys get to wash a car with Frank Sinatra?"

A Secret Crush

Tom Bahler: I had a huge crush on Shirley. She was a guest star on the Smothers Brothers show when I was on the show, and when she walked in, man, I thought she was such a fox! She was so beautiful. She was way older than me, but I didn't care. I was working on the show so I couldn't hit on her, but I wanted to! Later on, when we did *The Partridge Family*, I just liked her as a person. I was old enough to talk to her a little bit just to get a feel for her as a human being, and she was delicious, man. She was so nice, and so fun, and had a cool sense of humor. When we did *The Partridge Family* it was a joy to work with her. She remembered meeting me. She was that kind of person. She remembered people.

Run, Danny, Run!

Danny Bonaduce: I had broken some windows on Western Street, the same street that the Christmas episode was shot on. I was throwing rocks through them, playing around, and security started chasing me. I got into a golf cart and ran around, all through the commissary. The security guards were chasing me, and all of a sudden I heard this huge "STOP!" Everybody froze! Then we all kind of looked around like *Why are we freezing?* It was Sir Laurence Olivier. He gave me this motion to come toward him. So I went over to him, and I didn't know who he was. He said, "You're not supposed to be like other people. Otherwise, construction workers would be famous. Run!" I took off running. I don't think I've ever stopped since.

The 40-Year-Old Midget

Larry Rosen: Danny was the smartest kid. We'd give him these incredibly funny lines and he would read them at the table, and he had no idea what he was saying but we would get hysterical because he knew exactly what the tone was and how to read the lines. He'd say, "What does that mean?" We'd explain it to him, but he had this innate sense of humor that was wonderful, and captivating. We wrote to it all of the time, but 90 percent of the time he didn't know what the hell he was saying until we explained it to him.

when we're singin'

Bus Ride

Danny Bonaduce: The best time I ever had on that bus was once when David got kind of mad at me because I kept blowing my lines. We had become friends, and I think I was doing it on purpose to bug him, but I'm not sure. He'll tell you that I just flubbed my lines 22 times in a row, but most people will tell you that I didn't flub my lines that much. Whichever is right, I don't care—I either did it to bug him or I couldn't remember my lines. He was supposed to pull up about five feet forward and stop the bus. We'd back it up and do it again—pull up five feet forward, say the line again, pull up and back, do it again. Then one time he just kept going! We went out the gates, and we went into Hollywood. He just stole the bus! We didn't realize it, because we were living such protected lives, if you will. Not by knowledge, because all we did was work and sleep. So we drove to Hollywood Boulevard, and then the riot police came. Traffic stopped. We were driving in a psychedelic bus—David Cassidy and Danny Bonaduce—and it says *The Partridge Family* on the side of it! We're stopped at a red light, and we've got one of the biggest shows in the country and one of the biggest hits in the country, right? People went crazy! We rode it back to the studio escorted by the police. That was fun!

Mrs. Shirley Kinkaid?

Shirley Jones: I've been asked, and I knew you'd ask too, why I never had a romance with Reuben Kincaid. Please! He was my manager!

Reality vs. Psychosis

Suzanne Crough: I wasn't asked so much about whether we were really singing as much as I was treated as if the TV family was my real family. A certain percentage of the population really thought that Danny was my brother and Keith was my brother. They thought we were really a family, like reality TV of today. That percentage of people was kind of high, and still is by today's standards, which, to me, is like *Are you kidding me? Don't you know they have this big thing called a camera?* I remember once being at this hamburger place called Carney's on Sunset where I used to go a lot when I was growing up. I was with a friend, and it was just after I did a movie that was filmed as a reality documentary and won the Academy Award (*Teenage Father*, 1978). It had just aired on NBC. This lady walked up to me at the hamburger place and swung her purse and hit me! She told me I was such a bad mother, and how could I do that, and so on. I thought *Are you kidding me?* In some people's minds we were treated like our TV family was real, which was more strange than if they were going to think we were really singing.

Whole Milk Acceptance

Danny Bonaduce: My favorite memories from the times of *The Partridge Family* are things that ended up on our Christmas reel. It was a gag reel of outtakes. We were doing this scene once, and suddenly, in the middle of the scene while still delivering her line perfectly, Susan Dey just pours a gallon of milk over my head at the breakfast table. I'm sure I had done something wrong or screwed up a bunch of things, but whatever it was, she just dumped it over my head in one shot, and I wasn't expecting it at all. I mean, we were doing a regular scene and it was not called for in the script, so I don't know if they were mad at me for something I did earlier or kidding around with me, but all of a sudden I'm just covered in milk. At first I was mad. I was freaked and I kind of froze, like *What's happening?* Then I realized it was a practical joke—the kind you play on one of the adults. It's not something you do to one of the kids. At that moment I felt I had arrived. I was one of the adults that you could pull practical jokes on. *I guess I'm grown up now,* I thought. That's one of my favorites.

Hocus-Pocus

Danny Bonaduce: Shaun Cassidy was an amateur magician, and so was I. Shaun and I used to book kids' parties, birthday parties, and we'd do magic shows for kids. I don't think anybody really knows that. Dave Madden, by the way, is an excellent magician. It's still his big, big hobby. [Author's note: This interview was conducted before Madden's death.]

Jack Cassidy

Danny Bonaduce: Jack Cassidy was one of my heroes. I said that to Shirley Jones on a talk show one time. The host asked what I meant. I said it was just a kid's memory, and I'm not sure it's accurate, but you could knock on Jack

Cassidy's front door at 8:30 in the morning and he'd be wearing a red velvet smoking jacket, looked like James Bond with a martini in his hand, and he'd say, "Good morning." Jack was Errol Flynn. That was also the demise of Jack Cassidy, to be honest with you. He was somewhere between being an Errol Flynn and, for lack of a better term, Bruce Willis. Jack Cassidy should have been a superstar. He was either 10 years too early or 20 years too late. He was amazing, but at the same time he was just a scalawag. You know what I mean? He was just this damn swashbuckler, and he couldn't help himself.

Gardening

Danny Bonaduce: One time Jack paid me and Shaun [Cassidy] $10 to move these giant rocks. It was several tons of rock that was going to surround his pool. They were really heavy and I struggled to move them. When we were done moving them from one huge pile to the next, he said, "That's not where I told you to put them. Put them back." And he wouldn't pay me my 10 bucks until we did! I couldn't believe it, but at the same time there was something about Jack that I admired.

Go to Your Room!

Shirley Jones: Danny was always involved in funny moments, as you can well imagine, and I was always on his case. You know—"Would you please stop! Let's settle down now!" That kind of thing. He tells a story about me sending him to his room. It's true. I said, "Go to your room!" And he said, "What room?" Then I pointed up the stairs—which was simply a set!

The Look-alike

William S. Bickley: I remember every time I drove onto the lot—because my hair looked a little like David's, and I was in this '70s Camaro—the gate was always crowded with groupies, these teenage fans. I mean it was a horde of them all day long waiting for a chance to see David. And I swear it seemed like every single time I drove up to the lot, as I'd come to a stop, these four or five teenyboppers, teenage girls, would throw themselves on the hood of my car, and on the windshield, and it was like driving through Texas and having bugs on the windshield except they were girls! And their face would come

> straight across from mine in the windshield, and at that point they would see me and you would see this look of expectation melt into such cataclysmic disappointment! And I would often say, "I'm not him, I'm so sorry!"

Rock Us, Baby

David Cassidy's musical influences were heavily rooted in the blues and the music he grew up with through the '60s. He longed for the opportunity to record something reflective of his musical roots. *Cherish* was a huge success for him and opened the door for the record label to give him a little more control over his sound. Cassidy was driving full force to establish his own musical identity and *Rock Me Baby* was the next step in that process.

In May of 1972, while *Shopping Bag* was on the charts, Wes Farrell announced that his publishing company had bought out the main publishing arm for the Rascals, who'd had a No. 4 hit in 1967 with "How Can I Be Sure." The buyout price was not revealed, but the deal included more than 100 songs written by members of the group. Farrell also revealed that the Rascals had a stockpile of unrecorded material as well as their already released successes. He hoped to get hits with some of them on his own label, Chelsea Records. "We propose to exploit every outlet for this creative material," he said. One of the first outlets was *Rock Me Baby*.

A lot of time was spent thinking through exactly what songs Cassidy should cover. "We would listen for David," says Danny Janssen, who worked very closely with Farrell. "I don't think David even knows this. We'd listen to hundreds and hundreds of songs that came in from all over the world, and this nucleus of people picked the songs. Twenty songs at first, then 13 for the segments, then 11 for the album." But the choosing of songs for him rather than by him was exactly the thing that bothered Cassidy—not to mention that none of his chart successes to date included anything that he wrote himself. Some of that began to change with *Rock Me Baby*.

Cassidy loved the music of the Rascals and their singer-songwriting team Eddie Brigati and Felix Cavaliere. He was delighted to be able to choose "How Can I Be Sure" and "Lonely Too Long" for this album, now that he had convinced the powers at Bell Records to let him have some say in the design of his solo work.

"How Can I Be Sure" was the first single from *Rock Me Baby*—released in May 1972, six months ahead of the album itself. It was a screaming smash, especially in England. *Cash Box* declared, "His follow-up to 'Could It Be Forever' is a faithful re-interpretation of the Rascals hit complete with the continental flair. Should be a huge summer hit, rivaling if not surpassing 'Cherish.'" They were almost right on

when we're singin'

the money. In the States it only hit No. 25 on *Billboard* charts but the U.K. release was huge, surpassing the chart success of 'Cherish' and moving into the No. 1 slot, showing all signs that Cassidy star power in England was still on the rise. He recorded "Lonely Too Long," the other Rascals cover, as a rocker with a bluesy opening lick.

The title song of the album was written by Johnny Cymbal and Peggy Clinger, who were signed with Wes Farrell's publishing affiliate, Pocket Full of Tunes. The two had never had the success they would have liked with their Partridge Family songs, but Cassidy's rendition of "Rock Me Baby" put them on the map. Cassidy wanted this song. He felt connected to it. Initially Bell Records was hesitant because of concerns that some of the lyrics were too sexually driven for Cassidy's image. But despite objections it became the second single from the album, released in fall of 1972 just before the album itself, and going to No. 38 in the States and No. 11 in the U.K. Cymbal and Clinger also co-wrote with Wes Farrell "(Oh No) No Way," which appeared on the album.

There is a significant shift in songwriting style for the tracks written for the album. Kim Carnes and Dave Ellingson were friends of Cassidy's who had performed with him from the very start of his concert tours. They sang as background singers for Cassidy, even opening for him and doing some music of their own on occasion. Together the three of them had written "Some Kind of a Summer," inspired by a road trip from San Francisco to Los Angeles. It was released as a single—not by Cassidy but by the Sugar Bears, a Saturday-morning cartoon group created by the makers of the popular cereal. The song itself was still heralded. *Cash Box* reviewed it: "A good song is worth its weight in gold. Such is the case with this beautiful Dave Ellingson composition redone by the Sugar Bears. Warm and compassionate memories of a summer gone are the highlights of this track that should be hitbound in a matter of weeks." Carnes and Cassidy also wrote "Song for a Rainy Day," which appeared on *Rock Me Baby*.

Another *Rock Me Baby,* track, "Warm My Soul," is a Joerey Ortiz number that had been recorded for the Partridge Family but then cut. It offers a taste of something different for Cassidy, even though the musical arrangement still wasn't done the way he had envisioned—another hard reminder that Farrell still had final say.

Although it wasn't included on the album, Cassidy also recorded "Along Comes Mary," which had been a big hit for the Association during the '60s, during these sessions—not a surprising choice, given the success of "Cherish." Of the three cover tunes that were finally settled on for the album, "Go Now" by Larry Banks and Milton Bennett seemed perfect in another attempt to combine crooner Cassidy with bluesy Cassidy.

Many of the songs on the album reflect maturity and growth, including two from Adam Miller: "Soft as a Summer Shower" and "Song of Love."

WHITE COVERS

Miller recalls, "'Soft as a Summer Shower' is one I wrote with Wes. We were hack songwriters to a great degree, and to the extent that we had gifts. Basically we were sitting around the offices trying to think of ideas for songs and make them work. I don't think I was terribly good at it. I think the other guys were generally more successful with that than I was, but I felt that I should do my best for Wes." Miller felt much more connected to the songs he wrote for himself.

Cassidy also wrote "Two Time Loser," a contemplative song about an imaginary relationship. It was the first recorded song by Cassidy that he had written on the piano. Interestingly, both the singles released from this album featured Cassidy's self-penned songs on the B-sides. "Two Time Loser" appeared as the B-side on the "Rock Me Baby" single, and "Ricky's Tune," a popular album cut on *Cherish*, was the B-side of *Rock Me Baby*'s first single, "How Can I Be Sure."

The album reflects the same stellar musicianship fans of the era had come to know, with great work by the Wrecking Crew. "I saw that Wes was smart enough to give David an outlet to sing in a more adult way," says arranger Mike Melvoin, "and, needless to say, that allowed me to write in a more adult way too."

Well-known R&B singers Marnell McCall, Lisa Roberts, and Gwen Johnson were enlisted to help bring the soulful sound David Cassidy was after. Some of the regulars were back, too, including Jackie Ward—although she, too, was working with an R&B sound. "I didn't sing the same way as I did when I sang the Partridge Family songs," says Ward, "because I was singing a lower part. It wouldn't have been the same sound at all. It was a little more mature. My voice is more of an alto."

Rock Me Baby came out in October 1972, and critics and trade magazines applauded: "Being a transitional LP for the Partridges' (and America's) favorite son. The hard side—like that in the title tune and "Lonely Too Long." And the soft side—"How Can I Be Sure" and a tune he wrote with Kim Carnes, "Song for a Rainy Day." Another winning gentle track is Dave Ellingson's "Some Kind of a Summer" (both Kim & Dave sing backup for David on the LP as they do live.) Jim Gordon, Hal Blaine and Joe Osborn are among the musical luminaries helping David to rock right up the LP charts…a journey he can now take blindfolded."

Rock Me Baby served as a good next step for Cassidy. It had enough rock and blues to prove he was capable of different styles—just enough to allow his fans the opportunity to taste it and grow with him without alienating them.

For the first time FM radio play seemed like a possibility based on the music, but the image that defined Cassidy kept it from happening. The single release of "Rock Me Baby" was the second single from the album in America. A British pop group named Brotherhood of Man had also recorded the song, but "Cassidymania," as it was called in England, was so powerful that they held their version back from release.

when we're singin'

Wes Farrell told Ken Sharp, "We did recordings that I thought were a lot more grownup and a lot more sophisticated. They gave David the ability to have his own identity, his own presence. We didn't simplify it as we did with the Partridge Family. He couldn't have sung 'Rock Me Baby' as part of the Partridge Family."

Even so, Cassidy was never happy with Farrell's ultimate control over the solo albums. "He was so mad at Wes because he wanted to do R&B as a *single*," recalls John Bahler. "We did 'Cherish' and a couple of things that were hits for him, but he wanted to do R&B and Wes wouldn't do it." Farrell never believed R&B was the way to go with David Cassidy, likely because of the success they were currently having on the pop charts with the already-established sound. "Once a success formula is put into place, those looking at the business side of things rarely want to tamper with it," says Bahler.

The album reached No. 41 in the United States and soared to No. 2 in England. The *Cherish* album was still making fans scream in the U.K.—so much that the U.K. release of *Rock Me Baby* was delayed by Bell Records until *Cherish* cooled off a bit. It was a clever move by the record label, taking full advantage of the sales market. The delay also put *Rock Me Baby* in perfect alignment with Cassidy's third concert tour, the first to include Europe. Cassidy was hotter than hot overseas, and *Rock Me Baby*, his first attempt at some edginess, was fuel for the fire.

Liner Notes: *The Partridge Family Notebook*

Cover tunes became the focus for *The Partridge Family Notebook* even as the songwriters in the office cubicles were growing in number and trying to come up with more original material. "I think the creativity angle wasn't satisfactory anymore," recalls Tom Bahler, "and by doing covers, [Wes Farrell] could kind of lock David in to doing certain things, you know?"

Farrell had complete access to the Screen Gems/Columbia Music vaults, and with the huge success of *Cherish* (both the single and the album) followed by the Partridge cover of "Breaking Up Is Hard to Do" still resonating from summer, he was convinced he could launch more Partridge Family hits using cover tunes. Excluding the *Christmas Card* album, "Breaking Up Is Hard to Do" was only one of two covers recorded by the Partridge Family up to this point—the other one being "I Really Want to Know You," written by Barry Mann and Cynthia Weil. Farrell zeroed in on Mann & Weil, and *The Partridge Family Notebook* became a showpiece for some of their earlier work.

Mann and Weil were breakout songwriters of the '60s, having written songs that include "Kicks" for Paul Revere and the Raiders, "Shades of Gray" for the Monkees, and "You've Lost that Lovin' Feeling," co-written with Phil Spector for the Righteous

Brothers. They came from the same school of Brill Building songwriting as Gerry Goffin, Carole King, Howard Greenfield, and many others. By 1969 they had begun establishing themselves with music for films and Broadway, showcasing their talent to write music for dramatic storylines. By 1971, the vice president and director of professional activities at Screen Gems-Columbia, Irwin Schuster, said they were the "most talented songwriters in popular music today, and have been for over 10 years." Their pop chart success crossed with film work and hit soundtrack albums made their music a no-brainer for Wes Farrell, especially since they were Screen Gems writers. They also carried the kind of maturity David Cassidy had been wanting.

After careful study, Farrell selected three Mann and Weil songs that had garnered high-charting hits in the '60s for prominent slots on *The Partridge Family Notebook*. "Walking in the Rain," which had been a hit for the Ronettes, was a perfect choice, with its romantic imagery and pure declarations of love. "Looking Through the Eyes of Love," the first single from *Notebook*, captured the crooning side of Cassidy and made a brief showing on the *Billboard* charts.

The third, "We Gotta Get Out of This Place," was an odd choice given the marketing image of the Partridge Family. Constructed with dark lyrics and a grim undertone, the message of the song was difficult to sell on a show whose viewers were used to upbeat messages and intimate expressions of unrequited love. It is no wonder the song was never used on an episode.

"We Gotta Get Out of This Place" may have been something David wanted to do," John Bahler speculates. "To keep harmony in the family, Wes may have said OK. I'm guessing, but that's what my instincts tell me."

Notebook also serves as a showcase for the collaboration between Wes Farrell, Bobby Hart, and Danny Janssen. The three songwriters really began to dominate with album credits. *Notebook* is the first album to feature any one song credited to all three men, and there are two of them featured here. Their rock-driven "Friend and a Lover" and the speculative "Something's Wrong" are both written by the trio and appear alongside the more somber "Take Good Care of Her," which was written by Janssen and Hart without Farrell. "We were cranking them out," says Bobby Hart. "I mean the Janssen-Hart songs and the Farrell-Janssen-Hart songs—I remember doing them, and I remember we wrote some of them at the offices at Chelsea. I remember going over to Wes' house on the corner of Woodier and Sunset Boulevard in Beverly Hills and writing there with Wes. I remember having early morning breakfasts with Wes at the Beverly Hills Hotel, but specific memories of most of these songs are pretty sparse."

Another original track was Austin Roberts and John Michael Hill's "Maybe Someday." Roberts, who was a singer as well as a songwriter, had already established a rapport with Danny Janssen and Bobby Hart as the lead vocalist for the *Scooby*

when we're singin'

Doo, Where Are You? theme. He also had a big hit as a singer in 1972 with "Keep on Singing," written by Janssen and Hart and recorded on Farrell's Chelsea label.

"At the same time I was signed to Screen Gems there was an overlap for about a year where I also worked as a producer at Columbia Records," says John Michael Hill. "In addition to writing songs with Austin, I was also producing various acts." The Partridge Family had recorded Hill's song "Listen to the Sound." Their version was never released, although the song was recorded by a different artist, produced by Hill and released on Columbia. In 1972 Hill started his own jingle company. He is still active today, having written songs for filmmaker Quentin Tarantino and the hit TV program *That '70s Show*.

Adam Miller wrote two songs for *Notebook*: "As Long As You're There" and the gentle "Storybook Love," the latter co-written with Wes Farrell. Miller had established himself with the Farrell camp as an A-list songwriter.

Miller had lived outside the country before coming back for college. When he decided music was his passion, he quit school and moved to New York with a friend. He eventually did a few sessions with Les Paul, who was interested in him. Just about then, a wealthy Frenchman who had a strong desire to produce music, took an interest in Miller's music.

Miller was now a solo act, and had been playing clubs, and little venues, and together they produced some good material. "I guess some tapes that I had made came to Wes' attention and he called me in," says Miller. "We spoke—I actually was worried about the production, because I think at that point he had a few hits with the Partridges, and I was considering myself at that point as sort of a reflective, serious singer-songwriter, a little bit full of myself probably. I went and met with him and I asked him about the production. I didn't say anything negative, but I think he took a little mild offense at that, and he said, 'Well, perhaps we shouldn't continue talking.' I said OK and I went my own way.

"He called me back a couple of months later. We met and we struck up a relationship at that point, and I guess he had had by that time maybe one, maybe two hits with the Partridge Family. I signed with Wes, and he put me to work. In addition to my own stuff, he put me to work writing for everything he had going, which included the Partridge Family."

Miller reflects, "It was just a thrill to go there every day, and to write, and to be in that world, and to have the opportunity, and to have an audience for what you did. That was just a kick. A major, major kick, to be able to create something and have it actually materialize into something, I'm not a person who writes very well in a complete vacuum. And with the Farrell organization, you knew, with Wes, that somebody was going to be listening hard to what you did, and if they felt that it could be used someplace there were going to be a lot of opportunities to get it out there."

WHITE COVERS

Farrell released two solo albums with Miller: *Who Would Give His Only Song Away* in 1972, and *Westwind Circus* in 1975.

Johnny Cymbal and Peggy Clinger were back writing for *Notebook* with the energetic "Love Must Be the Answer"—complete with the signature Bahler la-la-las that every Partridge fan could sing along with. "I used to do those vocal intros all the time," says Bahler. "They immediately said 'Partridge Family.' David got to the place where he couldn't stand them. David just thought it was bubblegum. I never thought of it as bubblegum. Wes and I never approached it as bubblegum. We never approached it as rock and roll, either."

Cymbal and Clinger were a romantically involved couple drawn together by songwriting. He had a bit of a pop success with "Mr. Bassman" in 1963, and she was one of the original Clinger sisters who appeared regularly on the variety show circuit, appearing with Andy Williams, the Smothers Brothers, and others. Despite their individual success they were both artists searching for something more, and they found it when they met each other. Their love affair united them, especially with songwriting, and Wes Farrell was very impressed with their talents.

Farrell quickly signed them as resident writers for his artists, including David Cassidy and the Partridge Family. Farrell loved their songwriting so much that between fall 1971 and fall 1972, they wrote 24 songs and he recorded and released all of them—that is, until "Me Loving You."

The gorgeous "Me Loving You" is a Partridge Family outtake that came very close to being on *Notebook*. It was placed onto the original test pressings with 12 tracks rather than the usual 11, but ultimately it was the one song cut from the track list. It's the only one of the pair's five Partridge Family cuts that remains unreleased.

Cymbal and Clinger's songwriting success led them to their own album and single release, also out in the fall of '72. "God Bless You Rock and Roll" was released around the same time as *Notebook*. The duo went on to perform concerts, often appearing with other pop bands including Sly & the Family Stone.

The real standout on *Notebook*—the song that would prove to be an enduring fan favorite—was Tony Romeo and Ken Jacobson's "Together We're Better." Jacobson says of his influences, "I loved all of the old shows from the '40s and '50s when I was growing up—people like Jerome Kern, Irving Berlin, and George Gershwin." The influence is unmistakable in his only Partridge Family collaboration.

The recording sessions for season 3 were done in May and September 1972. *Notebook* was produced from these sessions, which were intense because of the rising demands on David Cassidy. Complicating things, Cassidy's time was now at a premium; he was doing more concerts and spending more time in the studio working on his solo albums. But the detail that went into the arrangements, no matter what the stress level became, was never compromised.

when we're singin'

John Bahler names the recording session dated May 1, 1972, which generated most of the songs for *Notebook,* as his all-time favorite memory and favorite day from his days with the Partridge Family. "We went in on a Saturday and we had 13 sides to cut," he says. "I think we started at nine or 10. Everything I had written was inspired and we just roared through it. It just so happened that everything I did for that session, Wes loved. We tripled everything, so everything you'd hear was three times. It was just one after another after another, and we cut all 13 tracks on that one day, and every one of them was a winner. It was such a great feeling. I just remember how proud of ourselves we were at the end of the day, knowing we had done a great job in such a short amount of time." Of the 13 tracks cut that day, six were included on *Notebook* and four on the next album, *Crossword Puzzle.* "Breaking Up Is Hard to Do" ended up a single, and the other two—"Me Loving You" and "Sunshine Eyes"— were never released.

"In those days," says Bahler, "you did albums usually in three sessions. You'd do four songs in three hours, or three songs in three hours. The rule of thumb was that you could record five minutes' worth of music in an hour.… So if you had an album with 12 songs, that would be three sessions of three hours each. Singers didn't go by the hour. We were paid by the song and by the number of songs. If we double-tracked or triple-tracked, we were paid extra for that.

"There was no specific reason to finish them all in that one day. I don't recall any pressure. We just went in there and they were all written, and we did it! It was really fun. In fact, I used to write at the top of the music "Supergroup." The four of us walked out of that session and we went out to get something to eat because we hadn't eaten all day. In those days when you sang, you didn't eat, because when you came back you'd be clearing your throat. Most of us ate one meal a day and that was late at night. We were also very skinny!"

Sales of *Notebook* were expected to be huge. *Billboard* and the other trades predicted major success. But sales failed to match expectations, serving as an unmistakable sign that the Partridge craze was slowing down in the U.S. Many factors played a role in this decline: First, the quantity of music released by David Cassidy and the Partridge Family in the past year was unheard-of for any artist. With *At Home with Their Greatest Hits, Rock Me Baby,* and now *Notebook* all released to store shelves over a three-month period in fall 1972, there was a huge amount of new Cassidy-voiced material to choose from, and *Notebook* was third in that string of releases. Fans were young, and parents who were usually footing the bill were most likely saying "pick one" if they hadn't done so already. *Notebook* didn't make store shelves in time for the Thanksgiving weekend, losing out on the biggest shopping weekend of the year.

Cassidy's *Rolling Stone* layout from earlier in the year may have taken a toll on the innocence factor, depending on who you talk to. There's also speculation that the album cover art was too bland from a marketing perspective, designed all in white with no photos—although the lack of front cover photos hadn't mattered on sales for *The Partridge Family Album* and *Christmas Card*. Bell Records had also made some serious internal shifts during the summer, and promotion of the album was likely handled differently by executives who were new to their roles. Beginning with *Notebook,* full-page ad placement in the trade magazines was discontinued on all Partridge Family albums and singles, but it was heavily amped up for David Cassidy's solo albums. *Tiger Beat's Official Partridge Family Magazine* also came to an end in the fall of '72, and *Notebook* was the first Partridge Family album that didn't receive publicity from that source.

The songs on *Notebook* received the least exposure on the show. While eight of the 11 tracks were used, they appeared less frequently and received less exposure.

Finally, there was the usual two-year span for teen idols, which had come full circle by September 1972, two months before *Notebook* was released.

The target audience was growing up. Two or three years' change is a big difference in the way teens and preteens think and feel. The cultural and social times were radically changing, too. Music was especially eclectic and ever-changing during the first part of the '70s and, though production on *Notebook* was top notch, it didn't reflect much of a change in style despite the choice of proven hitmakers for cover tunes.

U.S. fans may have been cooling off a bit, but those in England and Australia were just firing up, and doing so with a frenzy that would top the popularity of what had already happened in the States. A new peak of success was about to emerge overseas for the Partridge Family and David Cassidy, who were now a worldwide sensation.

Farrell was also stressed—really stressed. He had just launched his label, and Cassidy was becoming more and more resistant to the songs and arrangements Farrell was producing for him. Farrell was getting as burnt out as Cassidy.

The intensity with which Farrell had to work in order to manage all of his companies was beyond imagination. "One time they had to rush Wes to the hospital because he drank so much coffee he got caffeine poisoning," says Jean Inman. The incident happened during a Partridge Family recording session. "Shirley Jones rode with him in the ambulance," she says. "After that, he had a lifelong allergy to coffee. If he would have one sip of it, he'd get really sick." Adam Miller always felt Farrell had overextended himself with his organization during these years.

Notebook peaked at a mere No. 41 on *Billboard,* staying on the charts for only 16 weeks—the lowest numbers yet for a Partridge Family album. It was also the first one not to earn gold status based on sales. When *Notebook* failed to grab the fan base, Cassidy began pushing even harder for the music to change. He really believed that allowing the sound to change with the times would have helped keep it alive.

"Wes was trying to keep the music to what it was," says Shirley Jones, "and David wasn't happy. He wanted to go further, and that was a problem." Ron Hicklin agrees. "I think David felt at times that he could spread his talent out a little more and do more artistic and interesting things other than the bag we were singing in. I went through that with a lot of artists who had success in their day. Every time they wanted to change they fell, because they lost their audience. It didn't matter what they wanted to do. If they didn't gain a new audience that appreciated it, then they just lost the audience that they already had. We always observed those kind of things as we recorded with everybody that was out there—the Gary Lewises and the Bobby Shermans. In David's case he probably wanted to go beyond what the Partridge Family was doing, but he was doing a great job with it, and all of it was very successful."

"I remember when David started talking about wanting to do more R&B," says John Bahler. "You know the R&B arrangement of "I Think I Love You" that he does now? That's what he wanted to do then." John Bahler and Wes Farrell were both against it.

"Really, I love him to this day," Bahler says. He's such a great guy and a great talent, but he was pushing it. It just didn't work and it was pissing him off…. David talked to me about it, but I just didn't have the guts to say to him, 'That's not the right direction I think you should go.' In so many ways, and his own way, that's what Wes was saying." Some of the songs on *Notebook* reflect an attempt at some change, especially "We Gotta Get Out of this Place," but any move toward a new direction was slight. It was not embraced with the kind of commitment needed to really put something different out there.

Notebook has a slightly more adult contemporary feel than the earlier albums. The chart rankings for "Looking Through the Eyes of Love" illustrated the difference, peaking at No. 39 on *Billboard*'s pop charts but hitting an impressive No. 9 on the adult contemporary chart—the chart that had given good results for earlier Partridge Family songs including "I'll Meet You Halfway," "Doesn't Somebody Want to be Wanted," "It's One of Those Nights (Yes, Love)," and "Am I Losing You."

Whether or not *The Partridge Family Notebook* excited the buying public, it is artistically solid and a good pop–adult contemporary album in its own right. *Notebook* can be credited as the Partridge Family album that began to reach for a more mature sound but didn't jump into the musical waters of change quite deep enough.

Friend and a Lover, 2:29, Danny Janssen–Bobby Hart–Wes Farrell
The album's opener is also its first surprise. It's a very different sound—grittier, and a clear attempt at something new, especially given its placement as the first track on the album. It's far more rock and roll in nature, launching itself with a heavy, distorted fuzz guitar. The Partridge Family formula is still intact, but the arrangement reflects some experimentation. The tune bears a similarity to the lighter "Na

Na Hey Hey Kiss Him Goodbye" recorded by Steam in 1969. "Friend and a Lover" was released as the second single from the album four months after the album was released, after being singled out with praise by critics and trade magazines.

Cash Box reported: "David Cassidy and his musical TV family rock it up with another top 40 contender sure to please their leagions of fans."

Appears On: Season 3, episode 68, "Bedknobs and Drumsticks"
(February 9, 1973)

Walking in the Rain, 2:58, Barry Mann–Phil Spector–Cynthia Weil

Released as a single internationally but not in the States, "Walking in the Rain" soared up the British charts all the way to No. 10. Not bad, given that only the first three Partridge Family singles ever made it into the American Top 10. It was a clear indicator of the upward momentum happening in the U.K. The first of the three cover tunes, this is another Farrell-ized version of the Phil Spector "wall of sound," with heavy reverb on both the vocals and the drums. It was recorded by plenty of other groups—including Jay and the Americans, who had a No. 19 hit with it in 1969, and the Ronettes, for whom the song was written, taking it to No. 23 in 1964. It is the only Phil Spector-produced song to ever win a Grammy. Cheryl Ladd recorded a cover on a 1978 album, and the band Erasure covered it in 2003. It also marks the last Partridge Family hit single in the U.K.

Appears On: Season 3, episode 67, "The Eleven-Year Itch" (February 2, 1973)

Take Good Care of Her, 2:42, Danny Janssen–Bobby Hart

"Take Good Care of Her" was the only officially released Partridge Family song to be used on the short-lived 1974 cartoon series *The Partridge Family 2200 A.D.,* with different lead singers and new songs by Janssen and Hart. It was featured on two separate episodes but oddly never surfaced on an episode of the original series.

The tune is typical fare for Cassidy, a forsaken reflection on the lost love of a girl. His voice is out front without any reverb. For whatever reason, the track has a very wide stereo separation in an otherwise tightly mixed album.

Together We're Better, 2:38, Tony Romeo-Ken Jacobson

"He was my best friend, Tony was," says Ken Jacobson. And together these best friends wrote their only Partridge Family collaboration. An upbeat sleeper that has endured the test of time, "Together We're Better" was never released as a single in the States, but it was placed on the B-side of the U.K. release "Walking in the Rain." It showed up years later on the 2004 CD hits compilation *Come on Get Happy: The Very Best of the Partridge Family* after time had proven it a fan favorite and a lost opportunity for a hit single.

when we're singin'

The creative opening hook is a calliope, or an organ made to sound like one. There is also the subtle use of a 12-string acoustic guitar mixed within the song itself. The lyrics are much darker than one might notice at first because of the light and energetic melody. The song tells the story of two people who have a magic something when they are together, but the ways of the world interfere with their relationship. It played most memorably on an episode about a princess whose social class keeps her from her wish to go on a date with a normal American boy next door, and it was also chosen for the location episode at King's Island. Both times it was used as underscore rather than in the usual concert setting.

The title "Together We're Better" parallels Tony Romeo and Ken Jacobson's songwriting chemistry and ability to work together. Romeo rarely co-wrote, but he really wanted to write something for the Partridge Family with his longtime friend Jacobson.

"Tony said, 'Do you want to write a song with me for the Partridge Family?'" recalls Jacobson, "and I said 'Sure! Let's go!' Tony was just a wonderful, wonderful lyric writer. Tony came up with the title, and I believe that's how it all started, and then we sat down together. Whenever we wrote, we wrote pretty much together, not like some songs where one person is writing part of it separately. We didn't do that. We wrote this together. It wasn't lyrics first or music first. We sat down in a room and wrote this song very quickly. It wasn't one of those *Let's think about this for two months* things. This one was written quite fast. We always wrote either at his place or my place, walking around the room and sitting at the piano.

"We wrote this specifically for the Partridge Family, though it was not based on the show, or on any particular segment of the show. This was cooked up. We just sort of liked the sound of it, and decided we wanted to go for this kind of feel. The only thing I remember about the creative writing process is that we were both very happy with the way the words sat on the music. I always loved *"all alone we're fine, but united we're dynamite."* I still like listening to the marriage of words and music in that song. I know it was one of Tony's favorites."

Appears On: Season 3, episode 52, "Princess and the Partridge" (September 29, 1972); Season 3, episode 66 "I Left My Heart in Cincinnati" (January 26, 1973)

Looking Through the Eyes of Love, 3:03,
Barry Mann–Cynthia Weil

This was the last time the Partridge Family hit *Billboard*'s Top 40, and they did so just barely. "Looking Through the Eyes of Love" peaked at No. 39 the week of January 27, 1973, after entering the Hot 100 just before Christmas of '72.

Wes Farrell felt strongly about this song's potential as a hit. According to Cynthia Weil, it had been originally written for Gene Pitney, who had a Top 40 hit with it in 1965.

A self-deprecating, depressed character is reflected in the lead vocal on this track, with Cassidy singing as someone who feels like life's biggest loser—except in the eyes of his woman who loves him.

Cash Box had this to say: "Single culled from group's soon to be released 'Notebook' album is soft, meaningful ballad written by Barry Mann and Cynthia Weil. Needless to say, this is another top 20 disk from America's favorite family."

"Breaking Up Is Hard to Do" had proven that cover tunes could bring hits for the Partridges, and "Looking Through the Eyes of Love" was chosen as the first single from *Notebook* as a direct result of that success.

Appears On: Season 3, episode 60, "Whatever Happened to Keith Partridge?" (November 24, 1972)

Maybe Someday, 2:56, Austin Roberts–John Michael Hill

Sometimes songwriters put emphasis on the best way to say something once they figure out exactly *what* they are saying, making their approach more subtle. That's what John Michael Hill and Austin Roberts were aiming for with "Maybe Someday."

"I'm going to quote a really obscure composer here," begins Hill. "I believe it was Paul Hindemith who said that the whole thing with art is that you can't be so unfamiliar that your audience has no idea what you're doing, or so familiar that it is boring. You have to somehow walk that line where it's interesting yet not totally alienating. I think Joni Mitchell, for instance, does a fantastic job with that. For that matter, so does Steely Dan. They're unpredictable, and yet they're not crazy, you know?

"'Maybe Someday' was quite mainstream pop but then so was the Partridge Family, so it was kind of right for that. I was thrilled to find out it was being done by the Partridge Family, believe me, because they were a big deal! You know, it was cool to get something on the TV show. It was *very* cool to get something on an album! 'Maybe Someday' always seemed pretty commercial to me."

The song opens with a 12-string acoustic guitar and a lead guitar. Like "Looking Through the Eyes of Love," it evokes feelings of isolation and being misunderstood. It portrays lovers alone in the world, trying to find their way and grasping onto hope for the future. The minor key creates tension in the verses, then goes to a happier, more hopeful major key in the chorus. It is the same technique used with "I Think I Love You" and "I Woke Up in Love This Morning." Hill says Cassidy's vocal interpretation was right on the money.

Appears On: Season 3, episode 70, "Forgive Us Our Debts" (March 2, 1973)

We Gotta Get Out of This Place, 3:55, Barry Mann–Cynthia Weil

This is one of the oddest choices in all of the Partridge Family catalog, and the most obvious attempt on *Notebook* to reach for a more mature sound.

Opening with a bass guitar, the song stays true to its origins, bringing the organ in before the chorus, establishing a dark quality for the usually upbeat Partridges. The organ arrangement mixed with the background vocals brings out a sort of Ike and Tina vibe from the late '60s.

This song has been covered by countless other artists, including Grand Funk Railroad and Blue Oyster Cult. It was originally written for the Righteous Brothers on the heels of their success with Mann and Weil's "You've Lost That Lovin' Feeling." But when Mann won a recording contract for himself, his label wanted him to release it. Meanwhile, the Animals recorded it ahead of Mann, and their version, which came to be known as the definitive recording, hit No. 2 in England and (in a slightly different version) No. 13 in the States during 1965.

The song speaks heavily to social consciousness. During the Vietnam war, it was highly requested by soldiers, and many vets think of it as an anthem for Vietnam. Consequently it has been heard on the soundtracks of *Farenheit 9/11, China Beach, Tour of Duty,* and the BBC series *Privates.*

Whether this song was right for the Partridge Family or not is open to debate, but there is no arguing its credibility and craftsmanship. Barry Mann and Cynthia Weil were at the top of their game, and Wes Farrell clearly liked their work. "We mostly found out they had recorded our songs after the fact," says Cynthia Weil. 'We Gotta Get Out of This Place' has a long story, but nothing to do with the Partridge Family. I had no idea the Partridge Family even recorded this."

Storybook Love, 2:42, Wes Farrell–Adam Miller

Mike Melvoin provides another original opening hook, this time with a beautiful harp intro. A 12-string guitar replaces the usual harpsichord in the gentle fairy-tale opening. The folky-bluesy Adam Miller, whose songs had been well received on *Cherish* and *Rock Me Baby,* links his memories of Wes Farrell very strongly to this song:

"I think that 'Storybook Love' was another tune that was produced by another work session in the cubicle. *Let's go find a tune. Let's go find a line.* That kind of thing. I remember Wes really liking that song. I can see him right now sitting at the piano, singing that song and getting into it, you know, sort of enthusiastically embracing the whole idea, thinking it was good, and liking it a lot. I remember—I can see him right now. I remember Wes saying, 'Yeah, man, that's a good song. That one is really commercial too.' He would say that about various songs. Wes would be in a studio, or in a control room and he'd kind of let himself get carried away and say, 'Let's do this, let's do that,' and people would kind of scurry around to do it. I never really knew what chord I hit with him, but he liked this one. I think that he felt it was a good song for them, but I've got to tell you it was a product of the cubicle."

Farrell spoke highly of Miller in his Ken Sharp interview. "Adam was a very interesting writer. He added a different kind of approach to my writing which helped a lot. He was more like a James Taylor kind of writer."

Miller responds with a chuckle to the James Taylor comparison. "Mike [Appel] used to kind of poke fun at me a little bit," says Miller. "He and Jim [Cretecos] kind of poked fun at me because I had this hair all over the place. I remember Mike was talking about my hair all of the time. I think it was Mike and a couple of others who would indicate to me that I was going to give Wes this sort of authenticity—that part of my job signing on with Wes was to be his token serious singer-songwriter. I think that may have been what Wes was referring to. I was really quite different than anybody he had signed at that point. Most of the records he did and the acts that he worked with were sometimes his creations, and other times these folks were very, very polished show-business performers, people like Tony Orlando and Dawn, those sorts of acts. So anyway, I wasn't that. I was just kind of an introspective songwriter, you know, trying to do something that I imagined was interesting. But who knows?"

Appears On: Season 3, episode 74 "Me and My Shadow" (March 30, 1973)

Love Must Be the Answer, 3:10,
Wes Farrell–Peggy Clinger–Johnny Cymbal

Bright. Cheerful. Happy. A Spanish *yip* and effective upbeats. This is the second of Peggy Clinger and Johnny Cymbal's Partridge Family songs—produced at the same time their "Rock Me Baby" was racing up the singles charts for David Cassidy.

John Bahler had become a master at creating instantly catchy vocal intros. "Most of those intros that we became known for—that all came from God," says Bahler. "I have no idea where that came from. I'd sit down and it would just be there. I always felt when I said *inspired* that I was just the vessel. It just passed through me. It wasn't really me. I believe that happens. When the good stuff happens, it's not really you. You can take credit for it. You can take the money for it, but it comes from someplace else. I still experience that, even to this day. I'm over 70 years old and I still write."

"I liked that a lot," said Wes Farrell. "That song stays with me."

Appears On: Season 3, episode 54, "A Penny for His Thoughts" (October 13, 1972); Season 3, episode 59, "Ain't Loveth Grand" (November 17, 1972); Season 3, episode 62, "For Sale by Owner" (December 29, 1972)

Something's Wrong, 3:12,
Wes Farrell–Danny Janssen–Bobby Hart

Pure formula. Once again we get a minor key in the first verse, creating a haunting feeling that builds to the end of the verse. The theme is even more familiar—turmoil over a conflicted relationship.

when we're singin'

The Partridge Family music often incorporates a lot of differing styles, sounds, and musical surprises. "Something's Wrong" is repetitive and somewhat predictable, but it is still carried through with a smooth arrangement that reflects a well-practiced work process.

"Once we came up with the formula, for want of a better word, we executed it," says John Bahler. "I hate that word because it sounds like we rubber-stamped everything, and we didn't. Most of the arrangements I did were very inspired. The ones that weren't inspired were spotted by Wes Farrell immediately, and he would throw out nine-tenths of it. Then he'd throw ideas back at us and we'd work it out together."

"Something's Wrong" was never used on an episode, although it was released on 45 as a B-side.

As Long As You're There, 3:04, Adam Miller

Sometimes things end up far from where we intended them to go. Production of this song was one of those times.

Adam Miller again recalls working with Wes Farrell: "Wes would come in and tell us his recording schedule, and that we need this many songs by this time," says Miller. "Then we'd have to write a bunch of tunes and he would pick songs from whatever we came up with. This was a song that I wrote, and I thought it was a pretty well-written ditty. Just a little song. Just a little tune. I think it was probably better than many of the tunes I wrote in that environment.

"Well, Wes did something with this song, and brought something out of it that I really wasn't aware of when I wrote it. He arranged it just like Paul Simon's 'Mother and Child Reunion'! I think he even did background vocals that mirrored what Paul Simon had done. When I heard it I thought, *Oh, my God!* All of a sudden it sounded like 'Mother and Child Reunion'! I wasn't really aware of what I had done with the chord changes. Wes brought that whole rhythmic thing into it, and suddenly it sounded just like you took the tracks from 'Mother and Child Reunion' and plugged in different lyrics. Paul Simon had a very interesting little backup harmony on his tune, and I think Wes even had the Partridge Family backups arranged the same way. I was a little bit taken aback when I first heard it. If you listen to the tune, you'll see what I mean. It's very, very similar. I'm sure Wes said, 'Gee, Paul Simon had a really nice hook with that, and look! It's here, too! Let's just do the same thing!' This happened, either inadvertently or intentionally, throughout the music business all of the time. People would borrow heavily on things."

Appears On: Season 3, episode 62 "For Sale by Owner" (December 29, 1972)

Album Summary and Reviews

Total Running Time: 30:49
Original Release: November 1972, Bell 1111

With all of the TV exposure, plus the excellent hit-prone production of Wes Farrell, this album won't miss as a major seller. Best cuts: The current single, "Looking Through the Eyes of Love," "We Gotta Get Out of this Place," and "Love Must Be the Answer." Dealers should be aware that this is a Class-A-musically LP with such sidemen as Dennis Budimer, Tommy Tedesco and Hal Blaine sitting in. *Billboard, December 16, 1972*

The latest from TV's first family of song features a hefty helping of remakes: The Animals' "We've Gotta Get Out of This Place" along with The Ronettes' "Walking in the Rain" and the group's current single item, "Looking Through the Eyes of Love," originally famoused by Gene Pitney. Of the new material, "Friend and a Lover" is the highlight, having a very persistent beat and sing-a-long profile. Once again, the lead vocals of David Cassidy, the production expertise of Wes Farrell and the contributions of arranger Mike Melvoin combine to give their fans just what they've come to expect from the top charting team. *Cash Box, December 2, 1972*

The TV Partridge Family, featuring David Cassidy as vocalist, has fashioned another crackerjack contemporary pop album. Cassidy is in top form on such ballads as "Friend and a Lover," "Walking In The Rain," "Together We're Better," "Maybe Someday," "We Gotta Get Out of This Place" and "Love Must Be the Answer," among others. *Variety, December 6, 1972*

> **First Chart Appearance: December 9, 1972 (**Cash Box, *No. 105;* **Record World,** *No. 91);* **December 16, 1972 (**Billboard, *No. 138)*

MELLOW YELLOW
or ... The Partridge Family Crossword Puzzle

Shirley Goes Solo

"Larry Uttal, who was the head of the label, got this idea through the corporate chain—and because of the network's involvement—to do a single recording with Shirley," says music producer Bones Howe. "If he could get a hit record with her, the idea was to eventually do an album."

Uttal wanted to bring Shirley Jones into some segment of the pop music genre as a crossover artist. It was currently working extraordinarily well for Barbra Streisand, who, like Jones, had won her first round of fame doing movie musicals. Bell Records and Screen Gems went to work exploring the possibilities.

In 1971, after the first season was well underway, Jones went into the studio with music producer Bill Justis and recorded a few songs. Justis was a successful Nashville-based arranger and producer. He had arranged both country and pop music for stars including Johnny Cash and Charlie Rich. Country music was hot on the pop charts, and trade magazines took it so seriously that they devoted entire sections to country music. It seemed like an angle to explore for Jones.

The A-side of the single is the beautiful ballad "I've Still Got My Heart, Joe," written by Tony Macaulay, Roger Greenaway and Roger Cook. Greenaway and Cook were successful songwriters and performers who began in England. Together they had written "My Baby Loves Lovin'," a late '60s hit for White Plains, and Coke-jingle-turned-hit-single "I'd Like to Teach the World to Sing (In Pefect Harmony)," recorded by the New Seekers. The B-side selection has a quicker tempo, with Dickie Lee and Allen Reynolds' "Everybody's Reachin' Out for Someone." The single was released in June 1971. *Cash Box* chose it as a Pick of the Week, stating that it "makes a strong bid for sales recognition. Shirley Jones melds her original adult audience image with the teen potential gained as Mrs. Partridge to give her an across the board thrust." Despite the concerted effort by Uttal and Bell Records, the single failed to chart.

"Shirley was kind of an outline that needed to be filled in," explains Howe, who produced her second solo attempt with Bell Records. "She had this sweet voice, and I can understand why somebody would make a country record with her. She was one of those people that you could put in a cowgirl skirt and a cowgirl hat and you'd believe she was a cowgirl.

"When you bring an actress into the music business, a lot of people have opinions, particularly when the actress has a little cachet. Everybody at the record company has an idea. Somebody probably saw that Shirley has this sweet voice and that she could be a country singer, and they thought it was a good idea to start there. That has happened more than once, but it didn't work for her."

Uttal remained determined. In the fall of 1972 he decided to give it another try, this time, without the country tinge. Season 2 had just finished, and Jones had sung solo on the show to a warm reception on at least two occasions. She had also sung solo on the Christmas album, which sold hugely. Uttal sent her back into the recording studio, this time with Howe.

Howe was—and remains—a respected producer. He produced big hits for the 5th Dimension, the Association, and many other artists. It seemed a good idea to match him up with Jones.

"First, it was a matter of finding a song for her," says Howe. "'Ain't Love Easy' was a song I was thinking about for the 5th Dimension's Marilyn McCoo. It was just one of those songs that was always on the fence. Marilyn had listened to it once and wasn't crazy about it, so I just hung on to the song.

"Even though Shirley was an established actress, and musical theater actress at that, she was still unknown in the world of pop music. Part of the problem is that when you're working with an artist for the first time and they have no track record of hits, you don't get the best material from the publishers. You get the stuff that they've tried three or four times with other artists. It's just an understood thing. I always assumed if we had a hit record with Shirley, or if we even landed on the charts, there would be another chance for more.

"I met with her and I liked her a lot. First of all, she's very professional and just a sweet lady. She came right out and said to me, 'Look, I don't think I'm a pop singer, but if you could help me with this, it might be really, really good.' I just liked her for the pro that she was. I said, 'OK, let's take a shot and see what we can do.' I played several songs for Shirley, and this is the one that she and I agreed on."

The B-side of the single is the lovely "Roses in the Snow" with its winter imagery and gentle romantic theme. It was written by Randy McNeill, who had written a couple of songs for the 5th Dimension.

"'Roses in the Snow' was a song that I published," says Howe. "Shirley liked it. She said 'I can sing to that.' A lot of it was about what she felt she could sing. She liked the message of the song. It seemed appropriate for her. I had Screen Gems songs and I had all kinds of other songs to play for her, which I did, but somehow she felt connected to this one.

"Working with an actor is a completely different experience. My wife was an actress and I learned a lot about how to tap into the unconscious for creative things, and find things that work for them. By understanding that, you can identify with artists better. It was a process for me that was eye-opening. Musical artists like that are extremely professional. Shirley was a super pro because she'd been in front of the camera. She had done voiceovers and plenty of recording work, so a recording studio was home for her in a lot of ways. We talked a little bit about the environment and what it would be like in the studio. She said she didn't want to record live. So I said, 'That's fine. You don't have to record live. I just want you out in the room to sing along with the musicians so they get a sense of what the song is about,' and she did that. She was great. She walked out into the middle of the studio and it was like being on the set for her. She sang live in the room for the musicians, and they all loved that because most of the time they were recording for artists that they didn't see. That's the way a lot of records were made back then."

"Ain't Love Easy" was featured in season 3, episode 57, "A Likely Candidate," with Bert Convy in one of two guest appearances as Shirley's love interest Richard Lawrence. It was the third and final time Shirley was given an on-camera solo with the Partridge Family.

Bell Records still wasn't done trying with Jones. In 1973 she recorded "Walk in Silence," written by William O'Malley and Ronald Miller, with Miller producing. Miller had a lot of top 10 hits, with ballads for Motown recording artists including Stevie Wonder and Diana Ross—including Ross' "Touch Me in the Morning," which came out the same year. Miller also had a Broadway pedigree, having written lyrics for *Daddy Goodness* and *Cheery*. "Walk in Silence" was a perfect fit for Shirley Jones.

The music was arranged by Tom Baird and the recording engineered by the Partridge Family's own Bob Kovach. This time Jones' sound was deeper and darker than on the previous two attempts. "The World Is a Circle," from the 1973 musical *Lost Horizon*, was recorded for the B-side. Drastically different, the song features Jones with a full children's choir, something that had just hit big for the Carpenters on "Sing," released only a few months earlier. "Walk In Silence" was released but received barely any airplay. Jones says she remembers plans for an entire album and that enough songs were recorded for such a release—but it wasn't meant to be.

The fans who had originally followed Jones were young parents in the early '70s, and the new youth were tightly identified by their own music. The term *generation gap* had emerged, and even if Jones was TV's coolest mom, in the eyes of those buying the records, she was still a mom. Fans of her musical theater roots held fast to those memories, all the while buying Partridge Family and David Cassidy records for their children.

when we're singin'

Danny's Turn

Marketers do what marketers do—they try to make money. If the cool mom wasn't going to sell solo records, how about the sarcastic kid? Danny Bonaduce had an audience of his own. More scripts were written about his character than any other on the show because of his ratings popularity. It seemed reasonable to think that he might be able to sell records. *Danny Bonaduce* was released on Lion Records and promoted during the early part of 1973, in the show's third season.

"That album was completely done by a guy named Bruce Roberts," says Bonaduce. "It was produced by someone else, but written mostly by Bruce Roberts, who has written for everyone from Barbra Streisand to Cher. He's one of those unsung heroes who lives in a $15 million home, and Barbra Streisand won't go anywhere without him. Cher won't go anywhere without him. He's just one of those guys. They just hired him—this was before he broke that big—but most people still don't know his name."

Despite some heavy overdubs, Bonaduce pulled off his own vocals on the entire album. "I am, in fact, singing," he says. "I've always had a deep, gravelly voice, and there is one track where the higher notes were sung by a 25-year-old man, but it still includes my voice."

The first single, "Dreamland," one of the Roberts-penned songs, was backed with "Blueberry You" on the B-side. Bonaduce was naturally expected to make appearances promoting "Dreamland." One booking in particular stands out for him: "I was the grand marshal of the Macy's Thanksgiving Day Parade and I'm driving around—here's how bizarre my life is, dude—I'm riding in a gigantic snail. A huge three-story snail that's built around a car that this guy is driving from underneath it. He's looking out from whatever mesh is in front of the snail's eyes, which seems very dangerous now that I think about it. And they were going to put on a recording of 'Dreamland,' to which I'm going to lip-sync, because I'm the grand marshal. But on comes 'Blueberry You,' which I had sung exactly once in my life. So I'm lip-syncing as the grand marshal of the Macy's Thanksgiving Day Parade, and I'm sucking—in a giant snail! That's a fond memory of that album."

Advertising for *Danny Bonaduce* and the single "Dreamland" was launched at the top of the new year in 1973. But neither the single nor the album ever hit the charts. They tried a second time, too, releasing "I'll Be Your Magician" backed with "Fortune Lady" and releasing it during the spring but the interest just wasn't there. In the years since, the album has become a collector's item. "Lion Records paid people a nickel to take it," Bonaduce jokes, "and now it goes for like 70 bucks on eBay!"

Susan Dey's Recording Deal?

While the marketing forces tried to resurrect a solo career for Shirley Jones, invent one for Danny Bonaduce, and continually perpetuate the frenzied superstardom of David Cassidy, it seemed inevitable that someone would go after Susan Dey.

John Rosica, who was executive vice president of Bell Records for the West Coast satellite office during the Partridge Family years, was serving as a liaison between the studio and the record company. "I love Susan Dey," he begins, and launches into a favorite story. "There was a rumor that a record company—we didn't know which one—was going to offer her a contract. And since we had every one of the actors on the show, we were first refusal for any other record company—that was for everybody that was on the show.

"I was in and out of the studio all the time, and at the soundstage, mostly when I had to communicate with David. So I called her up and I said, 'We have to have lunch.' So I went and picked her up, went out and had lunch and said, 'I understand that you're going to make a record?' At that time, everybody wanted to do everything. What I mean by that is everybody thought they were a singer, comedians thought they were serious actors, etc. So I said, 'What do you think?' She said, 'I have no interest in that. I'm an actor. I don't want to be a singer.' I thought *Holy shit, this lady is really terrific!* And she was very insistent. She was just one of the most well-adjusted actors that I've ever met. She was funny, too. Hysterical. And just a very nice person. After the series went off the air I used to bump into her on airplanes all of the time and we would catch up. I must have bumped into her on cross-country flights a dozen times over the years."

Dey can still take credit for at least one solo recording of her own—in 1972 she recorded selections on an album titled *Girl Scouts of the USA*, a public service announcement on vinyl. Even if it was spoken, it still counts!

Music Videos

Even though solo careers were not working for anyone except David Cassidy, the fictional family band was still bringing in the audience every Friday night and selling millions of records with their smiling faces, matching crushed velvet outfits, and interactive chemistry. As simple as they look, the show's music segments were complex and time-consuming to film.

"Each week we had music, and we would actually pre-record the music first," says Shirley Jones. "I was the only one from the cast that was ever in the studio with David. It was just David, me, and the studio singers who were the actual Partridge Family voices. We would do the pre-record so that we would have time to work with the other kids on the playback. We would get the music ahead of time and look at the words."

"Our show shot for five days," says producer Larry Rosen. "It was a break in the normal routine of Columbia Pictures television and Screen Gems. Half-hour shows were usually shot in three days. We shot four days and rehearsed one day, so it was a five-day shooting schedule—which had never been done before, but we needed a day, or three-quarters of a day, just to do the song.

"We had a rehearsal on a Monday at nine in the morning, and we'd sit around a table and read the script. Then they were supposed to rehearse, but we didn't because it was the only day Shirley had to go to the cleaners, or to the dentist, or the doctor's, along with everyone else. It was the only day they had off. So we did very, very little rehearsing, unless it happened to be a complicated episode that required a lot of staging. Just a read-through was all we really needed so the cast had an idea of what the script was about, and we had an idea of how it sounded. If we had to do any rewrites it would be done that night, and we would start shooting on Tuesday morning."

There was never one specific day of the week slotted for the music, though they were usually shot all in one day. The goal with the music videos was to create believability, even though the general public learned very early on that only Jones and Cassidy were really singing. It was always important that the music complement the look and feel of the show. Episodes where the story actually revolved around the song required more focus. "In an episode like 'Soul Club,' we wanted the music to be credible so it would reach a broad audience. And other shows we simply wanted the mood of the piece to be complementary, so that it wouldn't take you out of the show or be unbelievable for this group to sing," says first-season producer Paul Witt. "Furthering the plot with the music was never truly a concern, or very rarely."

Shooting the musical sequences differed greatly from the rest of the show because they weren't driven by dialogue. "We were working to a playback," continues Witt. "These shoots were technically challenging in that we had to make it believable that these kids were playing. The kids were not musicians, so there was the use of hand doubles. We had to be very careful. There are all those stories about Danny strumming the bass, instead of picking it. I don't recall them specifically, but these were kids. A lot of them had never picked up an instrument before, so the video shoots were more technical and not easy to shoot at all."

David Cassidy's real-life ability to play the guitar added significant credibility to the musical sequences. Shirley Jones also knew what it took to sell the idea. But the complicated process of matching the music to the image took a great deal of effort on everyone's part.

Farrell was not on the set during the playback recordings. "We hired a number of people, and the only basic thing that they had to do on the set was to conduct tempo behind the camera so that the kid who was playing drums would not go out of tempo," he told Ken Sharp. "Brendan Cahill was the original first person. There were a couple of people."

The process of setting up for the musical sequences was much more difficult than it might be today. "In those days things were not digitized," says producer Mel Swope, "so when you're rolling, everything is synched up, and you were rolling big tracks. It was heavy-duty stuff, I think 16 tracks. Now you can do it digitally with such small equipment compared to then."

The cast had many impressive visitors on the set of the show, especially when they shot the videos. Even Elvis called up one day because his daughter was a fan of Cassidy's. Another day it was the U.S. secretary of state. "I got a phone call from the State Department one day, and they said, 'Henry Kissinger is coming to Los Angeles and he's a fan of *The Partridge Family*,'" says Rosen. "I said, 'You have to be kidding me!' They said, 'No, he is, and he would love to visit your set.' So I said, 'You name the day, and he'll be welcome!' So they gave us a day, and he came to the Burbank lot—and it turned out to be the day we were recording a song.

"Now, if you were ever on the stage when we recorded a song, it was hysterical because nobody played any instruments, and Brian had not a clue of how to play the drums. We had a drummer who would stand off-camera on his close-up and just raise his hands up and down exactly like he wanted Brian to do on the drums, and when there was a riff or something he would move his hands fast, so that Brian would hit the drums and the cymbal, and it would look like he was actually playing those drums when we did the playback. But if you were on the stage when David was trying to lip-sync to his own songs, and these sounds were coming out—Danny playing the guitar, which was just noise coming out of it because he didn't know how to play a guitar; Suzanne didn't know how to play her tambourine, or whatever the hell her instrument was, and Shirley was pounding on a dead piano. I don't know what the hell Susan was doing, and Brian was on those drums just banging horrible sounds in the background, all while David was singing, and Kissinger leaned over to me and said, 'Really?' I said, 'Wait till the show comes on the air. You'll be quite surprised at the sound you will hear!' But it was just a cacophony of noise, and none of it was recorded because we were just sending the track to postproduction."

Rosen continues, "Henry Kissinger had no idea that these people weren't actually playing their instruments like they were supposed to be. It was amazing that David could keep a straight face. Every music day he would just suffer through those noises and pretend they weren't there. He'd just keep lip-syncing to the track that we were playing, as loud as we could over the soundstage, to drown out the noise of the actors banging on those instruments. They had to do that because they had to look like they were playing. Danny couldn't fake like he wasn't hitting the guitar, and

when we're singin'

Brian couldn't fake like he wasn't hitting the drums. It was just insane on the stage. It was fun, and Kissinger had the best time! He said, 'I had no idea how movies were made!' He got a lesson that day."

On Lead Guitar!

David Cassidy knew what he was doing with the guitar. He could always be spotted on the set sitting around strumming his guitar off-camera, tinkering with his own ideas for songs and taking the music very seriously. He was equally concerned with the believability of the music videos and brought a distinctive charisma to those sequences.

On Bass Guitar!

On-camera bass player Danny Bonaduce knew so little of the instrument that castmate David Cassidy had to tell him to pluck the strings rather than strum them.

"The videos were more of a blocking thing," says Bonaduce. "We'd go through the songs at full volume, because if you could hear your own voice you felt silly, so the music was really loud. If you were trying to lip-sync and you could hear your own voice you were a little embarrassed, but if you didn't sing at all and just moved your lips, then it didn't look real. So those Marshall stacks of amps were real, and the Partridge Family music would blare out at concert level. You could sing your guts out, and nobody could hear that you didn't have any talent at all. I remember that we would be singing, and that sound would come out, and we'd just really rock and roll. I don't know who played the bass for me, but I heard he was world-class. I never met the musicians."

On Keyboards!

Shirley Jones and Susan Dey were both believable in their keyboard playing. They smiled, held rhythm, and looked like they were having the time of their life. Jones was on keyboards only from time to time. The primary job of making the keyboards and piano look believable belonged to Susan Dey. Dale McRaven recalls, "When she first came to the show and she was supposed to play the piano, she said she'd like some lessons or something, because she didn't know the first thing about playing the piano. She wanted to at least look like she knew what she was doing. So whoever handled this at Screen Gems sent her a package in the mail, a big envelope. She opened it up and she unfolded it, and it was a cardboard cutout of a keyboard! That's what they gave her to practice on! That was the help they gave her!"

On Drums!

Jeremy Gelbwaks and, later, Brian Forster had quite a big role in the musical sequences. They had to match the tempo to the actual recording, and visually it would be obvious if the drumming appeared off track. While the TV studio didn't provide any training for Gelbwaks, his parents signed him up for a few lessons during his days off. "I actually went to some studio in Hollywood that I suspect was designed to teach kids how to make it," recalls Gelbwaks. "I didn't take a lot of lessons. I took some. I used to listen to a lot of Buddy Rich. I actually liked him a lot." Gelbwaks never followed up with any interest in the music business. "Not much of a musician—wasn't then, not now."

Forster also took lessons, and this time the studio hired drum instructor Chuck Flores to work with him before and during shooting—a luxury Gelbwaks never had. "I have a funny story from the music side of things," says Forster. "One of my favorite bands is Little Charlie and the Nightcats. They're a blues/jump blues band. Unfortunately they've disbanded, but they played for like 20 years. Their drummer was a guy by the name of Dobie Strange. I really liked his drumming style. He had kind of a jazz-swing style, and he was one of the tightest drummers I have ever seen. I was at one of their shows, and during a break he comes off stage and I say to him, 'Hey, just wanted to let you know I really like your drumming.' And he says, 'Thanks a lot!' I said, 'Yeah, I used to play drums in a band,' you know, just totally tongue in cheek, and he goes, 'Yeah, what band was that?' I'm just practically laughing at this point. I go 'Well … the Partridge Family.' So he says, 'You must know Chuck Flores, then?' Now I'm floored! 'Chuck Flores!' I said, 'Yeah, I know Chuck Flores! He was my drum teacher!' He goes, 'Yeah I know that. I took lessons from him. I heard about you years ago!' So we became buddies at that point and he signed an album to me and he wrote 'To a more famous drummer, Dobie Strange.'"

Chuck Flores says, "I got a call, and they needed someone to coach Brian and to help him with the music, so I said 'sure!' So they would mail me a copy of the song for each week and I would make a little drum arrangement and then Brian and I would get together and we would play the song. His mother would drive him over to my house, or sometimes I would go over to his house. We would go over the whole arrangement.

"We would play the recording, and then the day of the shoot, of course the whole family would be on stage, and they would start playing the record, and I would be up on one of the tallest ladders I've ever seen in my life." Flores would then air-drum from atop the ladder while Forster watched him. "I would drum to my right, and he would be looking at me while they were taping, and he would see where I was playing and he would copy me. *OK, this is the part that he told me to play on the big floor tom-tom,* and then he would do that. And then I would move over to the hi-hat on my left, and then he knew that he was going to play the hi-hat on his left. We'd go through the whole song, and he nailed it. A couple of times we messed up, but nine times out of ten he would nail it on the first take. It was fun, you know? Because the music was good.

"And I was familiar with the real drummer, Hal Blaine. So I learned from that, because while I was doing this, I was learning about how Hal Blaine would approach a song. He would make kind of a drum arrangement for each song, and it would be different according to the way he heard the song for each week. Just from listening to Hal and the way he interpreted the song and the way he did it on the drums, I was learning as well as Brian."

"I've always had a musical bent to me," says Forster. "In college I was singing a lot. You had to take a minor in college as part of your degree, and I took a music emphasis. I sang in the local jazz group pretty much all of the years I was at school. I tried playing different instruments over the years, only to get sick of practicing. I took up guitar. I got sick of that. I took up piano first, before the Partridge Family, but I got sick of that. Voice was something I stuck with for a while. I like singing a lot."

On Tambourine and Cowbell!

Suzanne Crough, the youngest member of the band, played the tambourine and, from time to time, the cowbell. "The weirdest thing to me was the music day," begins Crough. "The outfits, the tights—those were kind of like the weird days, you know? On my own time I was actually getting keyboard and organ lessons. As far as lip-syncing, we would find out when we were supposed to *ooh* and *aah*. They'd work with us on the beat and stuff like that. I was petrified about the music thing. I mean, how can you really give me a cowbell lesson?"

And as for who really played the cowbells ... does it really matter?

Western Recorders, Studio 2

While most of the Partridge Family actors were learning how to pretend to play, the real musicians were learning the feel of the characters and the show so they could morph into a sound that would match the warm, positive portrayals created by those actors. And they did so at an unprecedented pace.

"You've got to remember that, at the time, an album a year was significant to the recording industry," said Wes Farrell of the overwhelming amount of music they produced.

"We did all the recording at Western Studios," said Farrell. "The sessions went very quick. The process of recording was rather simple. I can't tell you that it was technically complex. We used the best musicians, who had been responsible for numerous hits. They were some of the finest musicians of that time or any time. They were just super musicians."

Because the Partridge Family sessions had to be done in the evening due to the filming schedule of the TV show, the musicians would book double sessions on those particular days. David Cassidy especially respected the elite group of studio musicians—known collectively as the Wrecking Crew—who worked on the Partridge Family albums.

Guitarist Louie Sheldon recalls Cassidy's ambitious nature. "David was always at the sessions. He took it seriously—he was concerned in a good way that things were right, knowing that it was for a specific market. He always had this little bit of a serious side to him. He just definitely enjoyed that process of being there with the musicians and being a part of the record-making thing, as opposed to just coming in and putting down a track."

Another Wrecking Crew guitarist, Dennis Budimir, came from a jazz-influenced background but could play virtually any style of music needed. The late nights on the Partridge Family sessions are what stick out most for him. "We did them mostly at night, and most of us would have worked from eight or nine o'clock in the morning, so when we all got there we were pretty tired—and a lot of us were not real young; we were middle-aged or older. And I think we were in the booth listening to a playback and everybody loved what we were doing, and then I piped up and said, 'That sounds great, but now we all have to take a nap!'" Budimir laughs.

Joe Osborn and Max Bennett were the bass players on the Partridge Family records. While Bonaduce was too young to understand the level of musicianship behind him, Cassidy certainly understood. "An artist—you know the ones who are just totally into themselves—they don't even know who's there," says Osborn of the recording sessions. "They don't know what we've done that very week, but David appreciated the talent that was there, and that we were there to do for him. He understood that, and that made him just great to work with."

Bennett feels the same. "I just got a call from him not long ago, out of the blue. I was upstairs getting dressed and the phone rang. I picked it up and he said 'I bet you a thousand dollars you don't know who this is.' I looked on my phone and it was on there, and I said, 'David?' He said, 'How the hell did you know that?' We had a long talk. He had never really gave me his impressions about the band, but he wanted me to know how much he appreciated everything we played and how cool we were and what a great band it was."

Although both Osborn and Bennett played for the Partridge Family albums, sometimes Farrell would use one or the other when a certain kind of sound was needed. "Max played with his fingers, and his roots seemed to be jazz, and I played with a pick and I come from country roots. His style would fit more like an R&B feel or something with a busier line. Sometimes there would just be a style that I'd think *Max could handle this better than me."*

Hal Blaine was the foremost drummer in all of Hollywood and he played on every one of the Partridge Family albums. "One day I got a call from Mike Melvoin, who said we have some work to do on this new group that turned out to be the Partridge Family. I remember it being great fun because Thanksgiving and Christmas were coming up, and every year Hollywood had a Christmas parade. I lived in Hollywood, of course, and the Christmas parade is really a big thing there. All of the stars are in it. Well, at that time I had a wonderful antique car. It was a 1927 Rolls Royce convertible. Every year the parade officials asked me to pick somebody and drive them in the parade, so I asked Shirley if she and the kids wanted to go in the parade that year, and they all came along. It was great fun!"

"The people from the Partridge Family project were basically dominated by Wes Farrell," says Mike Melvoin, who played keyboards in addition to being the arranger, "so my impressions were of him—his motives, his abilities, his intelligence, his space, his way of doing business, his record savvy—all of those things were all right up in front. I started out as just the piano player, but it grew the more I found out about what he really needed—which he rarely would tell, but it was discernible. He was not as educated musically, so when it came to figuring out what to do musically he needed some guidance. The areas where he needed that help were the areas you would learn in becoming part of the partnership, part of the team."

Farrell was received by the musicians with mixed emotions. Some of them felt that he was rude and intolerable to deal with, while others held him in the highest regard for his ability to lead the group toward his vision.

Joe Osborn recalls, "He was very difficult. He'd be insistent about something that he wanted you to play, and not be able to communicate it well. It was just super irritating. Hal Blaine saved me one day. Wes was asking me to do something, and he was trying to hum something unintelligible. It just made no sense, and then he would say, 'Let me hear what that would sound like.' By now I am so angry at that guy, I can't even speak. I'm staring at Hal Blaine and finally Hal Blaine got it, and he said, 'Wes, why don't you go work with the guitar players for a while?' Just bailed me right out of that situation. I was ready to explode. So we had those moments. They're not fun, and it takes away from your creativity."

Before Farrell ever arrived at the sessions, the musicians were already playing with sounds, intros and styles based on the charts prepared for them by Mike Melvoin, who also played keyboards in the sessions. A lot of the opening hooks were created by the musicians right on the spot, before Farrell arrived. The better prepared everyone was, the quicker the sessions would go, and the less Farrell would have to get involved. Max Bennett recalls: "We tried to get as much done as we could before he got there because he'd try to redo the music. We would try to get everything really well organized with some good, unique ideas before he got there. I would say that probably 98 percent of it was done just by the guys saying 'Hey, how 'bout this,' or 'This sounds good' or 'Let's try this.' We just worked it out."

Louie Sheldon's experience with Farrell wasn't as stressful as some of the others'. "Wes took his work seriously, but always had a nice smile and wasn't hard on musicians. It was a pretty fun process as far as sessions go. We always had David Cassidy there giving us a guide vocal as we were doing a tune.

"The Partridge Family had its purpose. It had its market. I didn't compare it to other music because I knew what it was designed for. This was not heavy stuff—it was for a young audience, generally. You gotta keep it poppy. It's trite, you know? I thought it was good in that they had a theme and a concept. I thought it was really good. It's an interesting concept—a family of musicians and all that. It took some good writing to carry that off, and to be successful for as long as they were."

Sheldon continues, "It had that special thing for it—working for a TV show, knowing the music would be in it and that it would be successful. We always recorded at the same place on Sunset and Western, we always recorded with the same musicians usually, and it was always a fun session because of everyone there—David, Wes, and the other musicians. So it was always something I looked forward to. In the first session Tommy Tedesco was the other guitar player on it. Any time Tommy was in the group, you knew you were going to have a good time."

Sheldon had three young daughters, and they were all fans of Cassidy. He took them to the set once to meet him. Eventually Sheldon began producing records, including his first big hit with Seals & Crofts' 'Summer Breeze.'" As a result he wasn't able to play on the final Partridge Family album because of scheduling conflicts.

Max Bennett reflects, "What made the Partridge Family unique was the fact that they used great players to really make the music happen, you know? The music itself was very commercial, which it needed to be. It had to serve a purpose. Otherwise nobody would have paid much attention to it. It wouldn't have fit what was happening on the TV. So the ability of the band to use their professional expertise to make it happen, to put the music out to fit perfectly for whatever they wanted it to fit—that was the talent of all the guys that worked in the studios. The guys you never hear about—you know, as far as publicity and TV and all of that. Most of the people have no idea who these guys were, but that's just the way it was."

Of the more than 25 different session musicians who played on the Partridge Family albums, Max Bennett and Hal Blaine are the only two who are credited on every one.

when we're singin'

Weekend at Wembley

David Cassidy's third concert tour was the first to take him overseas, and it had more excitement surrounding it than any of the others so far. His set list was designed to promote *Rock Me Baby*, with previous hits thrown in. Cassidy was a big fan of Eric Clapton, and he would toss in a Clapton cover and maybe a few others from time to time.

This time he left the airport runway in his own personal jet, carrying his full entourage as well as an entire press corps that he invited along. Consequently, the press on Cassidy during this tour was all day, every day in its coverage. The tour started in Germany on March 3 and wrapped up on March 18.

One of the dates in Germany, at Offenbach, was canceled, reportedly from poor ticket sales in and around Frankfurt—where the TV show had not been airing. "Offenbach is only about six miles from Frankfurt," explains Tina Funk, a young German fan who eventually started the Just David Fan Club, which ran for 40 years. "*The Partridge Family* had just started airing on March 1 in that area. In my area *The Partridge Family* started airing earlier, in October 1972. I would not have known who he was without the PF being on TV, and I certainly would not have spent eight German marks on a concert ticket."

Cassidy played a few dates in France, also showing up on a broadcast of *Mélody Variétés*—which said a lot about his popularity in France, since hardly any English music was played on the radio there.

After France, he played several dates in Holland, Belgium, and Luxembourg. Cassidy was drawing extraordinary attention from the press but was discouraged that so much of it focused on the fans' excitement rather than his performances.

The fan response was newsworthy, though. The tour was filled with the kind of excitement that a Cassidy concert had become known for in the U.S., with teenyboppers crying in ecstasy over seeing their idol perform live. No one really knew how to deal with it. The European security people had never experienced anything like it.

The second half of the month was dedicated to dates in England. There was so much enthusiasm that additional dates were added at both Manchester and Wembley. Cassidy played four concerts in Manchester and then a whopping six sellout concerts over one weekend at Wembley, surpassing the record previously held by the Rolling Stones. Live footage from these performances was pulled for a TV special that aired in the U.K. titled *Weekend at Wembley*. The footage was the first time people could actually see just how frightening the experience truly was for Cassidy, and how dangerous it could get for the fans.

This tour was special for Cassidy in another way. Between his appearances at Wembley he met and spent some time with singer-songwriter Sue Shifrin. Over a decade later they reunited, married, and had a child together, Beau Cassidy. They were married for more than 23 years.

While he was in England Cassidy was invited to meet Queen Elizabeth, and he shocked everyone when he turned it down. The formality of such a meeting was uninteresting to him, and he already had plans to meet Sue Shifrin that same day. Cassidy has always joked through the years about how he stood up the Queen of England for lunch with Shifrin.

Bus Stop ...

The Musicality of David Cassidy

It was the choice to pursue music that drove David Cassidy more than anything else within show business during the four-year run of *The Partridge Family*. Though he began as an actor, he established himself internationally as a singer-songwriter and musician. David Cassidy has released more than 20 studio albums to date, including those with the Partridge Family.

Cassidy's live performances not only made bigger money for him than the television show but also revealed to fans who he was musically—that he could truly sing and play, and that he was the real deal as a live concert artist. Cassidy has played guitar, drums, piano, keyboards, and harmonica during his live shows. His smooth, breathy voice entranced millions of people during the '70s, and that sound eventually transformed into rock, blues, and Broadway musicals.

Cassidy's underrated voice, with its unmistakable sound and personality, is instantly recognizable. Here, those who have worked with him through the years share some of their thoughts:

John Bahler: He was great on stage, great on Broadway—he's just an awesome talent, and a great guy. I loved him. We didn't get to talk enough. We got fairly close when he was 19, and we've been friends through the years, and whenever we do get together it's like no time has passed at all. I'm not even sure if he knows to this day exactly what an impact he had. I would be surprised if to this day he knows how good he is. He's an American icon. One of a kind...

He was Elvis. He was his dad. He was Donny Osmond. He was a bunch of really energetic entertainers all rolled into one. What always used to surprise me in the very beginning is that he was Keith Partridge on the TV show but man,

when we're singin'

when he went out on his own, forget about it! You can't even bar the door. He was a different person. That's why kids just fell all over themselves for him. He was not only great looking, but he just knocked people's socks off.

I've heard of him talking about breaking the image. He's even said things to me like that. "Why couldn't we have done 'I Think I Love You' like this?" Meaning like the way he does it now. I just didn't have an answer for him then, because his head was in a different place. But my feeling about him all along, about him wanting to break the image, was really about him not knowing, really, who he is or who he was. He was so special and so different, but he never accepted that. He wanted to be something else. Isn't that true of a lot of performers?

I'm going to say this because I can relate to this: I think because David couldn't find anybody that sounded like him, rather than making him feel special, it made him feel weird. So we say things like "I want to sound like somebody else. I want to sound like a black artist. I want to do R&B and sound like…." That kind of thing. But nobody else sounded like him. Nobody did it like him. He was one of a kind, and I think that was not a pleasant thing for him when he was young. I think it was a curse. At least, he felt it was a curse. I think it was a demon that really hurt him a lot, both emotionally and professionally. Once he grew up and found out who he was, he became very, very successful doing what he does now. I still think that he thinks that he could have done it differently and done it better. He was obviously an unbelievable talent, because the public knows. You can't lie to them. If you've got it, they'll know. He's got it. I just don't think he had it the way he wanted it.

Paul Witt: David can sing his tail off! The kid can really sing. David loves music and has made it his career. He was serious about it from the get-go. He wanted to be heard. He wanted to have input—and I mean that in the most positive way. What was different about David's voice is that it had a clarity and purity to it that he might have felt a little constrained by. David always wanted to rock more than the family might have been capable of. It had to be believable within the concept of the show. A rough, growly rock voice or a strained Mick Jagger wouldn't have worked, but David had a real instrument.

Derek Lawrence: He's good ol' show biz! He knows his craft.

Shirley Jones: I saw him first perform live at Madison Square Garden in New York. That's where I first saw Shaun, too. Most of David's concerts were not in California. They were out of the country. He was all over England all the time, so I didn't have much of an opportunity to go where he was performing. He's still doing it and he's still doing it brilliantly.

Terry Cashman: I thought he was a very good singer. In those days you categorized him as a pop teen idol and all that stuff because he was such a good-looking kid. That was the market. He grew tired of that image, but I thought he did a terrific job.

Tommy West: Pure pop, with a touch of Broadway—he comes from that background. I thought he was a very underrated artist.

Bob Claver: It was just David in those recording sessions. There was a little bit from Shirley, but the only major player was David. He was a good break for the show. David, as a real singer, just gave the show so much more reality and so much more truth. Having him become a real singing star from the show made such a difference. I would put it at number one. David was the perfect young leading man. That's not so easy to find.

Brian Forster: He has that breathy quality that's good for a pop star and that kind of music. He has a very nice tone, a good range. Many years ago David was touring and he played in San Francisco. I had done an interview about a month prior with a radio station. They called me up and said, "Hey, David's in town—if we get a couple of tickets, will you go?" So here I am, out in the audience with these girls that are now around 40, bringing Partridge lunch pails to David and still swooning. Me and this producer from the radio program are just laughing our heads off because here I am standing right next to him going, "Um, I was in the Partridge Family too! Eh, never mind." (laughs)

Ron Hicklin: David was perfect for the bag. I think he was better for it than he wanted to be. He wanted to do material that was more important. He wanted to stretch out, but there was this demographic who was loving him, and this is how he was reaching them. So thank your lucky stars that you found this audience.

Harriet Schock: He's very soulful. I really like him as a singer. He's fabulous.

Danny Janssen: David was just this young kid caught between wanting to be a rock and roller and doing what he was doing. I'll tell you something funny about David Cassidy. I'm sitting out on the front deck of my beach house one time and these two young girls, probably about 12 years old, are out there laughing away, and I said, "What's so funny?" One of them said, "Do you know David Cassidy?" I said, "Aren't you Bob Dylan's daughter?" She said, "Yeah." I said, "Why are you asking me about David Cassidy when your dad is Bob Dylan?" She said, "I can see Daddy any old time!"

Jackie Ward: I really liked his voice. It was a very natural voice, and warm … very warm. Even for a young person there was a warmth there.

A lot of times young people can sing beautifully but they're still a little too young to have any concept of interpreting lyrics, and I think that he did a very, very good job of that. You are very comfortable with his voice. Sometimes people sing and you're not comfortable. The sound is either grating or you wonder if they're going to hit the notes. But with David it's there and it's a comfortable sound and you just like it. There is no mistaking it.

Mark James: He has a nice timbre, a nice tone, and he's got a nice range. It's a good commercial pop voice, and it's held up. You have to rank him with the best of the times.

Beverly Weinstein: Of all the bands we had—and we had some unusual ones and some loud ones—David was one of the nicest gentlemen. He was very, very, nice, and appreciative of anything you did. That was a pleasure. There was absolutely no ego there. I saw him at Radio City Music Hall once and it was phenomenal. He was an entertainer. As a live vocalist, he held his own. And to appear in Las Vegas for years and years and years is not something you can do without a fairly good voice.

L. Russell Brown: David Cassidy is probably one of the most underrated artists of all time. He had a great way of delivering a song as well as an indelible sound. That indelible sound is the critical part of a great artist's success. Rick Nelson had the special sound, and so did Elvis and Chuck Berry, and Paul and John had it, just as the Everly Brothers had it. I believe that David Cassidy was deceptively talented. Definitely talented."

Larry Rosen: David's voice applied a lot to his TV character. It was safe. It was pseudosexual. He could invite the female persona to be attracted to him and it gave off kind of a pheromone of its own that felt safe. It was like a moth going to a flame who knew it wouldn't get burned if it got too close. I think that was the essence of his character, and maybe even of himself. The voice that he projected was charming, and he had this great smile, great energy and confidence in himself. It was innocent, and it was full of the confidence of a young teenage boy who was learning what life was all about, making the mistakes that you make while developing into a man.

Rick Segall: Musically David has never been given the kind of respect he rightly deserves as an artist. In many ways the Partridge Family was a double-edged sword for him. Aesthetically, there's a very soothing quality to his voice. He had an expressiveness in the tonality of his voice that made them feel like *Oh, if you just knew me you'd love me.* There's a tenderheartedness in his voice. Men can connect to the same exact thing. There are a lot of guys who have never been given good examples of what it means to be a strong man, and at the same time tender-hearted. David was able to convey both.

Wes Farrell: He was there, man. He was a hundred-percenter. We were close. We were very close for a substantial period of time and we would talk when it was necessary to do so. I think he handled it all with a tremendous amount of professionalism.

Suzanne Crough: He's a good showman and he has a good voice. He's as good now as he was then. He is singing his own creations and he does it perfectly.

Jeremy Gelbwaks: In those days he had a teenage voice, but I saw him on Broadway in *Blood Brothers* and I thought it was pretty good. I left the business and went off and had a normal life. Guys like David who are out there, still trying things, making things happen, have balls on them. He has since gone out and played at places like B.B. King's Blues Club here in New York, and I think that's pretty gutsy. I hope he always sees a lot of success.

Included here are some thoughts from David Cassidy about his early music, taken from Ken Sharp's previously unpublished interviews in 1990 and 1992.

On the Partridge Family songwriters and musicians: I got to work with the greatest pop songwriters probably in history—and I really learned the craftsmanship. I learned how to write songs, and it really helped me to develop my own style. I think inevitably I'm a much better musician, singer, and player because I learned from the really great musicians that there is no musical prejudice. They don't feel the way young kids feel about music. They respect all of it. It really opened me up musically. I let go of all my musical prejudice.

On the Partridge Family songs he feels are the best: Songs in particular that stand out for me are a lot of the ones that they selected for the greatest hits CD [*The Partridge Family Greatest Hits*, 1989]. They selected the material pretty well. Stuff like "I Can Feel Your Heartbeat," most of the songs that Tony Romeo wrote. I think he is one of the best pop songwriters that I have ever heard or encountered, and I was fortunate enough to have him write songs for me.

On how it feels when today's artists cite him and the Partridge Family as an influence: It feels better than good because you know that your work has meant something. The fact that some people have come up to me a lot and said that they are a musician now, and the reason they are is because of my records and my music and watching [me] on television—that goes a long way. That means a lot.

when we're singin'

On playing guitar for the Partridge Family music videos: I was too busy at the time teaching everybody else how to stand and perform to worry about a song that I cut six weeks ago that I didn't even write. (laughs). You try and figure out the chords to "I Think I Love You." That will make you pull your hair out! There's a lot of chords and they are very intricate. They're certainly not your basic three-chord rock and roll song.

On *Creem* magazine's '70s polls that used to name Susan Dey as one of the top five keyboard players: (laughs.) Well of course in *Creem* magazine you would think so. It was mostly read by guys, and of course they would think that. She's one of the best-looking keyboard players I've ever seen!

On Partridge Family videos being likened to early MTV-style music videos: Oh yeah, they were definitely music videos. Every week we would perform songs that we recorded on film and cut them together and make little stories out of them. They were not terribly imaginative and inventive, but you couldn't within the framework of the show. It also wasn't intended—unlike the Monkees, where in the latter stages they got real gimmicky, we never did that. I think the producers didn't want to be compared to [the Monkees] for that reason. *The Monkees* also was never a successful television show. It was kept on the air after the first year even though it had really low ratings because they were making so much money from every other avenue—the records, the merchandising, and all that. *The Partridge Family*, on the other hand, had a huge demographic. A lot of adults. The demographics on the show were really broad. It was always a top 20, top 10 show until they changed the night for the last six months of the show.

On the first song he wrote that satisfied him: I was developing as a songwriter at the time. I had written a few other things—a bunch of things that were terrible. They were really so basic and naive and they sounded like a cross between rock and pop, trying to bridge the gap between the television thing that we were doing and my own interests. I think I stopped trying to be something and I just wrote. The first thing I wrote that I felt that about was "Ricky's Tune" on my first solo album. Although I wrote a couple of the Partridge Family songs, like "Love Is All That I Ever Needed," I think ultimately I didn't have the dimension which was necessary to write that kind of real innocent pop stuff. Wes Farrell really had a handle on that. He taught me a lot about songwriting. It was an invaluable experience. Tony Romeo, Gerry Goffin, Paul Anka—all of those people were great craftsmen and I got to learn a lot, but Wes was around more and was the catalyst and really taught me the most about how to commercially write pop songs.

On his first memory of hearing himself on the radio: It was "I Think I Love You." Like the first time you hear yourself singing on a record, I was more interested in hearing my voice back because I simply hadn't done it. I was playing live and singing live with a band that consisted of Hal Blaine and Joe Osborn, Larry Knechtel, Larry Carlton, and those guys. It was an awesome bunch of musicians and I was the singer. It was a pretty remarkable time being 19 years old—even though the music wasn't the kind of style I was really interested in and that I was interested in playing. I couldn't, nonetheless, deny the fact that it was good music.

On his favorite Partridge Family episode: There would be one that would stand out because it was so over the top, and that would be the Christmas show where I played this character called Sheriff Swell. I got my lollipop stuck in my hair! I mean, in this powdered blue suit—it was hysterical. In fact, Paul Witt, who had left the show, saw me on the lot and said, "I just saw a cut of the Christmas show"—and he was responsible for casting me—he said, "I just want to tell you your performance was brilliant." That, to me, even to this day remains one of the pieces of work that I'm proud of, because I was able to remove me and just go and be as free with that character as I could be. You know, we did some good work. I think that episode—and the episode that for me was my own personal struggle on the show to try and have my own age be reflected in the character, is the one where they finally got me to move out. Keith moves out and I got to talk about being in junior college as opposed to just being eternally in high school. We did some funny stuff on that show too.

On *Cherish* as his debut solo outing: It had a tremendous impact and it was very successful. It was the first attempt on my part to do everything I could to make a little bit different of a record—and them not wanting me to make a different record at all. The album was the first sign and glimpse that there was somebody else there who had deeper thoughts and different ideas and emotion, and musically perhaps had a little more of an edge. But they would only let me go two degrees, and that ultimately became our bone of contention. I wanted to make a different record every time and I wanted to reveal more about myself, i.e. the latter records *The Higher They Climb* and *Home Is Where the Heart Is*, and even *Dreams Are Nuthin' More Than Wishes*, though it isn't a hard-edged record—it's more of an introspective record. It was a record about what this person thinks and what makes him tick.

On *Dreams are Nuthin' More Than Wishes*, and singing about puppies: I don't mind singing about puppies if the songs are great. Imagination and

when we're singin'

> magic are one and the same, almost. It's like it can be anything. If there's a real creativity and imagination in the songs you can just about do anything. It's the execution and how well the song is written.
>
> **On "Summer Days" as a remake for *Dreams*:** It was more soulful, funkier. Unlike a lot of people who looked upon Tony Romeo as just a commercial writer, I think he's a romantic writer. He paints pictures with his lyrics. The greatest gift we as writers can do is paint a picture in somebody else's mind with our words. I learned a lot from Tony and I respect him a lot. "Summer Days" is another one of those songs that he wrote for me. He wrote a couple of songs specifically for me. He wrote "I Think I Love You." He wrote "Summer Days." He wrote "Sing Me."
>
> **On *Rock Me Baby* as a transitional album:** There's the beginning of a guy you can tell who's had some rock and roll influence there, and *Rock Me Baby* was one of those things. People didn't really like the album because it was so drastic in their brain of who I was. When I made that record, that was a tame record for me to make. The flack that I got about it was just "You can't be a rock star. You can't be *this* because you're *this* guy." That was the problem that I had.

The Price of Fame

By the end of season 3 David Cassidy had decided to call it quits. He announced that he was going to leave the show at the end of season 4.

The schedule of working on a series on top of his solo music career left him with virtually no time for himself, and superstardom had made normalcy impossible. "I remember so many days with David when we would be shooting," recalls Larry Rosen, "and I wanted to go to lunch with him, so I picked him up at the Burbank Ranch. It was only five minutes from the studio, but I'd have to put him in the back of my car, under a blanket in the back seat, and drive off the lot, because there were always 20, 30, 40, 50 kids, mostly girls, waiting for him every day. They'd wait for him to arrive and they'd wait for him to leave. They would never leave, and so I'd have to cover him with a blanket to get him off the lot just to go to a restaurant and sit down and have lunch."

Rosen continues, "David was a kid with such pressures on him. He would be on the road doing concerts on Saturday and Sunday, then he'd come back on Monday for a script reading. We'd start shooting Tuesday. Tuesday night, Wednesday night, and Thursday night he was recording songs and laying down tracks for the following week and working every day, until Friday. Then Saturday he was back on the road doing concerts and the whole cycle would continue to repeat. The kid never had a minute to himself. He was not able to go to a drugstore, or to the cleaners. He couldn't do anything without being spotted. He couldn't leave his house. It was a hellish life for him. There were times when he would come in late and exhausted, but Shirley would say to him, 'This is what you wanted. This is what you got. But when you're on the set—I know my lines. You better know yours!' She was good about that, thank God. He respected her, too."

"It's amazing that he got through it," adds Mel Swope. "I must say that he was a pro. He always had a good attitude. If I was directing a show and he had just come back from a concert, I took extra care. I'd ask myself, *Does he need a break? Do we need to shift things around a little bit to accommodate him a little without hurting the show?* Anybody that has any sense of empathy for a performer is going to do their best to try and make it work."

Wes Farrell told Ken Sharp of Cassidy, "I give him a lot of credit because he learned everything under very limited conditions. To begin with, we were on a very tight schedule—not only David, but myself as well. He had a 10-hour shooting day, and many days he had a five- and six-hour recording session. Plus he was not available Fridays, Saturdays, and Sundays, because once the records exploded he went on tour every weekend. He had a full card and I give him a lot of credit. He was a hundred-percenter. He never backed away from his commitment one iota. We did a lot to make it as easy as possible for all of us."

Liner Notes: *The Partridge Family Crossword Puzzle*

Mellow sounds and easy listening had taken firm hold on the pop charts by 1973, and they would hold steady through the remainder of the 1970s. Groups like Bread, America, and especially the Carpenters brought a romantic, relaxing style to the forefront of the musical culture. Where the Cowsills had become the '60s real-life family model for pop music, the Carpenters were now the top act, and, at least on the surface, their real-life brother-sister image was as wholesome as the fictional Partridge Family.

The style of *Crossword Puzzle*, with its fully intimate approach and soft rock vibe, was all part of the laid-back take-it-easy message moving to the forefront of '70s social culture, and it was only going to get stronger as the decade wore on.

As always, Wes Farrell and Bell Records had their finger on the pulse. Farrell studied the pop charts intently, like many other producers and performers of the day. Bobby Hart, for example, says, "When I played clubs I was basically an R&B singer. But I appreciated anything that was on the charts, and I made it my business for decade after decade to read the trades and to look at the top 100 and be familiar with every one of those songs—to analyze what had made them commercial, made them sell."

The Carpenters, in particular, shared many fans with the Partridge Family, and both were deeply loved by middle America. The intimacy of Karen Carpenter's articulate and charismatic voice was similar to David Cassidy's. Parents nurtured the idea of wholesome bands, especially coming out of the radical late '60s. Even music teachers were beginning to teach contemporary pop music to schoolchildren from the elementary levels on up, carefully choosing songs perceived as wholesome.

The songs planned for *Crossword Puzzle* reflect that same easy-listening pop sound of 1973. Most of the song choices and arrangements classify as slow-tempo ballads and heartfelt love songs. Very few up-tempo songs appear.

Crossword Puzzle is the black sheep of the Partridge Family albums, sometimes written off as a collection of session leftovers—which couldn't be further from the truth. *Crossword Puzzle* was released with as much effort, energy, and planning as every Partridge Family album that came before it.

The recording sessions for season 3 of the show took place in May and September of 1972, with the intention of generating material for two albums over the course of the season in addition to music for the show itself—the standard plan that had been followed every year. As Wes Farrell structured the music, sessions were conducted by season rather than being tied to a particular album. *Crossword Puzzle* was planned as the second album for season 3. It was developed with hopes of spawning more hits, even though it didn't turn out that way.

Bell Records initially announced that *Crossword Puzzle* was scheduled for release in late April 1973. Such a release would have made the album available before kids were out of school for the summer, but Bell held it back for two more months.

A few weeks earlier, in February 1973, even more changes at Bell Records had been taking place, with the announcement of a complete reorganization of the company's promotional department. All of it was happening because of the extraordinary success Bell was experiencing, but the rhythm in the handling of releases was affected.

At the same time, Cassidy was announcing his departure at the end of the following season. There were rumors that he might leave as early as midseason, which did not make for good publicity.

Amid all the uncertainty and upheaval, Bell released "Friend and a Lover" in the spring slot rather than an entire new album. It was the second single from *Notebook*, a song Farrell had co-written and one that the trade magazines liked. But it had the weakest showing and most dramatic drop on the charts of any Partridge Family single up to that point.

The television show was renewed for season 4 with Cassidy in place, and *Crossword Puzzle* was finally released in June 1973, only weeks after Bell signed Barry Manilow and Melissa Manchester as part of the new, soft rock evolution. But *Crossword Puzzle* spent only five weeks on the *Billboard* album charts, topping out at No. 167—a new record low for a Partridge Family album. No singles were released from *Crossword Puzzle*. It is the only Partridge Family album that didn't have a single released in the U.S. Bell Records National Promotion Director Noel Love explains it this way: "You follow the sales. You follow the acceptance with radio, and when radio doesn't want to play your new music, you kind of know you are over. No radio no sales. How are the kids going to hear it?" So what dictates the slowdown in radio DJs' enthusiasm? "Lack of sales. Lack of excitement for the new music from the music directors. New TV shows. Changing times." The announcement to move a hit show from its established TV slot to another night and time also sends signals. "On TV, when some other show gets bigger with music that's what happens. These things would cause radio DJs to back off."

Poor sales and weak chart positions often color the way an otherwise credible album is perceived, and *Crossword Puzzle* is often unfairly underestimated by both critics and even fans. It was also snubbed on most of the hits compilations that have come out since. But this album is full of great songs, especially love songs.

Completely gone are the cover tunes. More than any other Partridge Family album, this collection places Cassidy's breathy voice up front—comforting, relaxed, and instantly recognizable.

The content is especially dominated by the folk-influenced writing team of Terry Cashman and Tommy West. Of the eight songs that Cashman and West wrote for the Partridge Family—nine, if you count "Six Man Song Band"—only six made it onto an album, and three of those are on *Crossword Puzzle*. In fact Cashman and West's "Sunshine Eyes," which remains unreleased, was also considered for *Crossword Puzzle*. With four cuts, this songwriting team would have heavily dominated the album.

"Tommy and I were more into producing than anything else," says Terry Cashman. "We produced all of Jim Croce's records while we were also writing songs for Cashman and West. We did three albums together for ABC Dunhill Records at the same time that we produced Jim Croce." All of this was beginning at about the same time they started writing for Wes Farrell and the Partridge Family. By the time *Crossword Puzzle* was released, Croce's presence on the *Billboard* charts was strong; his album *Life and Times* was released in July 1973, within weeks of *Crossword Puzzle*.

Cashman and West had first teamed up around 1966, starting out with Gene Pistilli as Cashman, Pistilli & West. "We produced records, we performed, we sang, and we wrote songs," says Cashman. "There were types of songs we wrote that were more personal songs, which we ourselves recorded as singer-songwriters. Those songs are less pop, more folky and more personal. The songs we wrote for the Partridge Family were straightforward love songs. We had the ability to do that—to write all different kinds of songs. I wouldn't say that anybody in particular influenced us on those songs."

Tommy West says of his musical influences, "My favorite writer is Randy Newman. I can't come close to what he did. I love Gordon Lightfoot and a lot of those Canadian folkies. Joni Mitchell. I think Carole King is a genius. Paul Simon. But Randy Newman above and beyond anybody else."

Both "Come On Love" and "One Day at a Time" from *Crossword Puzzle* could have qualified if Bell wanted a single from the album, but Cashman and West's songs were again passed up as singles.

"That was a situation where Wes had his own publishing company," recalls Terry Cashman. "People like Tony Romeo, and whoever else was writing for Wes, tended to get the singles. Wes would push those songs because they were his writers, which is part of the business. We had our own publishing companies, but the deal was that any songs we wrote for the Partridge Family would be published by Screen Gems and Colgems. We are ASCAP writers so we get our royalties through Colgems."

Tommy West adds, "We also knew that none of our songs would be singles because of the politics of the game. Wes had writers who were signed to him. It's just my opinion, but I think they received a little bit of favoritism. The songs are terrific, don't get me wrong. Most of the songs that were turned in were very professionally written. I especially liked Tony Romeo's songs."

West continues, "We knew that David's TV character was a young late teenager, but we also tried to write songs that weren't juvenile. The songs we wrote were good, light-hearted—not bubblegum, but very pop-oriented tunes."

Both Cashman and West are proud of their work with the Partridge Family, and the craftsmanship of these songs endures. "The proof that I have is that they're still getting royalties, so somebody must be listening," says West.

Mark James is the songwriting newcomer on *Crossword Puzzle* with "It's a Long Way to Heaven." The combination of James' orchestral background and his love of the blues makes his work a perfect match for Cassidy's vocal interpretations and Bahler and Melvoin's arrangements.

Two new songs from Johnny Cymbal and Peggy Clinger show up on *Crossword Puzzle*: "I Got Your Love All Over Me" and the album finale, "It's You."

The Farrell-Janssen-Hart team was again significant with three cuts. In hindsight, and from a commercial standpoint, "Sunshine" was the most successful and important of their Partridge Family songs and the biggest miss as a single from *Crossword Puzzle*. However, it was released as a single in Japan, backed by Cashman and West's "Come On Love."

Tony Romeo is stronger than ever with his ballad "As Long as There's You," recorded the previous year. Romeo is also co-writer with Ralph Landis of the side 1 closer, "It Means I'm in Love with You"—which, incidentally is the longest song recorded by the group. It was also the last time Romeo worked with a co-writer on the Partridge Family.

The musicians are the solid standbys who worked on nearly every Partridge Family album. John Bahler's vocal intros are again well represented, as are Mike

Melvoin's arrangements. The packaging is vibrant and clever, with a crossword puzzle on the face of the bright yellow album jacket and the solution to the puzzle on the inside sleeve.

Given the ballad-like, easy listening sound of *Crossword Puzzle*, it seems natural to think Shirley Jones would be given a solo piece, but Farrell's instinct went against it. "I just think they were so afraid of going in any other direction than they had gone," says Jones. "They felt they had success and they didn't want to play with anything, and I understand that."

"I wasn't going anywhere else with the sound unless Wes asked me to," explains John Bahler. "He and I did a lot of projects together, all the way from teeny-bopper bubblegum to soul music, so we had a lot of experience together, and I can tell you that he certainly wouldn't have shied away from saying, 'I want to do something else on this.'

"You know, anything geared towards kids has a shelf life. If anything hurt sales, it was the fact that it had been on for a while. I don't think the situation between Wes and David helped any, and David quitting the show didn't help, either. That was really a shock to Shirley and the people on the show, but we weren't shocked at all—only because when we saw David and worked with him, he wasn't the same guy. He was worn out. They ran him ragged. He made a lot of money, but they burned him out. Plus he wasn't happy with the direction, and that happens a lot of times with stars. They get tired of doing what got them there. When they try to stretch out, sometimes it works, and sometimes it doesn't. Every star tries to reinvent themselves, and I think that's what David was wanting to do, and ultimately did."

By the time *Crossword Puzzle* was released, the lack of change was noticeable. One critic jabbed, "The puzzle's answers are as predictable as the musical formula used within. The only shift is to let David Cassidy dominate even more than ever."

Crossword Puzzle provided eight songs used on the show—seven during season 3. It's the album that fans bypassed, partly due to the changing times. It's also the album that can be looked back upon and re-examined by adult fans for its strong songwriters, especially the work of Cashman and West, and it serves as a nice showcase for Cassidy's voice. It was lost to the record store cutout bins fairly quickly, but it remains a solid offering with its own easy-listening identity.

One Day at a Time, 3:00, Terry Cashman–Tommy West

Wes Farrell was a master at sequencing. "Wes chose the order in which the songs appeared on the album," says John Bahler, "which is really important because you have to keep the listener going. You have to grab them in the beginning, and you have to make them want to listen to the next one. He was great at that." Cashman and West tunes were chosen as leads for both sides of the album.

when we're singin'

"The pacing of the songs is a thing they take a lot of time with," says Tommy West. "You don't want to have too many fast or slow ones in a row. When you put out an album by an artist, you want the radio guy to get the picture of the album within 30 seconds or a minute, so you usually choose something really commercial for the first track. Had they used 'Six Man Song Band' it would have been a perfect first song, because it's autobiographical to the Partridge Family."

"One Day at a Time" is itself a perfect album opener. It begins with a straightforward 12-string acoustic guitar that drives it amid an arrangement full of strings and brass. The energy is strong on this album opener.

Appears On: Season 3, Episode 57, "A Likely Candidate" (November 3, 1972); Season 3, Episode 63, "Aspirin at 7, Dinner at 8" (January 5, 1973)

Sunshine, 2:43, Wes Farrell–Danny Janssen–Bobby Hart

Gospel-tinged pop tunes were showing up all over the top 40 charts in the early and mid-'70s. Songs like Norman Greenbaum's "Spirit in the Sky" and Ocean's "Put Your Hand in the Hand" opened the decade in early 1970. By 1972 Australian Rick Springfield had landed on the pop scene with his breakout hit "Speak to the Sky." Even Broadway was showing a trend toward hip gospel with lavish productions of overwhelmingly popular musicals including *Godspell* and *Jesus Christ Superstar*.

"Sunshine" is a Partridge Family take on this style, emphasized most prominently on the first of three episodes in which it aired, showing the family singing to a church congregation. Probably the catchiest sing-along song from the album, it was licensed for use in a national campaign for 7UP, "100 Percent Natural," shortly after the turn of the millennium.

Danny Janssen says of the song's origins, "Well, this will sound dumb to you, but, see, I was never able to sleep at night. I still can't. I'm 76 and I mean I just cannot sleep. I don't know what it is. I'm lucky if I get two to three hours a night. But see, what happens is I go to sleep, and I ask God to just direct my feelings, you know? At that time, I'd keep a little tape recorder next to my bed, you know? And papers, pencils, and everything like that. My bed was also my study, so I'd just sit up and just work on these things. And if we had something we had to write for the series, or whatever it was, I'd pray about it. And then, during the night, it all came in a dream, and I just wrote it out. Every song—every single song, lyric for lyric—everything. I just hear it in my head. That's the way it was—I could hear all that stuff."

"Sunshine" was used three times on the series, signifying that all eyes were on it as a potential hit. But, like the album in which it appears, the song was given little notice, overlooked by all the Partridge Family hits compilations in the U.S. until 2005, when it was placed on the CD release *Come On Get Happy: The Very Best of the Partridge Family*.

Appears On: Season 3, Episode 59, "Ain't Loveth Grand" (November 17, 1972); Season 3, Episode 68, "Bedknobs and Drumsticks" (February 9, 1973); Season 4, Episode 94 "Morning Becomes Electric" (March 9, 1974)

As Long as There's You, 2:57, Tony Romeo

This beautiful love song is the most poignant of all the Tony Romeo offerings from the Partridge Family repertoire. The connection that Romeo had with Cassidy—the instinct through which he knew exactly what to write for Cassidy—has never been demonstrated with more strength. The storyteller-style lead vocal expresses the sense of isolation Cassidy was feeling at the time.

Opening with a 12-string acoustic guitar, this is another song with the verse in a minor key and the chorus in a major key, but with a less predictable composition. The chord progressions are interesting and quirky, a departure from the usual formula. The musical dynamics are some of the most emotionally evocative we have heard so far, and it brings out a new taste of maturity. This emotionally expressive song was perfectly placed into one of the most heartfelt sentiments of the series, a tribute to Shirley as Mother of the Year. If you listen closely, you can hear traces of the harpsichord, still a part of the Partridge Family sound.

Appears On: Season 3, Episode 51, "M Is for the Many Things" (September 22, 1972)

It's a Long Way to Heaven, 2:39, Mark James

For this beautiful ballad, John Bahler and Mike Melvoin opt out of the usual opening hook in favor of an orchestral opening—another parallel to the Carpenters' production, unsurprising since both Bahler and Melvoin also worked on the Carpenters' albums. The song features Cassidy in the lower register, going high in the chorus. Emotion and inflection permeate this song, whose flowing nature sets it apart.

Mark James mentions this song as his favorite Partridge Family song. "I liked the way David did that song," he begins. "I had just signed with Screen Gems. I left Memphis and I went to New York. It was a new thing for me. It was a bit like the Brill Building where you go in there and write, even though I had a studio at my house. They had pianos, and writers would go in there and write. I went in there to write this song, and I actually started writing the song, and it was Irwin Schuster who was responsible for getting it out. He worked at Screen Gems and he loved this song.

"It's a good ballad to sing. I think it's one of David's best vocals, too. This one started out as something unusual, and then I put it down and came back to it over a couple of days. The first part of the lyric came to me first, but the song came to me all the way through, as far as the verse and the chorus. But I was playing around with how to arrange it. The bulk of it, 50 percent of it, was there, but I didn't want to close the door on the rest of it too quickly. The best way to write a song is on the fly, but there are many ways to do it. With some kinds of songs you can sit down and a great, fantastic melody can come to you on the piano. You can try to write that, but it's not going to be as natural as if you wait a little while. Eventually that melody is going to tell you what it's trying to say."

"It's a Long Way to Heaven" was never used on any of the television episodes.

Now That You Got Me Where You Want Me, 2:45, Wes Farrell–Danny Janssen–Bobby Hart

Another ballad, this time with a catchy title and lyrics that demonstrate the skill of matching syllables to notes and choosing the right words with which to do it. "I like that one a lot," Wes Farrell told Ken Sharp. "I would have hoped that it might have come out a little stronger than it did, but I like the idea a whole lot." It was never used on any of the television episodes.

It Means I'm in Love with You, 4:00, Tony Romeo–Ralph Landis

When the cast was asked to learn the songs so they could lip-sync for the video sequences, they were often given a different version than the album cut. Usually the variation was simply a little bit shorter, timed to fit the show's available runtime slot for the music video and reworked with a cold-stop ending. The Screen Gems version of this song given to the cast for recording the video sequence has a completely different musical arrangement for the opening hook rather than the more predictable harpsichord opening on this version. The album tempo also picks back up here and carries the energy over to side 2.

Ralph Landis joins Romeo for another one-off songwriting partnership. Landis was a good friend of both the Romeo brothers and also wrote songs for Lou Christie and Richard Harris. "Ralph is my favorite human being that ever lived," says Frank Romeo. "He was a magnificent human being. He was an Amish guy and I loved him so much. As I'm speaking to you I'm looking at a painting that he did and that he gave to me. He worked in advertising and had a great job when he met my brother. He always wanted to be a country-western singer. He met Tony and quit his job and started working with Tony. He wrote some songs and everyone in our group considered Ralph the best of songwriters. He wrote country songs mostly. Very pure. I don't care who you are, you're going to start cheering up when you hear his songs. Tony was writing this with him, and wanted to submit it. I was just happy that Ralph was going to get a chance to write some lyrics and make some money. Anytime I can tell anybody that there was a man named Ralph Landis, I tell them that he was the most gorgeous creature in terms of his humanity. I can't tell you how wonderful he was."

The visualization is strong in this song, and it gets a little bluesy on the bridge. It seems the brass and strings are usually brought in later for Partridge Family songs.
Appears On: Season 3, Episode 58, "Swiss Family Partridge" (November 10, 1972); Season 3, Episode 69, "Everything You Wanted to Know About Sex … But Couldn't Pronounce" (February 23, 1973)

Come On Love, 3:43, Terry Cashman–Tommy West

The drums really drive this one. Danny Janssen, describing the legendary drummer Hal Blaine, says, "If you need 17-and-three-quarters-second crash cymbal, he can do it at 17-and-three-quarters second." The tempo here is very up and pop-punchy on an otherwise mellow album. The guitar at the end of the song is reminiscent of the end of an Elvis song, with the unique country-blues combination of finger-picking and flat-picking made famous by Elvis' lead concert guitarist, James Burton.

"Man, I learned from Hal Blaine," says bass guitarist and musical legend Joe Osborn. "He had already been there for a few years before I got into it, so I leaned on his experience heavily, and I got to know Hal. I learned how to follow him. Hal played on top of the beat, which I also have a tendency to do, or a little ahead of the beat, but without rushing."

Appears On: Season 2, Episode 48, "All's War in Love and Fairs" (March 10, 1972)

I've Got Your Love All Over Me, 2:39, Johnny Cymbal–Peggy Clinger

This lovely ballad sprinkles a little more harpsichord throughout, reminding us of the classic Partridge sound, along with a subtle tinkling of chimes. Held back from airing on the show during season 3, it appears toward the end of the series during the fourth season.

Appears On: Season 4, Episode 79, "Reuben Kincaid Lives" (October 13, 1973)

Let Your Love Go, 2:19, Wes Farrell–Danny Janssen–Bobby Hart

David Cassidy gets to play around in his favorite territory again, with a bluesy guitar and background vocals with a nice dose of soul. His love of the blues comes through on all the Partridge Family albums, stamping the group's catalog with his own style.

The music continues to mature, and "Let Your Love Go" is another Partridge Family experiment flavored with many seasonings. It also marks the third song from the album that was never featured on the show.

It Sounds Like You're Saying Hello, 2:54, Terry Cashman–Tommy West

This is the final song by Cashman and West to appear on any Partridge Family album. The arrangement surprisingly includes the most use of reverb—a mixing technique that

was slowly disappearing—on any song on the album. West remembers this lyric vividly with its catchy, lyrical flow as he sang it across the phone line during the interview.
   Appears On: Season 3, Episode 73, "Diary of a Mad Millionaire" (March 23, 1973)

It's You, 2:07, Johnny Cymbal–Peggy Clinger
So far the opening hooks have ranged from a tuba to a flute, a harp, a fuzz guitar, and big harmonic vocal arrangements. This time it's an a cappella whisper, putting Wes Farrell's me-and-you songwriting at the forefront and keying into the breathy, intimate quality of David Cassidy's voice. The song quickly opens up into another lovely ballad, bringing *Crossword Puzzle* to a close with the final Partridge Family song by Johnny Cymbal and Peggy Clinger and the final arrangement by Mike Melvoin.
   Appears On: Season 3, Episode 65, "Trial of Partridge One" (January 19, 1973)

Album Summary and Reviews

Total Running Time: 29:46
Original Release: June 1973, Bell 1122

With even greater television exposure—the half-hour TV show about the Partridge Family is moving into a better prime-time spot on ABC-TV network this next season—virtually all Partridge Family product has built-in sales guarantees. This particular LP focuses on David Cassidy fairly strong. And, though many may criticize Cassidy's vocal approach, he has something that appeals strongly to the younger demographic set. *Billboard, June 30, 1973*

Not a difficult one to figure out, this one is going straight to the top and should be the beginning of another string of Partridge hits. Leading the pack is what must be the single, "One Day at a Time," a solid, harmonious pop vehicle that just won't be stopped in its journey to the top of the singles charts. As usual David Cassidy shines and Shirley Jones fills the background with sweet vocals. Once again, the proper spelling is s-u-c-c-e-s-s." *Cash Box, June 23, 1973*

David Cassidy, Shirley Jones and other members of TV's Partridge Family have another bright Top 40 rocker. Here are "Come On Love," "One Day at a Time," "It Means I'm In Love With You," "It's You," "Sunshine" and "I've Got Your Love All Over Me." *Variety, June 27, 1973*

   First Chart Appearance: June 30, 1973 (**Record World,** *No. 125;* **Cash Box** *No. 124); July 7, 1973* (**Billboard,** *No. 177)*

THE FUNKY FINALE
or ... *The Partridge Family Bulletin Board*

Season 4: Reinvention

The Partridge Family never slipped significantly in the ratings, always managing to earn a respectable share of the audience. Even so, the fourth and final season saw many changes. The younger kids, Chris and Tracy, were getting noticeably older. Keith enrolled in college. The set was redecorated a bit, just enough to keep up with the look of the now-emerging mid-'70s.

Big shifts were also happening with the producers of the show. Larry Rosen, who had been a producer for seasons 2 and 3, announced his departure. Rosen had produced a pilot for ABC called *Bob and Carol and Ted and Alice*, based on the hit film of the same name. He left *The Partridge Family* after season 3 to produce the new show, but the project was never launched. He moved on to produce the short-lived series *The Girl With Something Extra*, starring Sally Field and Jon Davidson.

Dale McRaven left as story editor and William S. Bickley, who like McRaven had written many scripts for the show, took his place. "In those days there weren't big writing staffs," says Bickley. "There was usually just one writer or one team of writers, and you would get freelance scripts from other writers. But usually there was just the one entity, and that was Dale in the beginning. When Dale left he recommended me to replace him." McRaven still wrote a few episodes for season 4, most notably "The Last Howard," the final location episode.

Bickley, in another development, had received an offer he couldn't refuse halfway through the final season when he was offered a job on the new midseason show *Happy Days*. At that point Steve Zacharias became story editor for the remainder of the series on Bickley's recommendation. Associate producer Mel Swope, who had been with the show from the beginning, moved into the full-time producer position for the fourth season.

With Cassidy leaving the show the producers needed a plan to keep it alive, and they were working hard at coming up with solutions. Replacing Cassidy in the role of Keith Partridge was not an option. "Nobody can replace David. He's one of a kind," Swope told reporters in 1973, adding that the series newcomer "won't suddenly show up in a bedroom in the Partridge house. In other words, he won't be a member of the family."

when we're singin'

While the show was on location in Acapulco where they were shooting on board a cruise ship, the producers were working on a plan and began sharing it with reporters. Together, Mel Swope and Bill Bickley were given the task of finding that perfect replacement.

Johnny Whitaker was suggested while they were viewing *Tom Sawyer* one night on the cruise ship, but Swope said he had proved unavailable. Shirley Jones' real-life sons were also considered, but Jones was adamantly opposed.

The producers decided to experiment. They auditioned actors who couldn't sing and singers who couldn't act, and they aired a number of episodes that reflected both combinations. Bickley and Swope look back on the process: "We knew going into that season that David wanted it to be his last season," says Bickley. "We had a lot of lead time so we were making episodes while we were seeing people and trying to figure out what to do." Replacing Cassidy meant finding something or someone to take the show in a new direction and keep the audience tuning in.

One attempt came with an episode involving new character Alan Kincaid, Reuben's haphazard nephew. Alan Bursky was a stand-up comic who at 18 became the youngest comedian to ever appear on *The Tonight Show*. He had appeared twice in 1973 and was hired on *The Partridge Family* with an option for several episodes, but the idea was scrapped.

Dave Madden recalls this episode as a big flop. "He'd gone on the Carson show as being the youngest stand-up comic in existence. So they hired him for seven shows for *Partridge Family*. And they decided you can't just bring a guy in, so they had him be my nephew. After the first show with Alan, Shirley Jones went to the front office and said, 'It's him or me. Either you get rid of him or I take a hiatus and come back after he's gone.' So they had to pay him off for seven shows and that was all they did—the one show. He was just not any good. He was terrible. We would do a scene where he'd walk through a room 15 times before he could do it correctly. He had no experience as an actor and it showed."

"You would always hire someone with an option," explains Swope, "in case you wanted to continue in that direction. Either you exercise that option or you don't. It costs very little to do something like that.

"When you're fighting for your life to stay on another season, you do what you call a backdoor pilot, says Swope. "It's when you take an episode of an existing show and you change some of the elements so that it could stand alone as a pilot for a new series.

"We weren't doing a backdoor pilot in that sense, because it would have still been *The Partridge Family*, with a little different spin on it. When you're losing your star, this kind of backdoor pilot is one in which the episode has very little to do with the series, and it's a cheap way to do a pilot to present to the network in hopes you can keep the series. We tried a number of things."

On another occasion the show hired the Williams Brothers, twin nephews of Andy Williams, thinking they might get some positive audience reaction. Swope continues, "At the time, Andy Williams was very big in television, and his nephews were dabbling in music. They came in and they did an episode, which was just a way to say to the network, 'Here's a direction we can go.'" The Williams Brothers had released their debut album, *Meet Andy & David Williams*, in 1973, and it had done well with the teenybopper crowd over in England. Wes Farrell was signed to produce the twins' second album, *One More Time*, released later in 1973. Following that album, they released a single, "What's Your Name." When they appeared on *The Partridge Family* in January 1974, the producers felt "What's Your Name" was too slow for the show, so they used the B-side, "Say It Again." The young twins did little to stimulate the audience of *The Partridge Family*, and their appearance on the show was equally dismal for their recording career. The twins were not really comfortable as actors, either, so that didn't help. "What's Your Name" hit No. 92 on *Billboard*, and plans for the third album, already recorded, were scrapped. The Williams Brothers didn't release another album until 1987. "What's Your Name" and "Say It Again" weren't included on an album until 2002, when they appeared on CD as part of the previously unreleased album from 1974.

The producers eventually decided on the new plan. "We'll have David away at college next season and we'll need another singer for the group. So far we haven't come up with a winner," Swope announced in fall of 1973. "Because he sings, most people fail to realize he has as good timing and comedic ability as you're likely to find." The show auditioned actors from England, Australia, and all over the U.S. They needed someone who could handle both music and comedy, and they wanted a male that was about Cassidy's age. They auditioned hundreds of actors. As late as October 28 the producers had tested at least three young men but still didn't feel they'd found the right one yet.

Among the few names mentioned as possible replacements were the up-and-coming musical talent Rick Springfield, a new teen sensation out of Australia who was just hitting in the States. He had just been named Most Promising Singer of the Year by *16* and *Spec* when the *Partridge Family* producers took notice. He was being promoted heavily in the trades for his single "Believe in Me." Springfield had also just been cast as himself in the short-lived NBC animated series *The Magician* (later called *Mission: Magic!*) which premiered in the fall of 1973, the same time *The Partridge Family* returned to the air.

Bickley says, "We met with Rick Springfield, which would have been a good choice, but thank God for him he didn't do it. Rick is just a very good musician, very good singer. David was a very good singer too, but I think Rick Springfield had a much better career by not doing the show than he would have by doing it."

when we're singin'

Wesley Eure, a friend of Shaun Cassidy's, was a young actor and Hollywood hopeful who was discussed as a possible new actor for the show. Eure was popular with the teen magazines, and he could sing. He had done some recording with the Jacksons, been produced by Bobby Sherman, and been a member of a Mike Curb–produced Motown boy band. He auditioned for the replacement spot thinking that Cassidy was going to leave before the season was over. The premise was that Eure would play the new next-door neighbor and Keith Partridge's best friend, setting up the show for Cassidy's absence in the hoped-for season 5 renewal. The new character was reportedly planned to have a single father intended as a potential suitor for Shirley. Eure went on to star in the Saturday morning series *Land of the Lost* and the long-running soap opera *Days of Our Lives*.

Another actor who was considered, Michael Gray—as close to a dead ringer for Cassidy as one could imagine, complete with the brown shag hair—also became a Saturday morning celebrity during the '70s, starring as Billy Batson in *Shazam!*

"We brought in an English singer named Simon," recalls Mel Swope. Simon Fisher Turner became the next most talked-about addition to the show. Turner was popular in England, having played Ned East in the 1971 BBC-TV adaptation of *Tom Brown's Schooldays*, and in 1973 had just released his first album, *Simon Turner,* on UK Records.

Cash Box hinted in August of '73, "Almost every label would like to have a young superstar attraction a-la David Cassidy, Osmonds, Michael Jackson—and there's one around the corner who goes by the name of Simon Turner. He's English and he could take over Cassidy's spot on the Partridge Family if and when David leaves. He's been featured in every teen magazine for the past six months and the girls love him." But plans for Barton never came to fruition.

Then there was the little kid that sang," continues Swope. *"I can ride my bicycle,"* he sings with a little chuckle in his voice. He is referring to four-year old Ricky Segall, who came on in the first episode of the final season and was optioned for 10 episodes. "That was cute and all, but that wasn't going to save the show," says Swope. "Again, you're trying to do something to keep the show alive."

"What a dumb idea," says Bickley with a chuckle. "But he was a very cute and very talented little kid, you know. He was a little prodigy. You could say he was an Elvis prodigy. I don't know where kids like that come from, but he was very, very talented and very cute, and it was also a very odd sort of addition to the show. This is how desperate you can get when your star leaves. We were trying gimmicks to try and save the show, and we felt the water rising around our ankles at that point."

At one point reports and rumors began to circulate that Cassidy might leave before the end of the fourth season. It resulted in a press release from executive producer Bob Claver, making sure that all rumors were squelched. In August 1973, headlines read "Cassidy Stays a 'Partridge' in Fourth Season." The article elaborates, "David Cassidy will co-star in every episode of Screen Gems' ABC-TV comedy series 'The Partridge Family,' starring Shirley Jones, during its fourth season, clarifies exec producer Bob Claver. Contrary to industry rumors, Cassidy has one more year to run on his contract with the studio, Claver added. Rick Segall … will be playing a newly created role in the series and is not intended as a replacement for Cassidy. Claver also said that there is a search being conducted for a new teen actor to join the show, but he will be an additional character and will not replace Cassidy in the Keith Partridge role." Claver says, even today, that he would not have let Cassidy out of his contract early even if he did want to leave.

Another big change came with the switching of time slots. ABC decided to move *The Partridge Family* from Friday night at 8:30 to Saturday night at 8:00. The show had enjoyed a permanent home every week airing just after *The Brady Bunch*. The new day and time put *The Partridge Family* up against CBS's *All in the Family*, the nation's new powerhouse comedy—with many of its episodes written by Danny Bonaduce's father.

So why the move? "Because the network decided they were smarter than we were," laughs Swope. "When you have an audience in a time slot and you want to bring in a new show, you have an audience that's already there. That helps the new show get going. They were hoping that there was enough momentum behind *The Partridge Family,* forgetting the fact that the difference between a Friday night and a Saturday night for a family show is big."

Swope continues, "I don't know how that decision was made. You can talk to 10 network executives in the history of television, and they'll all say this was a good decision and this was a bad decision. They'll all contemplate the shouldas, wouldas, and couldas, and what might have happened if they made a certain decision, because there aren't any guarantees."

Swope thought the network had never given up on the show, right to the very bitter end. Bob Claver, on the other hand, feels the network essentially gave up as soon as Cassidy announced he was leaving, and put the writing on the wall when they moved the show opposite *All in the Family*. Dave Madden agreed. In the meantime, the first experiment for season 4 began with the arrival of Ricky Segall—Swope's "little kid that sang"—playing Ricky Stevens, the new little boy next door.

The Boy Shirley Temple

"Little Ricky Segall" grew up to be one of the nicest human beings one could ever hope to meet. His demeanor is heartfelt and his recollections are full of vivid memories and intellectual perspective. No one could possibly tell his story better than the man himself.

when we're singin'

"I think I became connected to *The Partridge Family* in a very providential way," begins Segall. "I was born in New York, and both of my parents were born and raised in Long Island, New York. My dad was in a band, and he was the lead singer, songwriter, and guitar player. They played around Long Island and were getting a name for themselves. My mom and dad went to the same high school and my mom knew him as the lead singer of the band. They fell in love and the band broke up.

"My mom had a fantastic singing voice. After I was born they went to Nashville to record a demo because they had somebody who potentially wanted to record them. At that time I was just about three or three and a half. Prior to that my parents would go performing in clubs in and around Long Island. I would cry if they wouldn't take me along, and I would also cry if they wouldn't let me get up on stage and sing. My dad had given me a brilliant diet of the Beatles, and the first song I ever sang was 'Hello Goodbye.' When I would sing with them, they were very celebratory of it, just because it was so much a part of who they were. Eventually my dad got the idea that the group wasn't just going to be him and my mom, but rather, the three of us. He called the band Family Portrait.

"My dad was very focused on songwriting. When we were in Nashville, they were recording their demo, and we took advantage of the time we had there and recorded me singing something. It turned out that one of the engineers in the studio heard me, and they knew Renée Valente. She was vice president of Columbia Pictures, and she was doing *The Partridge Family*. Renée and Columbia were on a nationwide search for what they were referring to as 'the boy Shirley Temple.' So this person sent them a copy of my demo and then Renée contacted my parents to ask if we would come to Los Angeles.

"I remember sitting on top of what was the bed of our hotel in Nashville looking out the window and my parents asking me if I wanted to go to Los Angeles, and I remember saying, 'Is that where Disneyland is?' That's all that mattered to me! So they said yes and I said, 'Yes! Let's go to Disneyland!' So then we got to L.A. and I screen tested and landed the part, and they signed my dad to write all the songs.

"I don't know how many other kids were up for the role, and I don't know how long the process took, because, for me, all that mattered was getting to Disneyland. I remember snapshots of it all very clearly. I remember the first day of shooting and the first episode I was on where my character was being introduced, and I remember it vividly and in color. My first and only memory is that I'm standing behind the door, which is the entry to the garage where the family is playing, and I'm going to come walking in. On the right hand side of the door frame there was this light. You could hear the dialogue going on behind the other side of the door. An assistant director said, 'When that red light comes on, that's your cue to walk in.' I remember standing there, hearing all the sounds—you know, "Quiet on the set!"—and getting ready, just looking at that light. Even now, retelling it to you, I can still feel that excitement waiting for that red light to go on.

"My memories are only very happy and good.... I was affirmed everywhere. I was too small to really comprehend it as a business, so the concept of ratings or how well the show was doing was beyond me. I knew it was being watched by people. I knew that I was going to be on as a regular. I think one of the reasons that they were looking for the quote-unquote boy Shirley Temple was because they were slotted against *All in the Family*. The inclusion of the boy Shirley Temple per se was an attempt to boost ratings. Of course *All in the Family* became a Smithsonian Institution exhibit.

"The entire cast welcomed me with open arms. Very much so. Everybody. I don't have a single negative memory of that entire time. That's carried over, even later on. Back in about 1991, '92, I was waiting tables in a restaurant in Tarzana and David Cassidy came in. I went up to him and I didn't even get to finish saying who I was when he recognized me, and he was extremely welcoming and happy to see me. It was a pleasant surprise.

"I don't believe anything happens by accident. I don't believe in luck. So it's a part of the ongoing fabric of my life and some of the early memories I have of my life. Very seldom does someone get to have memories like that, that—not only do you remember from your childhood—but you know that there's still a whole lot of people on the planet who have memories of your childhood, too. It's awesome."

"I think there are those people that are far enough removed that they kind of heard about *The Partridge Family*, but they confuse it with *The Brady Bunch*. And then there's the huge slew of people who didn't necessarily love the show but knew of it, and the minute you say 'Partridge Family' the most common response I get from people, the first thing they do is this: (sings) 'Hello world, hear the song that we're singin'! C'mon get happy!' That's the first thing they do! They'll sing the theme song! And if I tell them who I was, they first think I was the drummer who was replaced." Segall laughs. "They'll say, 'Oh you were the drummer!' I'll say 'No, no, no.' Even farther removed fans will be saying, 'Oh, you were the blonde kid with glasses.' I'll say, 'No, that was Oliver from *Brady Bunch*!'" He laughs again.

"Then there's the group of people who *really* loved the show, and they are the group who remember me. And the thing that they remember about me is the music. They're usually blown away that it's me because they're big fans of the show and they are star struck, and they will immediately go to 'The Bicycle Song' or 'When I Grow Up' or 'You Can Do It (Sooner or Later).' They'll go to one of those three songs and how that song impacted them when they were a kid. In all honesty I have never had anybody talk to me about the show from the group who remembers me and not bring up the songs I sang.

when we're singin'

"Real fans of the show, that is the link for them—the music. The whole nation was changing and had been ever since the British Invasion, and really before that with Elvis. Music had become the conscience of the country. This is something that differentiated *The Brady Bunch* from *The Partridge Family*. *The Brady Bunch* tried to do music, and I think the reason it didn't go as well for them was for one main reason: Everybody knew that Shirley Jones was musical. Everybody knew that David Cassidy was musical—and not just musical, but that these people were gifted. So the fact that Danny didn't play the bass, and the fact that Susan Dey might have been fudging the keyboards, that was kind of forgivable in light of the fact that the songs connected with people, and they knew there was an authenticity behind Shirley Jones and David Cassidy."

The addition of Segall was promoted heavily. He appeared in several photo sessions with the cast, and there were big articles in the trades announcing him as the newest addition to the show. When it came time for him to sing, that was promoted heavily, too.

"They never once pushed me," he says of his parents. "Not ever. My mom, who was typically the stage mom, was always on the set with me. Both of them always articulated themselves very clearly. 'Is this what you want to be doing?' they'd say. 'Because you don't have to.'"

To this day, casting executive Renée Valente and the Segall family are close friends, having maintained a meaningful relationship through the years since the nationwide search for "the boy Shirley Temple."

Bus Stop ...

Ricky Segall & the Segalls

"Ricky stole my act!" jokes Rick Segall Sr. of his son's sudden fame. When Ricky Segall landed the role on *The Partridge Family*, his mother and father shifted gears from Family Portrait's music and focused their support on the career of their only child.

History is always looking for reasons behind shows that fall into cancellation. It's easy to blame the new actors who come on to a show at the end as part of the problem, when really they were simply an attempt at a solution. Segall was embraced by the viewing audience worldwide, despite the show's impending cancellation months later. Rick Segall performed more songs on the show than any other musical guest star of the entire series. "The music that Ricky sang was so well received they wanted to release an album," explains his father, "so we made a deal with Bell Records." Bell Records VP Irv Biegel is the one who approached the family and got the ball rolling with Wes Farrell.

The album was recorded at the Record Plant, which is also where *Bulletin Board* had been recorded. Hal Blaine, Ben Benay, Dennis Budimir, and Michael O'Martian—all top-rate first-call studio musicians—appear in the credits. Segall Sr., who played guitar on the album, recalls some of the musicians and their skills with great respect. "The keyboardist, Michael O'Martian, was unbelievably exciting to be around. You don't get any better than that. He played two keyboards at one time—and I mean standard keyboards, not electronic. He rocked the whole room when he played."

Little Ricky's charisma was unmistakable. "As much as I was the face and the voice of those songs, the heart of those songs was my dad, who the world never had the opportunity to really know. I put my dad's songwriting capabilities up there with the best. If I listen to the song 'When I Grow Up,' I still get teary-eyed. There's two parts to that song that hit me emotionally, both melodically and lyrically. It's the part in the chorus where he writes (singing) 'Now I hope you see that we all can be anything we want to be.' That part has always been an exhortation and encouragement to keep dreaming. The song ends with 'When I grow up I think I'll be … I think I'll just be me.' That is a reflection of the writer. And what's awesome is that my dad and I have maintained the closest possible relationship that a dad and son can have."

Rick Segall Sr. proudly recalls, "I had somebody I met years later who was an attorney, and she told me she always wanted to meet the man who wrote that song because it was the reason she became an attorney. She said when she was young, she believed she could grow up and be anything she wanted to be."

It was "Sooner or Later" that was chosen for the season 4 debut episode, "Hate Thy Neighbor," and also the only single from his album.

"Sooner or Later' is one of my favorites," continues Rick Segall Sr. "It came out of the whole idea that if you want to do something, you can. It was something that I was singing to people in general, that Ricky related to and he took on as his own. He liked the idea that you can do it. He particularly enjoyed singing this one to the audiences when he was on *The Partridge*

when we're singin'

Family. He liked to make configurations with his thumbs and his hands, pointing his fingers and really selling the song. He was good at that. He emulated me and mimicked me, but nobody really knew that. He took it all unto himself in all aspects of his persona. That's part of what Renée Valente saw in him that she liked so much, because he was so engaging."

The B-Side of the single, 'Say, Hey Willie,' is another memorable Segall tune, from the episode about Danny joining a little league team. "Ricky and I played stick ball and Wiffle ball when he was a kid, and I loved Willie Mays. I still do. I wrote that as a tribute to Willie. It is something we would sing when we were playing Wiffle ball together. It was a family favorite, and it still is."

"The Bicycle Song" came out of a father's observations of his young son. "I was sitting on the front porch and he was riding his bicycle around in front of me. I wasn't on the bike with him, but I thought I would sing to him about what he was doing," says Segall Sr.

It's the cute "What Kind of Noise Do You Make?" that has the most endearing story of them all. Segall Sr. tells it: "His mother and I were putting Rick to bed for a nap, and a large bumblebee came by the window. I said, 'Oh look! A bee!' and Rick made the sound of a cow! His mother said, 'What's the matter with you? You're going to make him think you're crazy! Bees don't go 'moo!'"

Several songs from the album simply didn't fit into the show. "All I Want to Ask Santa Claus" was a quickly inspired cut. "I always wanted to write a Christmas song," says Rick Segall Sr. "In the middle of a recording session one day, Wes Farrell came out of the booth and said to me, 'You have to write a Christmas song. We have to have a Christmas song on this album.' Wes knew the value of a Christmas song. So I went home and began writing. If it was a Monday, I came back on Wednesday with a Christmas song. I really liked the idea of a child writing letters to Santa at the North Pole. They do that all the time, and that's what triggered the idea for this song." "What Would You Like To Be" was another LP-only release.

Segall Sr. pulled some songs for his son that had been composed years earlier. "Mr. President," which never appeared on the show but landed on the LP, was one of them. "This came out of my rock and roll days," says Rick Segall Sr. "It was originally intended for Family Portrait. It was an appeal to the president to help out the poor. 'A Little Bit of Love' is something I had written for his mother and I to sing. It had a nice country flavor to it and I just thought it would be really endearing if Rick sang it. The thing you have

> to understand about Ricky at that age is that he was a mimic, and he wanted to sing with his mother and I. Even at four years old he wanted to be part of the act. He just sang along, and he would sing lyrics he couldn't understand. If he could hear it, he could say it. If he could say it, he could sing it."
>
> The remaining songs from Segall's recording sessions included "Grandma (We Love You Just the Way You Are)," "If I Were a Monkey," "Just Loving You," and "A Secret in My Heart."
>
> *Ricky Segall & the Segalls* was produced fairly quickly without any duress. "The initial response was terrific," recalls Segall Sr. "The problem with Rick's album, and the reason it didn't succeed, was due to the folding of Bell Records."
>
> When Bell Records was absorbed by Arista, the new label didn't pick up the album. *Ricky Segall & the Segalls* was lost in the archives as quickly as it was produced, only to reappear in the collectors' market years later. Over the years, Partridge Family fans have added it to their collections. "About once every other year, I'll get a request from Germany or somewhere on the other side of the planet for an autographed picture," says Rick Segall. "When Danny tried to launch his TV talk show, *Danny!*, I was on that, and during the commercial breaks fans would come and talk to us and we would sign autographs. There was somebody there who had my *Ricky Segall & the Segalls* LP—unopened—that they wanted me to sign. I was flabbergasted!"

On Location: The Cruise

During the final season, the cast enjoyed another location shoot, this time on a cruise. It was the first time that a half-hour TV series filmed on a ship at sea. Mel Swope took great initiative in getting this episode off the ground.

"I tracked a man that I had met years before, and he was the head of the cruise line. I told them what I wanted to do, and that it would be valuable internationally for the cruise line, and they went along with it. They made a deal with Continental Airlines to charter a jet." The airline was arranged for one leg of travel. Sitmar Cruises owned the *Fairsea*, the ship used for the episode, and they invested $50,000 in transporting and housing more than 90 passengers made up of crew members, actors, and extras—many of them friends and family members of the cast. They were all flown to Acapulco in a charter Hughes Air West jet. They would board the ship and begin the cruise there.

Brian Forster recalls, "I remember getting on the ship when we arrived, and the tide differences down there were really different. The boat was down 10 or 15 feet from everything and we were wondering how we were supposed to get on the boat. Then suddenly this big wave comes in and brings the boat up to level and we were able to get on."

Like the location show at King's Island amusement park the year before, nonactors made up most of the extras. Friends and family of the cast were invited to go along. "A lot of times on those shows they'd recruit somebody's friend," says Forster. "Shirley had some friends along with her and they were asked to be extras because they kind of knew the business."

The first morning out to sea they headed north toward Los Angeles. First stop: Mazatlan. But many of them had to work, remaining on board shooting while others who were not needed that day visited the port.

Suzanne Crough says this was probably the most fun she had on any of the episodes. "This episode doesn't get talked about much. Brian and I weren't in it a lot, so we would go to the ice cream shop all the time. We'd go to the movies on the ship and had a lot of personal fun rather than professional fun. My parents and their best friends all came along, too. It was great for my parents. They had some other adults to interact with, and they had never been on a cruise before, either."

"This was another one with a little romantic thing that developed for me," says Brian Forster. "James Franciscus was also on the cruise, and he had his daughters and wife with him. Jamie Franciscus and I had a little romance on the boat," he laughs. "I saw her a couple times after that, and I spent a lot of time hanging out with them."

The musical sequence was shot on the boat near the pool, with extras placed all around. Unlike the hysteria at King's Island, the extras seemed more reserved. The group was made of Californians for the most part, many of them friends of the cast, so the overall level of fan worship was much lower. "I remember they just seem to be casually hanging around, not like the King's Island thing where people were literally frantic," says Forster. In addition to the crew and extras from L.A., paying passengers were used as extras. But many of them became bored with the experience, and some reports described them as a bit disgruntled.

Great effort was made to get the best shots, showing off the location and the ship at sea. "I remember going down the ladder onto a small boat so that we could shoot some shots of the whole ship in motion," recalls Mel Swope. "If it had been a car, you would have done a run-by, but when it's a ship it's hardly a run-by," he laughs. "I'm talking by radio with the captain, telling him when to turn the vessel around because we needed those establishing shots of the ship." The ship's captain initially refused to let the crew take the small boat out for shooting purposes, but Shirley talked him into it. The crew circled the *Fairsea* for 45 minutes shooting footage of the ship from a distance. "The cruise line was terrific," says Swope.

Shirley Jones also had her share of concerns over shooting on the ship. For years she had suffered from chronic motion sickness. So she went to see Romart, a famous

South African hypnotist, before leaving on the cruise, and she later told a reporter she never had any problems or any need for medication for the first time in her life.

"I couldn't tell you a thing about the episode, but I can tell you a behind-the-scenes story. Danny was a sweet, sweet kid—he was just a troubled kid. But the captain came to us and said, 'If you can't control that little redheaded kid, we're going to put him off at the next port,' laughs story editor William Bickley.

The episode came off successfully despite a day of rain that put them a bit behind schedule. The wind was also bad, so a lot of the sound for the exterior scenes had to be looped once back to the studio.

Did the episode have any influence with the viewing public or the network? Well, two years later ABC was developing a new series with Aaron Spelling called *The Love Boat*—and Bickley was eventually hired as a producer.

Bickley remembers the cruise as the moment he realized the vocal talent of David Cassidy. "I'll tell you, I saw him in the recording sessions, and I heard the records, and I liked his voice on all the—what we used to call bubblegum music. But when we shot the show on the cruise ship, one night in the ship's nightclub, Shirley got up and sang a lot of songs. Now, of course we all knew Shirley is an accomplished singer. We all know that. She sang several songs, and it was a wonderful little sort of mini concert. And then David got up and sang songs, and these were more like nightclub songs. Not the rock songs and all that, and I remember being stunned that he was such a good singer. Even though I had heard him sing 'I Think I Love You,' and all the others, which was all good. But singing these old standards was when I first realized, *Wow, this guy can really sing!* I mean, I knew a lot of singers back then who were very good at rock and roll, and country rock, and all of the music from that era, but when he got up and sang those standards—and I think he and Shirley sang some duets—I thought, *Wow, that cat can sing!*"

Dreams and Wishes

David Cassidy dreamed of doing an album under a different producer, feeling that with Wes Farrell controlling production there was not enough room for his own vision. He wanted freedom to expand and experiment in his craft, and he finally got his wish. A deal was put together with prominent producer Rick Jarrard to work with Cassidy on his third solo album, *Dreams are Nuthin' More Than Wishes*. Jarrard had produced some albums for Harry Nilsson and Jefferson Airplane that Cassidy really liked. But the freedom to get things his way came with a price. Bell Records had contracted with Farrell as the sole producer of all Partridge Family albums, so when Cassidy wanted to work with another producer, difficult negotiations ensued because Farrell had to be paid off. But Cassidy, for the first time, was finally getting the chance to express himself freely.

when we're singin'

Concept albums were becoming popular in the early '70s. Bookending the opening and closing of an album with a consistent melody or lyric was also being done frequently. Record albums were becoming thought of as art rather than a random collection of songs, and record companies had their hands full learning how to market these new kinds of albums. For their part, radio stations were playing a little bit of everything.

The album introduces itself with a short melody and lyric that meld into the first song, a wistful cover of John Sebastian's "Daydream," first recorded with the Lovin' Spoonful in 1966. Up next is the biographical "Sing Me," a gorgeous song loaded with images capturing Cassidy's childhood, written at Cassidy's request by Tony Romeo.

Sticking with personal memories, Cassidy next chooses "Bali Ha'i," a popular Rodgers and Hammerstein song from *South Pacific*, made famous as a Broadway musical in 1943 and a motion picture in 1958. Coincidentally, Shirley Jones had been given her first break with a small role in the Broadway production. Cassidy's first recording from musical theater is a standout on the album and a sign of things to come.

"Mae" was penned by Gary Montgomery, and "Fever"—made famous by Peggy Lee in the '50s—is another cover, a song that had stuck with Cassidy from the first time he heard it. It was recorded quickly, with a lot of improvisation, during the final moments of a session.

Wrapping up side one is a slowed-down version of "Summer Days." Cassidy wanted to make the song his own, so he recorded it completely differently from the Partridge Family version, giving Tony Romeo's work an alternate interpretation.

Side two opens with Harry Nilsson's "The Puppy Song," which was released as the second U.S. single from the album as well as a single in the U.K. While the single tanked in the U.S., it went all the way to No. 1 as part of a double A-side release in the U.K. The lyrics of "The Puppy Song" are the source of the album's title.

"Daydreamer," not to be confused with the opening album track, was written by South African songwriter Terry Dempsey. It was by far the most successful single released from this album.

Shel Silverstein and Bob Gibson co-wrote "Some Old Woman," loosely based on Elizabeth Cotten's "Oh Babe It Ain't No Lie." Silverstein had written several hits for Dr. Hook, including "The Cover of the *Rolling Stone*" and "Sylvia's Mother," and Johnny Cash's Grammy-winning "A Boy Named Sue." He was best known as the author of children's books *The Giving Tree, Where the Sidewalk Ends,* and *A Light in the Attic.*

Held back till the latter part of the album are "Can't Go Home Again" and "It's Preyin' on My Mind," both written by Cassidy, Kim Carnes, and Dave Ellingson. The three had become very close during these years, out on tour and hanging out together. Carnes and Ellingson were people Cassidy could relax around and be himself. Together, they had chemistry.

THE FUNKY FINALE

The final song, "Hold On Me," was written by Michael McDonald, who also played on every track on the album. McDonald went on to have a successful career with the Doobie Brothers and then as a solo act. The album ends by returning to the bookend title music.

The overall sound is radically different than anything we have heard so far from Cassidy. It feels distinctively less produced, with a more bluesy, folky, natural essence.

The shift in production meant different musicians and background vocalists, too, and a big reduction in background vocals.

The album jacket design reflects the essence of David Cassidy as well, with his own handwritten notes on each song and photography by his friend Henry Diltz. Even the texture of the album jacket is different, with a paper that feels soft to the touch. The trade ads that appeared in *Cash Box* and *Billboard* were designed with the same handwritten style.

A clever picture frame device on the front cover allows the buyer to remove the cover art—Bruno Piglhein's 1925 painting, "Pals," showing a child and a dog—to reveal a shot of Cassidy with his dog Bullseye. A gatefold opens to reveal Cassidy's handwritten notes on every track. The back of the jacket is a night shot of Cassidy in the pool at his home in Encino.

Dreams was explosively successful in England. It connected with British fans. The album and the two U.K. singles ("The Puppy Song" and "Daydreamer") were massive hits. Released in October 1973, *Dreams* made its first appearance on the British album charts in late November and was sitting at No. 1 by December 15, bumped out the following week by Elton John's *Goodbye Yellow Brick Road*. The double-A side single landed both "The Puppy Song" and "Daydreamer" at No. 1. "Daydreamer" was the 10th-best-selling single in the U.K. during 1973—arguably as big in the U.K. as "I Think I Love You" had been in the States.

Dreams was all but ignored by the U.S. fans, however. Bell Records plugged it hard, purchasing gorgeous full-page ads for both the album and the first U.S. single, "Daydream." Several articles on the album, its release and even the jacket design appeared in the trades, too. "Dreams" was given more push through the trade magazines than any other David Cassidy or Partridge Family album had ever received since the first album was released.

Cash Box reviewed the album: "The sweet vocals of David Cassidy are blended well within an elaborate production that makes his new LP a treat. Led by the single 'Daydreamer,' the album features the popular singer in a different light. His treatment of the Richard Liebert classic 'Fever' is sultry and seductive, and he handles up-tempo tunes like 'Some Old Woman' and 'Preyin' On My Mind' adroitly. 'Sing Me' is a good cut, and David's version of 'Bali Ha'i' is the LP's conversation piece. 'Mae' and 'Hold on Me' are the romantic-type ballads that have helped make the singer the star he is." More ads followed, and even press releases touting the album design and stating that the pull-out is "suitable for framing."

Within weeks of the disappointing showing of 'Daydream,' noted only for its remake-ability based on the Lovin' Spoonful's success, the second U.S. single, "The Puppy Song," was reviewed: "It's been a rocky road of late for David, hit-wise, but this cute, honky tonk Harry Nilsson tune should do much to change things for the better. Captures the laid-back 'Sweet Gypsy Rose' quality that folks seem to be picking up these days. Couple that with David's vocals and it powerfully spells 'hit.'"

But still no hit. Not even a dent. Meanwhile in England, the album and the singles were proving to be Cassidy's most successful endeavor yet. Only a week later, the U.S. trades were back pushing "Daydreamer" as a third single because of the giant reaction it was getting in England. It was on the flip-side of the U.S. single "Puppy Song," so Bell Records in the U.S. fired off a promo copy to the radio stations in hopes it might hit.

Cash Box again touted the work: "Not to be confused with David's recent cover of John Sebastian's 'Daydream,' this one is a smash and separate unto itself. Currently the top of the pops in England, the American reaction to the tune should make a matching pair on both sides of the Atlantic. Pretty ballad with changing uptempos prove that David is back and should re-acquire his pop stature again. His best in a long, long time." But shockingly the single never charted in the U.S.

By now there had been three aggressive attempts at a U.S. single release, and it was clear that neither the album nor the singles would be a hit. "I Think I Love You" introduced us to the Partridge Family with their first and biggest hit, topping *Billboard* at No. 1 for three weeks in a row in November 1970. It seems fitting that Cassidy's solo career would peak three years later, in the U.K., with another No. 1 also lasting for three weeks on the British charts. These two songs would remain Cassidy's highest charting hits of his entire career.

Dreams is Cassidy's favorite of his three Bell Records studio albums. He performed many of the songs from this album the following spring during his 1974 world concert tour, the last tour of the Partridge Family era. *Dreams* stands out as the strongest expression of his musical identity up to that point. It was also the final studio album for Cassidy as a solo artist on the Bell Records label, although he would go on to release a trio of highly credible solo albums on RCA. The passing of time brought out a greater appreciation of the work, and *Dreams* has become a beloved classic Cassidy album among the devoted fan base.

Liner Notes: *The Partridge Family Bulletin Board*

There are three stages of the Partridge Family's music. *Album* reflects the sounds of the '60s, with blended vocals that don't include David Cassidy. By *Sound Magazine*, the

THE FUNKY FINALE

sound most closely identified with the group has emerged, featuring Cassidy's breathy, intimate voice. That approach stays constant for the three albums that followed.

Bulletin Board marks the third stage, as the last studio album and the musical climax of the Partridge Family. It reflects several changes in sound, beginning with Cassidy's voice, now a bit more husky and soulful. The vocal and musical arrangements are also subtly different. The number of credited musicians has grown to 22—including horn, trombone, and saxophone players—compared to seven to 12 on the earlier albums. Guitar players Richard Bennett, Ben Benay, and Dean Parks appear for the first time alongside all the usual Wrecking Crew musicians, bringing a new influence to the sound.

Also new was the recording studio. The Partridge Family had come to call Western Recorders Studio 2 home, but for *Bulletin Board* they were at the newer, hip recording studio, the Record Plant. It had opened on the East Coast in 1968 and on the West Coast the following year. One of the first mix sessions held there was for the *Woodstock* soundtrack. By the '70s it was already legendary, having been the world's first studio to go to 24-track and, later, 32-track digital. The Eagles, Stevie Wonder, Fleetwood Mac, Jimi Hendrix, Frank Zappa, and many other artists would record there. It was fresh and happening.

The songs on *Bulletin Board* also reflect a change in themes and tones, especially those written by the three biggest Partridge Family songwriting contributors—Farrell, Janssen, and Hart. The album opens with a jolting musical intro on their "Money, Money," and the rambunctiously titled "Lookin' for a Good Time," which was chosen as the only single release (with "Money, Money" as the B-side). "I Wouldn't Put Nothin' Over on You" is the final Farrell-Janssen-Hart song on *Bulletin Board* and with the Partridge Family.

Farrell, Janssen, and Hart each had a different take on songwriting. Danny Janssen, with his quiet spiritual side, especially enjoyed the chemistry between the trio.

"Bobby was fun to be with and get together with every day. He had a house on Pyramid Drive. To me, there are certain homes that are like enchanted cottages. In those homes you can write great books. You can write great songs. You can do anything. Bobby had a house like that. When Bobby moved to Woodrow Wilson, I don't think we ever wrote a song together again."

Hart was focused strictly on the music business. His experience with the Monkees had primed him for the Partridge Family, and it also influenced his approach and his vision.

Farrell was creative but cramped as a songwriter, usually having to put his business hat on first. The Partridge Family had grown into a huge success, and so had his umbrella organization's many other businesses. Chelsea Records was becoming very successful, and by the time *Bulletin Board* was released, Farrell had launched a second record label, Roxbury.

when we're singin'

A lot of material was produced in an incredibly short time. In their 1993 interview, Ken Sharp pointed out to Farrell that some of the later songs had a lot of hit potential and it was sad they hadn't been more successful. Farrell replied, "Well, you know, you can't go back to what you did. You've got to keep stepping up and you hope that you're going to step up to a higher quality in production, and to a higher quality of competition. It's a growing process. If you keep somebody to where they've been at the beginning, it just becomes monotonous."

The different musical visions of Cassidy and Farrell had come to a boiling point by the time the fourth season's recording sessions began, to the point that they were not able to work together. Because of those tensions, *Bulletin Board* was produced by John Bahler, even though it was credited to Farrell.

"I mixed it," says Bahler, "but contractually Wes was the producer, so they just put his name on it and I didn't really care. I saw the writing on the wall. It wasn't going to last very much longer. I went in there to help Wes, because I was head of production for him at Chelsea. Wes and I had already been working together, and Wes said, 'You have to go in and produce David because he won't sing for me.' Any time he needed me, that's what I did. It wasn't the first time or the last time that Wes asked me to do that. It wasn't out of the ordinary that Wes asked me to do that, but I think the reason behind this particular album was because by then they weren't best of friends."

"Wes still did the tracks," continues John Bahler. "Normally Wes would do the tracks and David would be there at the same time and do a scratch vocal. Often we worked off that scratch vocal, but during the *Bulletin Board* sessions, David could not be in the same room with Wes. It would have become really ugly."

"I think the difference is that John understands what it takes to do it as a singer," says Tom Bahler of the disconnect between Farrell and Cassidy. "My brother is one of the best out there, man, and he understands. He and I both understand singers, and what it takes to do it. I'm not talking about the mechanics of singing. I'm talking about just emoting it. I think there was an understanding with David and my brother that wasn't there between Wes and David. They had different styles. I think David felt unappreciated by Wes. I mean Wes never said anything but lovely things about David, but it doesn't matter. Whatever it was, David felt that way. Wes had a real street side to him and David was anything but street."

In another point of difference, *Bulletin Board*'s vocal background arrangements did not showcase the signature vocal intros that had been part of the formula of the past three albums. Though the background vocals are still alive throughout each of the songs, the opening hooks were much more instrumentally driven.

The source of the changes, says John Bahler, was "probably pressure, and it was probably Wes trying to please everyone. I don't recall any conscious effort on my part to make any changes, although subconsciously I may have colored my creativity because I knew there were things that David didn't care for. He had mentioned them to me. He thought that the *ba ba ba*'s and all the vocal intros we were doing, that kind of made it the Partridge Family sound, was bubblegum. He didn't care for it. He really wanted to do something a little more hip. It was getting old. He was getting bored.

"David may have been right. I don't know. But my MO was always the producers'. They'd give me the song, and they'd offer their ideas, and then I'd go do what I do."

"In the beginning David didn't have any clout," says Jackie Ward, "but as he started having some hits and the show was a hit, he started gaining clout. When you have clout you can get your way a little more. I suspect that's when he was able to do things a little more the way he wanted to do them, and maybe have a little bit of say on what songs he wanted to do. That's the way the business works."

"Part of it was that they just didn't agree on material anymore," says John Bahler. "The more popular David became, the more power he had—at least seemingly so. In reality Wes was still the last word, and he had been right so much that there was really no reason to doubt him. That was my feeling. But David was young and aggressive and he wanted to move on. It was a shock to us, and we were also saddened because we had so much fun doing it."

"Wes really liked David, but David wanted to make a statement musically," says Tom Bahler. "In my opinion it was the wrong venue to make a statement, yet this was his shot to do it. You can't blame him for doing it. It's kind of like being at a concert. Rarely do bands play a new song on the tour. You know what I mean? It doesn't matter how good it is, man. People just want to hear their favorite song."

Tom Bahler continues, "Wes was very much like, 'No, dude. You're not doing this shit.' This was the Partridge Family. It wasn't a David Cassidy album. I think that's really when the rift started, and I think that's when Wes could see that this probably wasn't going to change. I think he [Cassidy] always put his heart and soul in everything, because he was a stone pro, but there was a disconnect. What I really felt happened, because of the Partridge Family, is that Wes became such a mega producer he was able to start Chelsea Records."

Mike Melvoin, who had served as musical arranger on all the previous Partridge Family albums, is absent from the credits on *Bulletin Board*, the result of a sudden rift in his relationship with Farrell. Melvoin recalls, "I had my family up in Big Bear in the snow.... He tried to call me back to L.A. and I refused to go. I said 'I'm up here, Wes, and I rented a house! You want me to leave my children and my wife up here in the snow and drive back to L.A. and do this record over a few days? Wes, please! That's nuts! I can't do that.' He took that as a mortal wound and never used me again." Newcomer Lenny Malaisky served as musical arranger for *Bulletin Board*.

Bell Records reported that Partridge Family albums were one of the most popular Christmas purchases every year. Given the incredibly short deadline to

when we're singin'

produce *Bulletin Board*, it was frantic getting it to store shelves in time. But they were able to release the album in October, just in time for the Christmas shoppers. The trades had positive reviews. Even *Variety*, which had dismissed the series in 1970, gave *Bulletin Board* a positive plug. But, like Cassidy's *Dreams* album, it was barely noticed.

The work of songwriter Mark James is most notably dominant, with three songs. James' influences were in R&B and blues, a style Cassidy loved, so it's not surprising this album contains a shift—even a subtle one—in that direction. His "Roller Coaster" is the perfect example of a new sound that may have worked for the Partridge Family had it kept going. "Where Do We Go From Here" and "Alone Too Long," the latter co-written with Cynthia Weil, are also James'.

James is originally from Houston, and brings a new style of writing to the catalog. In his early years, he was making a name for himself throughout the South, writing and singing with the Mark James Trio and breaking records for the most singles sold in New Orleans. Then he was suddenly drafted. When he came out of the military, it was his songwriting craft that received the most attention. He was soon asked to write extensively for B.J. Thomas.

"I became involved writing for Screen Gems because they heard my material," says James. "I went up there in 1971 and I signed with Screen Gems publishing and stayed with them for three years." It was during this time that James wrote the songs that were recorded for the Partridge Family.

"I was a guitar player originally," he says. "I played a lot of clubs, and I was raised on blues. I also come from a classical violin background. I played violin for six years, and I ran the orchestra in elementary, junior high—and then when I was about 11 or 12 I heard blues, and I thought, *I can't do that on a violin*," he laughs. "Houston was a big blues town. I got into that. A lot of blues, for me, is a feel. A lot of hit records are feel. Not only in the lyrics, but there's a lot of feel to great arrangements."

Of the Partridge Family's music, he says, "They were well-produced and very good." James' style played well against Melvoin's orchestral arrangements and Cassidy's feel for the blues."I felt the Partridge Family hit with all of the young people in the rock business. They had rock records, and they had ballads. I thought they did real well. They had a filter there that they had to abide by. Whatever they recorded had to tie in with their TV show. In some ways that was probably a restriction on them, but other than that they were right on."

Bobby Hart says of the Partridge Family's sound, "The only way you can judge it is by listening to the music. Obviously it was Wes' vision, not David's. But David brought so much to it. He brought the hit vocals, which made it possible to have good records. Without David's voice, they would've been in trouble. They also had the power of television behind them so it could go on for a while. I think David's voice was the biggest plus in the whole puzzle, and certainly the combination of the two made the music what it was. But it could've been better.

"As David gained more and more power, maybe the music got better. I don't know. Wes used musical arrangers. I think those records could've been a little more inventive, and more commercial in a good sense of the word, but he was just cranking them out. It was easy for him to turn them over to a musical arranger," explains Hart. "When you're doing music for a television show, it's hard not to fall into the trap that it's a hungry monster needing to be fed every week. It just stretches you too thin. You can't really make masterpieces when you're doing them at assembly-line pace."

Hart says that if he had produced the Partridge Family he would have aimed for a sound more like that of the Monkees. "Mike Melvoin did most of the arranging and it was a certain style that I don't know how to describe. It wasn't very commercial to me, but it became commercial because you had the power of television and a voice like David's, which I can't say enough about. He was the Micky Dolenz of the Partridge Family. When Tommy and I were given the project to produce the Monkees, even with the power of television behind it, we would have been in a lot of trouble if we didn't have Micky Dolenz. To me, that's what really saved it."

Hart was in the Partridge Family recording sessions from time to time and he remembers the atmosphere as professional. "David was always congenial, and whether he liked the songs we did for him or not, he was always very kind. He never said anything derogatory, never made any power play. He was always very friendly and very personable. I consider him a friend. I've seen him a few times over the years, and I'm always very happy to greet him and he's been the same, always very friendly in return.

"It looked like he was eager to please and do the best with whatever situation he'd been thrown into," continues Hart. "It was the opposite with the Monkees. They had more top writers on their table than anybody. They had this opportunity to have all the greatest songs, but because of the guys' ambitions to mold the music to their vision only, they really sabotaged themselves over the years whereas maybe with the Cassidy thing that might've made the songs and productions better."

Bulletin Board boasts another roster of brilliant artists and well-crafted songs. Covers from Barry Mann, Carole King, and Gerry Goffin are included, and newcomer Harriet Shock gives us the lyrical "That's the Way It Is with You."

Tony Romeo's one song on *Bulletin Board* captures the beginning and the end of the Partridge Family, as if he knew it would be his last time to write for the group that had put him on the musical map—the perfectly written "I'll Never Get Over You."

The two Farrell-Janssen-Hart songs making up the only single from *Bulletin Board*—"Lookin' for a Good Time" with "Money, Money" as the B-side—were drastically different from earlier Partridge Family songs. It was an obvious go-for-it moment to see if a true attempt at change might attract the buying public, since the Partridge Family's earlier, definitive sound was no longer selling. But radio stations and DJs still wouldn't touch it. They were definitely finished with the group.

"When it went cold, it went cold," says Harvey Cooper, former Bell Records vice president of West Coast operations. "David and I became very good friends because I was with him all of the time. I took him around to all of the radio stations. We travelled together on the West Coast. I'd been to his house. I'd been to the studio. We got to know each other. He's a very nice young man and I liked him a lot.

"There came a time where the music wasn't so hot, and somebody had to relay that message to him in some way. So I took him around to all of the radio stations to let him speak to all of the program directors on the West Coast."

Cooper didn't enjoy doing this. "It was a kiss-off tour. In the nicest way, we were trying to let him down easy. They wanted me to take David around so he could get an understanding of what was going on, the real picture. They were trying to get the last out of it, and you know, they were telling him the truth. They were very nice to him, respectful, and the message was clear.

"Then they wanted me to do the same thing around the country, because we were close, and nobody else wanted to do it. It's not a pleasant thing to do. I refused. It started out on the West Coast, where I took him for a tour of the West Coast stations, and then they wanted me to go to the Midwest, and then into the East, and I said, 'Look, I already did this—it's very painful for me,' and I said, 'Get the Midwestern guy to do it. I don't want to do it all over the country. It's a dirty job. I did it out here, and no thank you.' They said, 'Well, if you don't go, we're going to have to let you go.' And I said, 'You don't have to! I quit!'" And he did.

Bell Records promoted *Bulletin Board* with some cross-marketing on the album cover announcing the new time slot for the show. It made for a good attempt at reaching some of the fans who might have been buying the music but not watching the show.

The tensions between Wes Farrell's and David Cassidy's visions resulted in something positive: a creation of musical work that holds up over time in spite of the conflict—and maybe even as a direct result of the two strong-willed talents. Cassidy's soul was evident in every song, whether he actually felt that way or not.

Bulletin Board was the final hurrah. It finally accomplished some of the change Cassidy wanted. It has grit and groove in ways we have not yet heard. *Bulletin Board* succeeds where *Notebook* failed but it happened too late in the game to win commercial success. It seems to go after a male audience with some of its writing style and themes. It showcases Cassidy's voice, and it was finally referred to by some of the critics as "adult."

It's also a return to recording cover tunes, with four of them, more than any earlier album. But unlike *Notebook,* where the covers were drawn from songs that had been incredibly successful hits in earlier versions, the covers here had been

THE FUNKY FINALE

much less successful—several of them were barely recognizable. Still, ten of the 11 songs on *Bulletin Board* appeared on the final season of the show.

It's hard to say if the music could have gone on without the show, even though it stands alone on its merits. The branding with the visual image was fiercely ingrained. *Bulletin Board* was nearly invisible. There was no sign of it on *Billboard*'s Top 200 album charts. The album hit the *Cash Box* charts only for a brief showing, peaking at No. 124. It charted on *Cash Box* for a total of eight weeks, falling off on December 29, 1973. It was the last time the Partridge Family would ever chart. Three days later the world moved forward into 1974, welcoming the changing times and changing sounds of the mid-'70s.

Bulletin Board would remain the most difficult Partridge Family album to find for years and years, until the Internet came along. Even today, it commands a high price on CD. But *Bulletin Board* continues to be a favorite album for many fans, leaving us with a strong finish and happy ending to our favorite TV garage band.

Money, Money, 2:31, Wes Farrell–Danny Janssen–Bobby Hart

The opening piano licks are purposefully direct and sudden, raw and harsh. Cassidy jumps out of the gate with a new sound, and even the background vocals have a sharper, more abrasive sound. There's an edge to it. Right up front, "Money, Money" is an example of the songwriters focusing on a more relatable situation for men than for women—a rare approach for the Partridge Family.

The song plays well on the episode in which it aired, featuring a story about Laurie entering a beauty pageant to make a statement against superficiality. The change in Cassidy's voice is instantly noticeable here. It is the sound he would carry into his RCA years in the mid- to late '70s.

"'Money, Money' is a very infectious song," said Wes Farrell. "I love that song. That stands out very clearly to my thinking. It could have been a single."

Appears On: Season 4, Episode 90, "Queen for a Minute" (February 2, 1974)

Roller Coaster, 2:22, Mark James

Before he became a commercial success as a songwriter, Mark James—who wrote Elvis' "Suspicious Minds," B.J. Thomas' "Hooked on a Feeling," and the Grammy-winning "Always on My Mind"—had recorded his own album, the self-titled *Mark James*. It was his Bell Records debut album. "Roller Coaster" was released as the first single from his album, with a full-page ad appearing in the trades in May 1973.

"Atlantic was clamoring for that album," says James. "They wanted it. That was an album that really and truly needed a marketer who knew how to do it. The manager I was co-producing with made the mistake of actually giving that to Bell Records, which was really a TV-oriented company. They were doing things like Tony Orlando

& Dawn and Marlo Thomas. They were good at selling records from their shows and good at public appearances.

"Atlantic would have done a great job with that album," he continues. "It had a lot of good songs on it, but we went with Bell Records. I loved Larry Utall [president of Bell], but what I mean is that sometimes you're at the wrong place at the wrong time."

Wes Farrell was quick to snatch up "Roller Coaster." It seemed a perfect fit for the Partridge Family and David Cassidy's maturing voice. The father-son theme was something Cassidy could immediately relate to as he struggled to maintain a relationship with his own father, and his interpretation is passionate. This is a great song on so many levels, and perfect for Cassidy.

"Life is just that—*like a roller coaster,* you know?" says James. "It starts off kind of slow, but as you go along, as you get older, you have these hills and valleys and it starts speeding up." The song's title came to James first, and the melody followed suit. "I like a lot of the different parts of this song," he says. "The song flows well, and it goes into a driving thing in the chorus. It could be recorded as a lot of things—it could be jazz, it could be rock and roll, it could be R&B. But I think it's relatable, and it's got a great melody. It has that chord progression which captures the feel of the whole idea and keeps it going. I think it leans to R&B, but not necessarily."

The musical arrangement includes a heavy use of the Clavinet—recognizable as the same keyboard Stevie Wonder uses in "Superstition." "Roller Coaster" was recorded in the late summer sessions for season 4, only months after James released it as a single from his album. "Roller Coaster" was an obviously strong track. It, showed up again as a single for Blood, Sweat & Tears, appearing on the charts in September 1973 around the same time *The Partridge Family* was back on the air.

"I think artists need to try new things to keep them happy and keep them excited about their career and what they're doing," says James. "If you don't keep testing yourself, you're not going to grow. I think the Partridge Family fans realized that. You need to do new ventures like this. I don't care who the artist is—if it's Elvis Presley or anybody—they get excited when they go out of their little realm, try new things, and surprise people: *Who is that? Is that the Partridge Family? WOW!*"

"'Roller Coaster' is one of those songs that could be a huge hit," says James. "In the music business, sometimes you're at the wrong record company at the wrong time. Your backbone is in the marketing to get it out there. Sometimes it just doesn't happen, and then all of a sudden doors open up and you hit with something, and people say, 'Where have you been all of your life?'"

"Roller Coaster" has been recognized over time as a fan favorite. It appears again on the final Partridge Family album, the 1974 compilation *World of the Partridge Family*. It shows up years later on the 2005 CD *Come on Get Happy: The Very Best of the Partridge Family* CD and again in 2013 on *Playlist: The Very Best of the Partridge*

Family. Mark James says he really likes David Cassidy's interpretation of the song and the arrangement that went with it. It is one of his favorites.

Given its consistent placement on the hits reiusses, "Roller Coaster" proves to be the Partridge Family single-that-should-have-been from *Bulletin Board*. Regardless, it gets the distinguishing mark as the song featured in the final concert performance of the Partridge Family's last episode of the series.

***Appears On:** Season 4, Episode 84, "A Day Of Honesty" (November 17, 1973); Season 4, Episode 96, "...---... (S.O.S.)" (March 23, 1974)*

Lookin' for a Good Time, 2:12, Wes Farrell–Danny Janssen–Bobby Hart

Continuing to leave innocence behind, another edgy offering by the songwriters gets an almost spooky interpretation by David Cassidy. It's a story song about a boy trying his hand at the wild side of life. Story songs were huge in 1973, and Bell Records had scored big earlier in the year with the haunting "The Night the Lights Went Out in Georgia."

Hand clapping and other interesting choices round out the sound. It's the third song in a row with some edge, and the third in a row to seem more relatable for a male audience. Chosen as the only single release from this album and the last for the Partridges, it was a risk worth taking even though it never even bubbled under Billboard's Top 100. The U.S. single itself is quite hard to find in the collector's market today, though international copies can be found more easily.

"That was cookin'," recalled Wes Farrell. "That had a lot of edge to it. We were trying to step up."

Cash Box gave the song a smash review: "David Cassidy, Shirley Jones and the Partridge gang have always supplied good times musically and this is no exception to that rule. This one builds slowly and is a bit more progressive that much of their past material, but that Partridge sound is most definitely in evidence. Chalk up another smash for the TV recording artists."

The lyrics to this song have been misprinted over and over through the years, beginning with the first printing that appeared in the Japanese release of *Bulletin Board*. Skip the lyric sheet, put on your headphones and listen closely to the events that took place at Barefoot Joe's, the setting of this dark, and not-so-innocent story song.

***Appears On:** Season 4, Episode 89, "Danny Drops Out" (January 26, 1974)*

Oh, No, Not My Baby, 2:38, Gerry Goffin–Carole King

This song showcases the arrival of Carole King's work on a Partridge Family album. It's a perfect Partridge mid-tempo-to-slow ballad, and with the rise of King as the most prominent female singer–songwriter of the early '70s, it was a credible choice. King wrote this song with her then-husband, Gerry Goffin.

when we're singin'

"Oh No, Not My Baby" was first released in 1964 by Maxine Brown, who had a top 40 hit with it. Shortly after, in 1965, Manfred Mann had a hit with it in England. By late October 1973 Rod Stewart's cover was hitting the *Billboard* charts, leaving little chance for a Partridge Family release.

In spite of a new element—a sitar in the opening—"Oh, No, Not My Baby" returns to familiar territory, primarily in the vocal arrangement. With the exception of this song, side 1 represents something new and experimental. Side 2 is a stronger return to the classic Partridge sound, and the album's edge would have come off stronger if side 1 had not been broken up with the more familiar old-style arrangement heard here.

There have been several covers of this song since the Partridge Family, including one by Cher, who recorded it in 1992 as a follow up to "The Shoop Shoop Song."

Appears On: Season 4, Episode 80, "Double Trouble" (October 20, 1973)

I Wouldn't Put Nothin' Over on You, 2:51, Wes Farrell–Danny Janssen–Bobby Hart

With a nod to the times, the Farrell-Janssen-Hart trio seem to be playing off of Elton John, whose similar "Honky Cat" had risen to No. 8 on the *Billboard* charts in late 1972.

"I Wouldn't Put Nothin' Over on You" also seems similar to the *Shopping Bag* cut "Hello, Hello"—a fun inclusion and something different.

"I remember it had a funky edge to it," said Farrell. "That's a style of writing which I always enjoyed."

Appears On: Season 4, episode 79, "Reuben Kincaid Lives" (October 13, 1973); Season 4, episode 92, "Miss Partridge, Teacher" (February 23, 1974)

Where Do We Go from Here?, 2:36, Mark James

Side 1 of *Bulletin Board* ends with this mature song from Mark James, with very little background vocal work. Wes Farrell's absence is obvious, for better or worse. The song includes some high notes for Cassidy, and the guitar at the end is riffing, improvisational, and original. Mark James' own interpretation of this song also appears on his self-titled solo LP *Mark James*.

James says, "The opening lyric really comes out hard-hitting, and you can play with this song musically too. When the song hits the chorus, it's open to possibilities for all kinds of different musical arrangements. Mainly, and number one, it had a blues feel to it. It's a pop thing with an R&B feel. The main thing I try to do with my songs, musically or lyrically, is to try and reach both young and old. I try to find something within it that reaches you." "Where Do We Go from Here" is the only song from the album that never appeared on the show.

How Long Is Too Long, 3:41, John Bahler–Tony Asher

"I was never involved in the Partridge Family songwriting until the very last album," says John Bahler, "and I hit my head one day and said, 'What am I doing? I can write a song!'

"Tony Asher is my best friend in the whole world. He also happens to be Paul McCartney's favorite writer. In fact, Paul McCartney told Tony that the whole *Sgt. Pepper* album was an idea that came from listening to *Pet Sounds* by the Beach Boys, for which Tony had written something like 10 of the 12 songs. The lyrics that Tony Asher writes are just spectacular—'Wouldn't It Be Nice,' 'Caroline, No,' 'God Only Knows,' to name just a few.

"When I went to work for Wes as head of production at Chelsea Records he and I had several hits. Wes came to me one day and said, 'You know I used to do commercials when I was in New York, and I'd really like to start a commercial arm.' I said, 'Well, the best guy I know is working for an ad agency now, but I'll call him and see if he's interested.' So I called Tony and said 'This is what's up. Are you interested?' He said, 'Hell, yes!' So he got out of that and he came on board as head of the commercial division for Wes.

"Toward the end of that period, while we were both still working for Wes, one day I said to Tony, 'Why in the hell don't *we* write a song?' He said, 'Yeah! Great idea!' So I went home that night and 'How Long Is Too Long' came to me. I don't know what it was, but I'm playing the piano and it just came to me. I went in the next morning and I told Tony I had this idea. So I sat down and played and I sang, 'How Long Is Too Long,' and I was just *la la*-ing through the rest of it, so he said, 'That's cool, but what do you mean by *how long is too long*?' And I said, 'You're the lyricist! You figure it out! I don't know what I mean by that! It just sings well!' He went, 'Oh, OK,' and he went home and came in the next day with the song! He's amazing!"

Bahler continues, "It ended up on the last studio album, and it also ended up on a greatest hits album—and it wasn't even a hit!" (It was included on the first CD hits collection, *The Partridge Family Greatest Hits*, released by Arista in 1989.) "I always wondered why that song ended up on the greatest hits. I finally found out that somebody who was one of the big executives at the record label back then claimed this song was his favorite Partridge Family song. So when they did the greatest hits he just stuck it on there! Isn't that neat?"

Cassidy's voice moves toward blues-rock on the song—the only Partridge Family song by Tony Asher, and one of only two for John Bahler.

Appears On: Season 4, Episode 82, "The Diplomat" (November 3, 1973); Season 4, Episode 93, "Keith and Lauriebelle" (March 2, 1974)

I'll Never Get Over You, 2:59, Tony Romeo

Tony Romeo's final Partridge song appears to be a follow-up to his groundbreaking "I Think I Love You." The opening hook is almost a complete melodic reversal of the hook in the earlier song, with a similar style all the way through. Cassidy's tone, pleading, and sense of longing translate evocatively. "I'll Never Get Over You" was used in the fourth season's opening show, right at the top of the episode.

"I know it was written about the end of a relationship," says Frank Romeo. "My brother's melodies are very, very much like old Italian melodies. They sound like the kind of songs my grandmother would have sung—melodies that are familiar almost from the moment you hear them. They weren't complicated melodies, and there is great merit to the lyrics, which were magnificent lyrics to these melodies. Think about 'I Think I Love You,' for example. That melody is very simple, but that's a very Italian, sort of operatic, melody if you think about it, even Russian. I heard someone once say they thought 'I Think I Love You' had Russian heritage because all of Tony's melodies were very Old World–influenced."

Appears On: Season 4, Episode 75, "Hate Thy Neighbor" (September 15, 1973); Season 4, Episode 87, "Art for Mom's Sake" (January 12, 1974)

Alone Too Long, 3:10, Mark James–Cynthia Weil

Mark James teamed up in a one-time collaboration with Cynthia Weil to write this gorgeous love song, perfect for Cassidy as it plays to his strengths, reflecting back on the more traditional Partridge Family style.

"I'm really a self-writer," says James. "I've been that way for years. As a matter of fact, I had to learn how to be a co-writer. In this case, I was approached by Screen Gems and they said, 'Cynthia has a lyric and she'd like to write with you,' and I said I wanted to do it.

"Mostly when I write with somebody, we write lyrics and music together. Both of you are just trying to capture something, you know? And if somebody's got the spirit, you let them alone. I try to write down everything the other writer says, because sometimes it happens that way, too. You need to capture that spirit and let them run with it."

James continues, "That little office at Screen Gems had a piano, and they took us in there and closed the door. Cynthia pulled out these lyrics and I looked at the lyrics for a minute and just dove into the song. I almost played the song all the way through in one shot. That one just happened. It just flowed all the way through. It took us about 15, 20 minutes on that one. It was very quick. When I was writing the music, I didn't change any of her lyrics. I just worked off of them. Cynthia is easy to work with. She is a great writer, professional writer, and a lot of fun, too. We had fun writing this."

"Alone Too Long" appeared in the season 4 ABC commercial promos for the show's new slot on Saturday nights. And although perfect for Cassidy and the Partridge Family, it was also released the same year by B.J. Thomas on his *Songs* album released through Paramount with an arrangement very similar to the Partridge version. Thomas' version was titled "I've Been Alone Too Long."

Appears On: Season 4, Episode 76, "None but the Onely" (September 22, 1973)

THE FUNKY FINALE

I Heard You Singing Your Song, 2:38, Barry Mann

Barry Mann wrote this song for himself to sing, and it appeared on his album, *Lay It All Out,* released in January 1971. It was recorded again the following year by Punch, a sunshine-pop band that drifted over to Bell Records to record two singles after getting nowhere with their 1971 self-titled LP on A&M.

Punch's rendition of this song was one of those two Bell Records singles, both produced by Bones Howe and arranged by Bob Alcivar in 1972. Like the album, the single never managed to make a dent on the pop scene, despite the groovy look and vibe.

Bahler's arrangement is almost identical to the Punch arrangement, which was a perfect Partridge throwback sound. The rhythms are playful and upbeat, mid-tempo with plenty of classic Partridge *ba-dah-dahs, oohs,* and *ahhhs* serving as a final tribute to the layered harmonies that brought David Cassidy and the Partridge Family full circle.

According to Barry Mann's wife, Cynthia Weil, Mann's inspiration for composing this song was Carole King.

Appears On: Season 4, Episode 83, "Heartbreak Keith" (November 10, 1973); Season 4, Episode 91, "Danny Converts" (February 9, 1974)

That's the Way It Is with You, 3:04, Harriet Schock

"'That's The Way It Is with You' was a cut on my first album, *Hollywood Town,*" says singer-songwriter Harriet Schock, "which I recorded for 20th Century Records. In this case, I think my publisher, Colgems, got it to the Partridge Family. I think it really became popular when they did it on their TV show. I don't think my album was out yet when they recorded it.

"I was in love and I just wanted to be with the guy all the time," she continues. "So I guess the lyric reflects that—a book you can't put down, a song you have to hear over and over—I remember a columnist once said that I think in analogies. I believe it's the only way to explain a feeling to someone who may or may not have had the same feeling. Contrary to popular belief and contrary to the way many songwriters write, I guess I simply wrote the song based on my own experience. I did not have another artist in mind. In fact, I've had a lot of covers in the 35 years I've been writing songs, and in no case was I writing for the cover artist. In those days, every one of the cuts on all three of my albums was getting airplay. I suppose they either heard it on the radio like Helen Reddy did with 'Ain't No Way to Treat a Lady,' or my publisher gave them a copy of the demo."

Schock didn't know Wes Farrell, David Cassidy, or any of the people involved in the television show or recordings, but she values how they handled her song. "They were quite true to my original, so, of course I liked it! My fondest memory is just how soulful David Cassidy is when he sings a melody. I loved his interpretation. It was as

when we're singin'

close to R&B as a pop song sung by a white singer and written by a white girl can get. I was in heaven. I haven't always been that lucky with covers of my songs."

"He sings the melody precisely but very soulfully," continues Schock. "I absolutely love his voice, but even more than that, I love his musicality, his soulfulness. I'm so thrilled to have had a cut with someone who totally gets where the song is coming from and where it should go."

With plenty of phrasing challenges, this is one of only two songs on the album that contains any semblance of John Bahler's usual vocal opening hooks.

Shock's version came along a year later when her album was released in 1974. But it was the single from that album, "Ain't No Way to Treat a Lady," that put her on the map as a songwriter when Helen Reddy recorded it in 1975.

Appears On: Season 4, Episode 85, "Al in the Family" (November 24, 1973)

Album Summary and Reviews

Album Summary: Total Running Time: 28:42
Original Release: October 1973, Bell 1137

Televisions have long been tuned into this delightful musical family and record players around the world have played their joyful music for years, and this new LP promises to keep those machines running for a long time to come. "Money, Money" is a strong uptempo rocker and "Roller Coaster" is surprisingly funky and moves steadily with David Cassidy's lead vocals superbly accented by Shirley Jones' multi-tracked harmonies. "Lookin' for a Good Time" is a great pop tune with a catchy melody and Cassidy does a beautiful job on the Goffin-King 60's hit "Oh, No, Not My Baby." *Cash Box, November 3, 1973*

The Partridge sound is moving like a constant ball of energy. "I Wouldn't Put Nothin' Over On You," with a catchy arrangement and sweet, tight harmonies, contrasts with the question and answer sound of "Where Do We Go From Here." David Cassidy's soft but forceful vocals are dominant. Wes Farrell's powerful production matches the sweep of the new material. LP is fine adult fare. *Billboard, November 10, 1973*

David Cassidy is again featured in a surefire collection of Top 40 material by this TV family. Notice "Where Do We Go from Here," "I Wouldn't Put Nothin' Over on You," "How Long Is Too Long," "That's the Way It Is with You," "Money, Money" and "Alone Too Long." *Variety, November 14, 1973*

***First Chart Appearance: November 10, 1973** (Cash Box, No. 161)*

ACROSS THE POND, DOWN UNDER, AND BACK
or ... The World of The Partridge Family

Cancellation

As 1974 rolled around, the second half of the fourth season was airing. None of the attempts put forward in replacing David Cassidy with someone or something new was taking hold. "We were fighting to keep the show alive," says producer Mel Swope. "I never got the impression from the network that they were going to walk away from the show. Now whether somebody at the network thought, *Hey, without David Cassidy we don't have a show*, I don't know. But there was never a sense that they were giving up on us. If that would have happened, then the studio would have said at that point 'We'll do 10 bottle shows' [inexpensively produced episodes], and they didn't do that. That sends a message to the network that we're not giving up because you're not giving up. Every time you run a promo for a show it helps to generate the audience, so you're pushing the promotion department of that network to make sure you're seen by the audience, and that's a big part of the cooperation between the network and the studio. They are demonstrating they are behind you by promoting the show—whether it's print ads or a 10-second spot or a one-minute spot."

Television promos were running throughout the season. *TV Guide* featured an article on Shirley Jones as late as March 9, 1974 (two weeks before the final episode aired), in which she plugs the wholesome quality and general likeability of the show as one that all families dream of having—including her own. The article also hints that *All in the Family* was winning the ratings race against the Partridges.

"The critics were writing about it in advance to help the show," adds Swope. "I must say, the critics at that time were good. I remember I called one near the end of the show when the ratings were falling, and I said, 'Look, I'm going to be straight with you. We're fighting for our lives. Anything you can do, any good things you can say about the show so we can continue to build the audience, is something I would really appreciate.' I had never done that before. He was one of the top critics, and he followed through. He could have said, 'Hey, I'm busy. Don't bother me.' He didn't say he was going to do anything, and he didn't say he wasn't, but the next time he did his editorial, it was just very positive about the show."

when we're singin'

The Partridge Family was old-school in its design. "Each show was a stand-alone episode," says Swope. "There was no reference to what happened the previous week, or what was going to happen the next week. When you shoot episodes and you're four episodes ahead at the top of the season, by the end of the season you can choose which episodes are going to air when. The decision point with the network for renewing is also an important factor in deciding when to air which shows." He explains the importance of scheduling wisely during the sweeps periods, when viewership is measured: " You're going to use the strongest shows where the audience is going to be, because during the sweeps there's a lot of promotion. If there's another show you can air after sweeps, that's what you're going to do. Let's say they ordered 22 episodes with an option for six more. They have to give you enough notice to write those last scripts. They didn't cut us off with *The Partridge Family*. They gave us our final script order in terms of the last show that was aired."

The presence of Ricky Segall was the first sign of change when *The Partridge Family* began airing in the fall. In an attempt to do battle with *All in the Family*, the network ran promo ads of Segall wearing boxing gloves and promising "to deliver a knockout blow to Archie Bunker this fall." Even Shirley Jones was promoting the show heavily. "I feel we will do well opposite *All in the Family*," she told reporters. "We have our audience and they have theirs. Never the twain shall meet. And Saturday has been a weak one for the network. *Partridge* is one of its strongest shows, so it's probably a good move. I have no feeling of uneasiness going against *All in the Family*. But I have always been an optimist." Jones liked doing television and wanted to see the show continue. She said that she would like to have her own series again someday, preferably in situation comedy.

Earlier in the season, Jones had been more concerned about the writers' strike that was going on the summer of 1973 and its potential to slow things down for the show. Bob Claver was equally as concerned. "We have two good workable scripts for *The Partridge Family* and nine others that could be fixed by a writer if he could come to work," he told reporters. "There is talk of directors striking next and more talk, that if that happens, the studios will shut down. I wouldn't be surprised if the season didn't start till next January."

The move against *All in the Family* wasn't going so well for the Partridges. By December 1973, the network announced a planned scheduling move. The same announcement stated that David and Andy Williams, nephews of the more famous Andy Williams, were the official replacement for David Cassidy. Their episode was planned to air January 19, 1974.

But the January episode fell flat. Finding a replacement for David Cassidy was proving next to impossible. The show was never moved away from its slot against

All in the Family. Eight more episodes aired after that, none of them involving an attempt to replace Cassidy.

Looking back, executive producer Bob Claver felt differently than Swope about the way the network was looking at the show's future. He felt the upcoming cancellation was an obviously predictable one. "We were in such bad shape by then," says Claver. "We were down to the Ricky Segall time, which I thought was maybe the worst idea ever in the history of casting. It wasn't the young actor's fault, though. It was so silly, but sometimes they get desperate and they do crap like this at the end when they're going to get canceled. It never works. Can you imagine a kid who's six or seven years old coming in and changing this? I don't think so."

Claver continues: "Once they went to Saturday night, the show was over. I don't care who they hired. They could have hired the Pope. It wouldn't make any difference. They put us up against *All in the Family*, and that show was one of the biggest shows in television. They don't want to have to eat up a couple shows to find out it's over, so they knew that putting *Partridge* next to *All in the Family* was a very safe move for the network. Once that happens, as far as the network's concerned, you're not coming back. It was over, and it was too bad, because we'd have liked to keep going. But it had a good run." In a twist of fate, Claver and *All in the Family*'s Carroll O'Connor were good friends and had once worked as partners in a restaurant together.

In those days before the big series finales, when a series came to an end it simply ended. The last episode was simply scheduled, with no intention to wrap things up in any fashion. It was simply another day at the Partridge house, with a few subtly sentimental moments in the story.

Shirley Jones, Dave Madden, and Danny Bonaduce would have enjoyed seeing the show continue, while David Cassidy was burned out, Susan Dey was ready to move on, and Suzanne Crough and Brian Forster were simply willing to accept the show's demise. Bonaduce probably felt the loss more than any other, because this television family had become a family—even if manufactured—that he very much counted on for love and support.

Forster remembers feeling relief. "I think I was so glad I could finally go back and be a kid again and hang out with my friends again. At that point, my mom, who started me in commercials basically just to make money for college, was probably thinking, *OK, we don't need to do that anymore. We're good to go now*."

The final episode guest-starred George Chakiris, of *West Side Story* fame, as a suitor for Shirley. The episode was familiar fare, with Danny baiting Keith into an intervention on their mom's date, concluding with a lecture from Mom and a poignant scene in which Keith acknowledges Danny as an equal rather than a little brother. Although the episode did not set out any finality for the show, the moments were nice.

when we're singin'

Bus Stop ...

Laughing with Dave Madden

Dave Madden worked as a stand-up comic in his early show business years. His personality—every ounce of what you saw on the screen—came through immediately. Included here is a portion of the interview conducted in June 2011 for this book, reflecting the witty, dry sense of humor that embodied the late, great Dave Madden.

JM: Hello, Dave?

DM: Oh, what do you want now?

JM: (laughing, then rolling with it) Boy, for a manager who's been managing a successful band for 40-some years, you're pretty crabby!

DM: Yeah, I'm pretty crabby.

JM: (laughing) Well, thanks a million for doing this.

DM: I understand you've talked with Shirley Jones.

JM: I did.

DM: You're telling me they encouraged you on this—what has become known around the country as 'Miller's folly'?

JM: (laughing again—I think you get the idea) Boy, I wish I were that famous! There was only one book written on The Partridge Family *so far, so I thought I would give it a shot.*

DM: You say that because you haven't read my book!

JM: Actually, I did read your book!

DM: You did? Well that's two books that have been written about *The Partridge Family*.

JM: Yeah, that's true. There's a lot in there on The Partridge Family.

DM: Danny wrote a book. That's three. David wrote a book. That's four.

JM: Yeah, I guess I have to count all those too.

DM: Yeah, absolutely! Especially them, since they didn't have anything else to write about.

JM: I have a million questions here!

DM: Cut that down to about five.

JM: Let me start with the style of comedy. How does the style on **The Partridge Family** *compare to the style of today's shows?*

DM: Well, I don't know about style. The difference would be clean or not so clean, I suppose. There was a lot of cleanliness. I'll tell you how clean it was: One time there was a script where I had to say to Danny, "That's really rotten, Danny." The censors came up and said, "You can't say 'rotten.' This is family time and you *will* change that to 'terrible.'"

JM: You're kidding me!

DM: No, no, I'm serious. That's how clean things had to be. It was a clean world back then.

JM: Do you think that has something to do with the impact it has on a new young generation, or fans who keep following it?

DM: I don't know. The young generation talks to one another in four-letter increments. They go to motion pictures with lots of four-letter words in them.

JM: What do you think it is about The Partridge Family that people keep coming back to? In your book, you said this is the show that everybody keeps asking you about.

DM: I have no idea why they keep coming back to that. Of course I think we're talking about a very small percentage of people. It's like the terrorists in Afghanistan that make up about 1 percent of the population. Partridge Family fans make up probably a quarter of a percent of the population of the United States, but they're very vocal so as a result you get the feeling that a lot of people care.

JM: (laughs) You're right. The Partridge Family fans are vocal.

DM: So are Republicans. The Tea Party. Sarah Palin. The only people who get attention are the people who are vocal, and they know that. You don't hear anything about me because I'm not vocal. I just sit here with my bowl of soup and ignore the world.

JM: Well hopefully I can help you to be more vocal, because of course everyone in show business wants their manager to be Reuben Kincaid!

DM: Well, I don't understand that, either. Kincaid, if you analyzed him, which I don't imagine you have, was an absolute failure as a manager. He really was. He put them in the most awful places and they were supposedly big names. They had records out that were big hits and yet he had them working in these folk rooms. Kincaid misbooked them into places they weren't supposed to be. He was a terrible manager. I can't imagine anyone wanting him to even be near them if they were looking for a manager.

JM: (teasing him) But then you go 40 years later and all those records are being released on CD, so Reuben Kincaid must have done something right!
DM: No, no, no, no! You're mixing up fantasy with reality!
JM: (laughs) That's what we **Partridge Family** *fans do!*
DM: (laughs) No, I had nothing to do with the fact that any of the records are selling. They wouldn't even let me snap my fingers on those records. They let Shirley do her *doo-wa*'s so she could get a cut of the money for the recordings, but they wouldn't let me near them. And that is as it should be.
JM: (laughs) So you're not very musically talented?
DM: Well, no, I wouldn't really say that. I worked for years as a folk singer in clubs. This was all prior to Partridge—eight to 10 years before it came along. This was in the late '60s and early '70s when folk music was really hot. Sometimes I worked as a stand-up comic. Sometimes I worked as a folk singer. Sometimes I worked as both, depending on what they wanted.
JM: I know that you developed a close relationship with Danny Bonaduce during this show. What is the best quality that Danny brought out in you?
DM: Abusiveness. I never used to be abusive at all until I got around him. Now I'm compelled to beating my dog because of Danny.
JM: (laughs) What do you hope he learned from you?
DM: As time goes by, watching his career, I assume he learned nothing. That's what I assume. But no, most of the stuff he pulled off on his own.
JM: You said in your book that it was only on the **Partridge Family** *set that you produced lasting relationships with the cast and the production team. Why do you think that is?*
DM: Well, the fact that it lasted four years, and that it was a family-style show. I did *Alice* for seven years. I was on it longer than *The Partridge Family*, but *Alice* was an adult show. It was a taped show that we rehearsed for three days. We did it in front of a live audience and went home. We didn't have that much of a relationship. *The Partridge Family* was a film show. It took four or five days to do a single shoot with *The Partridge Family*, so we were around each other a lot more. I did *Laugh-In*, too, but it was ludicrous because, except for the joke wall and the cocktail party, we hardly saw one another because everyone was doing vignettes. You come in at 10 in the morning and there'd be a lighting man and a photographer and a director there, and you'd do two hours of blackouts about a doorknob or something. All by yourself, no one else around, and they'd take those, cut them up and use them on several shows. We

did sketches occasionally with one another, but there wasn't that much interaction on *Laugh-In*. *The Partridge Family* was really a family kind of thing. After four years and all those hours together, I guess we got hooked on each other.

JM: As an actor, who do you think grew the most as an actor in their four years on The Partridge Family?

DM: Me! Why would I say anything else?

JM: (laughs) Of course!

DM: Shirley Jones didn't grow. She was already an Academy Award winner when she went on the show. So you can't say her. Let's see … maybe David, I don't know.

JM: I recently found out about the band called the Reuben Kincaid. So what should I name my band now that Reuben Kincaid is taken?

DM: (laughs) I don't know if they're still around or not, but in fact this guy from the *Atlanta Constitution* sent me a great big almost full-page article about the Reuben Kincaid rock group that was in the paper there. I never got hold of them, which was probably wise, but I have not heard about them since. Rock groups that don't make it big normally fade from existence in a short length of time.

JM: Who was your favorite guest star on the show and why?

DM: Oh, Farrah Fawcett! Why? She was much sexier than anyone else. If somebody said, 'Who do you want to go out with tonight, Farrah Fawcett or Harry Morgan?' I wouldn't have too much trouble making a decision.

JM: (laughs)

DM: Favorite guest star … I don't know. We had so many in that four-year stretch. There were a lot of them. I'd need a list in front of me to pick them out, unless you absolutely don't believe in Alzheimer's at all.

JM: (laughs) You're sounding pretty good for Alzheimer's.

DM: See, Alzheimer's isn't always relative to the past. It's usually relative to yesterday. Like "What did you have for breakfast yesterday?" "Oh, did I have breakfast yesterday?" Like I know your name is … Bill or something.

JM: (laughs) I'm calling the doctor on you.

DM: Yeah, you should.

JM: What are your memories of the Christmas show?

DM: The Christmas show was a lot of fun, mainly because everyone got to play a different character than normal and to do a period piece, like a western. Also, the actor who played the old prospector, Dean Jagger, had been a favorite of mine. I got to sit and talk with Dean Jagger, and that was thrilling. He might be my favorite guest star.

JM: Were there any particular writers or directors you enjoyed working with?

DM: We had various directors. They kept changing them. I'm not sure why. Either they kept dying right after the show, which could be very possible, or they just didn't want to get stuck with the same director all the time. [Having more than one director] is not completely normal for sitcoms. *The Dick Van Dyke Show* had the same director for years. They wouldn't switch off at all. I have no idea why they did it on *The Partridge Family*. Just offhand I'd say we must have had 15 or 20 different directors over a period of four years.

JM: And a lot of writers too.

DM: Yeah, yeah, quite a few, but they accepted outside scripts.

JM: Do you think that was to the show's advantage or disadvantage?

DM: Disadvantage. I think it's a disadvantage not to have the same director, if he's a good director, and I think it's a disadvantage not to have the same group of writers, if they were good writers. If you're getting new writers to the show all the time, you have to constantly adapt the material to your style because they don't always write for you.

JM: You and Danny had a lot of comedic exchanges during season 1. There were less of them beginning season 2. Why was that?

DM: What I remember is this: They gave us four or five scripts during the hiatus period for us to look at. I read them, and they had a lot of scenes between Danny and I. Now at the same time the first year had gone by and they found out David Cassidy had not re-signed his contract. Obviously part of that renegotiation was to give him more to do. As a result they took all these scenes between Danny and myself and rewrote them for Danny and David.

JM: What's your opinion of the Partridge Family's music?

DM: My music is Frank Sinatra, Nat King Cole, Ella Fitzgerald—the music of the '40s. But I must say the Partridge Family was, for the most part, pleasing. I enjoyed it. It wasn't harsh. They called it bubblegum rock. Maybe it was made for simple minds like mine. I don't even know if it would be called rock and roll. It was something different. I don't know what it would be called.

JM: It seems more adult contemporary, or easy listening.

DM: You're right.

JM: What's your opinion of David Cassidy in concert?

DM: Well, the first time I heard David I went down the coast to one of those beach towns where he was performing in a club. The music was so unbelievably loud and pumped up, within 10 or 15 minutes I had a terrible headache and my ears physically hurt from the music. I had to go out of the room because I couldn't deal with it anymore. Now much later, in California I went to see David in an outdoor arena-style place. That was much more enjoyable. It didn't blast me out of my seat. I think he's a very good singer.

JM: What is the legacy of The Partridge Family?

DM: To be forgotten.

JM: (laughs) That doesn't seem to be happening.

DM: Well you have to give it enough time. Talk with me about 20 years after I'm in my grave and you'll find that nobody will know. I have a daughter who's in her early 30s who doesn't know who Gregory Peck is. Never heard of Clark Gable. That's what happens, you see.

JM: Speaking of your grave—I can't resist asking this. When I was reading your book, I laughed out loud over the story you tell about overhearing a conversation between two people trying to decide if actors are buried underneath their stars on Hollywood Boulevard. So I thought I'd ask you—would you prefer to be buried underneath your star in a standing, upright position?

DM: Uh, I think I'd kind of like to be buried head down so I can see where I was going.

JM: (laughs) That's great!

DM: But I don't have a star, so they'd have to create one to put me under it. There was an article emailed to me from a newspaper sporting article about a sports guy and a coach. They were comparing him to Reuben Kincaid. They had a picture of me there and everything. In the article, they started off talking about the Partridge Family and how they were managed by "the late Dave Madden." I thought, *That's a good idea. I ought to send that around to everybody and forget about Christmas cards from now on.* I thought, "The late Dave Madden." You're not that far off! Do you know how old I am?

JM: (laughs)

DM: You don't like to think about it. Neither do I. You ready for this? You sitting down? In December I'll be 80 years old. When I was your age I didn't think anyone lived to be 80 years old! When I was your age people didn't live to be 80 years old. That's something that has come along since then. That's insane. You see, something you'll find out later in life is that in your mind, you're still 22. It's only your body that becomes 80 years old. Your mind says, "No, I'm young and vital," and your body says, "Oh, no, you're not. Try walking without your cane." The aging process is ongoing and not necessarily thrilling. You'd only have to look at my address book. My address book is filled with doctors and dead people. You spend the early part of your life going to weddings and bar mitzvahs. You spend the latter part going to hospitals and rehabs and cemeteries.

JM: Was there ever any talk of a reunion episode?

DM: Yeah, they talked about it. Even wrote one once, but it was never produced because it was terrible. I think that reunion shows have about one value in the eyes of the American public, and that value lasts about two or three minutes. It's "what do they look like now?" Once they see you on the screen, that's all they care about. Then they'll switch over to *Seinfeld* or something. People from *The Partridge Family* wouldn't want to do it anyway. Danny would do anything. You could have a Brady Bunch reunion and he'd go to that.

JM: (laughs) Maybe they'll write a Partridge Family reunion where Danny plays all the parts?

DM: Yeah, maybe that! He'd do that, sure! Susan Dey wouldn't touch it. David would have mixed emotions about it. Shirley Jones would say, "Aw, what the shit? Let's go ahead. Let's make some money."

JM: (laughs)

JM: When they do these reunion TV shows they always do them in a one-hour format, which isn't the kind of program they were originally. Why don't they just put on the reunion show in a half-hour format to reflect the original script structure?

DM: Money, money. Everything is money. They don't care if it's too long, they just want to make money. Almost all of the reunion shows I've seen are from half-hour shows and the reunion is always an hour. It doesn't make a whole lot of sense from a logical point of view, but from a money point of a view they make more. I don't know anyone who stays around that long for a reunion episode. Three to five minutes. You have to be a masochist to stay with it longer than five minutes.

JM: Was there ever any talk of marrying Reuben off?

DM: Reubenoff? Was he a songwriter?

JM: (laughs) Of course. Prolific.

DM: There was talk of Shirley and Reuben getting married but that would've been fairly bizarre. Nice for me, though. I would've gone on a honeymoon with Shirley any time. But that, too, didn't make a whole lot of sense, because one of the main dynamics was the animosity between Danny and I—the fighting, the arguing, the bickering. You make me Danny's stepfather and that takes on a different edge. I could do that as his manager, but not as his stepfather. They also said, "Why don't we let him get a room upstairs in the Partridge family home so he can be around all the time?" We're talking about 1970, '71. You just didn't do that to a woman who isn't married and who is living with her children. You're going to put Reuben Kincaid in a room upstairs? It doesn't work. They talked about things like that but never did them.

JM: When you did the very last episode, did you know it was going to be the final episode?

DM: We knew it was the final episode, but it wasn't written as a final episode. It ended like every other show. Why they didn't decide to write an ending for it with Danny riding into the sunset with his dog or something, who knows? As a result it wasn't an "ending" kind of show.

JM: They did the same thing with **The Brady Bunch,** *too. There was no episode that ended the series. I wonder if maybe they hadn't quite figured out the concept of the series finale yet.*

DM: I don't know. I've never analyzed it, but it'd be an interesting thing to do a study on. That's your next book. It's called *Series Finales. Series Finales* by John Miller.

JM: Also known as **Miller's Follies.**

DM: *Miller's Second Folly*!

JM: (laughs) Was there any talk about having you make guest appearances on the short-lived Bobby Sherman show, **Getting Together?**

DM: No, but when the Brady Bunch started singing a little, I went to their producers and suggested we do a crossover episode where Reuben comes over and tries to sign the Brady Bunch to a contract. It would have been kind of interesting. He sounded interested but he never got around to doing it.

JM: That would've been very funny!

DM: Yeah, because we were on the same network so it wouldn't have been any problem.

JM: Were they looking for a David Cassidy replacement when they were bringing on the Williams Brothers and guests of that nature during the final season?

DM: I don't think that was the intent. The intent was to soup up the show. There's your lack of creativity. There were a lot of story lines left untouched, but they seemed to think they had run out of story ideas. Well, that's insane. It's demeaning to say that particular show could run out of story lines. You could have had that show on for 10 years. Run out of story lines? I could have come up with at least eight or ten story lines in a relatively short length of time.

JM: What might some of those have been?

DM: Well, one could've been a big management company trying to take over the Partridge Family and cut me out.

JM: That's a great idea!

DM: I thought it was a good idea but they didn't like that. I even mentioned that one to them—wrote a synopsis and everything. Didn't do any good. There were tons of ideas. To say that they ran out of ideas is a cop-out. David Cassidy didn't want to do the show anymore and they didn't want to do it without him. That's what it really came down to.

JM: What's your memory of Shirley learning how to drive the bus?

DM: Well it's not a matter of *learning*—the bus was like something out of World War II. Oh God, it was terrible. Imagine a big clunker bus like that, didn't have any kind of power steering— anytime she had to turn a corner we just crawled into a seat hoping she'd make it. I tried driving it and I'll tell you it was a *chore* to drive. We're lucky we weren't all killed.

JM: (laughs) That would've been headlines. "Partridge Family Killed on the Bus."

DM: Wouldn't it? I thought it would be a good way to end the series, actually.

JM: (laughs) Car crash and everybody's dead.

DM: Everybody's dead. (laughs) All at one time. Is that an ending? They did that one time with a radio soap opera that'd been on for 20 years. Back in those days a radio soap opera was sponsored by only one sponsor. They had one company sponsor each show. So this company called and said, "We're canceling the show, so wrap it up by Friday." This was like on a Monday. So Tuesday they were talking about a picnic. It was one of those sitcoms where everyone lived in some small town. So they build up a big thing about the picnic, then on Friday everyone got on the bus to go to the picnic and the bus went over a cliff. They actually did that. The sponsor was livid. People who'd been listening to the show for 20 years were livid. It was one of the great get-even things I've ever heard of.

JM: *The Partridge Family could've all gone to Muldoon's Point and slipped over the cliff!*

DM: That's right! Wouldn't that have been great? The kids wouldn't have appreciated that, I guess.

JM: *Yeah, you'd have scarred them for life.*

DM: (laughs) They wouldn't be singing their songs today, probably.

JM: *What's your favorite episode?*

DM: That's difficult to say. I like the Christmas show. We did a show the first season where we went to a prison to entertain. I thought that was utilizing the concept of a family of entertainers to a great extent, but later on they started running scared, not wanting to do anything that might offend the public who may have been wondering why the kids aren't in school, instead running around on a bus.

JM: *How would you describe each of the individual actors on the show?*

DM: I liked David. He and I got along very well. He was under a lot of pressure so I didn't bug him too much because he went off and made more money on weekends than he made during the show. He and I got along great.

JM: *Shirley Jones?*

DM: Well, I went to bed with her.

JM: *(laughs)*

DM: In my dreams, unfortunately. Shirley was a lovely lady. I liked her a lot.

JM: *Susan Dey?*

DM: I like Susan a lot too. She had her problems, but there again we got along extremely well. She and her boyfriend and me and my girlfriend went off and spent a weekend in Vegas once together. We went to see a couple shows. We were good friends and we had good fun. I've a picture of the four of us sitting in a booth in one of the showrooms but I don't know what ever happened to it. I talk with her and email with her all the time.

JM: *(laughs) What can you say about Danny that you haven't already said?*

DM: Nothing. Danny's a good kid in spite of all his problems. I like Danny. I used to call him every time something would happen and I'd make some comment about it. Was it in Vegas where he tried to pick up that transvestite? I called him and said, "Now Danny, that was clever.

That was really good. Now you gotta top that with something." I said, "I know a guy just outside of Palm Springs in Indio, California, who has a bull. I wouldn't ask you to ride it. A lot of people have rode bulls. But if you had sex with this bull and got pictures of it, I could promise coverage of it all over the country." He hung up on me.

JM: Brian Forster?
DM: Brian Forster. Now, there's a real enigma. He looks exactly like he did as a kid only now he has a mustache. Take little Brian Forster, put him in a suit, stick a mustache on him and you've got the Brian Forster of today. It's really bizarre. I'm not making this up. Forster became a race-track driver, which doesn't make any sense either. How could he see out through the windshield? He'd keep crashing into things.

JM: (laughs) And Suzanne Crough?
DM: I lived in Vegas for a couple years and Suzanne lived in a small town outside of Vegas. She and her husband had dinner with my wife and I a few times.

JM: I can't thank you enough for taking time to speak with me, Dave.
DM: You can thank me enough. Go ahead.

JM: (laughs) Your check is in the mail! I'll have to work on that star for you in Hollywood so you have some place to be buried.
DM: Well, I'm going to be cremated so it doesn't have to be a big star. Some little thing.

JM: Dave, thank you so very much.
DM: You're welcome.

To Australia, with Love

David Cassidy's world tour was a stadium tour that began in Auckland, New Zealand, with the first concert held at Eden Park on February 24, 1974. Henry Diltz went along, both as a photographer and a friend. "We spent about five days there so that he could acclimate and get over his jet lag before the first concert," says Diltz. "And Elton John was staying in the same hotel." John had started his tour in Asia and was arriving in Auckland the same time as Cassidy. He came to Cassidy's show and during the encore he came out on stage, took a seat at the piano, and performed with Cassidy, revving up the crowd even more.

Cassidy's next stop was Australia. The first concert in Sydney was held outdoors at a racetrack in sweltering hot weather. A television special was put together from

ACROSS THE POND, DOWN UNDER, AND BACK

some of the Sydney concert footage called *David Cassidy—To Australia with Love*, airing only in Australia later that year. The tour broke attendance records at the Melbourne Cricket Ground, with reports estimating as many as 65,000 people, and the emotions of the fans continued to grow with each new stop along the tour route.

While in Melbourne, Cassidy appeared as a presenter for the Logie Awards—similar to the Emmy Awards in the U.S.—where he met the Italian actress Gina Lollabrigida. Lollabrigida was fascinated by Cassidy. They met and spoke a little bit, then she came to his Melbourne show and introduced him to the audience. She was into photography, so she stood in the wings shooting him during the show. She told Cassidy that she wanted to shoot him nude for a book she was working on. He agreed to do it, and she posed him in a sheet with a bunch of fruit surrounding him. Nothing about it was very revealing, but Cassidy enjoyed doing it and they got along, enjoyed each other's company, and had some fun together.

The tour moved on to Japan and the Far East next. Fans went crazy for Cassidy in Tokyo, with the usual frenzied crowds that had to be contained. The Asian appearances were promoted by Kyodo Tokyo Inc. The concerts began March 18 with three nights in Hong Kong, followed by a show at Festival Hall in Osaka on March 24 and then traveling to the Sun-Plaza Hall in Tokyo for three nights of shows March 25–27 before concluding the series March 28 at Tokyo's Kosei Nekin Hall.

In between concert venues, Cassidy was often isolated with little access to the outside world. For the most part, he had to act as a recluse to avoid the emotionally charged fans. He couldn't leave his hotel room. He and Diltz learned how to pass the time.

"I remember a whole mob of little girls outside early in the morning singing 'We love you, David, we always will,' and you'd put the pillow over your head, thinking *Oh my God*. We couldn't sleep, and he couldn't leave the hotel in the daytime with all these little girls surrounding the hotel. So he was virtually a prisoner, in his sleep and all day long. So I would be up there with him, and we would play music, and the doorman would find young ladies in the lobby—older ladies, you know, in their twenties. Not teenyboppers. And he would bring them up to the room to have a drink with David and talk. We just had a great time.

"We had many days just hanging out. I would go out and buy postcards, and I'd buy really colorful postage stamps and we would have all these colored pens—I'm kind of a student of lettering—so we would have all these colored pens and these colored stamps and we would write postcards to our friends in all different colored pens, and then we'd put all these different colored stamps on them, which I would buy at the collection window at the main post office in town. That was always fun."

During the early '70s the energy crisis was at its peak in the U.S. The *Partridge Family* writers did an episode about it during the final season of the show, and even the Cassidy tour was affected. As one account described it: "A series of European

when we're singin'

dates on The David Cassidy World Tour '74 concert schedule, originally canceled because of the 'energy crisis,' has been reinstated with four countries back on the tour itinerary. Beginning in early May Cassidy will play Stockholm and Gothenberg, Sweden; Copenhagen, Denmark; Rotterdam, Holland; Nad Hamburg, Frankfort; and Munich, Germany. He'll perform for a total additional audience estimated at some 70,000 people reaching capacity at all of the halls. The seven-city swing follows a Cassidy visit to Paris where he'll tape a television special. He then travels to Glasgow, Scotland for a previously set Shawfield Stadium concert for some 15,000 on May 24 followed by the tour capper—a May 26 date at London's White City Stadium ... Cassidy presently is taking a breather at his home in Hawaii."

The final leg of Cassidy's tour returned to the U.K., the country that loved him the most. Earlier, Cassidy had gone into the studio with producer Michael Lloyd and recorded a new single titled "If I Didn't Care," an oldie from 1939 written by Jack Lawrence. The song was released in May 1974 and went to No. 9 on the British charts during the tour's time in England. The B-side featured Cassidy's self-penned "Frozen Noses." The single was never released in the States.

David Cassidy's live concerts had reached the point of hysteria very early on in his touring. Video clips and footage of public appearances again focused on the madness rather than the music. Cassidy himself was always asking fans nearest the stage to push back. Even during interviews, there was often a dangerous crush of fans trying to get closer to their heartthrob, and the media focused intently on them.

The entire '74 world tour was filled with teenyboppers who passed out at concerts. They were carried out on stretchers and sometimes taken to the hospital by ambulance. Countless security guards tried to control the fans, but the emotional state surrounding the tour only grew when Cassidy announced it would be his last.

One of the final concerts was held at White City Stadium in London on May 26. Tragedy struck amid the fans—as many as 1,000—who were treated for fainting and injuries. Bernadette Whelan, a 14-year-old girl with a heart condition, was crushed to death by the frenzied crowd. She spent four days in the hospital before she passed away.

Cassidy was devastated over Whelan's death. He finished his tour with one final show in Manchester and then retired from performing live. In a July 4 interview with Geraldo Rivera on *Good Night America*, Cassidy made clear that he was not retiring from music, just from touring. He wanted to continue to make records and grow artistically.

In the same interview, Cassidy announced that his next project, an album with David Bowie, was set to begin later in the summer. Only weeks earlier, Wes Farrell had announced that he was going independent as a distributor, cutting ties with RCA. Bowie had just produced a single by Lulu that was racking up sales and awards in England, and Farrell signed a deal with Bowie to distribute the single. But the Cassidy-Bowie collaboration never came to fruition.

ACROSS THE POND, DOWN UNDER, AND BACK

Cassidy Live! and *David Cassidy's Greatest Hits*

Following the close of the world tour was the successful release of *Cassidy Live!* in August 1974. Despite the massive sellouts worldwide, for many fans a live album was the only chance to hear their idol perform. The upcoming *Cassidy Live!* was announced in early August.

"Bell Records is rush releasing 'Cassidy Live!' by David Cassidy, recorded on location at his British concert tour," announced *Cash Box*. *Cassidy Live!* was made up of the live vocals recorded and extracted from his concert at White City Stadium, London. The album was produced by Cassidy and Barry Ainsworth, mastered and released very quickly. Cassidy recalled that one of the most difficult things about it was cutting out his voice telling the crowd to push back.

In those days it was a fairly cutting-edge move for a record label to release concerts as albums. The idea was only in its early stages, and *Cassidy Live!* is an electrifying sample of those early concert album releases. The album hit No. 9 on the British charts in August and spawned a hit single with Cassidy's live cover of the Beatles' "Please Please Me," which went to No. 16 earlier in July on the British charts." *Cassidy Live!* was released in the States with September reviews. *Cash Box* said, "This LP is positive testimony to the fact that the silver throated TV and recording star has what it takes to get down and make it in concert.... Cassidy weaves in and out of a number of styles flawlessly ... a sure shot LP if we ever heard one." The cover of "Please Please Me" was received equally well: "A Beatles classic, re-recorded by David is letter perfect contemporary style, culled from his latest 'Live' LP will be a stone smash all over again. Every element of high rock is in evidence (including the amazing crowd reactions) as international superstar David proves he's finally ready to crack American audiences. No Partridge references here. A new direction for David that's certain to score big points stateside. A real teaser." *Billboard* also plugged the album as a sure-shot success and a great chance for Cassidy to break out: "Cassidy may not have the constant chart singles he once enjoyed, but this set is proof that he is still very much a part of the general music scene. Recorded live in Britain, where his popularity is enormous, the LP could quite easily move him as strongly into the LP market as he was at one time in the singles market. Cuts vary from straight rock, fine ballads, and new arrangements of some familiar oldies. The vocals are more mature than ever, with strong orchestration and backing vocals helping the overall non-teenybopper effect. Should bring in a lot of new fans while retaining the old ones ... with his track record and TV success, Cassidy has a ready made audience." But again, the U.S. fans didn't take to it. It didn't help that Bell Records was undergoing a transition into Arista at this time and the album's promotion was somewhat lost in the shuffle.

when we're singin'

David Cassidy's Greatest Hits, the fifth and final Cassidy album on the Bell Records label, and one of Bell's last, was released in late November 1974 to nice reviews. *Cash Box* reported: "The TV and concert idol of millions of young American girls is featured on this new greatest hits package which is sure to be in demand this holiday season…. Featuring the catchy Cassidy vocals, this LP will obviously do well for the talented artist." In a year when greatest hits collections were extremely popular, it is shocking that this nice hits package did not do well. *Billboard* also touted the collection: "Cassidy used to draw a lot of laughs from so-called 'serious' music fans, but he sold a lot of records over the years and turned out some of the finest commercial singles to hit the AM airwaves. This package does indeed contain a fair sized amount of hits, both rockers and ballads, both of which are handled excellently. Recently 'retired' from singing, the set comes at the right time of year to make a perfect Christmas gift."

The front and back cover photos are especially striking, capturing the pure essence of David Cassidy and his shag hairstyle that defined a generation. The culminating collection combined a few Partridge Family hits—"I Think I Love You," "Doesn't Somebody Want to Be Wanted," "I'll Meet You Halfway"—with solo hits "Cherish," "Could It Be Forever," "Rock Me, Baby," "Daydreamer," "I Am a Clown," and "How Can I Be Sure." In a major mistake, "Could It Be Forever" was included on the track list, but "Blind Hope" was mistakenly included on the vinyl pressings in its place. "If I Didn't Care" and the live version of "Please Please Me" were also included as a representation of Cassidy's strong success in the U.K. and abroad. At the time, many young U.S. fans were unaware of overseas chart hits such as "Please Please Me" and "If I Didn't Care." *David Cassidy's Greatest Hits* was widely available through Columbia House mail-order record clubs for many years to follow. It was the last of a batch of LPs released with an actual Bell Records label on the record before Arista instituted its official new label.

Bus Stop …

The Most Inspired Fan Club

Tina Funk, a young German girl who was a big fan of the Partridge Family, had attended her first Cassidy concert in 1973. She made a lot of fan friends, and they began writing letters to one another. With Cassidy's second visit to Germany during the 1974 world tour, Funk began developing her correspondence extensively. It was the idea of friendship among fans that eventually led to the Just David Fan Club, which has gone on to become the longest-running David Cassidy fan club of all time.

Here, in her own words, is Tina's story:

"There was never really a conscious decision from my side to start a club. I was 14 years old in 1974 and very, very busy writing to all of my pen pals all over the world—I had 96 at that time, most of them in the U.K. and the U.S.A., but also one in Japan plus a few in the Netherlands and Denmark.

"In retrospect it was kind of funny because my knowledge of the English language was more than inadequate and the same could be said about my pen pals outside of English-speaking countries. When I recently moved, I found some of the correspondence and it made me smile to read it again and to remember how painstakingly those letters were written with the help of a dictionary and how very wrong some of the sentences were!

"All of my pen pals were David Cassidy or Partridge Family fans, and because there was so much more merchandise and information available to my friends in the U.S.A., U.K., and Japan, the letters centered around David. After a while, I found myself repeating the information I received from one pen pal to all the other ones. At that time all the letters were handwritten, so it was hard work and lots of repeats in every letter. To make things easier for myself, I decided in March 1974 to borrow my dad's old typewriter and to type the information on a matrice [the master sheet for a pre-photocopy page duplicating technique]. I could use the machine we had at school for free. Oh, no way to correct the matrice—because I was typing with one finger trying to find the correct keys, there were loads of typing mistakes in my text. That combined with the bad English certainly made for good reading.

"So once a month, I compiled all the information on David that I had, typed it up, duplicated it, and sent it out with much shorter letters to my pen pals when writing to them. Because that started in March 1974, I consider that to be the birth date of *Just David*, even though there was no club yet and no name.

"The following year, David signed a contract with RCA. In Germany, if you want to run an official fan club, you need the written permission of the artist's record company. By that time the idea had formed for me to make my information exchange a real club, especially since David's business fan club in the U.K. had just closed down. So when I heard about RCA, I contacted them and asked for permission to run a fan club for David Cassidy.

when we're singin'

"RCA responded almost immediately and sent me a letter saying they were granting me permission to run a club for their artist David Cassidy. I was thrilled with my official letter, although I had no idea how to start things. RCA also provided me with printed autograph cards that I could send out to fans. The problem was, after I sent all of my pen pals one card each no one else asked for an autograph.

"Soon after it was announced that David would come to Germany to promote 'I Write the Songs.' It was during my summer vacation from school so I was extremely excited, especially since RCA told me when David's plane was due. On that special day, I went to the airport and found myself among dozens of other fans who had also contacted RCA and been given the same information.

"When David arrived, it was like a blur. Everything happened so quickly. He was surrounded by two bodyguards—Gerry Slater and Billy Francis—and Henry Diltz, and before I knew it he was in the car on the way to his hotel. Three other fans and I jumped into a cab and asked the driver to follow the big Mercedes that was speeding away. The driver was laughing his head off at our excitement but did follow the car to the Hotel Vier Jahreszeiten in Hamburg. I remember to this day that the fare was 17 German marks and that we gave the driver a 20-mark bill because that was easier to divide by four!

"David was in Hamburg for three days and I was able to meet him several times—at the hotel, at a TV studio, and at newspaper buildings. I thought it would be better to also get his permission for the club I intended to run, so in very bad English I prepared a few sentences saying that David Cassidy was granting Tina Funk permission to run a fan club for him in Germany. On the second day, when David was returning to the hotel from some interview and was signing autographs, I shoved the piece of paper right under his nose and asked him to sign it because I wanted to run a fan club for him. He was so nice about it, did not laugh at me or my English but just glanced at my sentences and asked, 'Where do I sign?' When I was returning home that night with my precious permission by David himself, I felt like a million dollars.

"After three days, David was gone and I was eagerly waiting to get my rolls of film back with the photos I had managed to snap of him. I was absolutely delighted when I picked up my photos and discovered that although some were really far away and some were out of focus, there were a few photos that had turned out really well. Now I had my permission for the club, photos, and the answer to some questions that I had been able to ask David—one of which was "What brand of toothpaste do you use?" (If you've ever wondered about that, after he laughed out loud and told me that I must be a really clean girl, he answered "Crest.") I wanted to share the information as well as the photos with my pen pals, but of course that was not possible using a matrice.

"So I asked around and heard about this wonderful machine called Xerox. I had no idea where to find one, and print shops at that time were unheard of in Germany. So I started walking to our shopping area and walked down our shopping street asking in all kinds of stores for a Xerox machine. Finally I found one at a big department store called Hertie, only to find out that each copy would cost 50 pfennig, which was a fortune for me at that time. In fact, my whole monthly allowance would have bought exactly 20 copies. I walked the 50 minutes back home wondering about what to do, and had an idea. I contacted a few of my friends and asked if they would be willing to reimburse me for the costs of copying so that we could share the cost of the newsletter. The matrices were still free, but the price of the newsletter would depend on the number of pages that would have to be copied. Most of them agreed. Don't get me started on how difficult it was for us teens to transfer money at that time—it was all sent in letters or even in stamps that I sold to my parents and relatives.

"I very well remember how proud I was when I held the first real issue of the *Just David* newsletter in my hands in June 1975. Because I did not have any decent 8x10, the cover was a drawing of David that I had asked a German pen pal to make. The newsletter contained things David did in Hamburg, the questions he answered, some photos and—as a last page—a page from a *Tiger Beat* publication with four photos of David and the words *Just David* in the middle. I thought that was very clever and chose those words to be the fan club name. After all, this was a club about just David, and no one else. The first issue, and all following ones for the next few years, had a contest about who could draw the best picture of David to be used on the cover of the next newsletter. Prizes were always some of the memorabilia that I received from fans outside of Germany.

"I walked the 50 minutes to the department store many, many times, as I could only make the copies for the newsletter after I had already received the money for the copies from my pals. I wanted to send the newsletter out quickly and there were times when I came home from the store after almost two hours, only to be given another letter by my mother with money or stamps and have to turn around and walk back to the store. I can't believe how much free time I had back then.

"I also made some copies of my permissions to send to teen magazines, asking them to print my address for people who wanted to join a club for David

when we're singin'

or wanted an autograph card. I typed up an information sheet about the fan club on a matrice, saying that Just David offered monthly newsletters with the latest information on David, photos, song lyrics (at that time I actually listened to the songs and wrote down the words myself—I shudder to think how full of mistakes those written-down lyrics were), a raffle where you could win a great prize, answers to your David questions, and contact with other fans of David, so I was all set to send out the information as soon as the requests poured in.

"Not long after David left Hamburg, I had a call from RCA complaining that they were flooded with autograph requests for David after their address had been shown in *Disco '75* on TV, and could I please help them and come and pick up the letters to answer. Could I? You bet! It was still during summer vacation and I went to RCA several times to pick up and carry home literally sacks full of letters. My dad took a picture of me sitting on the floor of my room covered with letters from feet to neck! RCA also printed up more autograph cards for me to use. Those were really heavy to carry home—there were always 10,000 cards reprinted each time.

"So I spent most of my summer vacation sending out autographs of David. I read the requests carefully and if the letter said what a big fan of David's the sender was, I included an information sheet about the club with the autograph. A few months later Just David had 8,000 members. At that time I had no way of knowing that the fan club would be active for 40 years. It underwent many, many changes over the years, from matrices to photocopies, from 8x10 to a smaller format, from printing on one side to double-sided. The language went from German to a combination of German and English, then to two separate newsletters—one in German, one in English—then to just English with a separate German translation of the most important news. The changes over the years are too much to list," she concludes.

Just David lasted 40 years—longer than most print newsletters in the Internet age—and continued to deliver newsletters worldwide until spring 2015. Fans can still connect with the club on Facebook.

Liner Notes: *The World of the Partridge Family*

When change happens, so often it all seems to happen at once. The end of the Partridge Family was here. Everything and everyone was changing and moving on, ready or not.

The spring of 1974 brought not only the cancellation of the show but also the sale of Bell Records to Arista. Clive Davis, who was now in charge, wrapped up the Partridge Family contract with the 10th and final album, a compilation titled *The World of the Partridge Family*.

World was released on the Bell label and numbered as such, but in 1975, it was renumbered (AL 4021) and relabeled as Arista, although no new pressings of the vinyl were actually done. Like *David Cassidy's Greatest Hits*, the album was also made available through special mail-order record clubs, including Columbia House.

The World of the Partridge Family is an interesting title, if only as a tribute to the international impact the music had, especially for David Cassidy. The height of his fame overseas is often understated. When Cassidy hit in England, it was like a skyrocket. His image there was influenced much more by his music than by his television persona, giving his music career greater credibility. Even today you can walk into a card store in London and find his face on a greeting card next to images of Elton John, Marilyn Monroe, and Elvis Presley.

In England, the Bell Records division was led by Jack Leahy, and because Leahy believed in Cassidy's ability and appeal as a solo artist, he focused on promoting his solo albums and singles instead of the Partridge Family's music. While "I Think I Love You" was a hit in the U.S. it only rose to No. 18 on the U.K. charts. The show had not begun to air when the single was out, so it didn't have the TV show behind it as a marketing device. *Sound Magazine* was the biggest-selling Partridge Family album in the U.K, reaching No. 14–still modest compared to U.S. chart appeal. *Sound Magazine* never spawned a single in the U.K., either. "White Christmas," in 1973, was the final Partridge Family single released in the U.K.

Australia was a huge source of Cassidymania as well, sending "I Think I Love You" to No. 1 within weeks of it hitting in the United States. Jim Salamanis of Melbourne, whose 3,000-item Partridge Family memorabilia collection is thought to be one of the largest in the world, remembers, "We had our own Partridge Family bus in Melbourne! It used to go around all the beach areas, giving away records and memorabilia. Partridge Family records would fly out the door at record shops. The show was also broadcast in black and white here because we didn't get color TV until 1975."

"*Go-Set* magazine was an Australian magazine like *Tiger Beat*, which was the first to let us know David Cassidy was coming to Australia. David was like a house hazard here," laughs Salamanis. "The girls would almost faint at the mere mention of his name." Cassidy became an environmental spokesperson, as he had in England, and his photo appeared on giant "Keep Australia Beautiful" billboards and tram ads as late as 1977. "David's face was everywhere," says Salamanis. "Men would go to the barber shops and there would be posters in the shops of David that read 'Get your hair cut like his.'"

when we're singin'

The Partridge Family and David Cassidy also found a strong following in Asia. Albums were released in China and Japan. The Japanese versions were produced at the highest possible quality in terms of both sound production and cover art. Most featured gatefold designs with liner notes and were far superior in sound quality to those released in the U.S. or elsewhere. Albums were also released in Canada, Mexico, Brazil, Spain, Germany, Belgium, Holland, Greece, Malaysia, China, New Zealand and other countries.

The World of the Partridge Family includes the group's big hits and a few others that were considered important. Every track from *At Home with Their Greatest Hits* is included, and an additional nine tracks bring the song count to 20. It is the only two-record set released by the Partridge Family in the United States.

Unlike *At Home*, which had been released at the halfway point of the series, *World* was able to include later-emerging fan favorites. It was obvious that "Point Me in the Direction of Albuquerque" was a song with longevity, and "Looking Through the Eyes of Love" was the group's last top 40 song. The writing team of Cashman and West is well represented, with the inclusion of their first two songs—"She'd Rather Have the Rain" and "Only a Moment Ago"—both thought to be the best from this songwriting duo.

Wes Farrell's attempted hit "Friend and a Lover," which had squeaked in at No. 99 on the *Billboard* Hot 100, was included. Goffin and King's "Oh, No, Not My Baby," and Mark James' "Roller Coaster," representing the final album, *Bulletin Board* were also included. "Walking in the Rain" by Mann and Weil, which hit No. 10 on the British charts in 1973, appears. The Cowsills-influenced early sound of the group, without Cassidy's lead vocals, is represented with the very early recording of "I Really Want to Know You." Loved and hated by fans, the experimental "Hello, Hello" also earns a spot. The only album not represented is *Crossword Puzzle*.

Greatest hits albums were very popular in 1974. *John Denver's Greatest Hits* went to No. 1 in April, and Carpenters *Singles: 1969–1974* also went to No. 1 that year. An entire editorial appeared in *Cash Box* on the subject, titled "Greatest Hits as Great Sellers," noting: "The 'Greatest Hits' album, traditionally a popular gift giving item, once again looks to be one of the approaches labels will be keying on for strong sales. These albums, which are usually in the form of studio or 'live' versions of previously released material, have also proven helpful in stimulating the sales of artists' catalogs." But for whatever reason, neither *The World of the Partridge Family* nor *David Cassidy's Greatest Hits* ever appeared on any of the pop charts. Released in November 1974, *The World of The Partridge Family* is the band's 10th and final album, and its second hits retrospective. It's a nice showcase of the hits, plus a few important samplings of the band's style and experimentation.

During their four-year reign, the Partridge Family cranked out eight original studio albums and two compilation albums at a time when an album a year was considered ambitious. With an additional five David Cassidy solo albums also during those years, Bell Records released a combined total of 15 Partridge Family and David Cassidy albums between 1970 and 1974. That accomplishment remains one of a kind.

Side 1
I Think I Love You, 2:52, Tony Romeo
Point Me in the Direction of Albuquerque, 3:47, Tony Romeo
She'd Rather Have the Rain, 3:17, Terry Cashman–Tommy West
I Really Want to Know You, 2:55, Barry Mann–Cynthia Weil
It's One of Those Nights (Yes, Love), 3:24, Tony Romeo

Side 2
Doesn't Somebody Want to Be Wanted, 2:46, Wes Farrell–Jim Cretecos–Mike Appel
Hello, Hello, 3:57, Wes Farrell–Tony Romeo
I Can Feel Your Heartbeat, 2:05, Wes Farrell–Jim Cretecos–Mike Appel
Echo Valley 2-6809, 3:05, Kathy Cooper–Rupert Holmes
Breaking Up Is Hard to Do, 2:30, Neil Sedaka–Howard Greenfield

Side 3
I'll Meet You Halfway, 3:47, Wes Farrell–Gerry Goffin
Oh No, Not My Baby, 2:38, Gerry Goffin–Carole King
Brown Eyes, 2:44, Wes Farrell–Danny Janssen
Walking in the Rain, 2:58, Barry Mann–Phil Spector–Cynthia Weil
Only a Moment Ago, 2:33, Terry Cashman–Tommy West

Side 4
I Woke Up in Love This Morning, 2:41, Irwin Levine–L. Russell Brown
Friend and a Lover, 2:29, Wes Farrell–Danny Janssen–Bobby Hart
Am I Losing You, 2:22, Irwin Levine–L. Russell Brown
Roller Coaster, 2:22, Mark James
Looking Through the Eyes of Love, 3:03, Barry Mann–Cynthia Weil

Album Summary and Review

Total Running Time: 54:15
Original Release: November 1974, Bell 1319

The Partridge Family, for all the jokes pointed toward them, made some of the biggest selling AM records of their day and this repackage of two LPs concentrating primarily on Ms. Jones and Cassidy (one LP devoted primarily to him) includes

when we're singin'

the biggest hits as well as a host of others. Both Cassidy and Jones did have good voices and producer Wes Farrell used his true knack for the commercial market to help them along. With reruns of the TV show still going on, watch this one take off during Christmas. Best cuts: "I Think I Love You," "She'd Rather Have the Rain," "I Can Feel Your Heartbeat," "I Woke Up in Love this Morning," "Roller Coaster." *Billboard, November 23, 1974*

THE ALBUM COVERS
or ... The Partridge Family TV Dinner

Bell Records

Bell Records began in 1952, eventually sprouting two subsidiary labels, Mala Records and Amy Records. By 1961, Larry Uttal had folded his label, Madison Records, into the purchase of Bell Records, and by 1964 he absorbed the Amy and Mala subsidiaries. Uttal owned Bell Records independently until it was purchased by Columbia–Screen Gems in the late 1960s. He remained president and part owner of the company until its demise in 1974.

Beverly Weinstein was still in school when she started working at Bell Records. "There was about five of us working there in 1964," she says. "It wasn't a very big company. We were pressing records, and because we had hits from England it grew internationally very, very quickly. All of sudden there were 300 employees in something like two years' time." Weinstein came to be in charge of both the domestic art department and international production.

During the '60s, record labels varied in their promotional focus. There was a difference between a singles label that focused primarily on potential hits and an album label that dealt more with the bigger production of artists. Bell Records established itself as the master of producing hit singles, elevating president Larry Uttal to be one of the most powerful and successful names in the industry. Uttal was what they called in the old days a record lamp, meaning someone who knew all the angles. He knew the distributors and the disc jockeys and had relationships with them. Singles were his specialty, and he came to believe that certain groups, known as bubblegum groups, would sell extremely well as singles.

During the late '60s, Uttal cut a deal to sell the label to Columbia Pictures, though Uttal retained part ownership. "Columbia was not doing very well at the box office with their film division," says Weinstein. "They bought us, and they did so at a time when they were in a really serious debt service in terms of money. They enjoyed the income coming in from the label, but I don't think we really had that much backing in terms of growing and album artists.

"We just had so many hit singles. There were a lot of English hits. If you had a Rolling Stones, or a Beatles, or any of them who sold millions and millions of albums, the company would have been different. But then we would have been purchased by Polygram rather than Columbia. We had acts like Seals & Crofts and the 5th Dimension. You have to have album sales unless you have all these bubblegum groups that didn't sell big albums, but they sold a huge amount of singles."

In 1969 Bell Records began making changes. With a redesign of the company's logo, the next step became a realignment of executives within the company. The new focus came in the form of a serious plan that was put into motion to focus on album sales more intensely than ever before in Bell Records' history. The Partridge Family came right at the beginning of the shift in strategy. By early 1970, Larry Uttal had lined up an intelligent staff of experienced music industry people in all the right places. When the Partridge Family was given the green light, it was perfect timing for them. Bell Records began preparing for what would be one of their biggest promotions yet for a TV-related album.

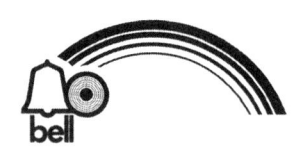

The Partridge Family was the first TV project pairing between Screen Gems and Bell. The public relations firm Bernie Ilson Inc. was hired, with costs exceeding $100,000 shared between ABC and Screen Gems, to promote the release of the Partridges' first album and single. The firm was known for its successful public relations campaigns for both the Monkees and the Beatles. A two-week hiatus was taken from filming the TV show so Shirley Jones and David Cassidy could go out on a promotional tour, launched with a kickoff party in Hollywood. They appeared in New York City, Boston, Chicago, Cleveland, Philadelphia, Pittsburgh, and Atlanta. They did local network TV show appearances as well as radio and print interviews. There were promotional parties with disc jockeys, magazine editors, record editors, and newspaper columnists. It was an aggressive campaign, and the first of its kind for Bell Records. Timing for the launch of the Partridge Family couldn't have been more perfect. By November *Cash Box* reported that the success of the Ilson campaign "can be measured in terms of the chart climb of 'I Think I Love You,' now among the Top 10."

The first full-page trade ad appeared in August 1970. It listed Shirley Jones as "Connie" because the character name had not yet been changed. In both July and August, several small ads, themed like a scrapbook, appeared in both *Billboard* and *Cash Box*. Sometimes multiple ads were placed on different pages of a single issue.

The Partridge Family generated millions of dollars for Bell. As the company became more focused on album sales, they also became more identified with music tied to television and film. Bell became known as the label best suited to succeed with TV-related artists and soundtracks for Broadway and motion pictures. A month before *The Partridge Family* first aired, Bell Records announced the best sales of their entire history. Album sales were up 92 percent.

In September 1970, Bell announced its first formal debut of album product under a new strategy: vice presidents would visit the top distributors all over the country to present eight diversified album releases. *The Partridge Family Album* was at the top of the list. The strategy was called the round trip approach, and it was so successful it resulted in over $1 million dollars in orders.

The Partridge Family albums were originally viewed as a marketing tool for the show but quickly established their own identities. They sold in the millions. Singles were also racking up dollars. By October of 1970, Bell Records announced "I Think I Love You" as the biggest-selling single in the label's history.

The launch of the Partridge Family was so successful that Bernie Ilson Inc. used it to establish bragging rights with other clients such as Madison Square Garden, The Ed Sullivan Show, and Motown Records.

Weinstein says, "I have to be honest—we never spent a lot of money on album covers. We spent it on promotion rather than album art, whereas other companies would rent planes and put up big elaborate productions. But Larry didn't feel it was important. He stayed in the best hotel suites, and we were all paid very, very nicely, but he didn't have a discipline in coming out of album sales or believing that sometimes you just have to spend. But I'll tell you, some of the best album covers don't cost a lot." Bell contracted with an advertising firm, the Music Agency, to design their trade ads for *Billboard*, *Cashbox*, and *Record World*. As vice president of art direction for Bell Records, Weinstein supervised the artwork created by the graphic artists at the Music Agency.

By 1973, during the last half of the Partridge Family's third season, and just before the release of *Crossword Puzzle*, Bell was still breaking records. "At one point we had the No. 1, No. 2, and No. 3 records on the hit charts all at the same time," says Weinstein ("The Night the Lights Went Out in Georgia," "Tie a Yellow

when we're singin'

Ribbon 'round the Ole Oak Tree," and "Little Willy," in April 1973).

Around the same time, when *Crossword Puzzle* was in the works, Uttal signed up-and-coming heavyweights Barry Manilow and Melissa Manchester, putting the focus on easy listening artists. It seemed the label could do no wrong with Uttal at the helm although he never won the support of Columbia. They had a lot of difficulties working together, and Uttal was often excluded from important meetings.

In 1974, still riding high, Bell Records was taken over by Clive Davis from Columbia Records and renamed Arista. Davis wanted to put his own stamp on the label, focusing on different kinds of artists. He did not want anything to do with music he deemed unsophisticated. Some of Bell's biggest hitmakers went with other labels—the 5th Dimension to ABC Records, and Tony Orlando & Dawn to Elektra. Davis held on to Manilow and Manchester, who became big stars on Arista. Bell Records' last No. 1 hit was Barry Manilow's "Mandy" in January 1975.

Meanwhile, Larry Uttal opened his own independent label, Private Stock, and several Bell Records employees—including Weinstein, Gordon Bossin, and VP of Sales Irv Biegel, who all had stock in the company—went with him. The company never found the right footing, however, and eventually closed.

The Music Agency

The Music Agency had been established as a PR and graphics firm for the music industry in 1968 by Jay Leipzig, a former executive with music publisher Big 3. Another Big 3 veteran, Joel Borowka, joined as CFO.

Art director Mary English was hired as the third member of the team, having some experience doing "instant album covers" for Lee Myles and Associates.

English took the lead on the graphic design for seven of the 10 Partridge Family albums. A graduate of New York University and the School of Visual Arts, English had developed a close working relationship and friendship with Leipzig and Borowka.

The Music Agency was a young company just coming into its own. In addition to the album covers, they created all the Partridge Family and David Cassidy ads that appeared in the trade magazines.

"I briefly did a stint there as a receptionist," recalls Dale Leipzig, Jay Leipzig's daughter, who was only 19 years old at the time. "I was there in 1971 for about a year. I worked directly with the team, and it was a very exciting atmosphere. I remember every Monday morning they had a staff meeting so that everybody could hit the ground running. You had the executives, and the creatives, and everybody who just grouped into Dad's office, sat down, and reviewed all of the big projects and ad placements that were happening for that week. There were times that we would walk over to Bell Records because they weren't that far away. The Music Agency was located at 888 Eighth Avenue, the third floor. Ironically I was reading Goldie Hawn's autobiography a couple of years ago, and I was absolutely flabbergasted to find out that she lived in that building. She moved out right before we moved in."

The Music Agency staff continued to grow during the early '70s, peaking at around 10 employees. But in 1978, the agency finally had to close. They had a client or two that went bankrupt and they were not able to sustain. "Most of the money that the Music Agency made was not through design of record albums," says Mary English. "That was done more as a courtesy. The substantial money was made by placing advertising in magazines, whether it was *Rolling Stone* or *Billboard*. Every album that we put out we made an ad for, and then we would pay for it to go into the magazines. Then the record company for whom we were doing the ad would reimburse the Music Agency. It was a small company, and this one client went out of business, going south of $200,000 that had to be paid back for the Music Agency to stay in business. When Clive Davis took over Bell Records he was a huge Music Agency fan and he did an awful lot for Jay and Joel before they had to throw in the towel. The money owed to the Music Agency just wiped them out."

The Album Designs

"I can tell you the Music Agency's philosophy was that you never, ever patronize a target audience. So even though you have a lot of preteens who were just going crazy over David—there was this whole hysteria around him—they still had a commitment to design artistically relevant art that had a very high level of integrity, and basically they were really more concerned with interpreting the music and the experience in a holistic way," says Dale Leipzig. Beverly Weinstein felt strongly about the talent of David Cassidy. After he became the focal point of the show, she felt that his face should be featured as large and as often as possible on the record covers.

As art director for Bell Records, Weinstein was responsible for the end product of each album design. She had thorough knowledge and experience in the printing processes of the day and she worked directly with the art directors at the Music Agency on every Partridge Family album design.

"They were basically design artists that were given projects," says Weinstein. "They would come up with three or four different designs, and we'd say, 'Go with this one and develop it a little further.' I'd sit and get the best photos I could that would project on a square album cover. It was a very combined effort—very, very combined."

when we're singin'

Weinstein, Uttal, and Leipzig spent a lot of time discussing the designs together. Weinstein says, "You talk about ideas and what have you, and then you give it to graphic designers. They're the ones that really come up with some guidance. It's not that I sat with a piece of paper and designed it. I didn't. Very often we'd have photo sessions, and I'd select the photographs that we liked and narrow it down." Weinstein was also in charge of the printing process.

The Partridge Family albums were well represented with a variety of colors, looks, and styles. Even after Cassidy became the breakout star, the album covers still maintained a balanced look with images of the TV family rather than large shots of Cassidy, and the stories behind each design are engaging.

Shopping in Manhattan: *The Partridge Family Album*

The original first title for the debut album was *Shirley Jones and the Partridge Family*, (leading Shirley Jones to believe she would be singing more leads) but when the assignment for the first album was given to the Music Agency, they were given free reign. None of the preconceived titles or ideas were thrust upon the company. The creative team went to work shaping the first album with a blank slate.

"The three of us at the Music Agency went to a meeting with Larry Uttal over at Bell Records," says Mary English. "We were told there was this TV show coming out and they were going to put out a record album to go with it. They said the show would be called *The Partridge Family*. So we went over to a theater at Columbia Pictures and we watched an episode of the show before we ever designed the album, which did not yet have a title."

It was Music Agency owner Jay Leipzig who came up with the album title after viewing the pilot episode. English says, "We thought, OK, we'll call it *The Partridge Family Album* and we'll make it look like a family album! That sounded like a good idea, right? Then I remember looking for that album cover!

"Jay and I, we went shopping together. We went to a number of stores in Manhattan, walking around on Sixth Avenue looking for scrapbook albums, and we finally bought this plain red album. It didn't even have the border on it! That was put on with press type."

Press type, sometimes known as Letraset after one of the main manufacturers, was a form of rub-down lettering sold on a piece of film. Graphic designers could get entire alphabets in various styles and designs, usually in gold and black, along with a selection of decorative characters.

The·Partridge·Family·Album

"The Partridge Family title lettering was also press type," says English. "I press-typed it out and traced over it directly onto this fake leather album cover. Then I painted over the letters in gold. It was all hand-painted. This was the olden days, believe me! There were no computers then! I traced the Partridge Family logo and painted it gold, and I press-typed the gold framing that went around the border of the album cover. Then we had a photo taken of the whole thing.

"We were given the Partridge Family logo, sent to us by the television people, and we put it on the cover. We were also given Shirley Jones' and David Cassidy's signatures, which were both featured on the cover design as well."

"If you notice on this album," says Beverly Weinstein, "Shirley Jones' name is a little bigger than David Cassidy's. It was a contractual thing that Shirley's signature had to be larger in size than David's, and rightly so. Shirley was a big artist and very big star, while David was still basically unknown. In the beginning the Partridge Family was 'Shirley Jones with David Cassidy and the Partridge Family.' It was a matter of billing."

The cover design did not include a photo of the group. "There wasn't that much photography available for the first album," explains Weinstein. "At that time they were really just building an audience. I don't think the TV show was in full swing yet."

"This was done in advance and it wasn't a big deal, you know?" English laughs as she thinks back to the surprising success of the album. "Who knew?"

The album contained a color photo insert that featured the entire cast in their red velvet outfits beside the bus. The photo was taken as part of the first session for the show, and the insert was handled by Beverly Weinstein after the album design was complete. Rumors through the years have laid claim that there was a contractual problem using photos of the cast in their red velvet outfits on the actual albums, but no one interviewed from the Music Agency, Bell Records, or even the producers of the show gives this rumor any merit. Bell Records' national promotional director Noel Love, is adamant that there would have been no problem using those outfits on the covers if they had wanted to, and Beverly Weinstein doesn't remember such a stipulation either.

The back cover was done in black and white, which was common in those days, and it is the only Partridge Family album to have liner notes. The notes appeared on the back cover and are thought to have been written by Music Agency CEO Jay Leipzig. Liner notes were still a popular feature on albums into the early '70s, and Leipzig wrote them for such artists as Melanie, Bobby Darin, and Melissa Manchester.

The Partridge Family Album design was well thought out. "As I recall, they gave us as much time as we needed on this one," says English. "It wasn't a pressure on that album. I would say it took roughly about two or three weeks for the mechanical of each album."

when we're singin'

In episode 4 of the show, Danny argues with Reuben about the design for their first album, stating emphatically that it has to have liner notes. The cover briefly seen on the show was not reflective in any way of the real first album, because the episode was shot before the design was done. Otherwise the company would have snagged any opportunity to promote the album. Visible images of actual Partridge Family albums do appear in later episodes.

Happy Birthday! *The Partridge Family Up to Date*

The Partridge Family's second album was bursting with color, tying in to the Mondrian-styled paint on the family bus. However, the design concept for the album had nothing to do with the multicolored bus or Mondrian. Those similarities emerged later.

The original concept was rooted in the birthdays of the cast. English wanted to line up all the actors across the album cover evenly, from left to right, in order of their birthdays. But the idea morphed into something else because of contractual legalities surrounding photo sizes.

"We were trying to think up ideas that might be interesting for the fans," explains Mary English. "So for the *Up to Date* album we thought, *Let's put their birthdays on it!* The next thing was figuring out how we were going to do it, because all of their birthdays were in different months. Now it was a question of taking the design priorities first. Could we do it in the order of when their birthdays happened? That didn't really work. We couldn't figure out a way to do that because by this time David and Shirley's photos had to be a certain size per contract with the record company. Different people's heads had to be a certain percentage of the other people. For example, Shirley Jones had to be x percent the size of David Cassidy's face. So I had to have my little proportion wheel and measure each photograph, making sure each face was the appropriate size. They were very concerned with the legal part of that. This was the tricky part. We had to keep those two a certain size and then the other children's pictures had to be a certain size, too. The dog wasn't required to be any certain size," she jokes. "We just stuck him in.

"So we went from that premise. We put David up toward the top because obviously he was the big sell, and then Shirley was placed to balance it. We didn't want to have the two of them next to each other for design purposes. The kids are sort of circling in between the two of them a little bit—Susan, and whatever that little pipsqueak's name is—Danny," she laughs. "And then the others.

"Because it's based on their birthdays, we thought, *How better to do that but as a calendar?* It just kind of fit the look to the title, rather than just calling it *Up to Date*. If you look at the design, the pictures actually did end up arranged in order of the numbers." English counts them out, going across the cover from left to right, tying each of the pictures together, placed in order of the cast members' birthdays.

"Then I did up this little design, which is all hand done—that was kind of cool at the time, you know? The colors are very early '70s, with that little bit of hand-done look. It's not psychedelic, but when I look at it I would date it to that period, you know? Late '60s, early '70s. It was of the time.

"Typography was so important to artists back in those days, and using numbers that were all different styles of type was considered very cool back in the day." She points out the examples on the cover. "See how they're all different? Some have serifs. Some are partly filled in. Some are all spacy. I was pretty fascinated with different styles of type.

"The type across the top that reads *The Partridge Family* is the same press type from the first album. I traced it and outlined the letters with a Rapidograph pen." But English was never happy with the title lettering on this album.

By using the same lettering from *Album*, they were experimenting in an attempt to create a set typeface to help mold the group's identity. By the second album, they were able to ease up on the initial requirements that Shirley Jones' credit be bigger than the others. "The legalese was so tricky," English emphasizes.

"They went with full color on the back side of the album design this time, which was another sign they were doing well," she adds.

John Zaccheo, who had just come on staff as an assistant art director, had an extraordinary talent for drawing. Recognizing the potential tie-in to the Mondrian-styled look of the bus, Leipzig asked Zaccheo to contribute the drawing of the bus on the back cover. He was given a photo still to work from.

"If you look in the back of the bus, I remember I drew a hammock inside the bus," says Zaccheo. "Now I'm going to tell you something that's really a lot of fun. If you look in the hammock you'll see my initials—JDZ—hidden in the drawing. I used to do that all the time! It was kind of a fun thing, sneaking my initials in there, and I don't think anybody at Bell Records ever knew I did it," he laughs. The same drawing with Zaccheo's hidden initials was featured in the trade ad for "Doesn't Somebody Want to Be Wanted."

Following on the success of *The Partridge Family Album*, another insert was included. This time it was a book cover for school kids to use on their textbooks, thought up by Larry Uttal, Jay Leipzig and Beverly Weinstein. Mary English remembers designing it from their instructions.

when we're singin'

"The book cover was printed by the same company that did our album covers," says Weinstein. "The *Up to Date* album design was a lot of fun to do because we were finally able to feature David in a big picture, because of David's breakout success. But we still had to live with *starring Shirley Jones, featuring David Cassidy*, even though David was the mainstay of the program."

After the first album, there were never any further albums with liner notes. "There just wasn't anything to say," says English. "I'm sure they could find something to say about the cast or the show or something, but I think there was probably a little bit of a disconnect, having the record company on the East Coast while the TV show was on the West Coast. They communicated well, but it's not as easy as walking down the street. Just like having to mail the photos cross-country."

It Takes a Lot of Good People: *The Partridge Family Sound Magazine*

"The Partridge Family music did not have a particular theme to it," Mary English reflects. "You know how albums from that era often have themes to them?" English and the other creative forces all felt they could create themes for these albums from the outside in, working through their graphic designs.

"This was a little bit unusual because very often the album designers are not involved in the concept of the package," says English. "That usually comes from the musicians or the band."

"We always had to come up with something we thought would appeal to kids of that age and that demographic. Mostly it was Jay, Joel, and myself sitting around thinking, *Oh, they want another album? What are we going to do? Hmmm ... I don't know. Let's think of something. How about if we make the cover look like one of those teen magazines? You know, like* Tiger Beat," she says. "David Cassidy was a superstar now, and his picture was all over them, so we thought, *Sure! Let's try that!* That's pretty much how it was done.

Promotional copies of "I Woke Up in Love This Morning" were pressed and sent out to radio stations before the album design was completed, and the notation on the promotional copies refer to the song as being "from The New Partridge Family Album." English responds strongly to the longstanding rumor that this was actually the original title of the album: "It absolutely was not! I remember Jay, Joel, and myself sitting around and coming up with this idea and then talking to Beverly about it. No, no, no!"

English designed the lettering for the title and the entire look of the cover based on the real magazines. "One style that they used on those magazines had that kind of block lettering with drop shadows. And then there was the subheadings of the stars, and lead teasers like *This Issue Features*. They would always have an interview with somebody and a photo story of somebody, so I did it just like those teen magazines. That was our prototype."

The back of the album reflects what might have been the inside pages of *Tiger Beat* or one of the other magazines from that era.

"I think we all kind of worked on the *Sound Magazine* a little bit," recalls John Zaccheo. "But I wouldn't say that any one of us took credit, though it belongs to Mary. We kind of played around with that one. I had all of these different photographs and I played around with them, putting them in some kind of an order, like you see." The contractual requirements on the size and proportion of each cast member's photo again played a heavy role in design limitations. "Mary was the one who actually did most of the album as far as the creative layout, putting the mechanical together, and getting it printed."

English had particular fun with a little piece of artwork on the back cover design. "I had to draw a picture," she begins. "See where it says *It takes a lot of good people*? I drew little pictures of the Bell executives," English chuckles. The drawings don't include any names attached, because they were just caricatures, done as sort of an in-joke, without their knowledge. "You can see these different executives that I'm talking about. The guy in the front with the glasses and the mustache is Gordon Bossin. He worked for Bell Records. He was a VP. To the right of him is Irwin "Irv" Biegal and to the right of him is Beverly Weinstein. That's me next to Gordon. I'm in the front row with the long blonde hair, which wasn't blonde, but I had long hair and I just did it like that," she laughs. "The bald guy with the square glasses is Larry Uttal, president of the record company. The black guy in the second row, in between myself and Gordon, is Oscar Fields—very hip, very cool guy. He was R&B. Joel Borowka is next to me on the left, and then Jay is beside him. Jay had the curly hair," she laughs. "I loved them both dearly." English says some of the little faces were made up, but most were based on real Bell executives and staffers, and Music Agency personnel.

when we're singin'

"My daughter is a young adult now, and she found a handbag that has this album design as the cover, including the little faces I drew. She looked at it and said, 'You really did draw those! That's still the way you draw people!'"

A Light Snow: *A Partridge Family Christmas Card*

When difficulties arose over photos, they often had everything to do with time and distance. Bell Records' art department and the Music Agency were on the East Coast, and the show was filmed on the West Coast. This was an era before fax machines or computers, so everything went through regular mail. Making it even more difficult, the photo shoots were done for multiple marketing purposes. There was never a photo shoot specifically for album artwork, except in the case of *A Partridge Family Christmas Card*.

"All of the photography was done in California and they would send us the photos," says English. "They were going to do a Christmas album, and we had no Christmas photographs to work with. So Beverly went out to California to art direct the photo shoot and oversee it. I remember being jealous because she got to go to California and I didn't. I was doing the artwork, but she had the title!" she jokes. "There was a time constraint on that one and we didn't have much time to take the photo. I mean it took maybe a week just to do separations for the printing process, so again we came up with creative design ideas.

"I think Jay and Beverly together came up with putting the card tucked into the front of the album cover. So I did a couple of different designs. The photo taken was specifically planned for the front of the Christmas card, to be placed inside the envelope, because that's what it would be like if you received a Christmas card from the Partridge Family—you would open it up and find a picture inside."

The green-and-white design was created with a can of artificial spray snow. "I had a piece of black paper and I sprayed it with the white snow, sent it out, and had a print made of it," says English. "That became the mechanical and the artwork for the cover. Then for the back I blew up their pictures and I traced the darkest parts of the photos and filled them in. I then had a high-contrast photo done and I made a stencil. I sprayed through the stencil to create the art for the back side of the cover. The art on the back side of the album design has more snowflakes. It's more dense because we wanted to see David and Shirley clearly.

"If you look on the back of the album, down in the lower left hand corner you'll see my signature—*English*. I signed the art on the back because I liked that art a lot! I thought, *I'm going to sign it and hide my signature in the snow. Probably no one will notice.* Oops!"

The title of the album on the front cover was done freehand. "That's my normal handwriting, with a few flourishes. That's still how I make my *As* when I write someone a letter," says English.

The red Christmas envelopes were given a holly design on the flap and placed face out, tilted into the card's slot cut into the front of the cover. The design was now complete. "We had a lot of freedom to come up with ideas," English says. "Beverly and Larry Uttal approved everything and nothing went out without it. No one forced ideas on us. It was always very much a collaborative thing."

Box Designs & Rain Boots: *The Partridge Family Shopping Bag*

As the design for *The Partridge Family Shopping Bag* was being developed, *Sound Magazine* sales were as hot as ever and the Partridge Family continued to sell in the millions. Bell wanted to do something more creative with the packaging. The budget was increased, making *Shopping Bag* the most expensive of the album designs.

The creative group came up with the shopping bag concept and the idea to include a special shopping bag insert as a tie-in to the merchandizing that was emerging from the show. John Zaccheo had come on staff at the beginning of 1971. Both he and Mary English submitted ideas for the design, and the agency decided to go with Zaccheo's concept.

"I remember Jay basically handed me a piece of paper that said *The Partridge Family Shopping Bag*," says Zaccheo. "He had a lot of copy on it that needed to be included in the design. He had written instructions that said to put *Free shopping bag inside* somewhere on the cover, and up in the corner it needed to say *Starring Shirley Jones and featuring David Cassidy*. Then there was the logo and the number of the Bell record, and then more copy for the back. I had to find places to put all of this copy! I started thinking about how I would do this in such a way that I could get all the faces, the credits, and everything else in the design, so once I came up with my idea, Jay said, 'Go for it!'"

"Prior to working for the Music Agency, I worked for a company in New York called Seidman & Lane," says Zaccheo. "We did a lot of box designing. Something that's very common in box designing is coming up with ways to open a box and be a little more creative with it. So we were talking about how we were going to get all the information and the photographs into this piece, and I suggested we just put an extra flap on it and open it that way. Not only that, but when you put the plastic bag inside, it will all tie together. That idea for the fold-down was from the experience I had in designing boxes and coming up with creative packaging.

when we're singin'

"If you look at the photograph on the inside fold-down flap, that was the same photo I used to create the cover art. I made a high-contrast shot of every one of the actors, but when I shot them I lost a lot of the base. So I had to go back with pen and ink and work on the photos themselves to try and make them look like who they were. I eliminated all the gray tones and just made everything black and white, so in reality I actually did paintings of each cast member. I thought it would be more interesting to do the high contrast on the cover, because it lent itself better to the design of the album, rather than just using photographs of them. It's more artsy. It has more of an artsy look about it. Then I used the family photo on the inside of the fold-down flap to reflect them as a group.

"The title artwork on the top front side of the cover that says *The Partridge Family Shopping Bag* was all hand done. It was something I created. If you notice the swirls and things used throughout the design, I was trying to repeat that style again for the title, tying the whole piece together. The handle design was also done to reflect the whole concept of the shopping bag."

Zaccheo also designed the plastic shopping bag insert. "I drew on my past experience working in advertising in creating the bag," he says. "We wanted something with great appeal in the sense that if you're walking down the street and you had that bag, everybody walking down the street would take notice of it because of the colors. It's almost like fireworks. You see all these things happening in the design, so it draws a lot of attention. The same was true for the album cover, which reminded me a lot of the group. They had this lively thing about them. That's how they performed. So if you think of music and rhythm and all these things, how do you create this sort of burst of sound and reflect it in the art? Use lively colors. I was using the primary colors, for the most part, to create an effect of brightness, so it would have an appeal like what you see when you're grocery shopping and looking for a product. When you see something on the shelf, you are likely more drawn to the product that has those kinds of colors than the product next to it that is not as flamboyant.

"The design has a lot of appeal, both through who they were and the concept of the shopping bag being a piece of memorabilia—something that was a keeper. For example, if you go down the street and you see a Macy's bag, you say, 'Oh, they just bought something from Macy's.' This was the same thing, at least when I was thinking about it. I wanted to come up with a bag that would say 'wow' rather than just a bag with a photograph on it. I thought, *Let's do something really wild! Let's do something really cool!*

"I think the shopping bag concept really worked. It was really a twofold idea. The design had a lot of energy in the bag as well as the cover, and the concept of the shopping bag all came from a marketing point of view. People were happy because it had this kind of energy for a cover. If you put it in a rack with a bunch of other albums it stood out like a sore thumb. Buyers would say, 'Oh, wow! There's a Partridge Family album cover!' It stands right out!

"The free shopping bag insert worked like getting a coupon, or getting something extra in a cereal box, you know? You buy the cereal and you get something extra. So if there was any question about buying the album or not, the answer would be *I'll buy it because it's got an extra little something in there.* We probably sold a number of pieces just based on the marketing part of it. It was part of making them famous on their TV show, but also making them famous for their music—especially David Cassidy and Shirley Jones." Zaccheo hid his name on the album cover in tiny lettering.

The *Shopping Bag* design was modified for release in other countries. The English version put an actual handle on the top of the album but cut the fold-down flap, and Germany released a special edition with a mustard olive-colored background for the cover art.

"I remember *Shopping Bag* very well," says Beverly Weinstein. "I remember exactly where those shopping bags came from. They came from Queens, across the river from Manhattan. It was a big order. Oh, God, we had shopping bags for everything! One time I found one of our vice presidents standing in a doorway on Broadway in a downpour, and he had two Partridge Family shopping bags over his new shoes," she laughs. "Yeah, it came in handy! We ordered a lot of them. That was a very, very popular album."

Doodling: *The Partridge Family at Home with Their Greatest Hits*

Having impressed with his *Shopping Bag* design, John Zaccheo was given the next design as well—*At Home with Their Greatest Hits*, a title that Jay Leipzig had worked up with Beverly Weinstein.

Zaccheo says, "Jay said we needed to come up with a cover where the Partridge Family is at home, so we were trying to think of ways to show the family inside a house. We had photographs of them all together, but we had to use them in some way that showed them inside a house. I remember seeing this particular color shot

when we're singin'

of them all together and thinking there must be some way I could use this and get them into some kind of a house, but I knew I had to make it a very simplistic house. It couldn't be anything other than that.

"We were just playing around with ideas, and I was just goofing off with a sketch. I showed it to Jay, and he said 'Jeez, that's really cool! That's a good idea!' So the whole thing just came together real quick, and in an hour or two I had come up with the whole design. It was one of those inspiration things that just happened. So Jay showed it to Beverly, who then gave approval, and Jay came back and said, 'OK, paint it!' I said, 'How much time do I have?' He said, 'Get it out as quick as you can.'

"I did that artwork on *The Partridge Family at Home* painting in one afternoon! I threw that together. I did the sketch the day before, and the next day I did the painting. It's almost primitive compared to the way I work now, but in those days I didn't have nearly the background I have today." (That background, by the way, includes work for Wentworth Gallery, the largest national gallery chain in the country, where he has created more than 650 paintings. President Obama is even a recipient of one of his works.)

"For the rest of it I simply took the front cover design and reversed it for the back side of the album, and I did it in black and white. Then I did all of the mechanicals and I came up with a typeface. I used press type for the album's title rather than hand drawing it, because I thought it was an interesting typeface for them from listening to the music and the whole concept of who they were."

the partridge family at home with their greatest hits
starring SHIRLEY JONES • featuring DAVID CASSIDY

"I can still remember playing those songs at the office over and over and over again. After a while you started singing along—at one point I knew all of the words to those songs! The audience for these albums was very youthful. It wasn't old people watching *The Partridge Family*, so I thought it was important to create the album so that it would fit the age group of the potential buyer. It couldn't be sophisticated in the sense you might imagine a sophisticated album design. It had to play on the youth. It had to play on the people watching them on TV.

"From my perspective, once again, I was doing two things. I was creating an artistic album cover, while at the same time creating a marketing image because Bell Records wanted to sell albums. It's another combination of both ideas, but I think creating the idea to have a fun album cover is more important than the marketing."

While *Shopping Bag*'s design was bold and very graphic, *At Home with Their Greatest Hits* had a quality much like an oil painting. "I had done a lot of illustration work, and every piece was always different. I tried not to repeat styles. I would do one thing, and then I would turn around and do something completely different. Jay use to tease me and say, 'What style are you going to use this time?' But I always tried to relate my design to the subject matter and tie it together. When I worked for Jay it was a lot of fun stuff. It wasn't like the serious kind of illustration work I had done earlier."

Zaccheo continues, "Everything seemed to fit together on this one. Rather than just painting a pretty landscape, it's almost surreal. It's make-believe. I was a bit older than the group. They were younger than me, but I really liked the music. I did the painting for the cover in a way that went along with how I thought about things at the time. It was reflective of the time period, the age of the buying public, and everything that I was at the time. It was very whimsical, with a Walt Disney quality to it, as if the life they were living was fun. They were having a good time in their surroundings, and everything about who they were and what they were doing was all about good stuff." The final touch was Zaccheo's signature hidden on the bottom fold of the album's edge.

By late 1972 Zaccheo was offered a position with Warner Brothers Music and Publications, where he became head creative director, going on to design album covers for Elton John, Gordon Lightfoot, and Neil Young, among others.

Shirley Jones says this album cover is her favorite because of the successful way it represents them all as a family.

The Palmer Method: *The Partridge Family Notebook*

Mary English dramatizes the brainstorming session behind *The Partridge Family Notebook*: "Well, what are we gonna do now? we thought. *Hmmm ... let's think. What do schools use?* I don't know whose idea it was to come up with the notebook, but I remember doing the comp for it and Beverly liked it. She showed everything to Larry Utall, and he liked it, too."

English wrote out the entire *Notebook* album by hand. Dale Leipzig remembers seeing English in action. "Mary had very beautiful lettering. Not only was she very good, she was very fast. She could just pump things out extremely fast, and get it right on the first time. I would watch her working sometimes, and she had a very sure hand. This is something that she would have done very quickly, to get that kind of consistent, bold sort of handwriting."

"It was done to look like a schoolchild's handwriting," explains English. "That wasn't really my style of handwriting. I can do many different handwritings. Many, many, many. Whatever you want, I can do. The *Notebook* was done to look like the kind of cursive that was taught in elementary school. In my day, every fourth grader was taught penmanship. It was a subject that we took. I believe it was called the Palmer Method. When you were growing up, did you have these green, poster-like things in the front of the classroom? That's what this design is on *Notebook*," she says. "It's that kind of script. We wanted to make it look just like it was a school child's notebook."

when we're singin'

The *Notebook* cover does not include a photo of the cast. "We just thought it would look cool," English says. "The layout was done by hand and it was intentional not to use a photo on this one. We had access to photos but they didn't need a photo. This is the way they wanted it to look. If they wanted to use a picture they would have, because they were still making money then," she says.

Notebook had a two-color cover, adding to the budget. "If you had to run something two-color it would cost you more than full color, because everything was going full color, so they had to stop the press in order to do two-color, and that cost more," says Weinstein.

"What's striking to me about this album is that it's a gutsy move, because it's very minimalist at a time when there wasn't a whole lot of minimalism in the market. Very unusual for that period," adds Leipzig.

"My favorite of them all is *The Partridge Family Notebook*. Why? I don't know why," laughs English. "Probably because it was all me. I love that it's different. It's not your typical record album cover. The design is more about what kids can relate to, rather than trying to be glitzy or rock and roll." The final touch was a three-hole punch along the left side of the album, done by a mechanical overlay with three dots that were photographed.

Larry Uttal's wife loved English's handwriting so much that she asked her to do the invitations for her daughter's wedding!

Breaking All the Rules: *The Partridge Family Crossword Puzzle*

This is the first story Mary English brings up in her interview. "The ol' *Crossword Puzzle*," she says. "They were going to release another album and they did not have a working title. So what would you think of as a thing? The Partridge Family *what*? You've done notebook, you've done teen magazine, you've done the album, you've done their birthdays, you've done the whatever-else-we-did! So what else do you want to know about the Partridge Family?

"Joel Borowka and I use to sit in the morning and he would do the *New York Times* crossword puzzle every day. I would kind of mosey into his office and do it with him, and we'd pick at it throughout the day. So someone suggested—and I don't remember who—that we do *The Partridge Family Crossword Puzzle*, and I remember having a difference of opinion with Joel.

"He said, 'Crossword puzzles are too hard to do. No one can write a crossword puzzle.' I said, 'Of course you can! I could do one, for heaven's sakes!' He said 'Ohhhh! OK, you think you can do one?' I said, 'I can! I *will* do one!'" They made a bet and soon the entire office was chipping in with clues!

"So I did up this design, and Jay was going over copy with me. I would ask for input on the questions and offer to put them in. Little did I know that there are rules for crossword puzzle making! I had no idea! First of all they have to be symmetrical. If you look at the design, this design is not symmetrical *at all*. And you very rarely have just one crossing letter. So this was not very good. This was not well done. Bad crossword puzzle!"

English laughs. "The only reason I know this now is because my husband constructs crossword puzzles for the *Times*. So I know what's wrong with it! He could probably give me a couple other reasons why it's so bad, but for a fan who knew the answers, we thought it would be a lot of fun."

The small black-and-white photos of David Cassidy and Shirley Jones were chosen as the type of photos you might see in a newspaper. "We thought it would look more newspaper-ish. You know, like a real crossword puzzle might look," says Mary. "Crossword puzzles are usually found in newspapers and we thought that take on it would be cool," says English.

It was the first U.S. cover to feature Cassidy and Jones without the other members of the cast. "We always had a big variety of photos available to us," explains Mary, "and we were able to get photos. I don't remember ever having a problem with that, but it would have taken away from the look of this cover," says English. "The reason the puzzle stands out, and David and Shirley stand out, is because it's not filled up with other things for the eye to look at. Artistically, we liked it."

"But we had to do color," she continues, "because we had just done the white *Notebook*. We had to jazz it up a little bit. And yellow, back in the day, was taught in art school as the color most people are drawn to, and the color they see the best when they see packaging." It was an intentional choice that each Partridge Family cover featured a different color.

The typeface and style were intended to reflect the look and feel of an actual newspaper. The puzzle answers were cleverly put on the inside liner sleeve so fans could pull it out and reference it when doing the puzzle. The back cover is a return to black and white—possibly because of a reduced budget based on *Notebook*'s relatively slow sales.

"If you notice, the group and the album title are almost always up at the top of the front of the album. That was for racking," Mary says, referring to the holding racks for retail display of LPs. "There's a certain spot on the album cover, about two-

when we're singin'

thirds of the way up, maybe a little bit less, where you wanted the title to be, because you want the title to show as people flip through the records."

As with all the albums, international packaging varied. The cover design for the Japanese *Crossword Puzzle* is completely different from the U.S. version, bearing no resemblance to a crossword puzzle in any way.

It featured David Cassidy's face making up most of the cover's available space, and it had a gatefold layout and a colorful orange block design on the back cover.

"My husband has one of the *Crossword Puzzle*s downstairs," says Mary English. "He was laughing because he couldn't believe some of these stories on how we came up with these album designs. You wouldn't believe how seat-of-the-pants this stuff was. We'd just sit around and brainstorm: Anyone have any ideas for the next album?"

Rush Delivery: *The Partridge Family Bulletin Board*

The concept for *Bulletin Board* was born of haste. Beverly Weinstein, illustrator John McKinzie (who had replaced John Zaccheo), and Mary English had literally a single day to produce a cover design. Scrambling for an idea they could execute quickly, they grabbed the bulletin board off the wall and quickly coined the new title. After all, they figured, a lot of kids had bulletin boards in their bedroom.

"I thought, *What the hell are we going to do?*" laughs Weinstein as she recalls racing down to the offices at the Music Agency the day she was given her 24-hour deadline. "I remember saying, 'Just pin things onto the bulletin board!'"

"And the artist went into the back, and he came out later with this piece of paper," says Weinstein. McKinzie wrote out all the songs and copy on paper from a yellow legal pad. "I thought it was so clever—that little piece of yellow paper," recalls Weinstein. "At this point we were so desperate. I remember this one distinctly because we were running out of ideas."

Meanwhile Mary English was working on a layout and looking for things around the office that they could use. "It was fun," she says. "We took some pictures and some things from the office and push-pinned them onto this bulletin board." She remembers poking around the board with push-pins, intentionally creating pin marks for added realism. "I remember working late on this one," she adds. "We were probably there till eight or nine o'clock that night."

English clipped a photo from a magazine with pinking shears to make it look like a postcard, and found a map. The "our new TV time" note was created on one of the office typewriters and pinned to the corkboard to promote the show's schedule change. John McKinzie cut out the title lettering from colored paper. They added a black-and-white photo of the cast, and the *Bulletin Board* rendering was ready for presentation.

The entire thing was photographed. "I literally held the bulletin board," says Weinstein of the moment they shot the picture. "This is my favorite one," adds Weinstein. "We just got hysterical over that one! It's funny how it all comes to be."

Arista in Charge: *The World of the Partridge Family*

By early 1974 the Bell Records takeover by Arista was in full gear. Clive Davis was at the helm and the final Partridge Family album ended up being "a quickie throwaway," in Mary English's words. Beverly Weinstein had left and Davis had hired Robert Heimall to take over as art director. With little interest in the release, they put together a two-album set featuring songs that reflected the best of the Partridge Family's four-year run. The cover features a photo that looks like it came from the same session as the one on *At Home with Their Greatest Hits*, with a grainy quality that suggests it may have been blown up from a print rather than a negative. The back has color headshots of each cast member along with a full track list.

The Best Worst Idea: *The Partridge Family TV Dinner*

When the graphic artists at the Music Agency prepared a presentation for a proposed Partridge Family album, they always included two or three concepts. One of the never-used ideas was Mary English's favorite Partridge Family submission: *The Partridge Family TV Dinner*.

"I loved this album cover!" says an animated English. No one else thought much of the idea, she recalls, but she was given the OK to develop it for presentation.

"The first thing I did was go out and buy a Swanson's TV dinner. You know the old Swanson's trays? I used one of those on the front cover. I wanted the album to look like a real Swanson's TV dinner. The heading across the top was done to mimic the style on a Swanson TV dinner box. The background color was a teal blue, and the image of the tray was flat and accurate to size. It wasn't angled or anything like that. It was one of those trays with the triangles, divided into parts. And then I showed the tray and what was in it.

when we're singin'

"I had David Cassidy's head coming out of the vegetable mix! Shirley's head was coming out of the mashed potatoes, and all the other little kids were at the bottom in the fried chicken!" English laughs. "I found these pictures and I worked them into the design by drawing. So if the picture didn't fit, I cut out as much vegetable mix as I could and I would hand draw whatever I couldn't find in photographs. Then the fried chicken was in the big tray slot and the little kids' heads were popping out of the fried chicken."

John Zaccheo remembers the kind of brainstorming session from which ideas such as this emerged. "We'd throw ideas out and some of them were way out and some of them were not so way out. Many times the ones that were so far out would be the ones that we'd go for." This wasn't one of them.

"It was a horrible idea," laughs English. "It was just horrible ... but I liked it! Beverly hated it! Beverly was very brief. I think she just shuddered, shook her head, and simply said 'No, that won't work.' But I was so proud, just so proud of that one. It was just their heads coming out of the food. I thought it was genius! The concept was TV-themed, and they were on a TV show, right? And kids eat TV dinners while they watch it, right? But no one else thought it was genius. Jay and Joel didn't like it either, but they always gave me a lot of freedom to go ahead and present whatever ideas I ever had. They were very good about that."

English kept the design for years and years, until she finally lost track of it. Now, as a treat for the group's fans, she has redesigned the comprehensive rendering for this book. "Thank goodness their publicist doesn't exist anymore," she laughs. "Ohhh ... horror of horrors! I still love it!"

THE LOST SONGS
or ... The Partridge Family Garage Sale

The Recording Sessions

"Ok, I had to go out to my files, into the garage," begins Ron Hicklin as he prepares to shed light on some of the Partridge Family's recording sessions and unreleased songs. Hicklin kept meticulous notes on all of the recording sessions.

Hicklin's session notes reflect all the songs that were recorded and planned for use on the show, an album, or both. The session vocalists came in for the last stage of recording the track, and the session notes include only the songs that were completely recorded. They do not include David Cassidy's vocal demos and rough cuts that never made it to the final stages of recording, nor do they reflect Shirley Jones' solo work on "Whale Song" and "Ain't Love Easy." "Stephanie" is also mysteriously missing from the session notes.

"When we did our sessions, David was not there," explains Hicklin. "Wes, John Bahler, and Mike Melvoin would gather ahead of time. Wes would pick the material, whether he wrote it or simply had an interest in the publishing. He would then discuss the chart with Mike Melvoin, and Mike would write the instrumental chart. Then John would write the vocal chart based on what they put down with David. So David's voice was already there when we would walk in to do our backgrounds. David was never recording live with us. In every one of these cases, when we walked in to sing on something, the lead was already there—other than the original pilot." [Author's note: *Christmas Card* is another exception.]

Just after the cancellation of the series, syndication made episodes available to the networks for reruns. *The Partridge Family* was initially very popular in syndication. At one time it could be seen as many as three times in one evening on different channels. When the show was first canceled from prime time, the background vocalists were noticing that they had not received royalty payments for the musical portions of the original first-run broadcasts. Hicklin took charge of the situation and wrote a few letters of inquiry in search of the missing payments.

"At the end of the original 96 Partridge Family broadcasts, the same thing happened with Screen Gems that happened with Colgems," says Hicklin. "We were paid for our work on the record albums, but we were never paid for the television

when we're singin'

SCREEN ACTORS GUILD   April 12, 1972
7750 Sunset Blvd.
Hollywood, California 90046
Mr. Phillip M. Dezen

Dear Mr. Dezen:

In answer to your letter of April 7, 1972, I respectfully submit the following:

These songs were recorded under AFTRA jurisdiction:

TITLE	RECORDING DATE
(12) (10) SOMEBODY WANTS TO LOVE YOU JOHN, TOM, RON & JACKIE	MAY 11, 1970
LEAD ME ON	5-11-70
(71) (9) I THINK I LOVE YOU	" " "
WE CAN MAKE EVERYTHING ALRIGHT	5-16-70
(11) THAT'LL BE THE DAY	" " "
(19) SHE'D RATHER HAVE THE RAIN	" " "
(16) ONLY A MONTH AGO	" " "
(5) I REALLY WANT TO KNOW YOU	" " "
(4) I'LL LEAVE MYSELF A LITTLE TIME	" " "
(2) (3) ON THE ROAD	" " "
ON THE ROAD (Re-recorded)	6-11-70
SINGIN' MY SONG	" " "
(7) TO BE LOVERS	8-4-70
(21) (14) (8) HEART BEAT (88)	" " "
(20) (3) POINT ME IN THE DIRECTION OF ALBEQUERQUE	" " "
(14) (3) BABY I LOVE, LOVE, I LOVE YOU	" " "
(17) BANDELA	8-5-70
BYE BYE BLACKBIRD	" " "
MY KIND OF MUSIC	" " "
(13) (16) THE LOVE SONG	" " "

374

THE LOST SONGS

- 2 -

	TITLE		RECORDING DATE
(8)	FIND PEACE IN YOUR SOUL	JOHN, TOM, RON & JACKIE	8-5-70
(12)	ALL OF THE THINGS		" " "
	COME ON DOWN		" " "
	BAD TIME		" " "
(88)	DOESN'T SOMEBODY WANT TO BE WANTED	JOHN, STAN, RON & Jackie	11-12-70
(22)	I'LL MEET YOU HALFWAY		" " "
(24)	I'M HERE, YOU'RE HERE		" " "
(23)	YOU ARE ALWAYS ON MY MIND		" " "
(18)	UMBRELLA MAN		" " "
	MORNING RIDER ON THE ROAD	JOHN, TOM, RON & JACKIE	11-13-70
	WARM MY SOUL		" " "
(18)	THERE'S NO DOUBT IN MY MIND		" " "
	LAY IT ON THE LINE		" " "
(36)(34)	RAINMAKER		5-4-71
(26)	ECHO VALLEY 2-6809		" " "
(44)(33)	I WOULD HAVE LOVED YOU ANYWAY		" " "
(39)	BROWN EYES		" " "
(27)	LISTEN TO THE SOUND		" " "
(90)(38)(89)	I'M ON MY WAY BACK HOME		" " "
(93)	ONE NIGHT STAND		5-5-71
(31)	TWENTY FOUR HOURS A DAY		" " "
(37)	IT'S TIME THAT I KNEW YOU BETTER		" " "
(31)(25)	I WOKE UP IN LOVE THIS MORNING		" " "
(91)	YOU DON'T HAVE TO TELL ME		" " "
(37)(30)	LOVE IS ALL I EVER NEEDED		5-11-71
	SUMMER DAYS (John & Tom Bahler ONLY)	JOHN & TOM	5-13-71
(33)(28)	SUMMER DAYS (Group) I believe the group was used in the final master.	JOHN, TOM, RON & JACKIE	6-7-71

when we're singin'

TITLE	RECORDING DATE
WHITE CHRISTMAS	JOHN, TOM, RON & JACKIE 8-25-71
SANTA CLAUS IS COMING TO TOWN	" " "
(42) LAST NIGHT	" " "
HELLO HELLO	" " "
(29) EVERY LITTLE BIT O' YOU	" " "
JINGLE BELLS	8-26-71
FROSTY THE SNOWMAN	" " "
(45) WINTER WONDERLAND	" " "
BLUE CHRISTMAS	" " "
ROCKIN' AROUND THE CHRISTMAS TREE	" " "
CHRISTMAS SONG	8-28-71
MY CHRISTMAS CARD TO YOU	" " "
SLEIGH RIDE	" " "
(45) HAVE YOURSELF A MERRY LITTLE CHRISTMAS	" " "
SLEIGH RIDE (Re-recorded)	9-4-71
(46) AS LONG AS THERE'S YOU	" " "
(41) IF YOU EVER GO	" " "
(43) ONE OF THOSE NIGHTS	" " "
(40) EVERY SONG IS YOU	" " "
(36) COME ON LOVE	" " "
(93)(50) GOD BLESS YOU, GIRL	" " "
(47) SOMETHING NEW GOT OLD	12-16-71
(48)(55) AM I LOSING YOU, BABY	" " "
(57) THERE'LL COME A TIME	" " "
(81) IT'S ALL IN YOUR MIND	" " "
(53) GIRL, YOU'VE MADE MY DAY	" " "
(58) I DON'T CARE	" " "

THE LOST SONGS

PARTRIDGE FAMILY RECORDS

SONG TITLE	GROUP	Session Dat
① "Let The Good Times In"	JOHN, TOM, STAN, RON & JACKIE	12/18/69
① "Together" → ⑧ ㉜	" " " " "	" " "
"What A Day"	" " " " "	12/21/69
㊽ "Lookin' Thru The Eyes of Love"	JOHN, TOM, RON & JACKIE	5/1/72
㊼ "Breaking Up Is Hard To Do"		" " "
㊾ "One Day At A Time" ㊽		" " "
㊷ "It's You"		" " "
"Me Loving You"		" " "
㊾ "Love Must Be The Answer" ㊺ ㊵		" " "
"Take Good Care of Her"		" " "
"We Gotta Get Outta This Place"		" " "
"Something's Wrong"		" " "
㊽ "Together We're Better" ㊼		" " "
㊺ "Sounds Like You're Saying Hello"		" " "
㊼ "It Means I'm In Love With You" ㊶		" " "
㊶ "Sunshine Eyes"		" " "
"It Means I'm In Love With You"	TOM, STAN, RON & JACKIE	5/23/72
㊾ "Story Book Love"	JOHN, TOM, RON & JACKIE	9/4/72
"Let Your Love Go"		" " "
㊿ "As Long As You're There"		" " "
㊻ "Sunshine" ㊵ ㊷		" " "
㊼ "Mayby Someday"	TOM, RON, JACKIE & JERRY	9/22/72
"Now That You've Got Me"		" " "
"It's A Long Way To Heaven"		" " "
㊻ "Walkin' In The Rain"		" " "
㊻ "I've Got Your Love"		" " "
㊼ "Friend And Lover"		" " "
㊽ "Money, Money"	JOHN, TOM, RON, & JACKIE	7/25/73
㊿ "I'll Never Get Over You" ㊵		" " "
㊻ "I've Been Alone Too Long"		" " "
㊼ "Oh No, Not My Baby" ㊹		" " "
"I Was Runnin' The Opposite Way"		" " "
⑰ "Somethin' Tells Me I'm Into Somethin' Good" ㊷ ㊶		" " "
㊼ "I Wanna Be With You" ㊽		7/26/73
㊵ "I Wouldn't Put Nothin' Over On You" ㊽		" " "

(over)

377

when we're singin'

```
⑨⑥ "I Heard You Singin' Your Song"  ⑦③   JOHN, TOM, RON & JACKIE    9/4/73
⑧① "Cryin' In The Rain"                                               "   "   "
⑨⑤ "Roller Coaster" ⑦④                                                "   "   "
⑦⑤ "Workin' On A Groovy Thing" ⑦⑥                                     "   "   "
⑧⑦ "Lookin' For A Good Time" ⑦⑨                                       "   "   "
⑧③ "How Long Is Too Long" ⑦②                                          "   "   "
⑦⑦ "That's The Way It Is With You"                                    9/5/73
    "Where Do We Go From Here"                                         "   "
⑥⑤ "When Love's Talked About"                                         "   "   "
```

shows. ASCAP handles members' rights for the record albums, and the Screen Actors Guild handles the television end of it. As members, if one of your performances is used in one way, it is covered by a certain code that everybody signs. If it's used in a different code, then you get paid appropriate scale for that, too."

"There's reruns of a television show, but that doesn't exist in records. There's no reruns of records. When we were paid for the record albums, we were paid a flat fee and that was the end of it. There's no royalty that we received beyond that. So it was important that we were on the cast list for the television shows, because it was our performances. Further, if they played the song twice on the TV show, you get paid a second time. So when we were done with the series we realized we weren't paid anything for the television shows.

"There should have been a Screen Actors Guild contract on every one of those television shows. So once again the ball was thrown to me and I went to Screen Actors Guild, and I said, 'The same thing's happening that happened on *The Monkees*. There's four of us involved here, and we're not going to go along with the kind of deal that I got for *The Monkees*. We need to do something about this.'

"So the Screen Actors Guild worked with me on it. I needed to know all of the songs, who was on what, what shows were played. Between John Bahler and I, we were able to gather the material. John sent me copies of all his contracts—all his after-records that he did—and I ended up writing a 25-page brief on all of this. I wrote out who was on what, what shows were entitled, what songs were in each one of those shows, who the personnel was in each song, what the recording dates were, all of that kind of stuff. I submitted it, and we ended up getting something like $100,000 for the television shows to be divided between the four of us. But from that point on I don't think it involved reuse. It was another situation where we weren't necessarily being paid for reuse, but at least we collected for the original-run broadcasts."

The Screen Gems Records

To help them prepare for the music performance portion of the show, the cast was given records to help them learn the words to the songs. These records were never intended to be heard by anyone outside the production, and only about 10 to 12 copies of each were pressed. Through the years diehard fans have clamored for these rarities, which include unreleased songs as well as different versions and mixes of the songs that were released.

There were nine main volumes of these Screen Gems records, each ranging from a single-sided LP to several full LPs. There were also some random one-off pressings of individual songs that did not appear on any volume but were thrown together quickly and passed on to the cast. On occasion, 45 RPM singles were also pressed. "These came from Wes," explains Bob Claver. "He brought them to the set, and he had them made so everybody had a copy. It's the same as learning a script. Everybody should have a comfort level for recording, so when they're getting the playback they have some clue as to what's coming up next."

"Wes would bring those to the office in a manila sleeve, and they'd have eight or nine songs on them," says Larry Rosen. "I'd take them home and I'd listen to them because I knew what all the episodes were that we were working on. As we developed the scripts, we would select what songs would go into which script, depending on the message of the song and if it related to the story. I'd pick a song. I'd show it to Bob, and I'd say, 'This is a song that I think works in the show,' and he would say 'Fine.' Then Wes would produce it for the episode in time to get it out on the soundstage for the lip-syncing sessions." All the Screen Gems versions are mixed in mono. "Anything that was planned for the show was always done in mono," explains John Bahler. "In those days they couldn't do stereo for TV."

Colagé

Wes Farrell was savvy and he was always looking for a new angle. Though he zeroed in on David Cassidy as the Partridge Family's potential lead singer, he thought there might be hit potential for the background singers too.

During one of the Partridge Family sessions he was recording the jazz standard "Bye Bye Blackbird," used in the first season of the show—a song that highlights the gorgeous harmonies of the background vocalists. Since the singers were uncredited, they were unknown as the actual voices of the Partridge Family. Wes came up with the name Colagé and released "Bye Bye Blackbird" as a 45 RPM single in September 1970 to test the waters.

"Colagé! That's us!" Hicklin says enthusiastically. "'Bye Bye Blackbird' was done as part of the Partridge Family situation, but Wes decided that it would be a good record all by itself. He just called the group Colagé and put the record out. I think he just bootlegged that into the Partridge Family session. I think it was just smuggled in, or it could have been intended for the Partridge Family but didn't utilize David or really depict the usual situation of the show. It was more about putting this record out as a kind of flyer to see what might happen. I can remember really liking the thing because it was an interesting thing that was just done by us."

"Wes could put another name to it, because David wasn't on it," explains Jackie Ward. "He could do that because it was his stuff. He produced it, so he could put any name he wanted on it. In a case like that, when you are not an organized group and you're a studio singer and you go in and you do the sounds for the producer, you get paid scale. You can negotiate for more, but generally it is scale, and you know that if they use you in another medium they have to pay for the conversion to that medium. However if you do a record, he owns it—lock, stock, and barrel. You have nothing to say about it. I'm assuming he owned it outright if he produced and had rights to what he produced. I don't know what his deal was with the record company, but that would be my guess."

The single was backed with the Appel-Cretecos lost song "My Kind of Music." The Bell Records single was numbered 920, only 10 numbers after "I Think I Love You." The single didn't resonate on the charts, and the Partridge Family took off, so that was the end of Colagé.

Liner Notes: *The Partridge Family Garage Sale*

Farrell originally planned to record 25 songs a year. He wanted to feature a new song every week on the show, while simultaneously releasing those songs on two studio albums a season. With about 25 shows in a season and 11 songs on each album as Farrell required, it was a good fit.

There were 31 tracks completed during season 1, 30 during season 2, and 25 during season 3. But only 17 tracks were recorded for the final season. There was only one Partridge Family studio album released during the final season rather than the usual two, but the producers still needed enough songs to fill out the rest of the season. Had *Bulletin Board* sold better, there likely would have been another album.

"Some of these songs were written to fit particular scripts that were planned, because of reasons in keeping with the format," Farrell explained to Ken Sharp in 1993. "Every song that was written was written with the view towards trying to capture a top-40-driven piece of work. Sometimes that wasn't the case. Not that we were doing any throwaway songs, but in some cases they just ended up favoring the concept of the show as opposed to the material as an important work. There's nothing that I'm ashamed of, but certain things in anybody's canvas of work will stick out."

More than 35 known lost songs—including outtakes, demos, sound cues, and alternate versions of songs that were part of the Partridge Family sessions—never made it onto an album, some not even having ever turned up on the show. Think of them as the lost tapes the family left behind in their garage back in 1974. Here are some tidbits, songwriter stories, and fun anecdotes on the tracks left behind.

THE LOST SONGS

Together (Havin' a Ball), 2:20, Shorty Rogers–Kelly Gordon
This masterful arrangement was done by the late, great Shorty Rogers. It was used in the pilot episode as both the first theme song of the series and a featured musical number. Variations and outtakes were recorded for use as sound cues on the show and used several times. "Together" best represents the choral sound that Rogers preferred, with a clever arrangement and meticulously layered harmonies. No one had ever heard the middle verse of this song until 2005, when it was released—complete with the missing verse—on the compilation CD *Come On Get Happy! The Very Best of the Partridge Family*. The lost lyric from the bridge, "taking care of business," harkens back to the original working title of the pilot, *Family Business*. This song was heard on the show more than any other unreleased song.

> **Appears On:** Season 1, episode 1 (pilot), "What? And Get Out of Show Business?" (September 25, 1970); Season 1, episode 3, "Whatever Happened to the Old Songs?" (October 9, 1970); Season 2, episode 35, "The Forty-Year Itch" (November 19, 1971); Season 2, episode 41, "Fellini, Bergman, and Partridge" (January 14, 1971)

When We're Singin', 1:05, Diane Hildebrand–Wes Farrell
When every theme song on the long list of those written for the show had been cast aside, Wes Farrell went to work himself with young songwriter Diane Hildebrand in an attempt to write one himself.

"I was brought into Les' office and asked if I would take on the assignment," recalls Hildebrand. "Lester Sill was the president of Screen Gems–Columbia Music at the time. They needed a lyricist, supposedly to write the theme song. Of course, a major Screen Gems TV show was always a plum, so I naturally said yes."

Hildebrand met Wes Farrell for the first time that day in Sill's office. "I didn't know Wes, but he was a powerhouse in those days. He was a New York kind of guy, in very classy suits, very good-looking and very charismatic, and a bit like a tank in a toy store. We were an odd pair—even just for writing. Him in his Armani and me in my flower-child jeans and T-shirt. He was polite to me, but I was a fly in the ointment, basically, and the night we wrote that song he basically wrote the song. I mean, I was sticking in my two cents as often as Wes would let me, but he so dominated the process that it was really all pretty much Wes Farrell. We'd discuss the idea and I, of course, had a concept that was very similar to the idea we used—sort of wholesome. But I was not very assertive. In fact, take into consideration this was in '69 or '70, so this was before feminism really took hold. I was about 24 years old. I was female and I was the only in-office female writer they had."

"When We're Singin'" was used only during the first season before the lyrics were rewritten. The new lyric, *"come on get happy,"* quickly became identified with

when we're singin'

the show. While you could hear both versions during the initial syndicated reruns, throughout the years there have been occasions when the first season theme song was edited out and replaced with "Come On Get Happy," leaving many to forget about it. The original theme song was reinstated for all the DVD releases, however.

Hildebrand feels the Partridge Family's music lives on with fans because of the message it sends. "It was positive and it was full of hope, and people need that. I think that music is such a benign and creative expression," she says. "I would let my own children watch this kind of a show because it was a single mother and I was, most of my child-rearing years, a single mother. It was full of hope. It was full of magic—I liked that about it."

Songwriter Stephen Dossick toyed around with a similar idea. His working title was "Voices Singing." He shared a little bit of it with Farrell the day of the pilot viewing and asked Farrell if he wanted to write it with him. "I have always felt the original theme song had a little bit to do with what I was going to do with the theme," says Dossick. "I mean it never got so far that I recorded it, but it was something that was in my head and I was sort of singing it to him a little bit. I really didn't get that far with it," he says. Coincidentally, Dossick has a vivid memory of meeting Tony Romeo that day. They sat next to each other. "He was reading *Variety*," says Dossick. "And he told me he wasn't going to write for this thing." How quickly that changed.

Often overlooked and forgotten as the first season theme song, "When We're Singin'" tells the story of the pilot episode in only 60 seconds, setting up the premise of the show like most TV theme songs of the era. David Cassidy delivers one of his early-style vocals, offering up a ride on the bus to the millions of new viewers as he sang *"there's nothing better than being together… when we're singin'."*

Appears On: Season 1, episode 15, "Mom Drops Out" (January 8, 1971)

Come On Get Happy, 1:05, Danny Janssen–Wes Farrell

Just before the start of season two, it was decided that a new theme song was needed. While several songs that had recently been completed for use on the show and the records were considered for the slot, it was a new lyric that was selected.

Wes Farrell's melody was kept intact. Danny Janssen rewrote the lyric. David Cassidy recorded a new vocal, and a harpsichord—reminding listeners of "I Think I Love You"—was added to the arrangement.

Cassidy has told the story in concert many times that he was literally called over to the studio to record this in a few short minutes, then never sang it again until 2000, when he opened another series of concerts beginning in Atlantic City.

In the years since, it has become so popular that it made its way onto a CD compilation as one of the group's greatest hits—despite the fact that it was never released in any format during the height of the Partridge Family's reign.

THE LOST SONGS

"That was specifically written to be the theme," said Wes Farrell. "I never wrote it as a song. After the first year something bothered me about the lyrics and I brought in another lyricist to change it in the second season. That came easier than others. It wasn't too hard. I play enough piano to write. I write the melody and the idea and then I bring in lyricists to complete it. It wasn't written to be a record. It wasn't written to be a hit song. As it turns out it became an infectious melody that has lasting power—but never in a million years was I sitting down at the piano to write a hit song. I was sitting down to write a theme."

"My favorite song is 'Come On Get Happy,'" says Rick Segall. "Not only because it was the theme song and it was the one everybody seemed to know, but it's also a really great message, you know? And every time somebody does it, they don't just say 'come on get happy'—they usually start singing it, very animated. (He sings the music leading into it). How can you do that and not kind of wiggle your head a little bit? Right?"

Jackie Ward adds, "I don't know that I would say I have a favorite song, but I have to say that I always felt that that theme song, 'Come On Get Happy,' just said it all. To me, I hear that and think, *Yes, that's Partridge!* That song was special in that regard. The show would come on the air and that's the first thing you hear, so I felt that song was special."

Favorite Partridge Family song of Rick Segall

Let the Good Times In, 2:51, Carol Bayer–Neil Sedaka

The original harmonies designed for the Partridge Family are demonstrated here with precision. If David Cassidy had not been brought into the fold as a singer, the blended harmonies and uncredited lead vocals heard here would have carried the group's entire catalog.

It is quintessential sunshine pop coming right out of the late '60s. The Partridge Family arrangement reflects more identifiable female voices than previous versions of this song, and Shirley Jones is prominently featured in the on-air music video version; listen for her bubbly *ba-de-la-la*'s. Until its 2005 release this was one of the most sought-after unreleased Partridge Family songs, despite the absence of a David Cassidy lead vocal.

The original cut by the Love Generation brought high hopes for a hit but was never released as a single. Tom Bahler remembers how much fun it was to dig it back out for the Partridge Family version. "I sang lead on that," said Tom Bahler. "That was before David was hired. It's funny to watch David on the show lip-synching over my voice."

"Let the Good Times In" was first released as the B-side of Hung Jury's first single, the sunshine-pop "Buses," released on Colgems in October 1967. The following year the Love Generation released it on their 1968 album *Montage*—the last of the three Love Generation albums on Imperial.

Appears On: Season 1, episode 1 (pilot), "What? And Get Out of Show Business?" (September 25, 1970)

when we're singin'

(Let the Lovelight in Your Eyes) Lead Me On, 3:09, Jack Keller–Ernie Sheldon

This was one of the first three songs laid down at the very first session. Jack Keller attended the initial viewing of the show with all the other songwriters and wrote this as a potential theme song submission as well as a regular album cut and TV music video. Separate female and male lead vocals were recorded as demos by Marty Kaniger, who later co-wrote "Whale Song," and Charlene, who recorded the demo for "I'm on My Way Back Home." Both versions were pitched to the show.

The recording was never used on the show and never appeared on an album. Even though the Partridge version has yet to surface as a release, the song was recorded by Tennessee Ernie Ford in September 1970, and later by Steve Lawrence and Eydie Gormé for their 1982 MGM Records album *The World of Steve & Eydie*. Petula Clark and Sacha Distel also recorded it on Polydor in 1973 in the U.K.

The Love Song, 2:25, Steve Dossick

Sometimes a demo can be so strong it outshines its mission.

"Over about six weeks I wrote a couple of songs, went into the studio and cut the demos and gave them to Wes," says songwriter Steve Dossick. "He liked one of the two for the Partridge Family." Wes had other ideas for "The Love Song."

Dossick tells the story: "Wes was annoyed with me. Wes wanted me to get more serious about 'The Love Song.' I wasn't that serious about the song and I didn't work on it as hard as I could have. A guy named Richard Perry was producing Barbra Streisand, and they were looking for her first pop single. Wes thought 'The Love Song' could have been her first single, but he wanted me to write a stronger second verse." At this time, Streisand was only known for her Broadway style and had yet to cross over to the pop charts. "All these guys knew each other," explains Dossick. "Perry knew Wes. They were about the same age. Perry was in New York and he was looking."

Farrell tried to get Dossick focused on the "The Love Song" and his work as a songwriter, but Dossick was caught up with girls and rock and roll. "One time Wes was sprawled out on a couch in his office," says Dossick, "and he says to me, 'I just want you to write songs. All I ask you to do is write songs.' He said, 'Do you know how much money I make? Do you know what my residuals are? My residuals are like a half a million dollars a year as a writer.' Wes financially did better than everybody.

"He was saying all this to me because all I was preoccupied with was my college girlfriend, who was a year behind me and had just broken up with me. I kept saying to him, 'But Wes, I'm heartbroken!'" Dossick laughs. "Wes was a very good guy. He was not malicious. He was a cool guy. The thing about Wes that sticks out is that everything he touched turned to gold. It was unbelievable."

THE LOST SONGS

"The Love Song" didn't receive any additional focus from Dossick and was never passed on to Streisand's manager. "If I had written a stronger second verse for 'The Love Song,' it might have been a song for her. Wes liked the idea and he liked the song. Knowing what I know now, I would have said, 'Let's rewrite it!'

"I could have written a beautiful melody," he says, "but I didn't appreciate it for what it was. I didn't show 'The Love Song' enough respect. I appreciated 'I'll Leave Myself a Little Time' a lot more.

"When I was initially thinking about this song, it had a feel to me like a French chanteuse kind of song. That's how I was hearing it. When I started to write that song, I wasn't thinking of it as a love song or a ballad. I was hearing the words in my head as if they were almost cynical. Do you remember the Beatles song 'You Know My Name (Look Up the Number)'? I was sort of playing with it in that manner before it took shape like a song. Then it started to take form, and I wrote it." Dossick's use of imagery on "The Love Song" is excellent, and he uses a lot of diminished chords, giving the impression of unresolved tone and suspense.

"The thing about songwriting, at least for me, is the words," he says. "Once you have a structure, you just try to get the words right. That's hard. Words are hard. For me to do that song right, there would be a stronger second verse lyrically and I'd write a bridge. It's kind of incomplete." This is the second and final Partridge Family recording by Dossick before he left his short-lived contract with Wes Farrell.

In fact, the video performance of this song is the last time Cassidy is seen lip-syncing on the show. The episode aired in early 1971, well after Cassidy had proven himself as a vocalist. He actually sang a verse of the song in an earlier episode, "Go Directly to Jail," but the only full version is done as a lip sync over the background vocalists. So why no Cassidy lead vocal?

The answer lies in the demo, which was sung by the then-unknown Carly Simon. "Wes heard 'The Love Song' as a song that a woman would sing," says Dossick. "That's why he was talking to me about Barbra Streisand."

"I spent less than a year with Wes and I left," says Dossick. "I wanted to do my own records. I was an artist. I took myself seriously and I wanted to write more serious songs." Dossick at one point came very close to breaking out as a songwriter. Time has changed his perspective on his Partridge Family contributions: "When I look at these song now—what a wonderful thing! We had produced great music!"

Established successfully today as a psychiatrist, Dossick picked up songwriting again in the early '90s, even completing songs that he'd begun writing 20 years earlier.

***Appears On:** Season 1, episode 10, "Go Directly to Jail" (November 27, 1970)*
Season 1, episode 16, "Old Scrapmouth" (January 15, 1971)

when we're singin'

Bye Bye Blackbird, 2:58, Ray Henderson–Mort Dixson

Ray Bolger and Rosemary DeCamp began guest starring on *The Partridge Family* as Shirley Partridge's parents as early as episode 3. The producers wanted to showcase Bolger and gave him this song to sing, backed up by the family. It seems fitting for Bolger, who came out of the same era as the song. The TV moment was a sentimental one, used as a resolution between the bickering grandparents.

Farrell knew the long and successful track record of this song and decided to use it for the A-side of his experimental single for Colagé, the alter ego of the Partridge Family singers. "Bye Bye Blackbird" continues to be recorded and has been used in films including *Sleepless in Seattle, Maxie,* and *Public Enemies*.

Appears On: Season 1, episode 3, "Whatever Happened to the Old Songs?" (October 9, 1970)

My Kind of Music, 2:46, Mike Appel–Jim Cretecos

Music triggers memories. In this case, the songwriter's memory of its own existence! "I had totally forgotten about "My Kind of Music" until you woke me up about it," says Mike Appel. He and Jim Cretecos had attended the special viewing of the pilot that Farrell organized. "Wes asked all the writers to work on a theme song, as well as songs for the TV series, at that initial viewing of the pilot. The inspiration for this song was that Wes wanted a song for the show's theme, or at the very least to be utilized in the show."

After deciding not to use the tune for the television theme song, Farrell found another use for it and placed it on the B-side of the Colagé single. "Wes may have thought he could get another single out of the Partridge Family sessions at no extra cost to him," speculates Appel. "I have no recollection of Colagé, the group, or the studio people who put that record together. I haven't heard this song in 41 years. I didn't think we even wrote it. I thought you had it all wrong—however, I was wrong for having that assumption the minute I heard it." Appel recognizes the song immediately upon listening to it and it takes him back in time with fond memories attached. "What I love about the song is the surprise chord changes that I'd forgotten we wrote," he says. "It was musically a bit more sophisticated than I thought it would be."

"My Kind of Music" never appeared on the show or any of the group's records.

Baby I Love, Love, I Love You, 2:22, Errol Brown–Tony Wilson–Derek Lawrence

What if David Cassidy is the center of the music industry? The path of this song and its writers makes for a great game of six degrees of separation, with David Cassidy at the center of several different musical currents and eras.

Derek Lawrence, one of the three songwriters, was a fledgling producer who was friends with Jack Leahy, who ran Bell Records U.K. The second writer, Tony Wilson, had come to England from Trinidad and was a postman along with singing and songwriting for his band, the Soul Brothers. He was also working for Lawrence as a session singer. Together they wrote and recorded "Come Back to My Lonely World" for Bell Records.

"Tony had just introduced me to this guy named Errol Brown," says Lawrence. "Errol was Jamaican, and he was a friend of Tony's. They both came to England around the same time, in the early '60s."

With Lawrence serving as producer, the three new friends put several recordings together. "Baby I Love, Love, I Love You" was first recorded and released in England on Bell Records U.K. featuring Tony Wilson. "I had written a lot and this was one of the songs I had sitting around at the time. Errol did a demo with Derek, and he liked it." It was assigned the B-side to "Come Back to My Lonely World," says Wilson.

"Baby I Love, Love, I Love You,' was one of the first two or three songs Tony and I ever wrote together," adds Lawrence. "I love the idea of a studio band that's there in the studio every day. So we'd stay in the studio most days and just write things, intentionally. We just wrote songs. It was much like the Brill Building in New York, but in Kingsway in London."

"We actually did it in reggae," says Wilson. "The only time I knew the Partridge Family recorded it was when I actually saw *The Partridge Family* on TV. I was quite surprised when they decided to use that one, especially in its reggae version.

"Baby I Love, Love, I Love You" eventually found its way to America through a series of connections. Lawrence explains, "That came about from a mate I used to meet in the park—a guy named Jack Leahy, who was running Screen Gems publishing in London. Through Jack, I met Lester Sill, my American partner. When we first started producing, for some reason or another, the records I would do were coming out in America rather than England.

"Since Screen Gems was my publisher in America, all of the records I published went to Lester Sill out in L.A. The Tony Wilson version was recorded in '69. Lester was very involved in the Partridge Family thing, and I guess he sent it to Wes and that's how it happened.

"Lester called me and said, 'Listen, I think that all this Tony Wilson stuff will be perfect for the Partridge Family.' They said, 'It's real pop!' But that was the only song that ever happened with the Partridge Family. He told me they were going to be recording it, but as far as we knew it wasn't coming out on their albums."

Cassidy's voice is really sped up on this one, giving it a punchy quality. We hear the clavinet and a bass guitar and drums, used to create a sort of congo effect. The sound is soulful, percussive, and begs to the blues and reggae.

The song came and went for the Partridge Family, making little impression. It was never released as a single, nor did it appear on any of the original albums. Its first

when we're singin'

release wouldn't come until 2005, as a bonus selection on the CD compilation *Come On Get Happy: The Very Best of the Partridge Family*. There were no other songs from this songwriting trio recorded by the Partridge Family, but all three were about to break out into their own phenomenally successful careers.

Another song Lawrence produced for Brown and Wilson was a reggae version of the Plastic Ono Band's "Give Peace A Chance" with rewritten lyrics.

When they went to John Lennon for permission to record with the new lyrics, he liked their version so much he insisted they record it on Apple Records. The band was named the Hot Chocolate Band by a staffer at Apple. "It was in *Melody Maker* and all the music press that Errol Brown and Tony Wilson are with Apple Records," remembers Wilson.

In light of Apple's instability in the wake of the Beatles' breakup, the group ended up with producer Mickey Most, who produced Herman's Hermits and the Animals, among others, for their second record. Most didn't like the name the Hot Chocolate Band. "He said, 'One Plastic Ono Band is enough,'" says Wilson. "So he just called us Hot Chocolate."

Hot Chocolate hit big internationally during the disco era, with dance hits like "Disco Queen" and "You Sexy Thing." Their staying power on the pop charts was phenomenal, with hits in the top 20 consistently for 10 years.

At the same time, Derek Lawrence had his own big break. Lawrence recalls, "Going back to Joe Meek and the Outlaws, I used guitarist Ritchie Blackmore on lots of records. I'm sure he probably played on Tony Wilson's record. Anyway, he came to me and said, 'Look, we've got these two guys who have a lot of money to play in a band. They know nothing about the business. Why don't you come and produce it?' And there was a deal made with them. That's how I came on as producer for Deep Purple."

Lawrence produced the first three albums by Deep Purple, including one of their biggest hit singles, "Hush"—a favorite of David Cassidy's, which he frequently performs in concert. Lawrence went on to produce other successful bands including Wishbone Ash, Fresh, and Angel. He produced the first album, released only in Japan, for the heavy metal hair band Quiet Riot.

Now where were we? David Cassidy performs "Hush" in concert, which was originally produced by Derek Lawrence, who also wrote "Baby I Love, Love, I Love You" with Tony Wilson and Errol Brown, who were founding members of Hot Chocolate. Take a breath.

So the Partridge Family connects to hard rock's Deep Purple and disco's Hot Chocolate in only two degrees of David Cassidy! Kevin Bacon, who has his own band called the Bacon Brothers (not to mention the '90s parlor game Six Degrees of Kevin Bacon) has said many times that David Cassidy was one of his musical influences. So can you connect Kevin Bacon to David Cassidy in six degrees or less?

"I'll tell you something even more strange," says Lawrence. "Back in the early days when I was really close to the boss at Screen Gems in England—he was a big mate of mine—he had me do some tracks in the studio with Sue Shifrin. I don't think anything ever happened with them. It was with Dimeback, who I left in the late '60s." Shifrin, of course, was married to Cassidy for more than 23 years and is the mother of Beau Cassidy. Now that's one very close connection in the six degrees of David Cassidy!

Appears On: Season 1, episode 3, "Whatever Happened to the Old Songs?" (October 9, 1970); Season 1, episode 15, "Mom Drops Out" (January 8, 1971)

Find Peace in Your Soul, 2:47, Bill Dorsey

How do abstract impressionist art and the craft of songwriting merge to result in a Partridge Family song?

John Bahler describes two directions that the show's musical staff undertook. "The biggest thing was obviously music for the albums. The other side of it was doing custom songs specifically for the show. Even the songs used on the records needed a custom arrangement for the show, like this folk song. This one, like so many, never made it onto an album because it wasn't really 'Partridge Family.' It wasn't really the sound we were after for the records. It was more for the drama of the show."

Bill Dorsey, who wrote this folky story song, began and ended his career painting impressionist art. Somewhere in between he began playing the guitar and eventually learned some piano. "I was learning all the chords and started writing," he says. "I operated as an island. I never jammed with anybody, or rehearsed with anybody. Most of my songs were written by the time I was 20. I was in Alaska and I built a guitar out of driftwood just to have a guitar because I needed to play songs.

"My first writings I did on a boat in Alaska and I sent them to Bobby Darrin's publisher," says Dorsey. He eventually ended up signed with the Sure Shot record label. He wrote for Epic Records and Columbia. "I started to do some writing about consciousness and reality, and it went off the deep end.

"When I was writing with Screen Gems, Columbia, I had only one desire, and that was to get something on the charts," says Dorsey. "I never did." But it wasn't for lack of trying. Dorsey approached songwriting from every angle, closely studying the chord structure of every hit song that came along. "What I started not liking is what I called the three-chord songs and the loud rock—the distorted rock. I didn't like the testosterone that was creeping in on music. And neither did Screen Gems."

Dorsey continued to experiment. "One of the things I got carried away with was mind paints. When I started writing lyrics, I searched and searched and searched for words that show up in songs that are easy to sing—words like *candle* and *memory*. And I'd color code them according to whether they were verbs, adjectives, prepositions, etc., and I later put them on blocks that plug together—on a prism-shaped box so you could plug together those three words. So you could create two blind sentences, instead of one sentence. And you'd go noun, verb, adjective, and you'd have another noun, verb, adjective on the other side. So you could switch words easily within a phrase." Dorsey would take certain phrases, like *over the rainbow*, and switch out one of the elements. If the preposition was on, say, a purple block, he'd turn the block and create *beyond the rainbow* or *into the rainbow*. "I mean, gee whiz, prepositions are powerful words," he explains. "So I was studying this stuff from a very mechanical aspect."

Screen Gems introduced him to Mickey Dolenz, and Dorsey got in on the tail end of the Monkees. He was involved in the creation of the TV special for the Monkees, titled *33 1/3 Revolutions per Monkee*. He wrote "String for My Kite" for Davy Jones to sing on the special. He also wrote "The Other Side" for Tiny Tim, which appeared on *God Bless Tiny Tim*.

Dorsey felt that often he would bury himself with the commercialism of his songs by using, in his words, "supposedly clever titles." But "Find Peace in Your Soul" was perfectly titled to its content, and both title and lyric grabbed the attention of Wes Farrell. Spiritually driven, this song fit the episode perfectly with its gospel sound and human lyric.

"I submitted some things to Roger Gordon. I was basically working for him. He submitted this one to the Partridge Family, and I didn't even know that the Partridge Family was going to record it," recalls Dorsey.

Exposure on a Partridge Family episode was always good for a songwriter. But verses were frequently cut as songs were edited for time—a big problem for a story song like "Find Peace."

"They left out the second verse, so it doesn't make sense," explains Dorsey, who could still recite every word of the missing verse. The song tells a story about stumbling upon a blind man's predicament. A full version, complete with all three verses, was finished but never used.

"Let's get it re-recorded!" jokes Dorsey. "Gee whiz! Fast! We'll put together a session and get the guys together again, and include the lost verse so it's complete! It doesn't make much sense with two verses."

Dorsey went on to be renowned within the world of impressionist art under the name William Ballantine Dorsey, setting records in the biggest auction houses in the East and Midwest.

Appears On: Season 1, episode 14, "The Red Woodloe Story" (January 1, 1971)

All of the Things, 2:14, Richard Klein

A filing error has left this song incorrectly credited for over 40 years. The story behind "All of the Things" and the related song "Stephanie" is an intriguing one.

"The story's a little different than I think you know," begins songwriter David Price. "Here's where it starts: The thing is, I wrote 'All of the Things.'"

Price explains: "Rick Klein and I were very good friends. We met working on *The Monkees* television show, and we lived together for a while. We remained good friends our whole life up until he passed away a couple years ago. Rick, as I recall, had bumped into Lester Sill, who ran Colgems Music. All of us had known Lester from the Monkees days. Lester told him that they were looking for material for the Partridge Family, so Rick said, 'Well, gee, let's write some stuff and run it by them.' So I had already written 'All of the Things' and performed it at the Troubadour, a club in Hollywood that used to have a talent night on Monday nights. I had performed 'All of the Things' there with Mickey Dolenz' sister, Coco. She and I sang it, and I didn't think a whole lot about it. I wasn't doing anything with the song, so I suggested to Rick that we submit this one. We put together one or two other things that we then took to Lester Sill for the Partridge Family, and they picked 'All of the Things.'

"I was listening to it the other day, and I think what may have happened is that Rick might have tweaked the lyrics to better fit the show, because I didn't write it for the Partridge Family. It was just a song I wrote. Eventually what happened with that song is that through some clerical error, Rick's name was put on 'All of the Things,' and I don't know if my name was even on it or not. But that story ends many, many years later.

"When 'All of the Things' got recorded by the Partridge Family, we were thinking, *Well, gee, that's great,* except they put it on one of the shows, but they didn't put it on an album. I received royalties over the years, pennies here and a dollar there for airplay, but nothing for a record. Then that whole thing with Bobby Sherman came around…"

TO BE CONTINUED below, under "Stephanie"!

Appears On: Season 1, episode 9, "Did You Hear the One About Danny Partridge?" (November 20, 1970)

Stephanie, 2:36, John Henning–Richard Klein–David Price

David Price continues the story begun under "All of the Things": "Rick called me up and said, 'Hey, they want to use the track but they want to rewrite the lyrics to match up with this storyline. Is that OK with you?' I said 'Sure.'

"'Stephanie' came about because the *Partridge Family* staff was planning an episode involving a girl named Stephanie who was planned as a romantic involvement for David Cassidy on the show. Stephanie was named for this supposed character on the show. So Rick and John Henning rewrote the lyrics but the music stayed the same. 'All of the Things' became 'Stephanie.' I really had nothing to do with it. They just called up and said, 'Hey, you mind if we do this?' And I said, 'Nah, go ahead.' So that's why "Stephanie" is credited with three writers. It's credited to me, Rick Klein, and John Henning. But I was just on there because I wrote 'All of the Things,' which was the melody and chord structure. That's the story of how those two songs came about." The Stephanie storyline never actually transpired as an episode on the show.

Price continues, "Now the whole David Cassidy–Bobby Sherman thing is interesting because I had heard that David Cassidy had been in the studio recording one of these two songs. I don't recall which, but I think it was 'All of the Things,' and Bobby Sherman came in with his manager, Ward Sylvester. Ward had also been the manager for the Monkees. The story I heard was that David said, 'Hey, let's come in and sing this together!' And so they went in and sang the song together, and there was this kind of *Hey, why don't we put this out together as a single?* sort of thing, since they were both massive teen stars. About the time everybody became really enthusiastic about it, Ward and David Cassidy's manager both agreed they didn't like the idea because they felt it would dilute each of Cassidy's and Sherman's individual rising stars. So they didn't put it out as a duo.

"Once again, Rick and I found ourselves going *Geez, how many near misses can you have on one stupid song?* I mean, that would have been a big moneymaker with the careers both those guys had at that point! If there had been a single that went out as David Cassidy and Bobby Sherman together, it would have sold millions!

"So the end of the story is that, over the years, I made minimal on the royalties from both those songs, because I was just getting television airplay royalties. It was only paid each time that particular episode aired. Rick moved to Phoenix many, many years ago, and I used to go over there and visit him. He wasn't making a whole lot of money then. He was kind of getting by on odd jobs, and I remember one time I was over there he said, 'You know, I've been getting all of the royalty checks for "All of the Things,"' and I said, 'That's OK.' I didn't think anything more of it, and that was the last connection I had with the song.

"My guess is that when Rick tweaked the lyrics on it, and they did all of the filing for it in publishing, they just put his name on it instead of mine," says Price. "Rock and roll history. That's how it goes."

When Price came to L.A. he first worked on *The Monkees* as a 5'10" stand-in for the 5'4" Davy Jones. "I crouched a lot!" Price laughs. He and Rick Klein became their head roadies in '66 and '67, and eventually went back to playing in bands after the Monkees petered out.

"I was just living down in Hollywood writing songs. 'All of the Things' had this kind of folky influence. I just wrote it because it came out of my brain that way. I guess I must have been feeling in a positive mood that day. I had never written with the thought of a hit record in mind. I just wrote whatever came out. This one just happened to be in three-quarter time, God knows why. When I was writing, particularly back in those days, I would be sitting around my little cheesy apartment in Hollywood with just my acoustic guitar, strumming away, and things would just come out," he says. "I was surprised that the Partridge Family did this song in the first place because it was in three-quarter time. Nobody was really doing three-quarter pop songs in those days. My first reaction when Rick said they were going to use it was *Oh, that's pretty interesting.*

"I think it's an emotionally positive song. It was a time when people wanted to feel good about themselves, and that's what it's about—*"good things are coming to me"*—it's optimistic.

"David Cassidy probably interpreted it better than any way I ever did," continues Price. "I was doing it just as a solo acoustic thing. I was pleased with the Partridge version. I thought it was interesting to hear it with full instrumentation, and David's a good singer. I think he sold the song very well, and I always felt he was a very talented guy."

There is an interesting use of a bluesy organ solo in the middle of the song, reminiscent of the '60s, suggesting a Ray Charles or Doors nod in the middle of the song. "What impresses me about the organ solo was that here you have this little pop tune about feeling upbeat and doing great, and then the organ solo comes in," says Price. "About halfway through the organ solo the guy starts playing some blues licks. Now all of a sudden there's this dominant seventh thing going on. I like it because it throws a little tension into the song. I think the organ part is really key to the arrangement. It's a very interesting little tag in the middle of that solo. It's very unexpected. Very cool. Credits to whoever came up with that." (Thank you, Mike Melvoin!)

"Listening to the song again makes me think of those times," says Price. "It makes me think of Coco Dolenz, who was, and still is, a great vocalist. I can still remember the two of us singing 'All of the Things' down at the Troubadour on Hootenanny Night. It was very well received. That's the first thing I think of—but I also think about Rick. He passed away a few years ago, and we were very good friends. I'm bittersweet over it. I think of him, and how much I miss him."

"Stephanie" is one of only two Partridge songs featuring the name of a girl as the song title. ("Bandala" is the other one.) There are several versions of "Stephanie" out there somewhere in the Screen Gems vaults, including one by Bobby Sherman.

Appears On: Season 1, episode 25, "A Knight in Shining Armor" (March 19, 1971)

Warm My Soul, 2:33, Joerey Oritz

David Cassidy rocks out! "Warm My Soul" was originally considered for episode 18, "Soul Club." It was also reportedly considered for single release, but ultimately it was unused even as an album cut.

If Cassidy was already unhappy when he had to record the spoken section in "Doesn't Somebody Want to Be Wanted," it must have added fuel to the fire when this song, which was the kind of exciting rock-oriented song he wanted to do, went unreleased.

when we're singin'

The mix opens with a distorted fuzz guitar and harkens back to the Temptations' "Ball of Confusion." The gritty, edgy arrangement—likely the reason it was not used—is as close to hard rock as the Partridge Family would ever get.

Nearly two years later the song was given to Cassidy for inclusion on his second solo album, *Rock Me, Baby,* and the arrangement was reworked. The new version appeared on the album, but the original remained in the vaults.

Twenty-six years later, in 1998, Cassidy was promoting his CD *Old Trick New Dog* when he put together a bonus compilation CD, *David Cassidy's Partridge Family Favorites*. Now quite rare, it was sold exclusively through the QVC home shopping network with the purchase of *Old Trick New Dog*—and it includes "Warm My Soul" in its original fuzz-rock rendition.

When Farrell looked back on his Partridge Family choices, he reflected on the subject of marketing and image and how they influenced his decisions. "I was held back," said Farrell. "See, my roots came from recording rock and roll, rhythm and blues, and things like that. You couldn't project a certain image of kids on stage who were family oriented. We were restricted to a lot of things. We had some real serious restrictions. There were some reasonable ones, too. All of a sudden someone couldn't break out into a real complex solo because nobody could perfect that image. There were a lot of things that I ended up taking off of some cuts because sight and sound didn't match up."

Listen to the Sound, 2:06, John Michael Hill

John Michael Hill looks back on the origins of "Listen to the Sound," which was uniquely inspired by a mechanical sound effect: "I know perfectly well what was in my mind when I wrote that song," says Hill. "I was very taken with 'Cecilia,' by Simon & Garfunkel. They used a certain kind of echo on it. This is really technical, but it was echo you could only easily get at Columbia Studios in New York. They had a little machine with several tape heads on it that you could adjust. In effect, what you got was a bold kind of Sun Records echo, only it was adjustable, unlike Sun.

On the opening hook of 'Cecilia,' part of that is an effect. I thought, *Wow! That effect is cool!* For 'Listen to the Sound,' I was definitely influenced by 'Cecilia,' mainly sonically, and so to some extent I was writing a song around the effect. I mean, 'Cecilia' was very simple. It was just like three chords. 'Listen to the Sound' is the same thing—very simple, and also just three chords. It's that slapback tape echo effect that was very key in 'Cecelia' that I thought was pretty neat, and so I tried to emulate that."

Hill didn't know that the song had appeared on an episode of the show until after the fact. "I was *very* happy to hear about it," he says. "I was always kind of sad that 'Listen to the Sound' didn't make it onto one of the albums."

Just before it aired on the show, "Listen to the Sound" was released as a single on Columbia Records by a group called Wool. Hill produced the single himself, and his intended echo effect can be heard in the opening hook. The Partridge Family version does not make use of the original sound effect that inspired the song. Before Wes Farrell set out to redo the theme song for season 2, "Listen to the Sound" was one of the songs considered for the slot.

Appears On: Season 2, episode 28, "A Man Called Snake" (October 1, 1971)

It's Time That I Knew You Better, 3:00, Terry Cashman–Tommy West

With the formulaic "getting to know the girl" theme and an organ interlude in the bridge, this song is every ounce a Partridge Family song.

Besides the version used on the show, with a David Cassidy lead vocal, there's an unreleased recording with a female lead vocal singing a demo-like rendition of the song, coming off a bit more folky. It can be found on the Screen Gems records, volume 3C. This version was intended for use on episode 39, "Where Do Mermaids Go?" guest starring Meredith Baxter, but it was ultimately not used.

Terry Cashman and Tommy West were both proud of this song and surprised it didn't make it to an album. "I think it's one of the better ones we wrote," says West. Cashman agrees. "It's a nice melody. It's a good song." West speculates, "By that time Jim Croce's records were released. We were recording our own albums for ABC Dunhill and producing Jim, so it was really a busy time and there was so much going on that it probably got lost in the shuffle." "It's Time That I Knew You Better" was considered for the new theme song in season 2, but again the duo's work was passed up.

And what about the mysterious female lead vocal on the Screen Gems record? It's not Jackie Ward. It's not Sally Stevens. And it's not a voice that either Cashman or West can recognize. Was there actually a scene using this song shot for the episode? Shirley Jones has a vague memory of a scene that may have been cut, where they were all sitting around singing. So who's voice could it have been? We'll probably never know for sure, but Meredith Baxter began her early studies at Interlochen Center for the Arts and her major was—you guessed it—voice.

Appears On: Season 2, episode 39, "Where Do Mermaids Go?" (December 31, 1971)

God Bless You, Girl, 2:58, Irwin Levine–L. Russell Brown

"'*God only knows what I'd be without you*' was the first time *God* was used in a record on the radio," says John Bahler of "God Only Knows," the song his friend Tony Asher co-wrote with Brian Wilson for the Beach Boys. "[Tony] almost came to blows with Brian Wilson out in the alley behind Wally Heider's [recording studio], because Brian said, 'You can't say *God* on the record!' Tony said, 'You're not saying it like

God damn, you're saying it like *God only knows what….*' After a huge argument they finally settled it, and the rest is history."

Though Bahler didn't seem to think it was of any concern in the early '70s, even for the Partridge Family, it's still a possible reason that Farrell left "God Bless You, Girl" on the cutting room floor. Since Farrell didn't use a single reference to God or anything spiritual on the entire *Christmas Card* album, he may have been playing it safe with his target audience. Farrell was after the broadest buyer market he could get.

"We always wrote hoping we'd get a single," says L. Russell Brown of himself and his co-writer Irwin Levine. "'Write me a great song,' Wes would say. 'Write me a great song, boys.'"

"'God Bless You, Girl' was another statement song. Unlike the story songs we wrote for Tony Orlando, we felt statement songs—professions of love—were the way we should approach David Cassidy. 'God Bless You, Girl' was Irwin's idea of the ultimate profession of love."

But Levine liked to write songs that were complex and open for interpretation. Brown explains, "Most of the time Irwin Levine was the fantasizer about things. A lot of times he was the person who was writing about situations of longing. He was into that. He knew how to state those things. Irwin was the impetus behind writing 'God Bless You, Girl.' When I sing 'God Bless You Girl,' I believe Irwin wrote that in a bittersweet way. You know? He didn't really mean it in such a nice way. It was like God bless you … for screwin' me over, God bless you … for breaking my heart."

But the man loved to fantasize, and he had songs for that. If you look deeper into them, you'll find deeper meaning." "God Bless You, Girl" was one of those songs that had that meaning.

"God Bless You, Girl" first appeared on the debut episode of the second season and was performed in an outdoor arena that resembled the Hollywood Bowl.

Appears On: Season 3, episode 50, "This Male Chauvinist Piggy Went to Market" (September 15, 1972); Season 3, episode 73, "Diary of a Mad Millionaire" (March 23, 1973)

I Don't Care, 2:39, Wes Farrell–Bobby Hart
Neither do we. Sometimes lost songs are lost for a reason.

Appears On: Season 3, episode 71, "The Partridge Connection" (March 9, 1973)

Sunshine Eyes, 2:35, Terry Cashman–Tommy West
This one would have fit nicely on *Crossword Puzzle,* with its gorgeous opening lick and its strength as a ballad. "I remember all the songs we wrote," says Tommy West, "though I don't particularly remember every lyric. They were all catchy songs with nice pop choruses and hooks. I guess that's why they were used. I always thought

'Sunshine Eyes' was a real commercial song. When you mentioned the title, I could immediately hear the chorus I had written."

"Sunshine Eyes" appeared in a memorable episode, with Arte Johnson guest starring as a home invader. Johnson performs the harmonica heard in the bridge of this song, arranged for the TV episode version. A complete version that includes the cut second verse can be heard on the Screen Gems record volume 6D.

Appears On: Season 3, episode 64, "For Whom The Bell Tolls ... And Tolls ... And Tolls" (January 12, 1973)

Whale Song, 3:38, Dan Peyton–Marty Kaniger

The story behind "Whale Song" reveals a plot that twists as frequently as a screenplay.

"We wanted to be songwriters," says co-writer Dan Peyton of the time he and writing partner Marty Kaniger were writers for Screen Gems Columbia Music. "Our contract called for us to write one song a week, so various things would come up and we would generate songs. We would write for our own band, but by this time the band wasn't really active, so Marty and I ended up focusing on writing as a team. We agreed to do everything 50 per cent."

Kaniger says, "Every writer over there wanted to give stuff to the Monkees and to the Partridge Family, and it was near impossible unless you were at the top of the pecking order. When it came to the Partridge Family, Wes Farrell obviously had first shot at everything, as far as writing. It was his material and pretty much his choice. So we were always suggesting when we came in with songs, 'What about the Partridge Family? What about the Monkees?' Then one day we got a call."

"They wanted to know if we were available to write a song for the Partridge Family, but the catch was that David wouldn't be singing the song. Instead it was going to be Shirley. I don't know how many other writers they asked before they asked us, but most of the writers just said, 'Nah, I gotta get the car washed,' you know? It just wasn't worth it for a lot of the writers because there wasn't going to be that much money in it. It would be done more for the glory of it all. No potential for a hit single, or at the very least, an album cut. But Dan and I figured work is work, and whatever comes along we would do a good job and move up the ladder there, so we said sure.

"It sounded interesting when they gave us the rundown on the show's storyline. They gave us a synopsis and at that point we wrote the song. They didn't just need a song that was going to be a good song for David, or a potential hit, or even a good album cut. They needed something specific to the actual story. It was made clear that the song would probably not make it to any of the Partridge Family albums, solo albums, or even singles for Shirley. We understood it was just going to be used in the show. It was good credit and it was work, and it just honed our craft as songwriters," says Kaniger.

when we're singin'

Dan Peyton remembers searching for an angle on the song. "The song was written in my bedroom in Pacific Palisades," he recalls. "Marty and I were both still living with our parents. We got together, and I remember sitting on my bed kicking around ideas. We were thinking about the atmosphere of the song and the general feeling of it and it was kind of a dilemma. We were sitting there for a long time thinking, *How do we get into this?* We told them we'd do it, but it was tough. Also, what do you say? It's one thing to come up with music that has the right feel for something like that, but it was another thing to decide if we should talk about the script. Do we talk about the mean guy who's going to hurt the whale? What do you say?

"So this idea came to me that I'm really singing about the whale and about the beauty of the whale song," continues Peyton. "Because the whale's sound is a gorgeous, haunting, beautiful sound. I think that is what gives people goose bumps when they hear it. The other thing is that we were sad at that time because the whale industry was killing them off. I remember thinking, *Wouldn't it be terrible if we lose them?* So that became a kind of subtheme in the song. And if that happens, *"Will the song of the man be the next song to go?"* I felt we had to say that. This song had a lot of elements in it that were timely.

"I remember singing some ideas to Marty and him saying, 'I think we're on the right track.' We came up with those three verses. There's no real bridge in it, and it's in three-quarter time, which would be a slow, melancholy kind of thing. It was right. They loved it. They absolutely loved it."

Then the plot turned.

The writers were told the song was going to include the actual sounds of real whales. "When we made our demo," begins Kaniger, "we took the Judy Collins song 'Farewell to Tarwathie' from her album *Whales and Nightingales,* which used whale sounds from *Songs of the Humpback Whale,* and we used those whale sounds for our demo. The intro to 'Whale Song' on our demo is about 20 seconds of just whales. As it turned out, our demo was exactly like the way Wes produced it for the Partridge Family."

"We made a tape," continues Kaniger, "and we took the 'Farewell to Tarwathie' song and recorded only the whales from the beginning of the song. Then we copied it to another tape recorder. We recorded it again, and again, and again, until we had probably 25, 30 feet of spliced quarter-inch tape with just the whale sounds so that it would run about 20 seconds before it would start to repeat.

"We did this at Dan Peyton's parents' house in his bedroom! We had the two tape recorders and we took that tape loop, ran it from one tape recorder, around the handle of the window, and with a broomstick, Dan wedged it in between the mattress and the bed frame, looping it around that, and it literally went around the whole room and back in the recorder again. It was the biggest Rube Goldberg thing. I wish we would have taken pictures of that. We put a sign on the door saying *Do not open the door* because if anybody had opened the door, the whole thing would have failed. All of the tape would have slacked. We couldn't run it too many times because those splices were not going to last long going over metal and wood.

"We recorded it onto a single tape, and we ran that as the beginning of the song. Then I came in with the guitar and did the vocal. We used the whale sounds in the beginning of the song, and we dipped it down and brought it back up in between verses a little bit. At the end we brought it back up as the guitar faded out, and that's pretty much what Wes ended up doing. On their version, I think they have an ending on it," says Kaniger.

Peyton and Kaniger then dubbed copies of the tape and passed it on to Farrell. Kaniger says, "Once the demo was handed in, Wes Farrell made a deal with the New York Zoological Society, who had whale sounds that could be used for the song, because there were copyright issues in using whale sounds from *Songs of the Humpback Whale*. The New York Zoological Society was also on board to donate proceeds for the cause, as well."

Kaniger continues, "I remember we were so excited. The New York Zoological Society had sent a tape for Wes to use. One of the people from Screen Gems called the day it arrived and said they received the package, so we went down to listen to it. Immediately we went 'Oh God! It's awful! It's awful!' They were not songs, and they certainly weren't pretty whale sounds! The sounds were just awful. They were very low, guttural sounds. It wasn't the kind of higher-pitched sounds that we had recorded on our demo. It really sounded awful. I mean it sounded like groaning and belching. It couldn't be used. Of course everybody was so disappointed, but they said, 'Well, let's give it to Wes. He'll figure it out.' And he did.

"We were down in Marineland when they filmed that show," says Kaniger, "and when I heard the final version of the song I said, 'That's certainly not what the Zoological Society sent us.' I know, because I had also received a copy of the final recording afterwards. It wasn't what we used. This was very nice. It was Wes' work and exactly what he needed to put on there."

The plot twists ... again!

"From what I remember," continues Kaniger, "Wes had gone over to the Elektra Studios in Hollywood on Ventura and La Cienega. He was doing some recording there and one of the engineers pulled some multitracks from the Judy Collins 'Farewell to Tarwathie' sessions. They had many tracks of just the whale sounds, and they just went through and used whatever they wanted to pull in and out. They found better sounds off of that! Then, for enhancement, I think Wes stepped up the whale sounds to get them to a better, higher pitch. That was not to be known because basically, he stole the whale sounds off of the Judy Collins multitrack! That's what we were told. We didn't know Wes that well. We met him a few times at the offices, but that's what we heard."

when we're singin'

Both writers to this day are very proud of this song. "It's one of my favorite songs that we ever wrote," says Kaniger. "It was at the time when we finished it, too. I thought we had a good melody. It was just a little guitar progression and it sounded so good on the 12-string. We liked the lyrics, and especially the subject matter. We really agreed with the environmental cause. Dan and I were both busy making music, so we weren't out there protesting that much, but if we could do something to draw people's attention for something like this, it was very satisfying."

Peyton says, "We hadn't expected the kind of choir in the background of the final version, but I like it because the whole family was involved in it. We thought for some time that it would make an interesting song in the environmental movement because it is very evocative, but nobody has ever picked it up. I think it still has something to say."

'Whale Song' led to an offer for work on the Bobby Sherman *Getting Together* series, and the two also wrote music for the motion picture *Getting Straight*. By the late '70s Peyton had left the music business and started a new career working in international relations. Kaniger continued in music, playing in a couple of bands—including Big Daddy, who in 2012 and 2013 fielded a successful Kickstarter campaign to fund a new album. The two reunite on occasion and have performed "Whale Song" a few times at the Cattle Company, a restaurant in Camarillo, California.

Tiger Beat and *TV Guide* both featured articles on the episode for which this song was written. Shirley Jones has always loved this song. It is her most memorable solo performance from the series, and she still receives requests for it. Screen Gems' top brass liked it so much it was planned to appear on *Sound Magazine*, but Wes Farrell argued against it because it didn't fit the commercial sound of the Partridge Family. Reporters were also announcing its probable release when the episode aired, dependent on the New York Zoological Society signing off on the use of the whale sounds.

One final note: Kaniger, through all these years, has been bothered by a transcription mistake in the lyrics. When Jones sings *"sing me a song of times that you knew, when the waters were clear and the sea birds, they flew,"* the intended lyric was actually *clean*, rather than *clear*, because *clear* is used in the following phrase—"*through a sky that was clear from the sea to the land.*"

Appears On: Season 2, Episode 31 "Whatever Happened to Moby Dick?" (October 22, 1971)

Ain't Love Easy, 3:18, *Carol Hall*

This was the second of three attempts to spawn a solo career for Shirley Jones in hopes of crossing her over to the pop charts. When Jones performed the song in the third season it was the last time she would sing solo on the show.

The song and the writer both seemed perfect for Jones, even if it didn't have the desired results. Carol Hall was in the early stages of her career, but she was rooted in the theater just as Jones was. Hall's first recorded composition was "Jenny Rebecca," picked up by Barbra Streisand for her album *My Name Is Barbra*. She since became best known for *The Best Little Whorehouse in Texas* and the song "Hard Candy Christmas," performed by Dolly Parton. Hall wrote often for children, with 10 years of work for *Sesame Street*. She also contributed several tracks to Marlo Thomas' *Free to Be ... You and Me*.

Appears On: Season 3, episode 57 "A Likely Candidate" (November 3, 1972)

My Best Girl, 2:42, Jerry Herman
Matters of the heart make us go that extra mile.

"My Best Girl" was originally written for the Broadway musical *Mame*; in fact, *My Best Girl* was the show's original title. *Mame* opened on Broadway in 1966 starring Angela Lansbury in the title role, though Herman had written the music and the show specifically with Judy Garland in mind. *Mame* closed in 1970 and spawned a 1974 film version with Lucille Ball in the title role.

"This song involves one of my favorite stories about my time on *The Partridge Family*," says producer Larry Rosen. "When I came on the show it was the beginning of the second season. Prime time TV was all about *The Partridge Family*, and David, and the group, and it was all wonderful—but I fell in love with Shirley.

"She's just such a delightful gal. She and I were both going through some private personal things with our marriages, and we used to hang out and have lunch on occasion and talk things out. She was also just the consummate professional.

"I used to go home at night and think about what we could do for her, and how we could showcase her. So one day I said to Claver, 'I'd love to give Shirley a solo somewhere in one of these episodes.' I've always been a fan of Broadway musicals. I used to produce *The Mike Douglas Show* years and years ago, and when I was in Philadelphia they brought *Mame* to town when it was in tryouts with Angela Lansbury. We had Angela on *The Mike Douglas Show* and I went to see *Mame* 15 times! The song from that show I loved the best was 'My Best Girl.' I loved that song so much it became one of my all-time favorites."

Rosen continues, "Ray Bolger and Rosemary DeCamp were the actors who played Shirley's parents on *The Partridge Family*. I had seen an episode from the first year of the show, before coming on as a producer, and I thought they were delightful. So I made it my business to make sure we did more stories with them, because they were such wonderful characters. During a second season episode we did one about the two of them breaking up after 50 years of marriage. So the story for the music was set up for the Partridge Family to perform one night and they would invite Shirley's parents, who weren't speaking to each other, to come to the concert.

when we're singin'

"This was an opportunity for me. I said to Claver, 'Bob, I want to do a solo song for Shirley. It's a song that's normally sung by a guy, and it's called "My Best Girl," from the musical *Mame*. The way I want to do it is to bring the parents into the nightclub and have Shirley introduce the song as something her dad always sang to her mother, and then Shirley will sing it as a solo performance.'

"Shirley had never heard the song before, so she and I got a pianist one day at the Columbia lot and I played her the song. She loved it! We worked on the song for about half an hour, and she did her solo with it. At the end of the song, in the scripted episode, Ray Bolger goes over to Rosemary and takes her hand and walks her out onto the dance floor and they sing as she does a reprise of the song. It was the song that brought them back together in the story, and it was Shirley's solo.

"I know that Shirley also did songs like 'Whale Song' as well, but that was still pretty much a Partridge Family song. I wanted to give Shirley one shot at doing a song as Shirley Jones, and this was it.

"People have always asked me what the highlights were from my time on *The Partridge Family*," adds Rosen, "and I always say that this is one of them. I wanted to give Shirley a solo on a song that happened to be one of my favorites for years. It worked so well into the episode, and she did it so beautifully."

Appears On: Season 2, episode 35, "The Forty-Year Itch" (November 19, 1971)

Let Me Call You Sweetheart, 1:36, Leo Friedman–Beth Slater Whitson

"Let Me Call You Sweetheart" is a popular old standard, published as sheet music in 1910 and first recorded by a group called the Peerless Quartet. It has been used on countless television shows, including *The Waltons*, which was airing during most of the same years as *The Partridge Family*.

According to Ron Hicklin's session notes, this was recorded on the same day as "My Best Girl." Television shows are planned right down to the second, and it's possible that this song was used as an alternate in case they needed to cut down on time. It's also possible that this performance was planned for another episode and never used.

Me Loving You, 2:16, Peggy Clinger–Johnny Cymbal

This beautiful ballad is a breathy Cassidy waltz and one of only four Partridge Family songs written in three-quarter time. A song like this was rare for the Partridge Family, and even more rare in commercial pop music. "Me Loving You" was mixed in both mono and stereo and made its way onto a test pressing of *The Partridge Family Notebook*, but ultimately it never appeared on a record or the TV show, making it a truly lost song. It was the only Partridge Family song by Cymbal and Clinger not to land on a record. But it can be found on Screen Gems Volume 6C.

THE LOST SONGS

I Was Running the Opposite Way, 2:02, Irwin Levine–L. Russell Brown

In the March 1972 issue of *Tiger Beat's Official Partridge Family Magazine*, there is a three-page spread advertising the much-anticipated release of David Cassidy's first solo album, *Cherish*. The spread features a complete track list for the album, including lyrics to all of the songs planned for inclusion.

"I Was Running the Opposite Way" is one of the songs announced for *Cherish*. The track was pulled from release, though. Strike one.

"I Was Running the Opposite Way" was later recorded and arranged for season 4, making it a possibility for *Bulletin Board*, but again it was passed up. Still it seemed predictable that it would appear on the television show, if not on an album. It was recorded for use on the show and placed on the Screen Gems records for the cast to learn. But it didn't make that cut either. Strike two.

L. Russell Brown says, "'I Was Running the Opposite Way' was one of many songs Irwin and I wrote while we both were signed to Wes. Unless it was a hit or it was used on the TV show or in an album, unfortunately we went on to our next tune. In order to remember hundreds of new songs, it's imperative that a writer blot other songs out of their minds. And that is the case with this song." Talk about a truly lost and forgotten song! Even the songwriter has dismissed it! Strike three—you're out!

I'll Be Your Magician, 2:04, Irwin Levine–L. Russell Brown

Originally demoed by David Cassidy for use in season 2, which could have led to release on *Sound Magazine* or *Shopping Bag*, "I'll Be Your Magician" later landed on Danny Bonaduce's solo album, a somewhat surprising choice because the lyrics are laden with the suggestive double meanings that Irwin Levine loved.

"I've written several magician songs," says L. Russell Brown. "I've always had a fascination with magicians. Levine and I wanted to write a song with a message that said *I will do anything to make you love me—I will even do magic*, and that is how this song came to be. I remember the song and always liked it."

Screen Gems use to advertise their catalog of music by putting three or four songs onto a vinyl pressing. The idea was to get other artists from other labels interested in licensing and recording a song. The Partridge Family version of this song was placed onto one of these pressings and shopped around, but it was never picked up by another artist. "I never knew that demo existed," said Brown after giving it a quick listen. "Obviously Wes Farrell produced it. Well done," he adds. Brown also teamed up with Billy Vera on another magician song, written for Lou Rawls, called "If I Were a Magician." He also wrote several other songs with similar themes. Aside from the industry pressing, the Partridge Family version was never used on either a record or the show.

when we're singin'

Crying in the Rain, 1:56, Howard Greenfield–Carole King
"Crying in the Rain" was originally recorded by the Everly Brothers in 1962 and peaked at No. 6 on the U.S. pop charts. The song was the only collaboration between Howard Greenfield and Carole King. They both worked for Aldon Music at the time of the song's composition, and a last-minute working arrangement put them together.

The Partridge Family's version is an excellent cover. It appeared at the top of episode 88, which introduced David and Andy Williams, nephews of the popular music and television star Andy Williams, in one of the attempted "replace David Cassidy" experiments for the hopeful season 5 renewal. The two brothers had just signed with Wes Farrell earlier that year. The Everly Brothers were Farrell's favorite recording act. Coincidentally the two Williams Brothers first began singing and harmonizing when they were young, listening to, and trying to imitate the Everly Brothers.

"Crying in the Rain" has been recorded by artists including Mickey Dolenz, Tammy Wynette, Crystal Gayle, and Art Garfunkel.

Appears On: Season 4, Episode 88, "Two for the Show" (January 19, 1974)

I'm into Something Good, 2:31, Gerry Goffin–Carole King
One of the fan favorites from season 4, this song was made famous by Herman's Hermits, who recorded it as their first single. It went straight to No. 1 in the U.K. and stayed on the charts there for two weeks before landing on the U.S. charts, where it peaked at No. 13 in the fall of 1964. The Partridge Family version captures the upbeat essence of the original recording and reflects Cassidy's ability to take a cover tune and make it his own.

The very first recording of this song was by Earl-Jean, former member of the group Cookies, going solo and hitting No. 38 on Billboard with it before Herman's Hermits made it famous. Since the Partridge Family recording in 1973, it has been used in a variety of feature films, and in 2010 it was used for an Australian McDonald's commercial.

Appears On: Season 4, episode 77, "Beethoven, Brahms, and Partridge" (September 29, 1973); Season 4, episode 85, "Al in the Family" (November 24, 1973)

Workin' on a Groovy Thing, 1:59, Neil Sedaka–Roger Atkins
David Cassidy's voice takes on a gritty, bluesy sound in the final year of the Partridge Family, and this song captures it well. The backing vocals also sound a little more mature, leaving some of the innocent sound behind.

Neil Sedaka was working to revive his solo career during the late '60s and early '70s. Despite his waning chart appeal in the United States, he was still very popular in the U.K. and Australia. He repositioned himself back on top with the support of his fan base, recording a new album of original material. The album was titled for the song *Workin' on a Groovy Thing*, which appeared as the opening track of side 2, recorded and released in 1969 by Festival Records in Australia. Oddly, the title song was never released as a single—in Australia or anywhere else. But in the States the 5th Dimension also recorded it that same year, in '69, on their *Age of Aquarius* album, garnering a No. 20 hit on *Billboard*'s Hot 100. The song played well as rhythm and blues—which likely appealed to Cassidy, who probably had a hand in choosing it.

Barbara Lewis released a version on her 1968 album *Working on a Groovy Thing*, and Patti Drew covered it in 1968, hitting No. 62 on the pop charts but doing better on the R&B charts at No. 34. Bola Sete, a Brazilian guitarist who had played jazz with Vince Guaraldi (of *Peanuts* fame) and Dizzy Gillespie, released it in 1970, also titling his album with the same name. Johnny Hammond, a soul and jazz organist, released it on his '71 album *Breakout*.

Appears On: Season 4, episode 86, "Maid In San Pueblo" (December 8, 1973), Season 4, episode 92 "Miss Partridge, Teacher" (February 23, 1974)

When Love's Talked About, 2:34, John Bahler–Wes Farrell

This is only one of two songs written by John Bahler, who remembers it as an idea mostly stemming from Wes Farrell. It was featured prominently on the season 4 location episode, which took the cast for a cruise along the Pacific coast. Both the episode and the song were quickly forgotten.

Appears On: Season 4, episode 81 "The Last Howard" " (October 27, 1973)

I Wanna Be with You, 2:29, Wes Farrell–Gerry Goffin

This is a rare Partridge Family leftover by the great Gerry Goffin, teaming up with Wes Farrell.

The song is very upbeat and lyrical. The opening is strong and Cassidy adeptly slams us with energy right off the bat. The quick lyric is reminiscent of Harriet Schock's "That's the Way It Is with You."

"I Wanna Be with You" was featured twice on the show during the last season, both times in episodes that featured a story about Danny.

Appears On: Season 4, episode 78, "The Strike-out King" (October 6, 1973); Season 4, episode 95, "Pin It on Danny" (March 16, 1974)

Lullaby...and Goodnight!

So often there was music used on the show that was intended simply as a sound cue rather than a featured musical presentation. "I Think I Love You" was rearranged into a classical version; "The Love Song" was heard as a sound cue; and "Together (Havin' a Ball)" is heard in several different short sound cue arrangements. Then there were all the special endings recorded for the TV versions of the songs.

when we're singin'

One verse of the classical composition best known as the Brahms lullaby was sung by David Cassidy during a season 3 episode in which he is trying to lull a horse to sleep. Though the scenario on the show is pure situation comedy, the moment is an episode highlight for fans of Cassidy's voice.

Other songs were used on the show for various purposes and recorded by other artists. "Say It Again" was sung by the Williams Brothers during their guest appearance, which was intended to stimulate interest in a new angle for the show. A comically bad version of "I Left My Heart in San Francisco" was recorded for the season 2 opener, "Dora, Dora, Dora," and sung by the actress Robyn Millan, and an intentionally butchered-up version of Mann and Weil's "You've Lost That Lovin' Feeling" was sung by Jackie Ward as another option for the same episode, but never used. Even "Because" by d'Hardelot and Lockton, published in 1902, showed up for about 10 seconds of Cassidy crooning at a biker's wedding!

"Ba Ba Ba" is noted by Hicklin as a completed recording, though it likely refers to a backing vocal that was probably discarded rather than any particular song. During the final episode of season 1, the cast and Bobby Sherman can be briefly seen and heard singing 'Ba Ba Ba,' using their real voices rather than lip-syncing. The melody is strikingly similar to Bobby Sherman's "Little Woman," which was then on the charts.

The female version of the lead vocal on "It's Time That I Knew You Better" was never used on the show, and Hicklin's notes also reflect outtakes "What a Day," recorded for the pilot, and "Bad Time," which was done during the same session that produced the songs for the Colagé single.

I Left My Heart in San Francisco — Season 2, episode 26, "Dora, Dora, Dora" (September 17, 1971)

Ba, Ba, Ba (a cappella) — Season 1, episode 25, "A Night in Shining Armor" (March 19, 1971)

Because — Season 3, episode 54, "A Penny for His Thoughts" (October 13, 1972)

Lullaby (Traditional) — Season 3, episode 61, "Nag, Nag, Nag" (December 8, 1972)

I Think I Love You (Classical version) — Season 4, episode 77, "Beethoven, Brahms, and Partridge" (September 29, 1973)

Say It Again — Season 4, episode 88, "Two for the Show" (January 19, 1974)

LIFE AFTER PARTRIDGE
or ... The Partridge Family Time Capsule

Moving On

The mid- and late '70s brought different struggles and opportunities to post-Partridge professionals as everyone moved on to their next gig.

Wes Farrell closed the Wes Farrell Organization in 1977 and moved to Florida. John and Tom Bahler continued to do vocal work. As Chelsea Records began its decline, John and Tony Asher started Asher/Bahler and Associates, also called Producer's Music Service, which produced jingles for commercials and various companies. Tom Bahler went on to become an established songwriter, penning hits such as Cher's "Living in a House Divided" and Michael Jackson's "She's Out of My Life." Jackie Ward and Ron Hicklin both continued to work as background vocalists. Ron particularly wanted to move into doing vocals for motion pictures and commercials, where there was a lot more opportunity than in making records.

The musicians known as the Wrecking Crew maintained their demand for work up into the '80s. The new sound of music was becoming heavily synthesized, changing the demand for live musicians, and those who did prefer organic sounds were playing their own instruments. The pace at which records were being made was also slowing down.

While David Cassidy attempted to take a breather, he signed with RCA for a three-album deal. His personal life took a difficult turn when his father, Jack Cassidy, died tragically in a fire at his penthouse apartment in 1976. The two had been estranged and had not spoken for nine months before Jack's death. Cassidy found great comfort in his relationship with his close friends and family, especially his brothers, as he struggled with his father's death. "I talked to David a lot," remembers Shirley Jones. "Jack was not an easy father. He didn't want David to be a rock star." There was a strong pulling together of the entire Cassidy family as they made their way through the grieving process.

Jones went on to do many made-for-TV movies, guest appearances, concerts, and albums. She married Marty Ingels in 1977, and by 1979 she had landed her own short-lived series, *Shirley*.

The other cast members all continued to work in the industry, for the most part. Dave Madden landed his next long-running gig as a semi-regular on *Alice*, which ran from 1976 to 1985.

when we're singin'

Susan Dey had the most successful post-Partridge television career. She made some films and made-for-TV movies and eventually landed several series, including the short-lived *Loves Me, Loves Me Not* in 1977, and *Emerald Point N.A.S.* in 1983. Her most long-running role was that of Grace Van Owen on *L.A. Law*, which ran from 1986 to 1992.

Danny Bonaduce struggled to keep afloat, for many years tagged as a child star gone bad. During the late '70s he guest starred on several series, including *Fantasy Island, Eight Is Enough*, and *CHiPs*, and did a few low-budget movies.

Suzanne Crough did a few made-for-TV movies and TV series guest appearances. She earned great respect for her work in the Academy Award–winning film short *Teenage Father*. The producers made special mention of Crough at the awards ceremony in 1978 while giving their acceptance speech. She also had a regular role on the short-lived series *Mulligan's Stew*. Like Jones, her family priorities came first. She eventually left the business to raise her children.

Jeremy Gelbwaks and Brian Forster enjoyed a return to normal childhood and regular schooling. They never went back into the professional world of acting but have taken part in the nostalgia that comes with having done a show of such longevity and influence. Gelbwaks says, "Even with my little minor character there, people pay attention to you in ways big and small that most people don't get to experience. If it's suddenly taken away, if all of a sudden it's not there anymore, it can be very confusing. I mean, I don't think I was in it long enough to get confused, but I will say the first year or so after leaving the program it was a little harder than later. I went off to a middle school in Virginia, and people knew who I was before I got there. It was a little bit scary."

Though his stint on the final season of *The Partridge Family* did nothing to save the show's ratings, little Ricky Segall benefited greatly. He went on to do toy commercials and guest spots on *The Tonight Show, Little House on the Prairie, Police Woman*, and *The Merv Griffin Show*, then drew on his years of tap lessons to become one of the Don Crichton Dancers on *The Tim Conway Show*.

The Partridge Family 2200 A.D.

During the last season of *The Partridge Family*, animated versions of the show's characters made guest appearances on *Goober and the Ghost Chasers* before being developed into the short-lived show *The Partridge Family 2200 A.D.*, an attempt to build on Hanna-Barbera's success with *The Jetsons*.

During each episode the cartoon family performs a concert number, just as the real actors did on the original series. Bobby Hart remembers that he and Danny

Janssen wrote the songs for the series—"a dozen songs, I think, which we probably wrote in about two weeks."

The show's 16 episodes ran from September 7 to December 21, 1974. All the cast except Shirley Jones and David Cassidy signed on to do voiceover work for the series, but Susan Dey left after two episodes to pursue other film projects.

"I didn't fancy myself a great actor, because Danny Partridge was so close to me," says Danny Bonaduce. "It wasn't hard for me to do *The Partridge Family*, but it was hard for me to do the Partridge Family cartoons where words like *yikes* were written into the scripts. They'd say, 'No, no, no, no! You're falling down a giant chute to a trap door and you have to go like this: YIIIIIIIIIIIIIIIKKKKEEESS!' Really? I was 12, man. I couldn't do that. That wasn't for me. I didn't care much for the Partridge Family cartoons, but it was extra money so I did it."

The Laurie House Album

In 1976, television commercials for a new Partridge Family album suddenly began showing up. Released by budget mail-order label Laurie House, the album—simply titled *The Partridge Family*—was a cheaply done record with an equally cheap and flimsy cover that was a rip-off of the *Up to Date* design with washed-out colors. The collection featured a poorly mastered rehash of the hits, with a few David Cassidy solo hits mixed in. The double album set was also available as an eight-track. It was forgotten as quickly as it was released but has since become a rare collector's item.

The Partridge Family/My Three Sons Reunion

The Partridge Family had been off the air for three years when the first reunion happened. *The Partridge Family/My Three Sons Reunion* was produced by Dick Clark Productions as a Thanksgiving special. It featured the casts of both shows sharing the spotlight and sitting down for a scripted get-together. By today's standards, the canned nature of the show is laughable.

David Cassidy sang two songs, "Strengthen My Love" (recorded for his upcoming series, *David Cassidy: Man Undercover*) and the standard "As Time Goes By," and Shirley Jones sang "He Touched Me."

Susan Dey taped a segment from the movie set where she was working on location. Suzanne Crough missed a day of taping because of a scheduling conflict with *Mulligan's Stew* and was spliced into some of the scenes, although she is missing from the final bows at the end of the show.

when we're singin'

David Cassidy: Man Undercover

In spring 1978 David Cassidy guest starred on the final episode of *Police Story*. The episode, titled "A Chance to Live," featured Cassidy as Dan Shay, an undercover officer working to bust a high school drug ring. The episode received the series' highest ratings in its five-year history, and Cassidy was honored with an Emmy nomination for Outstanding Lead Actor for a Single Appearance in a Drama or Comedy Series. The high ratings and nomination led to a spinoff series proposal.

David Cassidy: Man Undercover—his name was added to the title at the last minute for better recognition—was produced by David Gerber and *Partridge Family* veteran Mel Swope. The show's original plan included a musical element that was later cut. Before the premiere, *Variety* announced "Cassidy's NBC-TV Drama Series Angles Music for Disk Spinoff." The article detailed the plans: "The new David Gerber–Columbia Pictures Television series for NBC-TV, 'David Cassidy—Man Undercover,' already has a lot riding on its music…. The music is being designed to revitalize Cassidy's career as a recording artist, and maybe even turn up new songwriters and musical performers the way the same studio's 'The Monkees' and 'Partridge Family' series spotlighted Carole King, Gerry Goffin and Carol Bayer Sager, among others."

Cassidy and Gerber wrote the title theme to the series, "Hard Times," also intended for single release, and a follow-up love theme. It was part of a plan engineered by another Partridge Family veteran, Brendan Cahill, who was now the music supervisor at Columbia Pictures Television.

Cahill modeled the concept on the score (which he had helped produce) of *Midnight Express*, a dramatic film released only a month before *Man Undercover*. The plan was to incorporate commercial music into the show—some performed by Cassidy as part of the script storylines, and some by other artists to be used as theme and incidental music for individual episodes. One planned storyline sent Cassidy's character undercover as an auditioner for a disco job, while another put him undercover as a member of a rock group. The hope was to trigger interest in another merchandising spinoff, but these particular episodes were never produced.

Cassidy recorded a number of songs for the show, even though the theme song was the only one to end up on the air. In 1991, Curb Records released a limited number of copies in Japan of a CD that included 11 lost Cassidy songs from the *Man Undercover* sessions that included versions of "Junked Heart Blues" and "I Never Saw You Coming," songs first heard on his final RCA album, *Gettin' It in the Street*. The Curb Records collection was inaccurately titled *The Best of David Cassidy*. A different version of the CD was reissued by Curb in 1998 as *David Cassidy Classic Songs*, with only eight songs from the previous release, this time including "I Think I Love You." Again, the title was misleading to consumers.

David Cassidy: Man Undercover lost its footing early on, and reviews were moderate to unfavorable. *Variety* wrote, "A formula cop show without distinction … relies on the youth appeal of its star, and the standard elements of squealing tires and violence. The 'Police Story' touch of realism is that Cassidy plays a family man—loyal wife Wendy Rastatter and baby girl make three—and thus reduces the heartthrob appeal to teenyboppers…. The show has no special quality, so whether it works depends solely on Cassidy's appeal."

David Cassidy: Man Undercover did well in Japan, but poorly in the United States. It ran on Thursdays for 10 episodes, from November 2, 1978, to January 18, 1979. It was eventually canceled because of its poor ratings, though Mel Swope really believed in the show's possibilities.

"The network canceled the show too early," says Mel Swope. "Fred Silverman to this day will say he made a mistake on that one. It needed more time to catch on. It used to be that a show was given enough time and publicity to get the audience. Nowadays, as you can see, shows don't last very long. People get impatient."

The one single released from the recording sessions was "Hurt So Bad," backed with "Once A Fool." Written by Teddy Randazzo, Bobby Weinstein, and Partridge alum Bobby Hart, "Hurt So Bad" had been a hit in 1965 by Little Anthony & the Imperials. Cassidy's version was barely noticed, but a year later Linda Ronstadt scored one of her biggest hits with it.

The '80s: Partridge Who?

The 1980s were the bleakest of years for anyone who wanted more of *The Partridge Family*. Where puka shells and matching outfits were once cool, it was now all about punk, new wave, the moonwalk, and the Material Girl. The easygoing spirit of the '70s was left behind with platform shoes.

David Cassidy decided to return to the place where he had left off—England. He put together a record deal with Arista Records and released an album in 1985 titled *Romance*, produced by Alan Tarney. The album was a product of its time, sampling the electronic sounds of the '80s. Up-and-coming star George Michael can be heard singing backup vocals on the "The Last Kiss," and Basia sings on "Romance (Let Your Heart Go.)"

Alan Tarney co-wrote all of the songs with Cassidy except one. The album spawned several singles overseas, including "The Last Kiss," "Romance (Let Your Heart Go)," "She Knows All About Boys" and "Someone." "The Last Kiss" was the biggest success, peaking at No. 6 in the UK and charting all over Europe and Australia. The album was unavailable in the States until 2012, when Real Gone Music released it on CD.

when we're singin'

Cassidy also decided it was time to get back on stage and perform live again. In October 1985 he played at London's Royal Albert Hall. It was the first concert he had performed since 1974. The set list was made up primarily of songs from *Romance*, though several of his old hits were included. The concert was recorded and released as a double album set titled *David Cassidy's Greatest Hits Live* in 1986. Neither *Romance* nor *David Cassidy's Greatest Hits Live* was ever released on vinyl in the States.

Partridges vs. Bradys

In 1992 Susan Dey was asked to guest host *Saturday Night Live*. The catch? A garage band sing-off parody between *The Partridge Family* and *The Brady Bunch* with Dey playing Laurie Partridge. The sketch is classic *SNL*, especially when the camera catches Dey struggling to keep a straight face. It was finally the beginning of the return to cool for *The Partridge Family*.

As the decades passed, *The Brady Bunch* seemed to air in syndication continually while *The Partridge Family* faded.

"I think the big difference between Partridge and Brady Bunch is that they really included all of the kids in Brady Bunch and with us it was just so focused around the main characters—the top guys—and us little ones were just left out most of the time," says Brian Forster. Danny Bonaduce says, "In my opinion, *The Partridge Family* is a far better show because it brought you a higher quality cast," he says. "No offense to *The Brady Bunch*, but if you were to do a where-are-they-now story, you know immediately where three or four of us are from *The Partridge Family*, but you'll have to hunt for most of *The Brady Bunch*."

Executive producer Bob Claver agrees. "Kids like Susan got off as soon as the show ended and quickly landed other things and started nice careers. I don't understand it at all," says Claver of America's fascination with the Bradys. The actors on our show were better, easier to like, and funnier. That's not a bad combination. You've got a guy like David Cassidy and he can be cute and all the rest of it, but he's also very funny. He knows how to play comedy. Everybody on that show could." But yet the proof of the pudding is that *The Brady Bunch* is still running better than *The Partridge Family*. To this day, it's very successful."

Why has *The Brady Bunch* lived on so consistently in syndication while *The Partridge Family* has not? "From my experience in producing television, musical numbers are a good time to tune out and see what else is on, no matter how much you liked the band," says Danny Bonaduce, "because you have three or four minutes to get back to see the end of that song. Maybe the lack of syndication had something to do with the musical numbers."

LIFE AFTER PARTRIDGE

Some of the story lines on *The Brady Bunch* were very similar to those on *The Partridge Family*. "We go on a cruise. They go to Hawaii. We go to King's Island, Ohio. They go to King's Island, Ohio. We sang, so they're going to try to sing," says Suzanne Crough, laughing. But the Partridges are guilty of a little copycatting as well: Crough's Patti Partridge doll, introduced at the top of the second season, was an obvious attempt to cash in on the *Brady Bunch* success with Kitty Carryall.

"The songs and the authenticity of the musicianship was the big difference between the two," says Rick Segall. "David Cassidy was a real-life musical talent. Shirley Jones was also a musical talent. So the Partridge Family as a musical family capitalized on something that was very, very real about the people doing the show."

Dale McRaven reflects, "At the time the show was going on, people came to me and they said, 'You know *The Brady Bunch* is stealing your shows.' This is after the Brady Bunch became singers, which they stole from the Partridge Family itself, but, I said, 'Well, that happens.' I've written jokes, and comedians have called me up and said, 'You stole my joke,' and I didn't know the comedian and I didn't steal their joke. I just came up with the same joke—you know, that happens. And it happens where people will come up with the same idea, and I just kind of marked it off to that. And boy, like 10 years later I was in a different room and the TV was on. I never watched *The Brady Bunch*. I never watched much television at all because I was generally working, but I hear this dialogue, and it's dialogue I had written, but by actors I never wrote for! They stole one of my scripts that I had written, and they were doing the jokes! They didn't just take the idea, they took the dialogue too! Apparently, it happened on several occasions. If you were just a casual observer you may not see the similarity."

While it's fun to discuss *The Brady Bunch* as though there were a contest between the shows, they actually worked to support the same network, and most fans of one show tend to be fans of the other one, too.

The Lost Reunion

Nearly every show from the '60s had a reunion show in the '70s and '80s. *Gilligan's Island* finally saw the rescue of the castaways, and countless Brady revivals began soon after that show was canceled. In 1988, producer Larry Rosen began putting together a story premise and cast negotiations for a much-anticipated *Partridge Family* reunion show.

"When I was still with Columbia, the head of Columbia Pictures Television had a script deal with a writer," begins Rosen, "and he wanted to see if I was interested in producing a reunion show, or a show that would involve a Partridge Family concept, because he thought he could sell it in Europe. This writer and I came up with an idea that involved Keith and Danny, now grown up. Danny was now more like the Dave Madden character."

when we're singin'

The plot for the pilot called for Keith to travel to London for a performance, where he meets an exchange student and falls in love. With plans to get married, he calls up the rest of the family and they all go to London for the wedding—and, of course, some singing. The special was planned as a one-off with hopes that high ratings would merit a potential spinoff series.

"The rest of the pilot story involved the family falling into a situation where they meet up with this English band," continues Rosen. "It was these three guys who were part of an old rock and roll group. The family would bring them back to the States and it was going to become a kind of new Partridge Family." The idea was to spin off a new musical group over in London, then bring it back here, involving all of the original characters. In the end it was about launching this new group that Danny was going to manage."

"I just think we had the wrong writer," continues Rosen. "We needed Dale McCraven to do it, but the studio had this pay-for-play deal with this writer and they wanted to write it off on *The Partridge Family* deal. They said we had to use him so we did, and consequently it never went anywhere. The script was terrible. The guy was an awful writer, and we never got it launched.

"Another key element in all of it was Susan Dey. They would have wanted Susan to be in the movie, but Susan was involved with *L.A. Law* at the time and had no interest in going back to *The Partridge Family*. And so whether or not we had a good script, it still would have killed the deal if we couldn't deliver Susan, and I don't think, even with a good script, that we would have been able to deliver her.

"Susan had no interest. I didn't blame her. She had her whole career going at the time, and the last thing she wanted to do was be Laurie Partridge again, so the way we wrote the script was that Laurie was always out of town somewhere. The joke was that they were always trying to find Laurie and couldn't find her, but that wasn't satisfying to the studio. But needless to say, that wasn't the main thing. The main thing was the script wasn't very good. It would have been fun. We really tried to put that thing together."

"I was still under contract with the studio and I was six months pregnant when they put me under contract for the special," says Suzanne Crough. "We signed the contract and it was a good contract. It was lucrative."

Brian Forster says, "I remember at one point going into the producer's office and walking out and there was Dave Madden about to go in. We were all pretty excited about the idea of being able to work again, and we'd make a lot more money than we did the first time. My mom and I were especially happy about it because my family was all from England, and we were going to shoot this in London, so I thought I might get to see all my relatives and get paid to do it!"

"The reunion show has come up several times," says Danny Bonaduce. "I would still do it!," he says. "The Bradys were doing *The Brady Wives*, *The Bradys Get Married*,

LIFE AFTER PARTRIDGE

The Bradys Walk Down the Street, The Bradys Make Breakfast—it was obvious that the Partridge Family should do one, right? But the answer was always no. We were never going to do one. I think it was *Newsweek* magazine that quoted me as saying that if there were ever a Partridge reunion and there was no one there to stop me, I'd play my part and Laurie's! I'd still like to do it! I think it would be fun!" (Both Dave Madden and Suzanne Crough were still alive at the time of this interview, it should be noted.)

"They tried to get that going forever," adds Shirley Jones, "but one problem was the music. They couldn't use any of the music, and to have a family reunion we needed the music. Besides that, Susan Dey didn't want to be a part of it. I'm not sure, to be very honest with you, that David wanted to be a part of it, either."

By the '90s the new thing was movies poking fun at old television shows. Once again, *The Brady Bunch* went to the front of the line, making at least three feature films with young actors taking a satirical approach to the original characters, leaving the original cast members relegated to cameo appearances. "At one point, one of the studios was talking about possibly doing a Partridge Family film," recalls producer Paul Witt. "David called me. I hadn't heard about it. He said, 'Can you just see if you can find out about it and protect our legacy so we don't come off like buffoons?' The film was never made, which is probably a good thing."

'90s Retro

Where Susan Dey had made her way out of the Partridge image by reinventing herself on *L.A. Law,* David Cassidy did the same thing through his music. Cassidy has said on many occasions that it seemed like no one wanted to hear his name, and then suddenly when the '90s came around he was cool again.

In 1990 David Cassidy was back in a big way with his first U.S. album release in over a decade, simply titled *David Cassidy*. Fondly thought of by fans as "the comeback album," it gives insight to Cassidy's persona and musical expression at this point in his life. The album is some of his best work. Eight of the 10 songs were written by Cassidy and his future wife, Sue Shifrin, who had known him since his heyday in the '70s.

His first single, "Lyin' to Myself," put him back on the *Billboard* charts after a 15-year absence. The single rose to No. 27 on Billboard. *David Cassidy* was released on Enigma. Despite the potential for several more singles, as bad timing would have it the label went under as the album was just breaking out.

A year later, in 1991, Cassidy went back on tour for the first time since his England concert in 1985. The first regularly scheduled performance was held at Hershey Park, a small amusement park in Hershey, Pennsylvania, with two show-ings. Later concerts included Danny Bonaduce's standup comedy routine as an opening act. Both performers were well received.

Bonaduce has always credited Cassidy for giving him a chance to pull himself back up and start over again, and Cassidy has always professed his belief in his TV brother. The two actors share a special bond to this day.

"I couldn't get a job, and I was in a lot of trouble," says Bonaduce. "I was not a particularly reliable person, and when David gave me the job it was by necessity." Bonaduce admired Cassidy's professionalism, and from then on he showed up at every interview he ever had, and he showed up sober. "Because of that tour in the 1990s, I started my radio career, which paid for several homes, several families, several wives, and several children."

The initial success of the *David Cassidy* album brought the attention of another label, Scotti Brothers, which signed Cassidy for a follow-up album. *Didn't You Used to Be* was released in 1992 but didn't catch on with fans.

By 1998 Cassidy had formed his own label, Slammajamma Records, and released *Old Trick, New Dog*, featuring three revamped Partridge tunes along with some new original material. "No Bridge I Wouldn't Cross" was the clear standout, landing at No. 21 on the *Billboard* adult contemporary chart. *David Cassidy's Partridge Family Favorites* combined hits and unreleased songs on a CD available only through QVC as a special order packaged with *Old Trick, New Dog*.

In 1993 Cassidy went on the road in an updated Partridge Family bus to help promote Nick at Nite's first attempt at rerunning *The Partridge Family*. He met fans right on the bus and did promo spots. The syndicated return of *The Partridge Family* started off with great ratings but eventually fell off.

At about the same time, MTV aired a round of *Partridge Family* episodes in a 24-hour marathon called "Pile of Partridge." Again Cassidy signed on to help promote the event, making cameos on the bus at every commercial break.

By 1994 Cassidy was back on Broadway starring in the acclaimed musical drama *Blood Brothers*, featuring Petula Clark and his real-life brother, Shaun Cassidy. The success led Cassidy to Las Vegas, where he was named Entertainer of the Year in 1996 for his starring role in *EFX*. He was a creator for *The Rat Pack Is Back* and *At the Copa* as part of his continued success in Vegas.

Cassidy was spotted on numerous talk shows and prime-time guest appearances, and celebrities like Lisa Kudrow and Quentin Tarantino were acknowledging him as a favorite childhood celebrity. Rosie O'Donnell fawned over him, he kissed Little Richard on the *Tonight Show*, and Oprah Winfrey had him perform live for the now-fortysomething fans who were still screaming for him.

One special moment for Partridge Family fans was David Cassidy and Susan Dey's joint appearance as presenters on the 1990 MTV Awards. When they came out to present the award, Cassidy broke out into "C'mon Get Happy," joking with Dey about returning to the good old days. In England in 1993, Dey also turned out to pay tribute to Cassidy in a clip from *This Is Your Life: David Cassidy*, reminding him of the close friendship they had shared.

VH1 did documentaries on both Cassidy and the Partridge Family as part of their *Behind the Music* series. Documentaries also showed up on *Biography* and other TV news magazines.

The music began to re-emerge as well. The original Partridge Family studio albums began finding their way to CD as early as 1992, when Razor & Tie reissued *A Partridge Family Christmas Card* followed by *Album, Up to Date, Sound Magazine,* and *Shopping Bag*. After several years, the remaining studio albums were also released.

Nick at Nite New Year's Eve

In 1993 Brian Forster and Jeremy Gelbwaks were invited to appear as special guests on Kasey Casem's New Year's Eve countdown of television shows on Nick at Nite. It was the first time the two met, says Forster. "Their big angle for the show was that they were going to introduce the two Chrisses that never met before. Here we are filming this thing in a house in the San Fernando Valley. Before I arrived I was going, This is kind of silly. I arrived at the airport and they rented me a Mercedes, and I'm going, OK, I guess this is a bigger deal than I think it is, and I get back to the hotel and there's a little basket of fruit there and all this. Well, OK, what's going on here? It turns out we were like the main guests on that one because their other guests were people like the wardrobe guy from The Dick Van Dyke Show! So to have actual actors was a big deal."

Danny!

In 1996 Danny Bonaduce launched his own talk show, titled *Danny!* For the first episode, Bonaduce called up all his former castmates—including Jeremy Gelbwaks, who has made very few television appearances since his stint on the show—and asked them to join him for a Partridge Family reunion.

"My first contact with Danny after the show happened when he reached out to me and invited me to do his show in Chicago," says Rick Segall. "That was just fun! Whenever anyone asks me to do something related to *The Partridge Family*, two thoughts come to mind. The first one is that it will be fun, and the second one is that it's a privilege."

The pilot episode of *Danny!* began as the audience watched the cast arrive outside the studio in yet another replica of the famous Partridge Family bus—this time redesigned as a convertible! The reunion was entertaining, despite the fact that David Cassidy did not appear due to a scheduling conflict. There was a lot of energy and authentic happi-

when we're singin'

ness. Even Susan Dey called in, and she had a nice moment with Bonaduce. It was her last appearance in any kind of a Partridge Family reunion setting to date. There was no music during the reunion, but Bonaduce presented a table of memorabilia and even had a mock game show challenge between the cast members and the fans.

Partridge Pop Culture

The Partridge Family was being referenced in pop culture from the moment the show aired. One early memorable parody came from *Mad* magazine in April 1972, when the issue featured a comic strip titled "The Putrid Family" (starring Teeth Partridge). Two decades later, fans discovered their ability to find each other on the Internet. Fan sites and tribute sites dedicated to the Partridge Family were cropping up left and right, including the online cult oddity *Partridge Family Temple*. David Cassidy, Danny Bonaduce, Dave Madden, and Shirley Jones all launched their own sites over time. *Cmongethappy.com* became a fan-run website providing more information about the Partridge Family than any other source on the web. Currently there are more than a hundred Facebook pages dedicated to the show and its stars.

Partridge Family references still turn up from time to time in pop culture—such as an Oakland band called the Reuben Kincaid (which has nothing to do with Dave Madden, the Partridge Family or even Reuben Kincaid himself.) Another band, the Moses Gun, recorded "The Ballad of Reuben Kincaid" in 2012. Another Partridge-inspired musical endeavor, the Forever Family, which had Shirley Jones' support and involvement, was also created and promoted with the promotional slogan "You Either Get It, Or You Don't."

The Rerun Show, a short-lived comedy anthology series from 2002, parodied *The Partridge Family,* and "Come On Get Happy" has played in commercials for Dasani and in Volkswagen's 2013 Super Bowl ad. Even a Broadway musical titled after the song is in development.

Bus Stop ...

Sound Magazine, the Tribute Band

One long-lived reminder of the Partridge Family's influence in pop culture was the presence of the '90s tribute band called Sound Magazine. "Around 1989 I was at a used record store, just bebopping around with some friends, and all of a sudden over the in-house PA starts the Partridge Family music, which I had not heard since I was 10," says founder Howard Pattow. It was a newly released greatest hits CD, which he ended up buying the following week, unable to get the songs out of his head. "I was a little older now, and I was a musician and listening to them with fresh ears, I just marveled at how good they were, and how well-crafted, harmonic, and melodic." A new round of reissues in the early 90s inspired him: "The idea just hit me: *Wouldn't it be fun to put a band together and play these songs live?*"

He and a couple of other players put together a set list, then recorded their own instrumental and background vocal tracks. "We thought it would be more than impossible to find any girls who looked like Shirley Jones and Susan Dey who could play like Mike Melvoin," laughs Pattow. "We made these intricate, meticulously detailed tracks," says Pattow. "We actually contacted Wes Farrell's office and asked his secretary if we could get charts to the tracks, and we tried to get hold of John and Tom Bahler. I had conversations with Hal Blaine and Joe Osborn."

The group began playing in 1995. "Instrumentally, musically, it was live lead vocals, guitars, bass, drums, but we had a girl faking the keyboards and doing the Shirley Jones lip sync." When the bass player dropped out, the group recorded bass tracks to use in performance. "Now we had practically more music on track than music being performed live, but the beauty of that was the consistency of the performances was guaranteed. You didn't have to worry about your keyboard player making a mistake. It was perfect. So really, it was a sort of marriage of fake and real, which was the Partridge Family to begin with!

Their "Keith" was a live vocalist. Pattow played guitar, making him the de facto Danny, and their "Laurie" who faked the electric piano could actually sing. She was sometimes mixed into the tracks. Pattow says, "The song I loved, loved, loved was 'I'm on My Way Back Home.' My mother use to tell me that I would sing that song in the car. And 'Summer Days' is just a masterpiece. So we were kicking around ideas for the name [of the band] and we kept coming back to Sound Magazine." The band was named around Halloween 1993. Though clever, the title turned out to be a little too obscure. "More than one time we would be introduced as Sound Machine," says Pattow.

"When we first started playing, it was sort of an underground hipster retro kind of scene. It seemed to consist of women in their 40s who were in love with David Cassidy when they were little girls, and the other half of it was musicians in their 30s and 40s who loved music, who were coming to check out somebody trying to play Tommy Tedesco's guitar licks.

"We were about six months into it, and an agent that I had invited took me out to the sidewalk after the show and said to me, 'Listen, don't pay tribute to the Partridge Family—*be* the Partridge Family! Go out and get wigs, figure out who you're going to be, and everybody become those characters. Don't just be some band up on stage going *Oh, that song is like one of our favorites*. Take it to the next level. It'll make you much more bookable.' And he was right. The girl playing keyboards wasn't really Shirley at first. She was just kind of herself, and then bing! All of a sudden there's wigs!"

The group played clubs, some Las Vegas dates, and talent showcases. For one memorable Valentine's Day show, they teamed up with a Sonny & Cher tribute group.

Pattow remembers Ryan Cassidy attending a show at the Sunset Strip House of Blues, then coming backstage to congratulate the performers. "Everybody was hanging out and we were doing the after-gig schmooze, and he said, 'I can see you guys really like the music. It was really a lot of fun to watch.' And I said, 'Well, thank you. That was the intention—we never meant to be a mockery of the music. We wanted to put those songs up really well.' And the girl who was playing Shirley was in the room and he looked at her and he said to her, 'You've got my mom down!' And she just floated out of the room."

A phone call to the Chicago station where Danny Bonaduce worked led to Pattow suddenly being patched in live to Bonaduce's show. "He got me on the phone and goes, 'You've got a Partridge Family tribute band? So, what character do you play?' And I said, 'Well, we're not really doing characters. It's really more about the music, and we don't have a little redheaded kid playing bass,' and he said, 'Well, you said it's the Partridge Family, man!'"

He eventually met up with other cast members, as well. After sending numerous emails and faxes to Shirley Jones' office, he ran into her and Marty Ingels at Grauman's Chinese Theater. "So I just quickly introduced myself as the guy with the Partridge Family tribute band and they said, 'Oh, yeah! Keep sending us those faxes—we'll come eventually!'" He later received a letter and autographed picture. "She was very sweet and very nice about it," he recalls. "When we told David Cassidy that we were putting together a Partridge Family band, he gave me a look like he was either thinking *This guy's a genius* or *I'm going to call security*."

Pattow says the process of recording all the tracks gave him a new appreciation for the structure of the songs: "One of the things I really, really appreciated about the construction of the songs is how the orchestrations work with the basic tracks. Something like 'Echo Valley' I would notice that certain instrumentation would just be random little pieces of noise, but you put them together and they weave together, almost like an impressionistic painting. If you get close up, all you see are these dots of color, but as you stand back from it you see the big picture, and that's what these arrangements were like. I would start with a scratch piano track, just to have the song down, and then it was almost like putting up an empty Christmas tree—you start hanging your ornaments and stringing the garland and the tinsel, and then gradually it starts to come alive. There were some tracks that were incredibly, incredibly detailed, and we spent a lot of time looking for the right sound patches that matched what we heard.

"We got to play "My Christmas Card To You" on at least two Christmases, and that was one of those tracks that the people who knew it couldn't believe it, and the people who didn't know it were like, 'Wow, what song is that? That was a nice song!' It was fun to do that one, because it involved sound patches that we didn't normally mess around with. It had that Christmas-y French horn kind of thing going, and the background vocal section in the middle took forever to put together!

"It really opened the doors for me," says Pattow, who has since gone on to work with tribute bands for other groups, including Badfinger and Crosby, Stills & Nash. But he says of Sound Magazine, "It was the most fun because it was fresh and it was really coming out of nowhere, and it really was more about the music than it was about David Cassidy."

Audience members were more focused on their memories of the show, he recalls. "Let's eulogize the Partridge Family—'Oh, I love that show!" Then people just want to talk about the show, and 'Do you remember the one when the skunk was on the bus?' and that kind of seems to be where the conversation goes. Very few want to talk about Hal Blaine!

"Very seldom does anybody want to talk about the songs, and the music, which to me was the initial attraction. You don't really realize what's going on when you're a kid, but when I started listening to them with fresh ears, it was like *Pet Sounds* to me! Or the Association or the 5th Dimension or the Carpenters—any of those lush, swiftly produced pop records. It just got a bad rap because it was a bubblegum TV show. It was written off, not unlike

when we're singin'

> the Monkees, but in a different way because nobody knows who the unsung heroes are—Hal Blaine and Joe Osborn!
>
> Sound Magazine was invited to take part in a KISS tribute CD, recording "Shout It Out Loud" in the style of the Partridge Family. The track was mixed by Bob Exrin, the producer of the original KISS, who also produced *The Wall* for Pink Floyd. Pattow remembers, "In 20 minutes we mixed that track. We worked on the background vocals, and kind of spread the mix out. He ended up playing the track for Paul Stanley and Gene Simmons, and both went on record saying they loved it.
>
> "What is it about these groups that people want to come see?" he asks. "It's all very simple, really. It's music that people know, and it's not around anymore. When you go to a symphonic recital and you get to hear the Boston Pops doing Tchaikovsky, it's basically a tribute band. It's a band playing somebody else's material who is no longer around to do it for themselves, and you give the audience an idea of what it would have been like to hear this stuff when it was happening the first time. The difference between a cover band and a tribute band is that a tribute band is imitating the act, the look, the personality."
>
> Pattow describes Sound Magazine, which played from until around 2001, as "a little ahead of its time. If we had come out with it now, there would be much more of an audience for it," he says.

David Cassidy in the New Century

In more recent years, David Cassidy came to embrace his past, reshaping it into a new present. He began performing in concerts again around the turn of the millennium. In 2002 he released *Then and Now* with Universal Music, with re-recordings of original Partridge Family hits as well as a few new tracks. Music from the *Then and Now* sessions was also featured in the made-for-TV movie *The David Cassidy Story*, which aired in 2000 with Cassidy as executive producer. The Danny Bonaduce–produced *Come On Get Happy: The Partridge Family Story* made-for-TV movie aired only months before Cassidy's.

Cassidy called up all the original background singers and musical arranger Mike Melvoin together with as many musicians as he could get who had worked on the Partridge Family studio albums, and asked them to join him for *Then and Now*. He wanted to capture the original arrangements, duplicating them as closely as possible—right down to the vocal phrasings.

"I was conducting the Welk Orchestra at the time," recalls John Bahler. "When I talked to David he was so excited. He said, 'You have to come out here! I have Studio 2! I've got Mike Melvoin! Hal Blaine! Dennis Budimir!' and he's naming all these guys that did a lot of the original recordings. He said 'I'd have the original engineer, too, but he passed away. I would have Wes there too, but he's no longer with us either.'"

Both John Bahler and Tom Bahler quickly hopped on board. John, who was living in Branson, Missouri, jetted out to L.A. for the project. "Jackie Ward was there, too," John says, "but Ron [Hicklin] couldn't be there because Ron was in Europe with his wife on vacation, so we brought Randy Kranshaw in. He's an awesome talent. He's a trombone player as well, just like my brother, and so he approached the project the same way we did.

"I was standing there in the booth in Studio 2—the same place where we recorded all of the hits the first time—and we were setting up for the vocals. I laid out the arrangements of the tunes that David had picked for the show, and I was looking at one of them, just making sure everything was cool, and David came over and was looking over my shoulder and he said 'Wouldn't you love to know where the original charts for these are?' And I said 'These are the originals!' He just about hit the floor! He said 'What? You've got to be kidding me!' I said 'No—Janet found the box with all of my originals in it!' I'm such a pack ratter. He said 'I can't believe it!' He was blown away. He was absolutely blown away."

Bahler didn't, however, have original charts for "I Think I Love You," because it was one of the songs from the first Partridge Family session where he had quickly scribbled out an arrangement on scrap paper. For *Then and Now,* he had to write a new arrangement from the original recording.

John Bahler says, "The very first day we went in and recorded two or three songs. I lived in Missouri, so I was staying with my brother while we did this thing, and afterwards, driving back to his place, we were talking. I said 'Man, I'm whipped!' He said. 'So am I!' We both forgot how much that takes out of you! I was 60 years old when we did that, and my brother was 57. But the good news is that 30-some years after the fact, we sounded just as good as we did 30 years before! We really tried to recreate what we had done 30 years prior, and it sure felt good when we did it!"

Jackie Ward recalls, "I was just about getting ready to retire, and I hadn't been doing a lot of singing, so it was hard work. Being a singer and doing it properly is like an athlete. You do it so many hours every day and you do it, do it, do it. Otherwise it goes away. And as you get older, your voice changes. It gets lower. So it was a little harder for me to try to duplicate those songs because it was so many years ago, but I think everybody did a pretty good job. It was fun—it really was fun!"

Ward continues, "David was just a sweetheart because he was there a lot. That was one of the times we really got to see him more than we used to.... During the television show we would come in as he was leaving because he had to go to the set. This time that wasn't the case. We were doing the music first, and then they were doing the movie."

Cassidy was filled with energy during these sessions. "By the time we did *Then and Now*, I think David had grown up and matured," says John Bahler. "He realized he was an icon. He never said that to me, but I think he realized what an impact the Partridge Family had on the public, and what an impact he had as a solo artist, but he didn't know that when he was 20, 21, 22."

"I think he appreciates it more now than he could have possibly appreciated it the first time around," says Ward. "Back then he was ready to branch out. He was tired of doing the Partridge Family. I think now he can look back and recognize what a wonderful thing it was, and enjoy it more now than he did then. He realizes that music has a place in the history of recordings, and that it's special. I think he resented it back then because he couldn't do what he thought he wanted to do."

Mike Melvoin says of *Then and Now*, "It was like the conversation never stopped." *Then and Now* was released in 2002 and went platinum. The success of the CD spawned Cassidy's next album, *A Touch of Blue*, released in 2004, with slow-tempo covers of some of Cassidy's favorite songs arranged by Melvoin.

The Partridge Family background vocalists were drawing attention, too, as the now-adult audience grew interested in the faces behind the image. "*Eye on L.A.* came to my house in San Marino," says Ron Hicklin of one of the singers' reunions, "and wanted to film the actual real-life group that was the Partridge Family. They wanted to do the show from my house. The moment I got Mike Melvoin, John, Tom, Jackie, and myself together, the energy, the sense of humor, the sheer love of each other and what we had done over our careers just exploded. It felt so good."

But after the television crew began to script the interview, the authenticity of the moment was lost. "I was hoping they would capture all that energy on camera, because it was like winning a Super Bowl," says Hicklin. "But you can't recreate the feeling of victory that you have in those types of scripted situations. There was such a high being with each other again and feeling the energy we had together, the passion that was there—it's just magic."

In 2007 Cassidy released *David Cassidy Part II: The Remix*, with Partridge Family hits in dance mode. The CD was originally offered exclusively through Target department stores, then re-issued as *David Cassidy Dance Party Remix*.

In Search of the Partridge Family

In 2004 the original cast, minus Susan Dey, reunited to promote the VH1 reality show *In Search of the Partridge Family*, featuring a nationwide search for a new cast for an attempted reboot of the show. It ran for eight weeks.

Each episode focused on one particular character, and an actor from the original series appeared as a guest star. The initial launch was an episode covering the audition process, followed by individual episodes dedicated to the casting of Shirley, Keith, Laurie, and Danny. The two youngest characters, Chris and Tracy, and the character of Reuben Kincaid had been cast ahead of time.

The show tried to take the original casting concept one step further by searching out people who could act *and* sing. But the task proved challenging.

During the final episode, the new cast appeared alongside the original cast, who welcomed and congratulated them. The new Partridge Family performed their first song, though it was obviously prerecorded and lip-synced.

The new series failed to take off. Only one episode aired, "Exile on Wilshire Boulevard," in early 2005. That sole episode also marked the debut of the newest Partridge Family song, "Love Can Start a Revolution." "Come on Get Happy" and "I Think I Love You" were re-recorded as well. Most of the fans who were following the reality show missed the episode because it was poorly advertised.

Many of the new cast members resembled the original actors—with the exception of Leland Grant, who played the new Keith Partridge. But the script and production were poorly executed. Danny Bonaduce appeared in the pilot, but the new program failed to grab an audience. "They weren't actors," explains Shirley Jones. "This is my point. They could sing, but they weren't actors. You can't just pick people off the street and say, 'We want you to be a television star!'" The producers of the original show learned that the first time around when they met with the Cowsills. They were phenomenal singers with a full musical career—but they couldn't act. The reality show can, however, lay claim to casting the then-undiscovered Emma Stone in the role of Laurie.

"The little kids got screwed again!" says Brian Forster. "Instead of being part of the reality premise, where the viewers actually chose them, they were just cast ahead of time. They just lumped them in there! I have a distaste for reality shows in general, because reality shows ruined the careers of many actors who should be working. The whole premise of combining *American Idol* with *The Partridge Family* where week by week someone gets voted off was really silly, but at least there was some attempt to bring it back. It's good for us because it gets us publicity as the real actors."

Forster continues, "I think the cutest memory for me was the final episode. They had all of us back, alongside all of the new cast. The kid that was now playing the drums could not play the drums at all, and I'm laughing because I can't believe this. He's this little blonde kid about 10 years old, just like I had been, except I had a drum teacher who was at least going to show me what I'm supposed to do. Here we are, rehearsing, and now I am becoming the drum teacher! I was air drumming, trying to help him, and I'm going, 'OK, this is how we do it.' He's kind of watching

when we're singin'

me, and I'm thinking *Oh my God, this is such a flashback! And now I'm taking the instructor role!* Forster laughs. "It was fun!"

Ruby & the Rockits

The Cassidy brothers came together for a group project developed by Shaun Cassidy in 2009. The half-hour sitcom, *Ruby & the Rockits*, aired on ABC Family. Shaun Cassidy had found success as a writer after he exited the limelight as a performer. Though the entire Cassidy clan took part in the show, the star was young Alexa Vega, who was fresh off the box office smash *Spy Kids*. The premise was the launch of her character's singing career, following in the footsteps of her long-lost father, who shows up—played by David Cassidy—in the pilot episode.

Cassidy's television brother was played by another of his real-life brothers, Patrick Cassidy. Patrick played the more subdued suburbanite, and David the playboy who can't let go of the good old days when they were rock stars—a characterization that poked clever fun at his role on *The Partridge Family*. Shirley Jones made guest appearances as—you guessed it—Mom.

Moderately well received, *Ruby & the Rockits* premiered in July 2009 and was canceled in September after only 10 episodes. Aside from some comedic musical bits, the program didn't generate any new music from either David or Patrick Cassidy.

The Partridge Family Live in Concert?

When *The Partridge Family* premiered in 1970, promoters from all over the country were calling the studio wanting to book the group. In 2011, we finally saw the closest thing possible to a real-life Partridge Family concert.

"David and I had done the *Today* show together," says Danny Bonaduce, "and he had re-embraced *The Partridge Family*. That day he was just laughing at every joke I made, and I just looked at him and said, 'Why don't you come on my radio show when you're in Philly?' He said, 'I'm in Philly in three days!' So I had him on.

"Now, I don't have David on very much because he kind of makes me a little bit nervous, to be honest. When I see David, I see Elvis. When I see David, I see Paul McCartney. Having someone like Shirley on is more comfortable because she's like my mom! But when David's on, I stutter. It's my show and I'm in charge, but this is the guy who had the fan club bigger than the Beatles and Elvis combined at one point. That's still who I see.

"But he came on, and we were just chatting, fooling around, and then he said, 'Hey, you know I'm playing the Keswick Theater in Philadelphia in three months. I dare you to learn a Partridge Family song and come out on stage with me and play it on the bass!' So I thought, *It's four strings, how hard can this be?* The answer is really hard! *Really* hard!"

"I take dares all the time. That's how I ended up in the ring with Jose Canseco," laughs Bonaduce. "So the fact that David just came on and dared me in the middle of an interview made me take on the challenge." The only live performance Bonaduce had done with Cassidy at this point was a stand-up routine during the 1991 concert tour. This was the first time he was actually going to play an instrument and sing with Cassidy. "I knew I was going to do it several months ahead of time, but I really just wanted to go out and do stand-up comedy. I thought, *I'm going to add musical instruction to my day? Am I crazy? I'm one of the busiest guys I know! Do I really have time for this?*

"I was terrified about this show. David wanted it clean. My act is filthy. He wanted me to play the bass, and I don't know how! This was a lot of work for me, man! So I'm sitting there with an instructor going over these songs and I'm saying 'I don't know these songs!' I was kind of precocious at 10 or 11 years old. We were selling millions of albums! Why would I bother to take lessons if I can sell the albums without actually burdening myself?" he jokes.

"If you asked me the question 'Have you ever fantasized about …' and then just said almost anything, the answer is going to be yes," he adds. "I'd like to be a musician, but I think I missed that opportunity.

"I have often thought about how cool it would be to be a rock star and to get up on stage with David Cassidy and play. It was more so when I was 10, 11 years old—wanting to go out with him when he was filling Dodger Stadium, but I'm 50 years old now, and the idea of hitting the stage with David Cassidy has not been a recent concern of mine." Nonetheless, he had taken the dare and planned on going through with it.

"I was in New York pitching some reality shows that I had written, and in the middle of pitching *Danny does this, Danny does a fitness show, Danny does something else,* I started telling them about the fact that I was going on stage to play with David Cassidy for the first time ever. They didn't notice that I had slipped from pitching into casual conversation, and they thought I was pitching a show about me and David Cassidy hitting the road together. So later the package I received back from them about the shows they liked starts with 'David Cassidy and Danny Bonaduce together again! The new Odd Couple.' I didn't mean to pitch it as a show! I was just taking a break and telling them a funny story!"

The momentum for the concert was building and Bonaduce was practicing his bass religiously. Then his girlfriend had an idea for him to walk out in a red velvet suit. "Act like David lied to you and said it was a Partridge Family reunion show," he remembers her saying. "It will be so funny!"

when we're singin'

Bonaduce continues, "My first reaction to it was super negative. I've had to do some embarrassing things when I couldn't make a living. Around Christmastime, when I was really broke, I'd go to a K-mart opening in like Wichita and they'd put me in a tree in front of the store and I'd be Danny Partridge in a pear tree. I was so humiliated. But now that everything's going my way and life is wonderful I said, 'Absolutely. Find that suit! It's hysterical!' I realized people will probably get a kick out of it if I walk out there in that outfit.

"It was the only one they had left at the costume store and it was like a double extra-large and it was just filled with safety pins. The one thing I did to add my own touch to the outfit was that I didn't put a shirt on underneath. I thought I would do the first part of it, till he talks, dressed like the Partridge Family, then I'll take off the jacket and I will have all my tattoos showing, you know, with Richards and Mick Jagger, and this will make for two different interesting pictures."

David Cassidy had no idea what was coming. "I didn't even show the band ahead of time—but I walk out on stage and the piano player just busts out laughing. My bit was to act really mad, that David had lied to me, so it was really dark, and I look at the piano player and I go, 'WHAT?' Really, really mad, and you can tell he was terrified. He pulls back his head, and I couldn't hear what he said, but basically it was like, 'Nothing—it's great. I'm sure you look fine!' Then I stormed out on stage all mad at David for lying. It was one of my favorite parts of the show.

"So I'm waiting for David to say something, and there's almost six minutes where he keeps going to say something, and then he starts laughing and turning away. Finally he just goes, 'Nice outfit,' and then bursts out. And then I said, 'You lied to me! You said this was the Partridge Family!'"

Cassidy finally came back with a jab. "You've grown … (long pause) … and you're wearing Shirley's outfit," he said to Bonaduce. The audience roared.

After Bonaduce's explosive entrance, he and Cassidy played "Doesn't Somebody Want to Be Wanted" to big cheers from the crowd. Bonaduce says, "You can hear the audience cheering. I mean, they were so happy, and if you're a real performer, if you don't do this for anything but the love of the game … people cheering? Try and find something wrong with that! I'm a five-foot-six guy with the flesh of a Sharpei, and I go out there, I do something, and they cheer? That's a pretty good feeling.

"When we were done, David, on his way out the door, said, 'You have to learn another Partridge Family song, and soon!'"

Becoming Classic TV

By the millennium, the term *classic TV* was a household phrase. Cable network TVLand had become popular airing vintage shows. Beginning in 2003, the network hosted its own TVLand Awards honoring classic television and *The Partridge Family* was acknowledged with nominations during that inaugural year. David Cassidy and Shirley Jones were reunited, even singing "Come On Get Happy" together for the first time. Cassidy was the winner for Hippest Fashion Plate, Male. Susan Dey won the following year for Favorite Teen Dream, Female.

The nostalgia and innocence of *The Partridge Family* and other older shows make for a nice escape. No one of today's culture is fooled into thinking there is anything real about the premise of *The Partridge Family*. Instead, we simply wish it were real.

"It was a time when family shows like *Father Knows Best* and *The Brady Bunch* were on the air. There was an innocence about these shows," says producer Larry Rosen. "If it was *The Brady Bunch* it was the melding of two families. If it was *The Partridge Family* it was a family without a father that struggled to use their musical career to keep money coming in. Yet there was an innocence, a simplicity about their lives. Those shows have led to shows that became a lot more edgy. We never did edgy, controversial stuff."

"I'm not surprised by the impact," says fellow producer Paul Witt. "When kids and young people become attached to a show it can have a profound impact on them. The personalities of the younger boomers were forming when they were watching that show as kids, and they grew up with it over the years. We know the impact of television on children is profound. When they can identify with a character, whether it's a crush on David or Susan Dey, they hold those memories in their heads, and their hearts, and their gut. It's important to them."

"I get a lot of feedback from women my age," says Shirley Jones, "and even younger. They love the show. You know, a lot of the people your age don't know that I even did one movie," she laughs. "They know I did *The Partridge Family*, and from that standpoint it is wonderful for me. I would hope that new viewers can see what a nice family show it is, because you can't find them today. I mean, how can you sit with your whole family ranging from age five to 17 and watch a show together? It's impossible. I think shows like *The Partridge Family* and others of that era that are still hanging in there do so because of that quality."

Danny Bonaduce reflects: "There's a display in the Smithsonian Institution of pop culture. There's Archie Bunker's chair, there's Fonz's jacket, and then there's the Partridge Family lunchbox. For *The Partridge Family* to be in the Smithsonian it means it has to be important, but I cannot tell you why. Every boy wanted to be with Susan Dey, and every girl wanted to be with David Cassidy. The fact of the matter is, David Cassidy made puka shells important and the show could do almost no wrong for a while. I don't know why it was important, but I will agree that it was."

For Rick Segall, it was the lessons the show conveyed that are the source of its enduring appeal. "Like a lot of shows back then the stories told each week had

when we're singin'

a moral that featured a universal truth, even though it was light-hearted. It's two totally different worlds now, as far as programming.

"I think it all goes back to bubblegum music and David," says Brian Forster. "It's that fantasy within the music. All of these girls who are now 40 years old and they are still going, 'Oh, David,' which means he, and the music, were obviously a huge part of the success. When I do these autograph shows an interesting observation I make is that these people who are my age watched it when they were kids, and now their kids are watching it. It's fascinating to hear them say there's no good TV anymore, and that there's nothing like *The Partridge Family*. Just reality shows. Modern TV doesn't seem to appeal to a lot of these people. They like that innocence of those family shows.

"You never know how much negotiating went on behind the scenes," Forster continues, "but I think there were two people on the show that they didn't realize exactly what they had when the show first started. That was David and Danny. Obviously, they had plans for David, but I think they originally just thought of him as the bubblegum fluff guy. Then they found out this guy could really act. When they found out what they had with Danny, they found this little formula they could use between David and Danny and Dave Madden and Danny. They didn't have to worry about much else because it worked."

"It was a very successful show," says Bob Claver. "It stood out as very special. I had spent five years writing kids' shows with Bob Keeshan [Captain Kangaroo] so I had a lot of experience with that age group. The cast was really young, but it was a show where everybody, for some strange reason, turned out to be all the right people in the right place. The thing worked. There're a million reasons you could come up with, but mostly they had good chemistry together, and that's a big deal."

The magic didn't happen without discipline, though, and many talented professionals. "One of the goals was always maintaining high standards on the show," says Mel Swope. "We had a lot of support from the network and the studio, but we did our part to make sure we delivered the show on the budget they gave us. This is a challenge no matter what show you are working on."

Everyone interviewed for this book—especially the cast—was grateful in one way or another for their experience on *The Partridge Family*. "Believe me—and thank God—I'm so proud of *The Partridge Family*," says Danny Bonaduce. "I never, not for one day, take it for granted. People will say to me when they start interviews, 'I know you don't want to talk about *The Partridge Family*,' but I interrupt them and I say, 'Yes, I do! I couldn't be more proud! You're not even talking to me, you're not even interested in me, if I hadn't done *The Partridge Family*. I couldn't be more thrilled. So what is it you want to know?'"

Though Jeremy Gelbwaks' part on the show was short-lived, he also remembers it with good spirit. "It was fun," says Gelbwaks. "Even then I understood that not everyone got to do something like that. But I guess the most interesting memory for me is not the things that happened while we were making the show, but later in life when I was a teenager and moving around the country. Even as a young adult, I would meet people who had such great memories of the program. A Filipino guy once told me that he learned to play drums because he used to watch the show. There was a guy from Alaska that used to call me once in a while from a pay phone in Fairbanks, which was really more responsibility than I wanted to take, but I was glad to have given them some happy memories. It was so early in my childhood. I remember my parents bought their first color TV so we could watch the program in color. It had this impact on people. I didn't understand it at the time, but I am glad to have the experience. I think, had I realized then it was such a big deal, I might have been more disappointed about not doing it anymore."

Becoming Classic Music

The Partridge Family's music has lived on far beyond the scope for which it was envisioned, largely due to the professionals who cared so much about the musical side of production. The music stood on its own then and does so today. David Cassidy's solo career has also benefited from remixes and renditions.

"It started out with David as this wide-eyed 19-year-old kid who was just thrilled that he got to sing," says John Bahler. "He was so happy to be there. He was like a sponge, trying to learn, and he did. He learned a lot—not only on the set, but in the studio. He was there for nearly every facet. He wasn't always there for the backgrounds, but he was there when the tracking was done and he learned about production and recording."

Jackie Ward reflects, "When a record became a hit record it was very exciting. Anytime you can be a part of a hit record, it's exciting even if you're not a royalty artist, because you're still a part of it. This was exciting because the group was really instrumental and an integral part of the sound. The group made the whole thing happen. David's very good, but I still think it was the package of the whole that sold everything, and it was exciting for me to be a part of that. Sometimes it was not easy doing it. It was hard work, but it was still fun because you always wound up with a good product—and believe me, being a studio singer I can't tell you how many times you go in and you do something that is just awful, or even mediocre. You have to smile because you're in there getting your paycheck for that day's work and you just grin and bear it. You just grab the money and go home. You don't necessarily care whether anybody ever knows that you did it. You don't necessarily want to be associated with it. But it's fun when you can go in and you're doing something that is *good*, and you are proud of it."

when we're singin'

Ron Hicklin says, "When you were in that studio you were all recording together as equals. We didn't have to carry that burden of celebrity because we were only known within the industry. We'd walk in and pick up a piece of music and say, 'OK, here's who we are today.' We'd sight-read the music, record it, feel proud of the results, and move on. If it was successful, then we were back. If it wouldn't have been—if somebody would have been better, hungrier, younger, had a better attitude, God knows what—they might have be there in our place. I would always talk to the other singers and tell them that it isn't about the money you can make. It's about walking out and leaving that silver bullet there. It was about getting them to say 'Who *were* those people?' As long as we kept doing what we knew we could do, living up to the standards we set for ourselves and continuing to produce in that manner, we knew we would be there, and we had long, wonderful careers.

"The Partridge Family was an opportunity for those of us who had attained a certain level of proficiency in the studio to go in and make the most of it. The most enjoyable thing was moving from the pilot to the eventual four of us doing everything together. Enjoying my peers, the feeling of success we had working together, watching the pieces falling into place, whatever the circumstances were, we held together as a team. We shared the experience of that success—together. That is my fondest memory.

"The style that John Bahler created was good. The background vocals are very interesting, and they certainly weren't mixed way in the background. They are a vital part of the situation. I've got the Partridge Family classified with my adult contemporary section. The common denominator is that it's awfully good music. Few realize the circumstances under how it was all done. My God, we were moving fast—with the windows down!"

The last of the four principal background vocalists, Tom Bahler, cites the importance of great songs and songwriters to the Partridge Family's music. "Tony Romeo—that was the dude! I think Tony was golden for us. He was in the groove! The funny thing is that I was right there on the inside track. I'd just had a hit with Bobby Sherman's "Julie, Do Ya Love Me" and Wes was saying, 'Man, write for the Partridge Family!' I wrote and wrote and wrote, and I did not get it! Whatever it was, I was not on an emotional tie with it as a songwriter. As soon as I wrote something Wes would say, 'I love it—it's wrong. I love it—it's wrong.' So I never ever got a Partridge Family cut, and it was frustrating to me, but I was young. I really hadn't quite learned how to write to order. I wrote a bunch of songs that I would have liked the Partridge Family to record, but I don't even remember what they are. Once they were stillborn I just moved to the next one."

Having the right feel for a Partridge Family song was important on all counts. Nearly every songwriter who wrote specifically for the television band has said so. "I think it's terrific," says Tommy West. "It's a good body of work. It's focused, because most of the people who wrote did so with certain situations in mind. I think they should put all of those unreleased songs out."

Mike Melvoin led the way in creating arrangements that were cleverly crafted with sophisticated nuances. "My favorite memory is repeatedly walking into the room, sitting down in a group like that, and knowing that for at least the next three hours I'm going to be in the company of the world's greatest musicians," says Melvoin. "I am also quite proud that we were conscious of the fact that we were dealing with the tender and growing aesthetics of children, and that we didn't disappoint anyone in fulfilling their needs."

"Bubblegum—that word, or teenybopper, never came up in any conversation I had with Wes, ever," says John Bahler. "It was the family sound, and once we came up with it, it still was not a formula that was written in blood. Each song dictated what we did." Mike Appel adds, "What was special to me was that Toni Wine, Tony Romeo, L. Russell Brown and Irwin Levine, and Jim and I were so young ourselves at the time. So when you look back, it's very special."

"We were just trying to come up with hit titles and hooks," says Bobby Hart. "We weren't that interested in getting cuts on the TV show because we were only trying to write hits, or cuts for hit albums. As it turns out, all these years later, those songs continue to make money. Danny and I, and Tommy and I especially, were fortunate. Tommy and I were fortunate to be signed to a music publishing company that owned a motion picture studio and a television studio. We had a lot of material appear in both media, and those are the songs that hold up more than the income holds up. We were only trying to write hit singles, and those songs are the ones that have faded now, or continue to fade because there are less and less oldies stations that play those songs anymore. The songs that were wedded to visuals in a television show or a motion picture are the songs that continue to bring performance money because there's such a vacuum of content to put on television. There are all these new channels, and they're looking to fill them up with something."

The musicians also reflect on the distinct sound of the Partridge Family. Joe Osborn says, "There was a sound—the Mamas & the Papas, the 5th Dimension—all of that music is still alive. These oldies radio stations are very successful playing that and it's all they play. The sounds of those Partridge Family records and the songs are just part of that whole batch that will never die." "The people who wrote this music were hit wonders," adds L. Russell Brown.

"I thought there was some wonderful music in the show," says Shirley Jones. "At that time it wasn't my kind of music, but when I hear it again—when I hear it now—it's just wonderful music. Wonderful songs." Danny Bonaduce agrees. "My opinion of the Partridge Family music has changed. I still do not like 'I Think I Love You.'

when we're singin'

Since it was our biggest success and outsold the Beatles' "Let it Be," I think David will tell you what a wonderful song it is. The song I played live with him, "Doesn't Somebody Want To Be Wanted," except for the bizarre talking part, was a great song. "I Can Feel Your Heartbeat" is a great song. "I Woke Up in Love This Morning" is actually a great song. I remember singing *'went to sleep with ...'* and thinking it was the funniest thing in the world. To a 10-year-old that meant I slept with you. I thought that was the coolest thing in the world, because I was a little rebel.

"I did not understand the importance of the music then. I didn't know that Mike Appel, who discovered Springsteen, had a connection with the Partridge Family. When I met John Lennon I had no idea that he was a fan of David's, or that David Bowie, who is my ultimate hero, wanted to produce an album with David Cassidy, or that David Cassidy sang "I Write the Songs" before Barry Manilow, who didn't even like the song, nor did either of them write it. These are fascinating stories to me now, but I didn't care about any of that back then. I knew David didn't like the Partridge Family music, and if David didn't like it, then it wasn't cool. If David didn't like it, then I didn't like it. I just wanted David's approval. When other kids would pick fights and say 'My dad can beat up your dad,' or 'My brother can beat up your brother,' I would just say, 'My brother's Keith,' and I would just win! Conversation's over! It was a great experience growing up on that show."

Susan Dey has never professed to be a singer, nor has she ever spoken to the music of the Partridge Family. She is, however, a big supporter of music, especially grassroots music, and her desire to support meaningful causes has been a constant throughout her career. Heavily involved in her hometown community and surrounding communities, in 2013 she was asked by the town fire chief to help put on a battle of the bands for the sole purpose of creating a venue for musicians. "I just thought that was amazing," Dey said in an interview on a local TV station. "He didn't ask for a fundraiser for them. He wanted to promote the music of the region, and that's how it started. It's so important because everything is becoming so homogenized, and to bring back the focus on music as being something that is stimulating and cultural…. It's something where human beings are expressing themselves and it's through songwriting, and it's through sound that's unique…. If it's commercial radio or if it is commercial television it's fitting somebody's idea of what is the best way to make money. When you promote regional music … you say to young musicians and even older musicians that even though you may not be on the mainstream radio, we want to give you a venue and a focus."

"I owned the records on which I theoretically performed," laughs Jeremy Gelbwaks, "but I was a little young for the music, to be honest with you. It was music geared to teenagers, and I wasn't yet a teenager."

"We never tried to fake anybody out," says Bonaduce. "All the Partridge Family albums said 'The Partridge Family, featuring the voices of David Cassidy and Shirley

Jones,' and they were huge sellers. Anybody that's bitter about the Partridge Family who had anything to do with it has my complete permission to shut up! We had a great ride. We lucked out. So what if we didn't all really sing? Listen to my voice! What would I have sounded like on 'I Think I Love You?' It'd have been awful! Shirley was smart enough to do her *ooohs* and *aaaahs* and I'll bet she made several million dollars."

"As an adult I probably think like David does, because now my taste is varied," says Brian Forster. "I'm a mostly hard-rock guy, a blues guy, but I remember being in the fourth-grade classroom dancing around to 'I Think I Love You' going, 'This is great!' There were some songs that I really love, even now."

"It pleases me immensely that there's been a reflection upon that project from inception," said Wes Farrell. "It doesn't feel like 23 years—it feels like 23 days or 23 months. That's my first impression. I never hoped to do things in my life that were temporary. I guess in terms of a good judgment call, the quality was always what I aspired to bring to whatever I created, and if anything gives something the ability to sustain in time, it's quality. I don't think I've ever tried to go about doing anything where I gave less than a hundred percent."

The Partridge Family had become a group of its own after building an audience from the television show, and with the passing of time, now lives on in its own right. Although the show and the musical group were part of the same hatched egg, each had its own sphere of influence. "Where people make a mistake in music as it relates to motion pictures or television is forgetting to realize that if it isn't important in general—by itself—it will never be important to television or movies," said Wes Farrell. "It has to have its own merit and be able to stand alone."

Where Are They Now?

As of this writing ...

Shirley Jones continues to make appearances in film and television. She also does live concert performances now and then. She lives in Los Angeles. Just after the events of 9/11, Jones and her husband, Marty Ingels dedicated land they own in Big Bear, California, to start a memorial in honor of the victims. Fawn Park, as it was named, is the only 9/11 memorial on the West Coast. Ingels died in 2015.

David Cassidy still records and performs concerts both domestically and internationally. He occasionally appears on various television programs and has become a devoted advocate for Alzheimer's research after losing his mother, Evelyn Ward, to the disease in 2012. Cassidy lives in Fort Lauderdale, Florida. He has two children, Beau and Katie.

Susan Dey lives in upstate New York with her husband, TV producer Bernard Sofronski. She is an advocate for rape victims and supports her community by getting involved in local events supporting grassroots music and musicians. She has one daughter, Sara.

Danny Bonaduce and his wife, Amy, live in Seattle, where he currently hosts *The Danny Bonaduce Show* on KZOK 102.5. He has two children, Isabella and Dante.

Brian Forster enjoyed a long career in race-car driving. He has also worked as a science teacher as well as running his own winery. He currently resides in Sebastopol, California, with his wife, Lisa.

Suzanne Crough left the entertainment business completely after a few years doing movies, TV and specials post-Partridge Family. Crough, who was married with two children, passed away suddenly in April 2015 of a rare heart condition at her home in Laughlin, Nevada. She was 52 years old.

Jeremy Gelbwaks attended New York University and earned an MBA from Columbia University. He had his own consulting firm in New York City and then went on to work for a consulting firm specializing in manufacturing. He lives and works in New Orleans.

Dave Madden retired from his long and successful career in show business and lived his final years in Florida with his wife, Sandra. Madden had one daughter and one son. He passed away in 2014 at age 82.

Rick Segall continued to work as a child actor until age 16. Today he works as a pastor and worship leader in his church, and lives in Los Angeles with his wife and three children. He recorded an independent Christian album in 1999 and still writes and records.

Wes Farrell began reinventing himself with Christian music in the early '90s. He passed away in 1996 from cancer. He had three children, Sky, Wesley, and Dawn. He lived his final years in Florida with his wife, Jean Inman.

John Bahler still writes music and performs regularly. He is married to Janet Lennon, who is best known for her work as one of the Lennon Sisters. They live in Branson, Missouri, and sing professionally all over the country. He is also an accomplished photographer.

Tom Bahler went on to great success as a songwriter while continuing to work as a vocal artist. He recently completed his second book, titled *What You Want Wants You*, in 2014. He lives in New York City.

Jackie Ward retired after a long career as a session vocalist. She lives in Studio City, California.

Ron Hicklin is also retired and continues to work on various musical projects in his free time. He lives in Rancho Mirage, California.

What Is the Legacy of the Partridge Family?

Shirley Jones: Certainly it was the music. The music, and David Cassidy. He was the biggest star of that genre in his time.

Sandy Dvore, illustrator and animator: They were sort of the Beatles of television. Doesn't that sort of sound right to you? What the Beatles did for the world—that's what the Partridges did for television.

Adam Miller, songwriter: It was a marriage between the music and the show. It's kind of hard to describe, but when you're in that world and you are an inside part of it, even if you're on the periphery, it's quite a thrill!

Jackie Ward, background vocalist: I'm trying to think if … whether it needs a legacy. It was a period in time where it was one of the first television shows to produce a recording star with hit records. How many television shows and artists become stars because of the television show and then watch their records become famous? It's kind of special in itself.

William S. Bickley, producer: I was always trying to create the family I didn't have. I never wanted to write families that were mean to each other. I always wanted to write families that loved each other. Whether they fought or had their own foibles, the very base of who they were was that they really cared about each other and wanted to do the right thing for each other. As much of a fantasy as it was, with the Partridge Family, I was always trying somehow to get a family right. To me the Partridge Family was the first time I was writing for a family where I thought *I'm trying to write a family here that I would like to be a part of,* and I think the legacy is—if you can even call it a legacy—is that kids, maybe even mothers and fathers too, watched the show. Back then there were families that watched a show together. Now it's so fragmented that it's rare a family watches a show together. And I always liked to believe that watching that show sort of made families want to be better families, you know? And I think I formulated my philosophy, which is almost like the Hippocratic Oath: I wanted to either do good, or at least do no harm with whatever I put on television. And so for that half-hour families, kids, even parents could sort of live the family experience the way it should be, whether it was the way their family was or not. It was just a way to go visit a place where a family was the way families ought to be. And you know when you say, "Oh, is that a real family?" Well, it's probably not. I don't know anybody's family that was like that. Mine certainly wasn't. But it's nice to just believe that it's possible."

Ken Jacobson, songwriter: Feel-good. That's what the Partridge Family was all about!

John Bahler, vocal arranger, background vocalist: The first thing that comes to mind is that it was happy. It brings a smile to my face—not because I was a part of it and not because I was so proud of myself, but because the music itself makes you smile. My stepkids, who I raised, all listened to the Partridge Family. When they found out that I worked on it, I was the Big Kahuna! It was happy, clean, simple, fun music. We weren't cussing everybody out. We weren't trash-talking. We were just

when we're singin'

talking about happy things. Even the unrequited love songs were happy songs. You know what I mean? We have a saying in our family—if something is way too this or way too that, then the family was way too not real. They were a TV family, but in a Beaver Cleaver way, except it was in the '70s. It was clean-cut, fun, happy music that makes you tap your foot and smile.

Brian Forster: What made the show unique for its time was that it introduced a lot of things to TV. It had a lot of beginnings, like Laurie's role as a feminist or the widowed mother raising us as a single mom. A divorced mother would have been a little too radical for that time, but single parents raising kids was a big theme, and being the cool mom playing in the band while they are all touring together was revolutionary. In a lot of ways kids could relate to it because many were from broken homes, maybe a divorce or whatever, and I think it made the show more real. *The Brady Bunch* was like everything's perfect. I think *The Partridge Family* says that life's not always perfect, but we're still a family. Throwing the music into it was icing on the cake. I think another part of its legacy is that it was one of the first shows where the role of the merchandise was as huge as the show itself. It started with the albums, then the Partridge Family lunch pails, the dress-up dolls, the puzzles, and the comic books.

Danny Bonaduce: I remember Susan Dey saying something about the Vietnam War raging on as this Partridge Family show aired. I think she was trying to denigrate *The Partridge Family,* and instead I think she elevated it. We took your mind off the Vietnam War, which was the first war that spilled into your living room. Since then, Shirley Jones has conducted orchestras all around the country. David Cassidy makes millions of dollars touring around. I make a very comfortable living doing radio, and none of us could do that had we not had *The Partridge Family.* I would think that the greatest legacy of the Partridge Family would be that somebody, probably Bob Claver, found the right group of people.

Rick Segall: I think it's an ongoing legacy. It's very subjective to the minds of the people who either saw the show or didn't see the show. For those who didn't see it, it's something of an anomaly and kind of a pop culture item in that *Yeah, that was popular and isn't that a cool lookin' bus?* For the people who loved the show, I think it's as important to them as anything that's happened in American history.

There is that group of people for whom the show was impactful at their time of development. There are people who talk to me about how impactful the show was, and that they saw me as little Ricky and they wanted to be like me. I remember one person telling me that home life was so bad for them as a little kid, and their one rescue was to be able to escape and watch the Partridge Family. They will also tell me what the songs did for them. It's an imprint that was made on their hearts.

Ron Hicklin, background vocalist: For 11 years I did all of the music for *Happy Days, Laverne & Shirley,* sound-alike records, main title themes, little bridging cues—

but whatever bag it was, those stories are highlights that I begin speaking about by telling people that the four of us (Jackie, John, Tom and myself) were the background vocalists for the Partridge Family. When I speak to the Partridge Family, it's right there in the top two or three successes of what we have done. We were very proud to be accepted for the sound we created, whether anybody knew who we were or not.

Jeremy Gelbwaks: *The Partridge Family* was sentimental. It changed the way people think about TV. It changed the way people think about living in America, in ways big and small. We weren't the first family-oriented comedy, but we were the first with a single mother. *The Partridge Family* was able to come along with an idea and do it just differently enough from, say, *Family Affair*. We didn't invent anything new, but we took what was there and reinvented something, and brought it to a bigger audience. I don't think anybody working on the program understood the impact we would have. It's nearly 50 years ago, and here you are writing this book. Nobody's writing a book about *Family Affair*.

Paul Witt, producer: The legacy of *The Partridge Family* is complex in that it wasn't pure fantasy. Whether it was the Osmonds or the Cowsills, there were families out there making music. The Partridge Family made contemporary music a little bit more cuddly. I think it made parents feel more secure about their kids listening to it, because it was a time in which rock music was still considered threatening by a lot of parents. It was the social revolution during that era which included sex, drugs, and rock and roll almost at the starting point. *The Partridge Family* was able to bridge both ideas. It was able to make contemporary music comfortable and acceptable as part of family entertainment, and as such, I think that's an important part of its legacy.

Suzanne Crough: Whatever ends up lasting longest will be the legacy. Will the show always be known, or will the music always be heard? Probably a small portion of it lives on because of the music, in the sense that it has something to do with the actual show. But as far as the music by itself? No. The music was very influential, though. Can you tell me any other show that did that?

EPILOGUE

As a boy, I never heard my father speak about his achievements. I always knew he loved music from the excitement he would share with me as we listened to the classics of the '50s, '60s, and '70s. Our family road trips and vacations were filled from beginning to end with an anthology of the era, everything from Willie Nelson and Ray Charles to Eric Clapton, Aretha Franklin, the Beatles, the Stones, and the like.

When my dad would play these songs, though, he wouldn't just listen to them, he would obsessively dissect every aspect of them, telling my sister and me every little detail about each song—the story of how it was written, who wrote it, who produced it, who was in the studio, why they chose a particular style of instrumental arrangement. As a young kid I thought this was normal, and it was not till I was much older that I grew to understand that the storage facility full of gold plates were actually gold records of songs my dad wrote or produced, and that his stories were so detailed because he lived in and was a part of the music history of that era.

When my dad tragically passed away in 1996 at the age of 56, it was beyond devastating to my family and me personally. I was only 12 and had just begun to understand him as a man and his role in music history.

The gift that remained in his absence was his songs.

As I made my way through my teen years and college I became very fascinated and almost obsessed with music, and particularly the music of my father. Each song of his was like a story or lesson he had left for me. His work on the Partridge Family was but a small part of his catalogue, but it always stood out to me as remarkable—and in many ways underappreciated—music. Many of the lyrics from those songs really spoke to me as I made my way through life.

I could write an essay on his songs, but some stood out: The uplifting and aspirational nature of "Come on Get Happy" and "Sunshine." The lessons of "I'll meet you halfway, that's better than no way." The stories of love and life in "Money Money," "Twenty-Four Hours a Day," "Something's Wrong," "Hello, Hello," "Last Night," and "Rainmaker." The undeniable truth and honesty my dad must have felt when he wrote "Doesn't Somebody Want to Be Wanted."

when we're singin'

In listening to the songs countless times I learned a lot about my dad, and in the process was able to realize how good the lyrics and music were, how if you really listen and look past the TV show, the bus, and the characters, you will find music that possesses a quality, a wisdom, and a message so powerful that it has stood the test of time. People all over the world connected with it then, and they continue to connect with it over 40 years later.

Wesley J. Farrell
April 2014

AFTERWORD

A Tribute to Suzanne Crough

I shouldn't be writing this. I don't mean that *I* shouldn't be writing this; what I mean is, *no one* should be writing this. Suzanne was the baby of the family and although we're all older (really … it was 45 years ago?!), she was still the youngest and had no health issues. First we lost Dave, and now Suzanne... This is hard to write.

We all know that Suzanne and I were mostly inseparable on the show. I have often referred to our characters not as "Chris" and "Tracy," but as "Crizntracy"; in other words, one character. Our characters were not major ones on the show. (Someone once said, I think it was of the producers, that Chris and Tracy were nothing more than "talking props." Ouch! But that was basically true.) However, we were always there, at least in the song of the week, where our talents were there to shine! (Or not...

What about my relationship with Suzanne, not Tracy? Since we were not characters who got a lot of camera time in a typical week, we spent a lot of time together, whether it was in school, riding our bikes, playing badminton (I think her folks got that started…) or just exploring. Because of that, and because she was the only girl I was around constantly most of the year, she was one of my first serious crushes. At one point, we even had a "junior marriage" with a ceremony that she made up! My mom used to love telling the story of how I'd cry on Friday afternoons, saying, "I won't see Suzanne till Monday!" However, like most childhood romances, I moved on, as did she. The show moved on too and it was canceled, as we all know. She went on to do *Mulligan's Stew*, while I tried to catch up on "normal" life, going into the remainder of eighth grade and going surfing and skateboarding.

Fast forward to 1993 and we meet again in an interview for *People* magazine, where I find out that she married a CHP officer, had kids, and moved away from L.A. I also had moved away from L.A. to the San Francisco Bay area to start a career in car racing. I think we both had had it with the Hollywood scene and wanted to lead normal lives. By then, the stories of ex-child stars going bad were old news. (There was even one on our show!) We were boring, maybe, but at least we weren't in rehab or jail.

For a while there, it seemed like there was some sort of reunion show or article every five years or so; *People, The Today Show,* the *Danny!* show, and on and on. Suzanne and I even crashed *The Arsenio Hall Show* when we found out that they were advertising a Partridge Family reunion and didn't even contact us. I saw Suzanne's feisty side then and found I was a little feisty myself. We vowed we would stay in touch to make sure our voices were heard from then on.

Fast forward again about 10 more years, and we found out about the Hollywood Collector Show, an autograph show/convention that was held in the San Fernando Valley. We found out that they were glad to have us, Chris and Tracy! We had fans lining up for our pictures and autographs and were really happy to see us! We did one or two more shows, then went to New Jersey for the big one, called Chiller Theater. This show was geared towards the horror/goth genre, with people dressed like the characters on *The Walking Dead*, and here were Chris and Tracy! Again, people lined up to see us (and Mini-Me, and Adam West and the Soup Nazi…). Then the fun really started; I won't get into details, but let's just say that Chris and Tracy and the Soup Nazi had so much fun, the fire department had to be called! At the time, as it is right now, we told ourselves that it was a once-in-a-lifetime experience.

We did a few more shows and while they may not have been the gangbuster events they had been, it meant that I got to hang out with Suzanne, Bill, Sam, and Alex. I got to watch Alex blush when she got a birthday call from Orlando Bloom, thanks to an arrangement from Marty Ingels. I was able to introduce Suzanne to my future wife in New York during the *Today Show* taping. (And thanks to Bill and the never-empty martini, I almost didn't make the show….) I even got to see Suzanne become a grandmother.

Then I got the phone call… Scott, our partner in crime at the Chiller Show and in general, told me that Suzanne was found dead. I literally did not believe it … how was that possible? I respected the family's wishes and did not say anything to the media until I got the OK, but in today's world, that didn't matter; the news was out. I was in tears when I wrote the statement to the press, but after not saying anything at first, I guess they thought I didn't have anything to say. Shirley Jones and Danny Bonaduce were quoted, but not me. Now I've had my chance.

Suzanne, you will be missed by many; your family, your friends, your co-workers and the fans of the show. And me.

Brian Forster
"Chris Partridge"
August 2015

DISCOGRAPHY

Included is the complete Partridge Family discography as it was issued in the United States, arranged by release date. International (U.K.) reissues of complete albums on compact disc are also included. David Cassidy's solo work is not represented here, unless it was part of a U.S.-released Partridge Family compilation. All U.S.-issued CD releases containing Partridge Family compilations and/or unreleased songs are also included.

Chart positions in the trade magazines were based on actual sales. Release dates have been calculated based on the first chart appearance, and information shared by the staff of Bell Records.

1970

I Think I Love You/Somebody Wants to Love You
Released August 1970, Bell 910
Peak: *Billboard* No. 1 (three weeks), *Cash Box* No. 1 (three weeks), *Record World* No. 1 (four weeks)

Bye, Bye Blackbird/My Kind of Music
Released September 1970, Bell 920 (under artist name Colagé)

The Partridge Family Album
Released September 1970, Bell 6050
Peak: *Billboard* No. 4, *Cash Box* No. 6, *Record World* No. 7
Original formats: Vinyl, cassette, 8-track, reel-to-reel
Reissues: Razor & Tie Music Corp., 1993 (CD);
Buddah Records, 2000 (CD); 7T's Records, 2012 (CD)

1971

Doesn't Somebody Want to Be Wanted/You Are Always On My Mind
Released January 1971, Bell 963
Peak: *Billboard* No. 6, *Cash Box* No. 1 (one week), *Record World* No. 1 (one week)

The Partridge Family Up to Date
Released March 1971, Bell 6059
Peak: *Billboard* No. 3, *Cash Box* No. 3, *Record World* No. 3
Original formats: Vinyl, 8-track, cassette, reel-to-reel
Reissues: Razor & Tie Music Corp., 1993 (CD);
Buddah Records, 2000 (CD); 7T's Records, 2012 (CD)

I'll Meet You Halfway/Morning Rider on the Road
Released April 1971, Bell 996
Peak: *Billboard* No. 9, *Cash Box* No. 2, *Record World* No. 4

I Woke Up in Love This Morning/Twenty-Four Hours a Day
Released July 1971, Bell 45-130
Peak: *Billboard* No. 13, *Cash Box* No. 9, *Record World* No. 9

The Partridge Family Sound Magazine
Released August 1971, Bell 6064
Peak: *Billboard* No. 9, *Cash Box* No. 9, *Record World* No. 8
Original formats: Vinyl, cassette, 8-track, reel-to-reel
Reissues: Razor & Tie Music Corp., 1993 (CD);
Buddha Records, 2000 (CD); 7T's Records, 2013 (CD)

A Partridge Family Christmas Card
Released November 1971, Bell 6066
Peak: *Billboard* No. 1 (Christmas chart), *Cash Box* No. 19, *Record World* No. 79
Original formats: Vinyl, cassette, 8-track
Reissues: Bell Records, 1972 (vinyl); Razor & Tie Music Corp., 1992 (CD);
BMG Special Products, 2000 (CD)
Reissue peak: 1972 reissue, *Billboard* No. 9

It's One of Those Nights (Yes, Love)/One Night Stand
Released December 1971, Bell 45-160
Peak: *Billboard* No. 20, *Cash Box* No. 16, *Record World* No. 14

1972

The Partridge Family Shopping Bag
Released March 1972, Bell 6072
Peak: *Billboard* No. 18, *Cash Box* No. 16, *Record World* No. 8
Original formats: Vinyl, cassette, 8-track, reel-to-reel
Reissues: Razor & Tie Music Corp., 1993 (CD); BMG Heritage, 2003 (CD);
7T's Records, 2013 (CD)

Am I Losing You/If You Ever Go
Released April 1972, Bell 45-200
Peak: *Billboard* No. 59, *Cash Box* No. 31, *Record World* No. 35

Breaking Up is Hard to Do/I'm Here, You're Here
Released June 1972, Bell 45-235
Peak: *Billboard* No. 28; *Cash Box* No. 25, *Record World* No. 24

The Partridge Family at Home with Their Greatest Hits
Released August 1972, Bell 1107
Peak: *Billboard* No. 21, *Cash Box* No. 20, *Record World* No. 15
Original formats: Vinyl, cassette, 8-track, reel-to-reel
Reissue: Arista AL 5-8175, 1982 (vinyl)

Looking Through the Eyes of Love/Storybook Love
Released November 1972, Bell 45-301
Peak: *Billboard* No. 39, *Cash Box* No. 25, *Record World* No. 36

The Partridge Family Notebook
Released November 1972, Bell 1111
Peak: *Billboard* No. 41, *Cash Box* No. 33, *Record World* No. 37
Original formats: Vinyl, cassette, 8-track, reel-to-reel
Reissues: Buddha Records, 2000 (CD); 7T's Records, 2013 (CD)

1973

Friend and a Lover/Something's Wrong
Released March 1973, Bell 45-336
Peak: *Billboard* No. 99, *Cash Box* No. 92, *Record World* No. 67

The Partridge Family Crossword Puzzle
Released June 1973, Bell 1122
Peak: *Billboard* No. 167, *Cash Box* No. 105, *Record World* No. 95
Original formats: Vinyl, cassette, 8-track
Reissues: BMG Heritage, 2003 (CD); 7T's Records, 2013 (CD)

The Partridge Family Bulletin Board
Released October 1973, Bell 1137
Peak: *Cash Box* No. 124 (the group's last chart appearance)
Original formats: Vinyl, cassette, 8-track
Reissue: Collector's Choice Music, 2008
(CD; includes previously unreleased "Ain't Love Easy")

Lookin' for a Good Time/Money, Money
Released November 1973, Bell 45-414

1974

The World of the Partridge Family
Released November 1974, Bell 1319
Original formats: Vinyl, cassette, 8-track

1976 and Later

The Partridge Family
Released 1976, Laurie House LH 8014
Original formats: Vinyl, 8-track
Budget compilation available exclusively through mail order; includes both Partridge Family and David Cassidy songs

The Partridge Family Greatest Hits
Released 1989, Arista ARCD8604
Original formats: CD, Cassette
Includes previously unreleased "Come On Get Happy"

Tube Tunes, Volume One: The '70s
Released 1995, Rhino R2 71910
Original format: CD
TV theme song compilation that includes the unreleased "When We're Singin'"

David Cassidy's Partridge Family Favorites
Released 1998, Slamajama 812-2
Original format: CD
Available exclusively through Home Shopping Network with the purchase of David Cassidy's *Old Trick, New Dog*. Includes both Partridge Family and David Cassidy songs, some previously unreleased—including the Partridge Family's "Warm My Soul" and "It's Time That I Knew You Better"

David Cassidy & the Partridge Family: The Definitive Collection
Released 2000, Arista 07822-14640-2
Original format: CD
Includes both Partridge Family and David Cassidy songs; first CD release of "Breaking Up Is Hard to Do"

Come On Get Happy: The Very Best of the Partridge Family
Released 2005, Arista 82876-68199-2
Original format: CD
Includes previously unreleased songs including "Together (Havin' A Ball)," "Stephanie," "Let the Good Times In" and "Baby I Love, Love, I Love You"

Playlist: The Very Best of the Partridge Family
Released 2013, RCA 88837-12982
Original format: CD
Includes first stereo release of "Breaking Up Is Hard to Do"

SUGGESTED READING

David Cassidy, *Could It Be Forever? My Story*, 2007

Danny Bonaduce, *Random Acts of Badness: My Story*, 2001

Joey Green, *The Partridge Family Album*, 1994

Shirley Jones with Wendy Leigh, *A Memoir*, 2013

Shirley Jones & Marty Ingels with Mickey Herskowitz, *Shirley & Marty: An Unlikely Love Story*, 1990

Dave Madden, *Reuben on Wry: The Memoirs of Dave Madden*, 2007

Ken Sharp, *Sound Explosion! Inside L.A.'s Studio Factory with the Wrecking Crew*, 2015

ACKNOWLEDGEMENTS

My heartfelt thanks to all those interviewed for this book. The countless hours of your personal time that each of you gave to this project is tremendously appreciated. You have given the fans what they have wanted for so many years. Thank you Paul Anka, Mike Appel, John Bahler, Tom Bahler, Leslie Bell, Max Bennett, William S. Bickley, Hal Blaine, Danny Bonaduce, Caroline Boyce, L. Russell Brown, Dennis Budimir, Terry Cashman, David Cassidy, Lou Christie, Bob Claver, Harvey Cooper, Suzanne Crough, Neil Daniels, Henry Diltz, Bill Dorsey, Steve Dossick, Chip Douglas, Sandy D'Vore, Shelly Ellison, Mary Dee English, Stan Farber, Jean Inman Farrell, Wes Farrell, Wes Farrell Jr., Chuck Flores, Brian Forster, Tina Funk, Jeremy Gelbwaks, Don Glut, Bobby Hart, Ron Hicklin, Diane Hildebrand, John Michael Hill, Rupert Holmes, Bones Howe, Ken Jacobson, Mark James, Danny Janssen, Shirley Jones, Marty Kaniger, Russ Keller, Dale Laszig (née Leipzig), Derek Lawrence, Noel Love, Dave Madden, Dale McRaven, Mike Melvoin, Adam Miller, Sheila Molitz, Joe Osborn, Howard Pattow, Dan Peyton, Ken Poston, David Price, Mike Ragogna, Frank Romeo, Tony Romeo, Marshall Rogers, Larry Rosen, John Rosica, Jim Salamanis, Harriet Schock, Rick Segall, Rick Segall Sr., Ralph Senensky, Ken Sharp, Louie Sheldon, Sandy Siler, Bernard Slade, Sally Stevens, Colin Strayer, Mel Swope, Denny Tedesco, Jai Uttal, Renée Valente, Jackie Ward, Cynthia Weil, Beverly Weinstein, Tommy West, Tony Wilson, Toni Wine, Paul Junger Witt, and John Zaccheo.

This book wouldn't be possible without the hardworking team who contributed countless hours to help make this a reality: First and foremost a very special thank you to Ken Sharp. I will never forget your support, advice, and incredibly selfless generosity in letting your "lost" interviews be revealed in this book. Thanks to my good friend Tim "Voice of the Pirates" DeBacco, for your brilliant website design and execution, and the many, many hours you donated to this project; Mary Hertweck for helping to keep the Kickstarter campaign alive; Donna Spencer, an editor no writer should do without; Nick Cool and the Image Works for support with the photos when I went completely crazed; Kristina Danklef and Sourballpython for your brilliant graphic design and infectious enthusiasm from the day you joined this project; Tyler Cosma and Cosma Photography for your bail-out layout touch of genius and ability to pick me up when the sky looked dark, and for photographing hundreds of items (with your friendly assistant Jocelynne Samu); Jason Snyder for your bionic ear and lightning-fast transcribing skills; Steve Bodner for the two-day Partridge Family music marathon session; Keith Berger and Graphic Touch Letterpress & Binding Company for donating time, artwork and design, and product to the Kickstarter campaign; Alex Baker for additional transcribing; Barbara Pazmino and Tina Funk, for years and years of encouragement and support through the Just David Fan Club; Geoff Brown for your fact-finding skills; Louise Poynton for keeping things alive in the U.K.; Stacy Coffee-Thorne for spreading the word all over the Internet; Jane Reaburn for support through Davidcassidy.com; Denny Tedesco for your personal support, introducing me to the amazing Wrecking Crew musicians, and promoting our Kickstarter campaign on wreckingcrewfilm.com; David Thomas, my whimming attorney/filmmaker extraordinaire; the Rock & Roll Hall of Fame Library & Archives and the incredible staff who put up with me for over a year—Jennie Thomas, Anastasia Karel, William Jackson, and Andy Leach; The Ohio State University Library of Music and Dance and my undercover researcher Patty Werner; Brent Olynick, Kathleen Campbell and the Country Music Foundation, Nashville, TN; the I Think I Love You girls Brianna Miller, Jackie Witt and Andrea Davis; Seneca Printing Express; Insta-Copy of Salem, Ohio; the Salem News; the Cleveland Plain Dealer; Geri Dawson, Emma Brereton; and last but not least my Hollywood boys, Sam Hayes for teaching me so much; Scott Awley for priceless contributions of photos; and Scottie Gee Gerardi, for enthusiasm, help with graphic design and your work on the many photos seen in this book.

Special thanks to all those who donated items and personal autographs to the Kickstarter campaign, including 3 Moms Stitchin', Mike Appel, John Bahler, Tom Bahler, Max Bennett, Keith Berger and Graphic Touch Letterpress & Binding Company, Hal Blaine, L. Russell Brown; Dennis Budimir, Terry Cashman, Bob Claver, Harvey Cooper, Henry Diltz, Stephen Dossick, Mary Dee English, Brian Forster, Jeremy Gelbwaks, Glen Hanson, Bobby Hart, Ron Hicklin, Diane Hildebrand, Ken Jacobson, Marty Kaniger, Noel Love, Joe Osborn, Dan Peyton, David Price, Jackie Ward, and Beverly Weinstein.

There were many people who contributed photos of their memorabilia and Partridge Family/David Cassidy items for use in the book that were never used, simply because we ended up with different variations of the same photo. A very special thanks to Brian Forster for opening up your collection of rare acetates and records for use in this book, and taking the time and effort to personally photograph them. Your enthusiastic support is like no other. Thanks to Vreny Thrommen, Leslie Bell, and Tina Funk for the additional photos.

Last but not least I thank my loving family and friends. You were all there for me at 100 percent. Gale Colapietro, Adam Stevens, Patty & Jeff Werner, Ruth & Ed Mallinak, John & Novelle Miller, Joe & Kris Miller, Michael Miller, Joe & Brianna Miller, my pseudo-family Attila, Jaccie, Rick and Jocelynne Samu and Tyler Cosma; Ray Miller and Jessica Wood, Theresa Anne Miller, Donnie and Marylou Miller, Mary Lynne and Dick Macek, Cindy Jacobson; and Bob Miller, Joe Mokran, dancin' Carrie Mazzucco, Lindsay Moyer, the exuberant Jim Salamanis (the best Partridge Family friend the fan base could ever hope to find), my partner in crime Robert Forchione for your love and support (not to mention the endless computer backups!), and most especially to my loving parents, Ray Miller and Wilma C. Miller, who made love the rule of my life. My dear mother always wanted me to write. This one's for you, Mom. I love you and Dad both more than you could ever know.

Backers

This book was funded through Kickstarter.com and WhenWereSingin.com. More than 250 people backed this project to make this book a reality. From the bottom of my heart I'd like to thank all of you:

Jill Marie Adams, Connie Jensen Albrecht, Steve & Jill Alessandro, Judi Allio, Jeff Anderson, Araceli Ramirez Arevalo, Rosanne Arnold, Donald Arthurs, Scott Awley, Debbie Baker, John Barnhart, Leslie Lee Bell and Michael Feldman of the Forever Family "Starring Shirley Jones Ingels," Alain Bergeron, Cindy Collingwood Best, Jeff Bingham, Deb Blair, Robert Bober, Hal Bogart, Wade R. Boley, Aimee Bonomolo, George Bounacos, Mark Brammer, Barbara Brown, Geoff Brown, Joe Brown, Edwina L. Burke, P. Campen, Tsambiko Capperis, Chelsea Carbonell, Debbie Wilson Carr, Paula Chadwick, Robin Christman, Philip Clark, Bob Claver, Marina Clerin, Stacy Jo Coffee-Thorne, Gale Colapietro, Kim Conner, Linda Cooke, Susan Cope, Cheryl Corwin, Carol Cosenza, Tim & Debra Cosma, Tyler Cosma, Debbie Craver, Darryl Crickmore, Shirl Criss, Brian Curtis, Laurie Cull, Brian Curtis, Neelia Dahvid, Mark D'Alessandro, Carol D'Amico, Neil T. Daniels, Richard L. Daub, David Daum, Deborah Daum, Mandy J. Davies, Andrea "Hulapants" Davis, Chris Davis, Suzanne Davis, Tim DeBacco, John and Cathie DeFazio, Rich Derrico, Patrick Devine, Andrew Dobzyn, Dorri, Beth Duvall, Monica Dyce, Scott Edwards, Brad Ehlers, Rebecca Elder, Stephen Elders, Pam Elkins, Tuzy Ellis, Eugene Evans, Jan Evans, JoAnn Everett, Julie Faber, Dennis & Karen Falconer, Scott Falconer, Nancy L. Fediaczko, Robert Forchione, Astrid Frense, Richard Fronduto, Tina Funk, Connie Lynn Geho, Jeff Gehringer, Linda Glennon, Kim and Geoff Goll, John Gomolka, Jason Green, Mary Ann Greier, Tony Greier, Melanie Grimm, Kelly Guerriero, Joanna H., Becky Hall, John Hanibal, Rachael Hanna, Alison Hanson, Shirley Harker, Jeffery

Harlan, Shelly L. Haught, Lindsay Hawkins, Samson Stormcrow Hayes, Thomas E. Healey, Mary DeBacco Hertweck, Eddie Hicinbothem, Linda Higgins, LeAnne Hitchcock, Nancy Hoadley, Beth A. Holt, Joseph Hollis Holt, Sheila Jackson, Mary Evelyn James, Sandy James, Keith Jennings, Alan Jespersen, Sharon Jull, Jane Kaminski, Mish Kardachi, Shellie Ferancy Kearsey, Jennifer Adams Kelley, James Kontnier, Teresa Kremer, Bob Lamars, Karen Lambert, Richard Lancer, Dale Laszig, Edward Laszig, Julie Latz, Matthew Leipzig, John P. Lilly, LuAnn Littleton, David Lock, JoAnn Lowe, Lynne Madsen, Ed & Ruth Mallinak, Steven Martens, Casey Martin, Suzie Mason, Dr. Brian Mathie, Carrie Mazzucco, Machelle McDonald, Cecil & Marlene McEndree, Kimberlee McGuire, Ria Mclldufg, Dr. Lucio Mendonca, Jeannie Mercier, Mary Dee Merrell, Joe & Brianna Miller, Joe & Kristen Miller, John & Novelle Miller, Michael Miller, Raphael (Ray) Miller, Naomi Mills, Sam Misshula, Janet Mitchell, Lorina Moffett, Joe Mokran, Kerry Morrissey, Dana Moruzzi, Barbara Moyer, Jim & Ruth Newman, Angela Niebuhr, Mary Alice Noble, Colleen O'Mullen, Lisa Ortenzi, David Parks, Jane Parvin, Ellery Phillips, Frank Pinola, John Pitts, Gary Plamowski, Andrew Pollis, Diana Powell, Amy Poynter, Louise Poynton, Jane Reaburn, Tracy Reed, Dianne Reedy, Arthur Robillard, Jan Robshaw, Rock & Roll Hall of Fame Library & Archives, Pauline Ross, Marc Rubin, Jeffrey Ryan, Jim Salamanis, Attila and Jaccie Samu, Rick Samu, Baldassare Savona, Sandy Scanlon, Jean Schnur, Harriet Schock, Lenny Scolletta, Kate Sheely, John Sheldrake, Lynn Sherwood, Brian & Janice Shockey, Paul Sitkowski, Carolyn Slaven, Nicole Slaven, Jane Smith, Kenneth L. Smith, Tracy Soinger, Donna Spencer, Susan & Doug Spiker, William Stamper, Adam Stevens, Bill C. Storts, Dave, Lori and Tyler Stouffer, Colin Strayer, Sandie Strickland, David C. K. Swanson, Pam (Pixley) Swasta, Denny Tedesco, Joyce Thiel, Heidi Tittle, Mollie Turner, Kevin & Carrie Utt, Esther M. Rodriguez Vazquez, Maxine Vincent, the Vollmer family, Taffi & Greg Voorhees, Ida Wank, Ken Wank, Ken & Judy Warner, Valerie Weingart, Beverly Weinstein, Jeff & Patty Werner, Glen Wight, Mary Anne Wilkinson, C. Bruce Williams, Shelley L. Williams, Mary L. Wilson, Julie Winn, Jackie Witt, Sheraton Worley, Wendy Wright, Jeff Wunsch, Mark Wyckoff and Amy Shatzen, Frank A. Zamarelli, Nancy Z., and two anonymous donors.

SOURCES

Personal interviews by the author: Paul Anka, Mike Appel, John Bahler, Tom Bahler, Max Bennett, William S. Bickley, Hal Blaine, Danny Bonaduce, Caroline Boyce, L. Russell Brown, Dennis Budimir, Terry Cashman, David Cassidy, Lou Christie, Bob Claver, Harvey Cooper, Suzanne Crough, Neil Daniels, Henry Diltz, Bill Dorsey, Stephen Dossick, Chip Douglas, Sandy D'Vore, Shelley Ellison, Mary Dee English, Stan Farber, Wes Farrell, Wes Farrell Jr., Chuck Flores, Brian Forster, Tina Funk, Jeremy Gelbwaks, Don Glut, Bobby Hart, Ron Hicklin, Diane Hildebrand, John Michael Hill, Rupert Holmes, Bones Howe, Jean Inman, Ken Jacobson, Mark James, Danny Janssen, Shirley Jones, Marty Kaniger, Russ Keller, Dale Laszig (née Leipzig), Derek Lawrence, Noel Love, Dave Madden, Dale McRaven, Mike Melvoin, Adam Miller, Sheila Molitz, Joe Osborn, Howard Pattow, Dan Peyton, Ken Poston, David Price, Mike Ragogna, Frank Romeo, Tony Romeo, Marshall Rogers, Larry Rosen, John Rosica, Jim Salamanis, Harriet Schock, Rick Segall, Rick Segall Sr., Ralph Senensky, Ken Sharp, Louie Sheldon, Sandy Siler, Bernard Slade, Sally Stevens, Colin Strayer, Mel Swope, Denny Tedesco, Renée Valente, Jackie Ward, Cynthia Weil, Beverly Weinstein, Tommy West, Tony Wilson, Toni Wine, Paul Junger Witt, John Zaccheo. Unpublished personal interviews by Ken Sharp: David Cassidy, 1993 and 2013; Wes Farrell, 1993; Tony Romeo, 1993. David Cassidy, *Could It Be Forever? My Story.* Headline Book Publishing, 2007. David Cassidy with Chip Deffaa, *C'Mon Get Happy: Fear and Loathing on the Partridge Family Bus.* Warner Books Inc., 1994. Dave Madden, *Reuben on Wry: The Memoirs of Dave Madden.* BookSurge Publishing, 2007.

Additional Sources by Chapter

Prologue

Danny! Video recording of premiere episode, 1995.

Chapter 1

"100 Greatest Episodes of All-Time." *TV Guide,* June 25, 1997.
The Arsenio Hall Show. Video recording of episode airing July 13, 1993.
Billboard. October 8, 1966 (*Swingin' Country;* the Love Generation), October 10, 1970 (*Album* review).
Cash Box. May 3, 1969 (Boyce & Hart); May 10, 1969 (Wes Farrell); May 24, 1969 (Wes Farrell); July 19, 1969 (Boyce & Hart); October 10, 1970 *(Album* review); March 13 and 20, 1971; June 27, 1970 ("I'm on the Road"); August 22, 1970 ("I Think I Love You" review); January 9, 1971 ("I Think I Love You" sales); March 13, 1971 ("I Think I Love You"); March 20, 1971 ("I Think I Love You," *Album* sales).
Rock & Roll Hall of Fame Library & Archives, Cleveland, Ohio.
Lisa Sutton, liner notes, *The Partridge FamilyAlbum.*
Buddah Records reissue, 2000.
Variety, September 30, 1970. Review of first episode.
Joel Whitburn, *The Billboard Albums,* 6th edition, 2006.
Joel Whitburn, *Billboard Hot 100 Charts: The Seventies,* 1990.
Joel Whitburn, *Pop Annual, 8th edition* (1955–2011), 2012.

Chapter 2

"ABC Renews the Partridges." *Fresno Bee–The Republican,* December 6, 1970.

Michael S. Barrett, "Partridge Family Star Offers Good Times, No Messages." *San Bernardino County Sun,* September 21, 1970. David Cassidy assessment of the Partridge Family's music.

Tim Brooks and Earl Marsh, *The Complete Directory to Prime Time Network and Cable TV Shows 1946–Present,* 1999.

Billboard. March 27, 1971 *(Album* review); December 25, 1971 *(Bobby Jo and the Big Apple Goodtime Band).*

Cash Box. October 24, 1970 *(Album* and "I Think I Love You" sales); February 6, 1971 ("Doesn't Somebody Want to Be Wanted" review); February 27, 1971 ("New Partridge LP Spotlights Bell's Diversified Release"); March 6, 1971 (international appeal); March 20, 1971 *(Album* review); April 3, 1971 *(Up to Date* certification, "Doesn't Somebody Want to Be Wanted"); May 1, 1971 ("I'll Meet You Halfway" review).

Chevrolet model identification charts, General Motors. *1929–1954 Chevrolet Master Parts and Accessories Catalog,* p. 9; *1929–1957 Chevrolet Master Parts and Accessories Catalog,* pp. 9–10; *1958 Chevrolet Parts and Accessories Catalog,* no page number.

"For Shirley Jones, Life Is Beautiful." *Progress Bulletin,* Pomona California, December 27, 1970. First year winter break.

Janine Gressel, "David Cassidy Scores Hit in Concert Debut at Arena." *Seattle Times,* March 27, 1971. David Cassidy's first concert review.

Joyce Haber, "Will Success Spoil Young David Cassidy?" *Des Moines Register,* October 31, 1971. David Cassidy and Shirley Jones' involvement in *Getting Together.*

George Hetherington, "Nether Providence Graduates Greatest." *Delaware County Daily Times,* Chester, Pennsylvania, June 13, 1973. Bus painting prank.

"History of Superior Coach." Accessed online at superiorcoaches.com/about.

The Progress, Clearfield, Pennsylvania, October 13, 1973. Susan Dey interview.

Lisa Sutton, liner notes, *The Partridge Family Up to Date.* Razor & Tie CD reissue, 1993.

"Two Nights in Shining Armor." *San Bernardino County Sun,* March 14, 1971. Season 1 ratings.

Variety, March 31, 1971. *Album* review.

Joel Whitburn, *The Billboard Albums,* 6th edition, 2006.

Joel Whitburn, *Pop Annual,* 8th edition (1955–2011), 2012.

Joel Whitburn, *Top Pop Singles 1955–2010,* 2012.

Jeanne Wright, "Painted Bus Delights All." *Delaware County Daily Times,* Chester, Pennsylvania, June 7, 1973. Bus painting prank.

Chapter 3

Billboard, August 21, 1971. *Sound Magazine* review.

Cash Box. July 31, 1971 ("I Woke Up in Love This Morning" review); August 21, 1971 *(Sound Magazine* review).

David Cassidy Newsletter, November 13, 2006. Accessed online at davidcassidy.com/fansite/InPrintPages/DCNewsletter2006Nov.html. Most requested song.

Joyce Haber, "Will Success Spoil Young David Cassidy?" *Des Moines Register,* October 31, 1971. David Cassidy's invitation to play Madison Square Garden.

Lowell Sun, Lowell, Massachusetts, October 22, 1971. "Whale Song" possible release.

Ken Sharp, unpublished interview with Rupert Holmes, 2013.

Tiger Beat's Official Partridge Magazine: December 1970 (launch), May 1971 (Smile contest), August 1971 (Brian Forster).

Variety, September 22, 1971. *Sound Magazine* review.

Joel Whitburn, *Pop Annual,* 8th edition (1955–2011), 2012.

Chapter 4

"ASCAP Members Reign Over Most-Played Holiday Songs List," ASCAP, December 12, 2012. Accessed online at ascap.com/press/2012/1212-ascap-members-reign-over-top-ten-most-played-holiday-songs-list.aspx.

Billboard, December 4, 1971. *Christmas Card* review.

Tim Brooks and Earle Marsh, *The Complete Directory to Prime Time Network and Cable TV Shows 1946–Present,* 7th Edition, 1999.

Cash Box. February 6, 1971 (Grammy nomination); August 8, 1971 (David Cassidy concert review); August 29, 1971 (David Cassidy *Glen Campbell Goodtime Hour* appearance); September 11, 1971 (Christmas album promotion); October 16, 1971 ("Bell: Pre-Order Gold For 'Family'"); November 20, 1971 *(Christmas Card* review); December 11, 1971 ("The Necessity of Pre-Teen Stars"); December 25, 1971 (annual "best of" list).

Ace Collins, *Stories Behind the Greatest Hits of Christmas,* 2010.

Jeff Kunerth, "Story Behind Winter Wonderland." *Orlando Sentinel,* December 9, 2010.

David Lamb, "Making of Teen Idol, Cassidy, Strictly Big Business." *Anderson Herald,* Anderson, Indiana, December 29, 1971. Partridge Family Day, holiday album sales.

Ken Liebeskind, "Armonk Celebrates Frosty Day Dec. 10." *Armonk Daily Voice,* December 3, 2011.

New York Times, June 26, 1995. Tony Romeo obituary.

"Readers' Poll: The Best Christmas Songs of All Time," RollingStone.com, November 30, 2011. Accessed online at rollingstone.com/music/pictures/readers-poll-the-best-christmas-songs-of-all-time-20111130.

Lisa Sutton, liner notes, *Cherish.* Buddah Records CD reissue, 1993.

Joel Whitburn, *Christmas in the Charts (1920–2004),* 2004.

Chris Willman, "The History of a Popular Holiday Song." *Entertainment Weekly,* January 8, 2007.

Kim Wook, "Yule Laugh, Yule Cry: 10 Things You Didn't Know About Beloved Holiday Songs." *Time,* December 14, 2012.

Chapter 5

Billboard. March 4, 1972 (Ru-Da Music); March 25, 1972 *(Shopping Bag* review).

Cash Box. October 30, 1971 *(Cherish* preview); December 4, 1971 ("It's One of Those Nights" review); February 5, 1972 *(Cherish* review, David Cassidy tour announcement); March 18, 1972 *(Shopping Bag* and "Am I Losing You" reviews); May 27, 1972 (BBC series cancellation).

"David Cassidy Can't Get Happy after Winning 'Partridge Family' Lawsuit." Examiner. com, January 4, 2015. Accessed online at examiner.com/article/david-cassidy-can-t-get-happy-after-winning-partridge-family-lawsuit.

Robin Green, "Naked Lunch Box." *Rolling Stone,* May 11, 1972.

TV Guide, July 7, 1972. David Cassidy beach towel.
Variety, April 12, 1972. *Shopping Bag* review.
Joel Whitburn, *The Billboard Albums,* 6th edition, 2006.
Joel Whitburn, *The Comparison Book 1954–1982,* 2015.
Dwight Whitney, "It's Practically a Branch of the U. S. Mint." *TV Guide,* July 15, 1972. Merchandising, David Cassidy income sources.

Chapter 6

Billboard, September 16, 1972. *At Home* review.
Steven Bingen with Marc Wanamaker, *Warner Bros. Hollywood's Ultimate Backlot,* Bison Archives, 2014.
"Cameras Roll at Columbia Despite Studio Blaze." *Box Office,* February 9, 1970.
Cash Box. June 17, 1972 ("Breaking Up Is Hard to Do" review); June 24, 1972 (mislabeled DJ copies of "Breaking Up Is Hard to Do"); July 1, 1972 (first half 1972 artist rankings); July 22, 1972 (Bell Records restructuring); September 2, 1972 (*At Home* review, Bell promotional campaign).
"Fire Blazes on Burbank Sets." *Broadcasting,* February 9, 1970.
Joe Lapointe, "Who Is Sloopy and What Is She Hanging on To?" Bats: The Yankees, the Mets, and Major League Baseball *(New York Times* blog), October 5, 2007. Accessed online at http://bats.blogs.nytimes.com/2007/10/05/who-is-sloopy-and-what-is-she-hanging-on-to/?_r=0.
"Ohio's State Rock Song—Hang On Sloopy." Ohio History Central. Accessed online at ohiohistorycentral.org/w/Ohio%27s_State_Rock_Song_-_Hang_On_Sloopy.
"Susan Dey's Anorexia." *Woman's Day,* January 18, 1993, p. 6.
"The History." The Unofficial Columbia Ranch Site. Accessed online at columbiaranch.net/history.html.
Variety. February 4, 1970, "Fire Hits Ranch Lot"; May 6, 1970, "Col's 'Bewitched' Studio Hit by $500,000 Fire"; August 19, 1970, "Another Fire Ravages Col's Burbank Ranch"; September 13, 1972 *(At Home* review).
Joel Whitburn, *The Billboard Albums,* 6th Edition, 2006.
Joel Whitburn, *Billboard Top Adult Contemporary 1961-2001,* 3rd Edition, 2002.

Chapter 7

Billboard, December 16, 1972. *Notebook* review.
Tim Brooks and Earle Marsh, *The Complete Directory to Prime Time Network and Cable TV Shows 1946 to present,* 1999.
Cash Box. May 27, 1972 (Wes Farrell purchase of Rascals catalog; "How Can I Be Sure" review); October 14, 1972 ("Some Kind of a Summer" review); October 21, 1972 *(Rock Me Baby* album review; Johnny Cymbal & Peggy Clinger background); November 25, 1972 ("Looking Through the Eyes of Love" review); December 2, 1972 *(Notebook* review); March 17, 1973 ("Friend and a Lover" review).
"Danny of 'Partridge Family' Thrilled by Roller Coaster." *Times Record,* Troy, New York, August 14, 1972.
Lawrence Laurent, "Acting Career Began Early for Shirley Jones." *Sunday Gazette-Mail,* Charleston, West Virginia, August 13, 1972.
Variety, December 6, 1972. *Notebook* review.

Chapter 8

Billboard, June 30, 1973. *Crossword Puzzle* review.
Cash Box. June 26, 1971 (Shirley Jones single "I've Still Got My Heart, Joe"); June 23, 1973 *(Crossword Puzzle* review).
Panama City News-Herald, May 13, 1973. Shirley Jones single "Walk in Silence."
Variety, June 27, 1973. *Crossword Puzzle* review.
Tom Von Malder, *Crossword Puzzle* review. *Wheeling Herald,* Wheeling, Illinois, September 14, 1973.

Chapter 9

Nancy Anderson, *Waco Tribune-Herald,* Waco, Texas, October 28, 1973. David Cassidy's departure.
James Bacon, "'Partridge Family' at Sea." *The Daily Times-News,* Burlington, North Carolina, October 11, 1973.
Billboard. June 2, 1973 (Williams Brothers' *One More Time* album), November 10, 1973 (Bulletin Board review).
Cash Box. August 11, 1973 (rumors of show's post-Cassidy plans); August 25, 1973 (Simon Turner as possible replacement for Cassidy); September 22, 1973 (Rick Springfield); October 13, 1973 *(Dreams Are Nuthin' More Than Wishes* review); October 20, 1973 *(Dreams* cover); October 27, 1973 (Cassidy "Puppy Song" review); November 3, 1973 (Cassidy "Daydreamer" single review); November 24, 1973 *(Bulletin Board* and "Lookin' for a Good Time" reviews).
Roger Newcomb, "The Wesley Eure Interview, Part One." *We Love Soaps,* November 12, 2009. Discussion of Eure replacing David Cassidy.
Bill Pitzonka, liner notes, *The Williams Brothers, Andy & David.* Varese Sarabande reissue, 2002.
Variety, November 14, 1973. *Bulletin Board* review.

Chapter 10

The Bee, Danville, Virginia, September 13, 1973. Ricky Segall boxing gloves ad.
Billboard. November 23, 1974 *(World of* review); December 7, 1974 *(DC's Greatest Hits* album review).
Cash Box. March 2, 1974 (David Cassidy tour Asia schedule); May 18, 1974 (Cassidy tour reinstated European dates); July 27, 1974 (Cassidy planned collaboration with David Bowie); August 10, 1974 *(Cassidy Live!);* September 7, 1974 (Review of *Cassidy Live!);* September 14, 1974 ("Please Please Me" cover review); November 30, 1974, "Greatest Hits as Greatest Sellers"; December 7, 1974 *(DC's Greatest Hits* album review).
Gastonia Gazette, Gastonia, North Carolina, September 11, 1973. Jones' optimism regarding *All in the Family.*
Greeley Daily Tribune, Greeley Colorado, December 13, 1973. ABC announcement of schedule change and Williams brothers as replacement for David Cassidy.
Dick Lochte, "Life Is Not a Situation Comedy, but Sometimes Shirley Jones Wishes It Were." *TV Guide,* March 9, 1974.
Ogden Standard Examiner, Ogden, Utah, June 23, 1973. Bob Claver on writers' strike.

Chapter 11

Cash Box. June 27, 1970 (trade ads); August 8, 1970 (album sales before TV premiere); September 12, 1970 (Bell releases); September 26, 1970 (Bell strategy); October 17, 1970 (Bell's first million-dollar order); October 24, 1970 ("I Think I Love You" Bell's biggest-selling single); November 7, 1970 (Ilson PR campaign, trade ads).

Chapter 12

Lisa Sutton, liner notes, *The Partridge Family Up to Date.* Buddah Records reissue, 2000. "Warm My Soul" background.

"Marineland Background to 'Partridge Family.'" *Lowell Sun,* Lowell, Massachusetts, October 22, 1971.

Chapter 13

"*Partridge Family 2200 A.D.*" Cmongethappy.com. Accessed online at cmongethappy.com/2200.

Variety. October 25, 1978; November 8, 1978. *David Cassidy: Man Undercover.*

WSKG Public Media, *WSKG Web Original: Susan Dey (LA Law, The Partridge Family) and the Andes Battle of the Bands* by Joshua B, 2013.

Songs

"All of the Things," Richard Klein (BMI, Screen Gems–EMI Music Inc.)

"Come On Get Happy," Danny Janssen and Wes Farrell (BMI, Lovolar Music/ Screen Gems–EMI Music, Inc.)

"Could It Be Forever," Wes Farrell and Danny Janssen (BMI, EMI–Sosaha Music Inc./ Lovolar Music/R2M Music/Songs of Lastrada)

"Echo Valley 2-6809," Rupert Holmes and Kathy Cooper (ASCAP, Colgems–EMI Music Inc.)

"Every Song Is You," Terry Cashman and Tommy West (ASCAP, Colgems–EMI Music Inc.)

"God Only Knows," Tony Asher and Brian Wilson (BMI, Irving Music)

"I Think I Love You," Tony Romeo (BMI, Screen Gems-EMI Music Inc.)

"I Woke Up in Love This Morning," L. Russell Brown and Irwin Levine (BMI, Irwin Levine Music, Screen Gems-EMI Music. Inc.)

"I'll Leave Myself a Little Time," Stephen Dossick (ASCAP, Colgems¬–EMI Music Inc.)

"I'll Meet You Halfway," Wes Farrell and Gerry Goffin (BMI, Lovolar Music/ Screen Gems-EMI Music, Inc.)

"My Christmas Card to You," Tony Romeo (BMI, Screen Gems–EMI Music Inc.)

"She Loves You," John Lennon and Paul McCartney (BMI, GIL Music Corporation)

"Together We're Better," Tony Romeo and Ken Jacobson (BMI, Screen Gems–EMI Music Inc.)

"Whale Song," Marty Kaniger and Dan Peyton (BMI, Screen Gems-EMI Music, Inc.)

"When I Grow Up," Richard Segall (ASCAP Colgems–EMI Music Inc.)

"When We're Singin' Main Theme," Wes Farrell and Diane Hildebrand (BMI, Screen Gems–EMI Music Inc.)

"You Are Always On My Mind," Tony Romeo (BMI, Screen Gems–EMI Music Inc.)

PHOTO CREDITS

Collectors and fans were so generous in sharing images that I ended up with multiple copies of several images. I thank all those who provided prints, objects, and photography: Edna Albert and *Cash Box*, Scott Awley, John Bahler, Tom Bahler, Leslie Bell, Geoff Brown, Terry Cashman, Bob Claver, Michael Colavolpe, Nick Cool and the Image Works, Harvey Cooper, Suzanne Crough, Neil T. Daniels, Tim DeBacco, Henry Diltz, Mary Dee English, Brian Forster, Tina Funk, Scottie Gee Gerardi, Ron Hicklin, Diane Hildebrand, Marty Kaniger, Dale Laszig, *Los Angeles Magazine*, Dave Madden, Mike Melvoin, Sheila Molitz, Bill Morgan, Joe Osborn, Louise Poynton, Rock & Roll Hall of Fame Library & Archives, John Rosica, Jim Salamanis, Ken Sharp, Collin Strayer, Vreny Thrommen, Jackie Ward, Beverly Weinstein, and Nancy Witherell.

Color Insert

C1: *The Partridge Family Album* cover, photo insert, and 45 single from the collection of the author.

C2–5, Tracy's Scrapbook: All photos courtesy of Suzanne Crough

C6: *The Partridge Family Up to Date* cover, book cover, and singles from the collection of the author.

C7–11: Trade ads from the collection of the author; reprinted with permission of Edna Albert, with special thanks to the Rock & Roll Hall of Fame Library & Archives.

C12: Photos of Brian Forster and *The Partridge Family* set courtesy of Scott Awley. Photo of the Partridge Family bus from the collection of the author.

C13: Photo of David Cassidy and Susan Dey courtesy of Henry Diltz. Photo of the first season cast courtesy of Scott Awley. Photo of Danny Bonaduce courtesy of Dave Madden.

C14: *The Partridge Family Sound Magazine* cover and single from the collection of the author.

C15: Blue fan club single and fan club items from the collection of the author. Black and pink fan club singles and *Tiger Beat's Official Partridge Family Magazine* Issue No. 1 courtesy of Jim Salamanis.

C16: *Tiger Beat's Official Partridge Family Magazine* Issues No. 2, 3, and 4; David Cassidy yellow pin-up poster; *David's Private Photo Album;* and *Growing Up with the Partridges* courtesy of Jim Salamanis. *Dynamic David Cassidy, Susan Dey's Secrets on Boys, Beauty and Popularity,* and *David's Concert Tour* from the collection of the author. *The Partridge Family Fun Album* courtesy of Tina Funk.

C17: *Tiger Beat's Official Partridge Family Magazine* Issues No. 5, 6, 7, 8, 9, 10, 11, 12, and 13 courtesy of Jim Salamanis.

C18: *Tiger Beat's Official Partridge Family Magazine* issues No. 14 and 15 and four-fold poster of David Cassidy courtesy of Jim Salamanis. Life-size poster of David Cassidy from the collection of the author. Poster ad by Gemini and photo of David Cassidy Month window display reprinted with permission of Edna Albert, with special thanks to the Rock & Roll Hall of Fame Library & Archives.

C19: Cover of *Cash Box* from the collection of the author, reprinted with permission of Edna Albert.

C20: *A Partridge Family Christmas Card* and Christmas card insert from the collection of the author.

C21: Christmas photo of cast courtesy of Henry Diltz. Carlton Cards Partridge Family bus Christmas ornament from the collection of the author. U.K. Partridge Family and David Cassidy Christmas cards courtesy of Jim Salamanis. David Cassidy *Cash Box* cover reprinted with permission of Edna Albert, with special thanks to the Rock & Roll Hall of Fame Library & Archives.

C22: *The Partridge Family Shopping Bag,* plastic shopping bag insert, and singles "It's One of Those Nights (Yes, Love)" and "Am I Losing You" from the collection of the author.

C23: Remco toy bus, Johnny Lighting toy bus and Johnny Lightning model kit from the collection of the author.

C24: Bulletin board and David Cassidy push pins from the collection of the author. David Cassidy Roalex puzzle, pillow case, pencil case, and personality prints (sticker-poster) courtesy of Jim Salamanis. David Cassidy T-shirt and David Cassidy Poster Patch courtesy of Scott Awley.

C25: Remco Laurie doll, mini poster, and Patti Partridge doll from the collection of the author. Photo of unreleased David Cassidy doll courtesy of Jim Salamanis.

C26: Raisin Bran box, Snip N Pin photo, *Pictorial Album, Fun Book,* and *Paint and Color Album* from the collection of the author. Coloring books courtesy of Jim Salamanis. David Cassidy Halloween costume catalog illustration from the collection of the author. Halloween costume photo from Bill Morgan and Greg Davis, *Collector's Guide to TV Toys and Memorabilia Second Edition 1960s & 1970s,* used with permission of Bill Morgan.

C27: Susan Dey paper dolls; blue, gold, and green Partridge Family paper doll box sets; Partridge Family and Susan Dey paper doll expansion sets courtesy of Jim Salamanis. Orange Partridge Family paper doll box set and individual outfits from the collection of the author.

C28: Kate Greenaway white pants with bus design, denim shorts with yellow patch, tan pants, and brown purse courtesy of Jim Salamanis. Kate Greenaway denim shorts with bus design courtesy of Scott Awley. Kate Greenaway loose yellow patch and black sticker from the collection of the author.

C29: Kate Greenaway blue jeans with red pockets from the collection of the author. Kate Greenaway Clothing advertisement, red purse, white pants with toy design, and red jumpsuit courtesy of Scott Awley. Kate Greenaway white dress with bus pattern courtesy of Vreny Thrommen. Kate Greenaway blue jeans with yellow courtesy of Jim Salamanis. Kate Greenaway sales tags from the collection of the author.

C30: David Cassidy Beach Towel, Green Hi C label, individual Hi C photo labels of Shirley Jones, David Cassidy, Susan Dey, Danny Bonaduce, Suzanne Crough, and Dave Madden from the collection of the author. Brian Forster photo label and Partridge Family group photo courtesy of Scott Awley.

C31: David Cassidy Radio, Colorforms, and Partridge Family Tree Merry Motion badges from the collection of the author. Partridge Family charm bracelet, David Cassidy nickel-plated necklace, wristwatch, and lenticular photo cards courtesy of Jim Salamanis.

C32: Partridge Family Topps bubble gum card display box and wrapped wax packs courtesy of Tim DeBacco. Poster pack display box and wrapped wax packs from the collection of the author, with special thanks to Vreny Thrommen. Individual bubble gum cards with yellow, green, and blue borders; individual Topps posters of Shirley Jones, Susan Dey, David Cassidy, and Jeremy Gelbwaks; and David Cassidy Book cover from the collection of the author. Partridge Family comic book courtesy of Jim Salamanis.

C33: Partridge Family Song Books for *Album, Up to Date, Sound Magazine, Shopping Bag, At Home with Their Greatest Hits, Notebook,* "The Partridge Family Biggest Hits," "Simply

Bradley" guitar arrangements, "The Partridge Family Deluxe," and "The Partridge Family Complete" courtesy of Jim Salamanis. Partridge Family mystery book series Nos. 1–17, David Cassidy paperbacks *David, David, David, Meet David Cassidy, Young Mr. Cassidy, The David Cassidy Story, The David Cassidy Song Book, The David Cassidy Book,* and *The Partridge Family Cookbook* from the collection of the author.

 C34: David Cassidy white guitar courtesy of Scott Awley. David Cassidy red guitar courtesy of Vreny Thrommen. David Cassidy 1973 calendar courtesy of Jim Salamanis. David Cassidy 1974 calendar from the collection of the author. Partridge Family Lunch Box, metal Thermos and plastic Thermos from the collection of the author.

 C35: Partridge Family board game, David Cassidy giant jigsaw puzzle, 500-piece jigsaw puzzle, and David Cassidy 3-ring binder from the collection of the author. David Cassidy spiral notebook courtesy of Jim Salamanis.

 C36: Viewmaster sets "The Money Manager," and "Male Chauvinist," Talking Viewmaster, and Talking Viewmaster set "The Money Manager," from the collection of the author. Partridge Family and David Cassidy clocks courtesy of Jim Salamanis.

 C37: Photo of Partridge Family record cabinet box courtesy of Scott Awley. Record cabinet and bus sticker from the collection of the author.

 C38: *The Partridge Family at Home with Their Greatest Hits* and single "Breaking Up Is Hard to Do" from the collection of the author.

 C39: Partridge Family poster from the collection of the author.

 C40: Shirley Jones in concert photo, Shirley Jones concert poster, and photo of Partridge Family cast members reunited on *In Search of the Partridge Family* courtesy of Scott Awley. Susan Dey magazine cover courtesy of *Los Angeles Magazine*.

 C41: Photo of Wilma C. Miller, photo of the Barrow-Civic Theatre marquee, and poster of David Cassidy in concert at the Barrow-Civic Theatre from the collection of the author. Photo of David Cassidy in concert at the Barrow-Civic Theatre from the collection of the author, with special thanks to Jerry Sowden. Photo of Danny Bonaduce, photo of David Cassidy with Danny Bonaduce, and photo of the Keswick Theatre poster courtesy of Robert Forchione. Photo of Brian Forster and photo of Suzanne Crough courtesy of Michael Colavolpe.

 C42: Photo of *The Partridge Family Notebook* and singles "Looking Through the Eyes of Love," and "Friend and a Lover" from the collection of the author.

 C43: Screen Gems Records Volume 2A and 2B courtesy of Suzanne Crough; photos by Scottie Gee Gerardi with special thanks to Les Bell. Screen Gems Records Volume 3A, 3B, and 3C courtesy of Brian Forster; photos by Scottie Gee Gerardi, with special thanks to Brian Forster.

 C44: Screen Gems Records Volume 3D, Volume 4, Volume 5A and 5B, and Volume 6A and 6B from the collection of Brian Forster; photos by Scottie Gee Gerardi, with special thanks to Brian Forster.

 C45: Screen Gems Records Volume 6C, Volume 6D, and Volume 8 from the collection of Brian Forster; photos by Scottie Gee Gerardi, with special thanks to Brian Forster.

 Screen Gems Records Volume 7A, Volume 7B, and Volume 9 from the collection of Scottie Gee Gerardi; photos by Scottie Gee Gerardi.

 C46: Shirley Jones, "I've Still Got My Heart, Joe" and "Ain't Love Easy"; Danny Bonaduce, "I'll Be Your Magician"; Ricky Segall solo album from the collection of the author.

 Shirley Jones, "Walk In Silence" and Danny Bonaduce solo album from the collection of Scottie Gee Gerardi; photos by Scottie Gee Gerardi. Danny Bonaduce, "Dreamland" and Ricky Segall, "Sooner or Later" courtesy of Jim Salamanis.

C47: David Cassidy, "Cherish," "Rock Me Baby," "Dreams are Nuthin' More than Wishes," "Cassidy Live!" and "Greatest Hits" from the collection of Scottie Gee Gerardi; photos by Scottie Gee Gerardi. David Cassidy, "Cherish," "Could it Be Forever," "How Can I Be Sure," "Rock Me Baby," "Puppy Song," "Daydreamer," "Please Please Me," and "If I Didn't Care" from the collection of the author. "Daydream" from the collection of Scottie Gee Gerardi; photo by Scottie Gee Gerardi.

C48: *The Partridge Family Crossword Puzzle* and puzzle insert from the collection of the author.

C49: Photos of John Bahler, Tom Bahler, Jackie Ward, and Shirley Jones from the collection of the author. Photo of Ron Hicklin courtesy of Ron Hicklin. Photo of Music Agency staff courtesy of Dale S. Laszig (née Leipzig).

C50: Photo of Terry Cashman and Tommy West from the collection of Laura Fieber; copyright 2016 Laura Feiber. Photos of Johnny Cymbal and Peggy Clinger, of Tommy Boyce and Bobby Hart, of Adam Miller, and of David Cassidy courtesy of Edna Albert and the Rock & Roll Hall of Fame Library & Archives. Photo of Tony Romeo from the collection of the author. Photo of Diane Hildebrand courtesy of Diane Hildebrand; photo by Henry Diltz. Photo of Joe Osborn courtesy of Joe Osborn. Photo of Mike Melvoin courtesy of Mike Melvoin. Photo of Marty Kaniger and Dan Peyton courtesy of Marty Kaniger.

C51: Photos of Larry Uttal, Beverly Weinstein, Irv Biegel, Gordon Bossin, John Rosica, Steve Wax, Dave Carrico, Oscar Fields, Allen Cohen, George Goodman, Sheila Molitz, Richard Totoian, and Wes Farrell courtesy of Edna Albert and the Rock & Roll Hall of Fame Library & Archives. Photo of Dave Madden courtesy of Dave Madden. Photo of Harvey Cooper courtesy of Harvey Cooper. Photo of Bob Claver courtesy of Nancy Witherell. Bell Records cigarette lighter from the collection of the author.

C52: *The Partridge Family Bulletin Board* and single "Looking for a Good Time" from the collection of the author.

C53–C57: All photos by Henry Diltz, courtesy of Henry Diltz.

C58: *The World of The Partridge Family* from the collection of the author.

Singles "Am I Losing You" (Germany), "Breaking Up Is Hard To Do" (Lebanon), "My Christmas Card To You" (New Zealand), "I Think I Love You" (Yugoslavia), "I Woke Up In Love This Morning" (Spain), "Looking for A Good Time" (Germany), "Walking in the Rain" (Germany), "Sunshine" (Japan) courtesy of Jim Salamanis.

C59: Albums *A Familia Do Re Mi* (Brazil), *The Partridge Family Album* (Japan), *The Partridge Family Notebook* (Japan), *The Partridge Family Notebook* (Canada), *The Partridge Family Album of 14 Hit Songs* (Malaysia), *The Partridge Family Shopping Bag* (Greece), *The Partridge Family at Home with Their Greatest Hits* (Canada), *The Partridge Family Shopping Bag* special edition (Germany), *The Partridge Family Greatest Hits* (New Zealand), *The Partridge Family Crossword Puzzle* front and back (Japan), and *The Partridge Family Shopping Bag* (U.K.) courtesy of Jim Salamanis.

C60: "Keep Britain Tidy" ad, David Cassidy memo pad, David Cassidy iron-on transfer, Partridge Family board game (Greece) courtesy of Jim Salamanis. Photo of Cassidy poster on garbage can by Henry Diltz, courtesy of Henry Diltz. U.K. paperback book *The David Cassidy Story* and *The Big Four* collector book from the collection of the author. Partridge Family Laurie House album from the collection of Scottie Gee Gerardi; photo by Scottie Gee Gerardi.

C61: Partridge Family Fan Club wallet, David Cassidy ball cap, *The Partridge Family U.K. Annual*, Partridge Family New Zealand fan club record, Partridge Family stationary, David Cassidy stationery, cigar bands, stamps, David Cassidy key ring, David Cassidy scarf, "I Love

David Cassidy" flag, "Darling David" flag, and David Cassidy pop badge, courtesy of Jim Salamanis. David Cassidy stickers and David Cassidy sew-on patches courtesy of the author. David Cassidy Bikeathon and Cancer society pins courtesy of Scott Awley. David Cassidy concert ticket stubs from Madison Square Garden, Hollywood Bowl, Melbourne Cricket Grounds, Brisbane, Wembley, and White City Stadium courtesy of Jim Salamanis. David Cassidy concert ticket stubs from the Barrow-Civic Theatre and the Keswick Theatre from the collection of the author. David Cassidy concert ticket stub from Idora Park courtesy of Tim DeBacco.

C62: Partridge Family Bell Records promotional poster from the collection of the author.

C62–63: Two-page photo of David Cassidy and audience at the Melbourne Cricket Grounds, 1974, by Henry Diltz; courtesy of Henry Diltz.

C64: "The Partridge Family TV Dinner" comprehensive rendering from the collection of the author, courtesy of Mary Dee English. Partridge Family caricature photo from the collection of the author.

Chapter Images

Chapter 2

All images from the collection of the author.

Chapter 11

Keith ad (*Cash Box*, August 1, 1970), Tracy ad (*Cash Box*, August 8, 1970), Mom ad (*Cash Box*, August 1, 1970), Scrapbook cover ad (*Cash Box*, August 1, 1970), and "We Arrive In Las Vegas" ad (*Cash Box*, August 8, 1970) courtesy Edna Albert and the Rock & Roll Hall of Fame Library & Archives.

The Partridge Family Album album title: Original graphic design by Mary Dee English. From the collection of Scottie Gee Gerardi; additional graphic design for black and white layout by Scottie Gee Gerardi. David Cassidy and Shirley Jones signatures from album cover from the collection of Scottie Gee Gerardi, with additional graphic design for black and white layout by Scottie Gee Gerardi.

The Partridge Family Up to Date album title: Original graphic design by Mary Dee English. Drawing of the bus by John Zaccheo. From the collection of Scottie Gee Gerardi, with additional graphic design for black and white layout by Scottie Gee Gerardi.

The Partridge Family Sound Magazine album title: Original graphic design by Mary Dee English. From the collection of Scottie Gee Gerardi; additional graphic design for black and white layout by Scottie Gee Gerardi.

A Partridge Family Christmas Card album title, Mary Dee English signature: Original graphic design by Mary Dee English. From the collection of Scottie Gee Gerardi; additional graphic design for black and white layout by Scottie Gee Gerardi.

The Partridge Family Shopping Bag album title: Original graphic design by John Zaccheo. From the collection of Scottie Gee Gerardi; additional graphic design for black and white layout by Scottie Gee Gerardi. David Cassidy drawing: Original artwork by John Zaccheo. From the collection of Scottie Gee Gerardi; additional graphic design for black and white layout by Scottie Gee Gerardi.

The Partridge Family at Home With Their Greatest Hits album title: Original graphic design by John Zaccheo. From the collection of Scottie Gee Gerardi; additional graphic design for black and white layout by Scottie Gee Gerardi.

The Partridge Family Notebook album title: Original graphic design by Mary Dee English. From the collection of Scottie Gee Gerardi; additional graphic design for black and white layout by Scottie Gee Gerardi.

The Partridge Family Crossword Puzzle album title: Original graphic design by Mary Dee English. From the collection of Scottie Gee Gerardi; additional graphic design for black and white layout by Scottie Gee Gerardi.

The Partridge Family Bulletin Board album title, postcards: Original graphic design by Mary Dee English. From the collection of Scottie Gee Gerardi; additional graphic design for black and white layout by Scottie Gee Gerardi.

The World of The Partridge Family album title: Original graphic design by Richard Mantel. From the collection of Scottie Gee Gerardi; additional graphic design for black and white layout by Scottie Gee Gerardi.

"The Partridge Family TV Dinner" original graphic design by Mary Dee English. From the collection of the author; additional graphic design for black and white layout by Scottie Gee Gerardi.

Chapter 12

Recording session notes from the collection of the author, courtesy of Ron Hicklin.

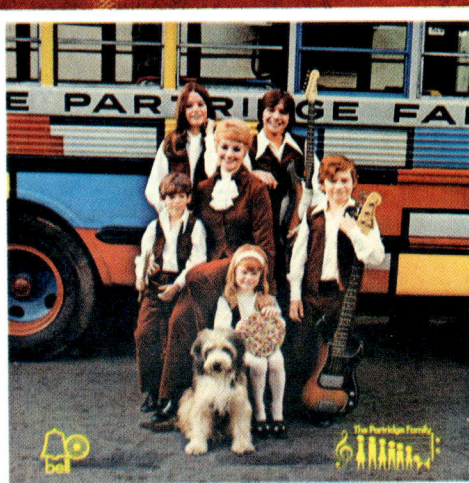

10 x 10" color photo insert included.

"I Think I Love You," the only single released from the first album.

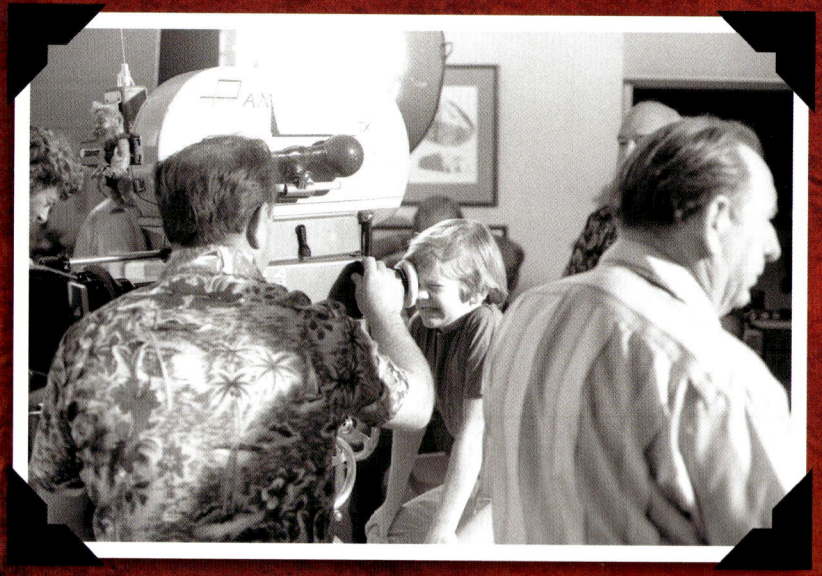

Brian, the filmmaker?

TRACY'S SCRAPBOOK

Soundstage 30 on the Columbia Ranch, home of the Partridge Family, located at the back of the bus. (Facing front is Soundstage 29.)

Bike riding on the Columbia Ranch. "San Pueblo High School" is visible in the background.

c2

Suzanne Crough

Posing for fun.

Friend or foe?

Hanging out on the back lot.

Rehearsing a scene.

Photos from the personal collection of SUZANNE CROUGH

Danny Bonaduce

Enjoying a game of badminton.

After a long bus ride.

Dave Madden, Shirley Jones, and David Cassidy's dressing rooms. Check out David's white Corvette!

Ray Bolger and Rosemary DeCamp as Shirley Partridge's parents.

Realizing Suzanne Crough had no living grandfathers, Ray Bolger told Suzanne "I'll be your 'grandfather.'" They shared that bond for the rest of their lives.

Book cover included.

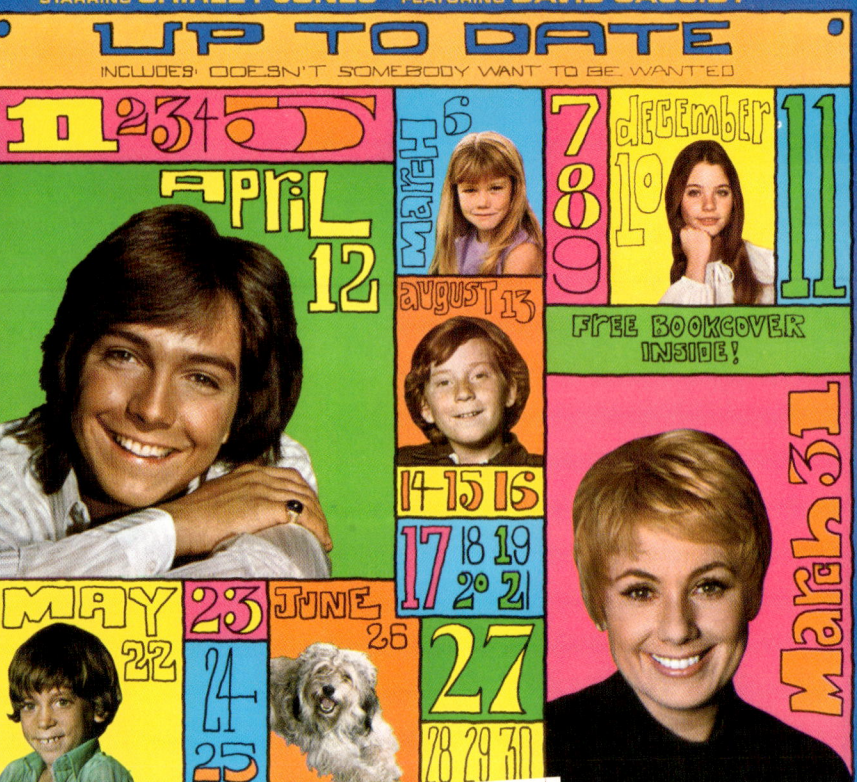

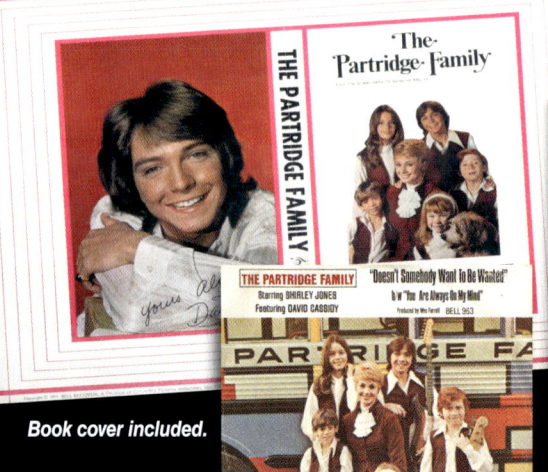

Singles released, "Doesn't Somebody Want to Be Wanted" and "I'll Meet You Halfway."

More Snapshots From THE PARTRIDGE FAMILY ALBUM

Featuring DAVID CASSIDY as "Keith"

Starring SHIRLEY JONES as "Connie"

THE PARTRIDGE FAMILY
Starring SHIRLEY JONES
"I THINK I LOVE YOU"
b/w "SOMEBODY WANTS TO LOVE YOU"
Produced by Wes Farrell
BELL 910

Bell Single #910
Produced by Wes Farrell
From The Screen Gems TV Series on ABC-TV

Our First Single!

Bell Records, A Division of Columbia Pictures Industries, Inc.

Full-page trade ads appeared in *Billboard* and *Cash Box*. This first ad appeared prior to the album's release during Bell Records' $100,000 promotional campaign.

August 15, 1970, *Cash Box, Billboard*

An alternate full-page color ad of the album's cover art (not pictured here) appeared in Cash Box, October 17, 1970, promoting the first album—the only album to receive two different full-page ads.

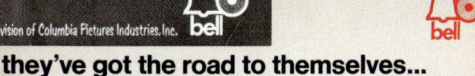

they've got the road to themselves...

THE PARTRIDGE FAMILY

The Partridge Family
starring SHIRLEY JONES featuring DAVID CASSIDY

their newest single
"DOESN'T SOMEBODY WANT TO BE WANTED"
produced by WES FARRELL

BELL #963
BELL RECORDS, A Division of Columbia Pictures Industries, Inc.

The same drawing of the bus is used on the back of *Up To Date*.

February 27, 1971, *Cash Box*
February 20, 1971, *Billboard*

everything you need to know about the family ∗

bell

The·Partridge·Family

starring **SHIRLEY JONES** featuring **DAVID CASSIDY**

November 10, 1970
"I Think I Love You"
RIAA Certified Gold Single

December 16, 1970
"The Partridge Family Album"
RIAA Certified Gold Album

March 11, 1971 —
"Doesn't Somebody Want To Be Wanted"
RIAA Certified Gold Single

March 25, 1971
"Up To Date"
RIAA Certified Gold Album

∗and their newest single—

"I'LL MEET YOU HALFWAY"

produced by **WES FARRELL**
Bell #996

From the Screen Gems Series on ABC-TV
BELL RECORDS, A Division of Columbia Pictures Industries, Inc.

This ad boasts the first four releases all went Gold.
May 8, 1971, *Cash Box, Billboard*

The little girl "sleeping" on the pillow is Carol L. Chavez (née Leipzig), Music Agency CEO Jay Leipzig's 8-year-old daughter.

August 14, 1971, *Cash Box*
August 21, 1971, *Billboard*

a million kids will soon wake up in love!

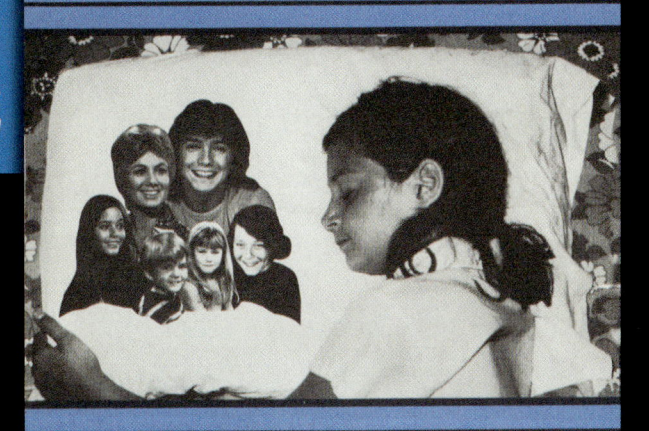

With The Newest Single Recorded By

THE PARTRIDGE FAMILY

Starring SHIRLEY JONES • Featuring DAVID CASSIDY

"I WOKE UP IN LOVE THIS MORNING"

Produced by WES FARRELL for Coral Rock Productions
BELL #45,130

BELL RECORDS
A Division of Columbia Pictures Industries, Inc.

Estimated Circulation: 1,000,000 Plus!...

A New Album To Match The Merchandising Savvy Of Partridge Family Fan Magazines!

THE PARTRIDGE FAMILY SOUND MAGAZINE

★ STARRING SHIRLEY JONES ★ FEATURING DAVID CASSIDY

INCLUDES
"I WOKE UP IN LOVE THIS MORNING"

Album Produced by WES FARRELL
For Coral Rock Productions, Inc.

BELL ALBUM #6064

BELL RECORDS
A Division of Columbia Pictures Industries, Inc.

The most critically acclaimed Partridge Family album.

August 28, 1971, *Cash Box*
September 4, 1971, *Billboard*

–we care enough to give our very best....

THE PARTRIDGE FAMILY'S NEWEST ALBUM

A Partridge Family Christmas Card

Starring **SHIRLEY JONES** Featuring **DAVID CASSIDY**

Produced by WES FARRELL for Coral Rock Productions

BELL STEREO #6066

BELL RECORDS A Division of Columbia Pictures Industries, Inc.

The number-one-selling Christmas album of 1971.

November 20, 1971, *Billboard*
December 4, 1971, *Cash Box*

A Shopping Bag made for more than marketing...

The first return to black and white full-page ads.
March 11, 1972, *Cash Box*
March 18, 1972, *Billboard*

The Partridge Family Shopping Bag

Starring **SHIRLEY JONES** Featuring **DAVID CASSIDY**

Another Unique Package To Carry On
The Partridge Family Tradition!

PRODUCED BY WES FARRELL
For Coral Rock Productions, Inc.
Bell Album 6072 Stereo

BELL RECORDS A Division of Co...

---

from our family–

...the best 2 minutes and 30 seconds of "breaking up" ever put together!

The Newest Single Recorded By

THE PARTRIDGE FAMILY
Starring DAVID JONES • Featuring DAVID CASSIDY

"BREAKING UP IS HARD TO DO"

Produced by WES FARRELL for Coral Rock Productions
BELL #45,235

BELL RECORDS
A Division of Columbia Pictures Industries, Inc.

The last of eight full-page Partridge Family trade ads to appear.
June 17, 1972,
Cash Box, Billboard

c11

On the set of The Partridge Family.

Brian in his "lucky" shirt.

Danny Bonaduce photographed by Dave Madden in Malibu – his favorite shot of Danny.

henry diltz

The legendary Partridge Family bus. 1955 Chevrolet 6800 Second Series Task Force with a coach by Superior.

c13

Sound Magazine's only single, "I Woke Up in Love This Morning."

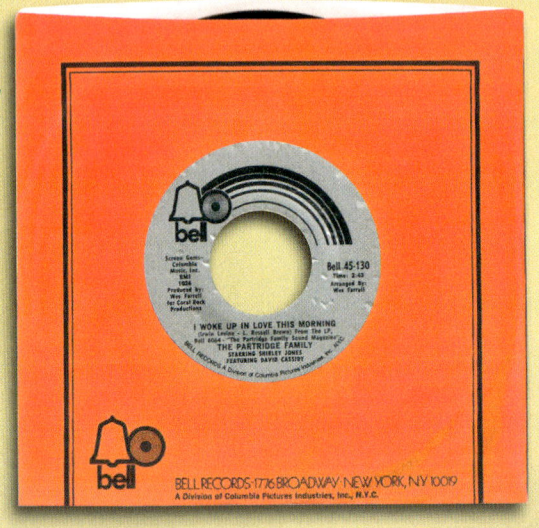

c14

**Issue No. 1
December 1970**

Items from the fan club kits.

PARTRIDGE FAN CLUB

It's easy--just substitute numbers for letters and you'll be able to decode the messages in TIGER BEAT and FaVE...

A-1	J-21	S-7
B-24	K-15	T-8
C-14	L-31	U-5
D-6	M-42	V-99
E-2	N-57	W-62
F-13	O-4	X-38
G-9	P-73	Y-20
H-11	Q-41	Z-10
I-3	R-33	

The secret decoder! 👉

c15

Issue No. 2
March 1971

Issue No. 3
May 1971

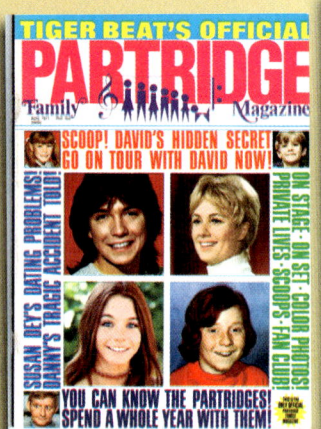

Issue No. 4
August 1971

Books and booklets available
through Tiger Beat mail order.

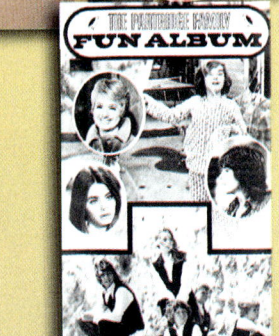

c16

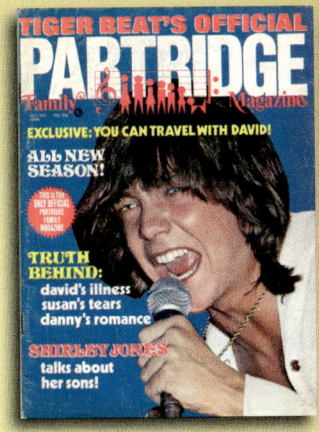

Issue No. 5
October 1971

Issue No. 6
November 1971

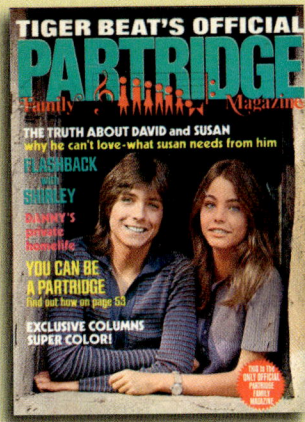

Issue No. 7
December 1971

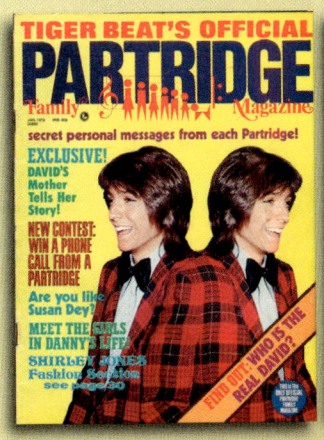

Issue No. 8
January 1972

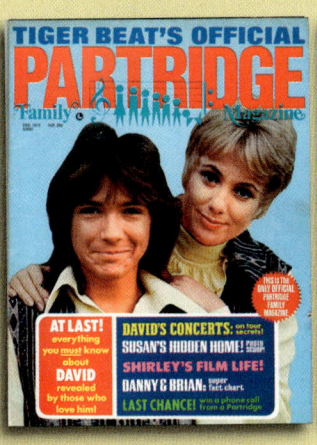

Issue No. 9
February 1972

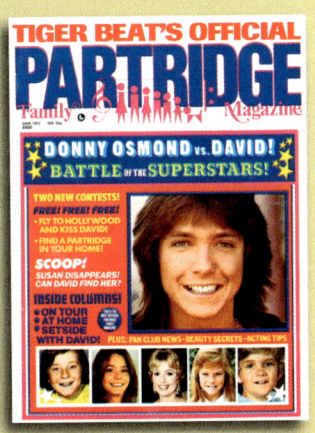

Issue No. 10
March 1972

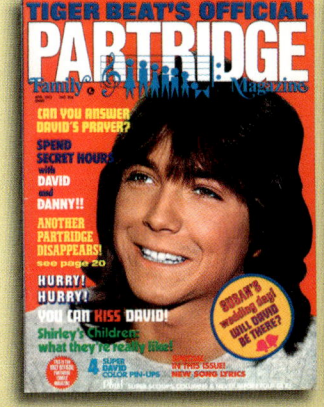

Issue No. 11
April 1972

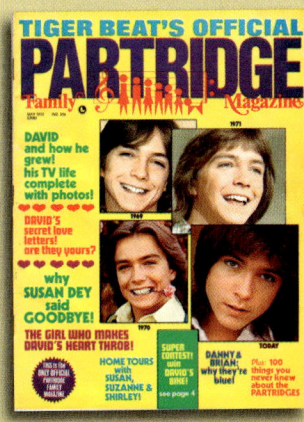

Issue No. 12
May 1972

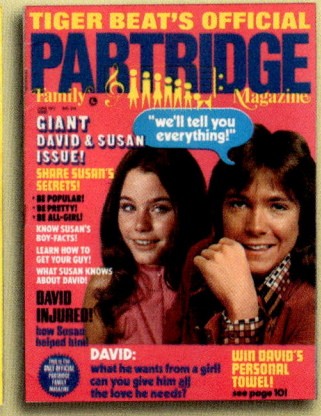

Issue No. 13
June 1972

c17

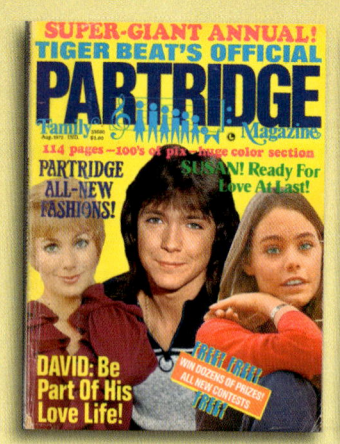

Issue No. 14
August 1972

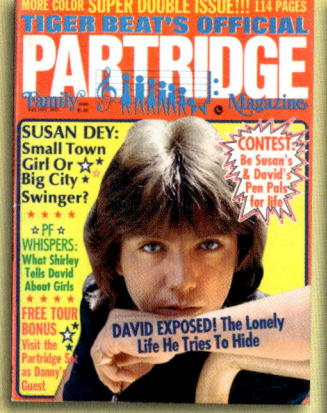

Issue No. 15
Fall 1972

One of four posters offered exclusively through Tiger Beat that created the largest David Cassidy poster in the world when pieced together from reverse. The same shot was used as the picture sleeves for singles: "Cherish" and "Could it Be Forever."

"Life-size" poster by Personality Posters, 20 x 56" U.S.

New Jersey chain Melody Records featured elaborate window displays as part of "David Cassidy Month" in February 1972.

c18

December 5, 1970 — One Dollar

Cash Box

A Task-Force For Convention Ideas and Proposals (Ed) Gavin Meet: Move Toward Unity & Humanization. MCA Dist. Corp.: It's A (Greater) Volume Business . . . CUC Music Pub Copyrights To Bienstock, Lieber & Stoller, Koppelman-Rubin. . .Vanguard's Top Price Yet For A Pop Act. . .Composer Guild Fights Pic Control. .

THE PARTRIDGE FAMILY: *HIT DIET ON FAMILY PLAN*

December 5, 1970, Larry Uttal (left) and Wes Farrell (right) pose with the cast!

A family photo, autographed by each cast member, included as insert.

henry diltz

Christmas cards
(only in the U.K.)

Cash Box

1971 In Review: Best Artists, Albums, Singles
in Pop, Country & Rhythm & Blues... Producers Of
Top 100 Hits... Top Hits, RIAA Gold Recordings
Through The Years... Complete Country-By-Country
Survey Of 1971's International Music Market...

Heirloom COLLECTION

the partridge family Music!

David Cassidy
on the cover,
Christmas Day 1971

The Partridge Family™

Christmas ornament plays
"Come On Get Happy."

© 2003 Carlton Cards

c21

Single releases,
"It's One of Those Nights (Yes, Love),"
"Am I Losing You."

Plastic shopping bag included.

Toy Bus, Remco, 1973. 16 x 8h x 7"d.

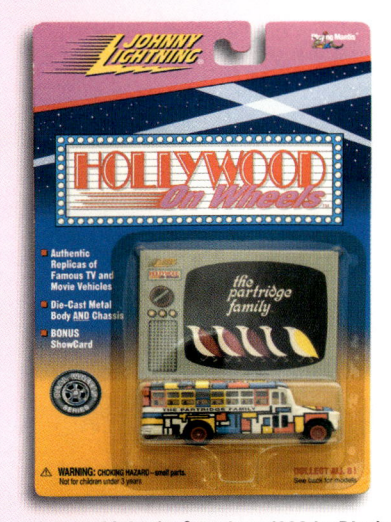

Johnny Lightning© toy bus model kit, 2001 by Playing Mantis© 1/64 scale comes with small screwdriver for assembly. Reissued in 2002.

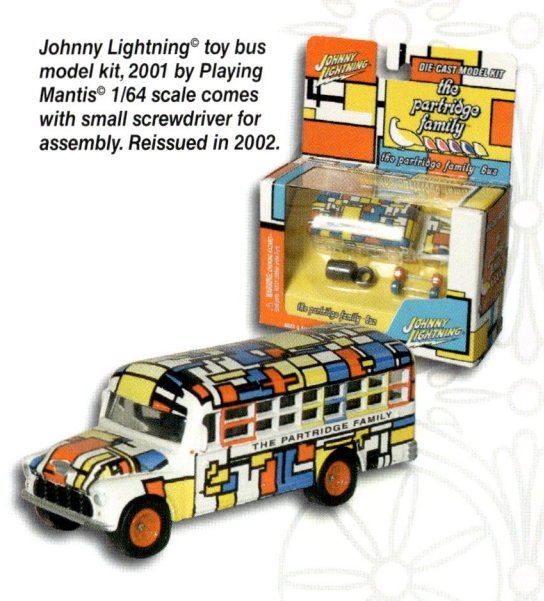

Johnny Lightning© toy bus, 1998 by Playing Mantis© 1/64 scale. Reissued in 2001.

c23

David Cassidy pillowcase, 1972.

T-shirt, 1972. Iron-on photo of David Cassidy. Sold as a mail-away premium.

Pencil case
Amalco Gift Co.
2-3/4 x 7-7/8" (U.K.)

Slide puzzle, the Roalex Company.

Poster Patch, Synergisms
3-1/2 x 4-1/2"

Kaymac Distribution Systems, Inc.
1971 8 x 13"

Bulletin board 18 x 24".

c24

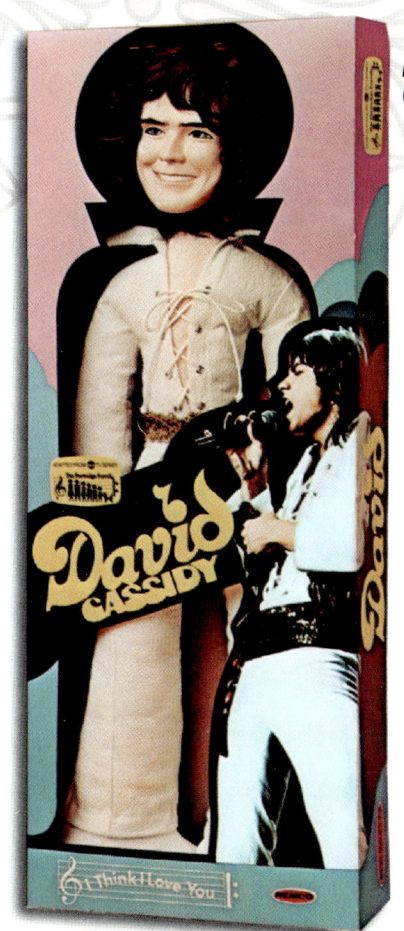

David Cassidy prototype doll (unreleased), 1973, Remco. 30" tall.

Poster 14 x 19"

Laurie Partridge doll, Remco, 1973. 19" tall. Mini-poster included.

Patti Partridge doll, Ideal, 1971. 16" tall.

c25

Cereal box. Four "Snip-n-pin" photos available.

David Cassidy Halloween costume, Kusan, 1973.

Artcraft, 1973.

Paint & color album, Artcraft, 1971.

Young Readers Press Inc., 1974.

1970

1971

1971

1972

1973

Coloring books, Saalfield / Artcraft.

c26

Box and expansion booklet, 1972.

Box and expansion booklet, 1973.

Susan Dey paper doll boxed sets featuring Kate Greenaway clothing designs! Artcraft and Saalfield.

1971

1973

1971

Paper Doll expansion booklets by Artcraft.

1972

1972

Paper doll boxed sets Saalfield Publishing Co.

1972

c27

The Kate Greenaway Collection
A Partridge Family clothing line for girls, with sew-on patches, stickers, and collectible designer tags! 1972.

c29

David Cassidy beach towel. Hi-C fruit drink mail order offer. 34 x 56" 1972.

Hi-C photos (8) found on inside of can labels. 1972.

c30

Pendant AM radio, Philgee International Ltd. 1973. (U.K.) 3½" diameter with 29" chain.

Nickel plated necklace.

Charm bracelet (Reuben's name spelled wrong–"Reuban.")

Wristwatch. 1972, 1.25" diameter. Alternate Partridge Family version also available.

Colorforms, 1972.

3-D lenticular photo cards, Merry Motion, 14 x 11". Postcard-size versions also available. 1971.

Merry Motion, 1971. Individual badges sold separately.

Bubble gum cards. Topps, 1971. First series (yellow), 55 cards, second series (blue), 55 cards, third series (green), 88 cards.

Comic books. 21 issues in all. Charlton, 1970–1973.

Book cover. 13 x 20" Lever Brothers mail-away premium. 1972.

Poster packs. Topps, 1971. 9½ x 18" posters, set of 24 available.

The David Cassidy Song Book. *Wise Publications, 1972. (U.K.) An alternate version,* The David Cassidy Book, *was issued separately with identical cover.*

Scholastic Books and Curtis Books. 1972.

Song Books
The Partridge Family Complete. *Arrangements by Dan Fox. 1971. Other song books also available. Screen Gems–Columbia Publications.*

Cookbook. Curtis Books, 1973.

Paperback mystery books. Curtis Books, 1970–1973.

c33

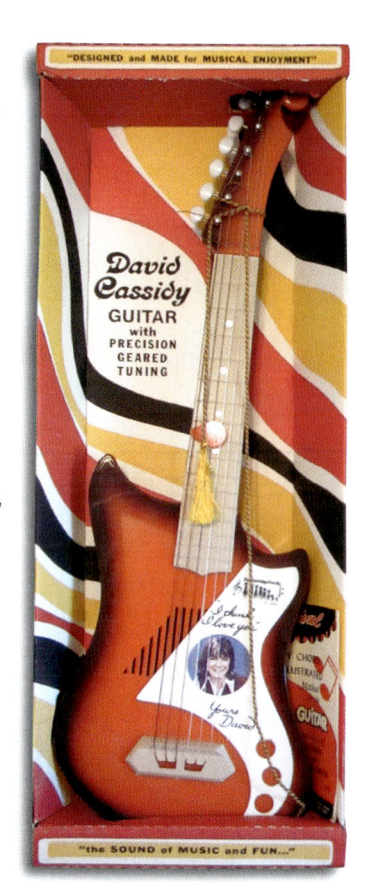

Guitars
Carnival Toys, 1973.
20" white guitar, (technically a ukulele!)
31" red guitar included a music book.

Calendars, APC. 1973 and 1974.

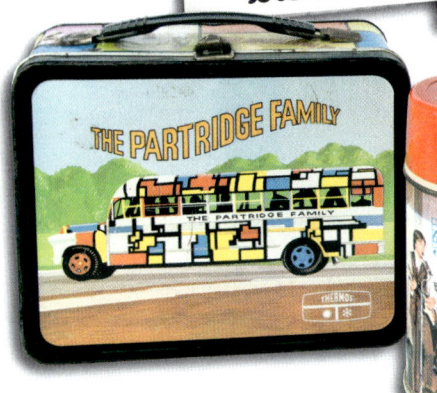

Lunch box. K.S.T., 1971. Metal lunch box with matching metal Thermos. Re-released in 1973 with a plastic Thermos.

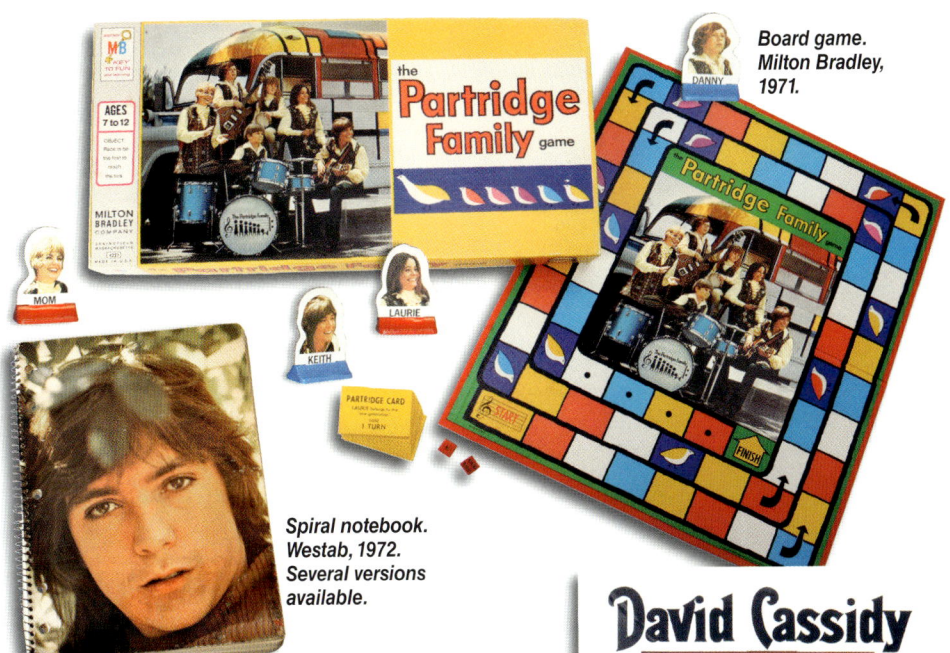

Board game. Milton Bradley, 1971.

Spiral notebook. Westab, 1972. Several versions available.

Jigsaw puzzle. APC, 1972. 500 pieces.

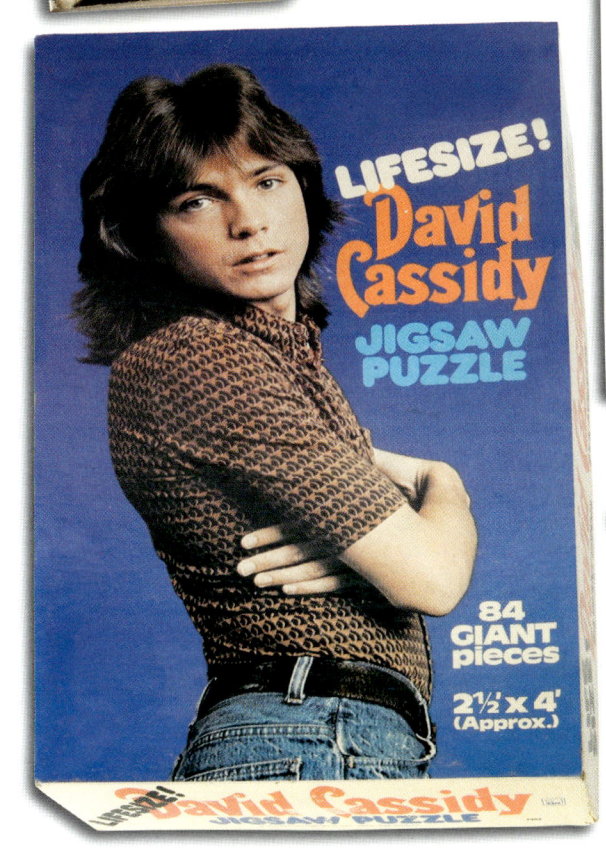

Life-size David Cassidy puzzle. APC, 1973. 84 giant pieces measuring 4–5" each.

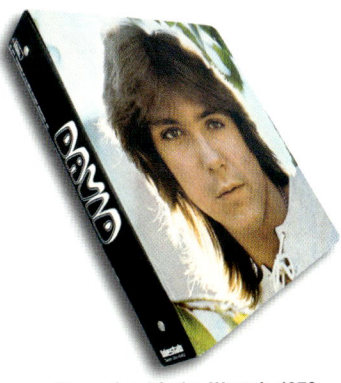

Three-ring binder. Westab, 1972.

c35

Talking View-Master reel "The Money Manager," 1971.

View-Master reels. GAF.
"The Money Manager," 1971.

"Male Chauvinist," 1973.

Clocks.
Time Setters, 1972.
Frames, cords, and hands
sold separately.

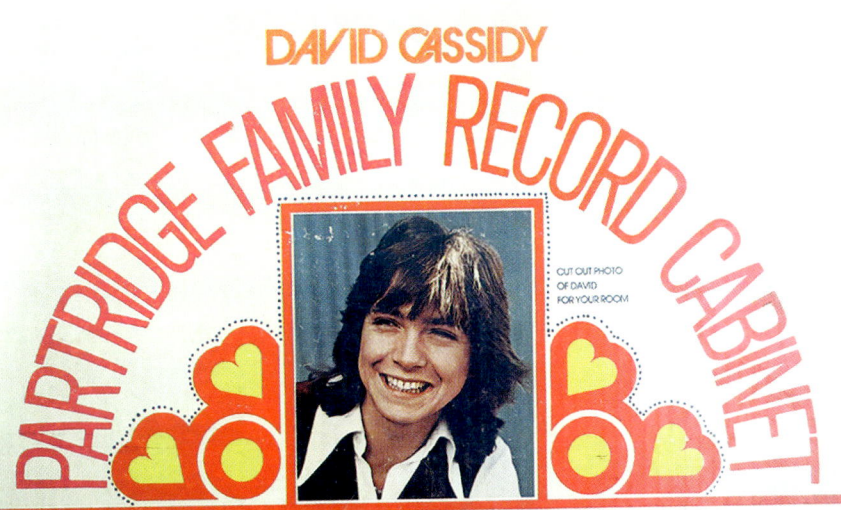

DAVID CASSIDY
PARTRIDGE FAMILY RECORD CABINET

CUT OUT PHOTO OF DAVID FOR YOUR ROOM

STORES OVER 200 45 RPMS AND 75 LP ALBUMS

EXTRA BONUS

DECORATE YOUR CABINET WITH THESE 4 FULL COLOR, 7" x 6" PRINTS OF DAVID & THE PARTRIDGE FAMILY

ALL HARDBOARD & WOOD CONSTRUCTION
25" WIDE/15" DEEP/22" HIGH
LIFT & SLIDE FRONT PANEL

ATF
AMERICAN TOY & FURNITURE CO., INC.
CHICAGO, ILLINOIS 60626

Record cabinet. American Toy & Furniture Company, 1972. 25" wide x 15" deep x 22" tall. Included four 7 x 6" color photo stickers. Original box pictured above.

One of four stickers, rare shot of bus before modifications.

Single release, "Breaking Up Is Hard to Do."

c38

One of the first official Partridge Family posters. 24 x 36" Poster Prints, U.S.

On tour through the years.

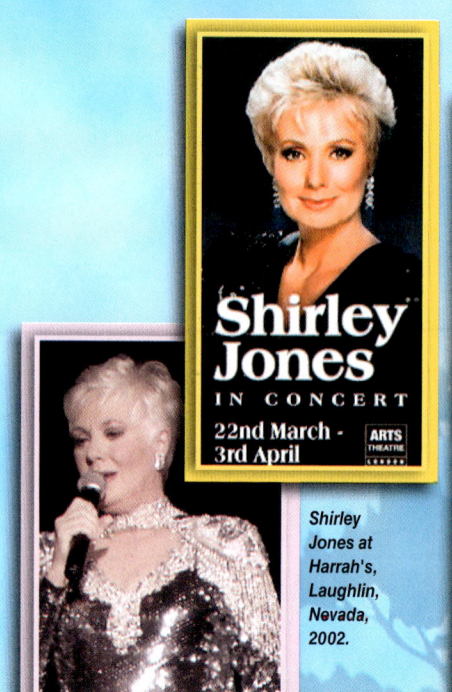

Shirley Jones at Harrah's, Laughlin, Nevada, 2002.

Susan Dey has fun with her past! March 1993.

Cast reunites on In Search of the Partridge Family, VH1, 2004, with host Todd Newton.

David Cassidy at the Barrow-Civic Theatre in Franklin, Pennsylvania, 2009.

David sang "Cry" at the Barrow for 79-year-old Wilma C. Miller by special request.

Danny, dressed in a rented crushed-velvet outfit, plays bass and sings "Doesn't Somebody Want to Be Wanted" with David for the first time at the Keswick Theatre in 2010.

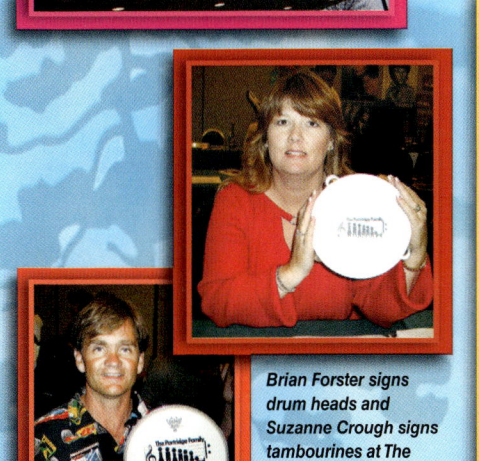

Brian Forster signs drum heads and Suzanne Crough signs tambourines at The Hollywood Show in 2005.

c41

The Partridge Family Notebook

Name: The Partridge Family
Starring: Shirley Jones
Featuring: David Cassidy

Subject: Music
Class: Bell 1111

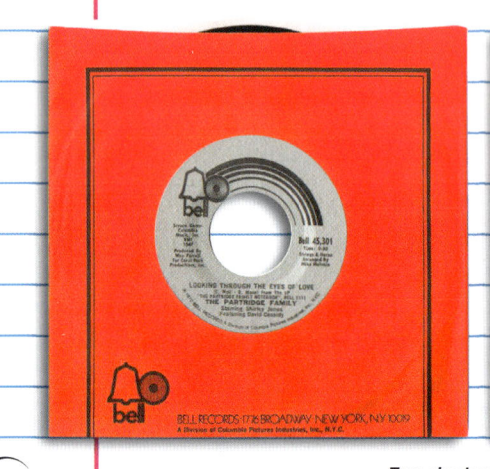

*Two singles released,
"Looking Through the Eyes of Love"
and "Friend and a Lover."*

The Screen Gems Records

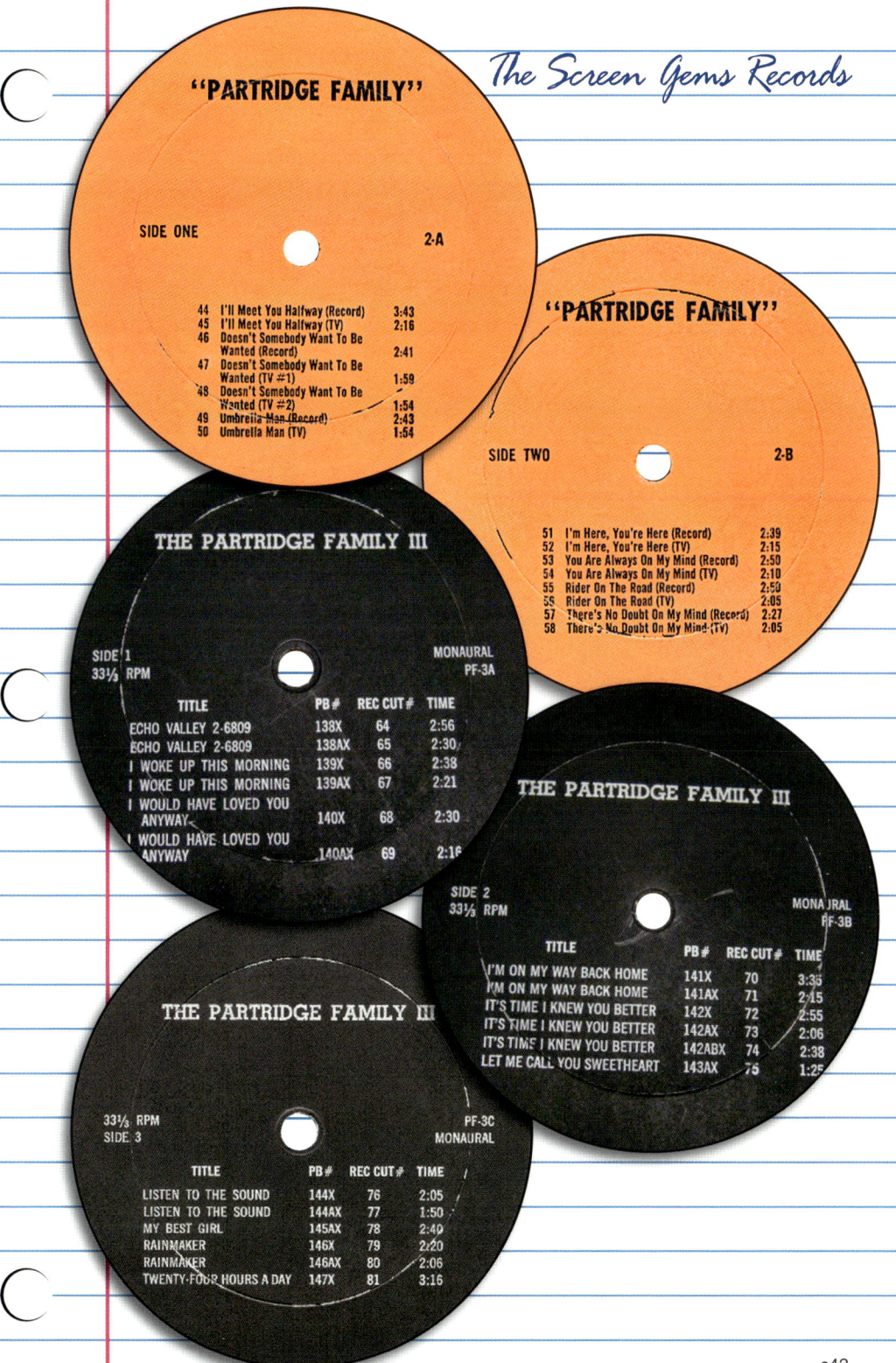

"PARTRIDGE FAMILY"

SIDE ONE   2-A

44	I'll Meet You Halfway (Record)	3:43
45	I'll Meet You Halfway (TV)	2:16
46	Doesn't Somebody Want To Be Wanted (Record)	2:41
47	Doesn't Somebody Want To Be Wanted (TV #1)	1:59
48	Doesn't Somebody Want To Be Wanted (TV #2)	1:54
49	Umbrella Man (Record)	2:43
50	Umbrella Man (TV)	1:54

"PARTRIDGE FAMILY"

SIDE TWO   2-B

51	I'm Here, You're Here (Record)	2:39
52	I'm Here, You're Here (TV)	2:15
53	You Are Always On My Mind (Record)	2:50
54	You Are Always On My Mind (TV)	2:10
55	Rider On The Road (Record)	2:50
56	Rider On The Road (TV)	2:05
57	There's No Doubt On My Mind (Record)	2:27
58	There's No Doubt On My Mind (TV)	2:05

THE PARTRIDGE FAMILY III

SIDE 1   33⅓ RPM   MONAURAL   PF-3A

TITLE	PB#	REC CUT#	TIME
ECHO VALLEY 2-6809	138X	64	2:56
ECHO VALLEY 2-6809	138AX	65	2:30
I WOKE UP THIS MORNING	139X	66	2:38
I WOKE UP THIS MORNING	139AX	67	2:21
I WOULD HAVE LOVED YOU ANYWAY	140X	68	2:30
I WOULD HAVE LOVED YOU ANYWAY	140AX	69	2:16

THE PARTRIDGE FAMILY III

SIDE 2   33⅓ RPM   MONAURAL   PF-3B

TITLE	PB#	REC CUT#	TIME
I'M ON MY WAY BACK HOME	141X	70	3:35
I'M ON MY WAY BACK HOME	141AX	71	2:15
IT'S TIME I KNEW YOU BETTER	142X	72	2:55
IT'S TIME I KNEW YOU BETTER	142AX	73	2:06
IT'S TIME I KNEW YOU BETTER	142ABX	74	2:38
LET ME CALL YOU SWEETHEART	143AX	75	1:25

THE PARTRIDGE FAMILY III

33⅓ RPM   SIDE 3   PF-3C   MONAURAL

TITLE	PB#	REC CUT#	TIME
LISTEN TO THE SOUND	144X	76	2:05
LISTEN TO THE SOUND	144AX	77	1:50
MY BEST GIRL	145AX	78	2:40
RAINMAKER	146X	79	2:20
RAINMAKER	146AX	80	2:06
TWENTY-FOUR HOURS A DAY	147X	81	3:16

c43

THE PARTRIDGE FAMILY III

33⅓ RPM
SIDE 4
PF-3D
MONAURAL

TITLE	PB#	REC CUT #	TIME
TWENTY-FOUR HOURS A DAY	147AX	82	1:47
WHALE SONG	148AX	83	3:25
COME ON GET HAPPY	149AX	84	:60
YOU DON'T HAVE TO TELL ME	150X	85	2:53
YOU DON'T HAVE TO TELL ME	150AX	86	2:15
YOU'VE LOST THAT LOVIN' FEELING	151X	87	:55
YOU'VE LOST THAT LOVIN' FEELING	151AX	88	1:04
YOU'VE LOST THAT LOVIN' FEELING	151ABX	89	1:03

THE PARTRIDGE FAMILY

PF-4
MONAURAL
33 1/3 RPM

	PB#	REC CUT#	TIME
Twenty Four Hours A Day	147ABX	90	2:30
I Left My Heart In San Francisco	152X	91	1:40
I Left My Heart In San Francisco	152AX	92	1:40
I Left My Heart In San Francisco	153X	93	1:28
Brown Eyes	154X	94	2:43
Love Is All I Ever Needed	155X	95	2:49
Love Is All I Ever Needed	155AX	96	2:19
One Night Stand	156X	97	2:58
One Night Stand	156AX	98	2:31
Summer Days	157X	99	3:15

THE PARTRIDGE FAMILY V

PF5-A
23:28
MONAURAL

REC. CUT #	P.B. #	TITLE	TIME
100	158X	HELLO HELLO	3:01
101	158AX	HELLO HELLO	1:55
102	159X	EVERY BIT OF YOU	2:56
103	159AX	EVERY BIT OF YOU	2:15
104	160X	LAST NIGHT	2:32
105	160AX	LAST NIGHT	2:06
106	161X	GOD BLESS YOU GIRL	2:54
107	161AX	GOD BLESS YOU GIRL	1:58
108	162X	IT'S ONE OF THOSE NIGHTS	3:26

THE PARTRIDGE FAMILY V

PF5-B
26:45
MONAURAL

REC. CUT #	P.B. #	TITLE	TIME
109	163X	IF YOU EVER GO	3:18
110	163AX	IF YOU EVER GO	2:07
111	164X	COME ON LOVE	2:57
112	164AX	COME ON LOVE	2:23
113	165X	EVERY SONG IS YOU	3:26
114	165AX	EVERY SONG IS YOU	2:01
115	166X	AS LONG AS THERE'S YOU	2:56
116	166AX	AS LONG AS THERE'S YOU	1:47
119	167X	HAVE YOURSELF A MERRY LITTLE XMAS	2:21
120	168X	WINTER WONDERLAND	2:10

1972-73 SEASON
THE PARTRIDGE FAMILY VI

MONAURAL   33 1/3 RPM PF-6A

	PB#	REC CUT#	TIME
AM I LOSING YOU	169X	121	2:25
BREAKING UP IS HARD TO DO	170X	122	2:36
GIRL YOU MADE MY DAY	171X	123	3:09
GIRL YOU MADE MY DAY	171AX	124	2:00
I DON'T CARE	172X	125	2:32

1972-73 SEASON
THE PARTRIDGE FAMILY VI

MONAURAL   33 1/3 RPM PF-6B

	PB#	REC CUT#	TIME
IT MEANS I'M IN LOVE WITH YOU	173AX	126	2:45
IT SOUNDS LIKE YOU'RE SAYING HELLO	174AX	127	2:25
IT'S ALL IN YOUR MIND	175X	128	2:16
IT'S YOU	176X	129	2:13
LOOKING THROUGH THE EYES OF LOVE	177X	130	3:20
LOOKING THROUGH THE EYES OF LOVE	177AX	131	1:54

1972-73 SEASON
THE PARTRIDGE FAMILY VI

MONAURAL 33 1/3 RPM PF-

	PB #	REC CUT #	TIME
LOVE MUST BE THE ANSWER	178X	132	3:16
LOVE MUST BE THE ANSWER	178AX	133	2:31
ME LOVING YOU	179X	134	2:15
ONE DAY AT A TIME	180X	135	3:17
ONE DAY AT A TIME	180AX	136	2:11

1972-73 SEASON
THE PARTRIDGE FAMILY VI

MONAURAL 33 1/3 RPM PF-6D

	PB #	REC CUT #	TIME
SOMETHING NEW GOT OLD	181X	137	2:54
SOMETHING NEW GOT OLD	181AX	138	2:21
SOMETHING'S WRONG	182X	139	2:30
SUNSHINE EYES	183AX	140	2:30
TAKE GOOD CARE OF HER	184X	141	2:24
THERE'LL COME A TIME	185X	142	2:27
TOGETHER WE'RE BETTER	186X	143	2:19

THE PARTRIDGE FAMILY VII
1973 SEASON

MONAURAL 33 1/3 RPM PF-7A

	PB no.	REC CUT no.	TIME
SUNSHINE	189X	144	2:30
STORYBOOK LOVE	190X	145	2:29
AS LONG AS YOU'RE THERE	191AX	146	2:35
LET YOUR LOVE GO	192X	147	2:17
FRIEND AND A LOVER	193X	148	2:10
IT'S A LONG WAY TO HEAVEN	194X	149	2:29

THE PARTRIDGE FAMILY VII
1973 SEASON

MONAURAL 33 1/3 RPM PF-7B

	PB no.	REC CUT no.	TIME
I'VE GOT YOUR LOVE ALL OVER ME	195X	150	2:22
MAYBE SOMEDAY	196AX	151	2:40
NOW THAT YOU GOT ME WHERE YOU WANT ME	197X	152	2:33
WALKIN' IN THE RAIN	198X	153	3:07
WALKIN' IN THE RAIN	198AX	154	2:34

THE PARTRIDGE FAMILY VIII
1973-74 SEASON

MONAURAL 33⅓ RPM PF-8

	P.B. NO.	CUT NO.	TIME
I WANNA BE WITH YOU	199X	155	2:20
I WAS RUNNING THE OPPOSITE WAY	200X	156	1:55
I WOULDN'T PUT NOTHIN' OVER ON YOU	201X	157	1:54
I'LL NEVER GET OVER YOU	202X	158	2:19
I'M INTO SOMETHING GOOD	203X	159	2:30
I'VE BEEN ALONE TOO LONG	204X	160	2:27
MONEY, MONEY	205X	161	2:30
OH NO NOT MY BABY	206X	162	2:30

THE PARTRIDGE FAMILY IX
1973-74 SEASON

MONAURAL 33⅓ RPM PF-9

	P.B. #	CUT #
1. CRYING IN THE RAIN	207X	163
2. HOW LONG IS TOO LONG	208X	164
3. I HEARD YOU SINGING YOUR SONG	209X	165
4. LOOKING FOR A GOOD TIME	210X	166
5. ROLLER COASTER	211X	167
6. THAT'S THE WAY IT IS WITH YOU BABY	212X	168
7. WHEN LOVE'S TALKED ABOUT	213X	169
8. WHERE DO WE GO FROM HERE	214X	170
9. WORKING ON A GROOVY THING	215X	171

c45

Gone Solo!

Shirley Jones recorded three singles during the Partridge Family years on Bell Records.
Danny Bonaduce recorded an album with Lion Records that garnered two singles.
Ricky Segall recorded one album with one single on Bell Records.

Of more than 20 albums to date, David Cassidy had five U.S. albums and seven U.S. singles on Bell Records including "Cherish," "Could It Be Forever," "How Can I Be Sure," "Rock Me Baby," "Daydream," "Puppy Song," "Daydreamer" (on flip side of "Puppy Song"). "If I Didn't Care" and "Please Please Me," released only in the U.K. also appeared on his U.S. Greatest Hits LP.

c47

c48

BACKGROUND SINGERS

John Bahler

Tom Bahler

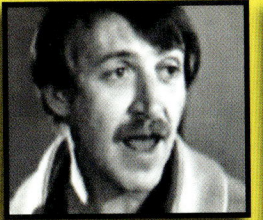

Ron Hicklin

Jackie Ward

and Shirley Jones!

THE MUSIC AGENCY

Left to right: Dale Leipzig, Mary Dee English, John Zaccheo, Jay Leipzig meeting with client.

MUSICIANS

&

Marty Kaniger & Dan Peyton

Terry Cashman & Tommy West

Mike Melvoin

Diane Hildebrand

Adam Miller

Peggy Clinger & Johnny Cymbal

Joe Osborn

Tommy Boyce & Bobby Hart

Tony Romeo

David Cassidy

SONGWRITERS

BELL RECORDS

Larry Uttal
President

Beverly Weinstein
Vice President
of Art Direction

Irwin "Irv" Biegel
Executive Vice President

John Rosica
Executive Director of
West Coast Operations

Gordon Bossin
Vice President of LP
Sales and Merchandising

Steve Wax
National
Promotion Director

Dave Carrico
Vice President of
Producer and Artist Relations

Allan Cohen
Vice President of
Financial Affairs

George Goodman
National R&B
Promotional Manager

Sheila Molitz
Production Coordinator

Richard Totoian
National
Promotion Director

Harvey Cooper
Director of West Coast
Promotional Activities

Oscar Fields
Vice President
of Singles Sales

Reuben Kincaid
Manager
Partridge Family

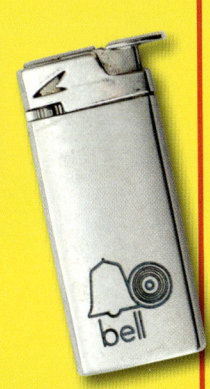

MUSIC PRODUCER

EXECUTIVE PRODUCER

Bob Claver

Wes Farrell
Owner, The Wes Farrell Organization

c51

THE PARTRIDGE FAMILY
Starring Shirley Jones · Featuring David Cassidy
BULLETIN BOARD

SONGS FOR OUR NEW ALBUM
Roller Coaster
Lookin' For A Good Time
How Long Is Too Long
That's The Way It Is With You
Where Do We Go From Here
I Heard You Singing Your Song
Money Money
Alone Too Long
~~I'd Never~~
I'll Never Get Over You
I Wouldn't Put Nothin' Over On You
Oh, No, Not My Baby

Memo:
Our New TV Time!
8 PM SATURDAYS
(7 PM Central Time)

BELL 1137

Single release, "Lookin' for a Good Time."

c52

Henry Diltz Gallery

Final location episode, season 4, aboard the Fairsea.

henry diltz

henry diltz

c53

David the musician.

Dinner on the cruise ship.

c54

Bad bunny!

Episode 81, "The Last Howard," aired four days before Halloween, 1973.

Cruising the Pacific on the Fairsea.

c55

David at home with his horses and dog Bullseye.

Guest starring on the Bob Hope Special, October 5, 1972.

c57

Germany  | Lebanon 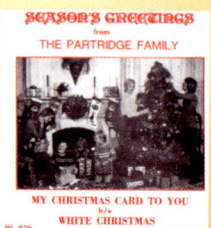 | New Zealand  | Yugoslavia

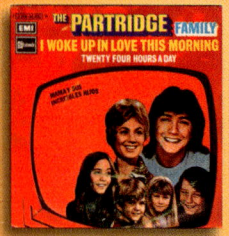

Spain 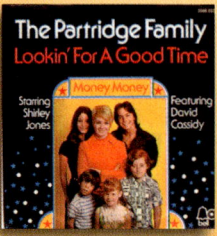 | Germany 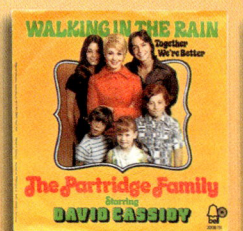 | Germany  | Japan (Sunshine)

c58   **International 45s**

Brazil    **Japan** 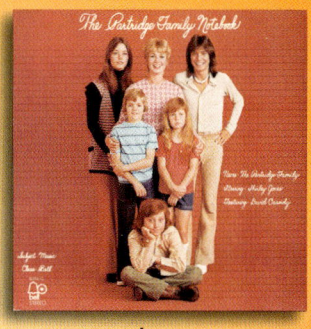   **Japan**

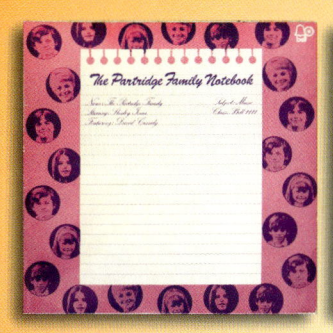

Canada    **Malaysia**    **Greece (Shopping Bag)**

Canada    **Germany** 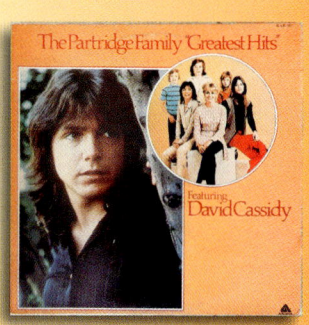   **New Zealand**

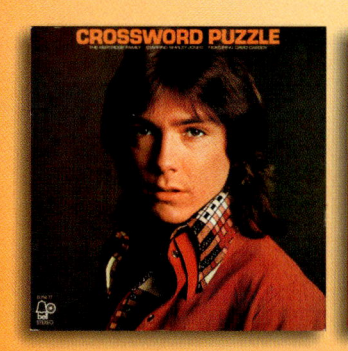

Japan (cover)    **Japan (back)**    **U.K.**

International LPs

c59

Collector's booklet
(UK)

Board game (Greece)

Peter Max–style
felt badges

"The Laurie House album"
TV mail order, 1976. U.S.

c60

Madison Square Garden

Melbourne

White City Stadium

Sew-on patches

Cigar bands

Stationery stamps

c61

The Partridge Family

AVAILABLE ON BELL / AMPEX STEREO TAPES • OPEN REEL • 8-TRACK CARTRIDGE • CASSETTE

In the beginning: The Partridge Family promotional team created this poster used strictly in retail outlets to break out the new group.

☞ 8-11-2 11-2-1-6 73-31-5-42-2 4-57 8-11-3-7 6-33-1-62-3-57-9 42-1-15-2-7
3-8 1 41-5-1-3-31, 57-4-8 1 73-1-33-8-33-3-6-9-2!

c62

In the end: David Cassidy broke attendance records at the Melbourne Cricket Grounds, Melbourne, Australia, March 10, 1974, captured in this iconic Henry Diltz photo.

The Partridge Family

Starring SHIRLEY JONES   **Featuring DAVID CASSIDY**

TV DINNER

FABULOUS TASTY HITS!
I THINK I LOVE YOU • C'MON GET HAPPY!
AND MANY MORE!

The "lost" album design. This comprehensive rendering was Art Director Mary English's favorite Partridge Family concept, but was never approved for development... Oh, what might have been!

the partridge family

Internationally renowned artist Glen Hanson created this Partridge Family caricature in 2010.